The Law and Special Education

The Law and Special Education

Second Edition

MITCHELL L. YELL
University of South Carolina

PEARSON

Merrill
Prentice Hall

Upper Saddle River, New Jersey
Columbus, Ohio

Library of Congress Cataloging-in-Publication Data

Yell, Mitchell L.
    The law and special education / Mitchell L. Yell.--2nd ed.
        p. cm.
    Includes bibliographical references and index.
    ISBN 0-13-110670-8
    1.   Children with disabilities--Education--Law and legislation--United States. 2.
Special education--Law and legislation--United States.   I.   Title.
    KF4210.Y45 2006
    344.73'0791--dc22   2006014357

Vice President and Executive Publisher: Jeffery W. Johnston
Senior Acquisitions Editor: Allyson P. Sharp
Editorial Assistant: Kathleen S. Burk
Senior Production Editor: Linda Hillis Bayma
Production Coordination: Lea Baranowski, Carlisle Publishers Services
Design Coordinator: Diane C. Lorenzo
Cover Designer: Ali Mohrman
Cover image: Corbis
Production Manager: Laura Messerly
Director of Marketing: Ann Castel Davis
Marketing Manager: Autumn Purdy
Marketing Coordinator: Brian Mounts

This book was set in ITC Century Light by Carlisle Communications, Ltd. It was printed and bound by
R.R. Donnelley & Sons Company. The cover was printed by R.R. Donnelley & Sons Company.

Pearson Education Ltd.   Pearson Education Australia Pty. Limited
Pearson Education Singapore Pte. Ltd.   Pearson Education North Asia Ltd.
Pearson Education Canada, Ltd.   Pearson Educatión de Mexico, S.A. de C.V.
Pearson Education—Japan   Pearson Education Malaysia Pte. Ltd.

10 9 8
ISBN: 0-13-110670-8

This book is dedicated to the memory of my mother and father, Vonnet and Erwin; to my in-laws, Vern and Delores Quam; and to my wife, Joy, and three sons, Nick, Eric, and Alex.

ABOUT
THE AUTHOR

Mitchell Yell, Ph.D., is a Professor in Special Education in the College of Education at the University of South Carolina in Columbia. For the past 12 years, Dr. Yell has conducted extensive research and presented numerous workshops on developing individualized education programs (IEPs), formulating legally correct special education policies, and adopting best practices in educating students with disabilities. His primary goal has been to extrapolate principles from legislation and litigation; communicate them to parents, teachers and administrators in clear, "nonlegalese" language; and assist teachers and school districts in the use of legally sound research-based policies and practices.

Prior to coming to the University of South Carolina, Dr. Yell was a special education teacher in Minnesota for 16 years. During this time he taught in elementary, middle, and secondary classrooms and special schools for students with learning disabilities, emotional and behavioral disorders, and autism.

He has published 60 journal articles and 12 book chapters and has conducted numerous workshops on special education law. He writes a column on education law for the journal *Preventing School Failure* and is the author of two textbooks published by Merrill/Prentice Hall titled *The Law and Special Education* and *No Child Left Behind: A Guide for Professionals.* He is also the lead author of the forthcoming textbook *Educating Students with Emotional and Behavioral Disorders in General and Special Education Classrooms,* also published by Merrill/Prentice Hall.

PREFACE

Federal laws mandating the provision of special education and related services to students with disabilities have been in effect since 1975. To understand the field of special education, it is important that we are familiar with the history and development of these laws. Because special education has become a highly litigated area, it is important that special education teachers, administrators, and associated staff know the requirements of these laws. Moreover, the laws are in a constant state of development and refinement; therefore, we need to be able to locate the necessary information to keep abreast of these changes. Thus, the purpose of this text is three-fold: (a) to acquaint readers with the legal development of special education; (b) to expose readers to the current legal requirements in providing a free appropriate public education to students with disabilities; and (c) to assist readers to understand the procedures to obtain legal information in law libraries and on the Internet and to conduct legal research using a variety of sources.

This textbook is written in the style of an educational textbook rather than a legal textbook. That is, rather than including passages from selected cases, legal principles from these cases will be presented. However, exposure to the written opinions is important, and readers are urged to locate and read them in a law library or on the Internet. Readers should note the wealth of materials on the Internet described in Chapter 3. For ease of use references are presented in accordance with the format described in the *Publication Manual of the American Psychological Association* (Fifth Edition) rather than in the standard legal format. Finally, legal terms are kept to a minimum, explained when used, and defined in the glossary.

A unique feature of this textbook is a homepage on the World Wide Web, titled *The Law and Special Education.* It contains links to the text of the Individuals with Disabilities Education Act (IDEA), the Individuals with Disabilities Education Improvement Act of 2004, Section 504 of the Rehabilitation Act, the Americans with Disabilities Act (ADA), No Child Left Behind (NCLB), the Family Educational Rights and Privacy Act (FERPA), and the corresponding regulations. Links to legal resources on the Internet are included on the page. The website also features a Special Education Law Blog. The primary purpose of the blog is to provide readers and instructors using the text with frequent updates regarding legal developments in special education. The website also presents an instructors' page, which includes presentations, suggestions for teaching, and a National Council for Accreditation of Teacher Education (NCATE) formatted syllabus. The URL of *The Law and Special Education* homepage is **http://www.ed.sc.edu/spedlaw/lawpage.htm**.

Acknowledgments

In writing this book I benefited from the help of many friends and colleagues. Thanks go to all of them. Terrye Conroy, the law librarian at the University of South Carolina, did a fabulous job assisting with the revisions to Chapters 2 and 3. David Rogers at St. Cloud State University in Minnesota and Elisabeth Lodge Rogers, special education director of the St. Cloud School District, did great work in Chapter 4. Thanks also to the reviewers of this text for their timely and helpful reviews: Sharan E. Brown, University of Washington; John Farago, The City University of New York; Dan Fennerty, Central Washington University; and Ken B. Heinlein, University of Wyoming. This is a better textbook because of their efforts. A hearty thank-you goes to Joseph Cross of the University of South Carolina law library, who was extremely helpful in the preparation of Chapter 2, and Delys Nast, who generously contributed her considerable talents in designing the homepage. Thanks also to Dr. Erik Drasgow and Dr. Bill Brown of the University of South Carolina for their helpful editorial feedback, and Antonis Katsiyannis and the many readers who made useful suggestions for the second edition. I would also like to thank Ann Davis and Allyson Sharp of Merrill/Prentice Hall, who have guided me through this endeavor with enormous skill, patience, and sound advice. Thanks also go to the giants on whose shoulders I perched, Frank Wood and Stan Deno of the University of Minnesota. Finally, I want to thank my wife, Joy, and our three sons, Nick, Eric, and Alex, for their love and our lives together.

EDUCATOR LEARNING CENTER:
AN INVALUABLE ONLINE RESOURCE

Merrill Education and the Association for Supervision and Curriculum Development (ASCD) invite you to take advantage of a new online resource, one that provides access to the top research and proven strategies associated with ASCD and Merrill—the Educator Learning Center. At **www.educatorlearningcenter.com**, you will find resources that will enhance your students' understanding of course topics and of current educational issues, in addition to being invaluable for further research.

How the Educator Learning Center Will Help Your Students Become Better Teachers

With the combined resources of Merrill Education and ASCD, you and your students will find a wealth of tools and materials to better prepare them for the classroom.

Research

- More than 600 articles from the ASCD journal *Educational Leadership* discuss everyday issues faced by practicing teachers.
- A direct link on the site to Research Navigator™ gives students access to many of the leading education journals, as well as extensive content detailing the research process.
- Excerpts from Merrill Education texts give your students insights on important topics of instructional methods, diverse populations, assessment, classroom management, technology, and refining classroom practice.

Classroom Practice

- Hundreds of lesson plans and teaching strategies are categorized by content area and age range.
- Case studies and classroom video footage provide virtual field experience for student reflection.
- Computer simulations and other electronic tools keep your students abreast of today's classrooms and current technologies.

Look into the Value of Educator Learning Center Yourself

A four-month subscription to Educator Learning Center is $25 but is **FREE** when packaged with any Merrill Education text. In order for your students to have access to this site, you must use this special value-pack ISBN number **WHEN** placing your textbook order with the bookstore: 0-13-219560-7. Your students will then receive a copy of the text packaged with a free ASCD pincode. To preview the value of this website to you and your students, please go to **www.educatorlearningcenter.com** and click on "Demo."

BRIEF CONTENTS

CONTENTS

CHAPTER FOUR

The History of the Law and Children with Disabilities

61

CHAPTER TEN   **Identification, Assessment, and Evaluation**   **249**

CHAPTER ELEVEN   **The Individualized Education Program**   **273**

CHAPTER FOURTEEN   **Disciplining Students with Disabilities**   **377**

CHAPTER FIFTEEN   **Additional Issues**   **419**

Note: Every effort has been made to provide accurate and current Internet information in this book. However, the Internet and information posted on it are constantly changing, so it is inevitable that some of the Internet addresses listed in this text book will change.

CHAPTER ONE

Introduction to the American Legal System

[Laws are] rules of civil conduct prescribed by the state . . . commanding what is right and prohibiting what is wrong.

Blackstone (1748)

Laws ensuring the provision of special education to students with disabilities are based on constitutional principles, written and enacted by legislatures and administrative agencies, and interpreted by the courts. It is through the interaction of the various components of the legal system, legislative and judicial, that special education law evolves. The purpose of this chapter is to examine the workings of the American legal system.

The American Legal System

Federalism

The American system is a federal system. That is, the government of the United States is comprised of a union of states joined under a central federal government. Federalism represents the linkage of the American people and the communities in which they live through a unique political arrangement. The federal government protects the people's rights and liberties and acts to achieve certain ends for the common good while simultaneously sharing authority and power with the states (Elazar, 1984). The U.S. Constitution delineates the nature of this arrangement in the 10th Amendment (see Appendix B for selected provisions of the U.S. Constitution) by limiting excessive concentration of power in the national government while simultaneously limiting full dispersal of power to the states. The national government, therefore, has specific powers granted to it in the Constitution; those powers not granted to the national government are the province of the states.

The Constitution does not contain any provisions regarding education. According to Alexander and Alexander (2002), this is not because the nation's founders had no strong beliefs regarding education. Rather, they believed the states should be sovereign in matters as important as education. Education, therefore, is governed by the laws of the 50 states.

Nevertheless, federal involvement has been an important factor in the progress and growth of education. The government's role provided under the authority given Congress by the Constitution's general welfare clause has, however, been indirect. In the earliest method of indirect federal involvement in education, the federal government made grants of land to the states for the purpose of creating and aiding the development of public schools. In addition to the federal land grants creating public schools, Congress in the Morrill Act of 1862 provided grants of land to each state to be used for colleges. In the land grants, the federal government had no direct control of education in the public schools or colleges.

The federal government has continued the indirect assistance to education through categorical grants. The purposes of the categorical grants have been to provide supplementary assistance to the state systems of education and to shape educational policy in the states. States have the option of accepting or rejecting the categorical grants offered by the federal government. If states accept the categorical grants, they must abide by the federal guidelines for the use of these funds. Examples of categorical grants include the National Defense Education Act of 1958, the Higher Education Facilities Act of 1963, the Vocational Education Act of 1963, the Elementary and Secondary Education Act of 1965, and the Education for All Handicapped Children Act of 1975 (now the Individuals with Disabilities Education Act). The role of the federal government in guiding educational policy has increased greatly through the categorical grants (Alexander & Alexander, 2002).

Sources of Law

There are four sources of law: constitutional law, statutory law, regulatory law, and case law. These sources exist on both the federal and state level. The supreme laws are contained in federal and state constitutions (i.e., constitutional law), and these constitutions empower legislatures to create law (i.e., statutory law). Legislatures in turn delegate lawmaking authority to regulatory agencies to create regulations that implement the law (i.e., regulatory law). Finally, courts interpret laws through cases, and these interpretations of law accumulate to form case law. Figure 1.1 illustrates the sources of law.

Constitutional Law

The U.S. Constitution is the basic source of law in our legal system. The Constitution (a) defines the fundamental rules by which the American system functions, (b) sets the parameters for governmental action, and (c) allocates power and responsibility among the legislative, executive, and judicial branches of government (Cohen, Berring, & Olson, 1989). The Constitution further defines the separation of powers between the legislative, executive, and judicial branches. Figure 1.2 illustrates the branches of government and their powers as created by the Constitution.

Federal statutes are based on provisions of the Constitution. The specific section of the Constitution that is the basis for special education (e.g., the Individuals with Disabilities Education Act and Section 504 of the Rehabilitation Act of 1973) is the provision that allows spending money to provide for the general welfare (Article 1, Section 8).

The Constitution can be amended by Congress and the states. Thus far, the Constitution has been amended only 26 times. The first 10 amendments, known as the Bill of Rights, describe the basic rights of individuals. The 14th Amendment is important because it has become the constitutional basis for special education. This amendment holds that no state can deny equal protection of the law to any person within its jurisdiction. Essentially, the equal protection clause requires that states must treat all similarly situated persons alike (Tucker & Goldstein, 1992). The 14th Amendment also states that persons may not be deprived of life, liberty, or property without due process of law. This amendment has played an important role in the right-to-education cases that will be explained in Chapter 4.

Figure 1.1
The Sources of Law

Figure 1.2
The Branches of Government

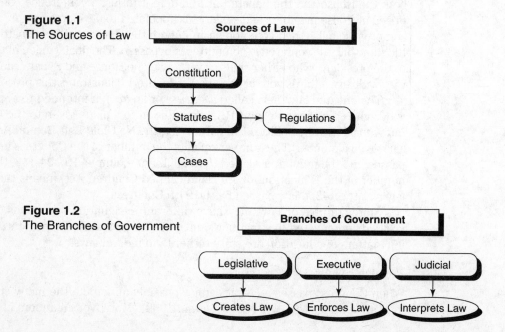

State Constitutions

All 50 states have their own constitutions. Like the U.S. Constitution, state constitutions establish the principle of separation of powers by establishing a lawmaking body (legislature), a chief executive officer (governor), and a court system. State constitutions tend to be more detailed than the federal Constitution. Often they address the day-to-day operations of the state government in addition to ensuring the rights of the state's citizens (Cohen et al., 1989). States cannot deny persons the rights found in the U.S. Constitution, but they can provide additional rights not found in the federal document. That is, they can provide more rights, but they cannot provide fewer.

There is no constitutional mandate regarding the provision of education by the federal government and, therefore, no constitutional right to an education afforded by the U.S. Constitution. The states, therefore, have the authority to mandate the provision of an education for their citizens. All states have educational mandates in their constitutions.

Statutory Law

The U.S. Constitution gives Congress the authority to make laws. The laws promulgated or created by Congress and state legislatures are referred to as *statutes*. The process of enacting laws is long and complicated. In Congress the formal process begins with the introduction of a bill by a senator or representative. The bill is assigned a number that reflects where it originated (House or Senate) and the order of introduction. The bill is then referred to the appropriate House or Senate committee. Most bills never pass this stage; some bills merely die, while some pass one house but not the other. If a bill passes both the House and the Senate but in different forms, a conference committee comprised of House members and senators is appointed to develop a compromise bill. The compromise bill is then voted on again. If both the House and the Senate initially pass the same bill, the conference committee is bypassed. The final version of the bill is sent to the president, who either signs or vetoes it. The House and Senate can override the veto with a two-thirds vote in each house. Figure 1.3 illustrates this process.

The enacted law (also called a *statute* or an *act*), if intended to apply generally, is designated as a public law (P.L.). In addition to a name given to the law (e.g., the Individuals with Disabilities Education Act, the No Child Left Behind Act) the law is also given a number. The number reflects the number of the Congress in which it was passed and the number assigned to the bill. For example, P.L. 94-142, the public law number of the Education for All Handicapped Children Act, means that this public law was the 142nd law passed by the 94th Congress.

State statutes or laws may have different designations or names, but they are created and enacted in a manner similar to federal statutes. Most statutes concerning matters of education are state rather than federal laws.

Regulatory Law

When Congress passes a law, it cannot possibly anticipate the many situations that may arise under that law (Cohen et al., 1989). Moreover, members of Congress do

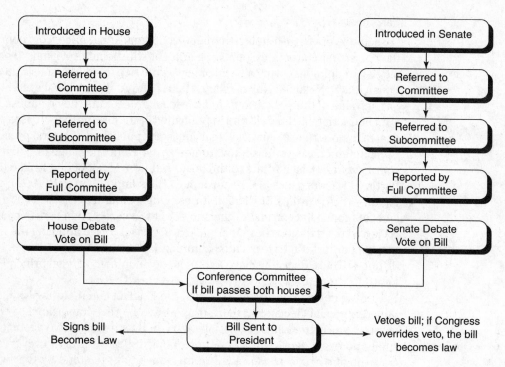

Figure 1.3
Creation of Law in the American Legal System

not have expertise in all areas covered by the laws they pass. The statutes passed by Congress, therefore, tend to be broad and general in nature. To fill in the details of the law, Congress delegates power to the appropriate administrative agencies to create specific regulations to implement the laws. These agencies are part of the executive branch of government. The regulations, also called *rules* or *guidelines,* that they create supply specifics to the general content of the law and provide procedures by which the law can be enforced. Regulations have the force of law. A violation of a regulation, therefore, is as serious as a violation of the law.

In addition to promulgating regulations, most administrative agencies have a quasi-judicial function, which means they can make rulings on the law and its regulations. These judgments may take the form of formal hearings or rulings on written inquiries. The agencies that often rule on special education matters are the Office of Special Education and Rehabilitative Services (OSERS) and the Office of Special Education Programs (OSEP). The Office of Civil Rights (OCR) of the Department of Education investigates and issues findings on claims of violation of Section 504 and, therefore, often investigates matters relating to special education.

Case Law

Case law refers to the published opinions of judges that arise from court cases where they interpret statutes, regulations, and constitutional provisions. The aggregate of published opinions forms a body of jurisprudence distinct from statutes and regulations (Black, Nolan, & Nolan-Haley, 1990). The American legal system relies heavily on the value of these decisions and the legal precedents they establish. Because only a small fraction of cases results in published opinions, these few cases take on a great deal of importance. If a judicial decision is not published, it has no precedential value.

The emphasis on case law comes to us from the English tradition known as *common law,* which refers to the legal tradition developed in England following the Battle of Hastings in 1066. According to Elias and Levinkind (1992), from this time forward the decisions of English juries, judges, and magistrates were written down and categorized according to the subject of the case. When courts heard cases, they reviewed the decisions in similar and earlier cases, often applying the legal principles developed in those cases. Thus, common law consists of court opinions in specific disputes. These decisions have led to the development of legal principles that are followed in later cases.

In the colonial period of America, the English common-law tradition was maintained. Judicial decisions, therefore, were of great importance. Over time, laws passed by Congress and regulations written by administrative agencies began to assume more significance (Elias & Levinkind, 1992). Courts, however, still follow the doctrine of *stare decisis,* a Latin phrase meaning "to stand by that which has been decided," in creating a body of case law.

Many areas of our law consist largely of common law or case law. In special education, this is especially evident. For example, laws involving the discipline of children with disabilities and the provision of extended school year services to special education students have been initiated by the courts.

Sources of Judicial Power

To understand the role of case law in the American legal system, it is necessary to become familiar with the sources of judicial power. Judicial power emanates from two sources; the first has been referred to as horizontal, the second vertical (Reynolds, 1991).

Horizontal Power.   There are essentially two types of horizontal power (Reynolds, 1991). The first is supreme power. In some areas of decision making, the power of the judiciary is virtually supreme. This is when the courts, especially the U.S. Supreme Court, act as the ultimate interpreter of the Constitution. The second type of horizontal power is limited power. Virtually all judicial decisions involve the interpretation of the laws of the legislative branch. The power is limited because the legislature has the final say as to the content of the law. If the legislature disagrees with a court's interpretation, it can change or alter the law or write another law. Figure 1.4 represents the horizontal power of the courts.

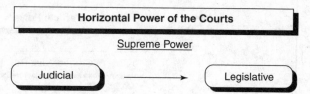

When court acts as the interpreter of the U.S. Constitution, they are virtually supreme.

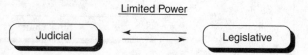

When the courts interpret the laws created by the legislative branch, the
legislature may change or alter the law or write another law if legislators disagree
with the court's interpretation.

Figure 1.4
The Horizontal Power of the Courts

An example of horizontal power was the passage of the *Handicapped Children's Protection Act* (1986) following the Supreme Court's decision in *Smith v. Robinson* (1984). The Education for All Handicapped Children Act (EAHCA) originally contained no mention of parents being able to collect attorney's fees if they sued schools to obtain what they believed to be their rights under the law. Undaunted by this problem, attorneys for parents sued school districts for these rights and also brought suit under other federal statutes to collect attorney's fees. In 1984, however, the U.S. Supreme Court held that attorneys could not collect fees under these statutes. According to the high court, because the EAHCA did not contain a provision for attorney's fees, fees were not available. In a dissent, Justice Brennan argued that parents should not be required to pay when they had to go to court to obtain the rights given to them in the law. He further suggested that Congress revisit the issue and write attorney's fees into the law. Congress did, and in 1986 passed the Handicapped Children's Protection Act (IDEA 20 U.S.C. § 1415(e)), which made possible the award of attorney's fees under the EAHCA and overturned *Smith v. Robinson.*

Vertical Power.   The vertical power of the courts lies in the hierarchical nature of the system. The hierarchy in most jurisdictions consists of a trial court, an intermediate appellate court, and a court of last resort. The vertical power of the courts is illustrated in Figure 1.5.

The first level of courts is the trial court level. Within the federal system, the trial courts are called district courts. The role of the trial court is essentially fact-finding. Litigants (i.e., participants in a lawsuit) may appeal the decision of the trial court to the next highest level of court, the intermediate appellate court. The decision of the appellate court is binding on all lower courts in its jurisdiction. The losing party in the appellate court may appeal the lower court's decision to the court of last resort. In most

Figure 1.5
The Vertical Power of the Courts

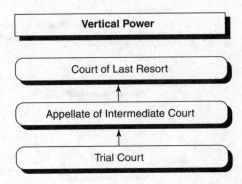

jurisdictions, the court of last resort (the highest level of court) is the supreme court. Decisions of the supreme court are binding on all lower courts, trial and appellate.

There are 51 separate jurisdictions in the United States: the federal courts and the 50 state courts. While the names of the courts may differ, the equivalent of the generic system described previously can be found in all 51 systems. A line of authority exists within the system, such that the inferior courts are expected to follow the decisions of courts superior to them. This line of authority is within a jurisdiction but does not cross jurisdictional lines. Therefore, a trial court in a certain jurisdiction is not obligated to follow the ruling of an appellate court in another jurisdiction. For example, a trial court in Minnesota is not obligated to adhere to an appellate court's ruling that is authority in South Carolina. A trial court in South Carolina, however, is obligated to follow a ruling of the appellate court with authority in South Carolina. Because lines of authority run only within a jurisdiction, it is important to know in which jurisdiction a particular decision occurs.

Court Structure

The generic model of the hierarchy of courts applies to both the federal system and the state jurisdictions. Figure 1.6 illustrates the generic model when applied to the federal judicial system.

In some states, the number of levels varies slightly, although the model is essentially the same. Questions involving state law are brought before the state courts, and questions involving federal law and constitutional issues are usually brought before the federal courts. The great majority of special education cases have been heard in the federal court system because most have concerned the application of federal law (e.g., the Individuals with Disabilities Education Act and Section 504 of the Rehabilitation Act).

Trial Court.   The trial court is the first level in the court system, the level at which the fact-finding process takes place. Matters of dispute are heard by a judge or jury, and the issues of fact are determined. When the facts have been determined, they remain constant. This means that if the case goes to the appellate court or the court of

Figure 1.6
The Federal Court System

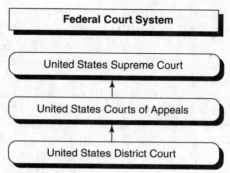

Federal Court System

United States Supreme Court

United States Courts of Appeals

United States District Court

last resort, the facts as determined by the trial court do not change, unless a higher court finds a procedural problem or bias in the fact-finding process. The facts of the case, once determined, cannot be appealed.

In addition to the facts of the case, issues of law arise at the trial court level. The judge makes determinations concerning the issue of law and applies them to the facts of the case. The rulings of the judge on the law, however, can be appealed to a higher court.

There are close to 100 trial courts in the federal judicial system. The federal trial courts are called U.S. District Courts. The geographic distribution of the district courts is based on state boundaries, with all states having between one and four district courts. All judicial districts have at least one and as many as three judges to share the federal district court caseload.

The role of the federal district court differs slightly in special education cases. Because the fact-finding process takes place at the administrative review process (i.e., the due process hearing or hearing by the state educational agency), the trial court takes on more of an appellate role and determines if the administrative agency or due process hearing officer correctly applied the law.

Intermediate Appellate Court.   Usually litigants have the right to appeal the trial court decision. The appeal will most often be to the intermediate appellate court. In an appeal, the appellate court reviews the decision of the trial court on the issues of law. The role of the appellate court is to ensure that the trial court did not err and to guide and develop the law within the jurisdiction (Reynolds, 1991). The appellate court determines whether the trial court's judgment should be affirmed, reversed, or modified. If the appellate court concludes that the lower court did not properly apply the law, the court may reverse the trial court's decision. If the appellate court determines that the law was not applied properly, but that the error was of a minor nature and did not affect the outcome, it may affirm the decision. Decisions of the appellate court develop law through the creation of precedents.

Because the facts are determined at the trial court level, the appellate court does not retry the case. The facts as determined by the trial court, therefore, are accepted by the appellate court. The primary concern of the appellate court is whether the trial court applied the principles of law correctly.

There is no jury at the appellate level, only the justices. Typically, the attorneys for each party exchange written briefs. Oral arguments may also be heard. An appellate court will usually consist of three or more judges who will then vote on the disposition of the dispute. Each federal appellate court is comprised of 12 judges, but typically cases will be heard by only 3 judges. By dividing judges in this manner, the courts can hear more cases. Occasionally all 12 judges on the appellate court will hear a case. A hearing by the full court is referred to as *en banc*.

There are 13 U.S. Courts of Appeals. The First through Eleventh Circuits cover three or more states each, a Twelfth covers the District of Columbia, and the Thirteenth, called the *Federal Circuit,* hears appeals from throughout the country on specialized matters (e.g., patents). The courts of appeal hear cases from trial courts in their jurisdictions. Their decisions become controlling authority in the court's jurisdiction.[*] Figure 1.7 shows the geographic jurisdictions of the federal appellate courts.

Court of Last Resort.   Litigants may file an appeal with the court of last resort. The court of last resort is called the Supreme Court in most jurisdictions. Because the courts of last resort are extremely busy, they cannot hear every case that is appealed. The courts, therefore, have the power to determine which cases they will hear.

The court of last resort has an appellate function. That is, it reviews the decision of the intermediate appellate court to determine if the law has been correctly applied. As with the intermediate appellate court, the court of last resort is not a forum for retrying the case. The decision of the court of last resort will be binding on all lower courts (trial and appellate) in its jurisdiction. The decisions of a court of last resort, therefore, are important sources of law.

The U.S. Supreme Court is the highest court in the land. The Court has nine justices, one designated as the Chief Justice. If a litigant decides to appeal a decision of an appellate court to the Supreme Court, the litigant files a petition for a writ of certiorari, usually called a *petition for cert.* This petition for cert essentially asks the Court to consider the case. The justices review the petitions, and if four of the nine justices decide to grant the petition, a writ of certiorari will be issued and the case will be heard. This is usually referred to as *granting cert.* If the Court decides not to hear the case, it will deny cert. When the Court denies cert, it does not have to explain why it is doing so. Because a denial can be for any of a number of reasons, it has no precedential value. If the high court denies cert, the lower court decision stands and may still exert controlling and persuasive authority.

---

[*]The U.S. Court of Appeals for the Eleventh Circuit was created in 1981 by taking Florida, Georgia, and Mississippi from the Fifth Circuit. Because there was no case law prior to that date, no controlling authority to guide court decisions (except decisions of the U.S. Supreme Court) was available in the Eleventh. To remedy this problem in the first case heard before the Eleventh Circuit Court, *Bonner v. Alabama* (1981), an en banc court ruled that all decisions of the U.S. Court of Appeals for the Fifth Circuit decided prior to September 30, 1981, would be controlling in the Eleventh Circuit.

Figure 1.7
The Federal Judicial Circuits

1st Circuit	2nd Circuit	3rd Circuit	4th Circuit	5th Circuit	6th Circuit	7th Circuit						
Maine	Connecticut	Delaware	Maryland	Louisiana	Kentucky	Illinois						
Massachusetts	New York	New Jersey	South Carolina	Mississippi	Ohio	Indiana						
New Hampshire	Vermont	Pennsylvania	North Carolina	Texas	Michigan	Wisconsin						
Rhode Island			Virginia		Tennessee							
			West Virginia									

Figure 1.7
Continued

8th Circuit	9th Circuit	10th Circuit	11th Circuit	D.C. Circuit	Federal Circuit
Arkansas	Alaska	Colorado	Alabama	Washington, D.C.	Washington, D.C.
Iowa	Arizona	Kansas	Georgia		
Minnesota	California	New Mexico	Florida		
Missouri	Hawaii	Oklahoma			
Nebraska	Idaho	Utah			
North Dakota	Montana	Wyoming			
South Dakota	Nevada				
	Oregon				
	Washington				

12

The U.S. Supreme Court grants cert to only a small number of cases, less than 1%. Cases that the Court hears will usually present an important question of constitutional or federal law or involve issues that have split the appellate courts. In the latter case the Supreme Court acts to resolve the conflict.

Precedence

The American system of law follows the doctrine of stare decisis. According to stare decisis, also referred to as *precedence,* courts are expected to follow the decisions of courts in similar cases. When a higher court applies the law to a specific set of facts, this decision controls decisions in similar cases in that and other courts. If the court does not follow the precedent, it must explain why that precedent does not apply or control in the particular case. Courts are not absolutely locked to every precedent, however, and can abandon earlier doctrines that are no longer useful (Valente & Valente, 2005). This doctrine helps to ensure uniformity, predictability, and fairness in court decisions (Reynolds, 1991).

A decision by a higher court controls the disposition of lower courts in the same jurisdiction. The lower court cannot make a decision contrary to decisions by the higher court. This is referred to as *controlling authority.* The decision of the supreme court in a jurisdiction controls the decisions of all lower courts.

Another type of authority may come from a court that is not controlling (e.g., a court in a different jurisdiction). This type of authority is called *persuasive authority.* A court is not bound to follow the precedent but does so because it is persuaded by the decision. For example, the decision of an appellate court in Minnesota will not control the decision of a court (even a lower court) in South Carolina, because they are in different jurisdictions. The court in South Carolina may find the decision in the Minnesota court to be persuasive, however, and use similar reasoning in arriving at its decision. An example of a special education ruling that has been extremely persuasive is the decision of the U.S. Court of Appeals for the Fifth Circuit in *Daniel R.R. v. State Board of Education* (1989). The reasoning in the Fifth Circuit's decision regarding the determination of the least restrictive environment for children in special education has been accepted by the U.S. Courts of Appeals in the Third, Ninth, and Eleventh Circuits.

Only published cases can be used for precedence. Only a small percentage—less than 10%—of cases decided by the U.S. District Courts are published. Approximately 40% of the decisions of the U.S. Courts of Appeals are published. All of the decisions of the U.S. Supreme Court are published.

Holding and Dicta

The holding of the case is the portion of the decision that controls decisions of lower courts in the same jurisdiction. The holding of the case is the actual ruling on a point or points of law. It usually consists of one or two sentences. The rest of the decision, judicial comments, illustrations, speculations, and so on, are referred to as *dicta,* plural form of *dictum.* The dicta are everything in the opinion except the holding. Dicta are not controlling but can be persuasive. They do not have value as precedent.

The Opinion

One of the judges of the appellate court or court of last resort will usually be appointed to write an opinion stating the ruling of the court and the court's reasoning for arriving at the decision. A written opinion usually contains a summary of the case, a statement of the facts, an explanation of the court's reasoning, and a record of the decision. The opinion of the court also lists the author's name and the names of justices who agree with it. A court's opinion may contain a concurring opinion or a dissent. A concurring opinion is written when a judge (or judges) agrees with the majority of the court on the ruling, but does not agree with the reasoning used to reach the ruling. A dissent is a statement of a judge (or judges) who does not agree with the results reached by the majority.

Dissents can be important. Because dissents are typically circulated among the justices hearing a case prior to writing a final opinion, they can serve to dissuade the majority justices from judicial advocacy, encourage judicial responsibility, and appeal to outside audiences (e.g., Congress) for correction of perceived mistakes by the majority (Reynolds, 1991). They can also serve as general appeals or appeals to higher courts or legislators to correct a perceived judicial error. Although dissents carry no controlling authority, they can be persuasive.

Dissents are sometimes used to appeal to a higher court or legislature to correct the court's action. An example of the latter is Justice Brennan's dissent in *Smith v. Robinson* (1984), discussed earlier. In his dissent, Justice Brennan disagreed with the Supreme Court's ruling that attorney's fees were not available in special education cases and appealed to Congress to revisit P.L. 94-142 and correct the Court's error. Congress did revisit the issue and passed the Handicapped Children's Protection Act in 1986.

The Law and Special Education

The four branches of law—constitutional, legislative, regulatory, and case law—often interact. Laws are sometimes made by one branch of government in response to developments in another branch. This can be seen clearly in the development of special education law.

Actions in the courts, such as *Mills v. Board of Education* (1972) and *Pennsylvania Association of Retarded Citizens (PARC) v. Commonwealth of Pennsylvania* (1972), created the right to a special education for children with disabilities under the 14th Amendment to the Constitution. Congress reacted to this litigation by passing legislation to ensure the educational rights of children with disabilities (P.L. 94-142). Regulations were promulgated to implement and enforce the law by the then Department of Health, Education, and Welfare. In response to the federal law, all 50 states eventually passed state laws and created state regulations ensuring the provision of special education to qualified children. The inevitable disputes that arose concerning the special education rules and regulations led to a spate of federal litigation to interpret the special education law. Some of this litigation, such as *Smith*

Figure 1.8
The Evolution of Law

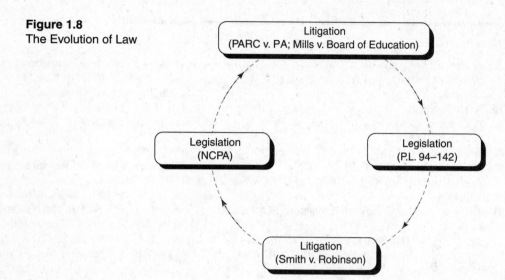

v. *Robinson* (1984), has led to more legislation. In 1986, Congress passed new legislation, the Handicapped Children's Protection Act (HCPA), to overturn the effects of *Smith v. Robinson.* This legislation, in turn, has led to more litigation to interpret it. Thus, the development of law is cyclical. Through the interaction of the various sources of law, special education law evolves. The interaction of the sources of law is depicted in Figure 1.8.

Summary

Special education is governed by an elaborate and extensive body of statutes, regulations, and court decisions. The U.S. Constitution and the state constitutions provide the foundations for special education. Congress and the state legislatures write statutes or laws that mandate and guide the provision of special education. These laws are implemented through the promulgation of regulations issued by administrative agencies such as the state and federal Departments of Education. Finally, laws and regulations are interpreted by the courts. The role of the courts is to apply the principles of the law to settle disputes. Although the courts do not initiate laws, their published decisions may result in judicially created principles known as *case law.* Legislation and litigation in special education have rapidly increased in the last decade. The effect of these judicial and legislative actions is that special education continues to evolve.

For Further Information

Davis, J. (1986). *Legislative law and process in a nutshell* (2nd ed.). St. Paul, MN: West Publishing.

Reynolds, W. L. (1991). *Judicial process in a nutshell* (2nd ed.). St. Paul, MN: West Publishing.

References

Alexander, K., & Alexander, M. D. (2002). *American public school law* (3rd ed.). St. Paul, MN: West Publishing.

Black, H. C., Nolan, J. R., & Nolan-Haley, J. M. (1990). *Black's law dictionary* (6th ed.). St. Paul, MN: West Publishing.

Bonner v. Alabama, 661 F.2d 1206 (11th Cir. 1981).

Cohen, M. L., Berring, R. C., & Olson, K. C. (1989). *How to find the law* (9th ed.). St. Paul, MN: West Publishing.

Daniel R. R. v. State Board of Education, 874 F.2d 1036 (5th Cir. 1989).

Elazar, D. J. (1984). Federalism. In *The guide to American law* (pp. 190–198). St. Paul, MN: West Publishing.

Elias, S., & Levinkind, S. (1992). *Legal research: How to find and understand the law* (3rd ed.). Berkeley, CA: Nolo Press.

Handicapped Children's Protection Act of 1986, Pub. L. No. 99-372. 20 U.S.C. § 1415.

Individuals with Disabilities Education Act, 20 U.S.C. § 1415(e) (1986).

Mills v. Board of Education, 348 F. Supp. 866 (D.D.C. 1972).

Pennsylvania Association of Retarded Citizens v. Commonwealth of Pennsylvania, 343 F. Supp. 279 (E.D. Pa. 1972).

Reynolds, W. L. (1991). *Judicial process in a nutshell* (2nd ed.). St. Paul, MN: West Publishing.

Smith v. Robinson, 468 U.S. 992 (1984).

Tucker, B. P., & Goldstein, B. A. (1992). *Legal rights of persons with disabilities: An analysis of federal law.* Horsham, PA: LRP Publications.

Valente, W. D., & Valente, C. (2005). *Law in the schools* (6th ed.). Upper Saddle River, NJ: Merrill/Prentice Hall.

CHAPTER TWO

Legal Research*

The material [on legal research] will not become meaningful or really useful to you . . . until you actually work through it. The great Zen koan of legal research is that you can't understand the materials without using them, and you can't use them very well without understanding them.

Johnson, Berring, & Woxland (1999, p. 126)

L egal research is the process of finding laws that govern activities in our society (Cohen & Olson, 2000). It involves finding statutes and regulations as well as cases that interpret them. It also involves consulting sources that explain and analyze the particular laws you find. Special education is governed by a specific set of rules and regulations at the national and state level. It is also among the most frequently litigated areas in education. The result is an extensive body of cases interpreting these rules and regulations. By accessing the law through legal research, educators will have a better understanding of the principles of law, the facts giving rise to these principles, and the application of those facts to situations they may encounter.

The purpose of this chapter is to describe the legal research process. Legal research requires the understanding of a variety of resources. These resources can be divided into three areas: primary sources, finding tools, and secondary materials. These resources differ in their legal authority. Some are controlling or mandatory, others are persuasive, and some are useful tools for finding still other controlling and persuasive materials. We will begin this chapter by explaining the primary sources: statutes, regulations, and case law. We will also discuss finding tools. Next, we will examine a few critical secondary sources, focusing on law reviews, legal journals, and loose-leaf services. We will end by presenting a strategy for conducting legal research.

---

*This chapter was written by Mitchell L. Yell, Ph.D., and Terrye Conroy J.D., M.L.I.S., of the University of South Carolina.

Primary Sources

Primary sources are actual statements of the law. There are three categories of primary source material: statutes or laws passed by either federal or state legislatures and signed into law, the regulations promulgated by administrative agencies to implement the statutes, and judicial decisions that interpret the statutes and regulations.

Enormous amounts of primary source materials available are issued chronologically rather than by subject. Resources used to locate these primary authorities are referred to as *finding tools*. Finding tools include the annotated codes, West's digests, and Shepard's citators.

Statutes and Regulations

Federal Statutes

Statutes are organized by topic and are published in a series of volumes called the *United States Code* (U.S.C.). The 50 numbered titles in the U.S.C. are divided into chapters and sections. Each title contains the statutes that cover a specific subject. For example, Title 20 contains education statutes, and the Individuals with Disabilities Education Act can be found in this title. Section 504 of the Rehabilitation Act can be found in Title 29, which contains labor statutes. The Americans with Disabilities Act (ADA) is in Title 42, which contains public health and welfare statutes. Some titles are published in one volume, while others have many volumes. A revised edition of the U.S.C. is issued every 6 years, with supplements issued during the interim years. Published by the U.S. Government Printing Office (GPO), the U.S.C. is considered the official version of federal statutes. The U.S.C. is now accessible on the GPO's website known as GPO Access at www.gpoaccess.gov/uscode; on the website of the Office of Law Revision Counsel of the U.S. House of Representatives at uscode.house.gov; and on Cornell Law School's Legal Information Institute's website at www.law.cornell.edu/uscode. Both the official print and Internet versions of the U.S.C. are unannotated.

There are two annotated versions of the *United States Code*. The first, published by West, a Thomson Company, is the *United States Code Annotated* (U.S.C.A.); the second is the *United States Code Service* (U.S.C.S.), published by LexisNexis, a trademark of Reed Elsevier Properties, Inc. The annotated code versions are useful because in addition to the actual text of the statutes, they contain information pertaining to each statute. For instance, the U.S.C.A. contains citations to the legislative history of each statute, cross-references to related statutes and regulations, research guides to other relevant resources published by West, and summaries of court cases that have interpreted each statute. The U.S.C.S. reprints the statutes and also examines relevant cases, provides citations to administrative materials, and includes references to secondary materials. Because the annotated versions of the U.S.C. have information that is more useful than simply the text of the statute, many researchers prefer to use the U.S.C.A. or U.S.C.S. rather than the official government code. Annotated codes are also updated more frequently than the official code.

Because federal statutes are frequently amended, it is important for the researcher to locate the most recent version. The annotated codes are published in hardcover editions, which are only reissued occasionally. In the back of each book, however, is a paper supplement called a pocket part that updates the hardcover book annually. It is important to check the pocket part to see if the statute being researched has been amended. When amendments and changes to federal statutes cannot be contained in only an annual pocket part, a separate softcover volume is issued (this volume sits next to the hardcover volume). Pocket parts only reprint the sections of the statute that have been changed (i.e., amended or repealed). If a particular section has not been changed, the reader is referred to the hardcover volume for the text of that section. It is also important to check the pocket part to the main volume for current cases interpreting the statute being researched. Although pocket parts are published annually, they cumulatively supplement the bound volumes, which may not be reprinted for some years. The annual pocket parts may also include references to current secondary sources, such as legal encyclopedias and law review articles, which analyze the statute being researched.

If the statute being researched is recent or currently pending in Congress, it will not be available in the annual pocket part. U.S.C.A is updated between pocket part publications via its Interim Pamphlet Service. West also publishes monthly its *United States Code Congressional and Administrative News* (USCCAN). LexisNexis updates its annual pocket parts for U.S.C.S. with the *U.S.C.S. Later Case and Statutory Service* and its monthly publication, *United States Code Service Advance*.

The text and summaries of current and pending federal legislation, as well as information on its status and history, is available through the Library of Congress's THOMAS website at thomas.loc.gov. Legislative documents may be searched on THOMAS by bill or public law number, keyword, subject, date, or sponsor. The House and Senate also maintain websites, which include information regarding pending legislation, at www.house.gov and www.senate.gov, respectively.

Several methods can be used to find federal statutes. The first method is to use the citation, the second is to use the popular name, and the third, when you only know the subject, is to use the annotated code indexes.

Finding a Statute by Citation. A reference to a primary law source is a citation. The citation tells where the law source is located. Citations are always written in standard form. Figure 2.1 is a citation for the Individuals with Disabilities Education Act.

The first number, 20, is the title number. The letters following the title number refer to the particular code; in this case, U.S.C. refers to the *United States Code*. The

Figure 2.1
Citation for the Individuals with Disabilities Education Act (Statute)

20 U.S.C. § 1401(20)

Title Number   United States Code   Section Number   Subsection numeral 1401 is the section number (§ is the symbol for section). In the U.S.C., the text of the IDEA begins at § 1400 and ends at § 1487. Title and section numbers will be constant in the three sources (e.g., the Individuals with Disabilities Education Act will appear in Title 20, §§ 1400–1487, in all three sources).

To locate federal statutes, find the maroon set of books labeled U.S.C. or U.S.C.A. or the black set of hardcover books labeled U.S.C.S. On the spine of the volumes, look for the title number (20). Below the title number on the spine of each volume is the subject of that title (Education) and section numbers contained in that volume. To find a statute with a citation to a particular title, section, and subsection, such as 20 U.S.C.A. § 1412(1), find the volume that contains the title (20) and section (1412) and turn to the subsection you need (1). The sections within each title are arranged numerically. Each volume of U.S.C., U.S.C.A., and U.S.C.S. includes a table of contents listing which subjects are covered by the various chapters within that title. The table of contents also has the beginning section number for each chapter. For instance, Chapter 33 of Title 20 addresses Education of Individuals with Disabilities and begins with Section 1400. Although the chapter number is not included in a citation for the U.S.C., it is useful for the researcher to know where a particular subject (chapter) is arranged within a certain title of the code.

Finding a Statute by Popular Name.   If the citation for a federal law is not available but the popular name (e.g., Individuals with Disabilities Education Act) is known, the statute can be found in the *Popular Name Table.* In most law libraries, the *Popular Name Table* is placed after the codes and provides the following information: the popular name, public law and statute at large numbers, date of passage, and the title and code section(s) where it was published in the U.S. Code. With this information, the researcher can locate the statute in U.S.C.A. or U.S.C.S.

Finding a Statute Using the Annotated Code Index.   If you know the subject of the statute but not the correct citation or its popular name, you may use the General Indexes to the annotated code to locate the statute. For example, if you did not know the citation and popular name for the Individuals with Disabilities Education Act, you could locate the General Index at the end of the U.S.C.S. and search under the topic "education" for terms such as "disabled persons," which would direct you to see "individuals with disabilities education," which would lead you to the Individuals with Disabilities Education Act. Every title of the annotated codes also has an index in the back of the final book in the series for that title. So if you happened to know that statutes relating to education were codified (arranged by subject) in Title 20 of the U.S.C., you could begin by searching the index at the end of that title in U.S.C.A. or U.S.C.S.

Once you find the statutes relevant to the legal issue at hand, you may wish to consult the annotations to both U.S.C.A. and U.S.C.S., if available, because the cases and secondary authorities included by each publisher differ. For instance, U.S.C.A. is known for including more case notes, while U.S.C.S. is said to focus more on administrative materials (Cohen & Olson, 2000).

State Statutes

Some states organize their statutes in volumes according to subject by name (e.g., education, health), while most states assign a title or chapter and section number to each subject, similar to the U.S. Code. Most collections of state statutes have indexes for all laws as well as for each subject. Citations for state statutes typically refer to the name, title, or chapter within which the statute is arranged, along with section numbers. State statutes, like federal statutes, are often changed. The hardcover volumes of state statutes are also updated by annual pocket parts, and some states publish interim pamphlets as well. State annotated codes usually include popular name tables along with other tables that cross-reference various information and resources.

All states now have the unannotated versions of their codes available on the Internet in some format. Many allow the researcher to search by keyword and to browse by title, chapter, or section. FindLaw provides links to the legislative websites for all states on its *Resources by Jurisdiction* page at www.findlaw.com/jurisdiction/.

Federal Regulations

Federal administrative agencies, such as the U.S. Department of Education, promulgate regulations to implement and enforce federal statutes. These regulations are published by the U.S. Government Printing Office in the *Federal Register,* issued daily, and the *Code of Federal Regulations* (C.F.R.). The C.F.R. is a multivolume set of paperbacks organized by subject, which is issued annually. Each of the 50 titles in the C.F.R. covers a general subject area. Titles in C.F.R. and U.S.C. do not always correspond. For example, the subject of Title 20 of the U.S.C. is education, but the subject of Title 20 of the C.F.R. is employee benefits. Regulations regarding education are found in Title 34. The C.F.R. provides, along with the text of the regulation, a reference to the statute that authorizes the regulation and the date of its publication in the *Federal Register.* Both annotated versions of the U.S.C. provide cross references to regulations. The *Index and Finding Aids* volume with the C.F.R. contains a "Parallel Table of Authorities and Rules," allowing the researcher to find regulations enacted pursuant to a particular statute.

Finding Regulations by Citation.   Regulations, like statutes, also have citations. The citation tells where the regulation is located. Citations are always written in a standard form. Figure 2.2 is a citation for the Individuals with Disabilities Education Act regulations.

The first number, 34, is the title number. C.F.R. stands for the *Code of Federal Regulations.* The numerals 300.1–300.756 refer to the section numbers of the IDEA regulations. To locate this federal regulation in a law library, find the paperbound set of books labeled *Code of Federal Regulations.* Every year the colors of the C.F.R. volumes are changed. The title number (34) can be found on the spine of the volumes. Section numbers of regulations contained in the volume are listed under the title number. The print versions of the *Federal Register* and C.F.R. are

Figure 2.2
Citation for the
Individuals with
Disabilities Education
Act (Regulations)

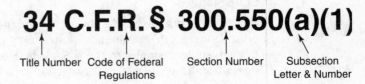

Title Number   Code of Federal   Section Number   Subsection
                    Regulations   Letter & Number

now available through the U.S. Government Printing Office on its GPO Access website at www.gpoaccess.gov/, which allows the researcher to retrieve a regulation by citation.

Finding Regulations by Subject.   If the citation for a federal regulation is unavailable, consult the annually revised *Index and Finding Aids* volume of the C.F.R. If the title in which the regulation will appear is known (e.g., education is Title 34), the "Table of C.F.R. Titles and Chapters" at the end of each volume of C.F.R. can be used to locate a particular regulation. The GPO Access version of C.F.R. at www.gpoaccess.gov/cfr allows the researcher to find regulations by subject through a keyword search of the entire C.F.R. or by searching an individual title.

Updating Regulations.   When the annual C.F.R. is published, the regulations in the volume are up to date. Like statutes, however, regulations are often changed in some way. It is important to consult current regulations. To determine if the regulation is up to date, consult the most recent issue of the monthly pamphlet entitled *Code of Federal Regulations List of Sections Affected* (abbreviated C.F.R.-L.S.A.). In the latest L.S.A., find the title and section number of the regulation of interest to see if there have been any recent changes. If changes have been made to the regulation, the affected sections will be noted. For changes made during the days following the latest available monthly L.S.A., check the back pages of the most recent Federal Register for the current month. The online version of L.S.A. is accessible from GPO Access's C.F.R. webpage at www.gpoaccess.gov/cfr. Its *Current List of C.F.R. Parts Affected* includes daily changes from the *Federal Register* since the last monthly issue of L.S.A.

GPO Access now also offers a prototype (unofficial) Electronic Code of Federal Regulations, or *e-CFR*, which incorporates amendments from the *Federal Register* within days at www.gpoaccess.gov/ecfr.

State Regulations

State regulations can be difficult to locate. Many states have administrative codes that may be located by consulting a general index. Usually, special education regulations will be subsumed under the broader category of education regulations. This is because special education regulations are typically promulgated by the state's department of education. In many states, regulations are published in loose-leaf form by the promulgating agency. Law libraries may carry only the regulations for their state. States publish proposed and final regulations in weekly, biweekly, and monthly registers. Unannotated state regulations and registers are also available on state government websites and can generally be browsed by section, chapter, or title and searched by keyword. Links to state regulations available online are also included on FindLaw's *Resources by Jurisdiction* page at www.findlaw.com/jurisdiction/. The Great Lakes Area Regional Resource Center (GLARRC) maintains the National State Policy Database, a collaborative project of the National Association of State Directors of Special Education and the Regional Resource and Federal Centers Network, on its website (128.146.206.233/resources/NSPD.cfm) where the special education rules and regulations from all 50 states are available. The GLARRC, however, cautions users that these files are not official legal files and that state educational agencies should be contacted to obtain official copies of each state's regulations.

Case Law

An important part of legal research is finding cases that interpret statutes and regulations. Cases are published in volumes in accordance with the level of court where they are decided for federal courts, and by geographical regions and levels of courts for state courts. These volumes, called *reporters*, are available in all law libraries.

Federal Cases

There are no official publications by the government for federal district or appellate court decisions. With the exception of electronic databases, the only source for decisions of the lower federal courts is the reporters published by West. West publishes federal cases in accordance with the level at which each case is decided. The published decisions of the U.S. District Courts are collected in a reporter called the *Federal Supplement* (abbreviated F.Supp.). West began publication of the *Federal Supplement, Second Series* (abbreviated F. Supp. 2d) in 1998 after the 999th hardcover volume of the *Federal Supplement.* There are currently more than 300 volumes of F.Supp. 2d. Decisions by the U.S. District Courts are appealed to federal courts of appeals, which are organized by circuits. Published decisions by the U.S. Courts of Appeals are collected in a series of hardcover volumes called the *Federal Reporter.* In 1924 the *Federal Reporter, Second Series,* began. This series (abbreviated F.2d) ran for 999 volumes. In 1994, volume one of the *Federal Reporter, Third Series* (abbreviated F.3d), was issued. There are currently 375 bound volumes of F.3d.

Appeals from the U.S. Courts of Appeals and from state courts of last resort are to the United States Supreme Court. The complete decisions of the U.S. Supreme Court are published in three different sources. The *United States Reports* (abbreviated U.S.) is the official report because it is printed by the U.S. government. The reporter published by West is called the *Supreme Court Reporter* (abbreviated S.Ct.). A third reporter, *United States Supreme Court Reports, Lawyers' Edition* (abbreviated L.Ed.), is published by Matthew Bender, a member of the LexisNexis Group.

The three reporters contain the same cases, but the latter two unofficial publications include editorial enhancements (e.g., synopses, related cases, and historical information). The *Supreme Court Reporter* is part of West's complete legal reference system called the National Reporter System, which arranges headnotes at the beginning of cases by topic and key number, while *United States Supreme Court Reports, Lawyers' Edition* provides editorial comments about each case and annotations referring to other cases on the same subject. Table 2.1 lists abbreviations for the federal court reporters.

There is a lag between the date that the case is decided and the publication of the case in a hardcover reporter. During this lag period, new cases can be found in weekly updates called *advance sheets*. Advance sheets may be found on the shelf at the end of the hardcover reporters.

The most recent slip opinions may also be kept in the reference section of law libraries located within that particular court's jurisdiction. Researchers who wish to obtain a copy of a court's written opinion as quickly as possible can obtain a copy directly from that court. The availability of the Internet, however, has made opinions accessible from official federal court websites on a daily basis. The Federal Judiciary's website at www.uscourts.gov provides links to the U.S. Supreme Court as well as all U.S. Courts of Appeals and District Courts. In fact, the U.S. Supreme Court website at www.supremecourtus.gov not only publishes slip opinions, but also includes transcripts of oral arguments within two weeks after the attorneys appear before the court. In addition, Northwestern University's Oyez Project maintains a website at www.oyez.org/oyez/frontpage, which provides audio files for listening to oral arguments made before the Supreme Court; and FindLaw, which includes petitions and briefs submitted to the Court along with links to lower court decisions on its site at supreme.lp.findlaw.com.

Table 2.1
Federal Court Reporters

Name	Coverage	Abbreviation
Federal Supplement	U.S. District Courts	F. Supp.
Federal Supplement, Second Series (1998–present)	U.S. District Courts	F. Supp.2d
Federal Reporter, Second Series (1924–94)	U.S. Courts of Appeals	F.2d
Federal Reporter, Third Series (1994–present)	U.S. Courts of Appeals	F.3d
United States Reports	U.S. Supreme Court	U.S.
Supreme Court Reporter	U.S. Supreme Court	S.Ct
United States Supreme Court Reports, Lawyers' Edition	U.S. Supreme Court	L.Ed

State Cases

The published appellate court decisions (intermediate and court of last resort) for each state can be found in that state's official report. Some appellate court cases can be found in regional reporters published by West. Many states have discontinued their official versions and rely solely upon West's regional reporters to publish their appellate court decisions.

The published appellate cases for each state and the District of Columbia can all be found in West's regional reporters. West divides the country into seven regions and publishes the appellate decisions of certain states together. Table 2.2 lists the states as they are arranged by region in West's National Reporter System. Separate reporters are published for California and New York. Advance sheets containing recent cases are also provided for the regional reporters between publication of the hardcover volumes. State court slip opinions can be found in local law libraries and directly from the state appellate courts. State appellate courts are also beginning to publish their slip opinions immediately on their judicial websites.

The researcher should keep in mind, however, that advance copies of federal and state court decisions will not include the editorial enhancements (e.g., synopses and headnotes with topics and key numbers) that the bound volumes of West's National Reporter System provides.

How to Find Cases

Cases are published chronologically rather than according to subject. A typical law library may contain more than 4 million cases. Without a means of accessing these cases, research would be a hopeless endeavor.

Table 2.2
West's Regional Reporters

Reporter	States
Atlantic Reporter	CT, DC, DE, MD, ME, NH, NJ, PA, RI, VT
Northeastern Reporter	IL, IN, MA, NY, OH
Northwestern Reporter	IA, MI, MN, NE, ND, SD, WI
Pacific Reporter	AK, AZ, CA, CO, HI, ID, KS, MT, NM, NV, OK, OR, UT, WA, WY
Southeastern Reporter	GA, NC, SC, VA, WV
Southern Reporter	AL, FL, LA, MS
Southwestern Reporter	AR, KY, MO, TN, TX
New York Supplement	New York Court of Appeals, Appellate Division of the State Supreme Court, and additional state courts (The highest court in NY is the Court of Appeals, the intermediate court is called the Supreme Court)
California Reporter	California Supreme Court and Intermediate Appellate Courts

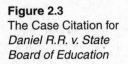

Figure 2.3
The Case Citation for
*Daniel R.R. v. State
Board of Education*

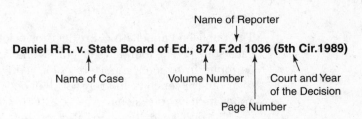

Finding Cases by Citation.   Every published decision has a citation that makes it possible to locate it in the reporters. Case citations follow a standard format. Figure 2.3 is a citation to a special education case.

The first item in the citation is the name of the case (*Daniel R.R. v. State Board of Education*). The name of the case will usually be two names separated by "v." (versus). The first name will be the plaintiff or the appellant. The plaintiff is the party that initially brought the suit seeking a remedy from the court. In the case of an appeal, the appellant is the party that appeals the decision of the lower court, whether the party was the original plaintiff or the defendant. The plaintiff in this case was Daniel R.R. The second name is that of the defendant (the party who has been sued and is responding to the complaint of the plaintiff). If the defendant appeals the ruling of the lower court, in most instances that party will become the appellant and in some states will then be listed first. The defendant in this case was the State Board of Education of Texas. Cases sometimes only have a phrase and one name, such as *In Re Gary B.* The phrase *in re* is Latin and means "in the matter of." Usually this means there was no opponent in the court proceeding.

The second element in the citation is the volume number of the reporter in which the case appears. The volume number of the *Daniel R.R.* case is 874. Volumes in reporters are numbered consecutively.

The third element of the citation is the name of the reporter. The reporter in which *Daniel R.R.* can be found is the *Federal Reporter, Second Series*, written as F.2d (called "Fed second"). F.2d contains cases heard by the U.S. Courts of Appeals; therefore, *Daniel R.R.* was heard by an appellate court.

The fourth element of the citation will be the page number on which the case starts. Thus, the *Daniel R.R.* decision can be found on page 1036 of volume 874 of the F.2d reporter.

The final element of the citation is the year of the decision. In researching cases, it is important to include the most recent ones. In federal cases, the level of court deciding the case will appear along with the year of the decision. *Daniel R.R.* was decided by the U.S. Court of Appeals for the Fifth Circuit in 1989. If the decision is from a federal district court, the state and judicial district of the case will be included. For example, in the case *Hayes v. Unified School District,* 699 F. Supp. 1519 (D. Kan. 1987), the court was the U.S. District Court for the District of Kansas. In the case *Espino v. Besteiro,* 520 F. Supp. 905 (S.D. Tex. 1981), the court was the U.S. District

Court for the Southern District of Texas. If cases can be found in more than one reporter, the names of all the reporters may be listed in this section of the citation. For example, a case decided by U.S. Supreme Court may appear in the three reporters (U.S., S.Ct., and L.Ed.) and all three "parallel" cites may be included in its citation. The landmark decision *Brown v. Board of Education* is often cited to include all three reporters as follows: *Brown v. Board of Education,* 347 U.S. 483, 74 S.Ct. 686, 98 L.Ed. 873 (1954).

Finding Tools

Several finding tools are designed to help the researcher locate primary sources. Finding tools include annotated codes, digests, indexes, legal encyclopedias, *American Law Reports (ALR)* annotations, and Shepard's citators. Because a comprehensive review of finding tools is beyond the scope of this chapter, only three such tools will be examined here: the annotated codes, West's digest system, and Shepard's citators.

The Annotated Codes

The annotated versions of the *United States Code—United States Code Annotated* (U.S.C.A.) and *United States Code Service* (U.S.C.S.)—are powerful research tools. In addition to the statutory language contained in the U.S.C., the annotated codes contain a wealth of information useful to the researcher. For example, West's U.S.C.A. contains information on legislative history; cross references to other federal statutes and regulations; references to the American Digest System topics and key numbers; citations to West's legal encyclopedias (*American Jurisprudence 2d* (Am Jur 2d) and *Corpus Juris Secundum* (CJS)) as well as other secondary sources, such as law reviews; guides to finding pertinent information in Westlaw's electronic database; and notes of relevant court decisions. The "Notes of Decisions" following the statutes in U.S.C.A. consist of abstracts of relevant cases that have interpreted the statute. Because judicial interpretations are crucial in understanding the law, the abstracts can be the most useful part of the annotated codes (Cohen, Berring, & Olson, 1989). The most current annotations are contained in the pocket parts to each volume and the interim pamphlets that update the annotated codes discussed earlier in this chapter.

The West Digest System

Another useful tool for locating cases is West's digest system. For each set of West's reporters there is a corresponding digest. Table 2.3 contains a partial list of West's digests and their coverage. West's digests are alphabetical indexes to case law, arranging headnotes of cases by topics and key numbers. To access the West digest system, the researcher must understand the topic and key number system.

Table 2.3
West's Digest System

Digest	Coverage
General Digest	Headnotes for all current cases in West's National Reporter System.
Decennial Digest	10 years' accumulation of headnotes from the General Digest (in two parts (5 years each) since 1976)
Modern Federal Practice Digest	Cases prior to 1961
Federal Practice Digest 2d	Covers all federal cases between 1961 and 1975 (closed)
Federal Practice Digest 3d	Covers all federal cases between 1975 and 1992 (closed)
Federal Practice Digest 4th	Covers all federal cases after 1992
U.S. Supreme Court Digest	All U.S. Supreme Court cases
State and Regional Digests	Most state cases are also included in both state and regional digests
Specialized Digests	Such as West's *Education Law Digest* covering cases reported in the *Education Law Reporter*

The West Topic and Key Number System

A case published in a West reporter follows a standard format. The first item on the page is the title of the case. For example, on the first page of the *Daniel R.R. v. State Board of Education* written opinion, Daniel R.R. is listed as the plaintiff-appellant and the Board of Education is the defendant. Following the title is the docket number (No. 88-1279), the court in which the case was heard (U.S. Court of Appeals for the Fifth Circuit), and the date the court's decision was handed down (June 12, 1989). Following this information is the synopsis of the case, written by an editor at West.

Next is the headnote section. A headnote is a one-sentence summary of a legal issue arising in a case. The headnotes are not part of the judicial opinion but are an editorial enhancement. Editors at West review judicial opinions and write the headnotes by isolating every individual issue of law that appears in the decision. Often opinions contain a number of legal issues and will, therefore, have a number of headnotes. *Daniel R.R.* contains 16 headnotes. Each headnote will appear as a boldface number (e.g., 1), followed by a topic (e.g., Federal Courts), an illustration of a key, and a number (e.g., 13.30).

The first numbers (e.g., the boldface 1) are in order and are used as a table of contents to the case. Numbers corresponding to the headnotes appear in the text of the case at the point where that legal issue is discussed. The term or phrase after the number (e.g., Federal Courts) is the topic where West has classified that legal issue.

Following the key illustration is the key number (13.30), a subsection of the topic. To find out what the key number stands for, you must consult a digest.

The key number system was designed by John Mallory and adopted by John West, who founded West Publishing Company in the late 1800s. At the time, cases were being published with no systematic way of accessing information. West developed a uniform classification system for legal issues raised in all published cases. Currently, the system consists of 450 topics and numerous subtopics, all classified under seven main divisions of law. Each of these topics is further broken down into subtopics, representing points of law. Each point of law is assigned a key number.

In the digests, every headnote, consisting of a topic phrase and number, is grouped with similar legal topics from every published case that deals with that issue. For example, number 2 of the 16 headnotes in *Daniel R.R.* is *Schools 148(2)*. "Schools" is a topic area (number 345 of West's 450 topic areas). The number 148 refers to a subtopic titled "Nature of Right to Instruction in General." The number in parentheses refers to a subtopic of 148, in this case 2, which is titled "Handicapped Children and Special Services Therefore." Depending on which digest is used, every headnote numbered 148(2) from every published state or federal case can be located quickly. The key number before the headnote (e.g., *148(2)*) will enable the researcher to locate every published state or federal case addressing instruction and special services for children with disabilities.

Using the Digest System

A number of different digests are published by West. Each digest contains headnotes for certain courts and is designed to fill a different need. The largest digests are the *Decennials* and the *General Digest*. This digest group, the *American Digest System,* contains headnotes from the published cases from all state and federal courts. The *Decennials* and the *General Digest* have been subdivided into smaller, more specific, digests (e.g., state, regional, federal, and specialized digests).

When using the digests to find cases, it is preferable to begin with the one that is narrowest in scope. For example, if the researcher is only interested in federal cases, the *Federal Practice Digests* should be consulted. The *Federal Practice Digests* also contain U.S. Supreme Court cases. If interested in U.S. Supreme Court cases only, the researcher should consult West's *U.S. Supreme Court Digest.*

Special educators will usually be interested in federal special education cases, so the appropriate digest will be the *Federal Practice Digest.* It contains headnotes from every case appearing in West's *Supreme Court Reporter* (S.Ct.), *Federal Reporters* (F.2d and F.3d), and *Federal Supplement* (F. Supp. and F. Supp.2d).

To access the digest system, the researcher will need to determine the relevant topic and key number(s). In the digests, the headnotes under each topic and key number are arranged by jurisdictions in chronological order, beginning with the most recent. The key number system is uniform in every digest West publishes.

The easiest way to find cases using a digest is to begin with headnotes from a case on point. In Figure 2.4 the *Daniel R.R. v. State Board of Education* decision is used as an example of how to access West's digest system using the topic and key

Figure 2.4
Using West's Digest System

Step 1: Locate the *Daniel R.R.* decision at 874 F.2d 1036 in the F.2d reporter.

Step 2: Read the headnotes at the beginning of the case and note the topic and key numbers. If the researcher is interested in the issue of law raised in headnote 2, locate Schools 148(2) in the appropriate digest.

Step 3: Whenever possible use the more specific digest; therefore, locate the *Federal Practice Digest* in the library.

Step 4: Locate the volume of the *Fourth Series* that contains the topic Schools, key number 148(2). The correct volume number is 84.

Step 5: Turn to the page that begins with headnotes that are keyed 148(2). Headnotes with the key number 148(2) from all federal court cases will be listed by jurisdictions in reverse chronological order (most recent first).

Step 6: Check the pocket part and white softcover supplements for the most recent cases.

numbers from a relevant case. Whatever case is used, the method of using the West digest system will be the same.

Cases can also be located by using the descriptive word indexes, the table of cases volumes, and the words and phrases volumes, all located at the end of each digest set, as well as by using the topical outlines at the beginning of each topic within the digest volumes. The digests also contain pocket parts and softcover supplements for recent headnotes.

Shepard's Citators

After a case of interest has been located, it is critical that the case be currently valid. That is, does it still have precedential value, or has it been overruled or reversed? Shepard's citators help researchers expand their research. A search of a case in Shepard's will direct the researcher to other cases and secondary authorities that have cited in it. The process of "shepardizing"® to find additional resources or to determine if a case has been reversed, overruled, or modified is an essential part of legal research. Shepard's citators are also available for other primary authorities (e.g., statutes and regulations) as well as for many secondary sources.

Shepard's citators were, until recently, the only option available to legal researchers. Although Shepard's remains the only print legal citator system, it now faces competition online. In 1997, LexisNexis, a Reed Elsevier trademark, purchased the Shepard's company. Shepard's citators then became available on the LexisNexis online database and ceased being accessible through Westlaw. In response, West Group introduced its own citator system, *KeyCite,* available exclusively online, which performs the same verification and research functions as Shepard's. Researchers should, nevertheless, know how to shepardize® cases in print because LexisNexis and West-law are online databases accessible by subscription only.

Once the citation for the case to be shepardized® is located in Shepard's, the citator lists every case that has referred to it. Shepard's also indicates whether the case was affirmed, modified, or reversed by a higher court and helps the researcher find other cases that have dealt with similar issues. For example, if the researcher is interested in least restrictive environment cases and has the citation for *Daniel R.R. v. State Board of Education*, *Shepard's Federal Citations* could be used to locate other federal decisions that have cited *Daniel R.R.* Because *Daniel R.R.* has proven to be a persuasive case, most subsequent federal cases on least restrictive environment have cited it. However, other least restrictive environment cases that do not cite *Daniel R.R.* will not be listed. To find those cases, the researcher would need to consult West's *Federal Practice Digest* using the topic and key numbers found in *Daniel R.R.* Another difficulty in using Shepard's is that every case, important or not, that cites the case being researched will be listed. This can result in numerous listings, especially for landmark cases that are cited frequently.

Another potential problem in using Shepard's is that it does not cumulate; that is, a volume of Shepard's will only cite cases covered by that particular volume year and will not include cases decided prior to that date. Therefore, the researcher may need to consult a series of Shepard's citators for full coverage of a case. For instance, there are hardcover volumes of *Shepard's Federal Citations* for every year since 1999. Thus, it is important that researchers look on the spine of each volume to see what years are covered. Furthermore, researchers consult the front cover of the soft-bound pamphlets under "WHAT YOUR LIBRARY SHOULD CONTAIN" to ensure all necessary volumes have been checked.

Law libraries carry many volumes of Shepard's citators. They can be distinguished by their dark maroon bindings. Separate gold and red softcover pamphlets update the hardcover volumes. *Shepard's Citations* are published for all state jurisdictions, for federal cases, and for U.S. Supreme Court cases. There are also Shepard's citators for regional reporters, state and federal statutes, federal administrative decisions, federal regulations, and law reviews. Shepard's case citators are organized according to the reporters that publish the cases. The first page of each Shepard's citator identifies the specific court reporters covered in that volume. Table 2.4 is a partial list of Shepard's citators.

Shepard's citators consist of page after page of columns of numbers and symbols. Figure 2.5 is a partial column of cases citing *Daniel R.R. v. State Board of Education* that appears in a 1995 bound volume of *Shepard's Federal Citations*. When shepardizing® cases, use the procedure shown in Figure 2.6 where *Daniel R.R. v. State Board of Education*, 874 F.2d 1036 (5th Cir. 1989), is used as an example. Shepard's groups the citing cases according to the circuit in which they were decided. For example, in Figure 2.5 the following citation appears under the *Daniel R.R.* case: f995F2d1207. This particular citation (from the Third Circuit) is to a page in *Oberti v. Board of Education* (1993). The citations in Shepard's include the volume number

Table 2.4
Shepard's Citators

Citator	Subject
Shepard's United States Citations	U.S. Supreme Court decisions
Shepard's Federal Citations	U.S. Courts of Appeals and District Court decisions
Shepard's United States Administrative Citations	Federal Administrative Decisions
Shepard's Code of Federal Regulations Citations	Code of Federal Regulations
Shepard's Law Review Citations	Selected Law Reviews
Shepard's Federal Statutes Citations	United States Code, U.S. Constitution, and Federal Court Rules
Shepard's state citators	Each of the 50 states, D.C., and Puerto Rico
Shepard's regional citators	Each series in the National Reporter Series, New York & California

in which the case appears (e.g., 995), the reporter (e.g., F.2d), and the page number of the citation (e.g., 1207). Shepard's citators may have numerous references to a particular citing case. In Figure 2.5 the *Oberti* case (995F2d) is listed several times. This is because the *Daniel R.R.* case is cited on a number of different pages of the *Oberti* decision.

The letters referred to in Steps 6 and 7 in Figure 2.6 represent the code that Shepard's has developed to give the researcher additional information. The letters and their meanings can be found at the beginning of every Shepard's volume. These abbreviations indicate the case's history and treatment. A few of the notations are listed in Table 2.5. The use of these notations is important in determining if the case is still good authority.

In the 1995 volume of *Shepard's Federal Citations,* the following citing case appears under the *Daniel R.R.* case: f933F2d1290. The *f* means that the citing case followed the *Daniel R.R.* decision. If no letters are present, it usually means that the case was cited but was not key to the decision of the citing case.

Shepard's gives the researcher the citation for every case that has cited the case of interest. However, cases usually deal with more than one legal issue. In a West reporter, the text of the case is preceded by the numbered headnotes corresponding to the issues addressed in that case. Some of the legal issues discussed in the case and written in a headnote may not be of interest to the researcher. For example, headnote 1 in *Daniel R.R.* concerns the issue of mootness, and headnote 16 concerns federal civil procedure. Headnote 4 deals with the court's interpretation of the continuum of alternative placements, and headnote 11 concerns the test the *Daniel R.R.*

Figure 2.5
A partial column of
cases from Shepard's

> Daniel R.R. v.
> Texas Board
> of Education
> 1989
>
> Cir. 1
> d 771 FS^{1}4
>   807 FS7864
>   807 FS14871
>
> Cir. 2
> 801FS^{11}171
> 801FS^{7}1173
> 801FS^{4}1176
> 801FS^{14}1178
> 839FS^{7}981
> 839FS^{11}982
> 839FS^{14}983
> 839FS^{15}983
> f 839FS987
>   839FS^{8}988
> f 839FS13989
>
> Cir. 3
> f 995F2d1207
>   995F2d^{1}1213
>   995F2d^{11}1215
>   995F2d^{13}1216
> d 995F2d^{12}1223

court used to determine if the school had complied with the IDEA's least restrictive environment principle. Cases that cite headnotes 4 and 11 would be of greater interest to researchers investigating least restrictive environment cases than would cases that cite headnotes 1 and 16 of the *Daniel R.R.* decision. Shepard's identifies the specific legal issues from *Daniel R.R.* discussed in the citing case by headnote. The superscript numbers to the right of the reporter (e.g., F2d) of the citing case refer to the headnotes of the case that is being shepardized®. For example, the citation 933F2d121290 means that on page 1290 the citing case discusses the issue identified in the 12th headnote of the *Daniel R.R.* decision.

Figure 2.6
Shepardizing® a Case

Step 1: Identify the citation of the case being shepardized®. The citation for *Daniel R.R.* is 874 F.2d 1036 (5th Cir. 1989). The parts of the citation needed for shepardizing are the volume number (874), the reporter (Federal Reporter, 2d Series), and the page number (1036). The name of the case is not required when shepardizing®.

Step 2: Find the volume that covers the reporter listed in the citation. The reporter used in *Daniel R.R.* was F.2d; therefore, the appropriate title will be *Shepard's Federal Citations.*

Step 3: Select the volume or volumes that contain citations for cases decided after the case being shepardized (1989). In addition to using the hardcover volumes, check the paperback pamphlets.

Step 4: Find the volume number of the case (i.e., 874 for *Daniel R.R.*) in Shepard's at the top corner of the page in bold type. Volume 874 will be listed in Shepard's as "**Vol 874.**"

Step 5: Under the volume, locate the page number of the case. The page number that is in the *Daniel R.R.* citation is 1036. Find 1036 in bold print. Page 1036 will be listed in Shepard's as "**-1036-**". Cases listed under -1036- have cited the *Daniel R.R.* decision.

Step 6: For information on whether the citation is worth reviewing, use the letters to the left of the citation. (e.g., *f* for followed, *e* for explained)

Step 7: Look specifically for letters such as *o* (overruled) and *r* (reversed) that affect the validity of the case being shepardized®.

Step 8: Notice the raised numbers to the right of the reporter abbreviation of each case cited, which represent the various headnotes of the *Daniel R.R.* case and the issues they address.

Step 9: Shepardize® all potentially useful cases in the appropriate Shepard's

As mentioned previously, Shepard's citators are also available electronically on LexisNexis, and KeyCite's citator system is available online through Westlaw. Electronic citators have distinct advantages over Shepard's citators in print. All citations are compiled in one database, thus eliminating the need to consult several bound volumes and paperback pamphlets. It is also unnecessary to consult more than one citator because all state, regional, and federal citations are combined. New cases are added daily and case names are included with each citation. Results can be narrowed by the researcher in several ways, to include by Circuit, headnote, treatment, and search terms. Both electronic citators have developed a system of symbols rather than abbreviations and the primary and secondary sources cited are hyperlinked for access within each of the databases.

Table 2.5
Shepard's Notations

Notation	Definition
A	Statutes
a	Case affirmed or adhered to on appeal
c	Reasoning of the decision is criticized
f	Case cited as controlling authority (followed)
o	Ruling in the case is overruled
r	Decision reversed on appeal
US cert denied	Certiorari was denied by U.S. Supreme Court

Secondary Sources

Secondary sources are materials that describe and explain the law. Because secondary materials are unofficial (i.e., not actual statements of law), they have no formal authority. They may, however, have significant persuasive authority.

In conducting legal research, it is often easier to begin with secondary sources. Secondary sources have two primary functions: They provide citations to primary source material (in this function they serve as finding tools), and they introduce the researcher to a particular area of the law by explaining the issues involved. Many secondary sources of information are available, including legal encyclopedias such as *Corpus Juris Secundum* and *American Jurisprudence 2d,* legal newspapers such as the *National Law Journal* and the *Legal Times,* legal periodicals and law reviews, loose-leaf services, and Internet resources. The following discussion will center on the secondary source materials that may be of greatest use to the educator: law reviews and loose-leaf services. Secondary sources are fully searchable through electronic databases such as Westlaw and LexisNexis, which are discussed more fully later in this section. Internet resources for both primary and secondary materials will be addressed in Chapter 3.

Legal Periodicals and Law Reviews

Because of their extensive coverage and footnoting to primary authorities and other secondary sources, legal periodicals, particularly academic law reviews, can be the best place to begin researching a legal issue (Berring & Edinger, 1999). It is not unusual to encounter pages in law review articles containing just a few lines of commentary and the rest footnotes, making them excellent case-finding tools. All accredited law schools in the United States produce law reviews. Law reviews are periodicals that contain articles on legal developments, legal issues, historical research, and empirical studies. Law reviews are usually edited by law students and include lengthy articles written by law professors, scholars, and practitioners along with shorter notes and comments authored by law students. Law review articles are often cited by legal scholars as well as by the courts and can have great persuasive authority. Student notes and comments, while not as prestigious, can be helpful sources for legal research.

Many law schools publish one or more specialized academic journals in addition to general law reviews. One example is the *Journal of Law & Education,* edited by the University of South Carolina School of Law and the University of Louisville's Louis D. Brandeis School of Law.

The H.W. Wilson Company publishes the *Index to Legal Periodicals* (ILP), which indexes several hundred legal periodicals dating back to 1908. Articles are indexed by author and subject. Each volume also includes alphabetical tables of cases and statutes. It is published monthly in paperback, except September, with a bound cumulative volume issued each year. H. W. Wilson also produces a CD-ROM version for information after 1981, but is most conveniently researched online through Wilson Web and to subscribers through Westlaw and LexisNexis.

Gale, a Thomson Corporation, publishes an index to legal materials called *Current Law Index* (CLI). This comprehensive index lists more than 800 general and specialty law journals from the United States, the United Kingdom, Ireland, Australia, and New Zealand. Articles are indexed by author/title and subject. Additionally, each volume of CLI contains alphabetical tables of cases and statutes. *Current Law Index* is available online as LegalTrac, which is part of Gale's InfoTrac system and is available through subscription on Westlaw and LexisNexis as *Legal Resources Index.* Information Access Corporation began printing CLI in 1980, so it is not possible to search for cases before that date.

Other online databases are available to university faculty and students using legal periodicals to research particular legal issues. LexisNexis provides abstracts and full text articles from more than 200 law reviews and legal journals (from 1989) to universities through its LexisNexis Academic database. For older articles not available on LexisNexis Academic, researchers can now consult Hein Online. Hein Online began in 2000 and is a growing digitized database of more than 500 journals from their inception. Created by William S. Hein & Co., Inc., in conjunction with Cornell University Information Technologies, it provides researchers with exact images of the earliest legal periodicals and other legal classics. Researchers may retrieve an article by citation, browse the issues of a particular journal, or search by author or full text via keywords and phrases.

Many law reviews across the country are now maintaining a web presence, and a growing number are including the full text of articles from recent issues on their websites. The U.S. Law Library of Congress, as part of its Guide to Law Online, maintains a website at www.loc.gov/law/guide/lawreviews.html, which includes links to electronic law journals as well as links to websites that list law reviews by law school and by subject.

Shepard's citators can be used to find journal articles that cite a particular case or statute and to shepardize® law review articles. The citators for each jurisdiction include select law reviews as part of their citing references. Shepard's also produces *Shepard's Law Review Citations,* which contains citations to articles from more than 150 law reviews, as referenced in other law reviews and in decisions of the federal and state courts.

Loose-Leaf Services

Loose-leaf services may contain analysis of legal issues and reprints of primary source material in specific subject areas. A loose-leaf service, therefore, may serve as both a finding tool for primary authorities and as a secondary source.

A loose-leaf service is a publication that is issued in a binder with removable pages. The publisher monitors legal developments in the subject area the service covers and regularly issues new pages to keep the publication current. The primary advantages of loose-leaf services are that the information is current (updated frequently) and that much of the information needed to conduct research on a particular topic has already been compiled for the researcher. Loose-leaf services may also include authorities not published in West's National Reporter System, such as decisions of trial courts and state and federal administrative agencies. There are two types of loose-leaf services: the newsletter and the interfiled formats.

Newsletter Loose-Leaf Services

In this format, a newsletter is issued regularly and added to the end of the binder. Often the newsletter monitors current information from a variety of sources. Newly released material does not replace but rather supplements the older material in the newsletter format. Examples of special education loose-leaf services that use the newsletter format are the *Individuals with Disabilities Education Law Report* (IDELR) and *The Special Educator* (TSE), published by LRP publications (www.lrp.com), and the *IEP Team Trainer* and the *IDEA Compliance Insider,* published by Brownstone Publications (www.brownstone.com).

Interfiled Loose-Leaf Services

In the interfiled format, new pages are sent frequently for insertion into the binder. The new pages are interfiled and the old pages are discarded. The interfiled format, therefore, is constantly being edited to reflect legal developments. Interfiled special education loose-leaf services include *Special Education Law and Litigation Treatise* and *Section 504, the ADA and the Schools,* both published by LRP Publications.

No two loose-leaf services are the same; therefore, the key to using such a valuable service for legal research is to read the instructions at the beginning of the particular publication used and to take advantage of its finding aids and indexing system.

Computers and Legal Research

Legal research is rapidly becoming computerized. The two primary computer-assisted legal research (CALR) systems are West's Westlaw system and Reed Elsevier's Lexis-Nexis. Two primary advantages of these systems are the enormous amounts of information they contain and the speed with which the legal researcher can access their databases and navigate between them. Westlaw and LexisNexis are very current, and their databases are updated constantly. Both systems contain full libraries of information, including cases from all jurisdictions, statutes, regulations, and administrative decisions, as well as a variety of finding tools and secondary source materials. Westlaw and Lexis also include table of contents and browse features that simplify searching within particular databases. Another key benefit of electronic research is the ease with which the researcher can move from one primary or secondary source to another through hypertext links to materials cited within the various documents. CALR, however, does not replace traditional legal research. Rather, it is used most effectively in combination with the printed resources available in the law library.

The Westlaw and LexisNexis systems are organized into distinct databases. To search Westlaw or LexisNexis, researchers specify the database they wish to search (e.g., U.S. Supreme Court decisions), then enter specific keywords designed to retrieve the desired information. Researchers can also use electronic systems to retrieve statutes, regulations, cases, and secondary materials by citation.

The primary difference between traditional legal research and computerized research is full-text keyword searching. In keyword searching, the researcher determines the keywords that are likely to be used in the document (e.g., statute or case) needed and uses them to call up the information.

In using the Westlaw or LexisNexis systems, the researcher first chooses the appropriate database within which to conduct the search. The Westlaw and LexisNexis services provide the researcher with a menu of databases. For example, if a researcher is investigating all federal cases regarding least restrictive environment, the researcher might choose "Federal Case Law" (Westlaw) or "Federal Court Cases" (LexisNexis) as the appropriate database.

The second step for the researcher using a CALR system is to formulate a query. The researcher formulates a query by determining the keywords needed in the documents retrieved. When the keywords are entered, the system will find all documents in the chosen database(s) that contain those keywords. For example, if the researcher searches the federal case law database and enters the keywords "special education" and "least restrictive environment," the computer will retrieve federal cases that contain those words. Both the Westlaw and LexisNexis systems allow the researcher to connect keywords using "and" or "or" so that only documents containing both keywords or either keyword will be retrieved from the database (referred to as *terms* and *connectors searching*). Both systems also allow the researcher to specify the position of the keywords relative to each other (e.g., the two words must appear in the same paragraph), to restrict the scope of the search (e.g., court opinions issued after 1990), and to have the search conducted on certain segments of a database (e.g., search only the synopsis of the court's opinion rather than the entire opinion). Keyword searches that are more general will usually result in a greater number of results, most of which may be irrelevant. When the query is more specific, the search will be more focused. There are instances, however, when relevancy rather than the specificity of terms and connector-type searches may be appropriate, and both Westlaw and LexisNexis have developed systems that allow the researcher to search using words as they would appear in a sentence (i.e., natural language), which produce such results.

Both Westlaw and LexisNexis are now accessible to subscribers via username and password through their respective websites at www.westlaw.com and www.lexisnexis.com, but can be impractical to use unless the researcher is a law student or a member of a law firm. Law schools generally subscribe to Westlaw and LexisNexis; however, access is limited to law students and law faculty. Other electronic research systems, such as LoisLaw (www.loislaw.com) and VersusLaw (www.versuslaw.com) are beginning to compete with Westlaw and LexisNexis, and some law schools now give professors and students access to all four. Although other university departments now subscribe to various online research systems for teaching and research purposes, more widely available today to faculty and students alike is LexisNexis Academic. LexisNexis Academic, which is part of university library databases across the country, enables students and faculty to access a wide range of news, business, reference, and legal information, including state and federal cases, statutes and constitutions, federal administrative law, and law reviews and journals.

The Internet has also become increasingly more valuable as a free resource for legal information. Although various websites, mostly government sponsored, are mentioned throughout this chapter, the Internet as a legal research tool is addressed more fully in Chapter 3.

Legal Research Strategies

This chapter has introduced the essential tools of legal research: primary sources, finding tools, and secondary sources. In addition to this information, a method for conducting legal research is required. The following three-step model may be useful.

Step 1: Analyze the Problem

The first task of the researcher is to analyze the problem and determine the most efficient manner in which to proceed. In the problem-analysis phase, Johnson, Berring, and Woxland (1999) suggest that the researcher (a) think about the answer that is needed for the research problem, (b) determine what it is that the research is to accomplish, and (c) decide what the ideal final product will look like. After analyzing the problem, the researcher must decide what legal sources will be needed to answer that question. Will the research question require information from statutes, regulations, current cases, historical information, an analysis of the law, or some combination of these? Will primary source material (i.e., statements of the law), secondary sources (i.e., interpretations of the law), or both be required? Answers to these questions will help focus the research and indicate where to proceed in the research strategy.

Step 2: Conduct the Research

In the second step, the researcher must locate relevant primary source materials. If a statute citation is available, the researcher can find case citations by looking up the statute in the annotated codes (e.g., U.S.C.A.) and reading the abstracts of relevant cases. Regulations may also be found in this manner.

Perhaps the most important element of step 2 is the location of one good case on the subject being researched. Once the researcher has one good case, West's digests may be accessed using the topic and key numbers in the case's headnotes. Additional cases may then be located and researched. Shepard's citators may also be used to locate additional case citations and secondary source materials.

If a statute or relevant case citation is not available, the researcher should begin with secondary sources. For example, locate a law review article on the subject. Law review articles are replete with statutory, regulatory, and case citations. Loose-leaf services are also useful in locating primary source material. In addition to references to primary sources, the secondary source materials supply the researcher with commentary and analyses of the law.

The ability to move between the sources of law and pull together the relevant information is critical in this stage of research. Analysis of legal issues requires the integration of both primary and secondary resources.

Step 3: Evaluate the Results

The final step of the research process is to evaluate the results. Has the researcher obtained enough information? Were the materials current? Was the analysis logically based on the legal sources located? Because the law is constantly changing, it is critically important that the research be current. Therefore, bringing the research up to date should be a continuous part of the process; sources should be updated as they are being used. It is also a distinct final step in evaluating the results of the research (Cohen et al., 1989).

Summary

Law refers to the rules that govern activities in society. Legal research is the process of finding these laws. It involves locating actual statements of the law (i.e., primary sources) as well as explanations and analyses of the law (i.e., secondary sources).

The primary sources include statutes, regulations, and cases. To varying degrees, the primary sources are the controlling authority; that is, these sources are the laws that govern the behavior of individuals and groups. These sources are available on both the federal and state level.

Primary sources for federal laws, regulations, and cases are the *United States Code,* the *Code of Federal Regulations,* and the various court reporters.

Finding tools are resources for locating primary sources. The purpose of finding tools is to allow the legal researcher to access the enormous body of primary sources. Examples of finding tools include the annotated codes (i.e., U.S.C.A. and U.S.C.S.), West's digests, and Shepard's citators.

Secondary materials discuss and analyze the primary sources. Although secondary sources do not have controlling authority, they can be influential and persuasive. Law reviews and loose-leaf services are examples of secondary sources. Electronic databases such as Westlaw and LexisNexis assist the researcher in retrieving both primary and secondary legal resources using full-text keyword searching; and the Internet is becoming increasingly more useful as a legal research tool.

Legal research requires the understanding of and ability to use primary sources, secondary sources, and finding tools. The researcher must also approach legal problems with a strategy. Although personal strategies vary, they will often include problem analysis, methods for systematically conducting the research endeavor, and an evaluation and updating phase.

For Further Information

The following texts are in-depth works:

Berring, R. C., & Edinger, E. A. (1999). *Finding the law* (11th ed.). St. Paul, MN: West Publishing.

Cohen, M. L., Berring, R. C., & Olson, K. C. (1989). *How to find the law* (9th ed.). St. Paul, MN: West Publishing.

Jacobstein, J. M., Mersky, R. M., & Dunn, D. J. (1998). *Fundamentals of legal research* (7th ed.). New York: Foundation Press.

Jacobstein, J. M., Mersky, R. M., & Dunn, D. J. (1998). *Legal research illustrated: An abridgment of fundamentals of legal research* (7th ed.). New York: Foundation Press.

The following texts are nontechnical works:

Berring, R. C., & Edinger, E. (2002). *Legal research survival manual.* St. Paul, MN: West Group.

Elias, S., & Levinkind, S. (2004). *How to find and understand the law* (12th ed.). Berkeley, CA: Nolo Press.

Johnson, N. P., Berring, R. C., & Woxland, T. A. (1999). *Winning research skills.* St. Paul, MN: West Publishing.

The following is a five-part videotape series:

Berring, R. C. (2000). *Legal research for the 21st century.* St. Paul, MN: West Group.

For more information on online legal research services, visit the following websites:

LoisLaw.com, Inc.: Law Office Information Systems: www.Loislaw.com

Reed Elsevier: LexisNexis: www.lexisnexis.com

West: Westlaw: www.westlaw.com

VersusLaw, Inc.: VersusLaw: www.versuslaw.com

References

Berring, R. C., & Edinger, E. A. (1999). *Finding the law* (11th ed.). St. Paul, MN: West Group.

Cohen, M. L., Berring, R. C., & Olson, K. C. (1989). *How to find the law* (9th ed.). St. Paul, MN: West Group.

Cohen, M. L., & Olson, K. C. (2000). *Legal research in a nutshell* (8th ed.). St. Paul, MN: West Group.

Daniel R. R. v. State Board of Education, 874 F.2d 1036 (5th Cir. 1989).

Johnson, N. P., Berring, R. C., & Woxland, T. A. (1999). *Winning research skills.* St. Paul, MN: West Group.

CHAPTER THREE

Legal Research on the Internet*

Remember my research mantra—find someone who has done the work for you.

Robert C. Berring (2000)

The Internet offers the legal researcher a wealth of information and can be a useful adjunct to the law library. In the preceding chapter, the fee-based online services of Westlaw and LexisNexis were introduced along with specific Internet versions of print resources. There are many other legal resources on the Internet, some of them fee-based, but most available at no charge to the researcher. Through these resources it is possible to monitor current legislation and regulations on a state and federal level, as well as developments in the courts.

The Internet is particularly useful because the researcher can access information quickly. For example, if the U.S. Court of Appeals for the Fourth Circuit announced a decision in an area of special education, it may be days before the final court opinion is available in a law library, and months before analyses of the decision appear in scholarly journals. Using the Internet, however, one can access the full opinion of the court within hours after it is announced. Analyses of the decision may be available almost as quickly. Similarly, when Congress passed the Individuals with Disabilities Education Improvement Act of 2004 reauthorizing the Individuals with Disabilities Act, the text of the new legislation was posted on the U.S. Library of Congress's THOMAS website that same day and within days the Council for Exceptional Children (CEC) had posted summaries, analyses, and a link to the new bill on its website.

---

*This chapter was written by Mitchell L. Yell, Ph.D., and Terrye Conroy J.D., M.L.I.S., of the University of South Carolina.

The purpose of this chapter is to introduce the reader to legal research on the Internet. First, we will examine features of the Internet that are particularly helpful to individuals doing legal research or those just trying to keep current on special education legal developments. Second, we will review some useful information sources on the Internet. Finally, we will discuss a strategy for conducting legal research on the Internet.

Prior to a discussion of the Internet, a caveat is in order. Currently the Internet contains much of interest to the legal researcher, but it is not a substitute for the law library. It is best viewed as a useful supplement to the law library, which houses federal and state laws and regulations, volumes of cases from federal and state courts (dating back many years), and legal journals and law reviews from across the country.

Today all state appellate and federal court systems maintain websites that may post their decisions daily; however, these opinions generally date back only 10 years or so and do not include the editorial enhancements contained in the print reporters and subscription databases. The same is true of state and federal statutes available online. The Internet versions of these laws will not include annotations that direct the legal researcher to regulations implementing them, nor will they provide cases that interpret them. Additionally, although peer-reviewed law reviews and legal journals are beginning to post recent issues on the Internet, the researcher must be prepared to evaluate the credibility and usefulness of the host of other information available on the World Wide Web.

Nevertheless, used appropriately, the Internet offers the researcher valuable and timely access to primary and secondary resources for use in the research process and offers today's researcher immediate access to information needed to stay abreast of developments in the law.

The World Wide Web

The World Wide Web (hereafter Web) has become the most flexible, commonly used, and rapidly growing component of the Internet. The Web is based on hypertext technology. Hypertext is essentially the presentation of text in which certain portions, called *links,* are highlighted in some manner. When highlighted text is selected, the user is linked to another website or document on the Web. Because the Web uses hypermedia, the linked document may be any combination of text, graphics, audio, or video.

To access documents on the Web, an individual user must have a web browser. A Web browser is software that locates and displays web pages. The two most popular web browsers are Netscape Navigator and Microsoft's Internet Explorer. One of the more useful features of the most commonly used browsers is the ability to save pages visited on the Internet. Bookmarks (or "Favorites" in Internet Explorer) are essentially address books or directories of web pages you have found useful. Once you have saved a webpage as a Bookmark or Favorite, you can return to it by merely selecting it from a list. These lists can also be organized by subject into folders. If you forget to bookmark a useful website and later decide to return to that site, the most popular browsers maintain a history list of recent websites visited and allow you to specify how long you wish to keep that list.

Internet Research Tools

Directories and Search Engines

Two widely used tools for locating pages of interest on the Web are directories and search engines. Directories divide websites into categories and subcategories allowing the researcher to continue clicking to narrow the search. Yahoo!, a well-known directory that now allows you to search as well as click through its subject headings, recently developed its own search engine technology to search the Web. Search engines index pages from the Web and enable the researcher to search using keywords and advanced searching techniques; some search engines also allow users to focus their research by searching within the results of their original query. Google, one of the most popular search engines today, recently announced that it now indexes more than 8 billion Web pages, which include hypertext as well as word processing, PowerPoint, and PDF (portable document format) documents. Figure 3.1 is a sample list of well-known directories and search engines.

Although directories and search engines are powerful Internet search tools, entering legal terms will generally yield many results, of which very few may be useful. However, legal search engines are growing in number. FindLaw's LawCrawler allows the researcher to limit searches of the World Wide Web to legal websites, federal or state government websites, the U.S. Constitution, the U.S. Supreme Court, FindLaw's legal dictionary, or legal news. You can also search FindLaw's directory of legal databases. Powered by Google, FindLaw's LawCrawler returns pages containing all the words in your query. You can exclude a word by using the minus sign and search for phrases by using quotation marks. For tips on retrieving better results, researchers should always consult the "Help" page of any search engine used.

LawCrawler is user-friendly and does an excellent job of searching legal resources on the free Internet. Over the past few years as greater amounts of special

Figure 3.1
Directories and Search Engines

All The Web www.alltheweb.com

AskJeeves www.ask.com

Alta Vista www.altavista.com

HotBot www.hotbot.com

Teoma www.teoma.com

Yahoo! www.yahoo.com

Google www.google.com

LawCrawler lawcrawler.findlaw.com

education legal information have become available on the Internet, LawCrawler has become a useful tool for the special education law researcher.

Online Communities

Electronic mail, commonly referred to as *e-mail,* allows one user on the Internet to send messages to other users on the Internet. It is an important tool for communicating with colleagues, researchers, and other Internet users. E-mail is also the foundation for discussion groups and newsgroups.

E-mail has made it easy to quickly and easily communicate and exchange information with others in a variety of ways. Discussion groups are a means of communicating simultaneously through e-mail with a group of recipients interested in similar information. To join a discussion group, you need only send a message to the host computer. The list program then puts your e-mail address on the distribution list, and all e-mail sent to the list is automatically sent to you along with the other list subscribers. Discussion groups exist for a large number and variety of topics. Commonly called *listservs,* discussion groups can be a great resource for locating relevant sites on the Internet and for establishing contacts. Monitoring listserv postings is also a means of staying up to date on legal developments.

A resource similar to discussion groups is the newsgroup or usenet, which is essentially an electronic bulletin board of various newsgroups where comments and responses are posted, creating a "thread" (online discussion) on a particular topic. Rather than reading individual e-mail messages, participants in newsgroups may open and browse discussions at their convenience. Figure 3.2 is a list of websites for locating and subscribing to general and law-related listservs and usenet postings.

Weblogs (Blogs)

A fast developing Internet tool for staying informed and for quickly and easily communicating information to others is the weblog, or *blog* for short. A typical blog is an electronic journal arranged in reverse chronological order that is updated frequently,

Figure 3.2
Internet Lists of Publicly Available Mailing Lists

Google Groups (access and create usenet discussion forums)
groups.google.com

LawLists (locate listservs, usenet newsgroups, and electronic newsletters)
www.lib.uchicago.edu/cgi-bin/law-lists

TILENET (newsletters, discussion lists, and usenet groups) www.tile.net/

CataList (catalog of public listserv lists) www.lsoft.com/lists/listref.html

LLRX.com (subscribe to law-related listservs) www.llrx.com/listtool.htm

usually daily. In fact, highly respected law professors, attorneys, and law librarians are beginning to maintain law-related blogs, or "blawgs," to present their opinions and analyses of legal issues (Moorman, 2004). The author of this textbook maintains a *Special Education Law Blog,* which is linked to the website for this textbook (www.ed.sc.edu/spedlaw/lawpage.htm).

  Free creation tools and hosting is available for those who wish to maintain a weblog, and weblog directories and search engines assist the researcher in locating blogs on particular topics. For instance, Google's *Blogger* allows you to create and publish your blog. *Blawg* maintains a searchable database of law-related blogs. *DAYPOP* indexes thousands of weblogs and news sites for you to search. And with *Bloglines* you can create and publish your own blog, consult its directory or search by keyword for other blogs of interest, and take advantage of its RSS aggregation system. RSS, which stands for "rich site summary" or "really simple syndication," collects news content, such as headlines from websites and blogs of interest. RSS is a format for delivering summaries of web content from newspapers, online magazines, and weblogs that change regularly. This information is described on DAYPOP's website as the "living web." In fact, government websites such as *ED.gov* have syndicated their sites to enable daily news updates through RSS readers. *ED RSS* delivers daily headlines of press releases, funding opportunities, and learning resources with links to *ED.gov* for the full article. You need only subscribe to a free RSS news reader and add *ED.gov* or any other website or weblog to your list to receive headlines. Figure 3.3 lists just a few of the many websites available for accessing weblogs and RSS aggregators.

Electronic Newsletters

ED.gov is one example of the accessibility of electronic newsletters. By selecting the link "Receive ED newsletters" on the U.S. Department of Education's website, you may search the archives or subscribe via e-mail to receive various weekly, biweekly, and monthly e-mail updates and newsletters addressing issues of interest to educators. For

Figure 3.3
Weblog and RSS Websites

> **Blogger (Google's free weblog creator)** www.blogger.com
>
> **Blawg (searchable directory of law or legal related issues)** www.blawg.org
>
> **DAYPOP (current events search engine that crawls the "living web")** www.daypop.com
>
> **Bloglines (search, subscribe, publish, and share news feeds and blogs)** www.bloglines.com
>
> **Big List of Blog Search Engines** www.aripaparo.com/archive/000632.html
>
> **RSS News Feeds for Law** www.virtualchase.com/resources/rss law.html

example, an electronic newsletter called *The Achiever* is devoted to information on the No Child Left Behind Act. It is now commonplace for professional associations and governmental entities to supply news of their activities through electronic newsletters and e-mail updates.

The Internet has developed into a rich source of timely information offering divergent points of view on myriad topics. Researchers should nevertheless keep in mind that as a research tool, information obtained through a search of the World Wide Web, as with any print resource, must first be evaluated for relevancy and reliability. Evaluating data is a part of any research project and will be addressed more fully later in this chapter.

Law-Related Resources on the Internet

A tremendous amount of law-related information is now accessible via the Internet. Unfortunately, an abundance of material directly related to legal issues in special education is not available, and some of what does exist tends to be updated rather sporadically. Nevertheless, many websites sponsored by commercial and nonprofit organizations, federal government agencies, and university law schools contain important material on the law and special education. This section will briefly review several of these resources.

The Law and Special Education

The Law and Special Education website is maintained by the author of this textbook. Its purpose is to (a) provide readers and instructors using the text with updates regarding legal developments in special education; (b) provide links to legal resources on the Internet; (c) provide access to special education statutes, regulations, and court cases, and (d) provide instructors with ancillary materials, such as presentations and a NCATE-formatted syllabus.

The Law and Education website is divided into five sections. The first, "Chapters of the Law and Special Education," is organized by chapters of the text. Developments in legislation, regulations, or court cases will be monitored regularly and posted on the page under the appropriate chapter title. Only legal developments after the publication of the text will be included in this section of the website. Because of the constantly evolving nature of special education law, it is important that instructors and readers be updated on a regular basis.

The second section allows users to link to pertinent special education statutes and regulations. The third section provides links to numerous law-related and special education resources on the Internet. Section four contains the Special Education Law blog. The purpose of this blog, which is written by the author, is to update instructors and students on developments and issues in special education law. Section five is the instructors' page, which includes presentations and a syllabus. Figure 3.4 contains the web address for *The Law and Special Education,* along with names

Figure 3.4
Websites Related to Special Education Law

> **The Law and Special Education** www.ed.sc.edu/spedlaw/lawpage.htm
> **Special Ed Connection** www.specialedconnection.com
> **Education Law Association** www.educationlaw.org
> **Wrightslaw** www.wrightslaw.com
> **The Council for Exceptional Children** www.cec.sped.org/

and Internet addresses of several other websites related to special education law and discussed in the following sections.

Special Ed Connection

Special Ed Connection is a fee-based Internet service maintained by LRP Publications. Special Ed Connection is designed to serve as a reference center for subscribers who need to stay informed on special education issues. It is organized by seven tabs at the top of its home page. The home page addresses the latest news and developments in special education. It includes a *What's New* link and a link to subscribe to its weekly e-newsletter, e-CONNECTIONS. The *Congressional Watch* link offers up-to-date summaries of key legislation affecting special education, and *SpeciaLinks* directs you to Internet sites covering various special education issues. The Special Ed Connection homepage also includes a link to its *Special Education Dictionary,* which includes explanations of more than 1,000 words and phrases relating to special education. The next five tabs provide in-depth coverage of specific topics related to special education, and the seventh tab, *Legal Research Center,* links subscribers to searchable full-text judicial decisions, administrative rulings, and briefs and pleadings. Special Ed Connection allows subscribers to search its entire website or particular databases, including state-specific content, from its homepage and offers other advanced searching capabilities, such as date limitations and results listed by age or relevance.

Education Law Association (ELA)

The Education Law Association (ELA), formerly NOLPE, is a nonprofit organization that brings together educational and legal scholars and practitioners with a special interest in education law. Founded in 1954, ELA became affiliated with the University of Drayton's School of Education in 1997. It is funded through membership fees, publication sales, and conference and seminar fees. From ELA's homepage, the researcher can click on *Links* and access legal search engines and directories, federal government websites, online publications, and links to other association websites that may be of interest to special education law researchers.

Wrightslaw

Wrightslaw is a website hosted by Pete Wright, an attorney who represents children with special needs, and Pam Wright, a psychotherapist with training in psychology and clinical social work. The site's advocacy and law libraries include links to cases, statutes and regulations, articles, newsletters, and other topical resources addressing special education law issues. The Wrightslaw law library is divided into four areas: *Legal News, Caselaw, Statutes and Regulations,* and *Articles and Reports.* The website's *Topics* pages provide A-Z links to subjects such as *IDEA Reauthorization News.* The IDEA Reauthorization News page directs researchers to free online newsletters and additional links to websites for up-to-date information on the Individuals with Disabilities Education Act. From the Wrightslaw website, you can subscribe to a free online newsletter, *The Special Ed Advocate,* read back issues from its archives, and order their books and other publications.

The Council for Exceptional Children

The Council for Exceptional Children (CEC) is the largest international professional organization dedicated to the education of students with disabilities. Its website provides news on legislation affecting special education and includes pages on *IDEA Laws and Resources* and *Public Policy and Legislative Information.* Its *Information Center on Disabilities and Gifted Education* page provides information on searching the U.S. Department of Education's ERIC (Educational Resources Information Center) database; links to laws, regulations, and other online resources; and instructions for subscribing to special education discussion groups, including several that address legal issues. The CEC website also includes information on its publications and professional development opportunities, a link to the National Clearinghouse for Professions in Special Education, and a form for subscribing to its free e-mail newsletter, *CEC SmartBrief.*

Government Resources Online

Many useful websites for researchers interested in special education law are either sponsored in whole or part by the federal government or are produced by the federal government for the purpose of providing government information to its citizens. Several such websites are described under the headings *Government Sponsored Websites* and *Government Publications.* Their Internet addresses are listed in Figures 3.5 and 3.6, respectively.

Government Sponsored Websites

The government sponsored websites described here serve as resource centers for those in the special education community and typically are maintained with the assistance of federal agency funds in collaboration with educational and other nonprofit organizations. Their Internet addresses are included in Figure 3.5.

Figure 3.5
Government Sponsored Websites

U.S. Department of Education www.ed.gov

Education Resources Information Center (ERIC) www.eric.ed.gov

National Dissemination Center for Children with Disabilities (NICHCY)
www.nichcy.org

Cornucopia of Disability Information www.codi.buffalo.edu

Discover IDEA www.ideapractices.org

Figure 3.6
Government Publications

Thomas Legislative Information thomas.loc.gov/

Law Library of Congress www.loc.gov/law/guide

Government Printing Office Access www.gpoaccess.gov

U.S. Courts: The Federal Judiciary www.uscourts.gov

State and Federal Government Information www.firstgov.gov

Disability Information disabilityinfo.gov

The U.S. Department of Education

The U.S. Department of Education maintains a website that can be useful to teachers, researchers, and students. *ED.gov* contains information on Education Department initiatives (e.g., the No Child Left Behind Act), resources for teachers and researchers, grants and funding opportunities, and Department of Education publications. It features sections for students, parents, teachers, and administrators. Its *Information Centers* section includes links to pages covering *Grants & Contracts, Financial Aid, Research & Statistics, Policy,* and *Programs.* Its Policy page includes links to legislation, regulations, guidance, and other policy documents relating to subjects such as *Special Education & Rehabilitative Services. ED.gov* also offers several electronic newsletters addressing various topics of interest to legal researchers (e.g., educational statistics, funding opportunities, and the No Child Left Behind Act).

Education Resource Information Center (ERIC)

The *Education Resources Information Center* (ERIC), sponsored by the Institute of Education Sciences (IES) of the U.S. Department of Education, maintains a publicly accessible centralized database of more than 1 million citations to journal and non-journal education literature dating back to 1966. Effective October 2004, more than 100,000 full-text non-journal documents from 1993 to 2004 that were previously fee-based only were made available for free through ERIC. ERIC now allows for the use of both basic and advanced searching techniques and enables researchers to limit their results by date range and publication type, as well as full-text availability.

National Dissemination Center for Children with Disabilities

The *National Dissemination Center for Children with Disabilities (NICHCY)*, funded by the Office of Special Education Programs (OSEP) of the U.S. Department of Education and operated by the Academy for Educational Development, is a national information and referral center that provides information on disabilities and disability-related issues. Services offered through NICHCY include specialists to answer specific questions; publications on a number of topics, including legal issues; and information searches. NICHCY's website maintains state lists of agencies and chapters of disability organizations and parent groups, a page with up-to-date information on IDEA, and recently launched *Research* and *A-Z Topics* pages.

Cornucopia of Disability Information (CODI) Directory

Cornucopia of Disability Information (CODI) is an Internet directory of disability information and library of electronic disability documents. The CODI directory addresses various disability related topics, which include such categories as *Legal Issues* and *Government Documents*. It is funded by state and federal funds and maintained by the New York Regional TRAID Center at the Center for Assistive Technology, University of Buffalo.

Discover IDEA

Discover IDEA is a mulitimedia package that is essentially a navigational tool to help teachers, families, service providers, administrators, and policy makers understand the IDEA. It includes a CD, resource guide, and webpage. From the CD, users connect to the Discover IDEA webpage, www.ideapractices.org, that has links to many IDEA-related resources, including the statute, regulations, training resources, topical documents, national studies, and state and national resources. The resource guide is a large notebook that contains a core module, which explains the IDEA and its history and lists annotations to research, information, and Web-based resources. Also included is a pathways guide, which includes information on the individualized education program, least restrictive environment, school climate and discipline, and state and district assessments. Additionally, the pathways guide includes connections to the law and other relevant materials. The project is a collaboration of the IDEA Partnership Projects, the Western Regional Resource Center at the University of Oregon, the National Information Center for Children and Youth with Disabilities, and the Education Development Center. The project is sponsored by the U.S. Office of Special Education Programs.

Government Publications

The primary sources of law (statutes, administrative regulations, and judicial decisions) were introduced in Chapter 2. Whereas all state governments now maintain websites that provide links to their primary sources available on the Web, special education law is governed largely by federal law. Following are several federal government websites that publish these resources on the Internet without the annotations or other editorial enhancements included with subscription online databases and print publications. Their Internet addresses are included in Figure 3.6.

THOMAS: Legislative Information on the Internet

THOMAS is a free Internet service maintained by the U.S. Library of Congress to provide users with federal legislative information. THOMAS began in 1995 at the inception of the 104th Congress and launched its updated site in January 2005 when the 109th Congress reconvened. THOMAS employs a sophisticated searching system that is easy to use. Updated daily as information becomes available, it is indispensable to researchers monitoring pending federal legislation. THOMAS provides researchers with the full text of the Congressional Record and the full text and status of all House and Senate bills, searchable by keyword or bill number. Figure 3.7 lists the major databases currently available on THOMAS. The THOMAS homepage also includes links of interest to the legislative researcher, including links for the U.S. Code, the executive and judicial branches, state resources, and historical documents. The updated version of THOMAS will incorporate changes designed to improve both its appearance and usefulness. The U.S. Law Library of Congress also maintains an annotated *Guide to Law Online*.

GPO Access

GPO Access is a service of the U.S. Government Printing Office that provides free electronic access to more than 2,000 databases of federal information. GPO Access's homepage includes a link to a comprehensive *A-Z Resource List* of official federal resources from all three branches of the government as well as links to databases by branch. For instance, its *Legislative Resources* links include pages that allow you to browse or search the *Congressional Record,* House and Senate Bills, Public and Private Laws, and the United States Code from the 104th Congress to present. Its *Executive Resources* links provide access to the Tables of Contents and searchable databases of the *Federal Register* and *Code of Federal Regulations* from 1994 to present as well as the Weekly Compilation of Presidential Documents from 1993 forward. Its *Judicial Resources* links provide access to online information for all the federal court systems.

U.S. Courts: The Federal Judiciary

Many sites on the Internet direct the researcher to the official federal court websites. However, the official Federal Judiciary website, *U.S. Courts.gov,* provides convenient links to the U.S. Supreme Court, U.S. Courts of Appeals, and U.S. District Court

Figure 3.7
THOMAS Databases

Congress Now

- House Floor This Week: 108th Congress: Measures expected to be considered this week on the House floor.
- House Floor Now: 108th Congress: Current Legislative Day.
- Quick Search of Text of Bills: 108th Congress

Legislation

- Bill Summary & Status: 93rd through 108th Congresses (1973–present)
- Bill Text: 101st–108th Congresses (1989–present)
- Public Laws by Law Number: 93rd through 108th Congresses (1973–present)

Congressional Record

- Most Recent Issue: Current Congress (108th)
- *Congressional Record* Text: 101st to 108th Congress (1989–present)
- *Congressional Record* Index: 103rd Congress, 2nd session; 104th Congress–108th Congress
- Roll Call Votes: 101st–108th Congress (1989–present)

Committee Information

- Committee Reports: 104th to 105th Congress
- Committee Home Pages: House and Senate: 108th Congress

systems for each state. Its *Court Links* page includes links for each Circuit as well as a map that is clickable by circuit. Each federal court website will generally include a link for slip opinions that can be browsed daily as well as a database of opinions dating back several years that may be searched by case name, number, or full-text keyword searches.

FirstGov

In addition to the government websites mentioned previously, in 2000, the U.S. government introduced *FirstGov*, a portal or gateway to state and federal government information administered by the U.S. General Services Administration. FirstGov offers a comprehensive search engine and a directory of links to millions of webpages from federal and state governments, the District of Columbia, and U.S. territories. It is also working with agencies to encourage portals organized around customer groups and topics. For example, its *Education and Jobs* page includes a link for *Disability Information,* which takes the researcher to the *DisabilityInfo.gov* website. The *DisabilityInfo.gov* site is organized by nine color-coded tabs at the top of its homepage, including one for *Education.* FirstGov can be useful for researchers who wish to search for information on a topic across state and federal agencies. Keep in mind that search engines such as Google and Yahoo! now allow you to limit your search results to government documents only.

Online Law Libraries

Another means of locating legal information on the Internet is by visiting an online law library. University law school websites generally include links to their law library sites, which provide online directories of legal resources. An advantage of using a local university law library is that often it will have information on state rules, regulations, and court decisions. Some university law libraries are also devoting their resources to projects of a much larger scale by maintaining websites that serve as excellent starting points for legal researchers. Following are examples of such Internet law libraries. Figure 3.8 lists their URLs.

Legal Information Institute (LII) Cornell University Law School

The Legal Information Institute is a nonprofit activity of Cornell Law School supported by grants, gifts, and the consulting work of its codirectors. LII is an internationally known provider of public legal information. Its databases include the opinions of the U.S. Supreme Court since 1992, with more than 600 earlier decisions of historic importance; the full United States Code; and a series of topical pages that serve as concise explanatory guides and Internet resource lists for about 100 areas of law. For instance, there are topics pages for education law and disability law.

JURIST Legal News and Research

JURIST is a legal news and legal research website provided as a public service by law professors and students at the University of Pittsburgh's School of Law. *Paper Chase,* its real-time legal news weblog, is dedicated to presenting important legal news and materials rapidly in an objective and ad-free format. *JURIST'S RESEARCH* tab links researchers to official government websites for U.S. and state judicial opinions and legislation; a quick reference guide to the constitutional and legal systems of countries around the world; and a guide to celebrated historic trials. The JURIST

Figure 3.8
Internet Law Libraries

Legal Information Institute www.law.cornell.edu/
JURIST Legal News and Research jurist.law.pitt.edu
University Law Review Project lawreview.org

website also includes a directory of legal journals based at law schools accredited by the American Bar Association.

Both Cornell's *Legal Information Institute* and *JURIST* are part of the Coalition of Online Law Journals, which supports the University Law Review Project, a website that provides full-text searching of online law journals and abstracts of new law review articles by e-mail. As further evidence that more scholarly material is becoming available on the Internet, Google recently announced that it has partnered with colleges, publishers, and library groups to allow researchers using its powerful search engine to limit their results to scholarly literature such as peer-reviewed papers.

A Strategy for Legal Research on the Internet

Research on the Internet demands an awareness of what you need and knowledge of where to look for it. Researching on the Internet is not the same as "surfing the net." Surfing the net brings to mind the image of persons sitting at their computers and jumping from link to link looking for anything that might pique their interest. Research, however, demands that users be focused, that they have a specific goal or question in mind, and that they proceed systematically to locate pertinent information on that question. It is also important for legal researchers to realize that the Internet does not replace the law library, but that it is a useful adjunct to it. The hard copies of reporters, books, journals, and texts available in law libraries are not accessible on the Internet; nor is the Internet's extensive collection of peer-reviewed analyses and commentaries found in law libraries.

Preparing for Research

The first step in conducting research is to focus yourself by developing a goal or constructing a research question. Once the question is firmly in mind, determine what information is required to find your answer. Decide what research can be done on the Internet and what needs to be done in the law library. With regard to Internet research, ask yourself what information will be needed and where it can be found.

Organizing Your Hard Drive or Data Disk

Prior to conducting research on the Internet, it is useful to organize your hard drive or a data disk so that you can download the information you locate and place it in an easily accessible location. For example, if you are conducting research on least restrictive environment and determine that you need the pertinent statutes from the IDEA, regulatory information from the United States Code, and the most recent cases from the U.S. Courts of Appeals, you might create a folder titled "LRE," with subfolders for statutes, regulations, and court cases. You can further divide your research into subfolders of cases decided by particular appellate courts and the Supreme Court. Subfolders may also be created for interviews and other pertinent information you find in discussion groups and newsgroups.

Remember to bookmark all websites where you find pertinent or potentially useful information. After a few sessions you may find that you have a large number of bookmarks. Fortunately, the popular browsers allow you to organize bookmarks into folders. Finally, remember to back up all your work.

Conducting the Research

Once you've determined what you need, begin a systematic search of the Internet. One final warning before you conduct your research: there is so much interesting information on the Internet that one can easily become overwhelmed and succumb to the temptation to explore. It is important to stay focused on your research. If you locate something of interest that is not pertinent to the task at hand, create a bookmark that you may return to later to assess the importance of that particular information to your research.

Locating Information

One of the most common ways of locating information on the Internet is through the use of what computer users call the *tree structure* (Rowland & Kinnaman, 1995). Tree structures refer to the structure of data on computers where there is an initial or root directory and branches of directories and subdirectories. In addition, the Web uses hypertext links that allow the researcher to jump directly to related information at another location.

A good starting point for legal research is one of the Web pages listed in the text or *The Law and Special Education* homepage. Once you access the pages, the hypertext links may be followed to find the related information. Finding resources on the Internet can also be accomplished by using search engines and directories.

Conducting an Internet Interview

Legal researchers often depend on the interview for information about a specific topic. The use of e-mail for conducting interviews is the latest and one of the most successful online research tools (Campbell & Campbell, 1995; Rowland & Kinnaman, 1995). The primary advantage of e-mail is that it allows asynchronous communications; that is, researchers can post their interview questions at their convenience and the persons being interviewed can answer the post at the most convenient time for them. Telephone tag, long-distance telephone bills, and the difficulties of arranging an interview time and place are eliminated with an online interview.

If you are doing research on an unfamiliar topic, finding a source for an interview on the Internet is not difficult. For example, you might subscribe to a listserv or find a relevant usenet group and monitor discussions to determine if your questions might be appropriate for posting. Prior to posting a question, have some basic information about your research area, which should have been developed through your research on the Web and in the library. This will help to ensure that your question is focused. When asking your question, clearly identify the purpose of your question and make certain it is tightly focused. Finally, suggest that the response can be made to your private e-mail. The advantage of getting a private response is that it will permit you to respond with follow-up questions or requests for more in-depth information.

Another method for locating contacts is through your library research. Perhaps you have come across the name of a university professor who has written an article in your research area, or in reading cases you found the name of a lawyer who has litigated in the area. Universities have pages on the Web that list the e-mail addresses of their faculty members, and law firms have websites that include the e-mail addresses of their lawyers. Locate the addresses of the persons you wish to interview and send them an e-mail asking if they would be willing to answer a few questions for you. Ask a few tightly focused questions in your initial e-mail, and wait for the professor or lawyer to respond.

The Internet is one of the best places to network with other researchers or persons knowledgeable about the area in which you are interested. When you have made contacts through discussion or usenet groups, save the addresses of the individuals in your e-mail address book. When using e-mail for interviews, however, be certain that you have done your research and that your questions are tightly focused and to the point. Questions that are unfocused or overly lengthy may be met with silence and sometimes with negative responses.

Evaluating the Data

Knowing when to stop collecting data can be a problem with any type of research, but it is a particular problem when researching on the Internet. This is because there is such a vast amount of information on the Internet that is always just a click away. It is far easier to keep collecting data when you only have to locate it and download it to your hard drive than when you have to go to the law library, copy it, and put your information in appropriate files for evaluation. Before getting on the Internet, do a thorough job of preliminary research so you know what you need. Go to the Internet, collect what you need while avoiding the fascinating sideroads, and then leave the Internet and evaluate your data. Keep what is useful and discard the irrelevant. As with any research, when evaluating data found on the Internet it is extremely important that you determine the credibility of the data you have collected. Consult checklists included in publications on Internet legal research (Levitt & Rosch, 2004). Visit websites devoted to legal research issues such as *Law Library Resource Xchange (LLRX)* (www.llrx.com) and *The Virtual Chase* (www.virtualchase.com), which suggest articles on evaluating Internet materials and provide topical research guides as well as up-to-date news and information on legal research strategies. Print out a copy of the information you use, keeping in mind that information available on the Internet can disappear as quickly as it appeared.

Summary

The Internet offers the researcher a wealth of easily accessible information. To access this data, the researcher needs knowledge of the various tools the Internet has to offer and skill in using these tools. As is true of all research, a strategy must be followed to derive the maximum benefit from the Internet. Be focused, avoid the many fascinating sites that may not be immediately useful, and know when to stop. Above all, it is important to realize that the Internet is not a panacea, nor is it a substitute for the law library. It is, however, an extremely useful tool for the legal researcher.

For Further Information

Biehl, K., & Calishain, T. (2000). *The lawyer's guide to Internet research.* Lanham, MD: Scarecrow Press.

Botluk, D. (2004). *The legal list: Research on the Internet.* St. Paul. MN: West Publishing.

Campbell, D., & Campbell, M. (1995). *The student's guide to doing research on the Internet.* Reading, MA: Addison-Wesley.

Halvorson, T. R. (2000). *The law of the super searchers: The online secrets of the top legal researchers.* Medford, NJ: CyberAge Books.

Kozlowski, K. (2001). *The Internet guide for the legal researcher: The complete resource guide to finding legal information on the Internet.* Teaneck, NJ: Infosources Publications.

Levitt, C., & Rosch, M. (2004). *The lawyer's guide to fact finding on the Internet.* Chicago: American Bar Association.

Rowland, R., & Kinnaman, D. (1995). *Researching on the Internet: The complete guide to finding, evaluating, and organizing information effectively.* Rocklin, CA: Prima.

For definitions of Internet-related terms, consult Webopëdia™ at www.webopedia.com.

References

Berring, R. C. (2000). *Legal research for the 21st century.* St. Paul, MN: West Group.

Brown v. Board of Education, 347 U.S. 483 (1954).

Campbell, D., & Campbell, M. (1995). *The student's guide to doing research on the Internet.* Reading, MA: Addison-Wesley.

The lawyer's almanac. (2004). New York: Aspen Publishers.

Levitt, C., & Rosch, M. (2004). *The lawyer's guide to doing research on the Internet.* Chicago: American Bar Association.

Moorman, P. (2004, November). Mining gold in the blogoshere: How to use web logs as reliable research tools. *AALL Spectrum,* 14–16.

Rowland, R., & Kinnaman, D. (1995). *Researching on the Internet: The complete guide to finding, evaluating, and organizing information effectively.* Rocklin, CA: Prima.

CHAPTER FOUR

The History of the Law and Children with Disabilities*

In these days, it is doubtful that any child may reasonably be expected to succeed in life if he is denied the opportunity of an education. Such an opportunity, where the state has undertaken to provide it, is a right that must be made available to all on equal terms.

Chief Justice Earl Warren, *Brown v. Board of Education* (1954, p. 493).

The educational rights of children and youth with disabilities were gained largely through the tireless efforts of parents and advocacy groups in the courts and legislatures of this country. The purpose of this chapter is to provide a brief chronology of these efforts. The history of special education law will be examined from the initiation of compulsory attendance laws to inclusion of students with disabilities. The effects of the civil rights movement on special education will be discussed, with particular attention paid to *Brown v. Board of Education* (1954) and the landmark cases of the equal opportunity movement. The manner in which these cases led inexorably to the legislation that ensured the educational rights of children and youth with disabilities will be explained. Finally, federal legislative mandates from Section 504 of the Rehabilitation Act of 1973 to P.L. 108-446, the Individuals with Disabilities Education Improvement Act of 2004, will be briefly examined.

---

*This chapter was written by Mitchell L. Yell of the University of South Carolina, David Rogers of St. Cloud State University, and Elisabeth Lodge Rogers of the St. Cloud School District in St. Cloud, Minnesota.

Compulsory Attendance

In our country, public education is viewed as a birthright. Public education leads to an educated electorate, which is necessary for a democracy to be viable (Levine & Wexler, 1981). A common misconception regarding public education is that it is guaranteed by the U.S. Constitution. In fact, education is not mentioned in the Constitution. Because the 10th Amendment to the U.S. Constitution requires that powers not specifically granted to the United States in the Constitution are reserved to the states, education becomes the responsibility of the states.

Rhode Island was the first state to pass a compulsory education law, in 1840; Massachusetts passed the second in 1852, with other states following suit. By 1918 compulsory education laws were in place in all states (Ysseldyke & Algozzine, 1984). Despite the enactment of compulsory education laws, however, children with disabilities were often excluded from public schools.

The Exclusion of Students with Disabilities

The continued exclusion of students with disabilities, notwithstanding the compulsory education laws enacted by the states, was upheld in the courts. For example, in 1893 the Massachusetts Supreme Judicial Court ruled that a child who was "weak in mind" and could not benefit from instruction, was troublesome to other children, and was unable to take "ordinary, decent, physical care of himself" could be expelled from public school (*Watson v. City of Cambridge,* 1893). Twenty-six years later, the Wisconsin Supreme Court, in *Beattie v. Board of Education* (1919), ruled that school officials could exclude a student with disabilities, even though that student had attended public school until the fifth grade. The student's condition caused drooling, facial contortions, and speech problems. School officials claimed this condition nauseated the teachers and other students, required too much teacher time, and negatively affected school discipline and progress. School officials expelled the student from school and suggested he attend a day school for students who were deaf.

In 1934, the Cuyahoga County Court of Appeals in Ohio ruled that the state statute mandating compulsory attendance for children ages 6 through 18 gave the State Department of Education the authority to exclude certain students (Winzer, 1993). This ruling was indicative of the contradiction between compulsory attendance and the exclusion of students with disabilities, a contradiction that was frequently present in legal rulings of the time on students with disabilities. The court stated that students have a right to attend school, and it noted the importance of education as evidenced by the compulsory education statute. Although the court acknowledged the conflict between compulsory education and the exclusionary provisions, it did not rule to resolve this conflict.

Despite compulsory attendance laws, states continued to enact statutes that specifically authorized school officials to exclude students with disabilities. As recently as 1958 and 1969, the courts upheld legislation that excluded students who school officials judged would not benefit from public education or who might be disruptive to other students. In 1958 the Supreme Court of Illinois, in *Department of Public Welfare v. Haas,* held that the state's existing compulsory attendance legislation did not require the state to provide a free public education for the "feeble minded" or to children who were "mentally deficient" and who, because of their limited intelligence, were unable to reap the benefits of a good education. In 1969 the State of North Carolina made it a crime for parents to persist in forcing the attendance of a child with disabilities after the child's exclusion from public school (Weber, 2002).

Parental Advocacy

Parents led the way in seeking educational rights for their children with disabilities. The parental advocacy movement reflected changes in the social climate of this country at the turn of the 20th century. The nation, having long ignored individuals with disabilities, focused on the need to humanely treat and educate these individuals, particularly children. In order to understand the impact parents had on legislation to protect the rights of children with disabilities, it is helpful to become aware of the evolution of special education in the first three decades of that century.

The White House Conference of 1910

The first White House Conference on Children in 1910 focused national attention on children and youth with disabilities. A primary goal of this conference was to define and establish remedial programs for children with disabilities or special needs. This goal reflected a broader societal shift in perspective on the treatment of children with disabilities. The conference led to an increased interest in educating children with disabilities in public school settings rather than institutionalizing them. As children with disabilities were moved from institutions to public schools, permanent segregated classes were formed in public schools to meet their needs. According to Winzer (1993), the move from institutions to public school settings resulted in changing primary placements of students with disabilities from isolated settings to segregated settings.

Public School Programming

The number of special segregated classes and support services in public schools increased significantly from 1910 to 1930 (Winzer, 1993). Public school educators believed that the segregated classes were beneficial to the children with disabilities because (a) smaller class size would allow more individualized instruction, (b) homogeneous grouping would facilitate teaching, and (c) the less competitive nature of these classes would improve the children's self-esteem.

Despite the increase in the numbers of special education classrooms, many children and youth with disabilities remained unidentified and continued to struggle in regular classrooms. Furthermore, many students with disabilities did not benefit from public school education because they had dropped out of school, been expelled or excluded from school, or were considered unteachable (Winzer, 1993). These problems led to a decrease in the growth of special education programs in the 1930s.

Many factors contributed to this decline in support for and provision of special education classes for students with disabilities. The country was in the midst of the Great Depression, and many, including public entities, were struggling with the resulting financial constraints. The public school system had been developed as an ideal for a democratic society. Compulsory education laws resulted in an increasingly heterogeneous student population, leading to a conflict between the democratic ideal and maintenance of order and high standards in public schools. The result of this conflict was to further separate children with special needs from the mainstream. Under increasingly grim conditions, the special classroom placements became as restrictive and custodial as placements in institutions had been (Winzer, 1993).

The Organization of Advocacy Groups

In response to the poor educational programming that their children with special needs had to endure in school as well as the increasing exclusion of children with disabilities from school, parents began to band together to advocate for their children's education rights. They came together to support one another and to work for change. In 1933 the first such group formed in Cuyahoga County, Ohio. The Cuyahoga County Ohio Council for the Retarded Child consisted initially of five mothers of children with mental retardation who banded together to protest the exclusion of their children from school (Levine & Wexler, 1981; Turnbull & Turnbull, 1997; Winzer, 1993). Their efforts resulted in the establishment of a special class for their children, sponsored by the parents themselves. Similar types of local groups were established throughout the nation during the 1930s and 1940s, although they did not begin to band together at the national level until the 1950s. These local organizations served several purposes. They provided an avenue of support for parents, offered a means to unite to make change locally, and set the stage for national advocacy movements on behalf of children and youth with disabilities.

The advocacy movement was critical to the development of special education services. The activities of interest groups were critical in terms of providing information, stimulus, and support to Congress when considering, developing, and acting on legislation. Congress cannot function without such interest groups (Levine & Wexler, 1981). Let's briefly trace the development of a few national groups that advocated for the rights of individuals with disabilities.

The National Association for Retarded Citizens

The National Association for Retarded Citizens (now ARC/USA, the Association for Retarded Citizens) was organized in Minneapolis, Minnesota, in September 1950. Forty-two parents and concerned individuals from 13 local and state organizations met to establish what has become a powerful and significant organization of parents, families, and other persons with an interest in improving services for persons with mental retardation. ARC's mission is to (a) provide information to concerned individuals, (b) monitor the quality of services for individuals with mental retardation, and (c) advocate for the rights and interests of individuals with mental retardation.

The Council for Exceptional Children

The Council for Exceptional Children (CEC) is a professional organization concerned with the education of children with special needs. Based in Reston, Virginia, CEC was founded in 1922 by faculty and students at Teachers College, Columbia University, in New York. This organization has been a longtime advocate for the educational rights of children and youth with disabilities and has been a leader in the movement to obtain these rights at the federal and state levels. The membership of CEC exceeds 60,000 people. The organization is a major force in (a) the development of innovative educational programming, (b) preservice and inservice teacher education, and (c) policy making and lobbying efforts for children and youth with special needs.

The Association for Persons with Severe Handicaps

The Association for Persons with Severe Handicaps (TASH) is another organization that has provided strong support for individuals with disabilities. TASH was established in 1974 and is comprised of teachers, parents, administrators, and related service providers. TASH disseminates information on best practices, publishes research reports, and supports the rights and humane treatment of persons with severe and multiple disabilities through active involvement in court cases (Siegel-Causey, Guy, & Guess, 1995).

Additional Advocacy Groups

Other advocacy groups founded primarily by and for parents and families of individuals with disabilities include the United Cerebral Palsy Association, Inc. (founded in 1949), the National Society for Autistic Children (1961), the National Association for Down Syndrome (1961), and the Association for Children with Learning Disabilities (ACLD) (1964). More recently, the Federation of Families for Children's Mental Health was formed after a group of 60 parents and professionals interested in children and youth with emotional, behavioral, or mental disorders met in 1988 (Turnbull & Turnbull, 1997).

The progress made in special education can be attributed in great part to the success of parents as advocates for their children. Parents have worked together, and continue to do so, at the local level by pushing local school boards, administrators, teachers, and legislators to provide appropriate educational programming for their children. Parent groups such as ARC and ACLD banded together with professional organizations to challenge state and federal governments in the courts and ultimately to establish federal legislation that mandated a free and appropriate education for all children with disabilities.

The Civil Rights Movement and *Brown v. Board of Education*

Every year hundreds of thousands of people immigrate to the United States. Many are escaping war or economic and political persecution. Many come not to avoid hardship, but to seek the promise of greater individual rights that are provided for the citizens of the United States under its Constitution. The civil rights that are protected under the Constitution and enforced by legislation, however, have not always been provided to all citizens on an equal basis.

In the 1950s and 1960s, the civil rights movement, which sought changes in society that would allow minorities, particularly African Americans, equality of opportunity, led to litigation and changes in legislation. This legislation provided greater constitutional protection for minorities, and eventually for persons with disabilities. A landmark case, *Brown v. Board of Education* (1954, hereafter *Brown*), was a major victory for the civil rights movement and became the major underpinning for further civil rights action. The *Brown* decision not only had a tremendous impact on societal rights for minorities, but also affected many aspects of educational law and procedure (Turnbull, 1993). Although it took time, the precedents set in *Brown* resulted in sweeping changes in the schools' policies and approaches to students with disabilities.

State-mandated segregation of the races in the schools denied black students admission to schools attended by white students. The plaintiffs maintained that the practice of segregating schools was inherently damaging to the educational opportunities of minorities, that segregated public schools were not—and could not be made—equal, and that segregated public schools violated black students' constitutional rights under the 14th Amendment. As an extension of this argument, the Court maintained that state-required or state-sanctioned segregation solely on the basis of a person's unalterable characteristics (e.g., race or disability) was unconstitutional. The high court also determined that segregation solely on the basis of race violated equal protections and denied children from minority backgrounds equal educational opportunity. This decision opened a number of legal avenues for those seeking redress for students with disabilities.

In *Brown,* the high court reasoned that because of the importance of education in our society, the stigmatizing effects of racial segregation, and the negative consequences of racial segregation on the education of those against whom segregation was practiced, segregated public schools denied students equal educational opportunities. This basic truth was considered by many to be equally applicable to those denied equal opportunity to an education because of a disability.

Parental Advocacy in the Wake of *Brown*

An outcome of the *Brown* case was that the equal protection doctrine was extended to a "class" of people, in this case racial minorities (Turnbull, 1993). Advocates for students with disabilities, citing *Brown,* claimed that students with disabilities had the same rights as students without disabilities. Advocates based their arguments on two main premises. First, they pointed out that there was an unacceptable level of differential treatment within the class of children with disabilities. Second, they argued that some students with disabilities were not furnished with an education, whereas all students without disabilities were provided an education. Thus, *Brown* became a catalyst for the efforts to ensure educational rights for children and youth with disabilities because if segregation by race was a denial of educational opportunity for black children, then certainly the total exclusion of children and youth with disabilities was also a denial of equal educational opportunity (Huefner, 2000). On the basis of the *Brown* decision, a series of court cases was brought on behalf of children and youth with disabilities by advocates and persons with disabilities in which they both challenged and sought redress for similar inequities.

The Equal Opportunity Cases

The *Brown* decision was important for students with disabilities because the concept of equal opportunity was applicable to them as well as to students of minority background. Sixteen years after the *Brown* decision, two seminal federal district court cases applied the concept of equal opportunity to children with disabilities. The two landmark decisions in which action was brought against state statutes and policies that excluded students with disabilities were *Pennsylvania Association for Retarded Citizens (PARC) v. Commonwealth of Pennsylvania* (1972) and *Mills v. Board of Education of the District of Columbia* (1972).

Pennsylvania Association for Retarded Citizens v. Pennsylvania, 1972

In January 1971, the Pennsylvania Association for Retarded Children brought a class action suit (hereafter referred to as *PARC*) against the Commonwealth of Pennsylvania in a federal district court. Specifically, the suit named the state's secretaries of Education and Public Welfare, the state Board of Education, and 13 school districts. The plaintiffs argued that students with mental retardation were not receiving publicly supported education because the state was delaying or ignoring its constitutional obligations to provide a publicly supported education for these students, thus violating state statute and the students' rights under the Equal Protection of the Laws clause of the 14th Amendment to the U.S. Constitution. Witnesses for the plaintiffs established four critical points. The first was that all children with mental retardation are capable of benefiting from a program of education and training. Second, education cannot be defined as only the provision of academic experiences for children (this legitimizes experiences such as learning to clothe and feed oneself as outcomes for public school programming). A third point was that, having undertaken to provide all children in the Commonwealth of Pennsylvania with a free public education, the state could not deny students with mental retardation access to free public education and training. A final stipulation was that the earlier students with mental retardation were provided education, the greater the amount of learning that could be predicted, a point related to denying preschoolers with retardation access to preschool programs available to children without disabilities (Levine & Wexler, 1981; Zettel & Ballard, 1982).

PARC was resolved by consent agreement specifying that all children with mental retardation between the ages of 6 and 21 must be provided a free public education and that it was most desirable to educate children with mental retardation in a program most like the programs provided for their peers without disabilities (Levine & Wexler, 1981; Zettel & Ballard, 1982). The decree, which was amended a year later, set the stage for continued developments regarding the educational rights of students with disabilities.

Mills v. Board of Education, 1972

Soon after the PARC decision, a class action suit was filed in the Federal District Court for the District of Columbia. This suit, Mills v. Board of Education (1972; hereafter Mills), was filed against the District of Columbia's Board of Education on behalf of all out-of-school students with disabilities. The action was brought by the parents and guardians of seven children who presented a variety of disabilities, including behavior problems, hyperactivity, epilepsy, mental retardation, and physical impairments. These seven children were certified as a class, thereby representing more than 18,000 students who were denied or excluded from public education in Washington, D.C. The suit, which was based on the 14th Amendment, charged that the students were improperly excluded from school without due process of law (Zettel & Ballard, 1982). The court held that because segregation in public education on the basis of race was unconstitutional, the total exclusion of students with disabilities was also unconstitutional. Mills resulted in a judgment against the defendant school board mandating that the board provide all children with disabilities a publicly supported education. In addition, the court ordered the district to provide due process safeguards. Moreover, the court clearly outlined due process procedures for labeling, placement, and exclusion of students with disabilities (Zettel & Ballard, 1982). The procedural safeguards included the following: the right to a hearing, with representation, a record, and an impartial hearing officer; the right to appeal; the right to have access to records; and the requirement of written notice at all stages of the process. These safeguards became the framework for the due process component of the EAHCA.

Additional Cases

The PARC and Mills decisions set precedent for similar cases to be filed across the country. In the two and a half years following the PARC and Mills decisions, 46 right-to-education cases were filed on behalf of children with disabilities in 28 states (Zettel & Ballard, 1982). The outcomes of these cases were consistent with those established in Mills and PARC. Notwithstanding the judicial success, many students with disabilities continued to be denied an appropriate public education (Zettel & Ballard, 1982). School districts continued to argue that sufficient funds did not exist, that facilities were inadequate, and that instructional materials and adequately trained teachers were unavailable. By the early 1970s, the majority of states had passed laws requiring that students with disabilities receive a public education. These laws, however, varied substantially and resulted in uneven attempts to provide education to these students. For these and other reasons, it became obvious to many that some degree of federal involvement was necessary.

Federal Involvement

Early Federal Involvement

The first significant federal involvement in the education of students with disabilities occurred in the late 1950s and early 1960s. Some of these early efforts included the Education of Mentally Retarded Children Act of 1958, in which Congress appropriated funds to train teachers of children with mental retardation, and the Training of Professional Personnel Act of 1959, which helped train leaders to educate children with mental retardation. In 1965, the Elementary and Secondary Education Act (ESEA) was passed and signed by President Lyndon Johnson as an important component of the war on poverty. This law was the first time the federal government provided direct funding to the states to assist in educating certain groups of students. As such, it was a precursor of direct aid for students with disabilities (Huefner, 2000). The purpose of the ESEA was to provide federal money to states to improve educational opportunities for disadvantaged children, including students with disabilities who attended state schools for the deaf, blind, and retarded. The following year an amendment to this act, Title VI of the ESEA, added funding for grants for pilot programs to develop promising programs for children with disabilities.

The Education of the Handicapped Act of 1970

In 1970, Title VI of the ESEA was replaced by the Education of the Handicapped Act (EHA). This law became the basic framework for much of the legislation that was to follow. The purpose of the EHA was to consolidate and expand the previous federal grant programs and to continue funding pilot projects at the state and local levels. The EHA provided funding to institutions of higher education to develop programs to train teachers of students with disabilities. Funds were also authorized for the development of regional resource centers to provide technical assistance to state and local school districts.

Section 504 of the Rehabilitation Act of 1973

In 1973 Congress passed P.L. 93-112, the Rehabilitation Act of 1973. Section 504, a short provision of this act, was the first federal civil rights law to protect the rights of persons with disabilities. Section 504 states:

> No otherwise qualified handicapped individual in the United States . . . shall solely by reason of his handicap, be excluded from the participation in, be denied the benefits of, or be subject to discrimination under any activity receiving federal financial assistance. (Section 504, 29 U.S.C. § 794(a))

In both language and intent, Section 504 mirrored other federal civil rights laws that prohibited discrimination by federal recipients on the basis of race (Title VI of the Civil Rights Act of 1964) and sex (Title IX of the Education Amendments of 1972). A "handicapped" person was defined as any person who has a physical or mental impairment that substantially limits one or more of that person's major life activities, or a person who has a record of such an impairment or who is regarded as having such an impairment.

The primary purpose of Section 504 was to prohibit discrimination against a person with a disability by any agency receiving federal funds. These agencies are any that receive funds, personnel services, and interests in property, whether receiving these benefits directly or through another recipient. Section 504 requires agencies that are the recipients of federal financial assistance to provide assurances of compliance, to take corrective steps when violations are found, and to make individualized modifications and accommodations to provide services that are comparable to those offered persons without disabilities.

The Education Amendments of 1974

The Education Amendments of 1974, P.L. 93-380, were amendments to the EHA. The law was greatly influenced by the *PARC* and *Mills* decisions. The EHA authorized the creation of the National Advisory Council on Handicapped Children. The purpose of the 1974 amendments was to require that each state receiving federal special education funding establish a goal of providing full educational opportunities for all children with disabilities.

P.L. 93-380 was significant legislation for both children with disabilities and children who are gifted and talented (Weintraub & Ballard, 1982). The amendment acknowledged students with disabilities' right to an education, provided funds for programs for the education of students with disabilities under Title IV-B, specified due process procedures, and addressed the issue of least restrictive environment. The Act, however, was not sufficiently enforceable in the eyes of many advocates for students with disabilities (Weber, 2002).

The Education for All Handicapped Children Act of 1975

Prior to 1975, the access of students with disabilities to educational opportunities was limited in two major ways (Katsiyannis, Yell, & Bradley, 2001; Yell, Drasgow, Bradley, & Justesen, 2004). First, many students were completely excluded from public schools. In fact, Congressional findings in 1974 indicated that more than 1.75 million students with disabilities did not receive educational services. Second, more than 3 million students with disabilities who were admitted to school did not receive an education that was appropriate to their needs (Yell, Drasgow, Bradley & Justesen, 2004). To address these problems, President Gerald Ford signed into law the most significant increase in the role of the federal government in special education to date on November 29, 1975— the *Education for All Handicapped Children Act* (EAHCA).

The EAHCA, often called P.L. 94-142, combined an educational bill of rights with the promise of federal financial incentives. The Act contained administrative and funding provisions providing that states develop policies assuring all qualified students with disabilities a special education. The EAHCA required participating states to provide a free appropriate public education for all qualified students with disabilities between the ages of 3 and 18 by September 1, 1978, and for all students up to age 21 by September 1, 1980. Furthermore, P.L. 94-142 mandated that qualified students with disabilities had the right to (a) nondiscriminatory testing, evaluation, and placement procedures; (b) education in the least restrictive environment; (c) procedural due process, including parent involvement; (d) a free education; and (e) an appropriate education.

The EAHCA delineated the educational rights of students with disabilities and also provided the promise of federal funding to the states. Funding would flow from the federal government to the state educational agencies (SEAs) and, finally, the local educational agencies (LEAs). To receive the funds, states had to submit plans meeting the federal requirements. Local school districts, in turn, had to have programs meeting the state requirements. Federal funding was to supplement state and local dollars and could not be used to supplant these funds. Additionally, 75% of the federal funds were to flow through the state to the local school districts. By 1985 all states had complied with the requirements of this act.

When the EAHCA was first enacted in 1975, the primary issue driving the passage of the law was access to education (Katsiyannis, Yell, & Bradley, 2001; Yell, Drasgow, Bradley, & Justesen, 2004). That is, far too many students with disabilities were (a) excluded from education, (b) segregated from their same-age nondisabled peers, or (c) placed in educational programs that were not appropriate for their unique needs. The EAHCA was successful in ameliorating these problems. Today the right to access to education for students with disabilities is assured. Clearly, the original purposes of the law have been met.

The Handicapped Children's Protection Act of 1986

Prior to 1984, there was no provision regarding attorney's. fees in the EAHCA. This meant that parents could not collect attorney's fees under the EAHCA when they had to sue school districts to ensure their rights under the law. Typically, attorneys who brought actions for parents under the law had to collect attorney's fees by using other laws (e.g., 42 U.S.C. 1983 and Section 504) to recover fees. This U.S. Supreme Court stopped this practice in the *Smith v. Robinson* (1984) decision. The high court held that because the EAHCA was the sole source for relief in cases brought under law, attorneys could not sue under other laws to collect their fees. The decision effectively made the recovery of attorney's fees impossible because the EAHCA contained no attorney's fees provision. Less than two years later, President Reagan signed the Handicapped Children's Protection Act of 1986 (HCPA; P.L. 99-372) into law. The HCPA amended the EAHCA, thereby granting courts the authority to award attorney's fees to parents or guardians if they prevailed in their actions pursuant to the law. The HCPA also overturned the Court's decision that the EAHCA was the sole source of legal relief and allowed the HCPA to be applied retroactively to cases pending or brought after the 1984 *Smith v. Robinson* decision. (For elaborations on attorney's fees, see Chapter 14.)

The Infants and Toddlers with Disabilities Act of 1986

Congress recognized the importance of early intervention for young children when it passed the Infants and Toddlers with Disabilities Act (ITDA) in 1986. This law, which became a subchapter of the IDEA (Part H), made categorical grants to states contingent on their adhering to the provisions of ITDA. The amendment required participating states to develop and implement statewide interagency programs of early intervention services for infants and toddlers with disabilities and their families (IDEA, 20 U.S.C. § 1471(B)(1)). With the consolidation of the IDEA in the amendments of 1997, Part H became Part C.

For purposes of the Act, infants and toddlers with disabilities are defined as children from birth through age 2 who need early intervention services because they are experiencing developmental delays or have a diagnosed physical or mental condition that puts them at risk of developing developmental delays.

Early intervention services are defined as developmental services provided at public expense and under public supervision that are designed to meet the child's physical, cognitive, communication, social or emotional, and adaptive needs (IDEA, 20 U.S.C. § 1472(2)). Early intervention services may include family training, counseling, home visits, speech pathology, occupational therapy, physical therapy, psychological services, case management services, medical services (for diagnostic or evaluation purposes only), health services, social work services, vision services, assistive technology devices and services, and transportation, along with related costs (IDEA, 20 U.S.C. § 1472(2)(E)). To the maximum extent appropriate, these services must be provided in natural environments (e.g., home and community settings) in which children without disabilities participate.

The infants and toddlers program does not require that the SEA assume overall responsibility for the early intervention programs. The agency that assumes responsibility is referred to as the lead agency. The lead agency may be the SEA, the state welfare department, the health department, or any other unit of state government. Many states provide Part C services through multiple state agencies (Weber, 2002). In these cases, an interagency coordinating council is the primary planning body that works out the interagency agreements concerning jurisdiction and funding.

The centerpiece of the ITDA is the individualized family services plan (IFSP). In states that receive Part C funds, all infants or toddlers with disabilities must have an IFSP. The plan is developed by a multidisciplinary and interagency team that includes the parents, other family members, the case manager (i.e., coordinator of the process), the person or persons conducting the evaluation, and other persons who will be involved in providing services (IDEA Regulations, 34 C.F.R. § 303.340).

The IFSP must be reviewed and evaluated every 6 months and revised every year if necessary.

The IFSP must contain

(1) a statement of the infant's or toddler's present levels of physical development, cognitive development, communication development, social or emotional development, and adaptive development, based on acceptable objective criteria,

(2) a statement of the family's resources, priorities, and concerns related to enhancing the development of the family's infant with a disability,

(3) a statement of the major outcomes expected to be achieved for the infant or toddler and the family, and the criteria, procedures, and timelines used to determine the degree to which progress toward achieving the outcomes is being made and whether modifications or revisions of the outcomes or services are necessary,

(4) a statement of the specific early intervention services necessary to meet the unique needs of the infant or toddler and the family, including the frequency, intensity, and the method of delivering services,

(5) a statement of the natural environments in which the early intervention services shall appropriately be provided,

(6) the projected dates for initiation of services and the anticipated duration of such services,

(7) the name of the case manager . . . from the profession most immediately relevant to the infant's or toddler's or family's needs . . . who will be responsible for the implementation of the plan and coordination with other agencies and persons, and

(8) the steps to be taken supporting the transition of the toddler with a disability to [special education] services. (IDEA, 20 U.S.C. § 1477(d))

Written consent of the parents is required prior to providing the services contained in the IFSP. The infants and toddlers amendment contains procedural safeguards similar to those in Part B. The primary area of differences between Part C and the rest of the IDEA is that Part C has a more flexible definition of eligible children, focuses on the family, and provides for coordinated interagency efforts.

The 1986 infants and toddlers amendments also created financial incentives for states to make children with disabilities eligible for special education at age 3. If a state lowers the age of eligibility, children with disabilities from age 3 to 5 will be entitled to receive all the procedural and substantive protections of Part B of the IDEA (Weber, 2002).

The Individuals with Disabilities Education Act of 1990

The 1990 amendments to P.L. 94-142, P.L. 101-476, renamed the EAHCA the Individuals with Disabilities Education Act (IDEA). The IDEA Amendments of 1990 substituted the term *disability* for the term *handicap* throughout the law. The law also used "people first" language (e.g., "student with a disability" rather than "disabled student"), to emphasize the person should precede the category of disability. The 1990 amendments added two disability categories, autism and traumatic brain injury. The law also added and clarified types of related services, assistive technology, and rehabilitation services.

IDEA 1990 also required that individualized transition planning be included in the individualized education programs (IEPs) of students with disabilities who were 16 years of age or older. The provision of transition services was a significant addition to the IDEA. Transition services refer to a

> coordinated set of activities for a student, designed within an outcome-oriented process, that promotes movement from school to post-school activities, including postsecondary education, vocational training, [and] integrated employment (including supported employment, continuing and adult education, adult services, independent living, or community participation). (IDEA Regulations, 34 C.F.R. § 300.18 *et seq.*)

Transition activities must be based on students' individual needs and take into account their preferences and interests. Transition services include instruction, community experience, the development of employment and adult living objectives, and acquisition of daily living skills and a functional vocational evaluation. Transition services may be either special education or related services.

Recent Federal Involvement

The IDEA Amendments of 1997

The Individuals with Disabilities Education Act Amendments of 1997, P.L. 105-17, were passed to reauthorize and make improvements to the IDEA. In passing the amendments, Congress noted that the IDEA had been successful in ensuring access to a free appropriate public education and improving educational results for students with disabilities. Nevertheless, the implementation of the IDEA had been impeded by low expectations for students with disabilities, an insufficient focus on translating research into practice, and too great an emphasis on paperwork and legal requirements at the expense of teaching and learning.

To improve the IDEA, Congress passed the most significant amendments to the law since original passage of P.L. 94-142 in 1975. The changes were seen as the next vital step in providing special education services by ensuring that students with disabilities received a quality public education through emphasizing the improvement of student performance. By adopting the 1997 amendments to the IDEA, Congress indicated that the goal of the amendments was to improve the effectiveness of special education by requiring demonstrable improvements in the educational achievement of students with disabilities. According to Eyer (1998), the passage of these amendments providing a quality education for each student with disabilities became the new goal of IDEA.

The No Child Left Behind Act

No Child Left Behind (NCLB) was signed into law by President Bush on January 8, 2002. The law is the most recent reauthorization of the ESEA. No Child Left Behind, which was a reaction to low academic achievement of America's students, dramatically expanded the role of the federal government in public education by holding states, school districts, and schools accountable for producing measurable gains in students' achievement in reading and mathematics (Yell & Drasgow, 2005). The purpose of NCLB was to increase the achievement of students in America's public schools. The law required states to establish rigorous systems that hold school districts and schools accountable for measurably improving student achievement. Moreover, the law required states and school districts to use numerical data to provide evidence of improved student outcomes (Yell, Drasgow, & Lowrey, 2005). Specifically, NCLB mandated that all public schools bring every student up to state standards in reading and math within a certain period of time, thus closing the achievement gap based on race, ethnicity, language, and disability.

Students with disabilities were included in NCLB. Specifically, Congress and the President believed that to ensure that instruction and achievement for students with disabilities is improved, and students with disabilities were not left behind, they had to be included in NCLB's accountability requirements. They also believed that if students with disabilities were excluded from schools' accountability systems, these students would be ignored and not receive the academic attention they deserved. This means that all students with disabilities must be assessed and the results of these assessments must be included in the data used to determine if a school and school district meet accountability requirements under the law. By including students with disabilities in NCLB's assessment and accountability systems, Congress made certain that schools would be held accountable for the educational performance of these students. (See Chapter 7 for an examination of NCLB.)

The President's Commission on Excellence in Special Education

In October 2002, President Bush created the President's Commission on Excellence in Special Education. The purpose of the commission was to recommend reforms to improve special education and to bring it into alignment with NCLB by requiring special education to be accountable for results and to rely on scientifically based programming. Accountability for results would mean that special education would be driven by increases in academic achievement and improved results for students with disabilities. Scientifically based programming would mean that special educators would only use instructional strategies and methods that were based on solid evidence.

The commission held 13 public hearings in which parents, teachers, administrators, researchers, and representatives of organizations testified about the state of special education. The commission concluded that special education had created an important base of civil rights and legal protections for students with disabilities; nevertheless, special education needed fundamental changes, a shift in priorities, and a new commitment to individual student needs. According to the commission, accountability for results must guide special educators and the ultimate goal of special education must be to close the achievement gap with nondisabled peers.

The commission issued its findings in a report titled *A New Era: Revitalizing Special Education for Children and Their Families.* The commission issued three major recommendations. First, special education must focus on results rather than process and be judged by the outcomes students achieve. Second, special education must embrace a model of prevention, not a model of failure. That is, rather than waiting for a child to fail before identifying a student as eligible and intervening, reforms must move the system toward early identification and swift intervention using scientifically based strategies and methods. Third, because special education and general education share responsibility for children with disabilities, both systems must work together to provide strong teaching and effective interventions using scientifically based instruction and strategies. The report of the President's Commission and the requirements of NCLB were important influences on Congress during work to reauthorize the IDEA.

The Individuals with Disabilities Education Improvement Act of 2004

On December 3, 2004, President Bush signed the Individuals with Disabilities Education Improvement Act (hereafter IDEA 2004), P.L. 108-446, into law. The U.S. Department of Education issued the regulations implementing the law on August 3, 2006. IDEA 2004 and regulations build on NCLB by emphasizing increased accountability for student performance. For extensive coverage of IDEA 2004, see Chapter 5.

The changes in IDEA 2004 are significant. Among the most important of these were changes in the IEP, discipline, and identification of students with learning disabilities. Additionally, IDEA 2004 requires that all special education teachers must be certified in special education and meet the highly qualified teacher requirements of the NCLB. The Individuals with Disabilities Education Improvement Act also adopted NCLB's requirement regarding the use of instructional strategies and methods that are grounded in scientifically based research. (See Chapter 5 for a description of the changes in IDEA 2004.)

Table 4.1 depicts the five most recent amendments to the IDEA.

State Education Statutes

As stated earlier in this chapter, education is the business of the states; however, with the passage of the EAHCA, special education became essentially federally controlled. States were not required to follow the EAHCA requirements, but by choosing not to adhere to the strictures of the law, a state would forfeit federal funding for special education. All states have chosen to comply with the federal regulations based on the EAHCA. States with special education programs in place were required to revise state law to comply with the EAHCA, and states that were not providing special education programs for children with disabilities were required to develop them. Some states developed statutes and regulations that expanded the federal special education requirements. The inclusion of children who are gifted and talented as eligible for special education services is one such example of states (such as Kansas and New Mexico) going beyond the requirements of the EAHCA. States set their own regulations specifying teacher certification regulations, teacher-pupil ratios, transportation time, and age-span requirements in the classroom. In addition, states were allowed some flexibility in funding mechanisms. States were required to distribute 75% of the federal funds to local educational

Table 4.1
Case Law and Legislation That Shaped Special Education

Date	Case Law & Legislation	Description
1954	Brown v. Board of Education	• Prohibited segregation in public schools on the basis of race
1965	Elementary and Secondary Education Act (P.L. 89-10)	• Provided federal funding to assist states in educating students as part of the war on poverty
1966	Amendments to the ESEA, Title VI (P.L. 89-750)	• Provided federal funding to assist states to expand programs for children with disabilities
1970	Education of the Handicapped Act (P.L. 91-230)	• Expanded state grant programs for children with disabilities • Provided grants to institutions of higher education to train special education teachers • Created regional resource centers
1972	PARC v. Commonwealth of Pennsylvania	• Required the state of Pennsylvania to provide students with mental retardation with a free appropriate public education
1972	Mills v. Board of Education of the District of Columbia	• Held that because segregation in public schools by race was illegal, it would be unconstitutional for the D.C. Board of Education to deprive students with disabilities from receiving an education
1973	Section 504 of the Rehabilitation Act (P.L. 93-112)	• Prohibited discrimination against otherwise qualified persons with disabilities in programs that receive federal funding
1974	Education Amendments (P.L. 93-380)	• Incorporated the rights from *PARC* and *Mills* into the law
1975	Education for All Handicapped Children Act (P.L. 94-142)	• Provided federal funding to states that agree to educate eligible students with disabilities as required in the EAHCA • Established the rights of eligible students with disabilities to a free appropriate public education in the least restrictive environment • Required schools to develop an IEP • Established procedural safeguards
1986	The Handicapped Children's Protection Act (P.L. 99-372)	• Allowed parents to recover attorney's fees if they prevail in a due process hearing or court case
1986	Education of the Handicapped Amendments (P.L. 99-457)	• Created federal financial incentives to educate infants (birth through age 2) using early intervention strategies • Required IFSPs for eligible children and their families • Extended the EAHCA's Part B programs to 3- to 5-year-olds in participating states
1990	Individuals with Disabilities Education Act (P.L. 101-476)	• Renamed the EAHCA the IDEA • Added traumatic brain injury and autism as new disability categories under the IDEA • Added a transition requirement to the IEP for students age 16 or older • Added language that states were not immune from lawsuits under the 11th Amendment for violations of the IDEA • Changed to "people first" language

(Continued)

Table 4.1
Continued

Date	Case Law & Legislation	Description
1997	Individuals with Disabilities Education Act Amendments (P.L. 105-17)	• Added new IEP contents and changed the IEP team • Added new disciplinary provisions • Required states to offer mediation to parents prior to due process hearings • Reorganized the structure of the IDEA
2004	Individuals with Disabilities Education Improvement Act (P.L. 108-446)	• Defined a "highly qualified" special education teacher • Removed short-term objectives requirement from IEPs, except for students with severe disabilities • Prohibited states from requiring school districts to use a discrepancy formula for determining eligibility of students with learning disabilities • Encouraged the use of a response to intervention model to determine if students were learning disabled

agencies; however, they could exceed the 75% allocation if they so desired. As the examples indicate, state statutes and regulations must meet the federal requirements as outlined in the EAHCA, though they may go beyond these requirements.

The History of Special Education Law: From Access to Accountability

The early history of special education law spans from the battles of parents and advocacy groups with schools, school boards, and state legislatures to ensure that children with disabilities were not excluded from public schools through the early court decisions and legislation. This history can be characterized as a struggle to ensure equal access for students with disabilities. These court decisions and the early legislation, culminating in the EAHCA in 1975, were profoundly successful. This law succeeded in securing access to public education for students with disabilities.

Building on these successes, legislation in the late 1990s and early 2000s began to focus on a new issue: ensuring that students with disabilities received beneficial and meaningful educational programs. Moreover, these laws required that schools and school districts be accountable for providing quality programming. Thus, the history of special education can fairly be characterized as a movement from access to quality and accountability. As President Clinton aptly stated on the 25th anniversary of the signing of the EAHCA (U.S. Department of Education, 2000):

Today I join millions of Americans in celebrating the 25th anniversary of the Individuals with Disabilities Education Act (IDEA)—a landmark law that opens the doors to education and success for more than six million American children each year. As we recognize this milestone, we know that education is the key to our children's future, and it is the IDEA that ensures all children with disabilities have access to a free appropriate public education. We have seen tremendous progress over the past 25 years—students with disabilities are graduating from high school, completing college, and entering the competitive workforce in record numbers—and we must continue this progress over the next 25 years and beyond.

President Bill Clinton, November 29, 2000

Summary

By the early 1900s, all of the states had compulsory education laws, yet the exclusion of children with disabilities was still widely practiced. The educational rights of children with disabilities were gained largely through the efforts of parents and advocacy groups. The civil rights movement, specifically the U.S. Supreme Court's decision in *Brown v. Board of Education* (1954), provided impetus for subsequent legislation and litigation granting students with disabilities the right to a free appropriate public education. Two seminal cases in securing these rights were *PARC v. Pennsylvania* (1972) and *Mills v. Board of Education* (1972). The early 1970s witnessed a number of federal legislative efforts to improve the education of students with disabilities. The major pieces of legislation to emerge in this decade were Section 504 of the Rehabilitation Act of 1973 and the Education for All Handicapped Children Act of 1975. The years following the passage of the EAHCA saw Congress attempting to improve the EAHCA through a number of amendments such as the Handicapped Children's Protection Act and the Individuals with Disabilities Education Act. In 1997, the Individuals with Disabilities Education Act Amendments made significant changes to the IDEA. Recent federal legislation that made profound changes in special education requirements includes the No Child Left Behind Act and the Individuals with Disabilities Education Improvement Act of 2004.

In this chapter we have provided a brief examination of the historical development of special education through case law and legislation. The struggle for equal educational opportunity for children and youth with disabilities has been arduous and, for the most part, successful. The history of special education law can be characterized as a movement to ensure access to education to one that seeks to ensure quality of educational programming. Although tremendous progress has been made as we enter the 21st century, much remains to be accomplished. Individuals with disabilities, their advocates, teachers, and all persons who desire fair and equitable treatment must continue to work toward attaining the goal of delivering a meaningful education for all children and youth with disabilities.

For Further Information

Ballard, J., Ramirez, B., & Weintraub. F. (Eds.). (1982). *Special education in America: Its legal and governmental foundations.* Reston, VA: Council for Exceptional Children.

Levine, E. L., & Wexler, E. M. (1981). *P.L. 94-142: An act of Congress.* New York: Macmillan.

Winzer, M. A. (1993). *History of special education from isolation to integration.* Washington, DC: Gallaudet Press.

References

Americans with Disabilities Act of 1990, 42 U.S.C.A. § 12101 *et seq.*

Beattie v. Board of Education, 172 N. W. 153 (Wis. 1919).

Brown v. Board of Education, 347 U.S. 483 (1954).

Civil Rights Act of 1964, 42 U.S.C. § 2000d.

Department of Public Welfare v. Haas, 154 N.E. 2nd 265 (Ill. 1958).

Education Amendments of 1972, 20 U.S.C., § 1681 *et seq.*

Education Amendments of 1974, Pub. L. No. 93-380, 88 Stat. 580.

Education for All Handicapped Children Act of 1975, 20 U.S.C. § 1401 *et seq.*

Education of the Handicapped Act of 1970, Pub. L. No. 91-230, § 601–662, 84 Stat. 175.

Education of the Handicapped Amendments of 1986, 20 U.S.C. § 1401 *et seq.*

Elementary and Secondary Education Act of 1965, Pub. L. No. 89-10, 79 Stat. 27.

Elementary and Secondary Education Act, amended by Pub. L. No. 89-750. § 161 [Title VI], 80 Stat. 1204 (1966).

Expansion of Teaching in the Education of Mentally Retarded Children Act of 1958, Pub. L. No. 85-864, 72 Stat. 1777.

Eyer T. L. (1998). Greater expectations: How the 1997 IDEA Amendments raise the basic floor of opportunity for children with disabilities. *Education Law Report, 126,* 1–19.

Handicapped Children's Protection Act of 1986, 20 U.S.C. § 1401 *et seq.*

Huefner, D. S. (2000). *Getting comfortable with special education law: A framework for working with children with disabilities.* Norwood, MA: Christopher-Gordon Publishers.

Individuals with Disabilities Education Act of 1990, 20 U.S.C. § 1401 *et seq.*

Individuals with Disabilities Education Act Amendments of 1997, 20 U.S.C. § 1401 *et seq.*

Katsiyannis, A., Yell, M. L., & Bradley, R. (2001). Reflections on the 25th anniversary of the Individuals with Disabilities Education Act. *Remedial and Special Education, 22,* 324–334.

Levine, E. L., & Wexler, E. M. (1981). *P.L. 94-142: An act of Congress.* New York: Macmillan.

Mills v. Board of Education of the District of Columbia, 348 F. Supp. 866 (D.D.C. 1972).

National Defense Education Act of 1958, Pub. L. No. 85-864, 72 Stat. 1580.

Pennsylvania Association for Retarded Citizens (PARC) v. Commonwealth of Pennsylvania, 343 F. Supp. 279 (E.D. Pa. 1972).

Rehabilitation Act of 1973, Section 504, 29 U.S.C. § 794.

Siegel-Causey, E., Guy, B., & Guess, D. (1995). Severe and multiple disabilities. In E. L. Meyen and T. M. Skrtic (Eds.), *Special education and student disability, an introduction: Traditional, emerging, and alternative perspectives* (4th ed., pp. 415–448). Denver: Love Publishing.

Turnbull, A. P., & Turnbull, H. R. (1997). *Families, professionals, and exceptionality: A special partnership* (3rd ed.). Upper Saddle River, NJ: Merrill/Prentice Hall.

Turnbull, H. R. (1993). *Free appropriate public education: The law and children with disabilities* (4th ed.). Denver: Love Publishing.

U.S. Department of Education. (2000, November 29). Education department celebrates IDEA 25th anniversary; progress continues for students with disabilities. Available at www.ed.gov/PressReleases/11-2000/112900.html.

Watson v. City of Cambridge, 32 N.E. 864 (Mass. 1893).

Weber, M. C. (2002). *Special education law and litigation treatise* (2nd ed). Horsham, PA: LRP Publications.

Weintraub, F. J., & Ballard, J. (1982). Introduction: Bridging the decades. In J. Ballard, B. Ramirez, & F. Weintraub (Eds.), *Special education in America: Its legal and governmental foundations* (pp. 1–10). Reston, VA: Council for Exceptional Children.

Winzer, M. A. (1993). *History of special education from isolation to integration.* Washington, DC: Gallaudet Press.

Yell, M. L. & Drasgow, E. (2005). *No Child Left Behind: A guide for professionals.* Upper Saddle River, NJ: Merrill/Prentice Hall.

Yell, M. L., Drasgow, E., Bradley, R., & Justesen, T. (2004). Critical legal issues in special education. In A. McCray Sorrells, H. J. Reith, & P. T. Sindelar,

Issues in special education (pp. 16–37). Boston: Allyn and Bacon.

Yell, M. L., Drasgow, E., & Lowrey, K. A. (2005). No Child Left Behind and students with autism spectrum disorders. *Focus on Autism and Other Developmental Disorders, 22,* 148–160.

Ysseldyke, J. E., & Algozzine, B. (1984). *Introduction to special education.* Boston: Houghton Mifflin.

Zettel, J. J., & Ballard, J. (1982). The Education for All Handicapped Children Act of 1975 (P.L. 94-142): Its history, origins, and concepts. In J. Ballard, B. Ramirez, & F. Weintraub (Eds.), *Special education in America: Its legal and governmental foundations* (pp. 11–22). Reston, VA: Council for Exceptional Children.

CHAPTER FIVE

The Individuals with Disabilities Education Act

We must recognize our responsibility to provide education for all children [with disabilities] which meets their unique needs. The denial of the right to education and to equal opportunity within this nation for handicapped children—whether it be outright exclusion from school, the failure to provide an education which meets the needs of a single handicapped child, or the refusal to recognize the handicapped child's right to grow—is a travesty of justice and a denial of equal protection under the law.

Senator Harrison Williams, principal author of the Education for All
Handicapped Children Act, *Congressional Record* (1974, p. 15,272)

On November 29, 1975, while traveling to China on Air Force One, President Ford signed the Education for All Handicapped Children Act (EAHCA). The EAHCA, often referred to as P.L. 94-142, was enacted to meet the educational needs of students with disabilities. The law was actually an amendment to the Education of the Handicapped Act and became Part B of that law. Part B offered federal funding to states in exchange for the states offering educational services to specified categories of students with disabilities. Moreover, the educational services states offered had to be provided in conformity with the requirements of the EAHCA. Amendments to the EAHCA enacted in 1990, P.L. 101-476, changed the name of the Act to the Individuals with Disabilities Education Act (IDEA). Amendments to the IDEA added in 1997 further clarified, restructured, and extended the law.

In this chapter I will provide an overview of the IDEA. First, I review the historical developments that led to the passage of the IDEA. Second, I examine the purpose, goals, and structure of the law. Third, I consider the major principles of the IDEA and how they affect the education of students with disabilities. Finally, I will examine the changes in the Individuals with Disabilities Education Improvement Act of 2004.

The Development of the IDEA

The genesis of the IDEA can be found in the (a) advocacy of various coalitions for children with disabilities, (b) litigation in the federal courts, and (c) federal and state legislation during the 1950s and 1960s (see Chapter 4). Many of the principles that were eventually incorporated into the IDEA can be traced to these court decisions and this legislation. As we have seen, advocacy groups played a major role in securing the principle of an equal educational opportunity for students with disabilities. The advocacy of these groups was aided through the support of national figures like President John F. Kennedy and Senator Hubert H. Humphrey.

Early Court Rulings and Legislation

Until the 1960s, the cost of educating students with disabilities was borne by state and local governments. During this period, very few teachers were being trained to work with students with disabilities, and extremely small amounts of funds were available to universities to support research (Levine & Wexler, 1981). With the passage of the Elementary and Secondary Education Act (ESEA) in 1965, and amendments to the ESEA in 1966 and 1968, the federal government began to provide funding to states to assist efforts to educate students with disabilities through various grant programs.

In 1970, the Education of the Handicapped Act (EHA) was signed into law. The EHA (a) consolidated the earlier grant programs under one law, (b) provided additional federal money to fund pilot projects in the states, (c) funded institutions of higher education to develop teacher training programs in special education, and (d) funded regional resource centers to provide technical assistance to state and local school districts.

The two seminal court cases in 1972, *Pennsylvania Association for Retarded Citizens (PARC) v. Pennsylvania* and *Mills v. District of Columbia Board of Education,* resulted in requirements that the Pennsylvania and D.C. public schools provide access to public education for students with disabilities. Moreover, these cases resulted in basic procedural rights being granted to students with disabilities. These cases influenced the federal government to amend the EHA in 1974. The Education Amendments to the EHA required each state that received federal funding to provide (a) full educational opportunities, (b) procedural safeguards, and (c) education in the least restrictive environment for students with disabilities. Nonetheless, advocacy groups believed that the law was not sufficiently enforceable and neither parents nor advocacy groups would be able to ensure that local school districts and states were meeting their obligations under the law.

Additionally, by the early 1970s, many states had their own statutes and regulations regarding the education of students with disabilities. Unfortunately, the efforts across states were uneven, and many believed that a more enforceable federal standard was needed. In fact, in late 1975 Congress reported that during this period approximately 1.75 million students with disabilities were excluded from public schools and 2.2 million were educated in programs that did not meet their needs (as cited in Weber, 2002). In response to these problems four bills were introduced in the Senate regarding the education of students with disabilities: S.896, introduced by Senator Jennings Randolph, to extend the life of the Education of the Handicapped Act for 3 years; S.34, introduced by Senator Ernest Hollings, to fund research on the problems of children with autism; S.808, introduced by Senator Mike Gravel, to provide federal funds for screening preschool children for the presence of learning disabilities; and S.6; introduced by Senator Harrison Williams, a comprehensive bill for the education of students with disabilities based on the *Mills* and *PARC* cases. The purpose of Williams's bill was to mandate that a free appropriate public education be available to all students with disabilities by 1976. These four bills were the subject of Senate hearings held in 1973. Eventually, conference committees agreed on a bill that would be known as the Education of the Handicapped Amendments of 1974, P.L. 93-380. The 93rd Congress, however, failed to act on this bill before adjournment.

The Passage of the IDEA

Because bills pending at the end of a final session of Congress die, Senator Williams had to reintroduce his bill, S.6, the Education for All Handicapped Children Act (EAHCA), in the next session. In April 1973 the Senate Subcommittee on the Handicapped held hearings on this bill in Newark, New Jersey; Boston, Massachusetts; Harrisburg, Pennsylvania; St. Paul, Minnesota; and Columbia, South Carolina. Even though the years since the passage of Title VI of the ESEA in 1966 had seen progress in the education of students with disabilities, the hearings on Senator Williams's bill indicated that significant problems remained.

The Senate passed S.6, and the House passed a similar bill, H.7217. When bills are passed in both houses of Congress, a conference committee is appointed to write a final bill by combining the two bills and ironing out any differences between them. In this situation, the conference committee resolved differences in the House and Senate bills and sent one bill, the EAHCA, to both houses of Congress. The Senate and the House approved the bill and sent it to the president for signing. On November 29, 1975, the 142nd bill passed by the 94th Congress, the EAHCA, was signed into law by President Gerald Ford. Federal regulations implementing the law took effect on August 23, 1977.

The EAHCA provided federal funding to states to assist them in educating students with disabilities. States wanting to receive federal funding were required to submit a state plan to the Bureau of Education for the Handicapped. The purpose of the plan was to describe the state's policies and procedures to educate students with disabilities in accordance with the procedures contained in the EAHCA. If the plan was approved by the bureau, the state was obligated to guarantee a free appropriate public education to students with disabilities in return for the federal funding they would receive. The federal funding that states received would be based on an annual count of all children and youth served under the law. The EAHCA made the federal government a partner with the states in educating students with disabilities who were covered by the law (Huefner, 2000).

All but one state, New Mexico, submitted a plan for federal funding under P.L. 94-142. New Mexico decided not to implement the Act nor accept the federal funds. An advocacy group for citizens with disabilities in New Mexico, the New Mexico Association for Retarded Citizens, sued the state for failing to provide an appropriate education for students with disabilities in the case *New Mexico Association for Retarded Citizens v. New Mexico* (1982). The association sued under Section 504 of the Rehabilitation Act of 1973, which prevents entities that receive federal funds from discriminating against persons with disabilities. The association maintained that the state discriminated against students with disabilities by denying them an appropriate education. (For elaborations on Section 504, see Chapter 6.) The association prevailed. The decision indicated that even though a state did not accept federal funding and the requirements attached to the funds (adherence to P.L. 94-142), it would still have to comply with Section 504, a civil rights law that contained no funding provisions. New Mexico, therefore, was required to provide a free appropriate public education to students with disabilities even though the state received no federal funding under the IDEA. New Mexico subsequently submitted a state plan to the Bureau of Education for the Handicapped, opting to implement the law and accept the federal funding. Following this action, all 50 states were participants in federal funding through the EAHCA.*

The Purpose and Structure of the IDEA

The IDEA was enacted to assist states in meeting the educational needs of students with disabilities via federal funding of state efforts. According to the U.S. Supreme Court, however,

> Congress did not content itself with passage of a simple funding statute. Rather the [IDEA] confers upon disabled students an enforceable substantive right to public education . . . and conditions federal financial assistance upon states' compliance with substantive and procedural goals of the Act. (*Honig v. Doe*, 1988, p. 597)

Purpose of the IDEA

In 1975 Congress stated that:

> Disability is a natural part of the human experience and in no way diminishes the right of individuals to participate in or contribute to our society. Improving educational results for children with disabilities is an essential element of our national policy of ensuring equality

---

*In 1990, Congress changed the name of the EAHCA to the Individuals with Disabilities Education Act (IDEA). For the remainder of this chapter I will refer to the law as the IDEA.

of opportunity, full participation, independent living, and economic self-sufficiency for individuals with disabilities. (20 U.S.C. § 1401 (c)(1))

Nonetheless, Congress also found that prior to the enactment of the EAHCA in 1975, the educational needs of millions of children with disabilities were not being met because many (a) children with disabilities were excluded from public schools; (b) children with disabilities who did attend public schools often did not receive an education that was appropriate for their needs; (c) children with disabilities were not diagnosed, which prevented them from receiving a successful educational experience; and (d) states and local school districts lacked adequate resources, which forced families to find services outside the public school system.

The purpose of the IDEA is to

> ensure that all children with disabilities have available to them a free appropriate public education that emphasizes special education and related services designed to meet their unique needs and prepare them for further education, employment, and independent living, to ensure that the rights of children with disabilities and parents of such children are protected, to assist states, localities, educational service agencies, and Federal agencies to provide for the education of all children with disabilities. (IDEA, 20 U.S.C. § 1400(d))

Rather than establishing substantive educational standards to ensure that the goal of the IDEA was fulfilled, Congress created an elaborate set of procedural safeguards. The purpose of these safeguards was to allow parental input into a school's decisions and to maximize the likelihood that children with a disability would receive a free appropriate public education.

Who Is Protected?

Students meeting the IDEA's definition of a student with disabilities receive the procedural protections of the law. Students with disabilities, determined to be eligible in accordance with the provisions of the IDEA, are entitled to receive special education and related services. The determination of eligibility is made on an individual basis by the multidisciplinary team in accordance with guidelines set forth in the law. The IDEA uses a categorical approach to define students with disabilities by setting forth categories of disabilities. Not all students with disabilities are protected; only those students with disabilities included in the IDEA, and only if those disabilities have an adverse impact on their education, are eligible to receive a special education. The IDEA categories are exhaustive.

Categories of Disabilities

The IDEA disability categories (see Figure 5.1) and regulations defining them can be found at 20 U.S.C. § 1401(a) and 34 C.F.R. § 300.7(a)(1)–(b)(13). The Office of Special Education Programs solicited public comments regarding the possible addition of a category for Attention Deficit Hyperactivity Disorder (ADHD) in the 1990 amendments to the IDEA. ADHD was not made a separate category; however, the OSEP did issue a policy memo stating that students with ADHD could be eligible for special education under

Figure 5.1
Categories of Disabilities

> Autism
> Deaf-blindness
> Deafness
> Hearing impairment
> Mental retardation
> Multiple disabilities
> Orthopedic impairments
> Other health impairment
> Emotional disturbance
> Specific learning disability
> Speech or language impairment
> Traumatic brain injury
> Visual impairment, including blindness

the categories of specific learning disability, serious emotional disturbance, or other health impairment (Joint Policy Memo, 1991). Students with ADHD may also be eligible for services under Section 504 of the Rehabilitation Act.

In the IDEA Amendments of 1997 the terminology "serious emotional disturbance" was changed to "emotional disturbance." The reason for this change was to eliminate the pejorative connotation of the term *serious*. The change was not intended to have substantive or legal significance (Senate Report, 1997).

States are required to provide services to students who meet the criteria in the IDEA. This does not mean that states must adopt every category exactly as specified in the IDEA. States may combine categories (e.g., many states combine deafness and hearing impairment), divide categories (e.g., many states divide the category of mental retardation in two or more categories, such as mild, moderate, and severe), use different terminology (e.g., *serious emotional disturbance* goes by a number of different terms such as *emotionally and behaviorally disordered* or *emotionally disabled*), or expand the definitions (e.g., Minnesota does not exclude students identified as socially maladjusted in their definition of emotional or behavioral disorders as does the federal definition). At a minimum, however, all students with disabilities who meet the appropriate criteria as defined in the IDEA categories must receive services.

Age Requirements

The IDEA requires that a program of special education and related services be provided to all eligible students with disabilities between the ages of 3 and 21. States are required to identify and evaluate children from birth to age 21, even if the state does not provide educational services to students with disabilities in the 3-to-5 and 18-to-21 age groups (IDEA Regulations, 34 C.F.R. § 300.300, comment 3). The duty to provide special education to qualified students with disabilities is absolute between the ages of 6 and 17 (Weber, 2002). If states do not require an education for students without disabilities between ages 3 to 5 and 18 to 21, they are not required to educate students in those age groups (IDEA, 20 U.S.C. § 1412(2)(B)).

If a special education student graduates with a diploma, successfully completes an appropriate individualized education program (IEP) leading to graduation, or voluntarily drops out of school, the school's obligation to the student ends (*Wexler v. Westfield,* 1986). If the graduation is merely used to terminate a school district's obligation, however, the district can be required to supply compensatory education, such as educational services beyond the age of 21 (*Helms v. Independent School District #3,* 1985).

Infants and Toddlers

An amendment to the IDEA was passed in 1986 (P.L. 99-457; The Infants and Toddlers with Disabilities Act). This amendment was originally added to the then EAHCA as Part H. Part H, which became Part C in the IDEA Amendments of 1997, provided incentive grants to states that provide special education and related services to children with disabilities from birth through age 2. At age 3, a child with a disability is entitled to receive services under Part B. When a child who receives early intervention services turns 3 years of age, the state is required to convene a transition meeting with the Part C lead agency, the local educational agency (LEA), and the parents to ensure that a smooth transition takes place.

This amendment is codified at 20 U.S.C. §§ 1541–1585. Regulations implementing this section of the IDEA, adopted in 1989, are codified at 34 C.F.R. §§ 303.1–303.653. Part C requires that participating states develop a statewide system of multidisciplinary interagency programs to provide early intervention services. The populations targeted for this program are infants and toddlers who:

(1) Are experiencing developmental delays . . . in one or more of the following areas:
    (i)   Cognitive development;
    (ii) Physical development, including vision and hearing;
    (iii) Language and speech development;
    (iv) Psychosocial development; or
    (v)   Self-help skills; or
(2) Have a diagnosed physical or mental condition that has a high probability of resulting in developmental delay. (IDEA Regulations, 34 C.F.R. § 303.16)

Infants and toddlers may be designated as developmentally delayed and receive special education services. It is not required that the children fit into a category of disabilities included in the IDEA to receive services.

States have an option of submitting plans to participate in Part C funding. To determine if a state has submitted a plan and is obligated under Part C, consult state statutes and regulations.

Structure of the IDEA

The IDEA is codified at 20 U.S.C. §§ 1400–1485. Originally the law was divided into nine subchapters. In the IDEA Amendments of 1997, the law was restructured into four subchapters. The structure of IDEA 2004 is depicted in Table 5.1.

Title I of the IDEA

Title I consists of four parts. Of these four parts, Part B contains the requirements that school personnel must be most concerned with in developing programs for students in special education. I next review the four parts of Title I.

Part A of the IDEA.   Part A is the section of the law in which Congress justifies the IDEA (Yell, Drasgow, Bradley, & Justesen, 2004). It contains findings of fact regarding

Table 5.1
The Four Parts of the IDEA

Part	Purpose	Contents
Part A	General provisions	Part A contains findings of fact regarding the education of students with disabilities that existed when the IDEA was passed. This section also contains definitions of terms that are used throughout the IDEA.
Part B	Assistance for education of all children with disabilities	Part B contains the information regarding the state grant program in which states submit plans that detail how the state will ensure a free appropriate public education to all qualified children and youth with disabilities who live in the state.
Part C	Infants and toddlers with disabilities	Part C provided categorical grants to states contingent on states adhering to the provisions of law, which required participating states to develop and implement statewide interagency programs of early intervention services for infants and toddlers with disabilities and their families.
Part D	National activities to improve education of children with disabilities.	Part D contains support or discretionary programs that support the implementation of the IDEA and assist states in improving the education of students with disabilities. Supporting research, personnel preparation, and professional development are especially important goals of Part D.

the education of students with disabilities that existed when the IDEA was passed. This section also contains definitions of terms that are used throughout the IDEA. These definitions are crucial. For example, the requirements necessary to be a highly qualified special education teacher are listed in Part A. The goals of the IDEA are also included in this part.

Part B of the IDEA.   Part B addresses educational requirements for students ages 3 through 21 and thus is the section with which special education teachers and administrators should be most familiar. Part B contains the information regarding the state grant program in which states submit plans that detail how they will ensure a free appropriate public education to all qualified children and youth with disabilities who live in the state. If the plan is approved, the state receives federal financial assistance. Part B also contains the procedural safeguards designed to protect the interests of children and youth with disabilities.

The IDEA was originally enacted to address the failure of states to meet the educational needs of students with disabilities (Tucker & Goldstein, 1992). The method chosen to accomplish this goal was federal funding for states submitting special education plans that met the IDEA's requirements. After the plan is approved, the state assumes the responsibility for meeting the provisions of the law. In addition to setting the formulas by which states can receive funds, the IDEA contains provisions to ensure that all qualifying students with disabilities receive a free appropriate education and that procedural protections are granted to students and their parents. These provisions are: (a) zero reject, (b) identification and evaluation, (c) free appropriate public education, (d) least restrictive environment, (e) procedural safeguards, (f) technology-related assistance, (g) personnel development, and (h) parental participation.

Readers should note that even though some scholars have divided Part B into major principles for discussion purposes (e.g., Katsiyannis, Yell, & Bradley, 2001; Turnbull & Turnbull, 2002; Turnbull, Turnbull, Shank, & Smith, 2004), neither the IDEA's statutory language nor the Office of Special Education Programs recognizes the division of the law into these principles (Yell, Drasgow, Bradley, & Justesen, 2004). It is, however, a useful tool for facilitating a thorough understanding of the law.

Zero Reject.   According to the zero reject principle, all students with disabilities eligible for services under the IDEA are entitled to a free appropriate public education. This principle applies regardless of the severity of the disability. According to the U.S. Court of Appeals for the First Circuit, public education is to be provided to all students with educational disabilities, unconditionally and without exception (*Timothy W. v. Rochester, New Hampshire, School District*, 1989).

The state must assure that all students with disabilities, from birth to age 21, residing in the state who are in need of special education and related services or are suspected of having disabilities and needing special education are identified, located, and evaluated (IDEA Regulations, 34 C.F.R. § 300.220). These requirements include children with disabilities attending private schools. This requirement is called the *child find system.* States are free to develop their own child find systems (IDEA, 20

U.S.C. § 1414(a)(1)(A)). The state plan must identify the agency that will coordinate the child find tasks, the activities it will use, and resources needed to accomplish the child find. School districts are usually responsible for conducting child find activities within their jurisdiction. The child find applies to all children and youth in the specified age range regardless of the severity of the disability. Furthermore, the child find requirement is an affirmative duty, because parents do not have to request that a school district identify and evaluate a student with disabilities. In fact, parents' failure to notify a school district will not relieve a school district of its obligations (Gorn, 1996). It is up to the school district to find these students. When students are identified in the child find, the school district is required to determine whether they have a disability under the IDEA.

A school district's child find system can take many forms. One method is the general public notice. School districts are obligated to notify the public as a means of locating children with disabilities. Additional methods that may be used to locate and identify children with disabilities include referrals, public meetings, door-to-door visits, home and community visits, brochures, speakers, contacting pediatricians, contacting day care providers, kindergarten screening, and public awareness efforts. If a school district becomes aware of or suspects that a student may need special education, an evaluation is required.

Identification and Evaluation.   In hearings on the original EAHCA, Congress heard testimony indicating that many schools were using tests inappropriately and therefore were making improper placement decisions (Turnbull & Turnbull, 2002). Sometimes schools placed students in special education based on a single test, administered and placed students using tests that were not reliable or valid, or used tests that were discriminatory. To remedy these problems, the IDEA includes protection in evaluation procedures (PEP). A fair and accurate evaluation is extremely important to ensure proper placement and, therefore, an appropriate education. The PEP procedures were incorporated into the IDEA to address abuses in the assessment process (Salvia & Ysseldyke, 1995).

IDEA 2004 made a few changes in the initial evaluation process. The statutory language makes it clear that a child's parents, the SEA, or LEA may request an initial evaluation. Moreover, when an LEA decides to evaluate a child for special education services and seeks consent from the child's parents, it must determine eligibility within 60 days of receiving consent or within the timeline that the state allows, if it is less than 60 days. The timeline does not apply, however, if the parents repeatedly fail to produce the child for the evaluation. (For elaborations on the identification of students with disabilities, see Chapter 10).

Free Appropriate Public Education.   The IDEA requires that states have policies assuring all students with disabilities the right to a free appropriate public education (FAPE). The FAPE requirement has both procedural and substantive components (Guernsey & Klare, 1993). The procedural components are the extensive procedural protections afforded to students and their parents. These protections ensure the parents' right to meaningful participation in all decisions affecting their child's education. The substantive right to a FAPE consists of

> special education and related services which (A) have been provided at public expense, under public supervision and direction, and without charge, (B) meet standards of the state educational agency (SEA), (C) include an appropriate preschool, elementary, or secondary school education in the state involved, and (D) are provided in conformity with the Individualized Education Program. (IDEA 20 U.S.C. § 1401(18)(C))

Special education is defined in the statutory language as "specially designed instruction, at no charge to the parents or guardians, to meet the unique needs of a child with a disability" (IDEA, 20 U.S.C. § 1404(a)(16)). Related services are any developmental, corrective, or supportive services that students need to benefit from special education (IDEA, 20 U.S.C. § 1404(a)(17)).

Public schools must provide special education and related services to eligible students at no cost. If a student is placed out of the school district by a school district, the home district retains financial responsibility. This includes tuition fees and related service charges. The only fees that schools may collect from parents of children with disabilities are those fees that are also imposed on the parents of children without disabilities (e.g., physical education fees, lunch fees).

The IDEA also acknowledges the rights of states to set standards for a FAPE. The IDEA requires that local school districts meet states' special education standards. These standards may exceed the minimum level of educational services provided for in the IDEA. For example, Massachusetts requires that schools provide a FAPE that will assure a student's maximum possible development (Massachusetts General Law Annotated, 1978), a standard greater than that contained in the IDEA. State standards may not, however, set lower educational benefits than the IDEA. (See Chapter 9 for an extensive discussion of the FAPE mandate).

One of the most crucial aspects of the substantive component is that the special education and related services must be provided in conformity with the IEP. An IEP must be developed for all students in special education. (See Chapter 11 for elaborations of IEP requirements.) The school district is responsible for providing the student's education as described in the IEP. The IEP must be in effect at the beginning of the school year and be reviewed at least annually (IDEA, 20 U.S.C. § 1414(a)(5)).

Least Restrictive Environment.   The IDEA mandates that students with disabilities are educated with their peers without disabilities to the maximum extent appropriate (IDEA Regulations, 34 C.F.R. § 300.550(b)(1)). Students in special education can only be removed to separate classes or schools when the nature or severity of their disabilities is such that they cannot receive an appropriate education in a general education classroom with supplementary aids and services (IDEA Regulations, 34 C.F.R. § 300.550(b)(2)). When students are placed in segregated settings, schools must provide them with opportunities to interact with their peers without disabilities where appropriate (e.g., art class, physical education).

To ensure that students are educated in the least restrictive environment (LRE) that is appropriate for their needs, school districts must ensure that a complete continuum of alternative placements is available. This continuum consists of regular classes, resource rooms, special classes, special schools, homebound instruction, and instruction in hospitals and institutions (IDEA Regulations, 34 C.F.R. § 300.551). (For a discussion of LRE, see Chapter 12).

Procedural Safeguards.   The heart of the IDEA lies in the procedural safeguards designed to protect the interests of students with disabilities (Tucker & Goldstein, 1992). The IDEA uses an extensive system of procedural safeguards to ensure that parents are equal participants in the special education process (IDEA Regulations, 34 C.F.R. § 300.500 *et seq.*). These safeguards consist of four components: general safeguards, the independent educational evaluation, the appointment of surrogate parents, and dispute resolution (i.e., mediation and the due process hearing).

The general safeguards for parents and students consist of notice and consent requirements. Specifically, notice must be given to parents a reasonable amount of time prior to the school's initiating or changing or refusing to initiate or change the student's identification, evaluation, or educational placement (IDEA Regulations, 34 C.F.R. § 300.504(a) *et seq.*). Parental consent must be obtained prior to conducting a preplacement evaluation and again prior to initial placement in a special education program (IDEA Regulations, 34 C.F.R. § 300.504(b) *et seq.*).

When the parents of a child with disabilities disagree with the educational evaluation of the school, they have a right to obtain an independent evaluation at public expense (IDEA Regulations, 34 C.F.R. § 300.503). The school has to supply the parents, on request, with information about where the independent educational evaluation may be obtained. When the parents decide to have the evaluation done independently, the district must pay for the cost of the evaluation or see that it is provided at no cost to the parents. If, however, the school believes its evaluation was appropriate, the school may initiate a due process hearing. If the result of the hearing is that the school's evaluation was appropriate, the parents do not have the right to receive the evaluation at public expense. Parent-initiated independent evaluations, when done at the parents' own expense, must be considered by the school. Results may also be presented as evidence at a due process hearing. Finally, a hearing officer can request an independent evaluation as part of a hearing; in this case the cost must be borne by the school.

When a child's parents cannot be located or the child is a ward of the state, the agency is responsible for appointing surrogate parents to protect the rights of the child. Employees of the school or persons with conflicts of interest cannot serve as surrogate parents. The method of selecting a surrogate parent must be in accordance with state law. The actual selection and appointment methods, therefore, are not determined by the IDEA. The IDEA does require that the surrogate parent must represent the child in all matters relating to the provision of special education to the child (IDEA Regulations, 34 C.F.R. § 300.514 *et seq.*).

When parents and the school disagree about identification, evaluation, placement, or any matters pertaining to the FAPE, either party may request a due process hearing. For example, if the parents refuse consent for evaluation or initial placement, the school may use the due process hearing to conduct an evaluation or place the child (IDEA Regulations, 34 C.F.R. § 300.504(b)(3)). The IDEA Amendments of 1997 require that states offer parents the option of resolving their disputes through the mediation process prior to going to a due process hearing. The mediation process is voluntary and must not be used to deny or delay parents' right to a due process hearing. The mediation process is conducted by a trained mediator who is knowledgeable about the laws and regulations regarding the provision of special education and related services. A mediator has no decision-making powers as do impartial due process hearing officers. Rather, the mediator attempts to facilitate an agreement between the parents and school officials regarding the matter in dispute. If attempts to mediate and reach agreement are not successful, either party may request an impartial due process hearing.

The due process hearing must be conducted by either the SEA or the LEA that is responsible for the education of the student. A due process hearing is a forum in which both sides present their arguments to an impartial third party, the due process hearing officer. During the hearing, the student must remain in the program or placement in effect when the hearing was requested. A school district cannot unilaterally change placement or program during the pendency of the due process hearing or judicial action. The IDEA provision that mandates the student's placement or program not be changed without the agreement of both parties is referred to as the *stay-put provision* (IDEA Regulations, 34 C.F.R. § 300.513). The stay-put provision may be abrogated in situations where a student with disabilities brings a weapon to school, uses or sells illegal drugs, or presents a danger to other students or to staff. (See Chapter 15 for elaborations on the stay-put provision and students with disabilities.)

Any party in the hearing has the right to be represented by counsel, present evidence, compel the attendance of witnesses, examine and cross-examine witnesses, prohibit the introduction of evidence not introduced 5 days prior to the hearing, obtain a written or electronic verbatim record of the hearing, and be provided with the written findings of fact by the hearing officer. Additionally, the parent may have the child present and may open the hearing to the public. Following the hearing, the hearing officer announces the decision. This decision is binding on both parties. Either party, however, may appeal the decision. In most states, the appeal is to the SEA. The decision of the agency can then be appealed to the state or federal court. (For elaboration on procedural safeguards, see Chapter 13).

Technology-Related Assistance.   The pervasive impact of technology on the lives of persons with disabilities was recognized in a report issued by the Federal Office of Technology Assessment in 1982 (Gibbons, 1982). The report identified a lack of comprehensive, responsive, and coordinated mechanisms to deliver and fund technology to improve the lives of persons with disabilities. In 1988, Congress passed the Technology-Related Assistance for Individuals with Disabilities Act (29 U.S.C. § 2201 *et seq.*). The purpose of the law was to establish a program of federal grants to states to promote technology-related assistance to individuals with disabilities. Assistive technology, as defined in the law, included both technological devices and services. Congress further recognized the importance of technology in the lives of children and youth with disabilities by incorporating the definitions of assistive technology devices and services from the Technology Act into the IDEA:

> The term "assistive technology device" means any item, piece of equipment, or product system, whether acquired commercially off the shelf, modified, or customized, that is used to increase, maintain, or improve functional capabilities of [children] with disabilities.
>
> The term "assistive technology service" means any service that directly assists a [child] with a disability in the selection, acquisition, or use of an assistive technology device. Such a term includes—
>
> (A) the evaluation of the needs of a [child] with a disability including a functional evaluation of the [child] in the [child's] customary environment;
>
> (B) purchasing, leasing, or otherwise providing for the acquisition of assistive technology devices by [children] with disabilities;
>
> (C) selecting, designing, fitting, customizing, adapting, applying, retaining, repairing, or replacing of assistive technology devices;
>
> (D) coordinating and using other therapies, interventions, or services with assistive technology devices;
>
> (E) training or technical assistance for a [child] with disabilities or, where appropriate, the family of a [child] with disabilities; and
>
> (F) training or technical assistance for professionals. (IDEA, 20 U.S.C. § 1401, 25–26)

These definitions were included in the IDEA; however, nothing in the law mandated that participating states provide assistive technology devices or services to students. Julnes and Brown (1993) noted that this was because assistive technology devices and services were implicitly required by the EAHCA prior to the inclusion of the assistive technology definitions in 1990. Regulations implementing these definitions support this contention. The regulations provide that:

> Each public agency shall ensure that assistive technology or assistive technology services, or both . . . are made available to a child with a disability if required as part of the child's—
>
> (a) Special education under § 300.17;
>
> (b) Related services under § 300.16; or
>
> (c) Supplementary aids and services under § 300.550(b)(2). (IDEA Regulations, 34 C.F.R. § 300.308)

The regulations indicate that assistive technology devices and services should be included in the IEP if necessary to provide a FAPE as a special education service or a related service or to maintain children and youth with disabilities in the LRE through the provision of supplementary aids and services.

The IDEA Amendments of 1997 added a requirement regarding technology and special education to the IEP. IEP teams are now required to consider whether students with disabilities, regardless of category, need assistive technology devices and services. In IDEA 2004, however, Congress said that schools did not have to provide or maintain surgically implanted devices. Because such a device is medical in nature, it cannot be considered an assistive technology device.

In 2004, President Bush signed the Assistive Technology Act of 2004. The purpose of the law was to expand access to technology for individuals with disabilities. The law assists students with disabilities in several ways. First, it requires that schools use assistive technology resources when they are necessary to improve transitions for students with disabilities. Second, it ensures that students with disabilities have better information and support when they apply for loans for assistive devices. Third, it will help to raise public awareness about the importance of assistive technology devices.

Personnel Development.   States are required to submit a plan to the U.S. Department of Education that describes the kind and number of personnel needed in the state to meet the goals of the IDEA. To receive funding from the state, school districts must also provide a description of the personnel they will need to ensure a FAPE to all students with disabilities.

The original EAHCA required states to develop and implement a Comprehensive System of Personnel Development plan that ensured that an adequate supply of special education and related services personnel were available and that these persons received adequate and appropriate preparation. IDEA 2004 eliminated the language requiring a comprehensive system of personnel development in each state. Instead it substituted the term *state personnel development grant* and required that states ensure that special education teachers and related services personnel meet state-approved or state-recognized certification/licensure requirements. Additionally, districts had to use 100% of their funding under these grants for personnel preparation and professional development activities. The purpose of the professional development activities, according to IDEA 2004, was to enable teachers to deliver scientifically based academic instruction and behavioral interventions to their students.

States must ensure that, by the end of the 2005–2006 school year, all special education teachers meet the highly qualified requirements of No Child Left Behind (see Chapter 8 on NCLB). Furthermore, emergency, temporary, or provisional certification or licenses cannot be issued in lieu of full state certification/licensing requirements; neither can state certification requirements be waived. Additionally, states must have a policy that requires school districts to have measurable goals to recruit, hire, train, and retain highly qualified personnel.

To ensure that these requirements are met, states must delineate current and projected needs for special education and related services personnel, and coordinate efforts among school districts, colleges, and universities to see that personnel needs are met and that professional development activities are offered. Grants are also made available to colleges and universities to train special education teachers (IDEA Regulations, 34 C.F.R. § 381).

The states must also have procedures for adopting promising practices, materials, and technology (IDEA Regulations, 34 C.F.R. § 382). Furthermore, states must be able to disseminate knowledge derived from research and demonstration projects to special educators. Finally, school districts must provide a description of special education personnel to the state to receive special education funding.

Parent Participation.   Since the early days of special education litigation, the parents of students with disabilities have played an important role in helping schools to meet the educational needs of their children. Key provisions of the IDEA that require parental participation are scattered throughout the law. Parents must be involved in evaluation, IEP meetings, and placement decisions. The IDEA Amendments of 1997 also required that schools give progress reports to the parents of students with disabilities as frequently as they give reports to the parents of students without disabilities. The goal of this principle is to have parents play a meaningful role in the education of their children and to maintain a partnership between schools and families. Parental involvement is crucial to successful results for students. Indeed, this provision has been one of the cornerstones of the IDEA.

Part C of the IDEA.   Congress recognized the importance of early intervention for young children when it passed the Education of the Handicapped Amendments in 1986, P.L. 99-457 (IDEA, 20 U.S.C. §§ 1471–1485). This law, which became subchapter H of the IDEA, made categorical grants to states contingent on states adhering to the provisions of law, which required participating states to develop and implement statewide interagency programs of early intervention services for infants and toddlers with disabilities and their families. With the consolidation of the IDEA in the amendments of 1997, Part H became Part C.

Part C is a discretionary or support program. In addition to extending Part B protections to infants and toddlers with disabilities and strengthening incentives for states to provide services to infants and toddlers (birth to age 3), this section also created a variety of national activities to improve the education of children with disabilities through investments in areas including research, training, and technical assistance (Yell, Drasgow, Bradley, & Justesen, 2004).

The IDEA defines infants and toddlers as children from birth through age 2 who need early intervention services because they are experiencing developmental delays or have a diagnosed physical or mental condition that puts them at risk of developing developmental delays. Early intervention services can be any developmental services, which are provided at public expense and under public supervision, that are designed to meet the physical, cognitive, communication, social or emotional, and adaptive needs of the child. Early intervention services may include family training, counseling, home visits, speech pathology, occupational therapy, physical therapy, psychological services, case management services, medical services (for diagnostic or evaluation purposes only), health services, social work services, vision services, assistive technology devices and services, transportation, and related costs. To the maximum extent appropriate, these services must be provided in natural environments (e.g., home and community settings) in which children without disabilities participate.

The infants and toddlers program does not require that the state educational agency assume overall responsibility for the early intervention programs. The agency that assumes responsibility is referred to as the *lead agency*. The lead agency may be the SEA, the state welfare department, the health department, or any other unit of state government. Many states provide Part C services through multiple state agencies. In these cases, an interagency coordinating council is the primary planning body that works out the agreements between the agencies regarding jurisdiction and funding.

Part D of the IDEA.   Part D is also a discretionary or support program. This section of the law contains provisions that are vitally important to the development of special education in the United States. The activities funded by Part D have also had a great effect on students in regular education and on the lives of all persons with disabilities. Figure 5.2 lists some of the Congressional findings and goals regarding the Part D programs.

According to the Office of Special Education Programs, Part D programs account for less than 1% of the national expenditure on programs to educate students with disabilities (OSEP, 2000). Nevertheless, programs funded by Part D have played a crucial role in identifying, implementing, evaluating, and disseminating information about effective practices in educating students with disabilities. Essentially, Part D programs support the other 99% of the federal expenditures to educate students with disabilities (OSEP, 2000). In IDEA 2004, three major Part D programs were authorized.

Subpart 1—State Personnel Development Grants.   Because personnel development and professional development are necessary to improve results for children and youth with disabilities, this subpart provides federal support for assisting state educational agencies to reform and improve their personnel preparation and professional development systems. This subpart authorizes funds for competitive grants to states to develop and implement personnel preparation and professional development. Personnel preparation and professional development are especially important goals of Part D. In fact one of the primary purposes of the IDEA, listed in Part A, is

> Supporting high-quality, intensive preservice preparation and professional development for all personnel who work with children with disabilities in order to ensure that such personnel have the skills and knowledge necessary to improve the academic achievement and functional performance of children with disabilities, including the use of scientifically based instructional practices. (IDEA, 20 U.S.C. § 1401 (c)(5)(E))

This subpart also authorizes formula grants that are given to states that apply and meet the requirements of the subpart. To apply for these grants, states must establish partnerships with school districts and institutions of higher education. The personnel preparation and professional development activities that are supported by these grants must (a) improve the knowledge of special and regular education teachers of the academic and functional needs of students with disabilities; (b) improve the knowledge of special and regular education teachers of effective instructional strategies and methods; and (c) provide training in the methods of positive behavioral interventions and supports, scientifically based reading instruction, including early literacy instruction, effective instruction for children with low incidence disabilities, and classroom-based

Figure 5.2

Congressional Findings on Part D of the IDEA

1) The Federal Government has an ongoing obligation to support activities that contribute to positive results for children and youth with disabilities, thus enabling those children to lead productive and independent lives.

2) Systematic change that benefits all students, including students with disabilities, will require the involvement of states, local educational agencies, parents, individuals with disabilities and their families, teachers, and other service providers so that they may develop and implement strategies that improve educational results for children and youth with disabilities.

3) An effective educational system serving students with disabilities should—

   a) maintain high academic achievement standards and clear performance goals for students with disabilities. Moreover, these standards and goals should be consistent with the standards and expectations for all students in the educational system and provide for appropriate and effective strategies and methods to ensure that all children and youth with disabilities have the opportunity to achieve those standards and goals;

   b) clearly define, in objective, measurable terms, the school and post-school results that children and youth with disabilities are expected to achieve; and

   c) promote transition services and coordinate interagency services so that they effectively address the full range of student needs. This is particularly important for children and youth with disabilities who need significant levels of support to participate and learn in school and the community.

4) The availability of an adequate number of qualified personnel is critical—

   a) to serve effectively children with disabilities;

   b) to assume leadership positions in administration and direct services;

   c) to provide teacher training; and

   d) to conduct high quality research to improve special education.

5) High quality, comprehensive professional development programs are essential to ensure that the persons responsible for the education or transition of children with disabilities possess the skills and knowledge necessary to address the unique needs of those children.

6) Models of professional development should be scientifically based and reflect successful practices, including strategies for recruiting, preparing, and retaining personnel.

7) Continued support is essential for the development and maintenance of a coordinated and high quality program of research to inform successful teaching practices and model curricula for educating children with disabilities.

8) Training, technical assistance, support, and dissemination activities delivered in a timely manner are necessary to ensure that parts B and C are fully implemented and achieve high quality early intervention, educational, and transitional results for children with disabilities and their families.

Figure 5.2
Continued

> 9) Parent training and information activities are of particular importance in—
>
>   a) playing a vital role in creating and preserving constructive relationships between parent and schools;
>
>   b) ensuring the involvement of parents in planning and decision making;
>
>   c) assisting parents in the development of skills that allow them to participate effectively in the child's education.
>
> 10) Support is needed to improve technological resources and integrate technology, including universally designed technologies, into the lives of children and youth with disabilities and their parents.

procedures to assist struggling children prior to referral to special education; and (d) provide training to special education personnel and regular education personnel in planning, developing, and implementing effective and appropriate IEPs. Additionally, these grants can be used for developing and implementing programs to recruit and retain highly qualified special education teachers.

Subpart 2—Personnel Preparation, Technical Assistance, Model Demonstration Projects, and Dissemination of Information.   This subpart provides federal support for (a) training personnel to work with students with disabilities using scientifically based instructional practices; (b) providing technical assistance to state and local educational agencies; (c) developing and implementing model demonstration projects to promote the use of scientifically based instructional practices; (d) conducting research to improve educational programs for students with disabilities; (e) conducting evaluations of exemplary programs for students with disabilities; (f) funding national programs that provide for technical assistance, dissemination, and implementation of scientifically based research; and (g) investigating and implementing interim alternative educational settings, preventing problem behavior by using positive behavioral interventions and supports, and employing systematic schoolwide approaches and interventions.

Subpart 3—Supports to Improve Results for Children with Disabilities.   This subpart provides federal support for (a) establishing parent training and information centers, (b) establishing community parent resource centers, (c) providing technical support to parent training and information centers, and (d) developing, demonstrating, and utilizing devices and strategies to make technology accessible and usable for students with disabilities.

Part D programs are often referred to as *support programs* because the primary purpose of these programs is to support the implementation of the IDEA and to assist states in improving the education of students with disabilities. The Part D programs, even though they constitute a small amount of the total federal expenditure for the IDEA, help to ensure that the field of special education will continue to move forward by translating research to practice and improving the future of students with disabilities (Yell, Drasgow, Bradley, & Justesen, 2004).

In 1976 the Department of Health, Education, and Welfare promulgated regulations implementing the IDEA. With every amendment to the law these regulations have been clarified, added to, or changed. The extensive regulations can be found at 34 C.F.R. §§ 300.1–300.754. Regulations implementing the original Part C—early intervention programs for infants and toddlers with disabilities—can be found at 34 C.F.R. §§ 303.1–303.670.

Title II of the IDEA

When the IDEA was reauthorized and amended in 2004 Congress added Title II, which established the National Center on Special Education Research. The center is located with the Institute of Education Sciences (IES) in the U.S. Department of Education. The center's mission is to sponsor research that (a) expands the knowledge base in special education, (b) improves services under the IDEA, and (c) evaluates the implementation and effectiveness of the IDEA.

The center is led by a Commissioner selected by the director of the IES. The commissioner of the center, along with the Assistant Secretary of the Office of Special Education and Rehabilitation Services (OSERS), develops a research plan. This plan is submitted to the IES director. This research plan will serve as a blueprint for all the center's research activities.

A central goal of the center is to identify scientifically based educational practices that support learning and improve academic achievement, functional outcomes, and educational results for students with disabilities. Additionally, the center seeks to sponsor research that will improve the preparation of special education personnel. Finally, the center synthesizes and disseminates research findings through the National Center for Educational Evaluation and Regional Assistance.

The IDEA and the Reauthorization Process

When Congress passes statutes that appropriate money, it may fund the statute on either a permanent or a limited basis. If a law is funded on a permanent basis, the funding will continue as long as the law remains unchanged—that is, unless the law is amended to remove funding or is repealed. Part B, the section of the IDEA that creates the entitlement to a FAPE and provides federal funding to the states, is permanently authorized. Congress may also appropriate funds for a statute on a limited basis. In this case, the funding period will be designated in the statute. When this period of time expires, Congress has to reauthorize funding or else let funding expire. The discretionary or support programs of the IDEA—Parts C and D—are authorized on a limited basis. In the past, funding for these programs has been authorized for periods of 4 or 5 years. Approximately every 4 or 5 years, therefore, Congress has had to reauthorize the IDEA, with the exception of Parts A and B.

Amendments to the IDEA

Since the passage of the original EAHCA in 1975, there have been numerous changes to the law. Some of these changes have been minor; for example, P.L. 100-630 in 1988 altered some of the statute's language, and P.L. 102-119 in 1991 modified parts of the infants and toddlers program. Some of the amendments, however, have made important changes to the law. These changes have expanded the procedural and substantive rights of students with disabilities protected under IDEA. Four acts that made significant changes to the then EAHCA were the Handicapped Children's Protection Act (P.L. 99-372), the Infants and Toddlers with Disabilities Act (P.L. 99-457), the Individuals with Disabilities Education Act of 1990 (P.L. 101-476), Individuals with Disabilities Education Act Amendments of 1997 (P.L. 105-17), and the Individuals with Disabilities Education Improvement Act of 2004 (P.L. 108-446; hereafter IDEA 2004). As amendments, the changes were incorporated into the Act and are not codified as separate laws. The last two reauthorizations were perhaps the most significant changes to the law since its original passage in 1975. The following sections briefly review these two reauthorizations.

The IDEA Amendments of 1997

The IDEA Amendments of 1997 (hereafter IDEA 1997) added several significant provisions to the law. Additionally, the IDEA was restructured by consolidating the law from eight parts to four, and significant additions were made in the following areas: (a) strengthening the role of parents, ensuring access to the general education curriculum; (b) emphasizing student progress toward meaningful educational goals through changes in the IEP process; (c) encouraging parents and educators to resolve differences by using nonadversarial mediation; and (d) allowing school officials greater leeway in disciplining students with disabilities by altering aspects of the IDEA's procedural safeguards. Additionally, these amendments required states to develop performance goals and indicators, such as dropout and graduation rates.

The Individualized Education Program

Congress believed that the IDEA had been extremely successful in improving students' access to public schools, and the critical issue in 1997 was to improve the performance and educational achievement of students with disabilities in both the special education and general education curricula. To this end, Congress mandated a number of changes to the IEP and the inclusion of students with disabilities in state- and district-wide assessments. Regarding the IEP, changes include the requirement that a statement of measurable annual goals, including benchmarks or short-term objectives, that would enable parents and educators to accurately determine a student's progress be included in the IEP. The primary difference in the statement of goals from that of the original IDEA is the emphasis on accurately measuring and reporting a student's progress toward the annual goals. The core IEP team was expanded to include both a special education teacher and a general education teacher. The original IDEA mandated that the child's teacher be a member of the IEP team but did not specify if the teacher should be in special or general education.

The 1997 amendments required that students with disabilities be included in state- and district-wide assessments of student progress. The amendments also required that the IEP team be the forum to determine if modifications or accommodations were needed to allow a student to participate in these assessments. The IEP, therefore, requires a statement regarding a student's participation in these assessments and what, if any, modifications to the assessment are needed to allow participation.

Disciplining Students in Special Education

Another significant addition of IDEA 1997 was a section addressing the discipline of students with disabilities. In hearings prior to the reauthorization, Congress heard testimony regarding the lack of parity school officials faced when making decisions about disciplining students with and without disabilities who violated the same school rules (Senate Report, 1997). To address these concerns, Congress added a section to the IDEA in an attempt to balance school officials' obligation to ensure that schools are safe and orderly environments conducive to learning and the school's obligation to ensure that students with disabilities receive a FAPE.

To deal with behavioral problems in a proactive manner, IDEA 1997 requires that if a student with disabilities has behavior problems, regardless of the student's disability category, the IEP team shall consider strategies—including positive behavioral interventions, strategies, and supports—to address these problems. In such situations a proactive behavior management plan, based on functional behavioral assessment, should be included in the student's IEP. Furthermore, if a student's placement is changed following a behavioral incident and the IEP does not contain a behavioral intervention plan, a functional behavioral assessment and a behavioral plan must be completed no later than 10 days after changing the placement.

School officials may discipline a student with disabilities in the same manner as they discipline students without disabilities, with a few notable exceptions. If necessary, school officials may unilaterally change the placement of a student for disciplinary purposes to an appropriate interim alternative setting, move the student to another setting, or suspend the student to the extent that these disciplinary methods are used with students without disabilities. The primary difference is that with students who have disabilities, the suspension or placement change may not exceed 10 school days. School officials may unilaterally place a student with disabilities in an appropriate interim alternative educational setting for up to 45 days if the student brings a weapon to school or a school function or knowingly possesses, uses, or sells illegal drugs or controlled substances at school or a school function. The interim alternative educational setting must be determined by the IEP team. Additionally, a hearing officer can order a 45-day change in placement if school officials have evidence indicating that maintaining the student with disabilities in the current placement is substantially likely to result in injury to the student or others and that school officials have made reasonable efforts to minimize this risk of harm.

The Manifestation Determination

If school officials seek a change of placement, suspension, or expulsion in excess of 10 school days, a review of the relationship between a student's disability and his or her misconduct must be conducted within 10 days. This review, called a *manifestation determination,* must be conducted by a student's IEP team and other qualified personnel. If a determination is made that no relationship exists between the misconduct and disability, the same disciplinary procedures as would be used with students without disabilities may be imposed on a student with disabilities. Educational services, however, must be continued. The parents of the student may request an expedited due process hearing if they disagree with the results of the manifestation determination. The student's placement during the hearing will be in the interim alternative educational setting (IAES). (For elaborations on the manifestation determination and IAES, see Chapter 14.)

Dispute Resolution

Congress also attempted to alleviate what was believed to be the overly adversarial nature of special education by encouraging parents and educators to resolve differences by using nonadversarial methods. Specifically, IDEA 1997 required states to offer mediation as a voluntary option to parents and educators as an initial process for dispute resolution. The mediator must be trained or qualified to conduct mediation sessions and knowledgeable regarding special education law. Furthermore, the mediator cannot be an employee of the LEA or SEA and must not have any personal or professional conflict of interest. The results of mediation sessions shall be put in writing and are confidential. If mediation is not successful, either party may request an impartial due process hearing.

Attorney's Fees

The 1997 amendments also limited the conditions under which attorneys can collect fees under the IDEA. Attorney's fees for participation in IEP meetings have been eliminated unless the meeting is convened because of an administrative or judicial order. Similarly, attorney's fees are not available for mediation sessions prior to filing for a due process hearing. Attorney's fees can also be reduced if the parents' attorney does not provide the appropriate information to the school district regarding the possible action. Finally, parents must notify school district officials of the problem and proposed solutions prior to filing for a due process hearing if they intend to seek attorney's fees.

Special Education and Adult Inmates

The 1997 amendments also provide that states may opt not to provide special education services to persons with disabilities in adult prisons if they were not identified as IDEA-eligible prior to their incarceration. If these persons had been identified and received special education services when attending school, however, states must continue their special education while they are in prison.

Charter Schools

The 1997 amendments also require school districts to serve students with disabilities who attend charter schools just as they would serve students attending the district's schools. Charter schools may not be required to apply for IDEA funds jointly in LEAs. Finally, school districts must provide IDEA funds to charter schools in the same manner as they provide funds to other schools.

The Individuals with Disabilities Education Improvement Act of 2004

On December 3, 2004, President Bush signed IDEA 2004 into law. The bill had almost unanimously passed both the U.S. House of Representatives and the U.S Senate. Figure 5.3 depicts the process that resulted in passage of the new law. Appendix A contains a table that depicts the major changes of IDEA 2004.

The primary goal of Congress in passing IDEA 2004 is to align IDEA with NCLB, thereby increasing accountability for improving student performance. Thus, IDEA

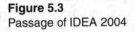

Figure 5.3
Passage of IDEA 2004

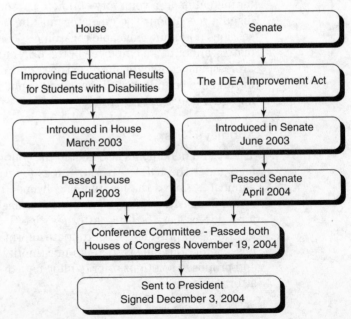

2004 includes measures to increase academic results for students with disabilities such as requiring the use of scientifically based practices. The law also defines highly qualified special education teachers in line with the definition in NCLB. Additionally, Congress sought to reduce the paperwork burden on teachers, expand options for parents, and reduce litigation.

Congress stated that the IDEA has successfully ensured access to educational services for millions of children and youth with disabilities. Nevertheless, implementation of the IDEA had been impeded by low expectations and an insufficient focus on applying scientifically based research on proven methods of teaching children and youth with disabilities. Specifically, Congress stated that having high expectations for students with disabilities and ensuring their access to the general education curriculum would assist them to be prepared to lead productive and independent lives. Moreover, IDEA 2004 sought to support high quality, intensive preservice preparation and professional development based on scientific research. Congress, in passing IDEA 2004, also sought to encourage schools to develop schoolwide approaches to reduce the need to label children as disabled and to provide assistance to all children who need it. Indeed, one of the major purposes of IDEA 2004 is

> providing incentives for whole-school approaches, scientifically based early reading program, positive behavioral interventions and supports, and early intervening services to reduce the need to label children as disabled in order to address the learning and behavioral needs of such children. (IDEA, 20 U.S.C. § 1401(c)(5)(F))

In IDEA 2004, Congress made significant changes to the law. Some of the areas affected include the IEP, discipline, assessment, attorney's fees, "highly qualified" teachers, scientifically based instruction, and funding. Readers should note that these are changes in the federal law. The U.S. Department of Education issued the regulations implementing IDEA 2004 on August 3, 2006. Many state departments of education will likely rewrite their regulations to conform to the federal law.

The Individualized Education Program

In IDEA 2004, Congress attempted to alter the IEP process so it (a) is easier for IEP teams to navigate, (b) involves less paperwork and meetings, and (c) increases accountability.

Changes in the IEP Development Process.   The IDEA requires that the IEP team must, at a minimum include (a) the student's parents; (b) the special education teacher; (c) a general education teacher (at least one, if a student has multiple general education teachers); (d) a representative of the local educational agency (i.e., school) who can provide, or supervise the provision of, special education services; (e) an individual who can explain the instructional implications of the evaluation results; and (f) others at the discretion of the student's parents or the school. IDEA 2004, however, allows a member of the IEP team whose attendance is not necessary because his or her area of curriculum or related services are not being modified or discussed at the meeting to be excused from attending the IEP meeting or other meetings if the student's parents and the local education agency agree that the person's presence is not necessary. To be excused the team member must submit a request in writing to the parents and the IEP team, and the parents and IEP team must agree with excusing the team member. This change may make it easier to schedule meetings.

Changes in the IEP Document.   The federal law no longer requires that benchmarks or short-term objectives be included in the IEP, except for students with severe disabilities who take alternate assessments. Rather, IDEA 2004 emphasizes the importance of writing measurable annual goals and then measuring progress toward each goal during the course of the year. Teachers must inform students' parents of their progress toward each annual goal at least every 9 weeks. If students are not making sufficient progress to enable them to reach their goals by the end of the year, instructional changes must be made to their instructional program.

Changes in the IEP Modification Process.   According to IDEA 2004, programming changes are proposed to a student's program after the annual IEP meeting has been held. The IEP team and a student's parents could agree to make the changes in a written document rather than reconvening the IEP team to make the changes. These modifications would then become part of the IEP. This is a significant change because previously an IEP team had to be reconvened to revise a student's special education program. Congress believed this would allow teachers to spend less time having to schedule, prepare for, and attend IEP meetings.

Three-Year IEPs.   IDEA 2004 allows up to 15 states to develop and implement 3-year IEPs. If the states applied to the U.S. Department of Education and were accepted for the pilot program, they could offer parents the option of developing a comprehensive 3-year IEP designed to coincide with natural transition points in their child's education (e.g., preschool to kindergarten, elementary school to middle school, middle school to high school). Parents had to agree to this option. States that did not apply for this pilot program are still required to develop and implement 1-year IEPs.

IEPs for Transfer Students.   When a special education student transfers from an in-state or out-of-state school district to a new school district, the accepting school is required to continue to provide the student with a FAPE. In other words, the new school must continue to provide services comparable to those described in the student's previous IEP. Moreover, the accepting school is required to consult with the student's parents regarding the services. If the student is from out of state, the new school is required to conduct an evaluation and, if appropriate, develop a new IEP.

Disciplining Students in Special Education

Congress made changes in IDEA 2004 designed to provide schools with greater flexibility to maintain safe educational environments while protecting the disciplinary safeguards that were extended to students with disabilities in the IDEA Amendments of 1997.

The Manifestation Determination.   IDEA 2004 keeps the manifestation determination mandate that requires LEAs to determine if a student's misbehavior leading to a suspension is related to the student's disability whenever schools suspend students with disabilities for more than 10 school days. This provision simplifies and strengthens the manifestation determination standard because a behavior could be determined to be a manifestation of a student's disability only if the conduct in question is "caused by" or has a "direct and substantial relationship" to the student's disability. Additionally, if a school fails to implement a student's IEP, a direct relationship would also exist. Many educators believe the new standard makes it easier for IEP teams to find that there is no relationship between a student's misbehavior and disability, thus subjecting a student with disabilities to the regular school disciplinary policies regarding suspensions and expulsions. Additionally, when a student with disabilities is suspended in excess of 10 school days or expelled, the law requires that he or she must continue to receive educational services.

Behaviors That Can Lead to a 45-Day Disciplinary Removal.   The IDEA Amendments of 1997 listed behaviors that could result in a student with disabilities being removed to an IAES for up to 45 calendar days, even in situations where the behavior is a manifestation of a student's disability. IDEA 2004 adds the offense of committing "serious bodily injury upon another person" to drugs and weapons offenses that were previously included. Additionally, the law changes the time that a student could be in an IAES from 45 days to 45 school days.

If a student with disabilities, therefore, engages in behavior that causes serious bodily injury to another person while at school, on school grounds, or at a school function, the school can place the student in an interim alternative setting for up to 45 school days. This can be done even when the misbehavior is related to his or her disability.

Stay-Put Provision.   Under the previous IDEA, when a student was disciplined and his parents filed for due process, the student had to stay put in his or her previous educational setting during the hearing. IDEA 2004 changes the requirement so that the stay-put placement is no longer the previous setting; rather, it becomes the IAES. Congress believed this change would remove the temptation for parents to litigate or file for due process, which was created by the old stay-put provision because it allowed students to remain in the pre-discipline placement during the hearing except in situations involving drugs or weapons.

Dispute Resolution

Congress attempted to reduce litigation in special education in two major ways when it enacted IDEA 2004. First, the law limits the time that parents can request due process hearings to 2 years from the date they knew or should have known about the issues that led to the due process request, and it imposes a 90-day limit for filing appeals. Second, the law creates a resolution session that school districts are required to hold in an attempt to settle the complaint that led the parents to request a due process hearing. This session must be held within 15 days of the request for the due process hearing. The representative of the school district is required to be at the meeting. A school district cannot send an attorney to the session unless the parents have an attorney. If the school district and parents decide to go to mediation and bypass the resolution session, they must agree to this in writing. If the school district and parents decide to go ahead with the process and reach an agreement regarding the issue, both parties most sign a binding settlement agreement.

Attorney's Fees

IDEA 2004 altered the attorney's fees provision by not allowing attorneys to be reimbursed for any actions or proceedings performed before a written settlement is made by the school district. Neither are attorneys allowed to receive reimbursement for attending IEP meetings, unless the meetings are ordered by a hearing officer. IDEA 2004 also allows courts to award attorney's fees to school districts, when parents' attorneys (a) file a compliant that is frivolous, unreasonable, or without foundation; (b) continue to litigate after the case is shown to be frivolous, unreasonable, or without foundation; or (c) bring a complaint or action to harass, cause delay, or increase the costs to the school district.

Eligibility of Students with Learning Disabilities

The regulations that implemented IDEA 1997 required that states use a discrepancy formula to determine if a student had a learning disability. This formula is used to determine if there is a severe discrepancy between a student's achievement, as measured by a standardized achievement test, and a student's ability, as measured by an intelligence test. This requirement was changed in IDEA 2004. States can no longer require school districts to use a discrepancy formula; instead, school districts may use a process that determines whether a student responds to scientific, research-based interventions.

Funding

IDEA 2004 allows states greater flexibility in their use of IDEA funds. For example, states can use their IDEA funds for technical assistance and direct services to provide supplemental educational services to students with disabilities who attend schools that have failed to make adequate yearly progress for 3 years in a row and are identified for improvement. However, these schools must have been identified for improvement solely because of the performance of the students with disabilities subgroup.

Additionally school districts may use as much as 15% of their IDEA funding for early intervention services to teach at-risk students who have not yet been identified as IDEA eligible. States may also establish risk pools by setting aside 10% of the reserve funding. The purpose of the state risk pools is to help schools pay for the high cost of teaching students with the most serious disabilities or unexpected increases in student enrollments.

Highly Qualified Teachers

IDEA 2004 defines a highly qualified special education teacher according to standards developed in NCLB. IDEA 2004 requires that all new special education teachers (a) obtain a bachelor's degree, (b) be certified by the state as a special education teacher, and (c) demonstrate competency of subject matter. Additionally, special education teachers cannot be highly qualified if they hold an emergency, temporary, or provisional certification.

Demonstrating subject matter knowledge for an elementary special education position requires that the teacher pass a rigorous state test of knowledge in the basic elementary curriculum. Demonstrating subject matter knowledge for a special education teacher who teaches a number of different subjects requires that the teacher pass a rigorous state test in the core academic subjects he or she teaches. However, Congress eased these requirements by letting experienced teachers meet NCLB's highly qualified requirements by passing a state's high, objective, uniform state standard of evaluation (HOUSSE). Additionally, if new teachers are certified in mathematics, reading, or science, they could also use HOUSSE requirements to demonstrate subject matter competency in the other subjects taught. The HOUSSE requirements must be met no later than 2 years after they are hired by a school district.

Teachers of students with severe disabilities, who would be assessed by using an alternative achievement measure, could demonstrate subject matter competency by passing an elementary test, if their students learn at the level of elementary school students, or by passing a test at their students' level of instruction. This level would be developed by individual states.

Funding of the IDEA

The federal government, through the IDEA, provides funding to assist SEAs with special education costs. To receive IDEA funds, SEAs must submit a state special education plan to the U.S. Department of Education. This plan must show that an SEA is providing free appropriate special education services to all students with disabilities residing in the state between the ages of 3 and 21 in accordance with the procedures set forth in the IDEA (this includes students with disabilities who have been suspended or expelled from school). States that meet the IDEA requirements receive federal funding.

A large portion of the federal IDEA funds received by the SEA must be distributed to school districts, or LEAs. The federal funds do not cover the entire cost of special education, but rather are intended to provide financial assistance to the states. Congress originally intended to fund 40% of states' costs in providing special education services through the IDEA. The actual level of funding to the states, however, has never reached this amount. In the first years following passage of the IDEA, federal funding reached approximately 12% of the total state expenditures on special education. From the late 1980s to late 1990s the federal IDEA expenditures equaled approximately 7% to 8% of total expenditures. The Omnibus Consolidated Appropriations Act Fiscal Year 1997, enacted in 1996, raised the federal contribution to close to 10%. With the passage of IDEA 2004 and the subsequent appropriations, funding levels reached approximately 19% of state expenditures.

In IDEA 2004, Congress announced that federal funding from 2004 to 2010 would increase each year so that IDEA would be fully funded in accordance with the original promise that Congress made in 1975. Readers should note that full funding means that the IDEA will reach the original funding goal of 40% of state costs. Additionally, the funding targets announced in IDEA 2004 were not mandatory.

Federal expenditures are computed on a state-by-state basis in accordance with the number of students with disabilities served (no adjustments are made either for the category of disability or for the setting in which a student is served). A state is responsible for counting the number of students with disabilities educated in special education. This is called the *child count.* The number is multiplied by 40% of the average per-student expenditure in public schools in the United States. The federal government caps the number of students in special education in each state that federal sources will fund. States cannot receive federal IDEA funding for more than 12% of the total number of school-age students in the state.

The funding formula remains based on the child count until federal appropriations reach $4.9 billion. Federal appropriations above that level will be allocated according to a population-based formula with an adjustment for poverty rates. When the trigger of $4.9 billion is reached, the new formula, based on the state's population (85%) and poverty level (15%), will apply to all excess appropriations. Congress capped the total increases a state could receive under this formula as no more than 1.5% over the federal funding from the previous year. Neither can states receive less than they did in fiscal 1997. The purpose of the caps and floors is to limit the increase in federal monies to states that gain from the formula change and to prevent large decreases in states that receive less under the new formula.

The federal money states receive must not be used to supplant state funds but to supplement and increase funding of special education and related services. This requirement, often referred to as the nonsupplanting requirement of the IDEA, ensures that states will not use IDEA funds to relieve themselves of their financial obligations, but that the funds will increase the level of state expenditures on special education. The state is ultimately responsible for ensuring the appropriate use of funds. IDEA regulations also grant school districts the authority to use other sources of funding to pay for special education services (IDEA Regulations, 34 C.F.R. § 300.600(c)).

The IDEA also requires that 75% of the federal funds received by the states be directed to the local schools and that 25% may be used at the state level. The majority of federal funding, therefore, flows from the federal to the state government and in turn to local school districts. To receive state funds, local school districts must have programs that meet the state requirements. States are required to establish management and auditing procedures to ensure that federal funds will be expended in accordance with IDEA provisions. States must also set up systems of fund allocation.

The amount of flow-through funds given to an LEA is in proportion to the district's contribution to the state total of students in special education.

The 25% of the federal monies that may be set aside for state agency activities may be used for administration and supervision, direct and supportive services for students with disabilities, and monitoring and complaint investigation (IDEA Regulations, 34 C.F.R. § 300.370(a)). States may, however, use only 5% of the federal funds they receive for administrative purposes. The states' administrative activities may include technical assistance to local educational agencies, administering the state plan, approval and supervision of local activities, and leadership activities and consultative services (IDEA Regulations, 34 C.F.R. § 300.621). The IDEA Amendments of 1997 capped the actual dollar amount of the 5% that may be used for administrative purposes at the fiscal 1997 level. States will also be given increases equal to the inflation rate or the increase in federal expenditures, whichever is less. If inflation is lower than the percentage increase in federal appropriations, states are required to spend the difference on improvements in services to students with disabilities.

States may also use up to 10% of the federal funds they retain to establish risk pools to reimburse school districts for the cost of educating students who require high cost services (e.g., residential placement, medically related services). For a school district to qualify for the reimbursement through the risk pool, the cost of serving a student must be three times greater than the school district's average per-pupil expenditure and must represent a significant proportion of the district's overall budget.

IDEA 2004 also gives school districts greater flexibility in determining how they will spend new federal special education funding. For example, districts can now divert much of their new special education funding under certain programs to other programs under No Child Left Behind. Additionally, states can spend a portion of the federal funds on special education activities such as administrative case management, early intervention students, and programming for at-risk students even if they are not in special education.

Monitoring and Enforcing the IDEA

The U.S. Department of Education is the federal government agency responsible for monitoring and enforcing the IDEA. The Office of Special Education and Rehabilitative Services (OSERS) is the specific department within the Department of Education that assumes these responsibilities. A subdivision within OSERS, the Office of Special Education Programs (OSEP), is responsible for (a) writing regulations that implement the IDEA, (b) conducting many of the activities authorized by Part D of the IDEA, (c) monitoring and enforcing the provisions of the law, and (d) providing technical assistance to states. Moreover, this agency is responsible for approving states' special education plans and releasing IDEA funds to the states.

One of the most important functions of OSERS and OSEP is to draft the regulations that implement the IDEA (Pitasky, 2000). The regulations that implement Part B of the IDEA can be found at 34 C.F.R. Part 300. When the IDEA is changed during the reauthorization process, the regulations are rewritten. Prior to rewriting the regulations, OSEP must have a public comment period. Additionally, the role of any agency that drafts regulations is to be consistent with the statute. In areas in which the statute is vague, the agency has authority to fill in missing details and clarify the law so that it can be implemented. As we discussed in Chapter 1, regulations have the force of law.

The Office of Special Education Programs also interprets the IDEA, often through the issuance of policy letters and interpretive guidance. In this respect, OSEP acts in a policy-making role. The Office of Special Education Programs does this by issuing documents that provide guidance on how to follow the law. For example in 1999, OSEP issued policy guidance on disciplining students with disabilities. The office also issues memoranda to explain particular issues or topics. Finally, OSEP will answer specific questions about the IDEA. Any interested person can send a question to OSEP, which will review the question and issue an opinion. These legal interpretations are not legally binding. Nevertheless, they are important. In fact, Zirkel (2003) asserted that in special education cases, the OSEP policy letters will be considered by hearing officers and judges. Pitasky (2000) noted that these interpretations are highly valuable to the special education community and should be studied carefully. She also stated that because of the issues of regulations and interpretation, OSEP has led the way in shaping and influencing special education law.

The Office of Special Education Programs monitors states to determine if (a) states and local school districts are complying with the strictures of the IDEA, and (b) IDEA funds are being spent in an appropriate manner. States may be forced to return funds that were spent improperly. Federal monies, once disbursed, can be withheld by the U.S. Department of Education if the state fails to comply with IDEA provisions. If the department withholds funds, this decision is subject to judicial review. The department also has the power to issue an administrative complaint requesting a cease-and-desist order and may enter into compliance agreements with a state that the federal agency believes is violating the IDEA (Weber, 2002).

States are required to monitor local school districts' use of funds. If a school district has failed to comply with the IDEA or the state law mandating a FAPE, the state may withhold funds until the district comes into compliance. If the school district wishes to contest the decision, it may request a hearing.

States must also have procedures to receive and resolve complaints regarding possible violations of the IDEA. Complaints can be filed by organizations or individuals, and states must investigate these complaints. Written complaint procedures help to fulfill federal requirements that states ensure that all special education programs conform to federal law (Weber, 2002).

Summary

In 1975, President Gerald Ford signed P.L. 94-142, the Education for All Handicapped Children Act. The law, renamed the Individuals with Disabilities Education Act in 1990, provides funding to states to assist them in providing an appropriate education, consisting of special education and related services, to students with disabilities. The IDEA uses a categorical approach to delineate students covered by the law by setting forth 13 categories of disabilities covered by the Act. Only those students with disabilities covered by the IDEA are protected by the Act. Additionally, the disability must adversely affect the student's education.

The IDEA sets forth several principles that states must follow in providing a special education to students with disabilities. The primary objective of the law is to ensure that all eligible students with disabilities receive a free appropriate public education specifically designed to meet their unique needs.

For Further Information

The following books analyze special education law, including the IDEA and Section 504. The publication by Weber is a loose-leaf service that is updated frequently.

Norlin, J., & Gorn, S. (2005). *What do I do when: The answer book on special education law* (yrs ed). Horsham, PA: LRP Publications.

Pitasky, V. M. (2000). *The complete OSEP handbook.* Horsham, PA: LRP Publications.

Weber, M. C. (2002). *Special education law and litigation treatise.* Horsham, PA: LRP Publications.

The following books explain the beginnings of governmental involvement in special education, offer an account of the IDEA from inception to passage, and provide interesting examinations of how a bill becomes law:

Ballard, J., Ramirez, B. A., & Weintraub, F. J. (Eds.). (1982). *Special education in America: Its legal and governmental foundations.* Reston, VA: Council for Exceptional Children.

Levine, E. L., & Wexler, E. M. (1981). *P.L. 94-142: An act of Congress.* New York: Macmillan.

References

Education Amendments of 1974, Pub. L. No. 93-380, 88 Stat. 580.

Education for All Handicapped Children Act of 1975, 20 U.S.C. § 1401 *et seq.*

Elementary and Secondary Education Act, amended by Pub. L. No. 89-750. § 161 [Title VI], 80 Stat. 1204 (1966).

Family Educational Rights and Privacy Act, 20 U.S.C. § 1232.

Gibbons, J. (1982). *Technology and handicapped people.* Washington, DC: Office of Technology Assessment.

Gorn, S. (1996). *What do I do when: The answer book on special education law.* Horsham, PA: LRP Publications.

Guernsey, T. F., & Klare, K. (1993). *Special education law.* Durham, NC: Carolina Academic Press.

Helms v. Independent School District #3, 750 F.2d 820 (10th Cir. 1985).

Honig v. Doe, 479 U.S. 1084 (1988).

Huefner, D. S. (2000). *Getting comfortable with special education law: A framework for working with children with disabilities.* Norwood, MA: Christopher-Gordon Publishers.

Individuals with Disabilities Education Act Amendments of 1997, Pub. L. No. 105-17, 105th Cong., 1st sess.

Individuals with Disabilities Education Act, 20 U.S.C. § 1400 *et seq.*

Individuals with Disabilities Education Act Regulations, 34 C.F.R. § 300.1 *et seq.*

Joint Policy Memo, (1991) 18 IDELR 118.

Julnes, R. E., & Brown, S. E. (1993). The legal mandate to provide assistive technology in special education programming. *Education Law Reporter, 82,* 737–749.

Katsiyannis, A., Yell, M. L., & Bradley, R. (2001). Reflections on the 25th anniversary of the Individuals with Disabilities Education Act. *Remedial and Special Education, 22*, 324–334.

Levine, E. L., & Wexler, E. M. (1981). *P.L. 94-142: An act of Congress.* New York: Macmillan.

Massachusetts General Law Annotated, Chapter 71B § 3 (West, 1978).

Mills v. Board of Education, 348 F. Supp. 866 (D.D.C. 1972).

New Mexico Association for Retarded Citizens v. New Mexico, 678 F.2d 847 (10th Cir. 1982).

Office of Special Education Programs. (2000). IDEA 25th anniversary website. Available at http://www.ed.gov/offices/OSERS/IDEA 25th.html.

Omnibus Consolidated Appropriations Act, FY97, Senate Joint Resolution, N. 63, 104th Cong., 2d session, *Congressional Record,* S12327 (1996).

Pennsylvania Association of Retarded Citizens v. Commonwealth of Pennsylvania, 343 F. Supp. 279 (E.D. Pa. 1972).

Pitasky, V. M. (2000). *The complete OSEP handbook.* Horsham, PA: LRP Publications.

Rehabilitation Act of 1973, Section 504, 29 U.S.C. § 794.

Salvia, J., & Ysseldyke, J. E. (1995). *Assessment* (6th ed.). Boston: Houghton Mifflin.

Sean R. v. Town of Woodbridge Board of Education, 794 F. Supp. 467 (D. Conn. 1992).

Senate Report of the Individuals with Disabilities Act Amendments of 1997, available at wais.access.gpo.gov.

Smith v. Robinson, 468 U.S. 992 (1984).

Technology-Related Assistance for Individuals with Disabilities Act, 29 U.S.C. § 2201 *et seq.*

Timothy W. v. Rochester, New Hampshire, School District, 875 F.2d 954 (1st Cir. 1989).

Tucker, B. P., & Goldstein, B. A. (1992). *Legal rights of persons with disabilities: An analysis of federal law.* Horsham, PA: LRP Publications.

Turnbull, A. P., & Turnbull, H. R. (2002). *Families, professionals, and exceptionality: A special partnership* (3rd ed.). Upper Saddle River, NJ: Merrill/Prentice Hall.

Turnbull, A. P., Turnbull, R., Shank, M., & Smith, S. J. (2004). *Exceptional Lives: Special Education in Today's Schools* (4th ed.). Upper Saddle River, NJ: Merrill/Prentice Hall.

Weber, M. C. (2002). *Special education law and litigation treatise.* Horsham, PA: LRP Publications.

Wexler v. Westfield, 784 F.2d 176 (3rd Cir. 1986).

Yell, M. L., Drasgow, E., Bradley, R., & Justesen, T. (2004). Critical legal issues in special education. In A. McCray Sorrells, H. J. Reith, & P. T. Sindelar, *Issues in special education* (pp. 16–37). Boston: Allyn & Bacon.

Zirkel, P. (2003). Do OSEP policy letters have legal weight? *Education Law Reporter, 171,* 391–396.

CHAPTER SIX

Section 504 of the Rehabilitation Act of 1973

[Section 504] is the civil rights declaration of the handicapped. It was greeted with great hope and satisfaction by Americans who have had the distress of physical or mental handicaps compounded by thoughtless or callous discrimination. These Americans have identified [Section] 504 with access to vital public services, such as education . . . they consider it their charter . . . it is a key to, and a symbol of, their entry as full participants in the mainstream of national life.

Senator Hubert H. Humphrey, principal Senate author of Section 504,
Congressional Record, April 26, 1977, p. 12,216

Section 504 is a brief section of the Rehabilitation Act of 1973. It is a powerful law that prohibits discrimination against individuals with disabilities. As such, it is a civil rights law. The statute holds that:

No otherwise qualified individual with a disability in the United States . . . shall, solely by reason of his or her disability, be excluded from the participation in, be denied the benefits of, or be subjected to discrimination under any program or any activity receiving Federal financial assistance. (Section 504, 29 U.S.C. § 794(a))

Because public school districts receive federal financial assistance, Section 504 protects students with disabilities from discrimination in public schools throughout the United States. Thus, all students with disabilities who attend public schools, whether or not they are protected by the IDEA, are protected under Section 504. Protection from discrimination includes, and extends beyond, the school's provision of an education to such areas as the provision of related services, participation in extracurricular activities, and architectural accessibility. In addition to covering students in

117

preschool, elementary, secondary, and postsecondary schools and institutions, Section 504 also applies to school district programs such as day care, afterschool care, and summer recreation programs (OCR Senior Staff Memorandum, 1990). Unlike the Individuals with Disabilities Education Act (IDEA), no federal funds are available under Section 504 to help school districts meet the requirements of the law.

Although Section 504 became law prior to the enactment of the IDEA, it seems that only in the last few years have educators taken notice of the statute. Champagne (1995) contends that the struggle of educators to stay abreast of rules and developments of the IDEA's many procedures made it difficult to enlarge their scope to Section 504. Additionally, because there was no federal funding, school personnel may have felt little motivation to meet the requirements of the law (Smith & Patton, 1998).

Parents and advocates for children and youth with disabilities, however, began requesting that schools provide their children with educational services and protection under Section 504 (Smith, 2001). An additional factor that may have influenced parents to request services under the law is that their children may have had disabilities that were not included under the IDEA (e.g., attention deficit hyperactivity disorder), but were covered under Section 504. Moreover, the increased activity of the Office of Civil Rights (OCR) of the U.S. Department of Education regarding school district compliance with Section 504 and increased litigation demanded that school district personnel and educators pay attention to the demands of this law.

The purposes of this chapter are to (a) provide an overview of Section 504 and (b) examine the effects of Section 504 on public elementary, secondary, postsecondary, and vocational schooling. First, I review the historical developments that led to the passage of Section 504. Second, I examine the purpose, goals, and structure of the law. Finally, I consider the major principles of Section 504 and how they affect the education of students with disabilities.

The Development of Section 504

In 1973, the first major effort to protect persons with disabilities against discrimination based on their disabilities took place when Congress passed Section 504 of the Rehabilitation Act. President Nixon signed the Act into law on September 26, 1973. Section 504 was seemingly out of place, located in a labor statute titled the Rehabilitation Act. Additionally, Section 504 had a rocky start to its existence (Zirkel, 2000).

What was to eventually become Section 504 was originally proposed in 1972 as an amendment to the Civil Rights Act of 1964 by Representative Vanik of Ohio and Senator Humphrey of Minnesota. Section 504 was passed later that year as an amendment to the revision of the Rehabilitation Act. The Rehabilitation Act provided for federally assisted rehabilitation programs for persons with disabilities. The law, however, was vetoed twice by President Nixon, primarily due to budgetary concerns. The following year it was rewritten and passed, and this time the president signed it.

Section 504 was originally written in the same antidiscrimination language as Title VI of the Civil Rights Act of 1964, which prohibits discrimination based on race and national origin, and Title IX of the Education Amendments of 1972, which prohibits discrimination based on gender. It was not clear, however, what protections were actually extended to persons with disabilities through the statute. Many believed the purpose of Section 504 was merely to correct problems in the rehabilitation of persons with disabilities, while others understood the law to be an extension of the Civil Rights Act of 1964. Because Congress failed to include any means to eliminate discrimination based on disability in Section 504, such as civil or criminal remedies, it seemed that the law was not a civil rights statute.

Amendments to Section 504 in 1974 and the Rehabilitation, Comprehensive Services, and Developmental Disabilities Act of 1978 clarified these ambiguities (Schoenfeld, 1980). The result of these clarifications was to extend civil rights protection to persons with disabilities by including all the remedies, procedures, and rights contained in the Civil Rights Act of 1964.

The issuance of regulations to implement and enforce Section 504 took an interesting route. Because of confusion over the original intent of Congress in passing Section 504, as well as political concerns (e.g., coverage of alcoholics and drug addicts), there was a 4-year delay in promulgating regulations to implement the law. A lawsuit was filed protesting the government's failure to issue the regulations under Section 504. In 1976, in *Cherry v. Matthews,* the Federal District Court of Washington, D.C., held that the Secretary of Health, Education, and Welfare (HEW)* was required to issue the regulations implementing the act. In the opinion, the court sarcastically noted that Section 504 was certainly not intended to be self-executing.

Because of the importance of Section 504, the HEW secretary for the Ford administration, David Matthews, felt that the incoming Carter administration should assume responsibility writing the regulations implementing the law. Matthews, therefore, left HEW without issuing the Section 504 regulations. The secretary of HEW in the Carter administration, Joseph Califano, also appeared to some to be stalling on the issuance of the regulations for political reasons. Angered at this lack of interest in moving the law forward through the issuance of regulations, advocacy groups for persons with disabilities began to exert political pressure on the new secretary. Demonstrations and sit-ins were held at regional HEW offices, and advocacy groups blocked Secretary Califano's driveway and various regional HEW offices with their wheelchairs. The weight of litigation and political pressure finally led to the issuance of the Section 504 regulations. According to Gerry and Benton (1982), "on May 4, 1977 the political system finally gave life to the promise of equal opportunity made in September 1973" (p. 47).

---

*HEW was later divided into the Department of Health and Human Services (DHHS) and the Department of Education (DOE).

The Purpose and Structure of Section 504

The Purpose of Section 504

Section 504 is a civil rights law that prohibits discrimination against individuals with disabilities in programs and activities that receive federal financial assistance. With respect to public schools, Section 504 requires administrators, teachers, school psychologists, and other school personnel to identify students with disabilities and afford these students educational opportunities equal to those received by students without disabilities. This means that students with disabilities should be allowed to participate in the same academic and nonacademic activities as their nondisabled peers (Smith & Patton, 1998).

Section 504 extends these protections only in programs or services that receive federal financial assistance. The Department of Justice defines a program receiving federal financial assistance as a program that receives "any grants, loans, contracts or any other arrangement by which the [school] provides or otherwise makes available assistance in the form of (a) funds, (b) services of federal personnel, or (c) real and personal property or any interest in or use of such property" (Section 504 Regulations, 28 C.F.R. § 41.3(e)).

In addition to elementary, secondary, and postsecondary schools that receive direct federal financial assistance, schools or programs that receive indirect federal financial aid (e.g., colleges where students receive federal education grants) are also covered under the statute. Section 504 does not apply to schools that receive no direct or indirect federal financial assistance.

Who Is Protected?

The original definition of persons protected under Section 504 was extremely narrow. The law protected individuals with the ability to benefit from rehabilitative services. Congress recognized that this definition was not appropriate for major civil rights legislation and in the Rehabilitation Act Amendments of 1974 developed a definition to clarify who was protected under Section 504. This definition is as follows:

> any person who (i) has a physical or mental impairment which substantially limits one or more of such person's major life activities, (ii) has a record of such an impairment, or (iii) is regarded as having such an impairment. (Section 504, 29 U.S.C. § 706(7)(B))

Section 504 only protects persons who are disabled as defined in the law. Let's examine the components of this definition.

Part 1 of the Definition: A Person Who Has a Physical or Mental Disability

The definition of a handicapping condition in Section 504 has three parts. Part 1 defines a person as disabled if that person has a physical or mental impairment that substantially limits one or more major life activities. This part has three components. The impairment must (a) be physical or mental, (b) affect a major life activity, and (c) be substantial. In *E.E. Black Ltd. v. Marshall* (1980), a federal district court commenting on the definition stated that the term *impairment* meant "any condition which weakens, diminishes, restricts, or otherwise damages an individual's health or physical or mental activity" (p. 1098).

Physical Impairment.   Regulations written for Section 504 in 1989 define physical and mental impairments as:

> (A) any physiological disorder or condition, cosmetic disfigurement, or anatomical loss affecting one or more of the following body systems: neurological; musculoskeletal; special sense organs, respiratory, including speech organs; cardiovascular; reproductive, digestive, genito-urinary; hemic and lymphatic; skin and endocrine. (Section 504 Regulations, 34 C.F.R. § 104.3(j)(2)(i))

The scope of physical impairment has been recognized as including those disabilities that substantially impair physical performance. Physical conditions that have been recognized by courts as constituting a disability under Section 504 include arthritis, asthma, deafness, blindness, diabetes, Crohn's disease, multiple sclerosis, paralysis, cerebral palsy, epilepsy, cardiac problems, Ménière's disease, chronic fatigue syndrome, kidney disease, Tourette's syndrome, and hyperthyroidism (Tucker & Goldstein, 1992; Zirkel, 2000). Physical characteristics or conditions, temporary or permanent, such as left-handedness, height, weight, strength capabilities, strabismus, and pregnancy, have generally not been considered to be under the purview of Section 504.

Mental Impairment.   The scope of mental impairments includes mental illness, mental retardation, and learning disabilities. The regulations for Section 504 define a mental impairment as:

> (B) any mental or psychological disorder, such as mental retardation, organic brain syndrome, emotional or mental illness, and specific learning disabilities. (Section 504 Regulations, 34 C.F.R. § 104.3(j)(2)(i))

In considering whether certain persons with psychological conditions (e.g., depression) are protected under Section 504, courts and OCR have tended to answer in the affirmative if the conditions are recognized by medical authorities as constituting a mental impairment (Tucker & Goldstein, 1992). For example, students with attention deficit hyperactivity disorder (ADHD) are protected under Section 504 if the disorder substantially affects a major life activity.

Mental impairments, however, do not extend to undesirable personality traits. In an employment-related 504 case, *Daley v. Koch* (1986), an applicant for a position of police officer was not hired when a police department psychologist determined that the applicant exhibited personality traits of poor judgment, irresponsible behavior, and poor impulse control. The court held that because the applicant had not been diagnosed as having a psychological illness or disorder, he did not have a disability under Section 504.

In the Rehabilitation Act Amendments of 1992, Congress added exclusions to Section 504. The term *impairments* specifically excluded individuals on the basis of homosexuality, bisexuality, transvestitism, transsexualism, pedophilia, exhibitionism, voyeurism, gender identity disorders, sexual behavior disorders, compulsive gambling, kleptomania, pyromania, or psychoactive substance abuse disorder resulting from illegal use of drugs (Section 504, 29 U.S.C. § 706(8)(E–F)).

The Americans with Disabilities Act (1990; hereafter ADA) further amended the definition of persons with disabilities in the Rehabilitation Act of 1973. Essentially, the definition was narrowed to exclude persons currently engaging in the illegal use or possession of drugs or alcohol. Individuals undergoing drug or alcohol rehabilitation and those who are not engaged in the illegal use of drugs or alcohol may be considered disabled under Section 504 if they are otherwise qualified.

Substantial Limitation of a Major Life Activity.   The definition of a disability in Section 504 also requires that the mental or physical impairment must substantially limit one or more major life activities. That is, just because a student has a disability under Section 504 does not mean that the student qualifies for protection under the law, unless that disability substantially limits a major life activity. This requirement was added by Congress to ensure that only persons with significant physical and mental impairments were protected under Section 504.

The question of what constitutes a substantial limitation of a major life activity has been the subject of considerable litigation and numerous guidelines from the OCR. It is clear, however, that when determining if a student is eligible for protection under Section 504, school district personnel must decide if an impairment substantially limits a major life activity for each student on an individual basis (*Letter to McKethan,* 1994).

The term *major life activity* means "functions such as caring for one's self, performing manual tasks, walking, seeing, hearing, breathing, learning, and working" (Section 504 Regulations, 34 C.F.R. § 104.3(j)(2)(ii)). This list is not intended to be exhaustive. From an educational perspective, a relevant life activity is learning. If a physical or mental impairment interferes with a student's ability to learn, the student is protected under Section 504. Smith and Patton (1998) point out, however, that learning, in and of itself, does not have to be affected for children to be eligible for protection under Section 504.

According to Smith (2002), *substantially limits* means that an individual is unable to perform a major life activity that the average person in the general population can perform. Additionally, it may mean that an individual is significantly restricted in the manner or duration in which he or she can perform the major life activity when compared to the manner or duration under which the average person can perform the activity.

Smith (2002) suggests that school personnel examine the following three factors to determine if a limitation is substantial. First, what is the nature and severity of the impairment? Here school personnel would determine if the impairment (a) is mild or severe, (b) results in failure or a student not achieving near expected levels, and (c) affects a major life activity, and if so, how? Second, what is the duration or expected duration of the impairment? Here school personnel would determine if the impairment (a) will be of such short duration that it will not cause a significant problem, and (b) will stop affecting the student even if there is no intervention Three, what permanent or long-lasting effect results from the impairment? School personnel would determine if the impairment (a) will be short or long in duration, (b) will have a significant effect without intervention even if the impairment is of short duration, and (c) will negatively affect a student's academic, social, emotional, and behavioral status if the impairment is long in duration.

Part 2 and 3 of the Definition: A Person Who Has a Record of Such an Impairment or Who Is Regarded as Having Such an Impairment

Part 2 of the definition protects persons who have a record of impairment. Under this part of the definition, a student who once had a disability but no longer does may not be discriminated against because of the past disability. This part of the definition also protects students who have been incorrectly classified as disabled (Zirkel, 2000).

Part 3 protects persons who are regarded as being disabled. Persons may be protected under Section 504 even if they do not actually have a disability, but are regarded as having one. The purpose of this rule is to protect persons who may have only minor disabilities or no disabilities at all from being discriminated against because of the stereotypical beliefs or negative reactions of others (Tucker & Goldstein, 1992).

The Office of Civil Rights defines being regarded as having a disability as meaning that the person:

> (1) has a physical or mental impairment that does not substantially limit major life activities but is treated by the [school] as constituting such a limitation; (2) has a physical or mental impairment that substantially limits major life activities only as a result of the attitudes of others towards such impairment; or (3) has none of the impairments [protected under 504] . . . but is treated by a [school] as having such impairment. (Section 504 Regulations, 34 C.F.R. § 104.3(j)(2)(iv))

These two parts of the definition are frequently misunderstood. Moreover, these parts of the definition generally only apply in the areas of employment and, occasionally, postsecondary education. In fact, they rarely apply in elementary and secondary education. According to OCR, many school officials believe that if someone (e.g., a student's doctor or parent) regards a student as having a disability or if a student has a record of a disability, he or she is automatically entitled to protection under Section 504. This is an incorrect assumption. These parts of the definition are insufficient to trigger Section 504 protections, in and of themselves. It is only when a student is discriminated against based on the perception that he or she has a disability (i.e., "regarded as") or because he or she had a disability (i.e., "has a record of") that a student is entitled to the protections of Section 504. For example, a school could discriminate against a student believed to have a communicable disease, even though the student does not have a communicable disease, by not allowing that student to eat lunch with the rest of the student body. This would violate the second part of the definition (i.e., regarded as). A school could also discriminate against a student who once exhibited serious behavior problems, but no longer had such problems, by not allowing the student to go on a field trip because of his or her history. This would violate the third part of the definition (i.e., has a record of). In both examples, a school taking these actions would be discriminating against the student and, therefore, violating the student's rights under Section 504.

The second and third parts of the definition, however, cannot serve as the basis of a free appropriate public education (FAPE) under Section 504. This is because the student who is regarded as having a disability or who has a record of a disability "is not, in fact mentally or physically [disabled], [therefore] there can be no need for special education or related aids and services" (OCR Memorandum, 1992). That is, only students with a current mental or physical disability are entitled to receive a FAPE. Students who are discriminated against in schools because they are regarded as having a disability or have a record of having a disability, however, may bring a claim of discrimination if a school district discriminates against them because of these perceptions.

Students with temporary disabilities may also be covered under Section 504 (Gorn, 1998). Neither the statute nor the regulations require that an individual must have a permanent disability for him or her to be protected under Section 504. If a temporary disability limits a major life activity for a period of time that will adversely affect a student's education, then it is likely that the student will be protected under Section 504 for the duration of the disability (Gorn, 1998). Although school personnel can only determine if a temporary disability qualifies a student for protection under Section 504, OCR decisions have held that a student with a broken leg who was confined to a wheelchair (*Sevier County School District,* 1995), a student with a broken dominant arm (*Georgetown Independent School District,* 1992), and illnesses (*Coppell Independent School District,* 1996) could qualify as disabled under the law.

Clearly, the definition of disability under Section 504 is broader than that under the IDEA (Zirkel, 1996). Whereas the IDEA requires that students have disabilities covered by the law and, as a result of their disability, require special education and related services, Section 504 does not have such specific requirements for protection. Students must have a disability that limits a major life activity (e.g., walking, seeing, hearing, learning).

Otherwise Qualified

Additionally, Section 504 protects only otherwise qualified individuals with disabilities from discrimination based solely on their disability. Persons who are not otherwise qualified, therefore, are not protected. In the final regulations, OCR used the term "qualified handicapped person" rather than the statutory language "otherwise qualified handicapped person." This was done because OCR believed that the statute, if read literally, might be interpreted as meaning that "otherwise qualified handicapped persons" included persons who were qualified except for their handicap. The actual meaning, according to OCR, includes all persons who were qualified in spite of their handicap.

Elementary and Secondary Schools.   With respect to elementary and secondary schools, students are qualified if they are

> (i) of an age during which nonhandicapped persons are provided such services, (ii) of any age during which it is mandatory under state law to provide such services to handicapped persons, or (iii) [persons] to whom the state is required to provide a free appropriate public education [students served under the IDEA]. (Section 504 Regulations, 34 C.F.R. § 104.3(k)(2))

A state is not required to provide services to students who do not meet the school's age requirements. All students of school age, however, are by definition qualified.

The otherwise qualified provision also applies to a school's extracurricular activities. Smith (2002) gives three examples of how the otherwise qualified provision of Section 504 would apply to students with disabilities who try out for such activities. First he gives an example of a student in a wheelchair who wants to try out for marching band. If the student was able to play an instrument, but the school did not let the student try out for the band, that would constitute discrimination. If, however, the student could not play an instrument, and the school did not let the student try out for the band, that would not constitute discrimination because the student was not otherwise qualified. In Smith's second example, a student with ADHD wanted to try out for the basketball team. If the coach let the student try out and he made the team, but the coach would not let him play on game days because the coach believed the student would present a problem, that would constitute discrimination. If, however, the student was cut from the team along with other students who were not sufficiently skilled, that would not be discrimination because the student was not otherwise qualified. In the final example a high school student with a severe disability wanted to join the Spanish club. If the only requirement for being in the Spanish club was that a student attend high school, then that student would be otherwise qualified and not allowing him to join would be discriminatory. However, if the requirement for joining the Spanish club was that the student had enrolled in and successfully passed a course in Spanish and the student had not taken Spanish, not allowing him to join the club would not be discriminatory because he was not otherwise qualified.

Postsecondary and Vocational Schools.   With respect to postsecondary and vocational schools, students with disabilities must meet the academic and technical standards requisite to admission or to participation in the educational program (Section 504 Regulations, 34 C.F.R. § 104.3(K)(3)). In postsecondary education and employment, the statutory language "no otherwise qualified individual with a disability . . . shall, solely by reason of his or her disability . . . " becomes particularly important. A student who is otherwise qualified is one who can meet program requirements, academic and technical, if provided with reasonable accommodations (auxiliary aids or services). The term "otherwise qualified" is intertwined with the concept of reasonable accommodations. Tucker and Goldstein (1992) state the relationship between "reasonable accommodation" and "otherwise qualified" as follows: "An individual with a disability is protected from discrimination under Section 504 only if he or she is able to perform in the . . . program at issue under existing conditions or with the provision of reasonable accommodations" (p. 5:1). *Reasonable accommodations* refers to the modifications of educational programs and facilities to make them accessible to persons with disabilities. If reasonable accommodations cannot be fashioned to permit the person with disabilities to participate in the program in spite of the disability, that person is not otherwise qualified (Dagley & Evans, 1995). The provision of reasonable accommodations will be examined in a later section of this chapter.

Summary of Section 504 Coverage

The definition of a disability in Section 504 is broad; it covers many types of disabilities as long as they affect a major life activity. Figure 6.1 illustrates the coverage of Section 504 (Zirkel, 2000).

Students in the inner circle are covered by the IDEA, thereby receiving double coverage under Section 504. By definition, students eligible for services under the

Figure 6.1
Coverage of Section 504

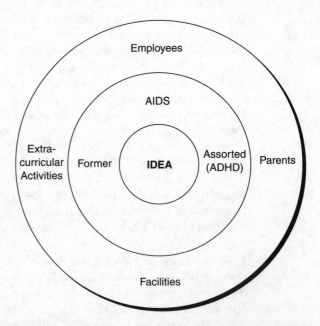

IDEA are disabled and, therefore, are also protected under Section 504. The second ring is comprised of individuals who meet the definition of having an impairment under Section 504. All students with disabilities meeting this definition are protected from discrimination by Section 504. This may include students with disabilities even if they are not eligible under the IDEA. Such disabilities may include ADHD, Tourette's syndrome, asthma, diabetes, arthritis, allergies, and AIDS. Technologically dependent children and those with alcohol or drug problems, if not currently engaging in the illegal use of drugs, would meet the definition of impairment. Students without disabilities who are treated as if they have disabilities are also protected. Students (e.g., disruptive students) whose main problem is poor impulse control, antisocial behavior, or poor judgment will not be covered if they do not have a physical or mental impairment that substantially limits their learning or another major life activity.

The final ring includes Section 504 coverage of facilities, extracurricular activities, parents, and employees. Section 504 also protects parents and employees who are disabled from discrimination. As the final ring indicates, Section 504 protections extend to extracurricular and nonacademic activities (e.g., graduation ceremonies, meals, recess, teams, clubs, sports activities). Finally, Section 504 requires that if a school operates a facility for students with disabilities, the facility must be comparable to facilities used by students without disabilities. This comparability mandate goes beyond the accessibility requirement. That is, even if a facility is accessible, it must also be comparable to those facilities for students without disabilities.

The Structure of Section 504

Section 504 is codified at 29 U.S.C. §§ 706(8), 794, and 794a. The federal regulations for Section 504 are divided into seven subchapters, which are listed in Table 6.1.

Major Principles of Section 504

Congress made a commitment to citizens with disabilities that "to the maximum extent possible, [persons with disabilities] shall be fully integrated into American life" (Senate Report, 1978). The regulations for Section 504 detail criteria for schools to follow. The rules and regulations are not as complex and detailed as those contained in the IDEA (Tucker & Goldstein, 1992; Zirkel, 2000). Section 504 regulations, however, are specific with respect to postsecondary education.

Protection from Discrimination

All students with disabilities are protected from discrimination in elementary, secondary, and postsecondary schools. Discrimination refers to unequal treatment of students with disabilities on the basis of their disability. For example, it is discriminatory for schools to provide academic or nonacademic programs or services for students without disabilities and not provide such services to children with disabilities.

Table 6.1
Subchapters of Regulations for Section 504

Subchapter	Purpose	Contents
1—Subpart A	General provisions	Purposes, definitions
2—Subpart B	Employment practices	Prohibits discrimination in employment practices
3—Subpart C	Program accessibility	Accessibility and usability of facilities
4—Subpart D	Preschool, elementary, and secondary education	Prohibits discrimination in preschool, elementary, and secondary programs receiving federal financial assistance
5—Subpart E	Postsecondary education	Prohibits discrimination in postsecondary programs receiving federal financial assistance
6—Subpart F	Health, welfare, and social services	Prohibits discrimination in health, welfare, and social services receiving federal financial assistance
7—Subpart G	Procedures	Procedures for ensuring compliance with Section 504

Similarly, Section 504 requires that individuals with disabilities have an equal opportunity to benefit from a school's academic or nonacademic programs or services as do their nondisabled peers. The concept of equivalency does not mean that services and benefits must be identical. Nor does it mean that the benefits or services must produce identical results. The benefits and services, however, must allow a student with disabilities an equal opportunity. As such, Section 504 requires that to ensure equal opportunity, adjustments to regular programs (i.e., reasonable accommodations) or the provision of different, and sometimes separate, services may at times be necessary. Protection from discrimination includes the requirement that schools ensure that (a) buildings and structures are physically accessible, (b) programs are accessible, and (c) children with disabilities are educated in comparable facilities.

Physical Accessibility

School academic and nonacademic programs, structures, and activities must be physically accessible to students with disabilities. Section 504 prohibits the exclusion of students with disabilities from programs because a school's facilities are inaccessible or unusable. Regulations to Section 504 require that:

> No qualified handicapped person shall, because a (school district's) facilities are inaccessible to or unusable by handicapped persons, be denied the benefits of, be excluded from participation in, or otherwise be subjected to discrimination under any program or activity. (Section 504 Regulations, 34 C.F.R. § 102.21)

For example, if a school has a chemistry classroom on the second floor, and the second floor is not accessible to students with wheelchairs, it would be discriminatory to deny a student in a wheelchair the opportunity to take chemistry because the chemistry classroom was not accessible to that student. It would be the school's responsibility to (a) move the chemistry classroom to an accessible location, or (b) make the chemistry classroom on the second floor accessible to the student.

Regulations state that "when viewed in its entirety," the program must be readily accessible and usable (Section 504 Regulations, 34 C.F.R. § 104.22). This means that school districts are not required to make all of their schools, or every part of a school, accessible to and usable by students with disabilities if its programs as a whole are accessible. However, a school district may not make only one school or a part of a school accessible when the result would be segregation of students with disabilities into one setting. For example, if a school district had a large high school campus with a number of buildings, only some of which were wheelchair accessible, the district would not have to make structural changes to all nonaccessible buildings. Administrators could reassign classes to the accessible buildings to accommodate students with disabilities. A district with only one wheelchair-accessible school, thereby requiring that all students needing wheelchairs attend only that school, would be in violation of Section 504 because students using wheelchairs would be segregated. School districts must meet the accessibility requirements of Section 504 even if they do not have students with mobility impairments.

The requirement of accessibility applies to all facilities within a school, such as classrooms, playgrounds, gyms, water fountains, swimming pools, parking lots, and restrooms. Schools can meet the physical accessibility requirements in various ways, including nonstructural alterations such as redesign of equipment, delivering services at alternate accessible sites, or assigning aides. Structural alterations are required only when there is no other feasible way to make facilities accessible. When school district personnel determine which of these means will be chosen to meet the program accessibility requirements, they are required to give priority consideration to methods that will allow the services to be provided in the most appropriate integrated setting. Districts must also inform persons with disabilities where they can obtain information regarding accessible facilities.

In school facilities that were built prior to 1977, programs and activities must be made accessible to and usable by persons with disabilities. Facilities constructed after 1977 must be in compliance with the American National Institute's accessibility standards. Schools constructed after January 1991 must meet the Uniform Federal Accessibility Standards (1984). No specific guidelines exist for playgrounds, but OCR has held that to meet the physical accessibility standards of Section 504, playgrounds must (a) allow student access, and be firm, stable, and slip resistant; (b) allow a range of activities that are accessible through the use of ramps and transfer systems; and (c) include a surface beneath the equipment that is firm, stable, slip resistant, and resilient (Gorn, 1998).

Program Accessibility

It is not enough that programs be physically accessible for students with disabilities if the student is unable to benefit from the program. Therefore, the program must also be accessible. This means that at times it may be necessary to make modifications or accommodations to programs so that students may benefit from them.

Reasonable Accommodations

A program receiving federal financial assistance is required to provide reasonable accommodations to otherwise qualified persons with disabilities. An educational institution or place of employment, therefore, must make modifications to the existing environment to eliminate barriers for persons with disabilities. Section 504 regulations, however, only define reasonable accommodation as it applies to employment. Reasonable accommodation as applied specifically to preschool, elementary and secondary schools, and postsecondary institutions is not addressed. This had led to disagreement and confusion regarding the reasonable accommodation standard. Dagley and Evans (1995) argued that even though the regulations suggest that reasonable accommodations are only required in the employment context, the judiciary has used the standard in making decisions regarding school district and postsecondary institutions' responsibilities under Section 504. This standard requires school officials to examine the individual needs of students with disabilities and make a professional judgment about what can and cannot be done to accommodate their needs (Dagley & Evans, 1995).

In *Alexander v. Choate* (1985), the Supreme Court held that Section 504 does not require that programs make substantial modifications, only reasonable ones. Modifications are substantial, and not required, if they impose an undue hardship on the program. Relevant factors in determining if modifications are reasonable include size, type, and budget of the program, as well as the nature and cost of the accommodation. Determining what constitutes a reasonable accommodation, as opposed to substantial accommodation, is difficult and subjective. What is reasonable varies given the specifics of a particular situation. The courts have offered some guidance, not so much by ruling what is reasonable but by ruling what is not reasonable.

Court Decisions Regarding Reasonable Accommodations.   The U.S. Supreme Court, in *Southeastern Community College v. Davis* (1979), held that reasonable accommodations are those that do not impose excessive financial and administrative burdens or require a fundamental alteration in the program. Courts and OCR guidelines have held that Section 504 does not require that schools create new and special programs but that they make reasonable modifications to eliminate barriers in existing ones. A federal district court, in *Pinkerton v. Moye* (1981), held that a school district did not have to establish a self-contained program for students with learning disabilities because that would have required a substantial modification to the district's programs. In *William S. v. Gill* (1983), the court ruled that a school district was not required to send a student to a private residential school if the costs at the private school far exceeded the costs at the public school. The school district was not obligated under Section 504 to send the student to the private school, since it represented a service not available to students without disabilities. Some courts, in determining whether a change in a program required a substantial modification, have asked whether the modification violates the basic integrity of the program. If it does, the change would not be reasonable.

Reasonable Accommodations in Schools.   The DOE's regulations to Section 504 suggest reasonable accommodations that might be made by postsecondary institutions to assist students with disabilities in obtaining an education (Section 504 Regulations, 34 C.F.R. § 104.44(a)). Although the regulations do not specifically address elementary or secondary schools, they offer guidance for the modification of school programs to accommodate students at all levels.

Academic adjustments are a category of accommodations. Accommodations needed to ensure that academic requirements do not discriminate on the basis of disability may include changes in the length of time needed to complete a degree, substitution of courses required to complete a degree, and adaptations in how courses are taught. Further, schools may not impose rules on students with disabilities, such as prohibiting tape recorders, that have the effect of limiting the students' ability to benefit from or participate in classes or programs. Academic adjustments that might be made include modifying methods of instruction, modifying materials, and altering environmental conditions.

Regulations also address the modification of examinations. Course examinations and evaluations should reflect students' achievement rather than their disability. Modifications, therefore, should be made to an examination if a student's disability will impair the student's performance on the test. Modifications to ensure that examinations do not discriminate might include giving tests orally, allowing the student to dictate answers, shortening the length of the test, allowing more time to take the test, altering the test format (e.g., multiple choice, essays), printing the test with enlarged text, and reducing the reading level of the test.

Comparable Facilities

When a school operates a facility for students with disabilities, the facilities and services must be comparable to regular education facilities and services. This mandate goes beyond the accessibility requirement. OCR does not intend to encourage the creation or maintenance of separate facilities, but clearly states that when separate facilities are used for students with disabilities, they must be comparable in attributes such as size, space, ventilation, furnishings, lighting, equipment, and temperature. This requirement is violated when schools provide separate facilities such as portable units and classrooms specifically for students with disabilities that are inferior to those provided students without disabilities. This does not mean, however, that the facilities must be identical. Additionally, the placement of students with disabilities in portable units that were designated solely for use by students with disabilities would be a violation of Section 504. If, however, the portable units were used equally by all students, in both general and special education, there would be no violation of Section 504.

Discrimination versus Legitimate Considerations Regarding Disabilities.   Protection from discrimination does not mean that the disabling condition cannot be considered by school administrators. In this respect, the definition of discrimination in Section 504 differs from the definition of discrimination in Titles VI (race) and VII (gender) of the Civil Rights Act of 1964. This is because disabilities may affect an individual's ability to perform in a program or job by impairing functioning, whereas race and gender virtually never tell anything about a person's ability to perform (Tucker & Goldstein, 1992). A school administrator, therefore, may consider a disability if it is a relevant factor. What is not permissible under Section 504 is discrimination against a person with a disability based solely on an illegitimate or unjustifiable consideration of the disability. For example, if school administrators deny a student with disabilities the right to participate in an academic or nonacademic program (e.g., extracurricular activities, recess, meals, field trips, transportation, groups or clubs) because of an erroneous conclusion that the disability would prevent the student from participating or because they failed to provide for reasonable modifications to allow participation, they may be guilty of discrimination. Additionally, schools will be seen as discriminating against persons with disabilities if they (a) deny opportunity to participate in or benefit from any program or service available to persons without a disability; (b) fail to provide aids and services that are provided to students without disabilities; or (c) provide different aids or services from those provided to students without disabilities unless those services are required to allow equal opportunity.

Avoiding Discrimination

Regulations to Section 504 (Section 504 Regulations, 34 C.F.R. § 104.22) list actions that schools may take to avoid discriminating against students with disabilities. Such actions may include (a) altering structure, (b) redesigning equipment, (c) reassigning classes, (d) assigning paraprofessionals, (e) conducting interventions in the general education classroom, and (f) modifying classroom methods, materials, and procedures. (For a detailed list of potential modifications, see Zirkel, 2000.)

An example of discrimination against students with disabilities based solely on the disability occurred in *Rice v. Jefferson County Board of Education* (1989). In this case, the Jefferson County Board of Education charged students with disabilities larger fees to attend after-school programs than they charged students without disabilities. The board justified the increased charges by maintaining that the school district had to provide care for the students with disabilities and that the additional costs of this care had to be passed on to these students. The court held that the board's action was discrimination in violation of Section 504, because the district failed to show that students with disabilities' attendance at programs created substantial additional costs for the district.

Discrimination in Postsecondary Education.   Colleges, universities, and vocational or technical schools may not exclude a qualified person with a disability from any aspect of the educational program or activities conducted by the school. According to Zirkel (2000), Section 504 claims most likely to arise in postsecondary education are in the areas of admissions and access to nonacademic programs or activities.

With respect to admission in postsecondary education, regulations to Section 504 protect qualified students with disabilities from being denied admission or discriminated against solely because of their disability. To protect persons from discrimination, a postsecondary school cannot inquire if an applicant has a disability. An important distinction between the responsibilities of elementary and secondary schools and those of postsecondary schools is that elementary and secondary schools have an affirmative duty to find students with disabilities, while in postsecondary schools students must self-identify. After admission, however, the institution may make confidential inquiries about the disability to determine accommodations that may be required. Postsecondary institutions cannot limit the number of persons with disabilities they accept.

Neither can postsecondary institutions administer admission tests that may reflect adversely on students with disabilities, unless the tests have been validated as predictors of success and alternative tests are not available. Admissions tests must be selected and administered to students with disabilities to reflect actual aptitude and achievement rather than reflecting the impaired skills.

Discrimination and Access to Nonacademic Programs and Services.   Another aspect of Section 504 involves access to nonacademic programs and services. Postsecondary institutions that provide housing to students without disabilities must provide comparable housing for students with disabilities. The housing must also be accessible. The regulations also require that the cost of housing to students with and without disabilities must be the same.

In physical education, athletics, intramural activities, and clubs the postsecondary institution must provide qualified students with disabilities an equal opportunity to participate. If separate or different facilities or teams are required, they must be in the most integrated setting appropriate and only if no qualified students with disabilities are denied participation in the integrated activities.

Counseling, vocational, and placement services must be provided to students with disabilities to the same extent as provided to students without disabilities. Additionally, qualified students with disabilities must not be counseled to more restrictive career options than are students without disabilities.

Often postsecondary institutions provide assistance to fraternities, sororities, or other organizations. If they do so, they must ensure that these organizations do not discriminate against or permit discrimination based on a disability. Furthermore, postsecondary institutions that provide financial assistance must not provide less assistance to students with disabilities than they provide to persons without disabilities. Neither can they limit the eligibility of students with disabilities.

Free Appropriate Public Education

Students with disabilities in elementary and secondary school are entitled to a free appropriate public education (FAPE) under Section 504 regardless of the nature or severity of their disabilities. This applies to all students with disabilities in a school's jurisdiction. A FAPE is required to protect persons with disabilities from discrimination (Section 504 Regulations, 34 C.F.R. §§ 100.6–100.10). School districts often have more difficulty meeting their FAPE obligations under Section 504 than they do meeting the physical accessibility and comparable facilities requirements.

Regulations implementing Section 504 define a free education as educational and related services that are provided at no cost to a student with disability, excluding fees charged to all students. Even when a school district places a student in another school, even if the school is not in the district's boundaries, the home school district retains financial responsibility for the student. If students are placed in programs where they will be away from home, the school is also responsible for room, board, and nonmedical care (e.g., custodial and supervisory care).

Regulations define an appropriate education as:

> The provision of regular or special education and related aids and services that are designed to meet individual educational needs of handicapped persons as adequately as the needs of nonhandicapped persons are met and that are based on adherence to procedural safeguards. (Section 504 Regulations, 34 C.F.R. 104.33(b)(1))

An appropriate education must be individualized. It may consist of education in general education classes with supplementary aids and services, or special education and related services in a separate classroom. Special education may consist of specially designed instruction in a classroom, at home, or in a residential setting, and may be accompanied by related services (e.g., psychological counseling, speech therapy) that are necessary for a student's education.

Section 504 also requires that related services be provided to students with disabilities in the general education classroom as well as to students in a special classroom when necessary. Related services in the classroom are required under Section 504 if they are necessary to provide an education comparable to that offered to students without disabilities.

The definition of appropriate education under Section 504 is one of equivalency. That is, the educational services designed to meet the needs of students with disabilities must do so as adequately as services designed to meet the needs of students without disabilities. To ensure this equivalency, Section 504 requires that the student's teachers must be trained in instructing the student with the particular disability and that appropriate materials and equipment must be available. The equivalency requirement also applies to nonacademic activities. Regulations require that nonacademic and extracurricular activities be provided in a way that affords students with disabilities an equal opportunity for participation. Nonacademic activities include counseling (personal, academic, and vocational), transportation, health services, special interest groups, clubs, and physical, recreational, and athletic activities.

Clearly, the FAPE requirement under Section 504 is more broadly defined than the FAPE requirement under the IDEA (Smith, 2002). To meet the FAPE requirement, the educational program of a student with disabilities must be developed by a group of knowledgeable persons based on evaluation data. Moreover, school districts should document the provision of a FAPE. When students are covered only by Section 504 and do not receive dual coverage under the IDEA, school officials still must develop an appropriate educational program.

There has been controversy over whether FAPE under Section 504 requires less than does a FAPE under the IDEA; however, this question remains largely unanswered (Dagley & Evans, 1995; Zirkel, 1996). For students with disabilities who are eligible for services under the IDEA, and thus also covered by Section 504, this question is not relevant because the FAPE standards for these students must conform to the standards of the IDEA. For students with disabilities who are eligible under Section 504, but not under the IDEA, the question is significant. Some court decisions have indicated that the standard for a FAPE involves the school making reasonable accommodations (*Southeastern Community College v. Davis,* 1979). OCR, however, seems to place a higher standard on school districts to meet the FAPE standard of Section 504 based on a student's educational needs (Zirkel, 2000). Zirkel (1996) contends that the applicable FAPE standard may be higher than that of reasonable accommodations. This higher standard is based on the statutory language requiring that commensurate opportunity or educational equivalency for FAPE be provided to students with disabilities under Section 504.

According to OCR (1988), many different elements comprise a FAPE. There are nondiscriminatory evaluation requirements, placement requirements, and periodic reevaluation of students served under Section 504. Schools must also adhere to procedural safeguards when developing and implementing a Section 504 plan. Additional information on school district responsibilities when developing a FAPE will be discussed later in the chapter.

Evaluation and Placement Procedures

The purpose of the Section 504 evaluation and placement requirements is to prevent misclassification and misplacement. Students with disabilities who are believed to need special education or related services must be evaluated prior to placement. According to Zirkel (2000), the matter of evaluation has been the subject of more OCR investigations than any other requirement of 504.

When determining placement for a student, the school must convene a group of persons knowledgeable about the student, the meaning of the evaluation data, and the placement options. Furthermore, the team must draw on information from a variety of sources. The group must establish procedures to ensure that all information gathered in the evaluation process is documented and considered. The team must be aware of different options for placement. Moreover, team decisions must be based on a student's individual needs. If a school seeks a significant change of placement, a reevaluation must be completed prior to the placement change. Even in cases where

a significant change of placement is not sought, schools must conduct periodic reevaluations of all students with disabilities.

Procedural Safeguards

Schools must establish a system of due process procedures to be afforded to parents
or guardians prior to taking any action regarding the identification, evaluation, or educational placement of a student with a disability who is believed to need educational
services. The Office of Civil Rights recommends, but does not require, compliance
with the procedural safeguards of IDEA as a way to ensure that the procedural safeguards of Section 504 are met.

Notice must precede any identification, evaluation, or placement action taken by
the school. Parents must also be notified of their right to examine educational
records. If there is a disagreement concerning an evaluation or placement action,
parents or guardians may request a due process hearing. Schools may also request
due process hearings. Hearing officers must be impartial and must have no personal
or professional conflicts of interest or connections with either school or student.

In the due process hearing, the parents have the opportunity to participate, present evidence, produce outside expert testimony, and be represented by counsel.
Parents may have the student present at the hearing and may open the hearing to
the public if they choose to do so. Following the hearing, the hearing officer reviews
all relevant facts and renders a decision. The decision of the officer is binding on all
parties but may be appealed to federal court.

The procedural rights of parents are listed in Figure 6.2.

School District Responsibilities Under Section 504

School districts and schools have two major responsibilities under Section 504:
(a) fulfilling general procedural responsibilities and (b) meeting educational obligations to students with disabilities.

Administrative Responsibilities

Schools districts' and schools' procedural responsibilities include (a) appointment of
a Section 504 coordinator, (b) public notification of the school's responsibilities under
Section 504, (c) establishment of grievance procedures, (d) self-evaluation, (e) staff
training, and (f) child find.

Appointing a Section 504 Coordinator

School districts with 15 or more employees must appoint a Section 504 coordinator.
The coordinator keeps the school district in compliance with the mandates of Section
504. Because this individual has many duties, it is important that the school district
ensure his or her thorough training. Although the special education director is frequently the Section 504 coordinator, Zirkel (1996) suggests that someone other than

Figure 6.2
Parental Rights Under Section 504

- Right to be notified of procedural rights under Section 504
- Right to be notified when their child is referred, evaluated, and placed
- Right to notification when eligibility is determined
- Right to an evaluation that uses information from multiple sources and is conducted by knowledgeable persons
- Right of the student to have access to equivalent academic and nonacademic services
- Right of the student to receive an appropriate education in the least restrictive setting, which includes accommodations, modifications, and related services
- Right to file a grievance with the school district
- Right to an evaluation prior to making a significant programming or placement change
- Right to be informed of proposed actions affecting the program
- Right to examine all relevant records and request changes
- Right to receive information in the parents' native language or primary mode of communication
- Right to periodic reevaluations
- Right to an impartial hearing when a disagreement occurs
- Right to be represented by counsel in the hearing
- Right to appeal the hearing officer's decision

the special education director—preferably a general education administrator—be appointed to fill this position. This is because assigning the special education director could serve to reinforce the erroneous belief of many general educators that Section 504 is a special education law when, in fact, it is primarily a general education law.

Notifying the Public of a School District's Responsibilities Under Section 504

The coordinator must keep the public and internal staff notified that the district does not discriminate on the basis of disability in employment, educational services, or treatment. It is advisable that the coordinator head a multidisciplinary team whose responsibilities include the identification, evaluation, and placement of students with disabilities.

Ensuring That Procedural Safeguards Are Afforded to Students and Their Parents

School districts must establish and implement a system of procedural safeguards. During the evaluation process, notification should be given when eligibility is determined, when an accommodation plan is developed, and before there is any significant modification of the student's program.

Establishing Grievance Procedures

School districts are required to set up grievance procedures and notify parents and guardians of those procedures. The Section 504 coordinator is responsible for establishing grievance procedures, which must include appropriate procedural safeguards. There is no procedure set forth in Section 504 detailing the requirements of grievance procedures. The mechanics of the procedure, therefore, are left to the agency.

Zirkel (2000) suggested that a Section 504 grievance procedure include the following steps. First have an informal discussion between parents and the Section 504 coordinator to attempt to resolve the dispute. Second, if the complaint is not satisfactorily resolved, parents should file a written grievance with the coordinator, who will then conduct an investigation and issue a written report. Third, if this action does not resolve the problem, the decision should be appealed to the school board. Finally, if a complaint to the school board does not resolve the problem, a complaint should be filed with OCR.

Conducting a Self-Evaluation

The coordinator should conduct periodic self-evaluations of the school district to ensure that all Section 504 mandates are followed. If the self-evaluation finds discrimination, the school district must take steps to correct the situation. If such remedial action is necessary, OCR has suggested that the agency seek the assistance of organizations representing persons with disabilities prior to undertaking the corrective procedures. The school district should also keep records of the self-evaluation process. The U.S. Department of Justice has published a technical assistance guide to conducting self-evaluations; it is available from the Coordination and Review Section, Civil Rights Division, U.S. Department of Justice, Washington, D.C.

Training Staff Regarding Their Responsibilities Under Section 504

Because of the lack of attention given to the requirements of Section 504, many general education teachers are unaware of the law's existence, let alone its requirements (Smith, 2002). An extremely important task of the Section 504 coordinator, therefore, is the training of staff in the meaning and requirements of the law. Zirkel (2000) includes the failure to conduct staff inservices on his "hit list" of Section 504 practices that school districts should avoid at all costs. It goes without saying that if teachers and other school staff are unaware of Section 504, they may inadvertently violate the law.

Developing a Child Find System

Section 504 requires that schools annually take steps to identify and locate children with disabilities who are not receiving an appropriate education and to publicize parental and student rights under the law. These duties, referred to as *child find,* require that school district officials locate and identify eligible students who reside in the school district. Thus, it is the responsibility of the school to identify and evaluate students who may qualify for special services under Section 504. This includes students transferring from other school districts, students in private schools, and homeless children. A school district may conduct screenings of students to comply with the child find requirements (Gorn, 1998). School districts have a great deal of leeway in determining how they will conduct screenings (*Letter to Veir,* 1993). When a child is identified as having a possible disability as a result of the screening process, the school district should conduct an expeditious and thorough evaluation of that student.

Educational Obligations

School districts' and schools' educational obligations to students with a disability under Section 504 include (a) identification, (b) evaluation, (c) programming, (d) placement, and (e) reevaluation.

Identification

As previously discussed, a student with a possible disability may be identified in the child find process. Most students who may be eligible for services under Section 504, however, are identified through a referral process. Referrals may be made by teachers, parents, school administrators, or other school personnel, although typically students are referred by teachers. Neither Section 504 nor its regulations specify a particular referral procedure; nonetheless, school districts should develop such a procedure and ensure that it is understood, and correctly used, by all school personnel.

School district officials need to know and define what will "trigger" a referral for a Section 504 evaluation (Goldstein, 1994). Figure 6.3 lists suggestions of the Council of Administrators of Special Education (1992) regarding problems that should trigger a Section 504 referral. School districts and individual schools should have a clear procedure for referring students under Section 504.

It is crucial that school district personnel and teachers understand that students may be eligible for services under Section 504 even if they do not qualify for special education under the IDEA. In fact, OCR has held that a blanket school district refusal to evaluate students who do not qualify under the IDEA is a violation of Section 504. It is advisable, therefore, that students with disabilities who have been referred for special education services under the IDEA should be referred for services under Section 504.

Identification and Evaluation

Following a referral, school personnel must decide if an evaluation for services under Section 504 is warranted. Prior to conducting an initial evaluation, a school must obtain parental consent (*Letter to Zirkel,* 1995) and provide parents with a notice of their procedural rights. The evaluation must be completed and an eligibility decision made before a student can receive services under Section 504. According to Gorn (1998), a school district should evaluate a student for Section 504 services when school personnel have a reason to believe that a student has a disability and needs such services. In the past, when OCR has found districts have not met their obligations, it has often been because the district did not properly evaluate a student (Gorn, 1998).

Figure 6.3
When to Refer Students Under Section 504

- A student has been referred for special education, but the decision was not to evaluate.
- A student has been referred for special education, but was determined not eligible.
- A student displays serious problem behavior.
- A student is being considered for suspension or expulsion.
- A student is being considered for grade retention.
- A student is not benefiting from instruction.
- A student returns to school after a serious illness or injury.
- A student is diagnosed by an outside source as having a disability.
- A student exhibits a chronic health condition.
- A student is identified as at risk.
- A student is considered a potential dropout.
- A student may be abusing drugs.
- A student is suspected of having a disability.
- A student is referred by his or her parents for evaluation under Section 504.
- A student is referred by his or her teacher for evaluation under Section 504.

Source: *Mesa Unified School District No. 4*, 1988.

Schools must convene a multidisciplinary team to interpret evaluation data and make programming and placement decisions. The team is to be composed of persons knowledgeable about the child, the evaluation, and the placement options. The multidisciplinary team that conducts evaluations and makes programming and placement decisions under the IDEA may also be used for evaluation and placement under Section 504.

The two primary purposes of the evaluation are to determine (a) if a student is eligible for services under Section 504, which involves deciding if a student has a physical or mental impairment and if that impairment results in a substantial limitation to a major life activity; and (b) what educational programming will be required to ensure that the student receives a FAPE.

Regulations to Section 504 regarding evaluations require that

(1) Tests and all evaluation materials have been validated for the specific purpose for which they are used and are administered by trained personnel in conformity with instructions provided by their producer;

(2) Tests and other evaluation materials include those tailored to assess specific areas of educational need and not merely those which are designed to provide a single intelligence quotient; and

(3) Tests are selected and administered so as best to ensure that, when a test is administered to a student with impaired sensory, manual, or speaking skills, the test results accurately reflect the student's aptitude or achievement level or whatever other factor the test purports to measure, rather than reflecting the student's impaired [abilities] except where those skills are the factors that the test purports to measure. (Section 504 Regulations, 34 C.F.R. § 104.35(b))

Additionally the evaluation that a school conducts must meet the following three criteria. First, the evaluation team must use a variety of assessment procedures and instruments to assess a student and draw upon information from this variety of sources. Second, schools should establish procedures to ensure that all information is documented and fully considered (Smith & Patton, 1998; Zirkel, 2003). Smith and Patton (1998) and Zirkel (2003) suggest that Section 504 coordinators develop evaluation forms that document the team's evaluation, data collection process, and decisions. Information on such forms should include (a) general referral information, (b) the rationale for conducting the evaluation, (c) eligibility criteria and determination, (d) placement decisions, (e) names of team members, (f) dates of recommended actions, and (g) projected review or reevaluation date. Third, schools must ensure that the evaluation is made by a team of persons, including persons knowledgeable about the student, the meaning of the evaluation data, and the placement options (Section 504 Regulations, 34 C.F.R. § 104.35). Readers should note that Section 504, unlike the IDEA, does not identify the specific individuals who must be on the Section 504 team, although the student's teacher should be included.

Two issues that may present difficulties for school districts when deciding if they should conduct evaluations are (a) parent referrals and (b) medical diagnosis. First, when a parent refers a student for evaluation under Section 504, and school personnel do not believe that the student will qualify, are they required to conduct an evaluation? The answer is no; if school personnel believe that a student who has been referred under Section 504 will not qualify, they are not required to evaluate him or her (Katsiyannis, Landrum, & Reid, 2002; Reid & Katsiyannis, 1995). Section 504 requires that in such situations the school district must inform the parents that they have the right to dispute the school's decision in an impartial hearing. It is advisable, therefore, that if a district denies a parent referral, it can demonstrate there was no evidence to indicate the child had a disability (Gorn, 1998).

Second, a medical diagnosis is not required as part of an evaluation (Zirkel, 2003). That is, school personnel should not decide whether or not a student is qualified as a student with a disability based on a medical diagnosis; nor should they require that parents provide a diagnosis from a physician or psychologist prior to determining a student's eligibility (Zirkel, 2003). If, however, a 504 team decides that a medical diagnosis is needed, the district must ensure that it is not charged to the parents (*Letter to Williams,* 1994). Further, Gorn (1998) suggested that when parents refer their child for services under Section 504, and they have a medical diagnosis that a child has a disability (e.g., ADHD), the district should conduct an evaluation, even though the school district is only required to do so if they believe the child has a disability. Similarly, if parents have an independent evaluation that indicates that a child has a disability and makes a referral based on that independent evaluation, the district would be well advised to conduct an evaluation.

Readers should note that Section 504 does not give parents the right to obtain an independent educational evaluation at public expense if they disagree with the school district's evaluation. However, OCR has ordered reimbursement of parents for the cost incurred in obtaining an evaluation when school districts have failed to evaluate a student (Gorn, 1998). Moreover, if a parent does have an independent evaluation, the school district should include the results of the evaluation in their decision-making process.

If an evaluation will be conducted, it must be completed in a timely manner (*Garden City Union Free School District,* 1990). In fact, delays in completing student evaluations from 61 to 185 days were found to be in violation of Section 504 (*Philadelphia School District,* 1992). Similarly, a 7-month delay between referral and evaluation and a 9-month delay between evaluation and placement were violations of Section 504 (*Dade County School District,* 1993). However, there are no specific timelines for conducting an evaluation. School personnel need to conduct an evaluation as soon as feasible after the decision to evaluate has been made.

Educational Programming

Based on the evaluation data, the team should design the services that a student will receive. A school provides a FAPE through regular education or special education programming or related aids and services. In the past OCR has found that school districts have failed to meet their FAPE obligations under Section 504 when they have (a) failed to provide a complete range of education and related services needed by a student, or (b) identified the complete range of education and related services a student needs but failed to provide them. Section 504 requires that school districts provide a FAPE to all eligible students, and there are sanctions when school districts fail to meet these obligations.

If an evaluation finds that a student has a disability under Section 504, a multidisciplinary team should develop an individualized educational program that provides a FAPE for that student. This plan can involve general education and related services or special education and related services. Furthermore, it is advisable that school personnel document this program in a formalized intervention plan (Fossey, Hosie, Soniat, & Zirkel, 1995; Katsiyannis, Landrum, & Reid, 2002; Reid & Katsiyannis, 1995; Smith & Patton, 1998). This Section 504 plan, sometimes called an *individualized accommodation plan,* should document (a) the nature of the student's disability and the major life activity it limits, (b) the basis for determining the disability, (c) the educational impact of the disability, (d) necessary accommodations, and (e) placement. Figure 6.4 is an example of a Section 504 plan.

Figure 6.4
Section 504 Plan

Section 504 Education Plan

I. Personal Information

Student's name: DOB: Age: Grade:

Address: Date of conference:

Date of implementation of Section 504 plan:

Parents or Guardians:

II. Referral Information

Date of referral: Source of referral:

Reasons for referral:

III. Section 504 Team

Coordinator: Teacher(s):

Principal:

Parents or Guardians:

Others:

IV. Evaluation Information

Dates of evaluation:

Results:

Impairment:

Major life activity affected:

V. Educational Services

VI. Accommodations

VII. Related and Supplementary Services and Aids

VIII. Placement

IX: Monitoring and Evaluation Procedures

X: Date of Review of Section 504 Plan

Section 504 regulations indicate that the development of an individualized education program (IEP) is one way to ensure that this requirement is met (Section 504 Regulations, 34 C.F.R. § 104.33(b)(2)). The IDEA requires IEPs for students in special education programs; however, using IEPs for students who are not IDEA eligible is not advisable. This is because it may result in confusion to parents and educators about whether the student is covered under IDEA or Section 504 (Huefner, 2000). Additionally, the IDEA's many requirements for IEPs are not necessary in 504 plans (Gorn, 1998).

The Section 504 plan should include accommodations and modifications to a student's educational program. The plan details the appropriate education that a student will receive and is the result of a multidisciplinary team planning process. Figure 6.5 contains a list of potential classroom accommodations.

Placement

The Section 504 team must also decide where students can receive their educational services. Placement options may include regular classrooms, regular classrooms with related services, or special education and related services. Special education may be provided in regular classrooms, special classrooms, at home, or in private or public institutions, and may be accompanied by related services. If the school district cannot provide the appropriate placement, it must assume the cost of alternative placements. The placement must allow for contact with students without disabilities to the maximum extent appropriate. This applies to both academic and nonacademic settings.

Least Restrictive Environment.   Regulations to Section 504 require that students with disabilities be educated along with students without disabilities to the maximum extent appropriate to the needs of the student. Additionally, the general education classroom is the preferred placement unless it is demonstrated that an education with supplementary aids and services in the general education classroom cannot be achieved satisfactorily and that the needs of the student would be better served by placement in another setting. OCR guidelines and rulings have specified that districts must document the reasons why more restrictive placements are needed when the student is removed from the general education classroom (or a less restrictive setting).

In making placement decisions to move students with disabilities to more restrictive settings, schools may take into account the effect of a student's behavior on students without disabilities if the effect is deleterious. In an analysis of final regulations, OCR stated that "where a handicapped child is so disruptive in a regular classroom that the education of other students is significantly impaired, the needs of the handicapped child cannot be met in that environment. Therefore, regular placement would not be appropriate to his or her needs and would not be required" (Section 504 Regulations, Appendix A, p. 384).

Neighborhood Schools.   Section 504 also requires that when a student with disabilities is placed in a setting other than the general education classroom, the school must take into account the proximity of the alternative setting to the student's home. However, schools are not required to place students in schools closest to their homes.

Figure 6.5
Examples of Reasonable Accommodations in Classrooms

Classroom Modifications
- Adjust placement of student (e.g., preferential seating).
- Alter physical setup of classroom.
- Reduce distractions (e.g., study carrel).
- Provide increased lighting.
- Schedule classes in accessible areas.

Academic Adjustments
- Vary instructional strategies and materials.
- Allow more time to complete assignments.
- Adjust length of assignments.
- Modify pace of instruction.
- Use peer tutors.
- Provide outline of lectures.
- Use visual aids.
- Use advance organizers.
- Highlight texts and worksheets.
- Tape lectures.
- Adjust reading levels of materials.
- Use specialized curricular materials.
- Provide study guides.
- Give tests orally or on tape.
- Allow more time to complete tests.
- Allow students to dictate answers.
- Alter the test format.
- Use enlarged type.
- Reduce the reading level of the test.

Auxiliary Aids and Devices
- Provide interpreters.
- Provide readers.
- Use audiovisual aids.
- Tape tests.
- Provide assistive technology devices and services, such as laptop computers, Braille readers, text enlargement devices, or alternative input devices.

If a school does not offer an appropriate program or facilities, a student may be transferred to another school. The home school will still retain responsibility for the student and must provide transportation.

Schools must also ensure that in nonacademic and extracurricular services and activities, students with disabilities participate with students without disabilities to the maximum extent appropriate to their needs. This requirement is especially important when students' needs require that they are educated primarily in a segregated setting.

Reevaluation

Unlike the IDEA there is no requirement in Section 504 that students be reevaluated every 3 years. Rather, Section 504 requires that students be reevaluated periodically or before a significant change in placement is made. If a school proposes a significant change in placement, the student must be reevaluated in a manner similar to the initial evaluation. In 1997, OCR defined a significant change of placement as a substantial and fundamental change in a student's educational program (*Harlowtown Public Schools,* 1997). Gorn (1998) states that generally if a student placement is changed so that he or she receives the same programming and services in a similar environment, that will not be a significant change in placement, thus triggering a reevaluation. Examples of significant changes that will trigger an evaluation include a placement change such as moving a student from a full-time general education placement to a full-time special education class (*Fairbanks North Star Borough School District,* 1994) and changes in educational programming (*Montebello Unified School District,* 1993). Additionally, transitions from elementary school to middle school to high school are considered changes in placement, which trigger the reevaluation requirement of Section 504 (*Mobile County School District,* 1992). Graduation may also be a significant change in placement, although graduation may only trigger the procedural safeguards and not reevaluation requirements (Gorn, 1998).

Regulations also state that reevaluations should be conducted periodically. No timeline for reevaluations is provided; however, regulations specify that conducting reevaluations in accordance with the more detailed requirements of the IDEA constitutes compliance with Section 504 requirements.

Enforcement of Section 504

The primary vehicles by which parents can bring actions against a school district are through (a) filing a grievance with the school district's grievance coordinator, (b) requesting a due process hearing, (c) filing a complaint to the OCR of the U.S. Department of Education, or (d) filing a suit in federal court.

Podemski, Marsh, Smith, and Price (1995) suggested that schools attempt to avoid complaints and hearings by (a) focusing on the child by making good faith efforts to provide appropriate programs; (b) involving the parents to the greatest extent possible; (c) conducting a thorough and individualized evaluation; (d) documenting all school and parent contacts, including phone calls, letters, face-to-face correspondence, sending important documents by registered mail; and (e) using mediation to resolve disagreements. Huefner (2000) argues that the best way for school districts to avoid legal liability under Section 504 is to take seriously the mandate not to discriminate against students with disabilities. If a parent files a complaint with OCR, Zirkel (2000) advises that a school attempt to reach a settlement with the complainant. This is referred to as *early complaint resolution* (ECR).

Filing a Grievance

Grievances can be filed with a school district's Section 504 coordinator if a parent, student, community member, or staff member believes that discrimination based on a disability has occurred. School districts must have a formal mechanism by which students, parents, or employees can file a grievance. Furthermore, the public must be notified regarding the grievance procedures.

Filing a Complaint with the Office of Civil Rights

Any person may file a grievance with his or her regional OCR office against a school district within 180 days of an alleged discriminatory action. All complaints filed with OCR are investigated as long as they have merit (OCR Complaint Resolution Manual, 1995). If a complaint has merit, OCR will investigate the complaint. The OCR investigation process is depicted in Figure 6.6.

The Pre-Determination Settlement Process

The first step in the OCR investigation process is the pre-determination settlement (PDS) process. OCR initiated the PDS process in an attempt to reduce its massive complaint load (Martin, 1993). Through this process the school can avoid an on-site investigation and essentially close the matter without admitting to a violation by agreeing to actions that resolve the complainant's issues to the satisfaction of OCR. If the complainant disagrees with the school district's actions, these actions can still be approved by OCR.

According to Martin (1993), the advantage of the PDS process is that it saves an enormous amount of time and expense for both the school district and OCR. The primary disadvantages are, first, that if the allegations are unfounded, there is no opportunity to dispute them, and second, that the school must develop a reporting and monitoring timeline to assist OCR in determining if the school district is fulfilling its commitment. Martin (1993) suggests that if the complainant's case against the school is strong, the PDS process is a more favorable option than the OCR investigation and possible finding of violation.

On-Site Investigation

If the PDS process is not successful, OCR will then go to the on-site investigation option. In the investigative process, OCR will request pertinent documentation and

Figure 6.6
The OCR Investigation
Process

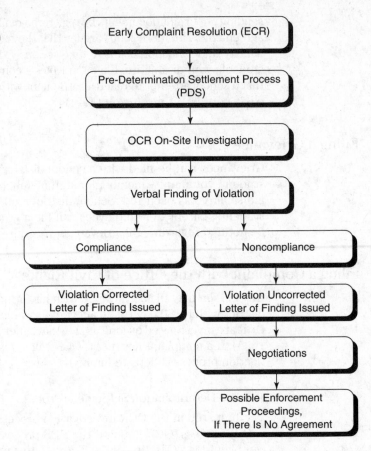

conduct staff interviews. These investigations are time-consuming and uncomfortable for school district staff. Following the investigation, OCR will issue a verbal finding of violation or a finding of no violation. If the finding is no violation, the matter is closed. If a violation is found to exist, however, the focus shifts to correction of the violation. Martin (1993) warns school districts that at this stage of the process OCR is not interested in discussing its legal findings or school district objections. Its focus is on the school district correcting the problem. If the district voluntarily complies to correct the complaint, and does so to OCR's satisfaction, the OCR will issue a letter-of-finding (LOF) violation corrected. If, however, the school does not comply to OCR's satisfaction, an LOF violation uncorrected will be issued. Following the issuance of this letter, OCR and the district attempt to negotiate appropriate corrective action. If there is no agreement, OCR can initiate enforcement proceedings to terminate federal funds to the school district. Terminations are unlikely to occur, however, and would only be imposed in the most egregious of cases. Any administrative decision, such as a decision to terminate, is subject to judicial review.

Filing for a Due Process Hearing

Parents may also request a Section 504 hearing to challenge a school district's actions. Individual states have policies regarding how Section 504 hearings will be handled. In many states when a student is covered under Section 504 and the IDEA, both issues will be handled in a IDEA due process hearing. If an issue involves a Section 504 issue only, it will be resolved in a separate 504 hearing. Huefner (2000) reports that some states train hearing officers to preside over 504 cases and separate training officers to preside over IDEA cases, whereas in other states IDEA hearing officers are trained to hear 504 disputes.

Filing a Suit in Federal Court

Often parents who file IDEA claims in courts also file claims under Section 504. In such situations, a court will first rule on the IDEA issue and then the Section 504 issue. If the issues are separate, a court will rule on the Section 504 issue. If a Section 504 lawsuit seeks relief under the IDEA, typically the claim must be first heard in a due process hearing. Courts have heard separate Section 504 cases if students were not also covered by the IDEA. In these situations, state law will determine if the parents can go directly to court or if they must exhaust administrative procedures (i.e., due process).

Although no private right of action is specifically mentioned in Section 504, case law holds that such a right exists. This is especially significant if the student seeks reimbursement or monetary remedies. Sources of relief available to the individual include injunctions (e.g., court orders to stop a certain practice, court orders to require specified changes in a student's program), attorney's fees, compensatory damages, reimbursement for costs incurred (e.g., tuition), and possibly monetary awards for damages. According to the U.S. Court of Appeals for the Eighth Circuit, monetary awards are only available in cases in which school districts act in bad faith or make gross errors in judgment (*Hoekstra v. Independent School District No. 283*, 1996). The U.S. Court of Appeals for the Sixth Circuit, however, ruled that punitive damages were not available under Section 504 (*Moreno v. Consolidated Rail Corporation*, 1996). Because Title II of the ADA, which applies to public schools, specifies the same remedies as Section 504, the Sixth Circuit decision implies that punitive damages are not available under either the ADA or Section 504.

Comparison of the IDEA and Section 504

The IDEA and Section 504 form much of the legal foundation of special education. The IDEA, with its detailed rules and procedures, is often considered the more relevant of the two laws to educators. In fact, Section 504 has been viewed by many as the less detailed version of the IDEA (Champagne, 1995). Although there is a great deal of overlap between the two laws, there are also distinct differences. Table 6.2 compares and contrasts the two laws.

Table 6.2

Comparison of the IDEA and Section 504

Component	IDEA	Section 504
Purpose of law	• Provides federal funding to states to assist in education of students with disabilities • Substantive requirements attached to funding	• Civil rights law • Protects persons with disabilities from discrimination in programs or services that receive federal financial assistance • Requires reasonable accommodations to ensure nondiscrimination
Who is protected?	• Categorical approach • Thirteen disability categories	• Functional approach • Students (a) having a mental or physical impairment that affects a major life activity, (b) with a record of such an impairment, or (c) who are regarded as having such an impairment • Protects students in general and special education
FAPE	• Disability must adversely impact educational performance • Special education and related services that are provided at public expense, meet state requirements, and are provided in conformity with the IEP • Requires an IEP • Substantive standard is educational benefit	• General or special education and related aids and services • Written education plan • Substantive standard is equivalency
LRE	• Student must be educated with peers without disabilities to the maximum extent appropriate • Removal from integrated settings only when supplementary aids and services are not successful • Districts must have a continuum of placement available	• School must ensure that students are educated with their peers without disabilities

150

Table 6.2
Continued

Component	IDEA	Section 504
Evaluation and placement	• Protection in evaluation procedures • Requires consent prior to initial evaluation and placement • Evaluation and placement decisions have to be made by a multidisciplinary team • Requires evaluation of progress toward IEP goals annually and reevaluation at least every 3 years	• Does not require consent; requires notice only • Requires periodic reevaluation • Reevaluation is required before a significant change in placement
Procedural safeguards	• Comprehensive and detailed notice requirements • Provides for independent evaluations • No grievance procedure • Impartial due process hearing	• General notice requirements • Grievance procedure • Impartial due process hearing
Funding	• Provides for federal funding to assist in the education of students with disabilities	• No federal funding
Enforcement	• U.S. Office of Special Education Programs (OSEP) (can cut off IDEA funds) • Compliance monitoring by state educational agency (SEA)	• Complaint may be filed with Office of Civil Rights (OCR) (can cut off all federal funding) • Complaints can be filed with state's Department of Education

Summary

Section 504 of the Rehabilitation Act of 1973 is a civil rights statute requiring that no otherwise qualified person with disabilities be excluded from participation in, be denied the benefits of, or be subjected to discrimination in any program receiving federal financial assistance. Although there are no funds available through Section 504, it is illegal for schools receiving federal funds to discriminate based on a student's disability.

Section 504 defines disabilities broadly. Students are protected under the statute if they have a physical or mental impairment that substantially limits a major life function, have a record of such an impairment, or are regarded as having such an impairment. The disability does not have to adversely affect educational performance, as is the case with the IDEA, and the student does not have to be in special education. Section 504 protects students with disabilities in both general and special education. All students protected under the IDEA are also protected under Section 504. The reverse, however, is not true.

In addition to offering protection from discrimination, Section 504 provides that schools must make reasonable accommodations—modifications to programs and services—if necessary to ensure that discrimination does not occur. Public schools are required to provide appropriate educational services to children protected by Section 504. The provision of general education and related services or special education and related services must be designed to meet the individual needs of students with disabilities as effectively as the education provided students without disabilities meets their needs. To provide an appropriate education, schools are required to follow a process to ensure equivalency. Schools are required to educate students with disabilities along with students without disabilities to the maximum extent appropriate.

With respect to educational matters, Section 504 is enforced primarily by the Office of Civil Rights of the U.S. Department of Education. When a discrimination complaint is filed, OCR will investigate. OCR can enforce compliance by terminating all federal funding.

For Further Information

Gorn, S. (1998). *What do I do when . . . The answer book on Section 504*. Horsham, PA: LRP Publications.

Smith, T. E. C. (2002). *The Section 504 trainer's manual: A step-by-step guide for inservice and staff development*. Horsham, PA: LRP Publications. (This is a useful manual for conducting staff development activities. It contains a script and transparencies.)

Smith, T. E. C., & Patton, J. R. (1998). *Section 504 and public schools: A practical guide for determining eligibility, developing accommodation plans, and documenting compliance*. Austin, TX: ProEd.

Zirkel, P. A. (2000). *Section 504, the ADA and the schools*. Horsham, PA: LRP Publications. (This book offers complete and thorough coverage of Section 504 and the Americans with Disabilities Act. It begins with the statutes and regulations, both in annotated and unannotated form. The annotated regulations include a comprehensive compilation of court decisions and administrative rulings on Section 504, ADA, and the schools. Sample forms and letters to help school districts comply with 504 and the ADA are included. Supplements and updates are issued annually.)

References

Alexander v. Choate, 469 U.S. 287 (1985).

Americans with Disabilities Act of 1990, 42 U.S.C. 12101 *et seq.*

Champagne, J. F. (1995). Preface. In P. A. Zirkel, *Section 504, the ADA and the schools.* Horsham, PA: LRP Publications.

Cherry v. Matthews, 419 F. Supp. 922 (D.D.C. 1976).

Civil Rights Act of 1964, 42 U.S.C. § 200d.

Congressional Record. (1977, April 26). Remarks of Senator Hubert H. Humphrey, principal Senate author of Section 504, p. 12,216.

Coppell (TX) Independent School District, 24 IDELR 643 (OCR 1996).

Council of Administrators of Special Education. (1992). *Student access: A resource guide for educators: Section 504 of the Rehabilitation Act of 1973.* Reston, VA: Author.

Dade County (FL) School District, 20 IDELR 267 (OCR 1993).

Dagley, D. L., & Evans, C. W. (1995). The reasonable accommodation standard for Section 504—eligible students. *Education Law Reporter, 97,* 1–13.

Daley v. Koch, 639 F. Supp. 289 (D.D.C. 1986).

Education Amendments of 1972, 20 U.S.C. § 1681 *et seq.*

E.E. Black v. Marshall, 497 F. Supp. 1088 (D. Hawaii, 1980).

Fairbanks (AK) North Star Borough School District, 21 IDELR 856 (OCR 1994).

Fossey, R., Hosie, T., Soniat, K., & Zirkel, P. A. (1995). Section 504 and "front line" educators: An expanded obligation to serve children with disabilities. *Preventing School Failure, 39*(2), 10–14.

Garden City (NY) Union Free School District, EHLR 353; 327 (OCR 1990).

Georgetown (TX) Independent School District, 19 IDELR 643 (OCR 1992).

Gerry, M. H., & Benton, J. M. (1982). Section 504: The larger umbrella. In J. Ballard, B. A. Ramirez, & F. J. Weintraub (Eds.), *Special education in America: Its legal and governmental foundations* (pp. 41–49). Reston, VA: Council for Exceptional Children.

Goldstein, B. A. (1994, May). *Legal and practical considerations in implementing Section 504 for students.* Paper presented at the National Institute on Legal Issues of Educating Individuals with Disabilities, San Francisco.

Gorn, S. (1998). *What do I do when . . . the answer book on Section 504.* Horsham, PA: LRP Publications.

Harlowtown Public Schools, 26 IDELR 1156 (OCR 1997).

Hoekstra v. Independent School District, 25 IDELR 882 (8th Cir. 1996).

Huefner, D. S. (2000). *Getting comfortable with special education law: A framework for working with children with disabilities.* Norwood, MA: Christopher-Gordon Publishers.

Katsiyannis, A., Landrum, T., & Reid, R. (2002). Section 504. *Beyond Behavior, 11*(2), 9–15.

Letter to McKethan, 23 IDELR 504 (OCR 1994).

Letter to Veir, 20 IDELR 864 (OCR 1993).

Letter to Williams, 21 IDELR 73 (OCR/OSEP 1994).

Letter to Zirkel, 22 IDELR 667 (OCR 1995).

Martin, J. (1993, April). Section 504 of the Rehabilitation Act of 1973. Paper presented at the international conference of the Council for Exceptional Children, San Antonio, TX.

Mesa (AZ) Unified School District No. 4, EHLR 312:103 (OCR 1988).

Mobile (AL) County School District, 19 IDELR 519 (OCR 1992).

Montebello (CA) Unified School District, 20 IDELR 388 (OCR 1993).

Moreno v. Consolidated Rail Corporation, 25 IDELR, 7 (6th Cir. 1996).

OCR (1988). Free appropriate public education for students with handicaps: Requirements under Section 504 of the Rehabilitation Act of 1973. Washington, DC: Office for Civil Rights.

OCR Complaint Resolution Manual. (1995). In P. A. Zirkel, *Section 504, the ADA and the schools.* Horsham, PA: LRP Publications.

OCR Memorandum Re: Definition of a disability, 19 IDELR 894 (OCR 1992).

OCR Senior Staff Memorandum, 17 EHLR 1233 (OCR 1990).

Philadelphia (PA) School District, 18 IDELR 931 (OCR 1992).

Pinkerton v. Moye, 509 F. Supp. 107 (W.D. Va. 1981).

Podemski, R. S., Marsh, G. E., Smith, T. E. C., & Price, B. J. (1995). *Comprehensive administration of special education* (2nd ed). Upper Saddle River, NJ: Merrill/Prentice Hall.

Rehabilitation Act of 1973, Section 504 Regulations, 34 C.F.R. § 104.1 *et seq.*

Rehabilitation, Comprehensive Services, and Developmental Disabilities Act of 1978, Pub. L. No. 95-062.

Reid, R., & Katsiyannis, A. (1995). Attention deficit/hyperactivity disorder and Section 504. *Remedial and Special Education, 16,* 44–52.

Rice v. Jefferson County Board of Education, 15 EHLR 441.632 (1989).

Schoenfeld, B. N. (1980). Section 504 of the Rehabilitation Act. *University of Cincinnati Law Review, 50,* 580–604.

Section 504 of the Rehabilitation Act of 1973, 29 U.S.C. § 794 *et seq.*

Senate Report No. 890, 95th Cong., 2nd Sess. 39 (1978).

Sevier County (TN) School District, 23 IDELR 1151 (OCR 1995).

Smith, T. E. C. (2001). Section 504, the ADA, and public schools: What educators need to know. *Remedial and Special Education, 22,* 336–343.

Smith, T. E. C. (2002). *The Section 504 trainer's manual: A step-by-step guide for inservice and staff development.* Horsham, PA: LRP Publications.

Smith, T. E. C., & Patton, J. R. (1998). *Section 504 and public schools: A practical guide for determining eligibility, developing accommodation plans, and documenting compliance.* Austin, TX: ProEd.

Southeastern Community College v. Davis, 442 U.S. 397 (1979).

Tucker, B. P., & Goldstein, B. A. (1992). *Legal rights of persons with disabilities: An analysis of federal law.* Horsham, PA: LRP Publications. Uniform Federal Accessibility Standards (1984), 49 31528.

William S. v. Gill, 572 F. Supp. 509 (E.D. Ill. 1983).

Zirkel, P. A. (1996). The substandard for FAPE: Does Section 504 require less than the IDEA? *Education Law Reporter, 106,* 471–477.

Zirkel, P. A. (2000). *Section 504, the ADA and the schools.* Horsham, PA: LRP Publications.

Zirkel, P. A. (2003). Conducting legally defensible Section 504/ADA eligibility determinations. *Education Law Reporter, 176,* 1–11.

CHAPTER SEVEN

The Americans with Disabilities Act

I now lift my pen to sign the Americans with Disabilities Act and say: Let the shameful walls of exclusion finally come tumbling down.

President George Bush, remarks on signing the Americans with Disabilities Act of 1990, July 26, 1990, *Weekly Compilation of Presidential Documents*, vol. 26, n. 30, p. 1165.

In 1990 President Bush signed P.L. 101-336, The Americans with Disabilities Act (ADA), into law. The ADA mandates protections for persons with disabilities against discrimination in a wide range of activities in both the public and private sector. The law focuses primarily on employment and public services. The impact of the ADA on special education services for students with disabilities in school districts is primarily limited to reinforcing and extending the requirements of Section 504 of the Rehabilitation Act of 1973 (Cline, 1994; Wenkart, 1993; Zirkel, 2000). Recall that Section 504 prohibits recipients of federal funds from discriminating against persons with disabilities in programs; under the ADA this prohibition against discrimination is extended to private employers and commercial entities that serve the public. In effect, the ADA extends the reach of Section 504 (Huefner, 2000).

The ADA also affects public education as an employer of persons with disabilities. Furthermore, public education is affected in the areas of public access and in the preparation of students with disabilities to take advantage of the law's provisions. Court decisions regarding the ADA and students with disabilities have been inconclusive regarding schools' responsibilities under the law (Zirkel, 2000). The courts, however, have tended to rule that the ADA is to be interpreted consistent with Section 504. Therefore, case law under Section 504 may be used by courts for guidance in interpreting similar provisions of the ADA (Osborne, 1995).

The ADA's effect on the provision of a free appropriate public education (FAPE) provided to students, especially when a school is in compliance with IDEA and Section 504, will be minimal (Wenkart, 1993). Moreover, no student-specific rights are granted in the ADA beyond those of Section 504. Wenkart (1993) conjectures that because nothing in the legislative history suggests an intention to enlarge the substantive rights of children with disabilities, the ADA may not add to rights already existing.

One of the few courts to address the relationship between the IDEA and the ADA, the U.S. Court of Appeals for the Tenth Circuit, ruled in *Urban v. Jefferson County School District R-1* (1994) that the placement rights of a student with disabilities is no greater under the ADA than under the IDEA. Congress believed substantive rights of students with disabilities to be adequately protected under the IDEA and Section 504. This does not mean, however, that public education is unaffected by the ADA. Areas of public education that are affected include employment, general nondiscrimination (which parallels the requirements of Section 504), communications, and program accessibility (Kaesberg & Murray, 1994). Additionally, an important area of difference between Section 504, the IDEA, and the ADA is that the ADA applies to private schools.

Pitasky (1997) asserts that the special education community needs to be aware of how the courts will apply the ADA to the school setting. Furthermore, Zirkel (2000) contends that it would be a mistake for school officials to think they will be in compliance with ADA because they adhere to the requirements of Section 504. School officials, therefore, should be aware of their responsibilities under both Section 504 and the ADA.

Finally, it is important that administrators, counselors, and teachers working with students with disabilities are aware of the content of the ADA because of the law's implications for the lives of the students they serve. When students with disabilities leave school and enter the workforce, they will need to engage in self-advocacy (Osborne, 1995). A duty of educators, aptly stated by Marczely (1993), is to inform students with disabilities and their parents of the "power and promise the ADA gives them, and the ways in which that power and promise can be productively used" (p. 207).

The purpose of this chapter is to briefly review the provisions of the ADA; the development, purpose, and structure of the ADA; and the school district's responsibilities under the law.

The Development of the ADA

Section 504 was the first federal effort to protect persons with disabilities from discrimination. Section 504 applied to the federal government, government contractors, and recipients of federal funds. Employers and public accommodations operated by the private sector and by state and local governments, however, were unaffected by the law. As a result, many persons with disabilities continued to suffer from discrimination in employment, education, housing, access to public services, and transportation. To rectify these continued inequities, President Reagan created the National Council on Disabilities, whose task was to recommend to Congress remedies for halting discrimination against persons with disabilities (Miles, Russo, & Gordon, 1992).

After 3 years of study, the council made recommendations to Congress that were to form the basis of the ADA. According to Miles et al. (1992), the bill, introduced in 1988, stalled in Congress because of congressional inaction, even though it enjoyed the strong support of President Bush and advocacy groups for persons with disabilities. In July 1990 the bill, recently arrived from the House-Senate Conference Committee, was passed by both houses of Congress. On July 26, 1990, the ADA was signed into law by President Bush on the White House lawn. The signing was witnessed by more than 3,000 persons with disabilities, reportedly one of the largest ceremonies in White House history (Burnim & Patino, 1993).

The Purpose and Structure of the ADA

In the introduction to the ADA, Congress reported that 43 million Americans had physical or mental disabilities. Congress found that discrimination against persons with disabilities persisted in employment, housing, public accommodations, education, transportation, communication, recreation, institutionalization, health services, voting, and access to public services (ADA, 42 U.S.C. §12101). Congress also found that persons with disabilities who had experienced discrimination had little or no recourse to redress such discrimination. Furthermore, this discrimination denied persons with disabilities the opportunity to compete on an equal basis and disadvantaged them socially, vocationally, economically, and educationally. Stating that America's proper goals in this regard were to assure persons with disabilities equality of opportunity, full participation, independent living, and economic self-sufficiency, Congress passed the ADA. Figure 7.1 lists examples of discriminatory practices that are prohibited by the ADA.

Figure 7.1
Discriminatory Practices

- Practices that deny a person with a disability the ability to participate in or cause a person to be denied the benefits from goods, services, facilities, or accommodations.

- Practices that provide an unequal benefit in goods, services, facilities, or accommodations on the basis of a disability.

- Practices that provide goods, services, facilities, or accommodations that, even though equal, are different or separate from those provided to persons without disabilities.

- Practices used in eligibility determinations for the use of goods, services, facilities, or accommodations that effectively exclude persons with disabilities through screening procedures.

- Practices that tend to segregate. Goods, services, and facilities shall be provided in settings in which persons with and without disabilities are integrated.

Purpose of the ADA

The primary purposes of the law are:

(1) To provide a clear and comprehensive national mandate for the elimination of discrimination against individuals with disabilities;

(2) To provide clear, strong, consistent, enforceable standards addressing discrimination against individuals with disabilities;

(3) To ensure that the federal government plays a central role in enforcing the standards established in the Act on behalf of individuals with disabilities; and

(4) To invoke the sweep of Congressional authority, including the power to enforce the 14th Amendment and to regulate commerce, in order to address the major areas of discrimination faced day to day by people with disabilities. (ADA, 42 U.S.C. § 12101)

The ADA extends the civil rights and antidiscrimination protections of Section 504 from the federal government, its contractors, and recipients of federal funds to employers, state and local governments or any instrumentality of the government, and any privately owned business or facility open to the public. The primary goal of the law, therefore, is that persons with disabilities will enjoy equal opportunity to fully participate in the life of the community and have an equal opportunity to live independently and enjoy economic self-sufficiency through the removal of the barriers that exclude them from the mainstream of American life (Turnbull, 1993).

Who Is Protected?

The ADA follows Section 504 in defining those individuals protected by the law. The Section 504 definition of persons with disabilities, therefore, applies to the ADA as well as to Section 504. In the ADA, a person with a disability is defined as having

(i) a physical or mental impairment that substantially limits one or more of the major life activities of such individual;

(ii) a record of such an impairment; or

(iii) being regarded as having such an impairment. (ADA, 42 U.S.C. § 12102 (2))

Physical and Mental Impairments.   The first part of the definition describes a disability broadly. ADA regulations mirror the language in Section 504 in listing physical or mental impairments. Protected disabilities include any disorder affecting body systems, including neurological (including traumatic brain injury), physiological, musculoskeletal, sense, respiratory, cardiovascular, digestive, or psychological systems. Regulations to the ADA require that whether or not a person has a disability, an assessment should be conducted without regard to the availability of mitigating modifications or assistive devices (ADA Regulations, 28 C.F.R. § 38, Appendix A). For example, a person with epilepsy is covered under the first part of the definition even if the effects of the impairment are controlled by medication. Likewise, a person with a hearing loss is covered if the loss substantially limits the major life activity of hearing, even though the loss may be ameliorated through the use of a hearing aid.

Persons with HIV and Tuberculosis.   The ADA includes persons with HIV (whether symptomatic or asymptomatic) and tuberculosis. If, however, a person with an infectious disease presents a "direct threat" (i.e., significant risk) of contagion or infection, he or she may be excluded from goods, services, facilities, privileges, advantages, and accommodations or denied a job if the threat cannot be eliminated by reasonable accommodations or modifications. The determination of a direct threat is made on an individual basis and relies on current medical or objective evidence to determine the nature, duration, and severity of the risk; the probability that injury will occur; and whether reasonable accommodations will alleviate the risk (ADA Regulations, 28 C.F.R. § 36.208).

For an individual to be covered under the ADA, the physical or mental disability must substantially limit one or more major life activities. These activities include caring for one's self, performing manual tasks, walking, seeing, hearing, speaking, breathing, learning, and working (ADA Regulations, 28 C.F.R. § 38, Appendix A). Persons are thus considered disabled under the first part of the definition when their "important life activities are restricted as to the conditions, manner, and duration under which they can be performed in comparison to most people" (ADA Regulations, 28 C.F.R. § 38, Appendix A).

Katsiyannis and Yell (2002) reviewed two U.S. Supreme Court cases that addressed the issue of when a disability is substantially limiting. The first case, *Murphy v. United Parcel Service, Inc.* (1999) involved an employee, Vaughn Murphy, who was hired by UPS to drive commercial vehicles. To drive commercial vehicles, Murphy had to pass the Department of Transportation health certification requirements. One of these requirements was that a driver must not have high blood pressure, which could interfere with the driver's ability to operate a commercial vehicle safely. Vaughn Murphy was hired despite having high blood pressure. When the error was discovered, Murphy was fired. A suit was filed under the ADA. Eventually, the U.S. Court of Appeals for the Tenth Circuit ruled that the employee's hypertension was not a disability because he functioned normally in everyday activities and as a result did not qualify for protection under the ADA. The case was appealed to the U.S. Supreme Court. The high court upheld the lower court's decision, concluding that Murphy was not substantially limited in the major life activity of working but rather was unable to perform only a particular job. The Supreme Court ruled that the fact that Murphy was only unable to perform this particular job, being a truck driver, was insufficient to prove that he was regarded as substantially limited in the major life activity of working. Because he was not disabled under the ADA, he was not protected under the law. Further, the Supreme Court reasoned that employees who could function normally when their impairments are treated do not qualify for protection under ADA. To be covered under the ADA a person must be presently substantially limited in his or her ability to work.

In a similar case, *Albertsons, Inc. v. Kirkingburg* (1999), a truck driver, Hallie Kirkingburg, was falsely certified as passing the Department of Transportation's vision standards for commercial truck drivers. His vision was correctly assessed in 1992, and subsequently, he was fired for failing to meet the basic vision standards. He eventually applied for and received a waiver allowing him to drive, but the company refused to re-hire him. The employee sued under the ADA. The district court dismissed the ADA claim. However, this decision was reversed by the Ninth Circuit. The circuit court found that Kirkingburg had established a disability under the Act by demonstrating that the manner in which he sees was significantly different from the manner in which most people see.

On appeal, the Supreme Court reversed the decision of the lower court, con-cluding that the extent of the limitation on a major life activity caused by the vision impairment was not substantial. The Court also observed that the appellate court erred in determining Kirkingburg's eligibility under ADA. The high court found that even though the ADA's standard that the physical or mental impairment must sub-stantially limit a major life activity, the circuit court had endorsed a new standard, a "significant difference" standard, which the circuit court believed was sufficient to meet ADA eligibility criteria. The Supreme Court disagreed, holding that different is not the appropriate standard. The ADA only protects persons with disabilities that are substantial.

Exclusions from Protection.   Physical or mental disabilities do not include simple physical characteristics, nor do they include environmental, cultural, economic, or other disadvantages (e.g., prison record, being poor). Neither are the following con-ditions included as disabilities: (a) age (although medical conditions resulting from old age are disabilities); (b) temporary,* nonchronic impairments such as broken limbs; (c) pregnancy; and (d) obesity (except in rare circumstances). Environmen-tal illnesses (e.g. multiple chemical sensitivity, allergy to smoke) are not considered disabilities under the ADA unless the impairment actually limits one or more major life activities.

The ADA specifically excludes certain individuals from its definition of a person with disability. Because courts had interpreted Section 504 as covering transsexuals and compulsive gamblers, Congress specifically excluded these individuals from coverage under the ADA (Tucker, 1992). Additionally, Congress acted to ensure that the ADA definition of disability would not include homosexuality, bisexuality, transvestitism, transsexualism, pedophilia, exhibitionism, voyeurism, gender identity disorders not re-sulting from physical impairments, or other sexual behavior disorders (ADA, 42 U.S.C. §12211(a)(b)). The law also specifically excludes persons with compulsive gambling disorders, kleptomania, or pyromania (ADA, 42 U.S.C. §12211(b)(2)).

Persons engaging in the illegal use of drugs, and any disorders resulting from cur-rent illegal drug use, are also excluded from protection under the ADA. Persons who have successfully completed or are participating in a supervised drug rehabilitation

---

*The word *temporary* was deleted from the final rules promulgated by the Equal Employment Opportu-nity Commission because it was not contained in the statute or the regulations. Whether a temporary im-pairment is a disability can only be determined on a case-by-case basis, taking into account both the impairment's duration and the extent to which the impairment actually limits a major life activity (ADA Regulations, 28 C.F.R. §38, Appendix A).

program and are no longer using illegal drugs are protected by the ADA. Persons who are discriminated against because they are erroneously believed to be engaged in illegal drug use are also protected. Furthermore, drug testing of employees is allowed under the law. The ADA effectively amends Section 504 to allow school districts to discipline students with disabilities for the use or possession of illegal drugs or alcohol in the same manner that students without disabilities would be disciplined (OCR Staff Memorandum, 1991).

Having a Record of a Disability or Being Regarded as Being Disabled.   The second and third parts of the definition essentially protect individuals when a negative or discriminatory action is committed against them based on a record of a disability or because they are regarded as being disabled. Persons covered by these two parts are those who have been subject to discrimination because they had a history of being disabled, and are treated in a discriminatory way because people still believe them to be disabled. Persons who are regarded as being disabled are subject to discrimination if a covered entity mistakenly believes that the person has a disability (*Murphy v. United Parcel Service,* 1999). It is this discriminatory treatment, which is based on false assumptions, that entitles these persons to protection. Examples of persons having a record of a disability include persons with histories of cancer, heart disease, or mental or emotional illness. Examples of persons regarded as having a disability include persons misclassified as having an impairment and those discriminated against because of the fears and stereotypes of others.

Structure of the ADA

The ADA is codified at 42 U.S.C. §§ 12101–12213. The law consists of five titles or subchapters. These titles are listed in Figure 7.2. The sine qua non of the ADA is the protection of persons with disabilities from discrimination based on their disabilities. The ADA language that prohibits discrimination varies slightly in Titles I, II, and III. Differences between the titles also exist in definitions and enforcement.

Titles of the ADA

The ADA consists of five titles, which we will briefly review in this section. The responsibilities of public schools under Title II and private schools under Title III will be emphasized.

Title I: Employment.   Title I of the ADA addresses employment. Employers, employment agencies, labor organizations, and labor-management committees are referred to in the law as "covered entities." These entities may not discriminate against any qualified individuals with disabilities, including employees or applicants for employment. Neither the U.S. government nor private membership clubs are covered entities. After July 1994, all employers with 15 or more employees are covered by Title I. Public school and private school employees are included under this title as long as the school employs 50 or more persons. Religious schools may give preference to applicants of the

Figure 7.2
The Americans with Disabilities Act

Title I—Employment
Title II—Public Services
    Subtitle A—General Prohibitions
    Subtitle B—Public Transportation
Title III—Public Accommodations and Services Operated by Private Entities
Title IV—Telecommunications
Title V—Miscellaneous Provisions

particular religion and may require that employees conform to its religious tenets (ADA Regulations, 29 C.F.R. §1630.16(A)).

Title I defines a qualified individual with a disability as "an individual with a disability who, with or without reasonable accommodation, can perform the essential functions of the employment position that such individual holds or desires" (ADA, 42 U.S.C. §12111(8)). To be protected by the ADA in employment, a person must have a disability and be qualified; that is, the person must be able to perform the duties of the job with or without the provision of reasonable accommodations. The qualified individual with disabilities must satisfy the requisite skill, experience, education, and other job-related requirements of the employment position. In essence, he or she must be able to perform the essential elements of the job. The Equal Employment Opportunity Commission (1992) suggests that employers follow two steps in determining if an individual with disabilities is qualified under the ADA. First, the employer should determine if the individual meets the necessary prerequisites of the job (e.g., education, work experience, training, skills, licenses, certificates, and other job-related requirements). If the individual with disabilities meets the necessary job requirements, the employer may go to the second step of the determination, which is assessing if the individual can perform the essential functions of the job with or without reasonable accommodations.

Reasonable Accommodations.   A reasonable accommodation is a modification to the job or the work environment that will remove barriers and enable the individual with a disability to perform the job. Reasonable accommodations include:

(A) making existing facilities used by employees readily accessible to and usable by individuals with disabilities; and

(B) job restructuring, part-time or modified work schedules, reassignment to a vacant position, acquisition or modification of equipment or devices, appropriate adjustment or modifications of examination, training materials or policies, the provision of qualified readers or interpreters, and other similar accommodations for persons with disabilities. (ADA, 42 U.S.C. §12111(9) *et seq.*)

When determining a reasonable accommodation, the employer should

(1) Analyze the particular job involved and determine its purpose and essential functions;
(2) Consult with the individual with a disability to ascertain the precise job-related limitations imposed by the individual's disability and how those limitations could be overcome with a reasonable accommodation;
(3) In consultation with the individual to be accommodated, identify potential accommodations and assess the effectiveness each would have in enabling the individual to perform the essential functions of the position;
(4) Consider the preference of the individual to be accommodated that is the most appropriate for both the employee and the employer. (ADA Regulations, 29 C.F.R. § 1630.9)

The ADA differentiates between reasonable and unreasonable accommodations. Accommodations that impose "undue hardship" on the employer (i.e., require significant difficulty or significant expense) are not required. Only those accommodations that are reasonable are required. Factors to be considered in determining if an accommodation would impose an undue hardship include (a) the nature and cost of the accommodation; (b) the number of persons employed; (c) the effect on expenses and resources; (d) the overall financial resources of the covered entity; (e) the number, type, and location of the employer's facilities; and (f) the type of operation of the employer.

Prohibition Against Discrimination.   Title I protects persons with disabilities from discrimination in "job application procedures, the hiring, advancement, or discharge of employees, employee compensation, job training, and other terms, conditions, or privileges of employment" (ADA, 42 U.S.C. §12112(a)). Discrimination, according to the ADA, involves limiting or classifying applicants or employees in a way that adversely affects the employment status of that person, participating in contractual arrangements that indirectly discriminate against disabled persons, or following administrative procedures that have the effect of discriminating against persons with disabilities. Employers can also discriminate by not making reasonable accommodations for a qualified person with disabilities unless these accommodations would result in undue hardship. Neither may employees discriminate against associates of the persons with disabilities (e.g., relatives).

Title I is not an affirmative action mandate. That is, employers need not hire employees with disabilities to redress past discrimination. If two equally qualified people apply for a job or a promotion, one with a disability and one without, the employer may hire or promote the applicant without disabilities, as long as the employer's decision is not related to the applicant's disability (Tucker & Goldstein, 1992). Employers have no obligations regarding Title I, however, when an applicant or employee is currently using illegal drugs.

Enforcement of Title I.   The ADA adopts the enforcement procedures in Title VII of the Civil Rights Act (ADA, 42 U.S.C. § 2000(e) *et seq.*). Powers of enforcement are given to the Equal Employment Opportunity Commission (EEOC), U.S. attorney general, and persons with disabilities who are subjected to discrimination. Clearly the ADA allows both administrative and individual enforcement of its provisions. Individuals, however, must exhaust administrative remedies before taking judicial action. Disability discrimination claims must be filed within 180 days of the alleged discrimination. EEOC will investigate the claim and attempt to reach a settlement between the parties. If these attempts are not successful, the individual has the right to go to court. The remedies available under the ADA are injunctive relief (i.e., court orders to stop discrimination), reinstatement, and compensatory damages (e.g., back pay). Moreover, if an employer is found guilty of intentional discrimination "with malice or reckless indifference," a plaintiff may receive compensatory and punitive damages. The ADA contains damage caps on punitive damages that prevailing plaintiffs can collect. In cases where the employer has made good faith efforts to reasonably accommodate an individual but has not succeeded in doing so, damages will not be awarded (ADA Regulations, 28 C.F.R. § 36.504 *et seq.*). When plaintiffs seek damages, they may ask for a trial by jury. The court in which the complaint is heard may, at its discretion, award attorney's fees.

Title II: Public Services.   Title II contains two subtitles: Subtitle A prohibits discrimination by state and local governments, and Subtitle B covers discrimination in public transportation. Title II protects all qualified persons with disabilities from discrimination by public entities. Public entities are any state or local government or any department or instrumentality of the state or local government. According to the Department of Justice, an entity is considered "public" if it (a) operates using public funds; (b) has employees who are considered government employees; (c) receives significant assistance from the government in terms of property or equipment; or (d) is governed by an independent or elected board (Tucker & Goldstein, 1992). Public schools fall under the purview of Title II.

To be protected under Title II, the individual with disabilities must be qualified. That is, the individual—with or without reasonable modifications to rules, policies, or practices; the removal of architectural, communication, or transportation barriers; or the provision of auxiliary aids and services—meets the essential eligibility requirements for the receipt of services or the participation in programs or activities provided by a public entity (ADA, 42 U.S.C. §12131 (2)).

Prohibition Against Discrimination.   Discrimination on the basis of disability is prohibited. Specifically, Title II prohibits discrimination in employment, like Title I, and in accessibility, like Title III. Title II requires that a qualified person with disabilities cannot be excluded from participation in or be denied the benefits of the services, programs, or activities of a public entity or be subjected to discrimination by a public entity. Public schools and colleges, although not specifically mentioned in Title II, are public entities, so reasonable modifications* will be required in employee hiring as well as in student programs.

---

*Titles II and III use the term *reasonable modifications* rather than *reasonable accommodations*. The terms, however, have similar meanings.

The statutory language and regulations concerning discrimination are similar to those contained in Section 504 and provide similar protections. The ADA, unlike Section 504, contains no separate coverage for public schools, nor does it contain specific student requirements that schools must follow.

Subtitle B, concerning transportation, is a detailed compilation of accommodations that are required in making transportation accessible for persons with disabilities. Public school transportation is expressly omitted from Title II (49 C.F.R. § 37.27 Appendix). Subtitle B is made up of two parts. Part 1 covers public transportation provided by bus or rail, excluding commuter services, or other means of conveyance with the exception of air travel. Part 1 covers new vehicles, used vehicles, remanufactured vehicles, paratransit services, new and altered facilities used to provide public transportation, and light or rapid rail systems. Part 2 concerns public transportation by intercity and commuter rail services covering accessible cars, new cars, used cars, remanufactured cars, new stations for use in intercity transportation, existing stations, and altered stations. The provisions of both parts require that intercity and commuter rail services be made readily accessible to and usable by individuals with disabilities.

Public entities must conduct self-evaluations to determine if they are in compliance with Title II. Additionally, covered entities must have information regarding adherence to Title II. Entities with 50 or more employees must keep a record of the self-evaluation available to the public for 3 years following the self-evaluation. Furthermore, they must have an ADA coordinator and establish a complaint procedure. Finally, when they make structural changes to comply with the ADA, they must develop transition plans regarding the changes to be made.

Enforcement of Title II.   Enforcement of Title II mirrors enforcement of Section 504, which incorporates similar remedies and procedures. The Department of Justice oversees compliance with Title II. Individuals may file a complaint with the appropriate agency within 180 days of the alleged discrimination or bring a private lawsuit to recover actual damages. Punitive damages, however, are not available against the government or a governmental agency. Under Title II the exhaustion of administrative remedies is not required before going to a court for relief.

Title III: Public Accommodations Operated by a Private Entity.   The purpose of Title III of the ADA is to prohibit discrimination by private entities that own public accommodations by providing persons with disabilities an equal opportunity to receive the benefits of goods and services in the most integrated settings. All privately owned businesses, facilities open to the public, and commercial facilities (even if not open to the public) are subject to Title III. If a business is a place of public accommodation fitting into one of 12 categories, it is covered. The examples provided of public accommodations in the ADA are illustrative, not exhaustive (ADA, 42 U.S.C. §12181 (7)). Figure 7.3 lists these categories.

Figure 7.3
Public Accommodations

- Places of lodging
- Bars and restaurants
- Places of exhibition or entertainment (e.g., concert halls, movie theaters)
- Places of public gathering (e.g., conference centers, lecture halls)
- Stores and shopping centers
- Service establishments, including barber shops, laundromats, hospitals, professional offices, and others
- Terminals and depots
- Cultural institutions (e.g., museums, galleries)
- Places of recreation (e.g., amusement parks, zoos)
- Places of education (nurseries and all schools from preschool to university)
- Places where social services are offered (e.g., day care centers, homeless shelters, food banks)
- Places for exercise or recreation (e.g., golf courses, health clubs, gymnasiums)

Private schools from "nursery to postgraduate school" are specifically covered under Title III (ADA, 42 U.S.C. § 12181 (7)). Title III also applies to private entities that offer examinations or courses related to applications, licensing, certification, or credentialing for secondary or postsecondary education, professional, or trade purposes (ADA Regulations, 28 C.F.R. § 36.102(a)).

Commercial facilities are covered under Title III. Commercial facilities are defined as facilities "that are intended for nonresidential use and whose operations will affect commerce" (ADA, 42 U.S.C. §12181(2) *et seq.*). Commerce is any means of travel, trade, transportation, or communication between states or between the United States and a foreign country.

Private residences, private clubs, religious entities, and public entities are exempt from the Title III mandates. Public schools, therefore, are exempt while private schools are not (Zirkel, 1993b). Private religious schools are also exempt under Title III.

Prohibition Against Discrimination.   Title III forbids discrimination against persons with disabilities on the basis of their disabilities. Two types of discrimination are addressed: overtly discriminatory practices on the basis of disability, and practices and structures that effectively discriminate against persons with disabilities whether or not there was intention to discriminate (Coupe, Ness, & Sheetz, 1992).

Title III also prohibits discrimination in privately operated public transportation services. These entities need not be primarily engaged in the transportation of people. Examples include shuttle services, student transportation systems, and transportation provided within a recreational facility (e.g., amusement park). Discrimination involves the imposition of eligibility criteria that serve to screen out persons with disabilities from using the transportation systems, failure to make reasonable modifications to ensure nondiscrimination, or failure to remove barriers to accessibility.

Requirements of Title III.   Businesses open to the public (i.e., public accommodations) must comply with the requirements regarding the provision of goods and services, the prohibition against discrimination, the construction of new buildings, and the alteration of existing buildings. Commercial facilities are required to comply with the new construction and building alteration requirements only.

Public accommodations must modify their operations if they are discriminatory unless they can show that to do so would fundamentally alter the nature of the business. Businesses open to the public must also take steps to ensure effective communications with persons whose disabilities affect hearing, vision, or speech. Auxiliary aids and services, such as interpreters and readers, may be used. Businesses, however, are not required to provide personal devices (e.g., hearing aids, eyeglasses) or personal services (e.g., assistance in eating) to individuals.

Architectural Accessibility.   Private entities operating public accommodations must remove architectural and structural barriers in existing facilities where the removal is "readily achievable" (i.e., easily accomplished and not unduly expensive or difficult). This obligation, however, does not extend to employee work areas within the public accommodations. If the removal of the barrier is not readily achievable, an obligation still exists to make goods and services available through alternative methods. Examples of alternatives to barrier removal include providing curb service or home delivery, retrieving merchandise from inaccessible shelves, and relocating activities to accessible locations (ADA Regulations, 28 C.F.R. § 36.305(b) *et seq.*). Figure 7.4 is a partial list of ways to remove architectural barriers. The list is not intended to be exhaustive.

The ADA provides no test for determining if the removal of these (or any other) barriers is readily achievable. The Department of Justice, and presumably the courts, will consider all claims that barrier removal is not readily achievable on a case-by-case basis. Factors in these determinations include the financial resources of the accommodation.

New Construction and Building Alterations.   Public accommodations and commercial facilities are required to comply with ADA regulations regarding new construction and building alterations. All new construction must be accessible; however, alterations to existing facilities must only be made to the extent that they are readily achievable. The ADA contains detailed specifications on making new construction accessible.

Enforcement of Title III.   Under Title III, persons who believe they have been subjected to discrimination may file a complaint with the Department of Justice.

Figure 7.4
Ways to Remove Architectural Barriers

- Installing ramps
- Making curb cuts in sidewalks and entrances
- Repositioning shelves
- Rearranging tables, chairs, and other furniture
- Repositioning telephones
- Adding raised markings on elevator control buttons
- Installing flashing alarm lights
- Widening doors and doorways
- Eliminating a turnstile or providing an accessible path
- Installing accessible door hardware
- Installing grab bars in toilet stalls
- Rearranging toilet partitions to increase maneuvering space
- Insulating lavatory pipes under sinks to prevent burns
- Installing a full-length bathroom mirror
- Repositioning the paper towel dispenser in the bathroom
- Creating designated accessible parking spaces
- Removing high-pile, low-density carpeting
- Installing vehicle hand controls

An individual may seek a court order to prohibit discrimination. Courts may award injunctive relief. Punitive damages, however, are not available (ADA, 42 U.S.C. §12188(b)(4)). In the area of transportation, claims may be filed with the Department of Transportation or with a court.

Title IV: Telecommunications.   Title IV of the ADA involves the provision of telecommunication services for persons with hearing and speech impairments. Many individuals with these disabilities are unable to communicate by telephone, thereby cutting them off from an extremely important mode of communication. Title IV amends the Communications Act of 1934 (Communications Act, 47 U.S.C. §151 *et seq.*) to require that phone companies (i.e., "common carriers") provide telecommunication services to allow persons with hearing and speech disabilities to communicate with persons without disabilities. To meet the ADA mandates, common carriers are required to establish systems of telephone relay services that connect telecommunication devices for the deaf to telephones. Title IV also requires that television public service announcements be close-captioned. Television broadcasters, however, are not required to close-caption television programs. Enforcement authority of Title IV was assumed by the Federal Communications Commission.

Title V: Miscellaneous.   The final title of the ADA contains a number of miscellaneous provisions. The following are some of the more important ones:

1. States are not immune from actions under the ADA (ADA, 42 U.S.C. § 12202). This provision of the law allows states to be sued under the ADA. Generally, if a law does not specifically allow states to be sued under the law, states will be considered immune from lawsuits under the doctrine of sovereign immunity. (See Chapter 14 for elaborations on sovereign immunity.)

2. Courts and administrative agencies may award attorney's fees to prevailing parties. Courts can also award expert witness fees (ADA, 42 U.S.C. §12205). The award of attorney's fees includes fees assessed against the plaintiff if the lawsuit is frivolous, unreasonable, or groundless (Tucker & Goldstein, 1992).

3. Retaliation and coercion against persons with disabilities seeking to enforce their rights under the ADA are prohibited. It is also illegal to coerce, intimidate, or threaten anyone attempting to help persons with disabilities exercise their rights under the ADA (ADA, 42 U.S.C. §12203).

4. The ADA does not invalidate or limit remedies, rights, and procedures of any federal, state, or local law whose protection for persons with disabilities is equal to or greater than the ADA (ADA, 42 U.S.C. §12201).

5. The ADA does not apply a lesser standard than Section 504 of the Rehabilitation Act of 1973 (ADA, 42 U.S.C. §12201(a)).

6. Where appropriate, parties are encouraged to seek to resolve disputes through some alternative method of dispute resolution rather than through litigation (ADA, 42 U.S.C. §12212). This provision is, however, completely voluntary.

7. An Access Board was convened to issue minimum guidelines for Titles II and III of the ADA. The board issued a volume of guidelines more than 130 pages long (see 36 C.F.R. §1191). These guidelines are intended to ensure that facilities are made accessible to persons with disabilities.

School District Responsibilities

Nothing in the ADA enlarges the right of students with disabilities to an appropriate education under either the IDEA or Section 504 (Wenkart, 1993). In fact, the ADA contains no specific student requirements such as the FAPE requirement of the IDEA and Section 504 or transition plans under the IDEA (Zirkel, 1993a). The ADA, however, will affect public education in other areas. In fact, schools may be liable for suits for remedies, possibly including monetary damages, when they violate the ADA (*Hoekstra v. Independent School District No. 283*, 1996). It is, therefore, important

Figure 7.5
School District Responsibilities

1. Appoint an ADA compliance coordinator (if more than 50 employees).
2. Conduct a self-evaluation that covers nondiscrimination provisions, employment, accessibility, and communication.
3. Develop transition plans to bring the school into compliance with ADA.
4. Maintain a file of self-evaluation, available for public inspection, for 3 years following completion of the evaluation.
5. Provide notice regarding services, programs, or activities of the school.
6. Know which students are protected under the ADA or Section 504.
7. Recognize that the ADA covers employees with disabilities.
8. Ensure that new construction is readily accessible and usable by persons with disabilities.

that school officials be aware of what constitutes compliance and noncompliance with the law. Figure 7.5 lists school district compliance requirements.

ADA Compliance Coordinator

School districts that employ 50 or more persons must have an ADA coordinator, and information should be made available on how to reach that person. The duties of the coordinator include coordinating ADA compliance activities, informing and involving the community, coordinating the school district's self-evaluation and transition plan, establishing a grievance plan, and investigating grievances (ADA Regulations, 28 C.F.R. § 35.107 *et seq.*). The ADA coordinator should also be responsible for informing interested persons regarding the services, programs, and activities offered by the school district. The coordinator should conduct staff inservice training to make employees aware of ADA requirements (ADA, 42 U.S.C. § 84.7(b)).

Self-Evaluation

The ADA requires that school districts conduct a self-evaluation. If a school has already completed a Section 504 self-evaluation, then the ADA self-evaluation will apply only to those policies and practices not included in the previous self-evaluation (28 C.F.R. § 35.105(d)). Provisions to ensure nondiscrimination, communication, employment, accessibility of programs and facilities, and staff training should be evaluated. Interested persons or organizations should be allowed to participate in the self-evaluation by submitting comments (ADA Regulations, 28 C.F.R. § 35.105 *et seq.*). The self-evaluation must be maintained for public inspection for 3 years. The description of the self-evaluation should include the names of interested persons consulted, a description of problems identified, and modifications to correct these problem areas.

Transition Plan

If areas of noncompliance with the ADA are identified, the school district must act to correct those deficiencies. If structural changes will be required to achieve program accessibility, a transition plan must be developed to guide completion of the necessary changes. This plan should identify accessibility problems and describe in detail methods to alleviate the problem.

The transition plan of the ADA is not to be confused with the transition plan required by the IDEA in the individualized education programs (IEPs) of students 16 or older. The ADA does not require transition plans for students with disabilities.

Prohibition Against Discrimination

The ADA's Title I requirements prohibiting discrimination against qualified persons with disabilities in employment applies to schools. School districts must also comply with the nondiscriminatory provisions of Title II. Additionally private schools are covered by Title III of the ADA, which requires that (a) programs, services, and activities should be provided in the most integrated setting feasible; (b) no written policies or procedures may exclude or discriminate; (c) school district contractors must not discriminate; (d) the use of criteria that screen out or have the effect of screening out eligible persons with disabilities are prohibited; and (e) modifications of policies, practices, and procedures that may discriminate must be made unless these changes will fundamentally alter the nature of the service, program, or activity.

Summary

In 1990, the Americans with Disabilities Act became law. The purpose of the law was to prohibit discrimination against persons with disabilities based on their disability. The ADA is similar to Section 504 of the Rehabilitation Act of 1973, but is larger in scope. Where Section 504 prohibits discrimination against persons with disabilities in programs receiving federal financial assistance, the ADA extends these protections to the private sector. The ADA prohibits discriminatory practices in employment, housing, and transportation. The ADA also legislates accommodations to facilities in order that they are free of barriers and accessible to persons with disabilities.

The ADA's effect on the provision of a free appropriate public education provided to students, especially when a school is in compliance with IDEA and Section 504, will be minimal. The ADA grants no additional student-specific rights beyond those contained in Section 504 and the IDEA. This does not mean, however, that public education is unaffected by the ADA. Areas of public education that are affected include employment, general nondiscrimination (which parallels the requirements of Section 504), communications, and program accessibility. Additionally, administrators, counselors, and teachers working with students with disabilities need to become aware of the content of the ADA, because of the law's implications for the lives of the students they serve. When students with disabilities leave school and enter the workforce, they will need to engage in self-advocacy. A duty of educators is the responsibility to inform students with disabilities and their parents of their rights contained in the ADA.

For Further Information

Americans with Disabilities Act: Law, regulations, and interpretive guidance. (1992). Horsham, PA: LRP Publications.

Equal Employment Opportunity Commission. (1992). *A technical assistance manual on the employment (Title I) provisions of the Americans with Disabilities Act.* Washington, DC: Author (available from the EEOC, 189 L Street NW, Washington, DC 20507).

Kaesberg, M. A., & Murray, K. T. (1994). Americans with Disabilities Act. *Education Law Reporter, 90,* 11–21.

Marczely, B. (1993). The Americans with Disabilities Act: Confronting the shortcomings of Section 504 in public education. *Education Law Reporter, 78,* 199–207.

Miles, A. S., Russo, C. J., & Gordon, W. M. (1992). The reasonable accommodations provisions of the Americans with Disabilities Act. *Education Law Reporter, 69,* 1–8.

Tucker, B. P. (1992). The Americans with Disabilities Act: An overview. *New Mexico Law Review, 22,* 3–112.

Wenkart, R. D. (1993). The Americans with Disabilities Act and its impact on public education. *Education Law Reporter, 82,* 291–302.

Zirkel, P. A. (2000). *Section 504, the ADA and the schools* (2nd ed.). Horsham, PA: LRP Publications.

References

Albertsons, Inc. v. Kirkingburg, 527 U.S. 555 (1999).

Americans with Disabilities Act of 1990, 42 U.S.C. 12101 *et seq.*

Americans with Disabilities Act Regulations, 28 C.F.R. §§ Parts 36–38.

Burnim, I., & Patino, L. G. (1993). Employment issues under ADA and Section 504. *The Americans with Disabilities Act: New opportunities for children and families.* Horsham, PA: LRP Publications.

Cline, D. (1994). *Fundamentals of special education law: Emphasis on discipline.* Arden Hills, MN: Behavioral Institute for Children and Adolescents.

Communications Act, 47 U.S.C. § 611 *et seq.*

Coupe, B. W., Ness, A. D., & Sheetz, R. A. (1992). The Department of Justice's final regulations implementing Title III of the Americans with Disabilities Act. *Education Law Reporter, 71,* 353–359.

Equal Employment Opportunity Commission. (1992). *A technical assistance manual on the employment (Title I) provisions of the Americans with Disabilities Act.* Washington, DC: Author.

Hoekstra v. Independent School District, 25 IDELR 882 (8th Cir. 1996).

Huefner, D. S. (2000). *Getting comfortable with special education law: A framework for working with children with disabilities.* Norwood, MA: Christopher-Gordon Publishers.

Kaesberg, M. A., & Murray, K. T. (1994). Americans with Disabilities Act. *Education Law Reporter, 90,* 11–21.

Katsiyannis, A., & Yell, M. L. (2002). Americans with Disabilities Act and the Supreme Court: Implications for practice. *Preventing School Failure, 47,* 39–41.

Marczely, B. (1993). The Americans with Disabilities Act: Confronting the shortcomings of Section 504 in Public Education. *Education Law Reporter, 78,* 199–207.

Miles, A. S., Russo, C. J., & Gordon, W. M. (1992). The reasonable accommodations provisions of the Americans with Disabilities Act. *Education Law Reporter, 69,* 1–8.

Murphy v. United Parcel Service, Inc., 527 U.S. 516 (1999).

OCR Staff Memorandum, 17 EHLR 609 (1991).

Osborne, A. G. (1995). Court interpretations of the Americans with Disabilities Act and their effects on school districts. *Education Law Reporter, 95,* 489–498.

Pitasky, V. M. (1997). *The special education desk book.* Horsham, PA: LRP Publications. Rehabilitation Act of 1973, Section 504, 29 U.S.C. §794.

Tucker, B. P. (1992). The Americans with Disabilities Act: An overview. *New Mexico Law Review, 22,* 3–112.

Tucker, B. P., & Goldstein, B. A. (1992). *Legal rights of persons with disabilities: An analysis of federal law.* Horsham, PA: LRP Publications.

Turnbull, H. R. (1993). *Free appropriate education: The law and children with disabilities* (4th ed.). Denver: Love Publishing.

Urban v. Jefferson County School District R-1, 21 IDELR 985 (D. Col. 1994).

Wenkart, R. D. (1993). The Americans with Disabilities Act and its impact on public education. *Education Law Reporter, 82,* 291–302.

Zirkel, P. A. (1993a). The ADA and its impact on the schools. *Proceedings of the 14th National Institute on Legal Issues in Educating Individuals with Disabilities.* Horsham, PA: LRP Publications.

Zirkel, P. A. (1993b). Our "disability" with the ADA. *The Special Educator, 8*(17), 251–253.

Zirkel, P. A. (2000). *Section 504, the ADA and the schools* (2nd ed.). Horsham, PA: LRP Publications.

CHAPTER EIGHT

The No Child Left Behind Act

The fundamental principle of this bill is that every child can learn, we expect every child to learn, and (schools) must show us whether or not every child is learning.

President Bush's remarks on signing the No Child Left Behind Act of 2001 at Hamilton, Ohio, on January 8, 2002.

On January 8, 2002, President Bush signed the No Child Left Behind Act (NCLB) into law. In a departure from the usual practice of signing bills in the Rose Garden of the White House, NCLB was signed at a ceremony at Hamilton High School in Hamilton, Ohio, the home of Representative John Boehner, Chairman of the House Education Committee. President Bush and U.S. Secretary of Education Rod Paige then embarked on a daylong tour to participate in ceremonies to celebrate the signing of the law in the home states of Republican Senator Judd Gregg of New Hampshire, Democrat Senator Ted Kennedy of Massachusetts, and Democrat Representative George Miller of California. These two senators and two congressmen had led the bipartisan congressional efforts to pass this legislation.

No Child Left Behind is a comprehensive and complex education law. It represented an unprecedented increase in the role that the federal government plays in education because the law dramatically increased federal mandates and requirements on states, school districts, and public schools. The NCLB also increased federal funding to states by almost 25% from the previous year. This law represents the most significant expansion of the federal government into education in our history.

Readers should note that to gain a thorough understanding of NCLB, it is important to understand how their state's Department of Education addresses and applies the requirements of the law. All states meet the goals of NCLB in their own unique way.

This chapter examines NCLB and its effect on the education of students in America's public schools, including its effects on students with disabilities. First, I review the historical developments that led to the passage of the NCLB. Second, I examine the purpose, goals, and structure of the law. Finally, I consider the major principles of NCLB.

The Development of the NCLB

The History of Federal Involvement in Education: From Assistance to Accountability

Our system of government is a federal system. The government of the United States is composed of a union of states united under a single central (i.e., federal) government. In this system, the federal government protects the people's rights and liberties, and it acts to achieve certain ends while simultaneously sharing authority and power with the states. The U.S. Constitution sets forth the nature of this arrangement in the 10th Amendment. The national government, therefore, has specific powers granted to it in the Constitution. Those powers not granted to the national government are within the province of the states.

The U.S. Constitution does not contain any provisions regarding education. Thus, the federal government has no authority to create a national education system, nor can it order states or local school districts to use specific curricula or adopt particular policies. Instead, the laws of the 50 states govern education.

The federal government's role in education has largely existed in the area of funding. The federal government's funding of education has never exceeded approximately 10% of the total amount of money spent on education. Therefore, 90% of all money expended on education is spent by states and local school districts. Nevertheless, federal involvement has been an important factor in the progress and growth of education.

The federal government's involvement has, however, been indirect. The earliest method of indirect federal involvement in education was through federal land grants, where the federal government provided land to the states for the purpose of creating and aiding the development of public schools. In the Morrill Act of 1862, Congress also provided grants of land to each state to be used for colleges. In the land grants, the federal government had no direct control of education in the public schools or colleges.

In more recent times, the federal government has continued the indirect assistance to education through categorical grants. The purpose of the categorical grants has been to provide supplementary assistance to the state systems of education and to shape educational policy in the states. States have the option of accepting or rejecting the categorical grants offered by the federal government. If states accept the categorical grants, they must abide by the federal guidelines for using these funds. Examples of categorical grants include the National Defense Education Act of 1958, the Higher Education Facilities Act of 1963, the Vocational Education Act of 1963, the Elementary and Secondary Education Act of 1965, and the Education for All Handicapped Children Act of 1975 (now the Individuals with Disabilities Education Act). The role of the federal government in guiding educational policy has increased greatly through the categorical grants (Alexander & Alexander, 2001). Perhaps the most significant of these early laws was the Elementary and Secondary Education Act (ESEA) of 1965.

The Elementary and Secondary Education Act of 1965

The ESEA of 1965 was passed as part of President Lyndon Johnson's War on Poverty. ESEA appropriated federal money to states to improve educational opportunities for disadvantaged children. Although Congress allocates funds to the ESEA annually, it must reauthorize the law every 5 or 6 years.

The first part of the ESEA, Title I, was the largest section of the law. The federal government developed a number of formulas to determine which schools would be Title I schools. These formulas involved data such as the number of students who were eligible to receive free or reduced-price lunch or the percentage of students within a school's attendance zone whose school was eligible to receive Title I funds. Schools could use these funds to supplement existing services paid for by local funds. Although the amount of federal money provided to the states fluctuated in the years following passage of the ESEA, the federal government's commitment to assisting states to ensure that equal educational opportunities were provided to economically disadvantaged students has continued. In fact, since the passage of the ESEA, the federal government has spent more than $400 billion to help states educate children and youth from disadvantaged backgrounds.

A Nation at Risk

During the Reagan administration, Secretary of Education William Bennett assembled the National Commission on Excellence in Education. In 1983, the Commission issued its report entitled *A Nation at Risk.* The uncompromising report, which was extremely critical of the nation's education system, ignited a firestorm of controversy (Wright, Wright, & Heath, 2004). According to the report, our nation was at risk because America's educational system was producing mediocre results and our students were falling further behind their foreign counterparts. In an often quoted statement, the commission wrote that "Our nation is at risk. . . . The educational foundations of our country are presently being eroded by a rising tide of mediocrity that threatens our very future as a Nation and as a people. . . . If an unfriendly foreign power had attempted to impose on America the mediocre educational performance that exists today, we might well have viewed it as an act of war" (p. 1).

The report called for a commitment to the following: (a) placing education at the top of the nation's agenda, (b) strengthening high school graduation requirements, (c) adopting higher, measurable standards of academic performance, (d) increasing time devoted to learning, and (e) raising standards for teachers. The document was an important factor in the origin of the current educational reform efforts.

The National Education Summit

In 1989, President George H. W. Bush convened the 50 governors as part of the first National Education Summit. The governors reached consensus regarding the state of education in America and the need for a national strategy to address the problems with public school education. As a result of this summit, eight educational goals were developed that were to be achieved by the year 2000 (see Figure 8.1). These educational goals became part of President Bush's education legislation, *America 2000*.

President Bill Clinton made many of these goals the centerpiece of his *Goals 2000: Educate America Act*. This Act created the National Education Standards and Improvement Council. This council had the authority to approve or reject academic standards that were developed by states. Because of opposition in Congress, the commission eventually was disbanded.

The Improving America's Schools Act of 1994

The federal role in education, however, continued with the passage of the Improving America's Schools Act (IASA) of 1994. This law was a reauthorization and revision of the ESEA. The central purpose of IASA was to implement standards-based education throughout the nation. In essence, IASA created a new framework for the federal role in elementary and secondary education, a framework in which the federal government not only provided aid to schools serving economically disadvantaged students

Figure 8.1
The Eight Goals of the National Education Summit

By the year 2000:
- Goal 1: Ready to learn. All children in America will start school ready to learn.
- Goal 2: School completion. The high school graduation rate will increase to at least 90%.
- Goal 3: School achievement and citizenship. All students will leaves grades 4, 8, and 12 having demonstrated competency over challenging subject matter.
- Goal 4: Teacher education and professional development. The nation's teaching force will have access to programs for the continued improvement of their skills and will have opportunities to acquire the knowledge and skills needed to prepare all of America's students.
- Goal 5: Mathematics and science. United States students will be number one in the world in mathematics and science.
- Goal 6: Adult literacy and lifelong learning. Every American will be literate.
- Goal 7: Safe, disciplined, alcohol-free, and drug-free schools. Every school in the United States will be free from drugs, violence, firearms, and alcohol and will offer a disciplined environment conducive to learning.
- Goal 8: Parental participation. Every school will promote partnerships that will increase parent involvement and participation.

but extended federal support to the states' implementation of local and state standards-based reform. The IASA was based on states developing challenging academic standards, creating and aligning assessments for all students, holding schools accountable for results, and increasing aid to high poverty schools (Cohen, 2002). In fact, many of the requirements introduced in IASA were revised by and retained in the NCLB (e.g., content standards, assessments, adequate yearly progress). Although states were able to develop their own system for addressing IASA requirements, they had to meet the requirements of the law to receive federal funds.

The National Assessment of Educational Progress

The National Assessment of Educational Progress (NAEP) is known as the nation's report card. It is a nationally representative and continuous assessment of American students' knowledge and skills. NAEP is an extensive data collection system that includes achievement tests in a number of areas, including reading and math (Reckase, 2002). The nation's report card does not provide individual student or school scores. Instead, it provides information about subject matter achievement, characteristics of the student population, instructional experiences, and characteristics of the school environment for populations of students.

In 2002, the NAEP results indicated that almost 70% of America's fourth-grade students could only read at a below basic or basic level. Approximately 30% of all fourth-grade students, therefore, could read at a proficient or higher level. This occurred despite massive increases in federal funding for education and decreases in class size (Wright et al., 2004). In fact, according to an investigation of the nation's educational system 20 years after the publication of *A Nation at Risk*, the Koret Task Force on K-12 Education (2003) reported that even though federal funding had risen over 50% since 1983, education outcomes had not improved, and the achievement gap between children from disadvantaged backgrounds and those from middle class backgrounds or above had not narrowed. These reports of low achievement in general and specifically in reading, despite large infusions of federal education funding to the states, led to a movement to include stronger accountability mechanisms to ensure that public schools show measurable improvement in student achievement.

The No Child Left Behind Act of 2001

When President George W. Bush took office, he announced that NCLB was the number one priority of his administration's domestic agenda. No Child Left Behind reauthorized the ESEA and also built on the foundation laid in IASA by including significant changes to the federal government's role in education. The most significant change was to require that all public schools bring every public school student up to state standards in reading and math within a certain period of time, thus closing the achievement gap based on race, ethnicity, and language (Cohen, 2002). An overwhelming bipartisan majority in both the House and the Senate passed the NCLB legislation. (The final version of the NLCB passed by a vote of 381 to 41 in the House and 87 to 10 in the Senate). The NCLB increased federal spending on education by almost 25%, and the law also significantly increased federal requirements and mandates on the states.

Summary of the Federal Role in Education

Although education is primarily a local and state responsibility, the federal government has been involved in providing funding to states. States and school districts provide approximately 90% of the funding, and they develop curricula and determine attendance, enrollment, and graduation requirements. Thus, the federal contribution to education is about 10%. Despite the low level of funding, the federal government's role in education has been an important one because it provides funds to assist states in critical areas such as the education of economically disadvantaged children.

Moreover, the federal role has evolved from one in which the government primarily provided federal assistance to the states to one in which the federal government is holding states accountable for improving learning outcomes and achievement of all students. This movement from assistance to accountability can be seen in the evolution of the ESEA.

In 1965, Congress passed the ESEA, which initiated several programs that focused on providing federal aid to assist states in providing educational programs for poor children. Congress has reauthorized this law over 4 decades. The two most recent reauthorizations to the Elementary and Secondary Education Act were the Improving America's Schools Act of 1994 and the No Child Left Behind Act of 2001. The purposes of these two laws were to (a) continue the federal government's commitment to ensuring equal access to education for poor and disadvantaged students, (b) promote educational excellence for all of America's students, and (c) hold schools accountable for the performance of their students. Since the publication of *A Nation at Risk* in 1983, the federal government has increased efforts to hold schools accountable for achieving educational results. These efforts, which required an increase in the role of the federal government in education, led to the passage of NCLB.

The Purpose, Goals, and Structure of NCLB

No Child Left Behind makes significant changes in the federal government's involvement in education and in the ways that schools will educate children in American schools. In the next section I will review the purpose, goals, and structure of the law.

The Purpose of No Child Left Behind

The primary purpose of NCLB is to ensure that students in every public school achieve important learning goals while being educated in safe classrooms by well-prepared teachers. To increase student achievement, the law requires that school districts assume responsibility for all students reaching 100% student proficiency levels within 12 years on tests assessing important academic content. Furthermore, NCLB requires schools to close academic gaps between economically advantaged students and students who are from different economic, racial, and ethnic backgrounds as well as students with disabilities.

To measure progress, NCLB requires that states administer tests to all public school students. The states set proficiency standards, called *adequate yearly progress,* that progressively increase the percentage of students in a district that must meet the proficiency standard. If a school district does not meet these proficiency levels, the law mandates that requirements be met and corrective actions applied.

No Child Left Behind has required a major shift in the ways that teachers, administrators, and state department of education personnel think about public schooling. NCLB is a controversial law that places educators under growing pressure to increase the achievement of all students and to narrow the test score gap between groups of students (Anthes, 2002). Moreover, educators will now be held responsible for bringing about these changes. Administrators and teachers will need to understand effective research-based instructional strategies and be able to evaluate student's instructional progress to make more effective instructional decisions. Clearly, NCLB puts more pressure on the public education system to increase student achievement for all students (Anthes, 2002).

The Goals of No Child Left Behind

The primary goals of NCLB are that:

- All students will achieve high academic standards by attaining proficiency or better in reading and mathematics by the 2013–2014 school year.
- Highly qualified teachers will teach all students by the 2005–2006 school year.
- All students will be educated in schools and classrooms that are safe, drug free, and conducive to learning.
- All limited English proficient students will become proficient in English.
- All students will graduate from high school.

These goals will pose great challenges for schools, school districts, and states. NCLB requires states to test students to ensure that these goals are met, and it holds schools, school districts, and states accountable for making demonstrable improvements toward meeting these goals. In an effort to assist states to achieve these goals, Congress significantly increased federal spending on education and gave states greater flexibility to use federal funds in ways that will be of the greatest benefit to individual school districts. Although we may debate about how realistic these goals are, and many have, we can all agree that these goals will require a fundamental change in the ways we measure student progress.

The Structure of No Child Left Behind

To achieve these goals, Congress created a massive and complex law. Every element of the law is intended to move all public school students progressively closer to the overall levels of proficiency set by their respective states. Public laws are divided into titles, which are major divisions of the law. The NCLB consists of 10 titles. These titles and the major parts of each title are listed in Table 8.1.

Table 8.1
The Titles of NCLB

Title of NCLB	Subsections
Title I: Improving the Academic Achievement of the Disadvantaged	a. Improving basic programs operated by local educational agencies (LEAs) b. Student reading skills improvement grants c. Education of migratory children d. Prevention and intervention programs for children and youth who are neglected, delinquent, or at risk e. National assessment of Title I f. Comprehensive school reform g. Advanced placement programs h. School dropout prevention i. General provisions
Title II: Preparing, Training, and Recruiting High Quality Teachers and Principals	a. Teacher and principal training and recruiting fund b. Mathematics and science partnerships c. Innovation for teacher quality d. Enhancing education through technology
Title III: Language Instruction for Limited English Proficient and Immigrant Students	a. English language acquisition, language enhancement, and academic achievement b. Improving language instructional programs c. General provisions
Title IV: 21st Century Schools	a. Safe and drug-free schools and communities b. 21st century community learning centers c. Environmental tobacco smoke
Title V: Promoting Informed Parental Choice and Innovative Programs	a. Innovative programs b. Public charter schools
Title VI: Flexibility and Accountability	a. Improving academic education b. Rural education initiative c. General provisions
Title VII: Indian, Native Hawaiian, and Alaska Native Education	a. Indian Education b. Native Hawaiian education c. Alaskan Native education
Title VIII: Impact Aid Program	There are no subsections in Title VIII
Title IX: General Provisions	a. Definitions b. Flexibility in the use of funds c. Coordination of programs d. Waivers e. Uniform provisions f. Unsafe school choice option

Table 8.1
Continued

Title of NCLB	Subsections
Title X: Repeals, Redesignations, and Amendments to Other Statutes	A. Repeals B. Redesignations C. Homeless education D. Native American Education Improvement Act E. Higher Education Act of 1965 F. General Education Provisions Act G. Miscellaneous other statutes

The following section briefly discusses the titles of NCLB with an emphasis on the titles likely to have the greatest impact on teachers, administrators, and parents.

Title I: Improving the Academic Achievement of the Disadvantaged

Title I is the largest portion of the NCLB. This part of the law authorizes grants to states that agree to adhere to NCLB requirements. The states distribute funds to school districts. The districts, in turn, distribute money to Title I schools, which are schools with large populations of disadvantaged or low-income students as determined by such measures as number of students on free and reduced-price lunch. Title I funds go for both schoolwide programs, which are programs that benefit an entire school population when more than 40% of the students are from low-income families, and targeted assistance programs, which are specialized programs for children who are failing or are at risk of failing to meet the state's academic standards. Approximately 90% of all public school districts and 60% of all public schools in the United States receive Title I funds (Wright et al., 2004), and thus may spend their funds on school-wide or targeted assistance programs.

The first part of Title I is entitled "Improving Basic Programs Operated by Local Educational Agencies." This section includes the provisions most often associated with NCLB, such as: (a) statewide content standards and assessments, (b) adequate yearly progress, (c) state and local report cards, (d) accountability for student performance, and (e) highly qualified teachers and paraprofessionals. The second part, "Student Reading Skills Improvement Grants," includes the Reading First grants and the requirements regarding scientifically based reading instruction and the essential components of reading programs.

In NCLB, Congress and the President recognized that "teaching young children to read is the most critical educational priority facing this country" (U.S. Department of Education, 2002, p. 1). No Child Left Behind, therefore, includes an ambitious national initiative designed to help all children become successful readers by grade 3. The initiative is called Reading First. President Bush called Reading First the academic cornerstone of NCLB.

Reading First is designed to ensure that states and school districts receive assistance to (a) establish research-based reading programs for students in kindergarten through grade 3 and (b) improve teachers' skills in using these effective instructional practices. The Reading First program is the single most ambitious effort ever undertaken by the federal government to improve the reading skills of America's students.

Three unique aspects of Reading First are that it (a) focuses on reading instruction that is supported by scientifically based reading research, (b) provides a large amount of money that states can receive to provide training to teachers and to implement professional development activities, and (c) emphasizes early identification of children at risk for reading failure so that effective early instruction can be provided.

The other parts of Title I focus on improving educational outcomes for migratory children, neglected or delinquent children, and children in institutions. This title also focuses on preventing school dropout. Additionally, this section of Title I authorizes the national assessment of Title I, provides financial incentives to school districts that develop school reform strategies for basic academics and parental involvement, and provides funds to participate in advanced placement courses.

Title II: Preparing, Training, and Recruiting High Quality Teachers and Principals

Title II provides grants to states to increase student achievement by improving teacher and principal quality. States that receive these grants will then make subgrants available to public school districts and state agencies of higher education for local projects to improve teacher quality. The purpose of Title II grants is to assist states to increase the number of highly qualified teachers in the nation's classrooms and the number of highly qualified principals and assistant principals in our schools.

When public school districts apply for NCLB funds from a state, they must submit a plan that addresses a range of key issues, including a description of the professional development opportunities they will make available to teachers and principals. School districts may use these funds for any of the following activities: (a) hiring highly qualified teachers; (b) providing professional development activities for teachers, principals, and paraprofessionals; (c) developing and implementing methods to recruit and retain highly qualified teachers, principals, and pupil services personnel; (d) providing merit pay; (e) establishing innovative professional development programs, which may include partnerships with institutions of higher education; (f) providing professional development activities on improving classroom behavior; (g) establishing programs for exemplary teachers, and (h) improving teachers' use of technology.

Financial incentives are also available to encourage teachers to get advanced degrees and certifications. Additionally, states may apply for grants to develop teacher and principal recruitment and to develop mentoring and training programs.

States are required to monitor school districts to determine if they are making progress on their teacher quality goals. If a school district does not make progress on its goals for 2 consecutive years, the district must develop an improvement plan to address the reasons it is not progressing. Additionally, when the school district is implementing the improvement plan, the state will assist the school district by providing technical assistance. If the school district fails to make progress after 3 consecutive years, the state must enter into an agreement with the district regarding its use of Title II funds. This plan must include strategies to help the district meet teacher quality objectives.

Title III: Language Instruction for Limited English Proficient and Immigrant Students

The purpose of Title III is to ensure that children and youth who are English language learners become proficient in English and in the core academic subjects. States and local school districts must establish goals for increasing the speaking, listening, reading, and writing skills of children and youth who are English language learners. Moreover, they must use research-based language instruction to teach these skills and must assess their abilities by measuring progress toward English proficiency. The title also authorized funds to recruit and train educators and to implement professional development programs to prepare teachers and principals to use research-based instructional procedures and curricula to increase English language proficiency in students. Professional development activities must be research-based and be of sufficient intensity that they meaningfully improve teachers' performance.

Title IV: 21st Century Schools

The primary purposes of Title IV are to (a) create safe and orderly schools, (b) protect students and teachers, (c) encourage discipline and personal responsibilities, and (d) combat drug use. To accomplish this, NCLB authorizes funding for grants to establish drug and violence prevention programs in schools. Programs that are funded under this title must use effective research-based programming that includes performance indicators and progress monitoring strategies. Schools must also have comprehensive plans to keep schools safe. Moreover, these plans must include measures such as schoolwide discipline policies, security procedures, drug and violence prevention programs, crises management plans, and student codes of conduct.

Title IV also provides funding to communities to establish or expand community learning centers that offer before- and after-school programs, summer enrichment programs, and family literacy programs. The services offered by the community learning centers can include: (a) academic enrichment, (b) tutoring, (c) remediation, (d) counseling, (e) recreation, and (f) technology education.

Title V: Promoting Informed Parental Choice and Innovative Programs

The major purposes of Title V are to (a) support educational reform, (b) fund school improvement programs that are based on research-based instructional practices, (c) meet the needs of at-risk students, and (d) improve student, teacher, and school performance. This title provides funds for school districts to develop innovative programs in such areas as programs for at-risk and high-need students, counseling, character education, gifted and talented programs, physical education programs, foreign language programs, arts programs, reading programs, economic programs, public charter schools and magnet schools, and smaller learning communities.

Title VI: Flexibility and Accountability

A major principle of NCLB is that states and school districts should have greater flexibility and control over how they use federal education funds. The philosophy behind local control is that school districts and state officials have a greater understanding of their needs than federal officials have; thus, school districts and state officials should have greater flexibility in deciding how to spend their money.

The major purposes of Title VI are to (a) give state and school districts flexibility in using federal funds, (b) encourage local solutions for local problems, and (c) help administrators improve student achievement. Part A of Title VI focuses on state assessments, state reporting systems, and student and school achievement. Part B of the law focuses on small rural districts and provides funding for teacher recruitment and retention, professional development, educational technology, and parent involvement programs. This title also describes the role of the federal government. Specifically, this subsection explains that the federal government will not control the instructional content, standards, or curricula of states and LEAs. It also requires states and school districts to equalize per-pupil spending. The subsection also delineates the role of the National Assessment of Educational Progress (NAEP) and NCLB. The NAEP assessments will be administered in reading and math every two years and will provide information about academic progress by race, ethnicity, socioeconomic status, gender, disability, and English proficiency.

Title VII: Indian, Native Hawaiian, and Alaska Native Education

Title VII consists of three subsections. Part A addresses educational programs for American Indian students. The major purposes of Part A are to (a) support Indian tribes, organizations, colleges, and universities; (b) assist states and LEAs to meet the unique educational, cultural, and academic needs of American Indian and Alaskan Native students; and (c) help these students meet challenging state academic achievement standards. In Part A, federal funds are available for innovative programs to improve the education of American Indians. These programs include: (a) remedial instruction, (b) research, (c) inservice training, (d) fellowships for American Indian students who attend college, and (e) centers for gifted and talented American Indian students.

Part B provides funds for school districts to develop innovative educational programs for Native Hawaiian students. Federal funds are available for the following types of programs for Native Hawaiians: (a) reading and literacy programs, including family literacy services; (b) programs for students with disabilities; (c) programs for gifted and talented students; (d) professional development for educators; (e) scholarships for college and graduate studies; and (f) community-based learning centers.

Part C recognizes the unique educational needs of Alaskan Native students, authorizes innovative educational programs, and supplements current programs for these students. Federal funds are available for the following types of programs for Alaskan Natives: (a) innovative educational methods and strategies, (b) professional development for educators, (c) home-based instruction for preschool children, (d) family literacy programs,

(e) math and science enrichment programs, (f) remedial programs, (g) dropout prevention programs, and (h) parenting education.

Title VIII: Impact Aid Program

The purpose of this title is to replace revenue lost because parents live or work on federal property. Federal funds are authorized for (a) providing support payments to districts with students whose families work for the federal government, (b) assisting students with disabilities, and (c) facilities maintenance.

Title IX: General Provisions

This title addresses many areas. It allows states to assume greater control over their use of federal funds through greater flexibility and the consolidation of funds. Additionally, Title IX requires that public school personnel consult with private school officials to ensure that students with disabilities attending private schools receive special education services and benefits under these programs. The services and benefits that private school children and their teachers receive must be equal to the services that public school students with disabilities and their teachers receive. Readers should note, however, that NCLB does not apply to students who attend private school or who are home schooled.

School districts receiving NCLB funds must certify that they do not have any policies preventing school prayer in public schools. Additionally, school districts that receive funds must provide military recruiters with access to students' names, addresses, and telephone numbers.

Perhaps the most recognized requirement of Title IX is the Unsafe School Choice Option. The purpose of the Unsafe School Choice Option is to allow parents, regardless of their income, the option of removing their children from a dangerous school setting. This option requires that states establish a policy to allow parents of children who are educated in unsafe schools to transfer to safe public schools. Under this requirement each state must (a) identify persistently dangerous schools, (b) identify the types of offenses that are considered violent criminal offenses, and (c) provide a safe public school choice option.

States must identify schools by using objective data such as the number of referrals to law enforcement, data concerning gang presence on school grounds, and results from student surveys on safety issues to identify unsafe schools. When a school is identified as persistently dangerous, the state must (a) notify parents of each student of the school's designation, (b) offer students the opportunity to transfer, and (c) transfer those students who exercise the choice option. Additionally, the school district in which the persistently dangerous school is located must develop a corrective action plan and submit it to the state. The plan must be implemented in a timely manner. Moreover, the state should provide technical assistance and monitoring during implementation of the plan.

There are two situations in which parents can exercise their option to move their child or children from an unsafe school. First, when a school is determined to be persistently dangerous, the student must be allowed to transfer to a safe school. Second, when a student becomes a victim of a violent crime at school, the student must also be allowed to transfer to a safe school. Each state's laws determine the types of offenses that the state considers violent criminal offenses. When a student has become the victim of a violent crime, the school district should offer the opportunity for that student to transfer to a safe public school within 10 calendar days. The state must allow students to transfer to a safe public elementary or secondary school, or public charter school, within the same district. To the extent possible, transfers that are allowed should be to schools that are making adequate yearly progress (AYP) and have not been identified as needing improvement or corrective action. States must certify NCLB compliance to the U.S. Department of Education, and NCLB funding is contingent upon states complying with this certification requirement.

Title X: Repeals, Redesignations, and Amendments to Other Statutes

This title of NCLB covers repeals, redesignations (i.e., redesignation involves rearranging the parts and sections of the act itself, which requires transferring and relettering), and amendments to other laws. Part C under this title is the McKinney-Vento Homeless Education Assistance Act of 2001. This Act requires that states ensure that homeless children receive an education equivalent to the education other children receive. Moreover, the law requires that states establish an Office of Coordinator of Homeless Children and Youth to ensure that homeless children and youth are not segregated nor stigmatized in public school programs.

The Major Principles of NCLB

No Child Left Behind will have a great effect on education in America. This section provides details on the major requirements of the law that will have the greatest effect on teachers, parents, and administrators: (a) accountability for results, (b) scientifically based instruction, and (c) highly qualified teachers and paraprofessionals.

Accountability for Results

No Child Left Behind focuses on (a) increasing the academic performance of all public school students and (b) improving the performance of low performing schools. It does this by requiring states to identify the most important academic content for students to learn and then assessing them to determine if they are learning this content.

Statewide Standards

The President and Congress believed that many schools operate without a clear set of expectations of what students should achieve in important academic subjects. In the NCLB, therefore, states are required to (a) establish their own standards of what students should know and be able to do and (b) provide guidelines to schools, parents, and communities that tell them what achievement is expected of all students.

Specifically, the NCLB requires states to develop academic standards for all students in reading–language arts, math, and science. Additionally, states are free to develop standards in areas other than those required by NCLB. For example, a state could develop standards in social studies, although social studies standards are not required by the NCLB.

The purpose of the state-defined standards is to provide guidelines to schools, parents, and teachers that tell them what achievement will be expected of all students. To reach the goal of having every child proficient on state-defined standards by the target date, the NCLB requires every state to develop academic content standards for all public schools. The purpose of the academic content standards is to identify the content information that all public school students are expected to learn.

States must also develop student achievement standards. These standards are explicit definitions of what students must know and must be able to do to demonstrate proficiency on the content standards (O'Neill, 2004). The achievement standards, therefore, must be aligned to the content standards. No Child Left Behind gives states a great deal of flexibility in determining these standards. States' achievement standards must include at least two levels of high achievement that indicate how well students are mastering the content standards. *No Child Left Behind* requires that these high levels be designated "proficient" and "advanced." States must also have a third level that designates students who have not attained proficiency on the content standards. No Child Left Behind requires that this level be designated "basic." Additionally, each state decides what scores on the statewide assessment separate the levels of achievement.

Statewide Assessments

The NCLB also requires that states implement a statewide assessment system that is aligned to the state standards in reading–language arts, math, and eventually science. The purpose of statewide testing is to measure how successfully students are learning what is expected of them and how they are progressing toward meeting these important academic standards. These tests must be valid and reliable and have adequate technical data. Moreover, the state tests enable stakeholders (e.g., teachers, administrators, parents, policy makers, and the general public) to understand and compare the performances of schools against the standards for proficiency as set by the states. Additionally, the tests must produce individual student reports.

All public schools must participate in the statewide assessment by testing 95% of their students. This includes testing at least 95% of students in each of the following subgroups: (a) low-income students, (b) students with disabilities, (c) limited English proficiency students, and (d) students from diverse racial and ethnic groups. The purpose of testing and reporting on the test scores by subgroups of students, called *disaggregating scores,* is to ensure that schools will be responsible for improving the achievement of all students. States, therefore, must report the assessment results within the state and for each school for all students, students in each subgroup, and also by migrant status and gender. The only exception to the disaggregation rule is when a subgroup is too small to yield statistically reliable information and when reporting such data may reveal personally identifiable information.

The results of these assessments are then reported to parents in annual report cards. States must include interpretive, descriptive, and diagnostic reports on all students. This information provides parents with data about where their child stands academically, thus allowing them to know if their child's school and school district are succeeding in meeting state standards. These assessments, therefore, are also used to hold schools accountable for the achievement of all students.

Statewide Assessments and Students with Disabilities.   Students with disabilities are an important part of a school's student body. They spend the majority of their time in the general education classroom and receive their instruction from the general education teacher. Moreover, the Individuals with Disabilities Education Act (IDEA) requires that students with disabilities should have access to, be involved with, and progress in the general education curriculum. Congress and the President believed that to ensure that instruction and achievement for students with disabilities is improved, all students with disabilities must be assessed and the results of these assessments must be included in the data used to determine if a school and school district make adequate yearly progress (AYP). They also believed that if students with disabilities were excluded from schools' accountability systems that these students would be ignored and not receive the academic attention that they deserve. By including students with disabilities in NCLB's assessment system, Congress made certain that schools would be held accountable for the educational performance of these students.

Students with disabilities are to be held to the standards for the grade in which the student is enrolled, although in some situations, accommodations or modifications may be needed to get a true picture of a student's achievement (Elliott & Thurlow, 2003; Thurlow, Elliott, & Ysseldyke, 2001). The NCLB, therefore, required that school districts provide students with disabilities access to appropriate accommodations if necessary to take the statewide assessment.

To receive these accommodations or modifications, students with disabilities must be eligible for special education services under the IDEA or services under Section 504 of the Rehabilitation Act. Each student's individualized education program (IEP) team or Section 504 planning team must determine how they will participate in the statewide assessment. The team may determine that a student will take (a) the regular assessment given to all students, (b) the regular assessment with state-approved accommodations, or (c) an alternate assessment. Readers should note that the IEP team or Section 504 team decides *how* the student will participate, not *whether* the student will participate.

If the team decides that a student will take the regular assessment with accommodations, they can only require accommodations that are approved by their state. Additionally, these accommodations should be consistent with accommodations that are provided during instruction. States must provide training and guidance to IEP and 504 teams on the appropriate use of testing accommodations.

Alternate Assessments.   If the IEP team decides that a student will take an alternate assessment, the next step is to select from at least two types of alternate assessments. One is aligned with the state's academic content standards, and the other is aligned with a state's alternate achievement standards. Only students with significant cognitive disabilities may take an alternate assessment based on alternate achievement standards. Neither NCLB nor its implementing regulations define a significant cognitive disability. A definition was deliberately not provided so that states would have flexibility in determining which students could take an alternate assessment. Out-of-level testing is considered a form of alternate assessment. All students who take an alternate assessment will either be scored as proficient or not proficient.

In either case, when the IEP is developed, the team must note that the student will take an alternate assessment and then include a statement explaining why the regular assessment is not appropriate and how the student will be assessed using the alternate assessment. Additionally, the parents should be informed of the consequences, if any, of taking the regular assessment with accommodations or taking the alternate assessment based on either the grade level standards or alternate achievement standards. For example, some states do not allow students who take the regular assessment with accommodations or the alternate to graduate with a regular diploma.

Adequate Yearly Progress

To receive federal funding under NCLB, states must submit accountability plans to the U.S. Department of Education. These plans must define the state's procedures for reporting school performance and their system for holding schools and school districts accountable for increasing student achievement. In accordance with the terms of NCLB, states must develop academic standards and tests to assess students' knowledge and skills in reading and math in grades 3 through 8. Furthermore, states must set state proficiency standards as goals that schools and school districts must attain within certain periods of time.

States develop a definition, called adequate yearly progress (AYP), to use each year to determine if schools and school districts are meeting the state standards. In the accountability plans submitted to the U.S. Department of Education, each state defined their AYP criteria for increasing student achievement to meet the 100% proficiency goal in reading–language arts and math by the 2013–2014 school year. In addition to all students in a school, schools are also required to report AYP data for the following subgroups: students who are economically disadvantaged, students from diverse racial and ethnic groups, students with disabilities, or students with limited English proficiency. To ensure that all students, and the students from each of the subgroups, are making progress toward reaching the 100% proficiency goal by the target date, the state must set specific targets for all students each year in reading–language arts and math. These specific targets are the AYP criteria.

Setting AYP Criteria.   To set AYP criteria, state education officials had to establish a starting point for measuring statewide student progress toward meeting proficiency on statewide standards in reading and mathematics. This starting point was the percentage of students in the state who scored "proficient" on the statewide test in the baseline year. The state education officials responsible for setting AYP targets had to go through three steps to choose the starting point. First, they determined the average percentage of students reaching proficiency in the lowest achieving schools in the state. For example, if only 16% of all students in the lowest performing school district in the state reached proficiency on the statewide test, the state used the figure of 16% to calculate the starting point. Second, state officials determined the percentage of students who achieved proficiency in the lowest achieving subgroup in the state. For example, of the disaggregated subgroups, if students with disabilities scored the lowest on statewide tests, then students with disabilities would be chosen for calculating the starting point. Third, state officials compared the proficiency scores of the lowest subgroup score and the lowest school district and then chose the higher score. If, for instance, the students with disabilities subgroup scored 20% and the lowest performing school district scored 16%, then 20% (i.e., the higher of the two scores) becomes the starting point or baseline for calculating AYP.

Once the starting point was established, the state gradually increased the percentage of students each year who must score at the proficient level so the state reaches the goal of having 100% of students scoring at the proficient level by 2013–2014. In setting AYP, most states either increased the required percentage of students who must be proficient in small increments each year or by slightly larger percentages every 3 years. This annual increase would be the measurable annual objective for each year, or AYP criteria. To make AYP, schools have to score at or above the criteria.

Figure 8.2 depicts an example of how AYP was calculated for reading–language arts in South Carolina. In this example, we will assume that the baseline level in 2001–2002 for the state was that 20% of students were proficient in reading–language arts and math tests as measured by the statewide assessment. Because 100% of the state's students and subgroups of students must be proficient in reading–language arts by 2013–2014, the state sets the AYP at slightly higher levels each year (e.g., 3%, 5%) so that the goal is met by the target date. To meet AYP, the required percentage of a school's students must achieve the target level each year on the statewide test in each year. In this example, only 20% of the students reached the proficient level in the 2001–2002 school year. The difference between the current 20% and the goal of 100% is 80%. When we divide the 80% increase by the number of years (12) until the state, school district, or school must reach the goal, we get approximately a 7% increase each year.

As we can see in this example the AYP for the 2004–2005 academic year is 40%. If 40% of a school's students, including students in the disaggregated subgroups, reach the proficiency level, the school has achieved AYP. If, however, 39% or less of a school's students have reached the proficient level, the school has failed to make AYP.

Readers should note that 100% of a state's students must reach 100% proficiency in both reading–language arts and math by the 2013–2014 academic year. In this example, I have only shown the South Carolina reading–language arts AYP; however, South Carolina, and all other states, had to calculate AYP for both reading

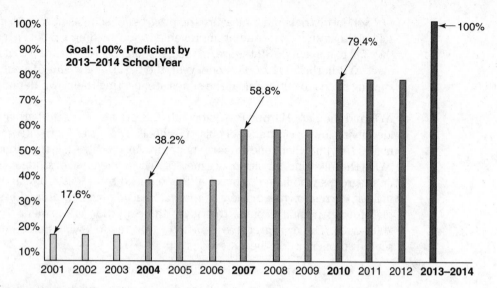

Figure 8.2
Calculating AYP

and math. This is because they may have different starting points and steps to reach 100%.

As can be seen in this example, for schools in South Carolina to make AYP in reading–language arts, their general student population and each subgroup of students must have the following percentages of students scoring "proficient" on the statewide test in reading–language arts in each of the following years. Note that education officials in South Carolina decided to step up the AYP criteria once every 3 years.

AYP criteria–17.6% of students meeting proficiency standard by 2001, 2002, & 2003

AYP criteria–38.2% of students meeting proficiency standard by 2004, 2005, & 2006

AYP criteria–58.8% of students meeting proficiency standard by 2007, 2008, & 2009

AYP criteria–79.4% of students meeting proficiency standard by 2010, 2011, & 2012

AYP criteria–100% of students meeting proficiency standard by 2013–2014

In addition to using assessments to determine AYP, states must use at least one academic measure to show progress. The states can select the indicator at the elementary level, but the indicator must be graduation rates at the secondary level. Schools can meet AYP if each group of students meets the state's annual measurable objectives and the school or school district meets the other indicator. For example, if Figure 8.2 represents the AYP criteria for the years between 2001 and 2014, and a school equals or does better than the AYP in a given year, and meets the other indicator the state has chosen, then they have met AYP.

School districts must measure the progress of schools in their district, rewarding schools that show substantial improvement and holding schools accountable when they fail to make AYP. States are, in turn, responsible for ensuring that school districts meet AYP. In the 2004–2005 school year, the U.S. Department of Education began reviewing states to determine if the states are meeting their own definitions of AYP.

AYP and the Safe Harbor Provision.   NCLB provides a "safe harbor" to avoid over-identifying low-performing schools. In schools where the aggregate group of students makes AYP, but where one or more subgroups fail to make AYP, the school will still make AYP if the following conditions are met: (a) The percentage of students in the subgroup or subgroups who failed to make AYP is reduced by at least 10%, and (b) that group makes progress on one or more of the state's academic indicators. Let's use the example of an elementary school that gives the statewide assessment to all students in 2004–2005. The disaggregated data show that the following percentages of students scored "proficient" on the statewide test:

- Students with disabilities–20% (80% failed to make AYP)
- All students (including all the disaggregated subgroups)–40%

The AYP cutoff for 2004–2005 is 38.2%; as a group the entire student body and all the other disaggregated groups scored at a level that meets AYP. However, as a group the students with disabilities did not meet the 38.2% proficiency level. Because all of a school's students and all the disaggregated subgroups must meet 38.2%, the school will not meet AYP because one of the disaggregated groups, students with disabilities, did not meet AYP.

In 2005–2006, these percentages of students in the two groups scored proficient on the statewide test:

- Students with disabilities–32% (68% failed to make AYP)
- All students (including all the other disaggregated subgroups)–45%

The AYP cutoff for 2005–2006 is still 38.2%. Again, as a group, all the school's students, including the other subgroups, exceed the AYP cutoff. Students with disabilities did not make the AYP cutoff; however, the school reduced the percentage of students failing to make AYP by 12% from the previous year. If the school's students with disabilities meet the other AYP indicator set by the state, then the school will make AYP. The school meets the AYP because the students with disabilities made more than a 10% gain from the 2004 to 2005 school year; therefore, the school reached the safe harbor criteria, despite the fact that the students with disabilities subgroup failed to make the required 38.2%.

AYP and Students with Disabilities.   In NCLB, the statewide assessment scores of all students with disabilities must be reported both as a subgroup and as part of the study body. Adequate yearly progress must be reported for the entire student body, then separately for students with disabilities. Congress's purpose in including students with disabilities with all students and then as a subgroup was to ensure that schools would be held accountable for the achievement of students with disabilities. Thus, schools and school districts would have to pay close attention to their instruction and educational progress.

Students who are assessed using an alternate assessment are also included in AYP. However, the federal government puts a cap on the number of students who pass the alternative assessment and can be counted as scoring proficient for purposes of determining AYP. This cap is currently set at 1% of the total school population at each grade level tested. This does not mean that there is a cap on the number of students with disabilities who can take an alternate assessment. Rather, it means that a school or school district can only include students who score proficient on the alternate assessment as proficient in the AYP calculation if the percentage of students comprises 1% or less of the total student population at their grade level. For example, in the fourth grade at Springdale School District, 1% of the students at that grade level took the alternate assessment and scored "proficient". Springdale School District could then count the students who scored proficient on the alternate assessment as proficient for AYP calculations. In the fifth grade, a total of 2% of the students at that grade level scored proficient on the alternate assessment. Because the amount exceeded the cap of 1% however, all the students above that cap must be included in the AYP calculations as failing to demonstrate proficiency. This is the case, despite the fact that the students were proficient on the alternate examination. Additionally, the 1% counts at the school district and at the SEA level but does not count at the individual school level. Therefore, a school that is small or has a higher percentage of students with significant cognitive disabilities may not be penalized for purposes of AYP because the numerical cap does not apply.

Although there is variation by state, the 1% cap across the total student population is approximately 9% of all students with disabilities. The U.S. Department of Education calculated this percentage based on incidence levels of students they believed had significant cognitive disabilities. Readers should note that the U.S. Department of Education did not define students with significant cognitive disabilities.

State educational agencies (SEAs) may request an increase in the 1% cap from the U.S. Department of Education. School districts may also request an increase in the cap from the SEA. Requests to have the cap raised must document that the school district's or SEA's incidence of students with significant cognitive disabilities exceeds 1% and that circumstances exist that increase the incidence of these students (e.g., community programs draw families of students with significant cognitive disabilities). The U.S. Department of Education expects that applications will request lifting the cap by small amounts (e.g., 2% or 3%).

What Happens When a School Makes AYP?

States are responsible for determining their own systems of requirements and rewards to hold all public schools and school districts responsible for meeting AYP. The state may set aside 5% of its Title I funds to reward the schools and teachers in the schools that (a) substantially close the achievement gap between the lowest and highest performing students and (b) made outstanding yearly progress for 2 consecutive years.

Although each state determines what the rewards will be, rewards often include some form of public recognition and monetary reward. States also can designate schools that have made the greatest achievement gains as "Distinguished Schools."

What Happens When a School Fails to Make AYP?

If a school fails to meet AYP, it will receive assistance to improve. The state will designate a school that has not achieved AYP for 2 consecutive years as "identified for improvement." When a school is first identified for improvement, the state provides technical assistance to enable the school to address the specific problems that led to its designation. The school, in conjunction with parents and outside experts, will develop a 2-year improvement plan. Although neither the law nor regulations specify who these outside experts may be, they will likely be faculty from institutions of higher education and private consultants who have expertise in research-based strategies in the areas in which the school needs help. The school personnel, state officials, outside personnel, and parents must develop a technical assistance plan. Figure 8.3 lists the required components of the technical assistance plan. This improvement plan must involve the school's core academic subjects that have the greatest likelihood of raising student achievement so that students meet the proficiency standards.

The statewide testing, therefore, helps schools identify subject areas and teaching procedures that need improvement. For example, if a school meets AYP in math but fails to do so in reading, school officials should target reading for improvement. Officials may decide to adopt a research-based reading curriculum or teaching procedure as a result of the information gained from statewide testing. The school district must help the school develop and implement the plan. Additionally, the school must set aside 10% of its Title I funds for professional development.

The NCLB also specifies corrective actions for schools that do not make AYP. States must determine if each public school and school district achieves AYP, even those schools and districts that do not receive Title I funds. When a school district fails to make AYP, the state must start the corrective action discussed previously. If a school does not make AYP, this information must be published and disseminated to

Figure 8.3
Components of a Technical Assistance Plan

The technical assistance plan must explain how the school will:
- Improve academics.
- Incorporate research-based strategies.
- Notify and involve parents.
- Use 10% of its Title I funds for professional development.
- Institute a new teacher mentoring program.
- Implement activities outside the regular school day (if necessary).

parents, teachers, and the community. The information must be made available in an easy-to-understand format.

What Happens If a School Fails to Make AYP for 2 Consecutive Years?

Title I schools that do not make AYP for 2 consecutive years are designated in need of improvement. In such situations, the state must continue to provide technical assistance to the school. Additionally, the school must offer the parents of students in the school the option of transferring to another public school within the district. The rationale behind public school choice is that providing parents a variety of options when their children attend a school that needs improvement will help to ensure that quality educational opportunities are available to all students.

When exercising the public school choice option, students may transfer to a public charter school or a public school within the district that has not been identified for improvement, corrective action, restructuring, or the status as persistently dangerous. All students who attend a school that has been designated in need of improvement may exercise the choice option. If it is not possible to offer a choice to all students, a school district must give priority to low-income students. Priority will go to the lowest achieving of the low-income students.

If more than one school within the district meets the NCLB's requirements, the school district must provide parents with a choice of schools. However, NCLB does *not* require the school district to offer the option to attend the specific school that the parent may want. Additionally, the district must provide the transportation.

When students with disabilities are involved in public school choice, schools may need to make specialized services available to allow them to take advantage of their opportunity to attend an eligible school (i.e., a school that is not designated as needing improvement) of their choice. School districts are not required to offer the same choices to a student with disabilities as they would to a student without disabilities because the school district may have to match the needs of the student with the ability of the school to provide those services. If a student with disabilities is attending a school that is identified in need of improvement and, therefore, has the public school choice option, when the district has an eligible school with the appropriate services available, the district may offer that choice to parents.

If a student with disabilities exercises the choice option, the new school becomes responsible for providing the student with a free appropriate public education. The new school may do this by either implementing the student's old IEP or Section 504 plan or by developing a new IEP or 504 plan.

If a school then makes AYP for 2 consecutive years, the "needs improvement" designation is removed. If students have chosen to attend another school during this period, they can continue to do so until they finish the top grade in the new school.

What Happens When a School Fails to Make AYP for 3 Consecutive Years?

If a school fails to make AYP for a third consecutive year, the school district will still be obligated to provide technical assistance to the school and to offer school choice. The school now also is required to offer supplemental educational services, which may include private tutoring, to low-income (i.e., Title I) students. The rationale behind supplemental educational service is that these services will increase the quality of the educational program the student receives.

Schools must provide these supplemental services in addition to instruction during the school day. These services, therefore, may take place before school, after school, on the weekends, or in the summer. Moreover, instruction and supplemental services must be research based and of high quality. The purpose of the services is to increase the academic achievement of eligible students, as measured by the statewide assessment system, and thus enable the student to attain proficiency in meeting the state's academic standards.

Parents can choose a provider of these services from a state-approved list. A service provider can be a nonprofit entity, for-profit entity, a local educational agency, an educational service agency, a faith-based organization, or a public school (including a public charter school), as long as it has not been identified for corrective action. Potential providers must meet state selection criteria, including: (a) having a demonstrated record of effectiveness in increasing the academic achievement of students in subjects relevant to meeting state standards, (b) being capable of providing supplemental educational services consistent with the school district's instructional program and the state's standards and achievement requirements, and (c) being financially sound. Additionally, providers must meet the requirements listed in Figure 8.4 before they can be added to the state-approved list.

When a school district is required to make supplemental services available, it must enter into an agreement with the service provider or providers. This agreement must (a) specify the achievement goals for students, (b) describe how students' progress will be measured, and (c) include a timetable for improving students' achievement.

Figure 8.4
Requirements of Providers

The provider must:

- Monitor students' progress and then furnish the information to parents and school districts.
- Ensure that content is consistent with the content provided by the state and school district.
- Ensure that instruction is aligned to state standards and is secular, neutral, and nonideological.
- Meet all applicable federal, state, and local health, safety, and civil rights laws.
- Meet the requirements of a student's IEP or Section 504 plan, if appropriate.
- Require written parent permission before disclosing the identity of any student who is eligible for, or receiving, services.

The agreement must also describe procedures for regularly informing a student's parents of his or her progress and how the provider will be paid. Additionally, the school district must implement the plan no later than the beginning of the next school year.

The school district is also required to provide an annual notice to parents about how they may obtain supplemental services and the identity, qualifications, and effectiveness of the providers. The school or school district must assist parents to choose the provider if requested to do so. When a student receives supplemental services, the school or school district must inform the parent of the student's progress.

For students with disabilities, the supplemental services must include (a) a statement of specific achievable goals, (b) a description of how a student's progress will be measured, and (c) a timetable for improving achievement that is consistent with a student's IEP. These statements of goals and progress monitoring statements must be consistent with a student's IEP or individualized services under Section 504. For students with disabilities who receive the supplemental services, these services are provided *in addition* to the instructions and services provided under the IEP or Section 504 plan. Supplemental services are not considered part of the IEP or Section 504 plan and are not intended to replace the services listed in those documents.

If a school district fails to provide supplemental services to students with disabilities while providing services to nondisabled students, the district would be discriminating against students with disabilities and thus be in violation of Section 504. Moreover, students with disabilities cannot be excluded by a provider from receiving supplemental services if accommodations and modifications can be made to enable the students to receive those services. If no provider is able to provide supplemental services with the necessary accommodations, the LEA would assume responsibility for providing the services. The school district is also responsible for ensuring that students with disabilities receive the supplemental educational services and accommodations.

What Happens When a School Fails to Make AYP for 4 Consecutive Years?

If a school fails to make AYP for a fourth consecutive year, the district must continue to (a) provide technical assistance, (b) make supplemental services available, and (c) offer public school choice. Additionally, the school is designated as needing corrective action. Figure 8.5 lists these corrective actions.

What Happens When a School Fails to Make AYP for 5 Consecutive Years?

If a school fails to meet AYP standards after 1 year of corrective action, which means it has not made AYP for 5 consecutive years, states are required to take corrective actions that involve major restructuring of the school. The restructuring plans should involve one or more of the changes to the school's governance structure that are listed in Figure 8.6.

The school district must continue to provide technical assistance, public school choice, and supplemental education services. Additionally, parents must be notified immediately when a school is identified for restructuring. During the restructuring period, the school must continue to offer parents the option of public school choice and supplemental educational services.

Figure 8.5
Corrective Actions

Corrective actions, at a minimum, must include one of the following actions:
- Replace the school staff members responsible for the school failing to make AYP.
- Implement research-based curriculum, including professional development activities.
- Decrease management authority significantly at the school level.
- Appoint an outside expert to advise the school.
- Extend the school year or school day.
- Restructure the school internally.

Figure 8.6
Restructuring Plans

Restructuring plans must include:
- Reopening the school as a public charter school.
- Replacing all or most of the school's staff, including the principal, who are responsible for the school's failing to achieve AYP.
- Entering into a contract with an entity, such as a private management company, to operate the school. The company must have a demonstrated record of effectiveness.
- Turning the operation of the school over to the state.
- Implementing other major restructuring arrangements that are consistent with NCLB.

What Happens When a School District Fails to Make AYP?

If an entire school district fails to make AYP, the state takes responsibility for helping the school district develop and implement an improvement plan and helps the school district implement corrective actions. The NCLB requirements regarding the school district's improvement plan and corrective action are the same as the requirements for schools. For example, when a school district is targeted for improvement, it has three months to develop or revise an improvement plan. The plan must be developed in consultation with parents, school staff, and other appropriate parties. Figure 8.7 lists additional required components of a school district improvement plan. The school district must implement the improvement plan no later than the beginning of the school year after it has been identified as in need of improvement.

Figure 8.7
Components of a School District Improvement Plan

A school district's improvement plan must include:
- Measurable goals and targets consistent with the AYP requirements.
- Extended learning time strategies.
- School district and state responsibilities under the plan.
- Effective parental involvement.

Figure 8.8
State Corrective Action Plans

States must implement corrective action, which includes:
- Deferring programming funds or reducing funds for administration.
- Implementing a new research-based curriculum.
- Implementing research-based professional development activities.
- Replacing school district personnel.
- Establishing an alternative governance structure.
- Appointing a receiver or trustee to administer the school district in place of the superintendent and school board.
- Abolishing or restructuring the school district.

If the entire school district does not achieve AYP for 4 years, the state must implement the corrective actions listed in Figure 8.8. The state may also authorize students in the school district to transfer to higher performing public schools.

What Happens When a State Fails to Make AYP?

The U.S. Department of Education will establish a peer review process to determine whether states are making their AYP goals. If a state fails to make AYP, it will be listed in an annual report to Congress. If a state fails to make AYP for 2 consecutive years, the U.S. Department of Education will provide technical assistance to the state.

If schools and school districts meet or exceed state proficiency standards, they will be eligible to receive academic achievement awards. These rewards, which are determined by each state, often consist of public commendations and recognition.

Scientifically Based Instruction

The second major principle of NCLB requires that states and school districts use scientifically based instructional programming to improve student achievement. In fact, the U.S. Department of Education calls instructional programs that are based on scientific research a major pillar of NCLB (U.S. Department of Education, 2002). Too often, schools have used programs and practices based on fads, fancy, and personal bias, which have proven to be ineffective (Carnine, 2000). Unfortunately, when ineffective procedures are used, it is at the expense of students. No Child Left Behind emphasizes using educational programs and practices that have been demonstrated to be effective by rigorous scientific research. In other words, reliable evidence shows that a program works. The law emphasizes scientifically based research because it (a) is not subject to fads and fashions, and (b) it makes teaching more effective, productive, and efficient (O'Neill, 2004).

No Child Left Behind requires the use of scientifically based research in all aspects of education (e.g., assessment, teaching, programs, instructional approaches, classroom management, monitoring student progress, professional development, technical assistance). The overarching goal of NCLB is to require schools, school districts, and states to rely on science when they make decisions about all aspects of education. The more than 700 pages of NCLB include more than 110 references to scientifically based research. O'Neill (2004) asserts that Congress's purpose in including so many references of scientific research in the law was to warn schools, school districts, and states that they must no longer rely on untested practices with no proof of effectiveness because reliance on such practices leads to widespread ineffectiveness and academic failure. Schools need to rely on evidence-based interventions to increase the academic performance of America's students. Moreover, scientifically researched practices must be the basis of technical assistance and support services provided to underperforming schools and professional development and personnel preparation programs in schools and institutions of higher education.

In the past few years, we have seen several national efforts to ensure that teachers across the nation use instructional procedures validated as effective by scientific research. For example, the National Research Council (2002) and the Coalition for Evidence-Based Policy (2002) issued reports stating that education will see progress only if we build a knowledge base of educational practices that rigorous research has proven effective. A central principle in NCLB requires that federal funds be expended to support *only* educational activities that are backed by scientifically based research.

Rod Paige, former Secretary of the U.S. Department of Education, noted that the intent of NCLB is to require that rigorous standards be applied to educational research and that research-based instruction is used in classroom settings (Paige, 2002). Furthermore, he asserted that states must pay attention to this research and ensure that teachers use evidence-supported methods in classrooms. NCLB demands the use of methods that really work: "no fads, not feel-good fluff, but instruction that is based upon sound scientific research" (Paige, 2002, p. 1). No Child Left Behind targets federal funds to support programs and teaching methods that have actually improved student achievement. For example, states must ensure that funds for Reading First activities go only to programs that are based on sound scientific research.

What constitutes sound scientific research? According to NCLB, scientifically based research involves the application of rigorous, systematic, and objective procedures to obtain reliable and valid knowledge relevant to educational activities and programs. Moreover, it includes research employing systematic empirical methods that draw on observation or experiments involving rigorous data analyses. The National Research Council (2002) reports that for a research design to be scientific, it must allow for direct, experimental investigation of important educational questions. No Child Left Behind defines scientifically based research as "research that applies rigorous, systematic, and objective procedures to obtain relevant knowledge" (NCLB, 20 USC § 1208(6)). This includes research that (a) uses systematic, empirical methods that draw on observation or experiment, (b) involves rigorous data analyses that are adequate to state hypotheses and justify the conclusions, (c) relies on measurement or observational methods that provide valid data evaluators and observers and across multiple measures and observations, and (d) has been accepted by a peer-reviewed journal or approved by a panel of independent experts through a comparably rigorous, objective, and scientific review. Figure 8.9 offers information on the U.S. Department of Education's Institute of Educational Sciences.

Reading First

Reading is an area in which NCLB specifies the research that should be used. Part B of Title I is entitled Student Reading Skills Improvement Grants. This section of NCLB contains the Reading First initiative. States can apply for Reading First grants under this initiative. This section of NCLB is a reaction to the problem of many children failing to master the essential and basic skills of reading (U.S. Department of Education, 2004). In fact, President Bush called Reading First the cornerstone of NCLB.

Figure 8.9
The What Works Clearinghouse

In 2002, the U.S. Department of Education's Institute of Education Sciences established the "What Works Clearinghouse" to provide a central, independent, and trusted source of scientific evidence on what works in education. The purpose of the clearinghouse is to assist schools, school districts, and states to incorporate scientifically based research into their programs. Based on its reviews, the clearinghouse issues evidence reports based on scientific standards. All of the research collected by the clearinghouse is available at its website: www.w-w-c.org/

Information on the department's Institute of Education Sciences is available at: www.ed.gov/about/offices/list/ies/index.html

Poor reading achievement is a critical problem for our children for three primary reasons. First, reading is the fundamental skill upon which all formal education depends, and if children cannot read well, they likely will fail in school (American Federation of Teachers, 1999). Second, children who do not learn to read early in their school careers will almost invariably continue to be poor readers (Torgeson, 2000). Third, poor readers tend to become less responsive to intervention as they grow older and their difficulties increase in scope and severity (Lane, Gresham, & O'Shaunessey, 2002; Torgeson, 2000).

Fortunately, the research is clear that the vast majority of poor readers can be taught to read (Fletcher & Lyon, 1998). We now have a compelling body of empirical evidence about how literacy develops, why some children have difficulty learning to read, what teachers need to do to prevent reading problems, and what constitutes best instructional practice in reading (Lyon, 2003). Research findings show that the best solution to the problem of reading failure is to allocate resources for early identification and prevention (Torgeson, 2000; Vaughn & Schumm, 1996). In fact, longitudinal studies by the National Institute of Health indicate that if we can identify young children who are at risk for reading failure and then use effective instructional procedures to teach reading, the failure rate can be reduced to 5% to 6%, even in the most disadvantaged areas (Lyon, 2003).

Research evidence clearly identifies the critical skills that young children need to learn if they are to become good readers (National Reading Panel, 2000). Moreover, teachers in reading programs throughout the nation have demonstrated that scientifically based reading instruction does work with all children (National Reading Panel, 2000). A key to helping children become proficient readers early in their school careers is to inform every teacher about the components of research-based reading instruction and how to implement them. To ensure that these instructional practices are actually used in classrooms, teachers will need to receive intensive competency-based inservice and preservice instruction in the science of teaching reading.

Three unique aspects of Reading First are that it (a) focuses on reading instruction that is supported by scientifically based reading research, (b) provides a large amount of money that states can receive to provide training to teachers and to implement professional development activities, and (c) emphasizes early identification of children at risk for reading failure so that effective early instruction can be provided. To ensure that all children in America learn to read well by the end of third grade, Congress and the President emphasized the importance of using scientifically based reading research. In other words, to teach reading successfully, Reading First requires that early reading instruction focus on instructional methods and strategies that have been proven to be effective for teaching young children to read.

The Five Research-Based Components of Reading Instruction

Reading First specifically requires that states ensure that the five essential components of effective reading instruction are included in their Reading First proposals. These five components were listed by the National Reading Panel as being essential for children to learn to read well. Specifically, the panel concluded that explicit and systematic instruction must be provided in (a) phonemic awareness, (b) phonics, (c) vocabulary development, (d) reading fluency, and (e) reading comprehension strategies (National Reading Panel, 2000).

States can apply for Reading First funds. The applications undergo a rigorous review by a panel of experts. States that receive the grants distribute grant funds to school districts that submit applications. States submitting grant proposals provide detailed and comprehensive plans outlining their proposals to use research-proven methods and strategies to teach reading. States that receive Reading First funds then distribute the funds to designated school districts. The state must ensure that all programs, strategies, and activities that are proposed meet the criteria for scientifically based reading research. *All* Reading First funds used by the states must be grounded in scientifically based reading research as described in NCLB. Table 8.2 lists the requirements of school districts that receive Reading First funds.

No Child Left Behind targets federal funds to support programs and teaching methods that are based on sound scientific research and have been shown to improve student achievement. As Dr. Russ Whitehurst (2003), the director of the Institute of Educational Science in the U.S. Department of Education, has aptly stated:

> I have a vision of a day when every child receives an education that is good enough, no child's future is crippled by a bad teacher, bad curriculum, or bad school, a day in which we figure out how to deliver an effective education to all children. When that day comes it will be because we have learned to ground educational practice in science, and when the education research community is able engage in a science that serves.

Highly Qualified Teachers and Paraprofessionals

The quality and skill of teachers are extremely important factors in student achievement (Whitehurst, 2003). Congress recognized the importance of having well-prepared teachers in public school classrooms when they included provisions in the NCLB requiring that all new teachers hired in programs supported by Title I funds must be highly qualified teachers beginning with the 2002–2003 school year. Additionally, the law requires that by the end of the 2005–2006 school year, all teachers in public schools must be highly qualified. The NCLB also requires that states ensure that paraprofessionals who work in the nation's public school classrooms must be highly qualified.

To ensure that only highly qualified teachers teach in public school classrooms, each state must develop a plan to ensure that all the state's public school teachers are highly qualified to teach core academic subjects in which they provide instruction by the end of the 2005–2006 school year. The NCLB regulations define core academic subjects as English, reading–language arts, mathematics, science, foreign languages, civics, government, economics, art,* history, and geography. If a teacher teaches in one of these core subjects, the NCLB highly qualified requirement applies

*No Child Left Behind includes "the arts" as a core academic subject; although it is up to the states to define what subjects constitute the arts.

Table 8.2
Components of Reading First Programs

Reading Component	Description
Reading assessment	• School districts must select and administer reliable and valid screening, diagnostic, and classroom-based reading assessments. • Assessments must measure student progress on the essential elements of reading instruction (i.e., phonemic awareness, phonics, vocabulary development, reading fluency, and reading comprehension strategies). • Assessments must identify students who are at risk for reading failure or who have problems learning to read.
Reading program	• School districts must adopt and implement a program of reading instruction that is grounded in scientifically based reading research and contains the five essential elements of reading instruction. • The reading program should include (a) sufficient time allocated for instruction, (b) explicit instructional strategies, (c) appropriate instructional sequences, (d) many opportunities to practice, and (e) materials that are aligned to the instructional program.
Instructional materials	• All instructional materials that the school uses must reflect scientifically based reading instruction. • Instructional materials may include any technological devices or services.
Professional development	• Schools must implement professional development activities for kindergarten through grade 3 teachers and kindergarten through grade 12 special education teachers. • The purpose of professional development is to prepare these teachers to implement instructional programs that teach the five essential components of reading instruction. • The professional development activities must prepare teachers to use screening, diagnostic, and classroom-based assessments to identify students who may be at risk of reading failure or have difficulty reading and to monitor their progress in their reading programs. • All professional development activities must be based on scientifically based reading research.

Table 8.2
Continued

Reading Component	Description
Evaluation and reporting strategies	• School districts must collect and summarize data to document the effectiveness of their Reading First program. • These data should be used to improve instruction by identifying those schools that are producing significant gains in reading achievement. • The school district must file a report to the state that details the data for all students and categories of students included in the adequate yearly progress definition of NCLB.

to him or her. If a teacher teaches in more than two of these core subjects, he or she must be qualified in all the subject areas taught.

No Child Left Behind also requires school districts that receive Title I funds to notify parents that they may ask their child's districts for information regarding a teacher's qualifications. Districts must comply with such a request. Specifically, parents may request information about whether (a) a teacher has met the state's licensing criteria for the grade levels and subject matters that he or she teaches; (b) the state has waived its licensing criteria to permit the teacher to teach on an emergency basis; (c) the teacher has a college major or graduate degree in which the teacher teaches; and (d) a teacher's aide provides services to their child, and if they do, the qualifications of the paraprofessional.

Additionally, NCLB requires states to hold school districts accountable if they do meet the teacher quality requirements of the law. Schools must provide notices to parents if their child's class has been taught for four or more consecutive weeks by a teacher who does not meet the highly qualified requirements. Moreover, if a school district does not make adequate progress toward their state's measurable goal for increasing the number of highly qualified teachers in the district for 2 consecutive years, the school district must develop an improvement plan to address the problem. Additionally, the state must provide technical assistance to the district to assist in developing and implementing the improvement plan. If a school district fails to make adequate progress for 3 consecutive years, it must enter into a cooperative agreement with the state to develop strategies and activities based on scientifically based research to meet the state's objectives.

Highly Qualified Teachers

NCLB specifies three basic requirements that public school teachers must meet to be highly qualified. First, teachers must hold a minimum of a bachelor's degree from a college or university. Second, teachers must have full state teacher certification or licensure for the area in which they teach. Third, teachers must be able to demonstrate subject matter competency in the core academic subjects in which they teach. Teachers can demonstrate subject matter competency by passing a state-administered test in each of the core subjects they teach. The structure and content of these tests are determined by the individual states.

Elementary School Teachers.   Elementary school teachers must hold at least a bachelor's degree and be fully certified by the state in the area in which they teach. To demonstrate their knowledge and abilities, they also must pass a test of subject matter knowledge. For elementary school teachers, this means passing a test of subject knowledge and teaching skill in reading–language arts, writing, mathematics, and other areas of the basic elementary school curriculum.

Middle and Secondary School Teachers.   Both middle school and high school teachers must meet the same NCLB highly qualified standards. Both must have at least a bachelor's degree and be fully certified by the state in the area in which they teach. Because states may have different requirements for certification in middle school and in high school, teachers need to contact their state department of education to determine the appropriate certification requirements.

To demonstrate their knowledge and abilities, they also must pass a state-administered test of subject matter knowledge. For middle and high school teachers, this means passing a test in each academic subject in which they teach. If a middle school or secondary school teacher provides instruction in more than one core academic subject, then he or she must be qualified in each area.

Special Education Teachers.   According to IDEA 2004, special education teachers must meet the same highly qualified standards as general education teachers. This is true for special education teachers who are new to the profession and experienced special education teachers. Special education teachers must meet three general requirements to meet the highly qualified standard of NCLB. First, all special education teachers must have a bachelor's degree. Second, special education teachers must have obtained a full state certification as a special education teacher or passed the state special education teacher licensing examination and hold a state license to teach as a special education teacher. This includes certification obtained through state-approved alternative routes to certification. States cannot waive special education certification or licensure requirements on an emergency, temporary, or provisional basis. Third, special education teachers who teach in elementary schools, middle schools, and high schools must pass a state-administered test of subject knowledge and teaching skill to demonstrate competency in the core academic subjects.

For elementary special education teachers this means competency in areas of the basic elementary school curriculum (e.g., reading–language arts, writing, mathematics). Special education teachers in middle and high school who provide instruction in core academic subjects must meet the requirements of NCLB for being highly qualified in every core academic subject they teach. This means they must take a state-administered test of content knowledge. This applies whether a special education teacher provides core academic instruction in a regular class-room, resource room, or another setting. For example, if a special education teacher provides reading instruction to students with learning disabilities, he or she must be highly qualified in reading.

Special education teachers in middle schools and high schools often teach many subjects to their students (e.g., math, social studies, science). Rather than specializing in one subject area like most secondary teachers, however, special education teachers often specialize in working with students with certain disabilities covered by the IDEA (e.g., children with autism, learning disabilities, or emotional disabilities). The NCLB requirements regarding being highly qualified in the core academic subjects they teach, nonetheless, apply to them. Therefore, if a special education teacher works with their students in core academic subjects, such as history, math, or science, he or she must be highly qualified in those subjects.

However, special education teachers may take part in some activities that do not require them to be highly qualified. Such activities include providing consultation to highly qualified teachers of core academic subjects, using behavioral supports and in-terventions, selecting appropriate academic accommodations, assisting students with study skills, and reinforcing instruction that a student has received in a core ac-ademic subject from a highly qualified teacher. Additionally, if a special education teacher team-teaches with a general education teacher in a core academic subject, the special education teacher must be certified or licensed to teach special educa-tion in the state but would not need to be certified in the subject as long as the gen-eral education teacher is certified in that subject.

Highly Qualified Teachers of Students with Significant Cognitive Disabilities. Special education teachers who teach core academic subjects to students with dis-abilities who are assessed using alternative achievement standards must meet the three requirements listed previously. That means teachers of students with severe disabilities, who typically will be assessed using alternate measures, need to hold a bachelor's degree and full state certification in special education and demonstrate competency in areas of the basic elementary school curriculum. In the case of a spe-cial education teacher who works with students with significant cognitive disabilities but who provides instruction above the elementary level (e.g., teaches at the high school level), the teacher must demonstrate subject matter knowledge appropriate to the level of instruction needed to effectively teach students. This level of knowl-edge is determined by the state in which the teacher works.

Highly Qualified Teachers and State HOUSSE Standards.   States have the option of developing a method by which teachers can demonstrate competency in each sub-ject they teach on the basis of a high objective uniform state standard of evaluation (HOUSSE). This standard must provide objective and coherent information about a teacher's attainment of core subject knowledge in the academic subjects in which he or she teaches. The state's HOUSSE criteria, which must evaluate a teacher's knowledge and ability, is available through each state's Department of Education.

Training and Professional Development Activities

The highly qualified teacher requirements of NCLB also includes funding for training and professional development activities. When a state or school district uses NCLB funds for professional development, the activities must meet the following standards. First, all professional development activities must be grounded in scientifically based research. When a district implements an approach to professional development, therefore, the district must ensure that the approach is supported by scientifically based research. Second, all activities must be linked to raising instructional quality. Third, activities must be of high quality, sustained, and intense, and they must have a classroom focus. This means that the professional development activities funded by NCLB may not be one-day or short-term workshops or conferences. Figure 8.10 lists professional development programs that are acceptable under NCLB (NCLB, 20 USC § 6623).

No Child Left Behind provides funding to states through the Teacher Quality Grants. The majority of these funds must be distributed to local school districts. These grants may be used for (a) providing scientifically based professional development activities for new and experienced teachers; (b) recruiting new teachers, including

Figure 8.10
Acceptable Professional Development Programs

Professional development activities should:
- Increase teachers' knowledge of the academic subjects they teach.
- Teach educators to properly implement new curriculum.
- Instruct teachers in classroom management skills.
- Teach educators to use proven instructional strategies that increase student achievement.
- Teach educators to use research-based language programs for English language learners.
- Train teachers to improve their teaching and student learning by using technology.
- Train teachers to use research-based methods for students with special educational needs.
- Teach educators to use data from assessments to increase student learning.
- Teach school personnel how to work effectively with parents.

teachers certified through alternative channels; (c) streamlining licensing requirements; (d) providing teacher support programs, including mentoring programs; (e) paying bonuses to retain teachers; and (f) measuring the effects of professional development programs on student achievement.

Highly Qualified Paraprofessionals

Paraprofessionals play a valuable role in providing services to public school students. This is especially true in special education. No Child Left Behind also requires that paraprofessionals who work in Title I schools must be highly qualified by the end of the 2005–2006 school year. To be highly qualified paraprofessionals must have a high school diploma or recognized equivalent. Additionally, paraprofessionals must have completed at least 2 years of college or an associate's degree or met rigorous quality standards by performing adequately on a designated state test. The state or local test should demonstrate that a paraprofessional has the knowledge of and ability to assist in teaching reading–language arts, writing, and mathematics or reading readiness, writing readiness, and mathematics readiness.

No Child Left Behind allows paraprofessionals to provide instructional support services only when they are directly supervised by a teacher. The teacher is also responsible for (a) planning all instructional activities implemented by a paraprofessional and (b) evaluating the achievement of the students who work with a paraprofessional. Figure 8.11 depicts the duties paraprofessionals may perform.

The NCLB definition of *paraprofessional* does not include individuals who perform only noninstructional duties, such as clerical tasks, playground supervision, translating services, or providing personal care services. If the paraprofessional performs only these duties and does not facilitate instruction, he or she does not have to meet NCLB requirements.

Figure 8.11
Appropriate Duties of a Paraprofessional

- Providing one-to-one tutoring (if scheduled when the student would not otherwise be taught by the teacher)
- Assisting with classroom management
- Assisting in computer instruction
- Conducting parent involvement activities
- Providing instructional support in a library or media center
- Acting as a translator
- Providing instructional support services under the direct supervision of a qualified teacher

Summary

No Child Left Behind is a comprehensive and complex law that increased federal education funding to unprecedented levels. In fact, NCLB represents the most significant expansion of the federal government into education in history. The law increases federal mandates and requirements for states, school districts, and public schools.

The law represents a logical step in a series of education laws passed by the federal government that were intended to improve the academic achievement of the nation's students.

Since the mid 1960s, the federal government has provided large amounts of money to states to assist them in improving educational programming for public school students. Beginning with *A Nation at Risk* (1983), officials in the federal government began to question the results that federal funding was having on the states' educational systems. Many believed that the evidence reported in *A Nation at Risk* clearly showed that the federal funds were not being spent on meaningful state activities designed to improve educational results. Moreover, legislators argued that the federal funds should be spent in a more effective manner.

The federal role in education began to expand with the passage of the Improving America's Schools Act of 1994, America 2000, and Goals 2000. These laws created a new role for the federal government in public and secondary education by tying government funding to the development of rigorous academic content standards by the states. Unfortunately, although states began to develop these standards, increases in student achievement were not occurring. No Child Left Behind's unique contribution was to expand the role of the federal government in public education by holding states, school districts, and schools accountable for producing measurable gains in students'

academic achievement. Specifically, NCLB was a reaction to low academic achievement in general, and reading in particular, among America's students. For the first time, the federal government requires states and school districts to use numerical data that provides evidence of improved student outcomes. Moreover, NCLB represents an emphasis on accountability and using scientifically based instructional methods and strategies.

No Child Left Behind is a powerful law that will directly affect education in America's public schools. Because of the strict accountability requirements of NCLB, it is vital that district administrators, principals, and teachers know exactly what the law requires of them. The consequences of failing to meet the requirements of NCLB are serious. Adhering to the requirements of the NCLB can be a daunting task; nevertheless, school districts must ensure that all district administrators, teachers, and staff are well trained in their responsibilities under the law. Moreover, preservice teachers need intensive training to prepare them to enter schools knowing and being able to use scientifically based instructional strategies and methods and be able to collect meaningful data to monitor students' progress.

Beyond doubt, this law will make profound changes in the ways educators work with students. For the first time, states, school districts, and schools are accountable for making improvements in students' academic performance.

Although Congress and the U.S. Department of Education will occasionally tweak the requirements regarding testing and other components, the major goals of NCLB, which are the use of scientifically based and researched educational practices and holding states, school districts, and schools accountable for increasing student achievement, will drive public school education for years to come. No Child Left Behind points educators toward accountability, which requires that schools improve student achievement in reading and math. To do so, educators must use scientifically based strategies and methods, which represent the primary tools that will allow schools to make meaningful changes in the academic achievement of their students. If the core of our educational practice becomes what the evidence shows us works in teaching, then we can make meaningful changes in our schools.

For Further Information on NCLB

Education Commission of the States. (2002). *No state left behind: The challenges and opportunities of ESEA 2001.* Denver, CO: Author. Available in PDF format at www.ecs.org/clearinghouse/32/37/3237.doc.

Learning First Alliance. (2002). *Major changes to ESEA in the No Child Left Behind Act.* Washington, DC: Author. Available at www.learningfirst.org.

O'Neill, P. T. (2004). *No Child Left Behind compliance manual.* New York: Brownstone Publishers.

U.S. Department of Education. (2001). *The achiever: An electronic newsletter that provides information on No Child Left Behind.* Free subscriptions available at www.ed.gov/news/newsletters/achiever/index.html.

U.S. Department of Education. (2002). *No Child Left Behind: A desktop reference.* Washington, DC: Education Publications Center. Available online at www.ed.gov/teachers/landing.html. The paper copy of this guide can be ordered online at www.edpubs.org or by writing to ED Pubs, Education Publications Center, U.S. Department of Education, P.O. Box 1398, Jessup, MD 20794-1398.

U.S. Department of Education. (2003). *No Child Left Behind: A toolkit for teachers.* Washington, DC: Education Publications Center. Available online at www.ed.gov/teachers/landing.html. The paper copy of this guide can be ordered online at www.edpubs.org or by writing to ED Pubs, Education Publications Center, U.S. Department of Education, P.O. Box 1398, Jessup, MD 20794-1398.

Wright, P. W. D., Wright, P. D., & Heath, S. W. (2004). *Wrightslaw: No Child Left Behind.* Hartfield, VA: Harbor House Law Press.

Yell, M. L., & Drasgow, E. (2005). *No Child Left Behind: A guide for professionals.* Upper Saddle River, NJ: Merrill/Prentice Hall.

For Further Information on Scientifically Based Research

Coalition for Evidence-Based Policy. (2002). *Identifying and implementing educational practices supported by rigorous evidence: A user friendly guide.* Washington, DC: Author. Available in PDF format at www.excelgov.org/displaycontent.asp?keyword=prppcHomePage

Graham, S. (Ed.). (2005). Special issue: Criteria for evidence-based practice in special education. *Exceptional Children, 71,* 130–207.

National Reading Panel. (2000). *Teaching children to read: An evidence-based assessment of the scientific research literature on reading and its implication for reading instruction.* Washington, DC: National Institute on Child Development and Human Development.

National Research Council. (2002). *Strategic education research partnerships.* Washington, DC: National Academy Press.

U.S. Department of Education, Institute of Education Sciences. (2003). *Identifying and implementing educational practices supported by rigorous evidence: A user friendly guide.* Washington, DC: Author.

References

Alexander, K., & Alexander, M. D. (2001). *American public school* (4th ed.). Edina, MN: Thomson/West Publishing.

American Federation of Teachers. (1999). *Taking responsibility for ending social promotion: A guide for educators and state and local leaders.* Washington, DC: Author.

Anthes, K. (2002, April). *Two states progress on preparing for NCLB.* Atlanta, GA: State Action for Education Leadership Project.

Carnine, D. (2000). *Why education experts resist effective practices: And what it would take to make education more like medicine.* Washington, DC: Thomas B. Fordham Foundation.

Coalition for Evidence-Based Policy. (2002). *Bringing evidence-based policy to education: A recommended strategy for the U.S. Department of Education.* Washington, DC: Author. Available in PDF format at www.excelgov.org/usermedia/images/uploads/PDFs/CoalitionFinRpt.pdf.

Cohen, M. (2002, February). Assessment and accountability: Lessons from the past, challenges for the future. Paper presented at a conference sponsored by the Thomas B. Fordham Foundation, *No Child Left Behind: What Will It Take?* Available in PDF format at www.edexcellence.net/ foundation/topic/topic.cfm?topic_id=5.

Commission on Excellence in Education. (1983). *A nation at risk: An imperative for educational reform.* Washington, DC: Author. Available at http://www.ed.gov/pubs/NatAtRisk/index.html.

Education Commission of the States. (2002). *No state left behind: The challenges and opportunities of ESEA 2001.* Denver, CO: Author. Available in PDF format at www.ecs.org/clearinghouse/32/37/3237.doc.

Elementary and Secondary Education Act (ESEA) of 1965, 20 U.S.C. §16301 *et seq.*

Elliott, J. L., & Thurlow, M. L. (2003). *Improving test performance of students with disabilities . . . on district and state assessments.* Thousand Oaks, CA: Corwin Press.

Fletcher, J., & Lyon, R. (1998). Reading: A research-based approach. In W. Evers (Ed.), *What's gone wrong in America's classrooms.* Palo Alto, CA: Hoover Institution Press, Stanford University.

Improving America's School Act (IASA) of 1994, 20 U.S.C. §16301 *et seq.*

Koret Task Force on K–12 education. (2003). *Are we still at risk?* Available at www.educationnext.org/20032/10html.

Lane, K. K., Gresham, F. M., & O'Shaunessey, T. E. (2002). *Interventions for children with or at risk for emotional and behavioral disorders.* Boston: Allyn & Bacon.

Learning First Alliance. (2002). *Major changes to ESEA in the No Child Left Behind Act.* Washington, DC: Author. Available at www.learningfirst.org.

Lyon, G. R. (2003, October 6). Speech at Family Service Guidance Center. Available at CJOnline/*Topeka Capital Journal,* www.cjonline.com/stories/041803/kan_educator.shtml.

National Center for Educational Statistics. (2001). *Dropout rates in the United States.* Available in PDF format at http://nces.ed.gov/pubs2005/2005046.pdf.

National Reading Panel. (2000). *Teaching children to read: An evidence-based assessment of the scientific research literature on reading and its implication for reading instruction.* Washington, DC: National Institute on Child Development and Human Development.

National Research Council. (2002). *Strategic education research partnerships.* Washington, DC: National Academy Press.

No Child Left Behind, 20 U.S.C. §16301 *et seq.*

O'Neill, P. T. (2004). *No Child Left Behind compliance manual.* New York: Brownstone, Publications.

Paige, R. (2002, November). Statement of Secretary Paige regarding Title I regulations. Retrieved August 2002 from www.ed.gov/news/speeches/2002/11/11262002.html?exp=0.

Reckase, M. (2002, February). Using NAEP to confirm state test results: An analysis of issues. Paper presented at a conference sponsored by the Thomas B. Fordham Foundation, *No Child Left Behind: What Will It Take?* Available in PDF format at www.edexcellence.net/foundation/topic/topic.cfm? topic_id=5.

Thurlow, M. L., Elliott, J. L., & Ysseldyke, J. E. (2001). *Testing students with disabilities: Practical strategies for complying with district and state requirements.* Thousand Oaks, CA: Corwin Press.

Torgeson, J. (2000). Individual differences in response to early intervention in reading: The lingering problem of treatment resistance. *Learning Disabilities Research and Practice, 15,* 55–64.

U.S. Department of Education. (2002). *No Child Left Behind: A desktop reference.* Washington, DC: Education Publications. PDF available at www.ed.gov/admins/lead/account/nclbreference/index.html.

U.S. Department of Education. (2004). The facts about Reading First. Washington, DC: PDF available at www.ed.gov/nclb/methods/reading/readingfirst.html.

Vaughn, S., & Schumm, J. S. (1996). Classroom interactions and inclusion. In D. L. Speech, & B. Keogh, (Eds.), *Research on classroom ecologies.* Mahwah, NJ: Lawrence Erlbaum.

Whitehurst, G. (2003). *The Institute of Education Sciences: New wine, new bottles.* Presentation at the Annual Conference of the American Educational Research Association. Available online at www.ed.gov/print/rschstat/research/pubs/ies.html.

Wright, P. D., Wright, P. D., & Heath, S. W. (2004). *No Child Left Behind.* Hartfield, VA: Harbor House Law Press.

Yell, M. L., & Drasgow, E. (2005). *No Child Left Behind: A guide for professionals.* Upper Saddle River, NJ: Merrill/Prentice Hall.

CHAPTER NINE
::

Free Appropriate Public Education

Free appropriate public education . . . evinces a congressional intent to bring previously excluded handicapped children into the public education systems of the states and to require the states to adopt procedures which would result in individualized consideration of and instruction for each child.

Justice Rehnquist, *Board of Education v. Rowley* (1982, p. 188)

P rior to the passage of the Education for All Handicapped Children Act in 1975 (now the Individuals with Disabilities Education Act or IDEA), the access of students with disabilities to educational opportunities was limited in two major ways (Yell, Drasgow, Bradley, & Justesen, 2004). First, many students were excluded from public schools. In fact, in the early 1970s Congress estimated that public schools in the United States were educating only an estimated 20% of all children with disabilities (OSEP, 2000). Second, more than 3 million students with disabilities who were admitted to school did not receive an education that was appropriate to their needs (Congressional Record, 1975). These students were often "left to fend for themselves in classrooms designed for education of their nonhandicapped peers" (*Board of Education of the Hendrick Hudson School District v. Rowley,* 1982, p. 191). Thus, many students with disabilities were excluded from school entirely, and many others were offered an education that was not appropriate to their needs.

To correct these inequities, Congress passed the EAHCA. The law offered federal financial assistance to states to aid them in the development and improvement of educational programs for students who qualified for special education under the Act. To qualify for assistance, states were required to submit state plans that assured all students with disabilities the right to a *free appropriate public education* (FAPE).

In the years following the passage of the EAHCA, the question of what exactly is a free appropriate public education had generated much discussion, controversy, and litigation. Although the *free* education and the *public* education parts of a FAPE have rarely been disputed, what constitutes an *appropriate* education for any given child has frequently been the subject of debate and litigation (Wenkart, 2000). This chapter examines the FAPE mandate, including the components of a FAPE and important litigation that has considered this mandate. In addition, I will discuss how schools can develop programs that meet the FAPE requirements of the IDEA.

The FAPE Mandate of the IDEA

Students who are determined eligible for services under the IDEA are entitled to receive appropriate special education and related services that consist of specially designed instruction and services provided at public expense. The law defines a FAPE as special education and related services that

(A) are provided at public expense, under public supervision and direction, and without charge,

(B) meet standards of the State educational agency,

(C) include an appropriate preschool, elementary, or secondary school education in the state involved, and

(D) are provided in conformity with the individualized education program. (IDEA, 20 U.S.C. § 1401 (a)(18))

The key to providing a FAPE is for school personnel to develop and implement a program based on a full and individualized assessment of a student that consists of specially designed instruction tailored to meet the unique needs of a child with a disability (IDEA, 20 U.S.C. § 1401(a)(16)). What constitutes an appropriate education, therefore, varies from student to student.

When writing the original IDEA, Congress understood that it would be impossible to define a FAPE in such a way that the actual substantive educational requirements were listed, so instead a FAPE is defined primarily in accordance with the procedures necessary to ensure that parents and school personnel would collaborate to develop a program of special education and related services that would meet the unique educational needs of individual students. Congress was specific in setting forth the procedures by which parents and school personnel, working together, would create programs to provide an appropriate education. Thus, the definition of a FAPE in the IEP is primarily procedural rather than substantive.

These procedural mechanisms included requiring school personnel to (a) provide notice to parents anytime their child's education program was discussed so they could participate in the discussions in a meaningful way, (b) invite parents to participate in meetings to develop their child's educational program, (c) secure parental consent prior to initiating evaluations of their child or placing their child in a special education program, (d) allow parents the opportunity to examine their child's educational records, and (e) permit parents to obtain an independent educational evaluation at public expense if the parents disagreed with the school's evaluation. Furthermore, if parents and school personnel cannot agree on a child's evaluation, programming, or placement, the parents can request mediation or an impartial due process hearing and even file a suit in federal or state court to resolve the issue (IDEA Regulations, 34 C.F.R. § 300.500–515). (See Chapter 13 for an elaboration of procedural safeguards.) The purpose of these procedural safeguards is to ensure parental participation and consultation throughout the special education process. Congress believed that requiring meaningful collaboration between parents and school personnel and providing protections for parents when collaboration did not occur would help to ensure that a FAPE would be developed and implemented for all students in special education.

Components of a FAPE

Several components make up a FAPE. Some of these elements have proven to be more controversial than others. Nonetheless it is important that school personnel understand that these are all important components and they must be considered in designing a FAPE.

Free Education

The special education and related services that are part of a student's educational program must be provided at no charge to parents or guardians of the student. Furthermore, the IDEA does not allow school districts to refuse to provide special education services because of the cost of those services. In enacting the IDEA, Congress specifically rejected limitations of federal funding as justification for denying a FAPE.

School personnel, however, may consider cost when making decisions about a student's special education program (*A. W. v. Northwest R-1 School District,* 1987; *Doe v. Brookline School Committee,* 1983; *Schuldt v. Mankato Independent School District,* 1991). The U.S. Court of Appeals for the Sixth Circuit, in *Clevenger v. Oak Ridge School Board* (1984), noted that "cost considerations are only relevant when choosing between several options, all of which offer an appropriate education. When only one is appropriate, then there is no choice" (p. 514). For example, if school personnel had to choose between two residential options for placing a student, and both options would be appropriate, the school district could choose the less expensive of the two placements.

The U.S. Court of Appeals for the Ninth Circuit, in *Department of Education, State of Hawaii v. Katherine D.* (1984), noted that school officials were often confronted with limited financial resources as the appellate judges ruled that school officials were required to provide an appropriate education, not the best possible education. According to the Office of Special Education Programs (OSEP) of the U.S. Department of Education, it is important that school personnel do not make FAPE decisions solely on the basis of cost of services, but that decisions be based on the individual needs of a student (*Letter to Greer,* 1992).

The regulations implementing the IDEA (IDEA Regulations, 34 C.F.R. § 300.301) clearly indicate that the free service provision of the law pertains only to the parents or guardians and does not relieve other governmental agencies, insurers, or third-party payers from valid obligations to pay for services. Title XIX of the Social Security Act, which established Medicare, was amended in 1988 to allow payment for covered services for eligible children and youth with disabilities, even if the services were incorporated into their special education programs (Social Security Act, 42 U.S.C. § 1396). Additionally, schools can often use private insurance companies as a funding source for costs related to a student's special education (Spaller & Thomas, 1994).

It should be noted that OSEP has stated that schools are not precluded from charging "incidental" fees to the parents of students with disabilities for items such as art or lab supplies or field trips. It is important that such fees are also charged to students without disabilities as part of their educational program (OSEP Policy Letter, 1992).

State Standards

The FAPE mandate of the IDEA includes the requirement that an appropriate education meet the standards of the state educational agency. This provision of FAPE acknowledges that providing an education to the citizens of a state is the responsibility of the state rather than the federal government. As we discussed in Chapter 5, provisions of the IDEA require states to submit special education plans that assure qualified students with disabilities the right to a FAPE. These plans, at a minimum, must meet the requirements set forth by the federal government in the IDEA. States, however, are free to impose more demanding standards than those contained in the federal law. When a state standard is more demanding, that standard must be applied (Tucker & Goldstein, 1992).

California, Massachusetts, Michigan, New Jersey, and North Carolina have FAPE standards considered by the courts to be more stringent than those of the federal government (Guernsey & Klare, 1993). Thus, schools in those states must meet the more demanding FAPE standards of their state laws. Interestingly, Arkansas and Iowa had higher FAPE standards than the federal government, but the state legislatures amended the state statutes to bring them into line with the federal standards.

The state standards requirement of a FAPE also specifies that the education must meet any standards required by the state, including licensure and certification requirements for teachers (IDEA Regulations, 34 C.F.R. § 300.153). Any additional educational requirements enacted by state legislatures must also be followed. If a special education teacher wants to teach in a state, therefore, the teacher must receive certification or licensure to teach in that state.

Appropriate Education

One of the most frequently disputed areas in special education involves the issue of what constitutes an appropriate education for a child. To ensure that each student covered by the IDEA receives an individualized FAPE, Congress required that an individualized education program (IEP) be developed for all students in special education. A FAPE is realized through the development of an IEP. The special education and related services a student receives are delineated in, and must be provided in conformity with, the student's IEP.

The school district in which the student resides is responsible for developing the IEP in collaboration with the student's parents. Thus, the IEP is both a collaborative process between the parents and the school in which the educational program is developed and a written document that contains the essential components of a student's educational program (Norlin & Gorn, 2005). The written document, developed by a team of educators and a student's parents, describes a student's educational needs and details the special education and related services that will be provided to the student (Bateman & Linden, 1998). The IEP also describes a student's goals and how his or her progress will be measured. The IDEA mandates the process and procedures for developing the IEP.

The law includes specific requirements regarding the IEP process. For example, participants in the meeting must include, at a minimum, a representative of the public agency, the student's teacher, and the student's parents. Other individuals may be included at the request of the parent or school district. It is the task of this team to formulate the student's special education program. The IEP must include the following six components: (a) a statement of the student's present level of educational performance, (b) measurable annual goals, (c) a statement of the specific special education and related services required, (d) a statement of needed transition services, (e) the date the special education services will begin and the anticipated duration of these services, and (f) appropriate objective criteria and evaluation procedures.

The IEP does not guarantee that a student will achieve the educational goals listed in the document, nor does it hold teachers or administrators liable if a student does not meet specified goals. The IEP, however, does commit the school to providing the special education and related services listed in the IEP and to making good faith efforts to achieve the goals. See Chapter 13 for elaborations on the IEP.

Related Services and FAPE

The provision of a FAPE sometimes requires that students with disabilities be provided with related services in addition to their special education services. Related services are defined in the IDEA as "supportive services . . . as may be required to assist a child with a disability to benefit from special education" (IDEA Regulations, 34 C.F.R. § 300.16(a)). (See Chapter 12 for elaborations on related services.) When related services are provided to a student with a disability, they must be included in the IEP, and they must be provided at no cost. Courts have ordered school districts to reimburse parents for the unilateral provision of related services when it has been determined that the service was necessary for educational benefit but was not provided by the school (*Max M. v. Illinois State Board of Education,* 1986; *Seals v. Loftis,* 1985).

The IDEA defines related services as:

Transportation, and such developmental, corrective, and other supportive services (including speech-language pathology and audiology services, interpreting services, psychological services, physical and occupational therapy, recreation, including recreation, social work services, school nurse services designed to enable a child with a disability to receive a free appropriate public education as described in the individualized education program of the child, counseling services, including rehabilitation counseling, orientation and mobility services, and medical services, except that such medical services shall be for diagnostic and evaluation purposes only) as may be required to assist a child with a disability to benefit from special education, and includes the early identification and assessment of disabling conditions in children The term *does not* include a medical device that is surgically implanted, or the replacement of such device. (IDEA 20 U.S.C. § 1402(26)(A))

The list of related services included in this definition is not exhaustive. With the exception of medical services (i.e., the services of a licensed physician) and medical devices (e.g., cochlear implants), there are no restrictions on IEP teams when they determine what, if any, related services a student needs.

Decisions regarding related services can only be made on an individual basis. The team that develops the IEP, therefore, is the proper forum to determine which services are required in order to provide a FAPE (*Letter to Rainforth,* 1990; *Letter to Shelby,* 1994). The IEP team, in addition to determining the types of related services to be provided, must include the amount of services provided. This is required so that the commitment of needed resources will be clear to the parents and other IEP team members (IDEA Regulations, Notice of Interpretation on IEPs, Question 51).

This is true for the type of related service and the amount of the services that are to be provided. Related services frequently complement the special education services a student receives, but related services can never be provided without an accompanying special education service (Pitasky, 2000). Some related services, such as speech therapy, may also qualify as a special education service. Nonetheless, related services cannot be included in a student's IEP if no special education is being provided to the student (Norlin & Gorn, 2005).

The most controversial of the related services has been complex health services provided to medically fragile students with disabilities. Difficulties have arisen when school districts attempted to distinguish school health services from medical services in providing the related services. School health services are "provided by a qualified school nurse or other qualified person" and are required under the IDEA (IDEA Regulations, 34 C.F.R. § 300.16). According to Lear (1995), the definition of school health services is extremely broad and may run the gamut from activities requiring almost no training (e.g., dispensing oral medication), to those requiring increased levels of training (e.g., catheterization), to those requiring extensive training and a substantial amount of time (e.g., tracheotomy care and chest physiotherapy).

When health care services must be provided by a physician, however, they are excluded medical services, not required related services. School districts have often argued that the established legislative and regulatory language that differentiates medical from health services simply on the nature of who provides the service (i.e., physician or nonphysician) is unjustifiable (Rapport, 1996). Proponents of this view argue that when the health services become extremely complex and burdensome to a school district, the health services become medical and, therefore, school should not be required to provide these services.

Medical services covered under IDEA are only those services provided by a licensed physician for diagnostic or evaluation purposes; all other medical services provided by a licensed physician are excluded. A school health service, or the services of the school nurse, may be required if (a) the service is necessary to assist a child with disabilities in benefiting from special education, (b) the service must be performed during school hours, and (c) the service can be provided by a person other than a licensed physician, such as a school nurse or some other properly trained school employee (*Letter to Greer,* 1992).

Litigation and Related Services

In 1984, the U.S Supreme Court issued a ruling in a case involving related services. The case, *Irving Independent School District v. Tatro* (1984), was to assume a great deal of importance because it was the first high court ruling regarding related services. Amber Tatro, an 8-year-old born with spina bifida, a condition that resulted in orthopedic and speech impairments and a neurogenic bladder, was in need of a procedure called *clean intermittent catheterization* (CIC) to be performed every 3 to 4 hours to prevent kidney damage. The evidence presented in the case indicated that a lay person could perform this medically accepted procedure with less than an hour's training. Although the school district found that Amber qualified for special education services under the IDEA, the district would not provide CIC services. Amber's parents unsuccessfully pursued a due process ruling to have the school train personnel to provide CIC services. In an action brought by the Tatros in federal district court, the court ruled in favor of the school district, holding that CIC was not required by the IDEA. The court held that CIC was a medical service that was excluded from the related services mandate. The Tatros filed an appeal with the U.S. Court of Appeals for the Fifth Circuit. The appellate court reversed the district court's ruling in holding that CIC was a supportive service, not a medical service, and thus had to be provided by the school. The Irving Independent School District then filed a petition of certiorari with the U.S. Supreme Court.

The Supreme Court decided to hear the case. The high court concluded that the requested CIC service was a supportive service within the legal parameters of IDEA because the services were necessary for Amber to attend school. Without the provision of CIC services, therefore, Amber could not benefit from her special education program. Further, the court ruled that CIC services were not subject to exclusion as a medical service. The Court agreed with the Department of Education's definition of school health services and medical services and found it to be a reasonable interpretation of congressional intent. The DOE had defined *related services* to include school health services provided by a qualified school nurse or other qualified person.

To assist lower courts and schools in determining whether a particular service was covered, the Court established three criteria: (a) the student must be IDEA eligible, (b) the service must be necessary to assist the child to benefit from special education, and (c) the service must be performed by a nurse or other qualified person (services performed by a physician are excluded).

In *Tatro,* the Supreme Court adopted a "bright-line test" for lower courts to follow when making related services decisions (Katsiyannis & Yell, 2000). A bright-line test is clearly stated and easy to follow (Thomas & Hawke, 1999). The bright-line that *Tatro* established was whether the services were provided by a physician. If the related services must be provided by a physician, the school district is not responsible for providing the services. However, if the services can be provided by a nonphysician, even if they are medical in nature, the school district is responsible for providing the services.

Despite the high court's ruling in *Tatro,* the controversy regarding school health services and medical services continued. In fact, a number of courts departed from the bright-line standard of *Tatro* and ruled that when numerous and complex health services were required for a particular student, they became medical in nature and were therefore not required under the IDEA. Thomas and Hawke (1999) referred to the standard developed by these courts as the "medical-services standard." That is, the administrative and medical complexity as well as the feasibility and cost of complex health services rendered them medical in nature. Appellate courts in other jurisdictions adopted the Supreme Court's bright-line test.

Because of the split in the circuit courts and the ongoing controversy on issues involving complex health services, it was inevitable that the Supreme Court would take a case on this issue. On March 3, 1999, the high court handed down a ruling in the case of *Cedar Rapids Community School District v. Garret F.* (1999; hereafter *Garret F.*). The case involved more complex and riskier procedures than those presented in *Tatro,* and the financial stakes were considerably higher. Garret Frey was paralyzed from a motorcycle accident when he was 4. He was ventilator dependent and could only breathe by use of an electric ventilator or with someone manually pumping an air bag attached to his tracheotomy tube. Garret also required tracheotomy supervision and suctioning, repositioning in his wheelchair, assistance with food and drink, ventilator checks, catheterization, and observations and assessments to determine if he was in respiratory distress or if he was experiencing autonomic hyperreflexia (i.e., increases in blood pressure and heart rate in response to anxiety or a full bladder). In his early school years, Garret's parents provided for his nursing care during the school day. Using funds from their insurance and proceeds from a settlement with the motorcycle company, a licensed practical nurse was hired to care for Garret's physical needs. When Garret was in middle school, his mother requested that the school district accept the financial responsibility for the physical care during the school day. School district officials refused the request, stating that they were not legally obligated to provide continuous nursing care. Garret's mother requested a due process hearing.

After hearing extensive testimony, Larry Bartlett, the administrative law judge (ALJ), issued a ruling that relied on the bright-line standard, in which he ordered the school district to pay for the services. The ALJ found that although Garrett was the only ventilator-dependent student in the district, most of the requested health services were already provided to other students. Whereas Garret needed a greater amount of complicated health care services than other students in special education, they were no more medical than the care in *Tatro*. Furthermore, the ALJ found that the distinction between health care services and medical services in the IDEA was that the former are provided by a qualified school nurse or other qualified person whereas the latter refers to services performed by a licensed physician. The ALJ, therefore, followed the bright-line standard. The school district appealed, and lost, in the district court and the U.S. Circuit Court of Appeals for the Eighth Circuit. The school district then appealed to the Supreme Court. The high court agreed with the lower courts that the requested services were related services because Garret could not attend school without them and that the services were not excluded as medical services. Therefore, the high court upheld the bright-line test established in *Tatro*. The Court acknowledged that the district may have legitimate concerns about the financial burden of providing the services Garret needs, but noted that its proposed cost-based standard as the sole test for determining the required services fell outside the Court's authority. Such a test would also challenge the IDEA's zero reject principle as Congress intended to open the doors of public education to all qualified children.

By reaffirming the bright-line test established in *Tatro,* the Supreme Court affirmed school districts' responsibility to provide any and all necessary health services to qualified students with disabilities irrespective of the intensity level or complexity. As long as the needed related service does not have to be provided by a physician, the service is considered a related service under the IDEA. This ruling also reaffirms the intent of Congress to ensure access to an appropriate education to all qualified students with disabilities and preserve the zero reject principle. The Court reasoned that this case was about whether meaningful access to the public schools would be assured, not the level of education that a school must finance once access is attained. Lower courts, such as in *Timothy W. v. Rochester (NH) School District* (1989), have also ruled on the necessity for school districts to provide FAPE to all qualified students with disabilities unconditionally and without exception. Without such a ruling, Garret F. would have not been able to access the education the school district provided.

Litigation and FAPE

The lack of a substantive definition of FAPE in the IDEA has led to frequent disagreements between parents and schools regarding what constitutes an appropriate education for a particular student. State and federal courts, therefore, have often been required to define FAPE (Osborne, 1992). This litigation is instructive. By understanding FAPE litigation schools can help ensure that they develop and implement appropriate special education programs for students with disabilities.

The FAPE litigation has evolved over the 30 years since the passage of the IDEA. Early court decisions set the standard of a FAPE as more than simply providing students access to education but less than the best possible educational program (Osborne, 1992). In *Springdale School District v. Grace* (1981), for example, the U.S. Court of Appeals for the Eighth Circuit held that FAPE did not require the state to provide the best education but instead required an appropriate education. The U.S. Court of Appeals for the Sixth Circuit, in *Age v. Bullitt County Public Schools* (1982), ruled that the existence of a better program did not make the school's proposed program inappropriate.

In 1982, a case from the U.S. Court of Appeals for the Second Circuit became the first special education case to be heard by the U.S. Supreme Court. In *Board of Education of the Hendrick Hudson School District v. Rowley* (hereafter *Rowley*), the high court considered the meaning of FAPE.

Hendrick Hudson School District v. Rowley, 1982

Rowley was the Supreme Court's first opportunity to interpret the FAPE mandate. The case involved the education of Amy Rowley, a student at the Furnace Woods School in the Hendrick Hudson Central School District. Amy was deaf and entitled to a FAPE under the IDEA. She had minimal residual hearing and was an excellent lipreader. The year prior to Amy's attendance at Furnace Woods, a meeting was held between her parents and school officials to determine future placement and services. A decision was made to place Amy in the regular kindergarten class to determine what supplemental services she might need. Several school personnel learned sign language, and a teletype machine was placed in the school office to facilitate communication between Amy and her parents, who were also deaf. A sign language interpreter was also present in the classroom. Following a trial period in the kindergarten placement, a decision was made that Amy would remain in the class, with the school providing a hearing aid. Amy successfully completed her kindergarten year.

As required by law, an IEP was prepared for Amy prior to her entry into first grade. Her IEP provided for education in a general education classroom, continued use of the hearing aid, instruction from a tutor for deaf children for an hour daily, and speech therapy three hours a week. The Rowleys requested a qualified sign language interpreter in all of Amy's academic classes. Because Amy's kindergarten interpreter believed that Amy did not need the services at that time, school officials concluded, after consulting with the school district's Committee on the Handicapped, that the interpreter was not necessary. The Rowleys then requested a due process hearing. The hearing officer agreed with the school district that the interpreter was not required by the IDEA, and the decision was affirmed on appeal by the New York Commissioner of Education. The Rowleys brought an action in federal district court, claiming that the district's refusal to provide a sign language interpreter denied Amy a FAPE.

The district court found Amy to be a well-adjusted child who was doing better than the average child. Nevertheless, the court ruled that Amy was not learning as much as she could without her handicap. The disparity between Amy's actual achievement and her potential convinced the district court that Amy had been denied a FAPE, which the court defined as "an opportunity to achieve [her] full potential commensurate with the opportunity provided to other children" (*Rowley,* p. 534). Moreover, because FAPE requirements were unclear, the court stated that the responsibility for determining a FAPE had been left to the federal courts.

The U.S. Court of Appeals for the Second Circuit, in a divided decision, affirmed the lower court's ruling. The U.S. Supreme Court granted certiorari to the Board of Education's appeal. The high court considered two questions: What is a FAPE, and what is the role of state and federal courts in reviewing special education decisions?

Justice Rehnquist, writing for the majority, stated that a FAPE consisted of educational instruction designed to meet the unique needs of a student with disabilities, supported by such services as needed to permit the student to *benefit* from instruction. The high court noted that the IDEA required that these educational services be provided at public expense, meet state standards, and comport with the student's IEP. Therefore, if individualized instruction allowed the child to benefit from educational services and was provided in conformity with other requirements of the law, the student was receiving a FAPE. The court noted that any substantive standard prescribing the level of education to be accorded students with disabilities was conspicuously missing from the language of the IDEA.

According to the Supreme Court, Congress's primary objective in passing the law was to make public education available to students with disabilities. Therefore, "the intent of the Act was more to open the door of public education to handicapped children on appropriate terms than to guarantee any particular level of education once inside" (*Rowley,* p. 192). The Court disagreed with the Rowleys' contention that the goal of the IDEA was to provide each student with disabilities with an equal educational opportunity. The Court stated that

> the educational opportunities provided by our public school systems undoubtedly differ from student to student, depending upon a myriad of factors that might affect a particular student's ability to assimilate information presented in the classroom. The requirement that states provide "equal" educational opportunities would thus seem to present an entirely unworkable standard requiring impossible measurements and comparisons. Similarly, furnishing handicapped children with only such services as are available to nonhandicapped children would in all probability fall short of the statutory requirement of "free appropriate public education"; to require, on the other hand, the furnishing of every special service necessary to maximize each handicapped child's potential is, we think, further than Congress intended to go. (pp. 198–199)

The high court, however, held that the education to which the IDEA provided access had to be "sufficient to confer some educational benefit upon the handicapped child" (p. 200). Therefore, the purpose of FAPE was to provide students with disabilities a "basic floor of opportunity" consisting of access to specialized instruction and related services individually designed to confer "educational benefit." Moreover, the high court specifically rejected the argument that school districts were required to provide the best possible education to students with disabilities (Wenkart, 2000).

The Rowley Standard

The Supreme Court developed a two-part test to be used by courts in determining if a school has met its obligations under the IDEA to provide a FAPE. "First, has the [school] complied with the procedures of the Act? And second, is the individualized education program developed through the Act's procedures reasonably calculated to enable the child to receive educational benefits?" (*Rowley*, pp. 206–207). If these requirements are met, a school has complied with FAPE requirements. The court cautioned the lower courts, however, that they were not establishing *any one test* for determining the adequacy of educational benefits.

Applying the two-part test to the *Rowley* case, the Supreme Court found that the school district had complied with the procedures of the IDEA, and Amy had received an appropriate education because she was performing better than many children in her class and was advancing easily from grade to grade. In a footnote, the high court noted that the decision was a narrow one and that it should not be read too broadly. The Court stated that the ruling should not be interpreted to mean that every student with a disability who was advancing from grade to grade in a regular school was automatically receiving a FAPE. Rather, the FAPE standard can only be arrived at through a multifactorial evaluation conducted on a case-by-case basis. The high court also noted that in this case the sign language interpreter was not required to provide a FAPE to Amy Rowley. The decisions of the district and circuit court were reversed.

The Supreme Court also addressed the rule of the courts in determining whether a school had provided a FAPE to a student. Regarding this role, Rehnquist wrote that

> courts must be careful to avoid imposing their view of preferable educational methods upon the states. The primary responsibility for formulating the education to be accorded a handicapped child, and for choosing the educational method most suitable to the child's needs, was left by the Act to state and local educational agencies in cooperation with the parents or guardian of the child. (*Rowley*, p. 207)

In special education cases involving FAPE, therefore, the courts' role is (a) to determine if the procedural requirements are being met; (b) to examine the substantive requirements of FAPE; and (c) to determine if the special education is providing educational benefit. In making this determination, courts should not substitute their judgments for the judgments of educators, because courts lack the "specialized knowledge and experience necessary to resolve persistent and difficult questions of educational policy" (*San Antonio ISD v. Rodriquez*, 1973, p. 42).

The Supreme Court ruled that students with disabilities do not have an enforceable right to the best possible education or an education that allows them to achieve their maximum potential. Rather, they are entitled to an education that is reasonably calculated to confer educational benefit.

In a 1993 decision in *Doe v. Board of Education of Tullahoma Schools*, the Supreme Court used an interesting metaphor to drive this point home. According to the court, the IDEA does not require school districts to provide the educational equivalent of a Cadillac to every eligible student with disabilities, but school districts are required to provide the educational equivalent of a serviceable Chevrolet to every student.

Post-Rowley Litigation

The first principle of the *Rowley* test establishes the importance of adherence to the procedural aspects of a FAPE. Clearly, a court could rule that a school district has denied a FAPE if the district has not adhered to the procedural safeguards in the IDEA. The second principle of the *Rowley* test is substantive. The principle requires courts to determine whether the IEP developed by the school is reasonably calculated to enable the child to receive educational benefits.

Procedural Violations of FAPE.   If a school fails to adhere to the required procedural mechanisms, and the failure results in harm to the student, the school could be found to be denying a FAPE on procedural grounds (Tucker & Goldstein, 1992). A number of post-*Rowley* decisions have ruled that, based on procedural violations alone, schools have denied a FAPE. In *W.G. v. Board of Trustees* (1992), the U.S. Court of Appeals for the Ninth Circuit ruled a school that had failed to include the classroom teacher or representative of a private school in developing an IEP had denied a FAPE to a student with disabilities. The court also noted, however, that procedural violations do not automatically require a finding of a denial of a FAPE. In *Tice v. Botetourt County School Board* (1990), the U.S. Court of Appeals for the Fourth Circuit ruled that a school had denied a FAPE because of a 6-month delay in evaluating a child and developing an IEP. Two decisions by the U.S. Court of Appeals for the Fourth Circuit also ruled that schools had denied students with disabilities a FAPE because of procedural violations. In *Spielberg v. Henrico County Public Schools* (1988), the school's determination to change a student's placement prior to developing an IEP violated the parents' right to participate in the development of the IEP and, therefore, violated the IDEA. In *Hall v. Vance County Board of Education* (1985), a school was found to have denied a FAPE because of its repeated failure to notify parents of their rights under IDEA.

Other post-*Rowley* rulings, however, have held that technical violations of the IDEA may not violate the FAPE requirement of the IDEA if they result in no harm to the student's education. For example, in *Doe v. Alabama Department of Education* (1990), the U.S. Court of Appeals for the Eleventh Circuit held that, because the parents had participated fully in the IEP process, a school's technical violation in failing to notify parents of their rights did not warrant relief. In *Doe v. Defendant 1* (1990), the U.S. Court of Appeals for the Sixth Circuit ruled that the failure of school officials to include a student's present level of educational performance and appropriate criteria for determining achievement of objectives did not invalidate the IEP when the parents were aware of this information. The school's procedural violations of inadequately notifying the parents of refusal to reimburse private tuition and failure to perform the 3-year evaluation in a timely manner were harmless errors because the parents had actual notice and their child's progress had not been harmed.

The Individuals with Disabilities Education Improvement Act of 2004 made it more difficult for attorneys to rely on procedural violations to win a case. This is because the law directs hearing officers to rule primarily on substantive grounds. The only exception is when procedural violations have impeded a student's right to a free appropriate public education, significantly impeded the parent's participation in the decision-making process, or deprived a student of educational benefits (§615(f)(3)(E)). The crucial determinant in ruling a procedural violation a denial of FAPE is the degree of harm caused to the student's educational program. Procedural violations that have not caused significant difficulties in the delivery of a special education have not resulted in adverse court rulings in the past, and the language in IDEA 2004 ensures that this trend will continue.

Substantive Violations of FAPE.   The second principle of the *Rowley* test—the determination of whether the IEP was reasonably calculated to enable a student to receive educational benefits—has proven to be a more problematic determination than the first principle. Early post-*Rowley* rulings appeared to indicate that an IEP was appropriate if the student obtained some educational benefit (Osborne, 1992). In these early rulings, the courts seemingly regarded IEPs as appropriate if a school was able to show that the IEP was developed to provide some educational benefit, no matter how minimal it might be. Cases that followed this line of judicial reasoning include *Doe v. Lawson* (1984), *Karl v. Board of Education* (1984), and *Manual R. v. Ambach* (1986). Recent decisions, however, have indicated that minimal or trivial benefit may not be sufficient and that special education services must confer meaningful benefit.

The U.S. Court of Appeals for the Fourth Circuit, in *Hall v. Vance County Board of Education* (1985), held that the *Rowley* decision required courts to examine the IEP to determine what substantive standards meet the second principle of the *Rowley* test. Additionally, the court cited *Rowley* as stating that this could only be accomplished on a case-by-case basis. The appeals court affirmed the district court's ruling that because the plaintiff, who had a learning disability, had made no educational progress in the public school, and because the IEP was inadequate, the school district had to reimburse the parents for private school tuition. The court noted that Congress did not intend schools to offer educational programs that produce only trivial academic advancement.

In *Carter v. Florence County School District Four* (1991), the U.S. Court of Appeals for the Fourth Circuit affirmed a district court's ruling that the school district's IEP had failed to satisfy the FAPE requirement of the IDEA. The IEP, which contained annual reading goals of 4 months' growth over a school year, did not, according to the district and circuit courts, represent meaningful growth, even if the goals were achieved. The case was later heard by the U.S. Supreme Court on a different issue. In *J.C. v. Central Regional School District* (1996), the U.S. Court of Appeals for the Third Circuit ruled that school districts must provide more than a de minimus or trivial education, and that districts are responsible for the adequacy of the IEP. In this case, the IEP developed for a student with severe disabilities failed to address important educational needs. Furthermore, the student had made little progress in the current program and had actually regressed in some areas.

The courts have not provided a precise definition to follow when determining whether the education offered is meaningful or trivial. This lack of precision appears appropriate because what constitutes a meaningful education to particular students can only be ascertained on a case-by-case basis. There can be no bright-line formula, no clear standard, that will apply to all students. It is clear that courts, when determining if the substantive requirements of a FAPE have been met, will look to the school's IEP to determine if a meaningful education designed to confer benefit has been provided.

Polk v. Central Susquehanna Intermediate Unit 16 (1988).   The U.S. Court of Appeals for the Third Circuit provided a thorough discussion of *Rowley* and the IDEA's requirement to provide a "meaningful" education in *Polk v. Central Susquehanna Intermediate Unit 16* (1988). In the decision, the court noted that because *Rowley* involved a student who did very well in the general education class, the high court was able to avoid the substantive second principle of the *Rowley* test and concentrate on the procedural principle. In other words, because Amy Rowley was an excellent student, the court really only had to examine the procedures the district followed. Clearly she must have been receiving an appropriate education if she was one of the top students in her class and had been advanced to the next grade. In the case before the Third Circuit Court, however, the substantive question of how much benefit was required to meet the "meaningful" standard in educating the plaintiff, Christopher Polk, was inescapable.

Christopher Polk was a 14-year-old with severe mental and physical disabilities. The severity of his disabilities necessitated physical therapy, but the school's IEP provided only consultative services of a physical therapist. Christopher's parents brought action under the IDEA (then the EAHCA), claiming that the school had failed to provide an appropriate education. A federal district court held for the school district, finding that the *Rowley* standard held that the conferral of any degree of educational benefit, no matter how small, could qualify as an appropriate education. The appellate court reversed the district court, declaring that just as

> Congress did not write a blank check, neither did it anticipate that states would engage in the idle gesture of providing special education designed to confer only trivial benefit. . . . Congress intended to afford children with special needs an education that would confer meaningful benefit. (*Polk*, p. 184)

The court also stated that the type of education that constitutes a meaningful education can only be determined in the light of a student's potential. Courts in *Board of Education v. Diamond* (1986), *Doe v. Smith* (1988), and *Hall v. Vance County Board of Education* (1985) all reached similar conclusions.

Cypress-Fairbanks Independent School District v. Michael F. (1997).   In this case the parents of Michael F. had requested an impartial due process hearing, claiming that the school had denied their son an appropriate education under the IDEA. The hearing officer ruled in favor of the parents. The school district appealed to federal district court. The district court reversed the decision of the hearing officer and ruled in favor of the school district. The district court based its decision on a four-part test devised by an expert witness in the case. The four factors were:

1. Was the program individualized on the basis of the student's assessment and performance?
2. Was the program delivered in the least restrictive environment?
3. Were the services provided in a coordinated and collaborative manner by key stakeholders?
4. Were positive academic and nonacademic benefits demonstrated?

The parents appealed the decision to the U.S. Court of Appeals for the Fifth Circuit. Using the four factors, the court ruled that the school district had (a) conducted a thorough assessment of Michael F., (b) developed an appropriate program tailored to his individual needs, (c) implemented the IEP as written, and (d) educated Michael in the least restrictive environment. The court ruled that Michael F. had received an appropriate education, thus affirming the decision of the lower court.

Houston Independent School District v. Bobby R. (2000).   The U.S. Court of Appeals for the Fifth Circuit in *Houston Independent School District v. Bobby R.* (2000) ruled that a student with learning disabilities received an appropriate education because the school had data to show that the student had received academic and nonacademic benefit. Moreover, the circuit adopted the four-part test used by the circuit court in *Cypress-Fairbanks*. To determine if academic benefits had been demonstrated, the court examined the school's testing data. Finding that Bobby's test scores had shown a good rate of improvement, even though it was not commensurate with his peers in general education, the court held that the student's progress should be measured in relation to his own degree of improvement rather than in relation to his nondisabled peers. The court ruled, therefore, that Bobby's IEP was reasonably calculated to provide him with meaningful educational benefit, thus meeting the requirements of the IDEA.

Methodology and FAPE

When is a particular methodology necessary to provide a FAPE? Moreover, who chooses what methodology schools will use when they educate children and youth with disabilities? This answer seemingly was answered in the *Rowley* decision when the Supreme Court asserted that methodological decisions were best addressed by educational authorities.

The methodology issue has been examined by several courts. In these cases, the courts have examined the question of the school's choice of teaching methodologies in regards to FAPE. The plaintiffs in three cases—*Boughham v. Town of Yarmouth* (1993; hereafter *Boughham*), *Lachman v. Illinois State Board of Education* (1988; hereafter *Lachman*), and *Peterson v. Hastings Public Schools* (1993; hereafter

Peterson)—brought actions against school districts, alleging a denial of a FAPE because the school districts had chosen particular educational methodologies the parents opposed. The school districts prevailed in all three cases.

The court in the *Lachman* decision stated that parents have no power under the IDEA to compel schools to choose a particular methodology over another. Similarly, the court in *Peterson* held that in a methodology case the court would still only review the second principle of the *Rowley* test. The court stated that if the IEP developed by the school is reasonably calculated to provide educational benefits to the student, the courts can require no more. Finally, the *Boughham* court, in holding for the school district, cited the Supreme Court's admonition in *Rowley* that courts should not get involved in making decisions about educational theory and methodology and should take care to avoid imposing their view of preferential educational methods.

In *Wall v. Mattituck-Cutchogue School District* (1996), the parents of an elementary student with learning disabilities brought an action against a school district in New York. The parents wanted their child taught reading using the Orton-Gillingham instructional procedure. The student, who was educated in a public school's self-contained special education classroom, was unilaterally placed in a private school that used the reading procedure. At a hearing, the parents did not challenge the appropriateness of the IEP; rather, they contested the school district's failure to offer the Orton-Gillingham program. The hearing officer found that the school district's program was appropriate. The parents appealed to federal district court. The court, finding that the student had made progress in the school district's program, affirmed the ruling for the school district.

In a federal district court in California, in a case called *Adams v. Hansen* (1985; hereafter *Adams*), the court found that the plaintiff, a student with "dyslexia," had shown little progress in a public school program. The court found that the child had progressed 4 months in total reading achievement and 8 months in math achievement in 2 years of public school instruction. Consequently, the student's mother had placed him in a private school. Finding that the student did not make sufficient academic progress in his 2 years in public school, but did so in the private school, the court ruled that the mother was entitled to reimbursement from the school district for tuition and travel expenses.

According to Huefner (1991), the court could have ended its analysis at this point. However, it went on to consider the educational methodology offered in the private school as opposed to the public school's educational methods. The court was impressed by testimony that the student had a "specific language disability [involving] all three learning modalities—auditory, visual, and sensory-motor" (*Adams*, p. 863)—but no relative strengths and weakness in the three modalities. Because of this "lack of relative strength" the court stated that the student needed an intensive "structured sequential simultaneous multi-sensory approach" (p. 864) that could not be provided in the public school. The *Adams* case, which was not appealed, seemingly went beyond the scope of judicial review as set forth in *Rowley*.

The cases reviewed seem to offer little encouragement to plaintiffs seeking to have the courts require schools to use favored educational procedures or methodologies. As held by the Supreme Court in *Rowley*, "once a court determines that the requirements of the [IDEA] have been met, questions of methodology are thus left for resolution by the states" (p. 207). The *Adams* case, however, indicates that courts may find it difficult to ignore comparisons between a public school's methodology and one used in a private school if only the latter results in significant progress. Huefner (1991) contended that in such situations, if a student was making meaningful progress in the public school's program, the courts would uphold the methodology even if it had been less effective than the alternative methodology.

FAPE and Lovaas Therapy

Several treatment cases have been brought by parents of children with autism to obtain reimbursement for individual programs using Lovaas treatment. Many of the rulings in these cases have seemed to run counter to the Rowley admonition that methodology is best left to the educational authorities

These cases involve a treatment program that was developed by Dr. O. Ivar Lovaas in the early 1960s. Lovaas viewed autism as a constellation of behavioral deficits and excesses and developed a method of working with young children with autism that consisted of highly structured lessons to be taught in one-to-one training formats by trained therapists. The system, based on the principles of applied behavior analysis, was an intensive program that focused on changing a child's individual behavior excesses and deficits. The training is targeted toward preschoolers, preferably younger than 3, and can take as long as 2 or 3 years. It requires 40 hours per week of intensive one-to-one work with the child and usually is initially conducted in the child's home. Lovaas treatment is expensive, generally ranging from $12,000 to $20,000 a year.

In recent years many school districts have been confronted by parental demands to provide Lovaas treatment for the children, often in their homes or to reimburse parents for the expenses they incur as a result of securing the therapy (Mandlawitz, 1996). Several of these cases have reached the due process level, and a few have been decided in the courts.

A few administrative rulings by the state educational agencies (SEAs) of Maryland (*Frederick County Public Schools*, 1995), Connecticut (*In re Child with Disabilities*, 1995), and North Carolina (*Sherman v. Pitt County Board of Education*, 1995) awarded reimbursement for parents who had provided Lovaas programming in their homes. In all three cases the schools were found to have offered inappropriate programming, while the Lovaas educational programming was held to be appropriate.

In an SEA decision, an administrative law judge determined that a school district's educational program for a student with autism was inappropriate and ordered the district to reimburse the parents for a program of home-based Lovaas therapy and rewrite the student's IEP (*Independent School District No. 318*, 1996). The district's program consisted of 8 hours per week of instruction in a classroom with a low student-teacher ratio, speech and language therapy, and occupational therapy. The home-based program consisted of 35 hours per week of Lovaas programming. The school district incorporated aspects of the Lovaas program in the school program and agreed to teach the student sign language. Additionally, the student was placed in a general education kindergarten with a full-time aide. The district, however, refused to have its teachers and staff trained in the Lovaas method and to incorporate the method into the student's educational program, as the parents requested. The parents requested a due process hearing and reimbursement for the Lovaas programming. The hearing officer ruled for the parents. The hearing officer determined that the school's IEP was not appropriate because it failed to provide any educational benefit. The parents' home-based program, however, was appropriate. The ruling, in addition to requiring that the parents be reimbursed for the cost of Lovaas training, ordered the school to have the aide trained in the Lovaas method, and also ordered that the IEP be rewritten to include Lovaas programming, monthly consultation with Lovaas consultants, computer training, and extended school year services.

A few court cases have also addressed Lovaas treatment and FAPE. In *Delaware County Intermediate Unit #25 v. Martin and Melinda K.* (1993), a federal district court ruled that a school-provided program for children with autism was inappropriate. The school had offered a 10-hour-a-week program based on the principles of the TEACCH method of educating students with autism, developed at the University of North Carolina by Dr. Eric Shopler. According to the court, the school district's program was inappropriate because it offered only 10 hours per week of TEACCH therapy, even though the program developers recommended 30 hours per week. The court also found that the Lovaas program was appropriate and ordered that the school reimburse the parents for program costs and expenditures and pay for an additional year of the Lovaas program. The court noted that if the school district had increased the TEACCH program's intensity to recommended levels and provided a mainstreaming component to the program, the court would have been faced with a battle between the TEACCH and Lovaas programs, "a contest between two teaching methodologies, either of which would be appropriate under the IDEA. At that point, the Court will yield to the educational agency" (p. 1212).

In *Union City School District v. Smith* (1994), the U.S. Court of Appeals for the Ninth Circuit upheld a lower court ruling that the Union City School District had failed to provide a FAPE to a child with autism. The school district had placed the child in a classroom for students with communications disabilities with supplemental behavioral therapy counseling, even though the district had a program for children with autism. The parents removed their child from the public school program and placed him in a program at Lovaas's clinic at the University of California at Los Angeles. The court awarded the parents reimbursement for tuition and travel expenses. In its decision, the appellate court noted that had the school offered an appropriate special education in the program for autistic youngsters, the parents would not have won reimbursement.

A federal district court in New York awarded the parents of a child with autism reimbursement for 40 hours a week of Lovaas training weekly in *Malkentzos v. DeBuono* (1996). The case involved a 3-year-old child with autism. The New York Department of Health (DOH) had written an individualized family services plan (IFSP) that provided the child with 23 hours of structured play activities without a behavioral therapy component. The child's parents requested that the IFSP be revised to include 40 hours of weekly Lovaas programming. The DOH denied the request, stating that there was a lack of certified behavioral therapists. The parents provided the programming at their own expense and requested a due process hearing to challenge the appropriateness of the IFSP. The hearing officer ruled in favor of the DOH, citing a shortage of qualified personnel to provide additional behavioral programming. The federal district court reversed the hearing officer's decision, holding that the New York DOH had failed to provide a FAPE under the IDEA. The court awarded the parents reimbursement for the amount expended in providing the Lovaas treatment and ordered the state to either fund continued training for 40 hours per week or reimburse the parents for securing the programming. Noting that the IDEA did not require that the DOH provide any particular program, provide the best possible program, or maximize the potential of the child, the court held that the IFSP had not adequately addressed the plaintiff's autism and was therefore inappropriate. The court found that the parents had provided convincing evidence that the DOH program was not reasonably calculated to provide educational benefit and that the child might have suffered imminent damage under the plan. The court also cited the Supreme Court's decision in *Florence County School District Four v. Carter* (1993) in holding that the parents were not required, as a prerequisite to being reimbursed, to use certified therapists for the Lovaas programming. The case was appealed to the U.S. Court of Appeals for the Second Circuit. The circuit court held that the district court's order of reimbursement for the private therapy and prospective relief were improper. Because the child had aged out from Part H (now Part C) of the IDEA and was no longer eligible for services, the court declared the claim moot. That is, the case was legally insignificant because the court's decision would no longer have any practical effect on the controversy.

Despite the fact that the Lovaas programming prevailed in the decisions reviewed, the three courts noted that it was because the Lovaas programs were appropriate while the schools' programming was inappropriate. The states' programming was found to be inappropriate for various reasons, including (a) lack of intensity of the programming, (b) inappropriate focus of the programs, and (c) lack of individualization.

Counter to the court decisions favoring Lovaas treatment, SEAs have denied parents reimbursement for Lovaas programming when the school offered appropriate programming. This indicates that in contests of two appropriate programs, the SEA will prevail (*Central Susquehanna Intermediate Unit 16,* 1995; *Chester County Intermediate Unit 23,* 1995; *Fairfax County Public Schools,* 1995; *Tuscaloosa County Board of Education,* 1994).

The case law on the methodology issue is clear: As long as the school offers an appropriate program, the choice of educational methodology is up to the school district. In situations involving Lovaas therapy, however, the rulings indicate that when a school district's programming does not show results and is compared with the Lovaas method, which does collect evidence of progress, it is likely that judges will favor the Lovaas programming. To prevail in such situations, school districts need to provide a FAPE that results in meaningful educational benefit and must have formative evaluation data to show that a student is making meaningful educational progress in the school's programming (Yell & Drasgow, 2000).

Extended School Year and FAPE

The IDEA does not specifically address the provision of special education programs that extend beyond the traditional school year of approximately 180 school days. The regulations written in 1999 define an *extended school year* (ESY) as special education and related services provided to a student with a disability beyond the normal school year FAPE (IDEA Regulations, 34 C.F.R. § 300.309). The regulations also require that a school district must ensure that ESY services are available as necessary if an IEP team determines, on an individual basis, that these services are needed to provide a FAPE. Furthermore, the regulations prohibit school districts from limiting extended school year services to particular categories of disability or unilaterally limit the type, amount, or duration of these services

The requirement that school districts provide ESY when necessary to provide a FAPE originated with the courts. In a number of cases, parents and advocates contended that extended breaks in educational programming could result in severe regression of skills and subsequent failure to recoup lost skills within a reasonable period of time. When self-sufficiency skills are lost, ESY services may be needed to provide a FAPE. ESY services are only required when the lack of such a program will result in denial of a FAPE. ESY is not, therefore, required for all students with disabilities. When found to be necessary, these services must be provided at no cost to the families. Additionally, ESY services must be offered, when necessary, even if the school district does not ordinarily provide summer school programming or other educational services outside of the regular school year (Gorn, 1996). The determination of whether a student with disabilities must be provided with ESY programming must be made on an individual basis.

The courts have clearly stated that if ESY services are required to ensure the provision of a FAPE, they must be provided (*Alamo Heights Independent School District v. State Board of Education,* 1986; *Cordrey v. Euckert,* 1990). SEA and local educational agency (LEA) policies that provide only the traditional number of school days have consistently been struck down by the courts (e.g., *Alamo Heights ISD v. Board of Education,* 1986; *Armstrong v. Kline,* 1979; *Bales v. Clark,* 1981; *Battle v. Commonwealth of Pennsylvania,* 1980; *Cordrey v. Euckert,* 1990; *Crawford v. Pittman,* 1983; *Georgia ARC v. McDaniel,* 1983; *Johnson v. Independent School District No. 4,* 1990; *Yaris v. Special School District of St. Louis County,* 1984). These policies have been overturned because the inflexibility of the traditional school year prohibits consideration of the rights of students to an individualized education or because the ESY services were determined to be necessary for students to receive a FAPE.

Many courts have based their decisions on the regression/recoupment problem (Boomer & Garrison-Harrell, 1995; Osborne, 1995; Tucker & Goldstein, 1992). In these cases, the students had regressed to such a degree on important skills during an extended break in educational programming that it took an inordinate amount of time to recoup the lost skills. Therefore, the student requires an ESY program to avoid regression. Courts have held that regression may be in a number of areas, including academics, emotional or behavioral status, physical skills, self-help skills, or communication (*Cremeans v. Fairland Local School District*, 1993; *Holmes v. Sobol*, 1991; *Johnson v. Lancaster-Lebanon Intermediate Unit 13*, 1991). Very young children (i.e., birth to 3 years of age), covered under Part C, must also receive ESY services if needed to provide a FAPE. Additionally, in some situations in which a student with a severe disability regresses in skills quickly when there is a break in services, ESY services have been awarded not only for summer break, but for shorter breaks during the school year as well (Pitasky, 2000).

In the ESY cases, school districts have not been ordered to provide these services because students would benefit from them but because they would be harmed by an interruption of special education services. It is important, however, that school districts be flexible in making ESY decisions and not rely solely on regression/recoupment considerations (Gorn, 1996). That is, criteria for determining extended school year should take into account individual factors and particular circumstances that may merit inclusion in an ESY program in addition to regression/recoupment.

In *Johnson v. Independent School District No. 4* (1990), the U.S. Court of Appeals for the Tenth Circuit gave some direction to school districts in making ESY determinations. According to the court, factors involved in determining if ESY is necessary to provide a FAPE may include the degree of impairment, the ability of parents to provide educational structure in the home, the availability of resources, a determination whether the program is extraordinary or necessary, the student's skill level, and areas of the curriculum in which the child needs continuous attention. The court also noted that in using the regression/recoupment analysis, schools "should proceed by applying not only retrospective data, such as past regression and rate of recoupment, but also include predictive data, based on the opinion of professionals in consultation with the child's parents" (p. 1028).

Students who are determined to have disabilities under Section 504 but not under the IDEA must also be provided ESY services if it is a necessary element to a FAPE. A number of OCR rulings have indicated that ESY programming can be required under Section 504 (*Baltimore (MD) City Public Schools*, 1986; *Clark City (NV) School District*, 1989).

Katsiyannis (1991) recommends that SEAs and schools develop ESY policies. Included in his recommendations for developing ESY policies are the following: (a) clearly define the ESY program and objectives; (b) develop eligibility criteria; (c) generate a systematic referral process; and (d) construct a detailed plan for monitoring and data collection. He also suggests that LEAs provide inservice training on ESY programming for all administrators and teachers.

Determining Student Placement and FAPE

One of the critical determinations in providing a FAPE to students with disabilities is placement, which refers to the setting in which a FAPE will be delivered. Placement, however, refers to more than just the setting. It also includes factors such as (a) facilities, (b) equipment, (c) location, and (d) personnel required to deliver the special education and related services specified in an IEP (*Weil v. Board of Elementary and Secondary Education,* 1991). The placement decision must be made by a group of knowledgeable persons, typically the IEP team. School districts must ensure that parents take part in all placement decisions. Parents must be involved in the entire decision-making process. Additionally, the parents must be provided with all the necessary information needed to help them make an informed decision. School officials, therefore, cannot make a placement decision unilaterally (Lake, 2002). Prior to deciding on a student's placement, the student must have been evaluated and his or her IEP developed.

Determining Placement

To choose the setting in which a student will be placed, IEP team members must draw on a variety of informational sources, including aptitude and achievement tests, teacher recommendations, physical condition, social or cultural background, and adaptive behavior, to provide the information needed to make the determination (IDEA Regulations, 34 C.F.R. § 300.533(a)(1)). Additionally, the information that the team uses should be documented (IDEA Regulations, 34 C.F.R. § 300.533(a)(2)). According to OSEP, no single factor should dominate decision making regarding placement; rather, all factors are to be considered equally (OSEP Policy Letter, 1994).

One such factor is parental preference regarding their child's placement. Although parental preference is an important consideration in the decision, according to the Office of Special Education and Related Services (OSERS), it is not the most important factor (*Letter to Burton,* 1991). The U.S. Court of Appeals for the Seventh Circuit, in *Board of Education of Community Consolidated School District No. 21 v. Illinois State Board of Education* (1991), held that a court may consider parental hostility as a factor in making placement decisions. In this case the parents had objected with such hostility to the school's proposed placement that the court found that the proposed placement had been undermined. The lower court had held that the parents of a student with behavioral disorders had essentially "poisoned" the proposed placement in the mind of the youngster, thereby assuring failure in that setting. The court, therefore, ruled that the school district would be violating the IDEA by implementing a program that would not benefit the student. The appellate court affirmed the lower court's decision in a 2 to 1 ruling.

The circuit court applied the *Rowley* test to the case. The court stated that the school had met the procedural principle but had not provided a FAPE because by not considering the negative effects of parental hostility, the school had failed to propose an education reasonably calculated to benefit the student. The dissenting judge stated that parental hostility to the proposed placement was not an appropriate factor to consider in applying the *Rowley* test and that the school district had fully satisfied the requirements of *Rowley.* According to the dissent, there was not the slightest evidence that the school district's proposed placement would not have provided educational benefit; further, the lower court's decision had improperly surrendered the school's educational authority to the parents.

The decision was appealed to the U.S. Supreme Court, which decided not to hear the case. Although this decision was met with fears that the circuit court had given parents the absolute right to dictate the educational program for their child, Zirkel (1992) contends that the majority decision may not spread widely beyond the Seventh Circuit. According to Zirkel, the dissent was strong and may be viewed as the correct decision by many. In addition, the majority decision held that parental hostility was a factor to consider, but not the only factor.

Placement Factors

When an IEP team makes a placement decision, it must consider three important factors. First, the IEP team must make the placement decision based on a student's IEP (IDEA Regulations, 34 C.F.R. § 300.552(a)(2)). Placement decisions can only be made after the IEP has been developed and in accordance with its terms (Appendix A to 34 C.F.R., Part 300, Question 14). Thus, a student's placement cannot be determined prior to writing his or her IEP. Only after the IEP has been written can the team determine where a particular student's needs can be met (Gorn, 1996, Lake, 2002). In fact, in *Spielberg v. Henrico County Public Schools* (1988), a decision to place a student prior to developing the IEP was held to be a violation of the IDEA. Placing a student in a particular setting prior to determining the student's program, therefore, would be putting placement ahead of his or her individual educational needs. According to Lake (2002) such a decision would be a serious mistake that may lead to a denial of a FAPE. The IEP is often developed and the placement determined in the same team meeting; therefore, the IEP and placement decision are actually two separate components of the special education decision-making process.

Second, a student's educational placement must be determined at least annually (IDEA Regulations, 34 C.F.R. § 300.552(a)(1)). This means that the IEP, including the student's placement, should be reviewed at least once a year. Either the parents or school personnel may request a placement review more frequently than annually if necessary.

Third, the placement must be made in conformity with the least restrictive environment (LRE) requirement of the IDEA (IDEA Regulations, 34 C.F.R. § 300.533(a)(4)). According to the LRE requirement, a student must be educated to the maximum extent appropriate with students without disabilities. Removal of the student from the general education environment occurs only when education in general education classes with the use of supplementary aids and services cannot be achieved satisfactorily (IDEA Regulations, 34 C.F.R. § 300.550). To ensure that the LRE mandate is met, school districts are required to ensure the availability of a continuum of alternative placements from which to choose the LRE (IDEA Regulations, 34 C.F.R. § 300.551).

The FAPE and LRE requirements of the IDEA are interrelated. LRE refers to the relative restrictiveness of the setting in which a student with disabilities is educated. The preferred environment is as close to the general education environment as is appropriate. Depending on what special education services an IEP team determines to be required for students to receive a FAPE, however, the LRE may be a more restrictive setting than the general education classroom. For example, a team could decide that a special school is the least restrictive and appropriate placement for a student. (See Chapter 12 for elaborations on the LRE requirements.)

In addition, the placement should be as close to home as possible. Unless otherwise indicated in the IEP, students should be placed in schools they would be attending if they did not have a disability. This is not an absolute right so much as it is a preference. If placements in home schools will not provide a FAPE, schools may place students in more distant schools (*Hudson v. Bloomfield Hills School District*, 1995).

Schools cannot unilaterally change students' placements. Placement decisions must be based on an existing IEP, so any change of placement must be supported either by that IEP or by a new IEP. If the school determines that a change in placement is necessary, the parents must be notified (IDEA Regulations, 34 C.F.R. § 300.504(a)(1)) and be included in the decision-making process.

Graduation and FAPE

A student is no longer eligible for a FAPE under the IDEA when (a) he or she reaches the maximum age to receive services under the IDEA (usually 21 years old), or (b) he or she graduates from high school with a regular diploma, whichever comes first (Pitasky, 2000). When students are no longer eligible for a FAPE, the school district's obligation to them ends. When students graduate with a graduation certificate, a certificate of attendance, or a special education diploma, rather than a regular diploma, they remain eligible to receive special education services (IDEA Regulations, 34 C.F.R. § 300.122(a)(3)(i)(ii)) and are entitled to receive a FAPE until they age out of IDEA eligibility.

Before a student in special education can properly graduate, the student's IEP team should meet to determine if the student is ready to graduate. Several factors must be determined. First, the student must have achieved his or her IEP goals. It should be noted that if a student has met the school's regular high school graduation criteria, the school can graduate the student even if he or she hasn't met the IEP goals. However, if a student has met his or her IEP goals but not the graduation requirements, a school district would not be required to award the student a diploma. If a student has graduated but has not achieved the IEP goals, however, the student may claim that he or she did not receive a FAPE and is entitled to receive compensatory educational services. Second, the parent must receive a written notice because graduation is a change in placement and the procedural safeguards of the IDEA apply. Third, although the IEP team is not required to conduct an evaluation of the student prior to his or her graduation with a regular diploma and termination from IDEA services, the IDEA 2004 requires that the IEP team provide the student with a summary of his or her academic achievement and functional performance. This summary must include recommendations on how to assist the student to meet his or her postsecondary goals (IDEA 20 U.S.C. § 1414(c)(5)). According to Richards and Martin (2005), the rationale for this section is to provide practical recommendations to help a student with future employment, additional training, or postsecondary schooling.

Readers should note that graduation requirements are determined solely by the state and the school district. Nevertheless, the IEP plays an important role in a student's graduation. For example, the IEP team could use the state's and school district's graduation requirements as a basis for planning transition services or writing annual "goals" (Gorn, 2000). Additionally, if graduation is contingent on a student completing an exit examination, the IEP team's role is to make decisions about the necessity of having the student testing with accommodations. Although it may be unlikely, if a student has graduated with a regular diploma but could still benefit from special education services and has not aged out, the school district could continue to provide the student with special education services. In such a situation, the IEP team would still have the responsibility of determining a FAPE for the student.

IDEA 1997, IDEA 2004, and FAPE

When the EAHCA was passed in 1975, Congress intended that the law open the doors of public education for students with disabilities. Thus, the emphasis of the original law was on access to educational programs rather than any level of educational opportunity (Eyer, 1998, Yell & Drasgow, 2000). Although IDEA had been dramatically successful in including children with disabilities in public education, Congress believed that the promise of the law had not been fulfilled for too many children with disabilities (H.R. Report, 1997). The underlying theme of IDEA 1997 and IDEA 2004, therefore, was to improve the effectiveness of special education by requiring demonstrable improvements in the educational achievement of students with disabilities. Indeed, a quality education for each student with disabilities became the new goal of IDEA in 1997 (Eyer, 1998) and in 2004. As Eyer (1998) aptly stated,

> The IDEA can no longer be fairly perceived as a statute which merely affords children access to education. Today, the IDEA is designed to improve the effectiveness of special education and increase the benefits afforded to children with disabilities to the extent such benefits are necessary to achieve measurable progress. (p. 16)

The IDEA requires that schools further the educational achievement of students with disabilities by developing an IEP that provides a special education program designed to confer measurable and meaningful educational progress in the least restrictive environment. Moreover, school districts are also required to provide instruction that is grounded in scientifically based research. In fact, school districts may be vulnerable to special education lawsuits if they don't offer programs that are based on scientific research (Norlin & Gorn, 2005). This is especially true of reading. Figure 9.1 provides a list, published by the U.S. Institute of Education Sciences, of criteria for studies to be scientifically based.

Additionally, IDEA 2004 instructs hearing officers to make their decisions on substantive grounds based on a determination of whether a student received a FAPE (IDEA, 20 USC § 1415(f)(3)(E)(i)). This section of the law does not negate the importance of following procedural requirements of the IDEA; however, it does require that hearing officers attend first and foremost to the educational benefits received

Figure 9.1
Criteria for Scientifically Based Instruction

Educational programs proven to be effective by research should:

1. Use systematic, empirical methods that come from observation or experiment.
2. Involve data analysis to test a hypothesis.
3. Rely on measurements and observational methods that provide reliable and valid data from various observers.
4. Evaluate using experimental or quasi-experimental designs.
5. Present experimental research studies in full detail.
6. Clarify the methods used in the research, so that the research can be replicated.
7. Be published in a peer-refereed journal or endorsed by a panel of independent reviewers.

by the student. In cases in which a procedural violation is alleged, a hearing officer may only rule that the student did not receive a FAPE because the procedural violation (a) impeded the student's right to a FAPE, (b) impeded the parent's opportunity to participate in the IEP process, or (c) caused a deprivation of educational benefits (IDEA 20 USC § 1415(f)(3)(E)(ii)). Clearly, IDEA 2004 continues the trend to improve the effectiveness of special education and improve results for students with disabilities that Eyer noted in IDEA 1997 (Eyer 1998).

The reauthorization of the IDEA in 2004 reemphasizes the importance of developing and delivering special education programs that confer meaningful educational benefit. In other words special education programs must lead to real results. To ensure that students actually benefit, IEP teams must ensure that programs are (a) based on student needs, (b) meaningful and contain measurable annual goals, (c) grounded in scientifically based practices, and (d) measured on an ongoing basis to ensure that students make progress. Furthermore if the data show that a student is not progressing, the IEP team must make changes to a student's program and continue to collect data to monitor progress.

Summary

A free appropriate public education consists of special education and related services, provided at public expense, that meet the standards of the state educational agency and are provided in conformity with the IEP. The U.S. Supreme Court, in *Rowley* (1982), ruled that a FAPE does not require schools to maximize the potential of students with disabilities. Rather, a FAPE is a specially designed program that meets the individual needs of students and allows them to receive educational benefit. The Supreme Court provided lower courts with a two-part test for determining a school's compliance with the FAPE mandate. First, the court must determine whether the school has complied with the procedures of the Act. Second, the court will examine the IEP to ascertain if the IEP was reasonably calculated to enable the child to receive educational benefits. If these requirements are met, a school has complied with FAPE requirements. Subsequent lower court rulings indicate that the schools must offer a meaningful level of educational benefits. According to the *Rowley* decision, courts are to give deference to educational determinations made by school officials. Educational procedures and methodology, therefore, are the responsibility of the schools. It is the responsibility of the courts to determine compliance with the IDEA.

A student's FAPE is realized through the development of an IEP. In determining the special education and related services to be provided to students, a knowledgeable group of persons, which must include a representative of the school, the student's teacher, and the parents of the child, formulate the IEP. The IEP delineates the special education and related services to be provided by the school. Once the IEP has been developed, decisions concerning students' placements are made. Placement decisions must be in conformity with the LRE rules of the IDEA, which require placements in general education settings when appropriate.

The courts have consistently struck down policies that do not consider students' individual needs when making educational programming decisions. An example of such a policy is one in which the school year length cannot be extended beyond its usual length. If an IEP team determines that an extended school year is needed to provide a FAPE to a student, the school must make the services available.

For Further Information

Huefner, D. S. (1991). Judicial review of the special educational program requirements under the Education for All Handicapped Children Act: Where have we been and where should we be going? *Harvard Journal of Law and Public Policy, 14,* 483–516.

Katsiyannis, A. (1991). Extended school year: An established necessity. *Remedial and Special Education, 12,* 24–28.

Norlin, J., & Gorn, D. (2005). *What do I do when . . . The answer book on special education law* (4th ed.). Horsham, PA: LRP Publications.

O'Hara, J. (1985). Determinants of an appropriate education under P.L. 94-142. *Education Law Reporter, 27,* 1037–1045.

Osborne, A. G. (1992). Legal standards for an appropriate education in the post-*Rowley* era. *Exceptional Children, 58,* 488–494.

Pitasky, V. M. (2002). *What do I do when . . . The answer book on placement under the IDEA and Section 504.* Horsham, PA: LRP Publications.

Richards, D. M., & Martin, J. L. (2005). The *IDEA amendments: What you need to know.* Horsham, PA: LRP Publications.

Wenkart, R. D (2000). *Appropriate education for students with disabilities: How courts determine compliance with the IDEA.* Horsham, PA: LRP Publications.

References

A. W. v. Northwest R-1 School District, 813 F.2d 158 (8th Cir. 1987).

Adams v. Hansen, 632 F. Supp. 858 (N.D. Cal. 1985).

Age v. Bullitt County Public Schools, 701 F.2d 233 (1st Cir. 1982).

Alamo Heights Independent School District v. State Board of Education, 790 F.2d 1153 (5th Cir. 1986).

Armstrong v. Kline, 476 F. Supp. 583 (E.D. Pa. 1979), aff'd. in part and remanded sub nom.

Battle v. Commonwealth of Pennsylvania, 629 F.2d 269 (3rd Cir. 1980), cert. den. *Scanlon v. Battle,* 452 U.S. 968 (1980), further decision, 513 F. Supp. 425 (E.D. Pa. 1980), 629 F.2d 269 (3rd Cir. 1980).

Bales v. Clark, 523 F. Supp. 1366 (E.D. Va. 1981).

Baltimore (MD) City Public Schools, EHLR 311: 42 (OCR 1986).

Bateman, B. D., & Linden, M. (1998). *Better IEPs: How to develop legally correct and educationally useful programs.* Longmont, CO: Sopris West.

Board of Education v. Diamond, 808 F.2d 987 (3rd Cir. 1986).

Board of Education of Community Consolidated School District No. 21 v. Illinois State Board of Education, 938 F.2d 712 (7th Cir. 1991).

Board of Education of the Hendrick Hudson School District v. Rowley, 458 U.S. 176 (1982).

Boomer, L. W., & Garrison-Harrell, L. (1995). Legal issues concerning children with autism and pervasive developmental disorder. *Behavioral Disorder, 21,* 53–61.

Boughham v. Town of Yarmouth, 20 IDELR 12 (1993).

Bremen High School District No. 228, 257 EHLR 195 (OCR 1981).

Carter v. Florence County School District, 950 F.2d 156 (4th Cir. 1991).

Cedar Rapids Community School District v. Garret F., 526 U.S. 66 (1999).

Central Susquehanna Intermediate Unit 16, 2 ECLPR 109 (SEA PA 1995).

Chester County Intermediate Unit 23, 23 IDELR 723 (SEA PA 1995).

Clark City (NV) School District, 16 EHLR 311 (OCR 1989).

Clevenger v. Oak Ridge School Board, 744 F.2d 514 (6th Cir. 1984).

Cordrey v. Euckert, 917 F.2d 1460 (6th Cir. 1990).

Crawford v. Pittman, 708 F.2d 1028 (5th Cir. 1983).

Cremeans v. Fairland Local School District, 633 N.E. 2d 570 (OH App. 1993).

Cypress-Fairbanks Independent School District v. Michael F., 118 F.3d 245 (5th Cir. 1997).

Delaware County Intermediate Unit #25 v. Martin and Melinda K., 831 F. Supp. 1206 (E.D. Pa. 1993).

Department of Education, State of Hawaii v. Katherine D., 531 F. Supp. 517 (D. Hawaii 1982), aff'd. 727 F.2d 809 (9th Cir. 1984).

Doe v. Alabama Department of Education, 915 F.2d 651 (11th Cir. 1990).

Doe v. Board of Education of Tullahoma City Schools 9 F.3d 455 (6th Cir. 1993).

Doe v. Brookline School Committee, 1983, 722 F.2d 910 (1st Cir. 1983).

Doe v. Defendant 1, 898 F.2d 1186 (6th Cir. 1990).

Doe v. Lawson, 579 F. Supp. 1314 (D. Mass. 1984), aff'd. 745 F.2d 43 (1st Cir. 1984).

Doe v. Smith, EHLR 559:391 (N.D. Tenn. 1988).

Elizabeth v. Gilhool, 558 EHLR 461 (N.D. PA 1987).

Eyer, T. L. (1998). Greater expectations: How the 1997 IDEA amendments raise the basic floor of opportunity for children with disabilities. *Education Law Report, 126,* 1–19.

Fairfax County Public Schools, 22 IDELR 80 (SEA VA 1995).

Florence County School District Four v. Carter, 114 S.Ct. 361 (1993).

Frederick County Public Schools, 2 ECLPR 145 (SEA MD 1995).

Georgia ARC v. McDaniel, 511 F. Supp. 1263 (N.D. Ga. 1981), aff'd. 716 F.2d 1565 (11th Cir. 1983), 740 F.2d 902 (11th Cir. 1984).

Gorn, S. (1996). *What do I do when . . . The answer book on special education law.* Horsham, PA: LRP Publications.

Gorn, S. (2000). *What do I do when . . . The answer book on assessing, testing, and graduating students with disabilities.* Horsham, PA: LRP Publications.

Guernsey, T. F., & Klare, K. (1993). *Special education law.* Durham, NC: Carolina Academic Press.

Hall v. Vance County Board of Education, 774 F.2d 629 (4th Cir. 1985).

Holmes v. Sobol, 18 IDELR 53 (W.D.N.Y. 1991).

House of Representatives Report on P.L. 105-17 (1997), available at wais.access.gpo.gov.

Houston Independent School District v. Bobby R., 200 F.3d 342 (5th Cir. 2000).

Hudson v. Bloomfield Hills School District, 23 IDELR 612 (E.D. Mich. 1995).

Huefner, D. S. (1991). Judicial review of the special educational program requirements under the Education for All Handicapped Children Act: Where have we been and where should we be going? *Harvard Journal of Law and Public Policy, 14,* 483–516.

Independent School District No. 318, 24 IDELR 1096 (SEA MN 1996).

Individuals with Disabilities Education Act, 20 U.S.C. § 1400 *et seq.*

Individuals with Disabilities Education Act Regulations, 34 C.F.R. § 300.533 *et seq.*

In re Child with Disabilities, 23 IDELR 471 (SEA CT 1995).

Irving Independent School District v. Tatro, 468 U.S. 883 (1984).

J.C. v. Central Regional School District, 23 IDELR 1181 (3rd Cir. 1996).

Johnson v. Independent School District No. 4, 921 F.2d 1022 (10th Cir. 1990).

Johnson v. Lancaster-Lebanon Intermediate Unit 13, 757 F. Supp. 606 (E.D. Pa. 1991).

Karl v. Board of Education, 736 F.2d 873 (2nd Cir. 1984).

Katsiyannis, A. (1991). Extended school year policies: An established necessity. Remedial and Special Education, 12, 24–28.

Katsiyannis, A., & Yell, M. L. (2000). The Supreme Court and school health services: *Cedar Rapids v. Garret F., Exceptional Children, 66,* 317–326.

Lachman v. Illinois State Board of Education, 852 F.2d 290 (7th Cir. 1988).

Lake, S. E. (2002). *The top 10 IEP errors: How to avoid them, how to fix them.* Horsham, PA: LRP Publications.

Lear, R. (1995). The extent of public schools' responsibility to provide health-related services. In *Proceedings of the 16th Annual Institute on Legal Issues of Educating Students with Disabilities.* Alexandria, VA: LRP Conference Division.

Letter to Burton, 17 EHLR 1182 (OSERS, 1991).

Letter to Greer, 19 IDELR 348 (OSEP, 1992).

Lunenberg School District, 22 IDELR 290 (SEA VT 1994).

Malkentzos v. DeBuono, 923 F. Supp. 505 (S.D.N.Y. 1996).

Mandlawitz, M. (1996). Lovaas, TEACCH, and the public system: The court as referee. *Proceedings of the 17th National Institute on Legal Issues of Educating Individuals with Disabilities.* Alexandria, VA: LRP Publications Conference Division.

Manual R. v. Ambach, 635 F. Supp. 791 (E.D. N.Y. 1986).

Max M. v. Illinois State Board of Education, 684 F. Supp. 514 (N.D. Ill. 1986).

Norlin, J., & Gorn, D. (2005). *What do I do when . . . The answer book on special education law* (4th ed.). Horsham, PA: LRP Publications.

Office of Special Education Programs. (2000). IDEA 25th anniversary website. Available at www.ed.gov/offices/OSERS/IDEA 25th.html.

Osborne, A. G. (1992). Legal standards for an appropriate education in the post-Rowley era. *Exceptional Children, 58,* 488–494.

Osborne, A. G. (1995). When must a school district provide an extended school year program to students with disabilities? *Education Law Reporter, 99,* 1–9.

OSEP Policy Letter, 20 IDELR 1155 (OSEP, 1992).

OSEP Policy Letter, 21 IDELR 674 (OSEP, 1994).

Peterson v. Hastings Public Schools, 831 F. Supp. 742 (D. Neb. 1993).

Pitasky, V. M. (2000). *The complete OSEP handbook.* Horsham, PA: LRP Publications.

Polk v. Central Susquehanna Intermediate Unit 16, No. 16, 853 F.2d 171 (3rd Cir. 1988).

Rapport, M. J. (1996). Legal guidelines for the delivery of special health care services in school. *Exceptional Children, 62,* 537–549.

Richards, D. M., & Martin, J. L. (2005). The *IDEA amendments: What you need to know.* Horsham, PA: LRP Publications.

San Antonio ISD v. Rodriquez, 411 U.S. 1 (1973).

Schuldt v. Mankato Independent School District, 1991, 937 F.2d 1357 (8th Cir. 1991).

Seals v. Loftis, 614 F. Supp. 302 (E.D. Tenn. 1985).

Section 504 Regulations, 34 C.F.R. § 104.33(a).

Sherman v. Pitt County Board of Education, 93 EDC 1617 (SEA NC 1995).

Social Security Act, 42 U.S.C. § 1396.

Spaller, K. D., & Thomas, S. B. (1994). A timely idea: Third party billing for related services. *Education Law Reporter, 86,* 581–592.

Spielberg v. Henrico County Public Schools, EHLR 558:202 (E.D. Va. 1988).

Springdale School District v. Grace, 494 F. Supp. 266 (W.D. Ark. 1980), aff'd., 656 F.2d 300, vacated, 73 L.Ed. 2d 1380, 102 S.Ct. 3504 (1982), on remand, 693 F.2d 41 (8th Cir. 1982), cert. den. 461 U.S. 927 (1983).

Thomas, S. B., & Hawke, C. (1999). Health-care standards for students with disabilities: Emerging standards and implications. *Journal of Special Education, 32,* 226–237.

Tice v. Botetourt County School Board, 908 F.2d 1200 (4th Cir. 1990).

Timothy W. v. Rochester School District, 875b F2d. 954 (1st Cir. 1989).

Tucker, B. P., & Goldstein, B. A. (1992). *Legal rights of persons with disabilities: An analysis of public law.* Horsham, PA: LRP Publications.

Tuscaloosa County Board of Education, 21 IDELR 826 (SEA AL 1994).

Union City School District v. Smith, 15 F.3d 1519 (9th Cir. 1994).

Wenkart, R.D. (2000). *Appropriate education for students with disabilities: How courts determine compliance with the IDEA.* Horsham, PA: LRP publications.

W.G. v. Board of Trustees of Target Range School District No. 23, 960 F.2d 1479 (9th Cir. 1992).

Wall v. Mattituck-Cutchogue School District, 24 IDELR 1162 (E.D.N.Y. 1996).

Waltham (MA) Public Schools, 20 IDELR 37 (OCR 1993).

Weil v. Board of Elementary and Secondary Education, 931 F.2d 1069 (5th Cir. 1991).

Yaris v. Special School District of St. Louis County, 1984, 661 F. Supp. 996 (E.D. Mo. 1986).

Yell, M. L., & Drasgow, E. (2000). Litigating a free appropriate public education: The Lovaas hearings and cases. *Journal of Special Education, 33,* 206–215.

Yell, M. L., Drasgow, E., Bradley, R., & Justesen, T. (2004). Critical legal issues in special education. In A. McCray Sorrells, H. J. Reith, & P. T. Sindelar, *Issues in special education* (pp. 16–37). Boston: Allyn and Bacon.

Zirkel, P. A. (1992). A special education case of parental hostility. *Education Law Reporter, 73,* 1–10.

CHAPTER TEN

Identification, Assessment, and Evaluation

The goal of all evaluations, whether district initiated or independent educational evaluation, is to aid the parties to develop an appropriate program to meet the child's needs.

M. K. Freedman (1996)

Assessment is the process of collecting data for the purpose of making decisions about students (Salvia & Ysseldyke, 2004). It is, therefore, an integral part of the learning and teaching process in special education (Kauffman, 2001; Reschly, 2000). The Individuals with Disabilities Education Act (IDEA) requires that before a student is placed in a special education program, he or she must be evaluated or assessed to determine (a) whether the student has an IDEA disability; (b) if the student requires special education and related services because of his or her disability; and (c) the nature and extent of the student's academic and functional needs that will be addressed in the individualized education program (IEP).

According to Yell and Drasgow (2001), the assessment/evaluation process answers the who, what, and where questions in special education. That is, the primary purposes of this process are to answer (a) *who* should receive special education services (i.e., classification and eligibility decisions), (b) *what* instructional services and monitoring a student will need to confer meaningful educational benefit, and (c) *where* the student's special education services can be most effectively delivered.

The evaluation of a student is an incredibly important part of the process that leads to the development of a FAPE for a student. It is important because the goals of a student's educational program, the special education services he or she will receive, and the monitoring of a student's progress is based on the evaluation data. As Huefner

(2000) noted, "It is difficult to overstate the importance of a full [assessment] of the child prior to the development of the IEP. An accurate evaluation of the child's strengths, weaknesses, and current levels of performance is the basis of all that will follow" (p. 156).

The evaluation process must be individualized, which means that the procedures and methods of the evaluation must address a student's unique needs, rather than being a general assessment that can be used interchangeably with all students. Deficiencies in a school's evaluation process and procedures are a serious matter, especially if the school has reason to suspect the student may have a disability. Such deficiencies can lead to the deprivation of a free appropriate public education (FAPE) and possible court action (Gorn, 1996). The assessment is the keystone upon which a student's IEP, and therefore FAPE, is based (Yell & Drasgow, 2001).

The purpose of this chapter is to examine federal statute, regulations, and cases as well as administrative rules and guidelines involving the identification, assessment, and evaluation of students with disabilities for determination of eligibility for and placement in special education. The issues of minimum competency testing and the inclusion of students with disabilities in accountability efforts will also be discussed.

Definition of Assessment

According to Salvia and Ysseldyke (2004), assessment is the process of collecting information for the purpose of making decisions about students. The information collected may include test data, work samples, and the results of observations, interviews, and screenings. Assessment in special education involves decisions in several areas, including prereferral classroom decisions, entitlement decisions, programming decisions, and accountability/outcome decisions (Salvia & Ysseldyke, 2004).

Prereferral Decisions

Prereferral classroom decisions are made by the classroom teacher prior to formally referring a student for special education. Teachers may use assessment tools to assist them in making decisions regarding prereferral interventions. Prereferral interventions are used in the general education classroom to attempt to ameliorate the problem prior to referral to special education. Informal prereferral assessments may include classroom tests, daily observations, and interviews.

Entitlement Decisions

The second category of assessment decision involves so-called entitlement decisions. Entitlement decisions are those identification and classification decisions, based on individualized assessment, that are used to identify students as having disabilities and to determine if they require special education and related services. Salvia and Ysseldyke (2004) include screening, referral, and eligibility decisions under entitlement decisions.

Screening is the process of collecting data to determine whether more intensive assessment is necessary (Ysseldyke & Algozzine, 1995). Screenings are typically done with all students in a particular school or school district. Students scoring below a certain cutoff point on the screening instrument(s) are considered for further assessment. When screenings are conducted in this manner and not conducted selectively with individual students, they are not subject to the rules and regulations of the IDEA (IDEA Regulations, 34 C.F.R. §300.500(3)(b)) or Section 504. If they are conducted with an individual or a small group of individuals to determine interventions or placements, however, they do require parental consent (*Letter to Holmes,* 1992).

Referral decisions usually involve a determination by a teacher or parent that a student may need special education. The Individuals with Disabilities Education Improvement Act of 2004 (IDEA 2004) states that either a parent of a child or personnel from the state educational agency, another state agency, or the school district may initiate the referral request. Usually a teacher who completes a referral form brings a student to the attention of a school's multidisciplinary team (MDT). The referral is a formal request made to the MDT to evaluate a student for the presence of a disability. Although school districts may have procedures regarding referrals, referrals are not subject to the federal special education laws. Following a student referral, the MDT determines if the student requires further assessment to determine eligibility for special education. The final type of entitlement decision, therefore, is the determination of eligibility. Evaluations for eligibility are subject to the rules and regulations of the IDEA.

Programming Decisions

Programming decisions are based on evaluations of students and are used in (a) planning individualized instruction, (b) writing goals, and (c) monitoring student progress. These decisions become the basis of a student's IEP. Far too often, unfortunately, evaluations of students for special education services focus exclusively on the eligibility using standardized tests and ignores the informal tests, curriculum-based assessments, and direct observations that will lead directly to a student's educational programs.

Accountability/Outcome Decisions

The final area of assessment decisions in special education, according to Salvia and Ysseldyke (2004), involves accountability/outcome decisions. Accountability/outcome decisions involve the collection of assessment data to evaluate curricula, specific programs, and the schoolwide, statewide, or national performance of students. Currently, federal special education laws do not cover accountability and outcome data of this sort. A number of court cases, however, have addressed these macro assessments, especially as they involve minimum-competency testing.

The Assessment/Evaluation Process

When a parent, personnel from a state educational agency or other state agency, or personnel from the school believe a student may have a disability, the student is usually referred to a school's MDT. This team, which is typically composed of an administrator, special education teacher, regular education teacher, and a school psychologist, is responsible for deciding if the student should receive a complete evaluation. If the answer is yes, then the team must (a) conduct a full and individualized assessment of the child and (b) coordinate the collection of educationally relevant information. Based on the assessment data, the team then decides if the student has an IDEA disability and requires special education and related services.

If the MDT decides that the student is eligible for special education services, the team must determine the student's specific individual needs. In this respect the assessment serves as an indicator of the student's needs as well as a baseline by which the team can measure student progress in the program. Without such a baseline the MDT and the IEP team cannot show if a child made educational progress.

If the MDT determines that a student is eligible for special education services under the IDEA, an IEP team is formed to plan the student's academic and functional program. Of course, this process culminates in the development of an IEP for the student. The IEP, which is a written document that serves as a blueprint for a student's educational program as determined by the IEP team, constitutes a student's FAPE. The IEP begins with the present levels of performance statement, which describes a student's academic and functional needs as determined in the assessment. These statements lead directly to the goals and special education services. All areas of need identified in the assessment must be included in the present levels of performance. Then all need statements in the present levels of performance lead to a goal, a service, or both. Because the entire program is based on the assessment, it must be thorough and individualized to produce an IEP that results in a FAPE.

According to Yell and Drasgow (2001), to ensure that a thorough assessment is conducted for each student, the IDEA mandates procedural and substantive requirements schools must follow when conducting the assessment. *Procedural requirements* include such things as involving the student's parents in the assessment and conducting the assessment in a timely manner. *Substantive requirements* refer to the manner in which the assessment is conducted. These requirements compel school personnel to assess a student in such a manner that an educational program can be developed that confers meaningful benefit to the student. The procedural and substantive requirements of the assessment form the framework that guides the MDT team in assessing a student and, in turn, guides the development of the student's IEP. We next discuss the procedural and substantive requirements for conducting the assessment.

Procedural Requirements

To ensure that the MDT conducts an appropriate assessment, the IDEA includes rigorous procedural requirements that must be followed during the assessment process.

Strict adherence to these procedural requirements is extremely important because major procedural errors by an MDT may render an IEP inappropriate in the eyes of a hearing officer or judge (Bateman & Linden, 1998; Yell & Drasgow, 2001). When procedural violations are detected in the assessment process, hearing officers and judges scrutinize the effects of the violations. If the violations interfere with the development of the IEP, and a student did not receive an appropriate education as a result, the IEP and the student's program of special education will be ruled invalid. Thus, school districts must meet their procedural responsibilities when conducting the assessment. The law's procedural requirements are listed in Table 10.1

Substantive Requirements

A thorough and individualized assessment that (a) addresses all areas of a student's needs, (b) was conducted by knowledgeable persons, and (c) results in the development of an IEP that confers meaningful educational benefit to a student will meet the substantive requirements of the law. The following four elements are necessary to ensure that an assessment meets the IDEA's substantive requirement (Yell & Drasgow, 2001). These elements are also depicted in Table 10.2.

First, the assessment must be a *full and individualized examination* of a student's needs. This means that the assessment must provide an in-depth look at every potential area of deficiency. Reschly (2000) contends that best practice requires individualization of the assessment. Individualization involves matching assessment carefully and precisely to (a) the referral concerns, (b) the nature of the problem, (c) the characteristics of the student, and (d) the student's learning and behavior patterns. Additionally, the assessment must be matched to parental concerns.

Assessing all students in a similar manner by using a standard battery of tests is the antithesis of this requirement (Reschly, 2000). Properly conducted assessments, therefore, should consist not only of standardized tests (e.g., standardized achievement test, standardized intelligence measure), but should also include interviews, direct observations, curriculum-based measures, curriculum-based assessments, and other similar measures. If the assessment is incomplete, the IEP and, thus, the student's special education program will not provide an appropriate education.

Second, a *team of knowledgeable persons* must make decisions regarding the process and results of the assessment. This means that a team of school personnel, parents, and other professionals use the assessment data to assist them to determine eligibility and make classification decisions based on their well-informed judgments. Furthermore, people who make these educational decisions should have expertise in the specific areas being assessed. For example, if the team needs a functional behavioral assessment, at least one team member should have expertise in this area. If a school district's personnel do not have the necessary knowledge, experience, and expertise to conduct a functional assessment, the district must ensure its personnel are trained or hire outside consultants to conduct the assessment. In sum, assessment information should inform the decision-making process but not determine it. Teams should not rely on formulas or quantitative guidelines alone to make their decision.

Table 10.1
Procedural Requirements

Key Points	Explanation
Consent	• The school must obtain consent for the initial assessment and for any reevaluations conducted. • The school may use mediation or due process procedures to secure permission to evaluate, if parents refuse consent.
Parent participation	• The school must include parents in the initial assessment. • The student's parents may participate in the reevaluation process.
Assessment tools	• The school is required to use a variety of assessment tools to gather relevant, academic, and functional information about the student, including information provided by the parents. • The assessment team must use technically sound instruments that assess students in all areas of the suspected disability, including cognitive, behavioral, physical, or developmental factors. • The team may not use a single procedure as the sole criterion for determining eligibility or planning educational programs. • The tests must be nondiscriminatory. • Tests must be administered in the student's native language or mode of communication, unless it is not feasible to do so.
Standardized tests	• The tests must have been validated for the specific purpose for which they are intended. • The tests must be administered by trained personnel. • The tests must be administered in accordance with the instructions provided by the producer of the test.
Assessment process	• The student must be assessed in all areas of the suspected disability. • The assessment must be sufficiently comprehensive to identify all the student's educational needs, regardless of disability. • The assessment must provide information that directly assists the team to determine the educational needs of the student.
Statewide assessments	• The students in special education programs must participate in state- and districtwide assessments of achievement. • Testing accommodations and alternate assessments, if needed, must be provided to students with disabilities.
IEP team	• The IEP team must consist of someone qualified to interpret the instructional implications of the assessment results.
Reevaluation	• The assessment data must be reviewed every 3 years. • The team determines that no additional data are needed to assess continued eligibility. The school does not have to conduct a new assessment, unless the parents request it.

Table 10.2
Substantive Requirements

Key Points	Explanation
Full and individualized assessment	• The school must conduct a full and individual assessment to determine whether a student has a disability under the IDEA and to determine the student's educational needs. • The assessment should assist the IEP team in planning a student's program of special education, related services, and supplementary aids and services.
Team decision making	• The assessment team must include professionals with expertise in the student's disability and the student's parents. • The team makes the decisions about the conduct and results of the assessment. • The parents of a child with disabilities being evaluated must be allowed to participate in the process.
Link between assessment and intervention	• The results of the assessment must lead directly to intervention. • The areas of need identified in the assessment must be addressed in the student's IEP through the goals, special education services, or both.
Data collection	• The IEP must include data collection methods that can be used to determine if a student is making progress toward meeting his or her goals. • The student's progress toward his or her goals must be assessed, and the results of the assessment must be reported to parents at least as often as students in general education receive report cards.

The IDEA requires the exercise of professional judgment when making eligibility and instructional planning decisions and total reliance on formulas is not legal (Bateman & Linden, 1998).

Third, the *assessment information must lead to intervention.* If the assessment reveals an area of educational need, the first task of a student's IEP team is to review and use the assessment data and to determine the student's educational needs. These needs are then written into the IEP in statements in the present levels of educational performance section. These statements describe the student's performance in areas that are adversely affected by his or her disability. The purpose of the present level of performance statements is to identify these areas of need, academic and nonacademic, so that an appropriate educational program can be devised.

The IDEA requires that the performance statements in the IEP lead directly to education planning. Each present level of performance statement, therefore, must lead to a measurable annual goal and a special education service, or in some cases, only a special education or related service (e.g., counseling). Academic or nonacademic needs that are described in the assessment phase must be addressed in the student's educational program. Failure to directly link assessment and intervention is a primary reason that school districts lose in due process hearings when their IEPs are challenged (Yell & Drasgow, 2000).

Fourth, the IEP team must *collect meaningful data to monitor student progress.* The assessment is the baseline by which we develop our instructional or behavioral programs. The IDEA requires monitoring a student's progress during instruction (i.e., formative evaluation), so that we can modify a student's program if necessary. The assessment process is not just about following procedures; it is about developing special education programs that lead to meaningful educational progress. Indeed, a student's progress is the critical determinant of a FAPE (Eyer, 1998; Yell & Drasgow, 2001).

Teachers must continuously collect meaningful data to document student progress toward IEP goals and, thus, to document the program's efficacy. This means that the data must be collected over the course of instruction so that student progress is continually monitored. Appropriate data will provide objective evidence of student performance, which can be used to guide instructional decisions. Schools can meet the FAPE standards by collecting meaningful data and by demonstrating that these data were used to guide their instructional decisions.

Protection in Evaluation Procedures

Regulations that implement the IDEA require schools to evaluate students when a disability is suspected. The regulatory language of the IDEA on conducting evaluations is comprehensive and detailed. It is the responsibility of the schools to locate and evaluate students with special needs in accordance with these regulations. It is, therefore, important that schools be aware of the procedural requirements of both laws.

Child Find

All states must ensure that all students with disabilities, from birth to age 21, residing in the state who are in need of special education and related services or are suspected of having disabilities and in need of special education are identified, located, and evaluated (IDEA Regulations, 34 C.F.R. § 300.220). These requirements, located in Part B of the IDEA, include children with disabilities who are attending private schools, migrant children, and homeless children. This is called the *child find system.* This child find program may include (a) public awareness programs, (b) mailings to parents, (c) television and radio advertisements, and (d) coordinated activities with local service agencies, such as hospitals and clinics to identify children and youth with disabilities (Bartlett, Weisenstein, & Etscheidt, 2002). Part C includes similar child find requirements.

Parental Consent

In a reasonable amount of time prior to conducting an evaluation, the school must notify the parents in writing of its intent to conduct an evaluation and obtain their consent to proceed. The notice must be understandable to the general public and must contain an explanation of the parents' due process rights as well as descriptions of what the school is proposing and the evaluation procedures to be used. If the parents refuse to consent to the evaluation or fail to respond to a request to evaluate a child, the school may use hearing procedures to get permission to conduct the evaluation. The school district, however, is not required to request a hearing (*Letter to Ackenhalt,* 1994). Similarly, if the school refuses a parental request to conduct an evaluation, the parents may also challenge the refusal through the IDEA's hearing procedures.

Following parental consent for preplacement evaluation, the IDEA does not require that consent be obtained for subsequent evaluations, even when the school uses additional assessment procedures following the initial evaluation (*Carroll v. Capalbo,* 1983; *Letter to Tinsley,* 1990). This is because parental consent is for the entire evaluation process, not for individual parts (*Letter to Graham,* 1989).

Prereferral Evaluation

Prereferral evaluations have become an important component in the referral process (Salvia & Ysseldyke, 2004). Prereferral interventions are conducted in the general education classroom to attempt to ameliorate or remediate the problem prior to referral to special education. These interventions are typically based on informal prereferral evaluations such as classroom tests, daily observations, and interviews. Because of the informal nature of prereferral assessments and interventions, they are not subject to the strictures of the IDEA. It is important, however, that prereferral interventions not have the effect of delaying the referral of an eligible student (Bateman & Linden, 1998).

Preplacement Evaluation

A school's MDT determines the need for an evaluation based on referral or screening that indicates that a student may have a disability. Referrals from teachers or parents typically will lead to an evaluation by the school; in fact, according to Algozzine, Christenson, and Ysseldyke (1982), approximately 92% of all referrals lead to a full evaluation. Following consideration of the referral, the MDT may choose not to conduct an evaluation if there is no reasonable basis to suspect that a disability exists (Gorn, 1996; *Letter to Williams,* 1993). If a school declines a parental request to evaluate a student, the district must notify the parents in writing of the refusal. The notification must include the reasons for the refusal and inform the parents of their due process options (OSEP Policy Letter, 1994). Although refusing a parental request to evaluate is an option, a school district invites court action and possible remedies for violation of the IDEA if it is later determined that a student did have a disability requiring services under either law.

Comprehensiveness of the Evaluation

The IDEA requires that prior to the initiation of special education placement or services, a comprehensive and individualized evaluation of the child's educational needs be conducted. The evaluation must include all suspected areas of need, including, when appropriate, health, vision, hearing, social and emotional status, general intelligence, academic performance, communicative status, and motor abilities (IDEA Regulations 34 C.F.R. § 300.532(f)). Additionally, a school district must conduct an assistive technology evaluation if needed (*Letter to Fisher,* 1995).

After a student is identified during the screening or referral process as possibly having a disability, the MDT team must conduct the evaluation in a timely manner (Kelly, 1981). IDEA 2004 established a timeframe of 60 days to complete an evaluation after receiving parental consent. This timeframe does not apply, however, if a parent fails to produce the child for the evaluation. Many states have chosen their own time limits for conducting an evaluation. Typically, such time limits will be between 30 and 45 days. Delays in preplacement evaluations may result in due process hearings, court actions, and the possible imposition of remedies such as tuition reimbursement, attorney's fees, or compensatory education (*Bartow (GA) County School District,* 1995; *Chicago Board of Education,* 1984; *Foster v. District of Columbia Board of Education,* 1982; *Letter to Williams,* 1993).

Qualifications of Evaluators

The evaluation is conducted by members of the MDT, which must include at least one teacher or specialist in the area of the child's suspected disability. When a learning disability is suspected, the team must also include the student's general education teacher or a person qualified to teach students with learning disabilities, as well as a person qualified to conduct an individual diagnostic examination of the student, such as a school psychologist. The team's evaluators must be qualified in assessing and evaluating children with disabilities. Additionally, the Office of Special Education Programs (OSEP) has stated that evaluators must meet the qualification criteria established by the producer of the evaluation instrument (OSEP Policy Letter, 1995a).

Parental participation in the evaluation process is allowed, although it is not required (OSEP Policy Letter, 1993a). Parents may inquire about the qualifications of the examiner; therefore, OSEP recommends that school districts have written criteria for evaluators (OSEP Policy Letter, 1995a).

Evaluation Materials and Procedures

The IDEA details the specific requirements of the evaluation procedures and materials in a legally correct preplacement evaluation (IDEA Regulations, 34 C.F.R. § 300.532). Figure 10.1 lists the requirements of the IDEA regarding the selection of evaluation materials and procedures to follow in conducting the evaluation.

The evaluation materials must be provided and administered in the child's native language or other mode of communication unless it is not feasible to do so. This requirement is especially important when evaluating a student with limited English proficiency. According to the IDEA, a student's native language is the language normally used by the student's parents (IDEA Regulations 34 C.F.R. § 300.12). The reasoning

Figure 10.1
IDEA Evaluation Material and Procedures Requirements

1. Test and other evaluation materials must be
   - provided and administered in the student's native language or mode of communication unless not feasible to do so.
   - validated for the specific purpose for which they are used.
   - administered by trained personnel in conformity with instructions.
2. The evaluation must be tailored to access specific areas of educational need.
3. The evaluation must be designed to reflect the student's aptitude or achievement level rather than reflecting the student's disabilities, unless intended to do so.
4. No single procedure is used as the sole criterion to determine FAPE.
5. Decisions are made by a multidisciplinary team, including one person knowledgeable in the area of suspected disability.
6. The student is assessed in all areas of suspected disability.

behind this regulation is that the tests used must reflect a student's actual ability rather than his or her fluency in English. If a student is bilingual and shows age-appropriate English proficiency, however, the school district may test the student in English even though English may not be the student's native language. English may also be used in testing even when it is not the language used by the student's parents (*Greenfield Public School,* 1994; IDEA Regulations, 34 C.F.R. § 300.12, Note (1)). The term *mode of communication* refers to the means of communication normally used by individuals who are deaf, blind, or have no written language, and may include Braille, sign language, oral communication, or technologically enhanced communication (IDEA Regulations, 34 C.F.R. § 300.12, Note (2)).

Tests used for preplacement evaluation must be validated for the specific purpose for which they are being used. A valid test is one that measures what it purports to measure (Salvia & Ysseldyke, 2004). The IDEA, however, does not set forth rules or regulations regarding the determination of test validity. Presumably, tests validated by their publishers will fulfill this criterion (Norlin & Gorn, 2005).

Additionally, the evaluation must be designed to assess specific areas of educational need rather than merely providing a single intelligence score. Assessment instruments must be selected and administered to ensure that they accurately reflect the student's aptitude or achievement levels, rather than the student's impaired skills (unless they purport to measure the impaired skills). Finally, no single procedure can be used as the sole criterion for placement or determining the appropriate program. The selection of the evaluation materials is left to the school district or state as long as the aforementioned criteria are met.

Figure 10.2
Written Report for Specific Learning Disability

1. The MDT shall prepare a written report of the evaluation results consisting of
   - whether the student has a specific learning disability
   - what the basis for making the determination is
   - what relevant behavior was noted during the observation
   - whether educationally relevant medical findings apply
   - whether there is a severe discrepancy between achievement and ability that is not correctable without special education
   - whether environmental, cultural, or economic disadvantage affects the child's ability to learn
2. Team members shall certify in writing whether the report reflects their conclusions. If it does not, the dissenting member must submit a separate statement.

IDEA 2004 does not allow a state to require that a school district take into consideration a severe discrepancy between achievement and ability when determining eligibility. Furthermore, an observation of a student in the general education classroom and the preparation of a written report of the evaluation results are required (IDEA Regulations, 34 C.F.R. § 300.542–543). Figure 10.2 lists the IDEA's requirement for the written report.

Special Rules for Eligibility Determination

When making the eligibility decision, IDEA 2004 does not allow a student to be determined to have a disability if the determining factor is lack of appropriate instruction in reading, including instruction in the essential components of reading instruction: phonemic awareness, phonics, vocabulary, fluency, and reading comprehension. Neither can the determining factor be lack of instruction in math or limited English proficiency.

In IDEA 2004, Congress prohibited states from requiring that school districts use a discrepancy formula to determine if a student has a learning disability. Rather, Congress encouraged schools to use an assessment process that establishes if a student responds to scientific, research-based interventions. This has been referred to as a *response to intervention* model.

Nondiscriminatory Evaluation

The IDEA requires schools to select and administer tests that are not racially or culturally discriminatory. This requirement, however, is not specific and does not provide guidance to a school district in determining if an assessment measure is discriminatory or whether local norming to adjust for economic deprivation or discrimination is required (OSEP Policy Letter, 1992).

An area of particular concern in special education has been the overrepresentation of minority students. Much of this concern has focused on the selection of discriminatory evaluation materials and procedures, especially the use of tests that result in a global score indicating an intelligence quotient (IQ). The primary concern has been that IQ tests, when used for making placement decisions, may result in the overreferral of minority students or students from economically disadvantaged backgrounds.

Larry P. v. Riles, 1979

In *Larry P. v. Riles* (1979; hereafter *Larry P.*), a federal district court in California banned the use of standardized IQ instruments to evaluate African American students for placement in classes for students with educable mental retardation (EMR). The court ruled that such tests contained racial and cultural bias and discriminated against students from racial minorities. The decision was affirmed by the U.S. Court of Appeals for the Ninth Circuit. In 1986, the *Larry P.* ban was expanded to include IQ testing of African American students for all special education placements.

Parents in Action on Special Education (PASE) v. Hannon, 1908

Shortly after the first *Larry P.* decision, a federal district court, in *Parents in Action on Special Education v. Hannon* (1980), arrived at a different conclusion regarding standardized IQ tests. According to the court, the Wechsler Intelligence Scale for Children (WISC), the WISC-R, and the Stanford-Binet IQ tests were not racially or culturally discriminatory. The court further held that they could be used in the special education placements of African American children. The court also found that the school district had not used the IQ tests as the sole basis for special education placement, thereby complying with the IDEA.

Crawford v. Honig, 1994

The *Larry P.* ban on IQ testing for purposes of placing African American students in special education classes was vacated in 1994 by the U.S. Court of Appeals for the Ninth Circuit in *Crawford v. Honig*. The action was brought by African American students who sought to have standardized IQ tests administered in special education evaluations so that they could qualify for special education for students with learning disabilities. A federal district court consolidated the case with *Larry P.* and vacated the 1986 modification, which had prohibited IQ tests in all special education placements. The court, however, left the original ban against using IQ tests to place African American students in EMR classes in effect. The *Larry P.* plaintiffs, the superintendent of public instruction, and the California State Board of Education appealed the decision to vacate the modification to the Ninth Circuit court. The appellate court affirmed the lower court's ruling, stating that the 1986 modification inappropriately expanded the scope of the original injunction because the modification was not supported by factual findings. The appellate court decision did not address the underlying facts of *Larry P.,* only the propriety of extending the original ban on IQ tests. In fact, the court indicated that the discriminatory nature of IQ tests was a disputed issue of fact to be addressed in future *Larry P.* proceedings.

Nevertheless, the decision of the appellate court seemed to indicate that the IDEA does not prohibit the use of IQ tests per se in special education evaluations. This holding affirmed a position taken by the Office of Special Education and Rehabilitative Services (OSERS) a year earlier, that the appropriate use of IQ tests is not prohibited (*Letter to Warrington,* 1993). According to Gorn (1996), IQ tests can be a valuable part of the evaluation process as long as they are valid, are not racially or culturally discriminatory, and are not used as the sole criterion for placement.

Interpretation of Evaluation Data

When the evaluation is completed, the MDT must draw on the results of all the instruments used, as well as other information provided in the decision-making process. The law requires that professional judgment be relied on; sole reliance on formulas or quantitative guidelines is not permitted (Bateman & Linden, 1998).

Drawing on the information gathered during the evaluation process, the MDT first determines a student's eligibility—that is, whether a student has a disability covered under the IDEA. Second, the MDT determines whether, because of the disability, a student requires special education and related services. Regulatory guidelines for interpreting evaluation data are reported in Figure 10.3.

School districts have been cited for determining students were not eligible for services under IDEA but then failing to assess them for eligibility under Section 504. This problem has occurred frequently with students having Attention Deficit Disorder (ADD) or Attention Deficit Hyperactivity Disorder (ADHD) who were ineligible for services under the IDEA (*Anaheim School District,* 1993; *Calcasieu Parish*

Figure 10.3
Interpreting Evaluation Data

When interpreting evaluation data, the MDT must

- draw on information from a variety of sources, including aptitude and achievement tests, teacher recommendations, physical condition, social or cultural background, and adaptive behavior.

- ensure that information is documented and carefully considered.

- ensure that decisions are made by a team, including a person knowledgeable about the student, the meaning of the evaluation data, and the placement options.

- ensure that the placement decision is made in accordance with LRE requirements.

(LA) Public School District, 1992; *LaHonda-Pescadero (CA) Unified School District,* 1993; *Petaluma City (CA) Elementary School District,* 1995).

The IDEA (IDEA Regulations, 34 C.F.R. § 300.543) require that the MDT's decision be documented in written form. The IDEA further states that team members must certify that the final team decision reflects their conclusions. If team members disagree with the team decision, they may attach a separate report detailing their views. Finally, the IDEA does not address whether the decision must be by majority vote, although it does not have to be unanimous. In a policy letter, OSEP stated that the school district was required to comply with the decision made by the MDT as a whole (*Letter to Greer,* 1992). OSEP did not further elaborate on what "as a whole" meant, nor has it defined how many people, at a minimum, are required on the MDT.

Medical Diagnosis and Eligibility Determination

Multidisciplinary teams may use a medical diagnosis as part of the eligibility determination, when appropriate. It is clear, however, that a medical diagnosis cannot be used as the sole basis for eligibility determination (Joint Policy Memorandum, 1991). Furthermore, a medical diagnosis may not be required as part of an evaluation, although if an MDT believes a medical diagnosis is necessary, it must be provided at public expense (*Letter to Parker,* 1992; *Response to Veir,* 1993). Although schools do not have to consult a physician when determining eligibility and services for a student with ADD or ADHD, the MDT must have someone on the committee with specific knowledge of how to identify and treat the disorder (*Letter to Shrag,* 1992).

Reevaluation

The educational needs of students with disabilities change over time. The IDEA, therefore, requires that students in special education be reevaluated every 3 years. A reevaluation is a comprehensive evaluation conducted on a student already in special education. The reevaluation is usually similar to the original preplacement evaluation, and it must meet the same procedural requirements under the IDEA as did the original evaluation (IDEA Regulations, 34 C.F.R. § 300.534). The reevaluation, however, does not have to be identical to the preplacement evaluation; it can consist of different assessment procedures so long as they address the student's current educational needs (*Letter to Shaver,* 1990).

The IDEA requires that eligible students be reevaluated more frequently than every 3 years if necessary or if requested by the student's parents or teacher (IDEA Regulations, 34 C.F.R. § 300.534). Regulatory language is unclear as to when it may be necessary to reevaluate more frequently than every 3 years. A ruling in *Corona-Norco Unified School District* (1995) found that more frequent evaluations may be warranted when there is a substantial change in the student's academic performance or disability. Reevaluations must also be conducted prior to any significant change in placement under Section 504, although the IDEA does not have a similar requirement.

A federal district court has used the Section 504 regulation (Section 504 Regulations, 34 C.F.R. § 104.35(a)) as authority for requiring a reevaluation under the IDEA when a school district made a significant change in placement (*Brimmer v. Traverse City Area Public Schools,* 1994). A reevaluation is also required when a school is contemplating the long-term suspension or expulsion of a student with disabilities. (For elaborations on suspension and expulsion, see Chapter 14.)

If a full and complete reevaluation is not needed to collect additional information, the reevaluation should focus on collecting information about how to teach the student in the most appropriate manner. If an IEP team determines that additional data are not needed, the team must notify the student's parents of the determination, the reasons for it, and the parents' right to request a full evaluation.

Informed parental consent is required for a school to conduct a reevaluation. Until the IDEA Amendments of 1997, parental consent was not required. This requirement does not apply, however, if the school district can demonstrate that reasonable steps were taken to obtain consent but the parents failed to respond. When a parent requests a reevaluation, the student must be reevaluated unless the district challenges the parents' request in a due process hearing (*Letter to Tinsley,* 1990).

IDEA 2004 does not require a complete reevaluation when a student graduates from a regular high school or ages out of IDEA eligibility. Instead the student's IEP team must provide a student with a written summary of his or her academic achievement and functional performance, which should include recommendations on how to assist the student to meet his or her academic and functional goals.

Independent Educational Evaluations

An independent educational evaluation (IEE) is an evaluation conducted by a qualified examiner who is not employed by the school district responsible for the education of the student in question (IDEA Regulations, 34 C.F.R. § 300.503). Parents have the right to request an IEE at any time during their child's education. On the parents' request, the school district must provide information about where the IEE may be obtained. Furthermore, although the school district is under no obligation to accept the results of the evaluation, it must consider the IEE as part of its decision-making process. School district responsibilities regarding the IEE are listed in Figure 10.4.

The IDEA allows parents to obtain one IEE at public expense if they disagree with the school district evaluation. Parents may also request an IEE if a school does not evaluate for assistive technology devices or services (*Letter to Fisher,* 1995). The school, however, may initiate a due process hearing if it believes the school district's evaluation is appropriate. If the hearing officer's decision is that the school had conducted an appropriate evaluation, the parent is not entitled to have the evaluation paid for by the district.

Apparently, the school district may choose whether it will fund the IEE in advance, pay the examiner directly, or reimburse the parent (Gorn, 1996). This issue is not addressed in the IDEA. However, if the refusal to fund the IEE in advance denies

Figure 10.4
Independent Educational Evaluation Requirements

1. Schools must, on request, provide parents information on where to obtain an IEE.

2. If parents disagree with the school's evaluation, they have the right to an IEE at public expense.

3. If school personnel believe their evaluation is appropriate, they may initiate a hearing. If a hearing officer finds the evaluation appropriate, parents are still entitled to IEE, but not at public expense.

4. The results of the IEE, even if paid for by the parents, must be considered in the special education decision-making process.

5. The results of the IEE, even if paid for by the parents, may be presented as evidence at a hearing.

6. A hearing officer may request an IEE as part of a due process hearing. This IEE must be performed at public expense.

the parent the right to seek an IEE, the parent may seek relief (*Edna Independent School District,* 1994). In situations where the school district refuses to fund the IEE, the parent must prevail at a due process hearing to secure the public funding.

Parents should notify the school district when they disagree with the school's evaluation and plan to request an IEE at public expense. The school district must respond within a reasonable amount of time and either agree to fund the IEE or request a hearing to show that its evaluation was appropriate. Typically, school districts will challenge an IEE when they believe their evaluation was appropriate or when the IEE obtained by parents did not dispute the district's evaluation (Freedman, 1996). If parents have obtained the IEE to provide additional information or more meaningful information, they will not have a claim for public funding (*Millcreek Township School District,* 1995), nor will public funding be ordered if the findings of the independent evaluator are consistent with the district's findings (*Brandywine School District,* 1995). The criterion for public funding, therefore, involves the appropriateness of the district's evaluation. IEEs are typically funded when the district has been negligent in conducting the evaluation, when the evaluation was inadequate, when all sources of information were not considered, or when major procedural safeguards were not followed (*Carbondale Elementary School District 95,* 1996; *Douglas School District,* 1993; *Livingston Parish (LA) School Board,* 1993).

If the parents already have secured an IEE and requested payment, the district might contend in a hearing that the IEE was inappropriate, deficient, or conducted by an unqualified examiner. In a policy letter, OSEP stated that a district may disqualify an independent evaluator chosen by a parent and may refuse to pay if the evaluator does not meet the district's criteria (OSEP Policy Letter, 1995b).

A school district may establish a fee structure for the IEE that the parents cannot exceed (OSEP Policy Letter, 1995b). The purpose of the maximum fee set by the school district is to eliminate unreasonable and excessive fees. School district limitations on the parents' choice of an independent examiner, the location of the IEE, and the fees for the evaluation will be upheld as long as they are reasonable (Gorn, 1996). The school district, however, must allow the parents the opportunity to demonstrate that unique circumstances justify an IEE that does not fall within the district's fee structure (OSEP Policy Letter, 1993b).

When parents initiate an IEE, the results of the evaluation must be considered by the school district in decisions regarding the education of the evaluated student. The district is not, however, obligated to accept or act on the recommendations made in the IEE. Although the IDEA does not detail what *consider* means in this context, the U.S. Court of Appeals for the Second Circuit, in *T.S. v. Board of Education of the Town of Ridgefield and State of Connecticut Department of Education* (1993), used the definition "to reflect on or think about with some degree of caution" (p. 89). The parents in this case argued that the school's MDT had not considered the IEE when only two members of the team had read the IEE prior to the meeting. The court rejected the argument, finding that nothing in the IDEA suggested that all team members had to read the IEE to consider it. The circuit court's decision indicated that it is important that a school district document consideration of the IEE. According to Gorn (1996), school districts should (a) document how the IEE was made available to the MDT or IEP team; (b) record the findings of the IEE and the team's review and discussion of the report; and (c) put any reasons for disagreement with the IEE in writing. OSEP has stated that the school does not need to document the results of the rejected IEE on the IEP (OSEP Policy Letter, 1993c), but that the school should review the IEE and discuss its results in all programming and placement decisions (OSEP Policy Letter, 1995b).

Freedman (1996) stresses the importance of actively listening to and addressing parents' concerns when confronting parental requests for an IEE. Preventive actions and cooperative participation are crucial. Figure 10.5 is Freedman's advice to schools regarding the IEE.

Accountability Efforts and Students with Disabilities

The early 1980s witnessed a series of reports that alerted the public to a crisis in American education and led to calls for improving the educational system. The publication of *A Nation at Risk* (National Commission on Excellence in Education, 1983) was especially influential in leading to calls for educational reform. The widespread criticism of the public school system and the perceived need to reform education led to efforts to increase accountability in our educational system. One result of this movement was the No Child Left Behind Act (NCLB) of 2001. Three tools adopted to increase accountability in education are (a) development of standards and outcomes for America's students, (b) the use of student assessments through the adoption of statewide testing, and (c) the use of minimum competency tests.

Figure 10.5
Freedman's Advice Regarding IEEs

- Remember that the goal of all evaluations, whether the school district's or an IEE, is to develop an appropriate program for the student.
- When an IEE is clearly and substantively wrong in its recommendations and facts, correct the record in writing.
- Consider all sources of information and attempt to find an appropriate balance between the district's recommendations and the IEE.
- Remember that IEEs are a pivotal part of the procedural safeguards granted to students with disabilities and their parents.
- Establish a cost structure for IEEs and notify parents in writing that if they believe a more costly IEE is warranted, they must inform the district of these unique circumstances.

From "Independent Educational Evaluations: Love 'em or Hate 'em, but Do 'em Right" by M. K. Freedman, 1996, in *Proceedings of the 16th Annual Conference on Special Education Law,* LRP Publications. Adapted with permission.

This has had, and will continue to have, a profound effect on the education of students with disabilities. How the NCLB-driven state standards and state assessments affect students with disabilities is addressed in Chapter 8 on NCLB. This chapter briefly examines the use of minimum competency tests.

Minimum Competency Tests

The purpose of minimum competency tests (MCTs), or school exit exams, is to ensure that students attain minimum proficiency in tested academic areas before they graduate from high school. MCTs are seen as a means to restore meaning to the high school diploma, since students must show a certain level of skill development and knowledge before receiving one. Advocates believe that these tests will help to establish educational standards, provide an incentive to learning, and give the public an opportunity to assess the effectiveness of schools. Critics raise concerns over the unsound psychometric properties of such tests, the narrowing of the curriculum caused by teachers teaching to the test, and the disproportionate impact of the use of these tests on students from economically disadvantaged backgrounds, racial minorities, and students with disabilities (Thomas & Russo, 1995).

Twenty states now require that students in high school pass exit or graduation examinations to receive a diploma (Stateline.org, 2005). The states are Alabama, Alaska, Florida, Georgia, Indiana, Louisiana, Maryland, Massachusetts, Minnesota, Missouri, Nevada, New Jersey, New Mexico, New York, North Carolina, Ohio, South Carolina, Tennessee, Texas, and Virginia. Four additional states, Arizona, California, Idaho and Utah, will phase in exit exams by 2006. Washington will have a high school exit exam by 2008.

All states with exit exams allow multiple re-test opportunities for students who do not initially pass, and states also provide alternate tests for students with disabilities.

Litigative challenges to these examinations have shown that states clearly have the legal prerogative to require them. Courts are reluctant to intervene in educational affairs, and both state and federal courts have overwhelmingly recognized the right of states to determine the effectiveness of their educational programs through methods such as exit examinations. For example, in an important court challenge to MCTs, the U.S. Court of Appeals for the Fifth Circuit, in *Debra P. v. Turlington* (1981), found that an MCT used in the state of Florida had been demonstrated to be instructionally valid, was not discriminatory, and could be used in the determination of diploma awards. The court praised Florida's efforts to improve the quality of education. The decision was affirmed by the U.S. Court of Appeals for the Eleventh Circuit in 1984 (*Debra P. v. Turlington*). In a case heard in the Seventh Circuit, *Brookhart v. Illinois State Board of Education* (1983), the court stated that the use of MCTs to ensure the value of the diploma was admirable and that the court would only interfere with educational policy decisions if needed to protect a student's individual statutory and constitutional rights. *Brookhart* was important in that it was the first case to address a state's decision to deny diplomas to students receiving special education who had failed to pass the state's MCT. The court, in analyzing the plaintiff's claims under the Education for All Handicapped Children Act (EAHCA), held that the denial of diplomas did not deny the student a FAPE and was, therefore, legal. The court also ruled that the use of MCTs did not violate Section 504 because the state, although required to provide reasonable accommodations, was not required to modify the test so substantially that the purpose of the test would be vitiated.

Thomas and Russo (1995) note that students with disabilities tend to perform more poorly on MCTs and, thus, are ineligible for a diploma more frequently than do students without disabilities. Claims of discrimination in violation of Section 504 and denial of a FAPE in violation of the IDEA, however, are unlikely to be successful. Thomas and Russo further contend that states giving MCTs are not required to establish separate standards or prepare individualized MCTs for students with disabilities. These authors conclude that parents should be made aware of the general use and content of MCTs. Moreover, the IEP team should consider including MCT content in the student's IEP.

Including Students with Disabilities in Accountability Efforts

No Child Left Behind has led to a burst of activity in the area of developing standards and assessments for students. Standards are statements of criteria against which comparisons can be made. The purpose of educational standards is to guide instruction regarding what students should know and be able to do. In addition to developing standards and assessments in reading and mathematics as required by NCLB, many states have developed standards and outcomes in other academic content areas as well as in health and physical education, the arts, and vocational education (Shriner, Ysseldyke, & Thurlow, 1994). An area of concern in the development of standards has been how to include and address the needs of students with disabilities. Various options for including students with disabilities include setting separate standards, maintaining a single set of standards but allowing a range of performance relative to them, allowing standards to be demonstrated using alternative measures (e.g., portfolios), excluding students with disabilities from assessment, and using the IEP as a document and process in linking the student's program to the local, state, or national standards (Shriner et al., 1994). If the last option is used, the IEP team will be charged with preparing IEPs that are aligned to these standards.

The IDEA Amendments of 1997 require that students with disabilities participate in state- and districtwide assessments of student progress, with or without accommodations, whichever is appropriate for individual students. Furthermore, NCLB requires that school districts disaggregate assessment data by subgroups, including students with disabilities. States must report to the public on the assessment of students with disabilities with the same frequency and detail as they report on the assessment of students without disabilities. They must also report the number of students with disabilities participating in statewide regular assessments and, eventually, the numbers participating in alternative assessments. The data on the performance of students with disabilities must be disaggregated when reporting to the federal government.

The IEP meeting is the proper forum for considering whether students with disabilities can appropriately participate in regular assessments or whether they need modifications in the administration of the state tests. According to Ysseldyke, Thurlow, McGrew, and Vanderwood (1994), the IEP should list any accommodations of the test or testing situation. Possible testing accommodations include altering the manner in which the assessment is presented (e.g., use of magnifying equipment, signing of directions), the manner of student response (e.g., using a computer for responding, giving responses orally), accommodations in setting (e.g., testing alone in a study carrel, testing with a small group), and time (e.g., more frequent breaks during testing, extending the testing session over several days). If an IEP team decides that a student will not participate in a particular state- or districtwide assessment of achievement, the IEP must include a statement of why the assessment is not appropriate and how the student will be assessed.

Summary

Before a student can be placed in special education or related services, the student must be identified as having a disability and needing special education services to meet his or her individual needs. The evaluation is important in identifying a student as eligible for special education and crucial in the development of the student's FAPE.

Parents' written consent is required prior to conducting an initial evaluation. After permission is received, the evaluation must be conducted in a timely manner. The MDT must then make eligibility decisions based upon the evaluation data. If the parents refuse consent and the MDT believes the child needs special educational services, the school district may go to a due process hearing to obtain permission to conduct the evaluation.

The evaluation must be individualized and conducted in all areas related to the suspected disability. The MDT's charge is to use the results of the evaluation to determine if the student is eligible for services under the IDEA or Section 504 and to further determine if, because of the disability, the student needs special education and related services to meet his or her needs.

The IDEA Amendments of 1997 required that students with disabilities participate in state- and districtwide assessments. This requirement

remains in IDEA 2004. Furthermore, states are required to report on the assessments of students with disabilities under NCLB. IEP teams must determine if students in special education can participate in such assessments or if they require modifications in administration of these assessments. The IEP must also list any testing modifications needed. If the team determines that a student cannot participate in regular assessments, the IEP must include a statement of why the student cannot participate and how the student will be assessed.

For Further Information

Bateman, B. D., & Linden, M. A. (1998). *Better IEPs: How to develop legally correct and educationally useful programs* (3rd ed). Longmont, CO: Sopris West.

Salvia, J., & Ysseldyke, J. E. (2004). *Assessment in special and inclusive settings* (9th ed.). Boston: Houghton Mifflin.

Shriner, J. G., Ysseldyke, J. E., & Thurlow, M. L. (1994). Standards for all American students. *Focus on Exceptional Children, 26*(5), 1–19.

Shriner, J. G., & Spicuzza, R. J. (1995). Procedural considerations in the assessment of children at risk. *Preventing School Failure, 39,* 33–38.

References

Algozzine, B., Christenson, S., & Ysseldyke, J. E. (1982). Probabilities associated with the referral to placement process. *Teacher Education and Special Education, 5,* 19–23.

Anaheim School District, 20 IDELR 185 (OCR 1993).

Bartlett, L. D., Weisenstein, G. R., & Etscheidt, S. (2002). *Successful inclusion for educational leaders.* Upper Saddle River, NJ: Merrill/Prentice Hall.

Bartow (GA) County School District, 22 IDELR 508 (OCR 1995).

Bateman, B. D., & Linden, M. A. (1998). *Better IEPs: How to develop legally correct and educationally useful programs* (3rd ed). Longmont, CO: Sopris West.

Brandywine School District, 22 IDELR 517 (SEA Del. 1995).

Brimmer v. Traverse City Area Public Schools, 22 IDELR 5 (W.D. Mich. 1994).

Brookhart v. Illinois State Board of Education, 697 F.2d 179 (7th Cir. 1983).

Calcasieu Parish (LA) Public School District, 20 IDELR 762 (OCR 1992).

Carbondale Elementary School District 95, 23 IDELR 766 (SEA Ill. 1996).

Carroll v. Capalbo, 563 F. Supp. 1053 (D.R.I. 1983).

Chicago Board of Education, EHLR 257:568 (OCR 1984).

Corona-Norco Unified School District, 22 IDELR 469 (Cal. 1995).

Council of Chief State School Officers. (1996). *Viewing the landscape: States' assessment practices.* Washington, DC: Author.

Crawford v. Honig, 37 F.3d 485 (9th Cir. 1994).

Debra P. v. Turlington, 644 F.2d 397 (5th Cir. 1981).

Debra P. v. Turlington, 730 F.2d 1405 (11th Cir. 1984).

Douglas School District, 20 IDELR 458 (SEA SD 1993).

Edna Independent School District, 21 IDELR 419 (SEA Tex. 1994).

Eyer, T. (1998). Greater expectations: How the 1997 IDEA Amendments raise the basic floor of opportunity for children with disabilities. *Education Law Reporter, 126,* 1–19.

Foster v. District of Columbia Board of Education, EHLR 553:520 (D.D.C. 1982).

Freedman, M. K. (1996). Independent educational evaluations: Love 'em or hate 'em, but do 'em right. In *Proceedings of the 16th Annual Conference on Special Education Law.* Horsham, PA: LRP Publications.

Gorn, S. (1996). *What do I do when... The answer book on special education law.* Horsham, PA: LRP Publications.

Greenfield Public School, 21 IDELR 345 (SEA Mass. 1994).

Guernsey, T. F., & Klare, K. (1993). *Special education law.* Durham, NC: Carolina Academic Press.

Huefner, D. S. (2000). Getting comfortable with special education law: A framework for working with children with disabilities. Norwood, MA: Christopher-Gordon Publications.

Individuals with Disabilities Education Act (IDEA), 20 U.S.C. § 1400 *et seq.*

Individuals with Disabilities Education Act Regulations, 34 C.F.R. § 300.1 *et seq.*

Joint Policy Memorandum, 18 IDELR 116 (OSERS 1991).

Kauffman, J. M. (2001). *Characteristics of emotional and behavioral disorders of children and youth* (7th ed.). Upper Saddle River, NJ: Merrill/Prentice Hall.

Kelly Inquiry, 211 EHLR (EHA 1981).

LaHonda-Pescadero (CA) Unified School District, 20 IDELR 833 (OCR 1993).

Larry P. v. Riles, 495 F. Supp. 926 (N.D. Cal. 1979), *aff'd in part, rev'd in part,* 793 F.2d 969 (9th Cir. 1986).

Letter to Ackenhalt, 22 IDELR 252 (OCR 1994).

Letter to Fisher, 23 IDELR 565 (OSEP 1995).

Letter to Graham, 213 EHLR 212 (EHA 1989).

Letter to Greer, 19 IDELR 348 (OSEP 1992).

Letter to Holmes, 19 IDELR 350 (OSEP 1992).

Letter to Parker, 19 IDELR 963 (OSEP 1992).

Letter to Shaver, 17 EHLR 356 (OSERS 1990).

Letter to Shrag, 18 IDELR 1303 (OSEP 1992).

Letter to Tinsley, 16 EHLR (OSEP 1990).

Letter to Warrington, 20 IDELR 593 (OSERS 1993).

Letter to Williams, 20 IDELR 1210 (OSEP 1993).

Livingston Parish (LA) School Board, 20 IDELR 1470 (OCR 1993).

Millcreek Township School District, 22 IDELR 1011 (SEA PA 1995).

National Commission on Excellence in Education. (1983). *A nation at risk: The imperative for educational reform.* Washington, DC: U.S. Government Printing Office.

Norlin, J., & Gorn, S. (2005). *What do I do when . . . The answer book on special education law.* Horsham, PA: LRP Publications.

OCR Policy Letter, 20 IDELR 1073 (OCR 1993).

OSEP Policy Letter, 18 IDELR 741 (OSEP 1992).

OSEP Policy Letter, 20 IDELR 1219 (OSEP 1993a).

OSEP Policy Letter, 20 IDELR 1222 (OSEP 1993b).

OSEP Policy Letter, 20 IDELR 1460 (OSEP 1993c).

OSEP Policy Letter, 21 IDELR 998 (OSEP 1994).

OSEP Policy Letter, 22 IDELR 563 (OSEP 1995a).

OSEP Policy Letter, 22 IDELR 637 (OSEP 1995b).

Parents in Action on Special Education v. Hannon, 506 F. Supp 831 (N.D. Ill. 1980).

Petaluma City (CA) Elementary School District, 23 IDELR 245 (OCR 1995).

Reschly, D. J. (2000). Assessment and eligibility determination in the Individuals with Disabilities Education Act of 1997. In C. Telzrow & M. Tankersley (Eds.), *IDEA Amendments of 1997: Practice guidelines for school-based teams* (pp. 65–104). Bethesda, MD: National Association of School Psychologists.

Response to Veir, 20 IDELR 864 (OCR 1993).

Salvia, J., & Ysseldyke, J. E. (2004). *Assessment in special and inclusive settings* (9th ed.). Boston: Houghton Mifflin.

Section 504 of the Rehabilitation Act of 1973, 29 U.S.C. § 794 *et seq.*

Section 504 Regulations, 34 C.F.R. § 104.1 *et seq.*

Shriner, J. G., Ysseldyke, J. E., & Thurlow, M. L. (1994). Standards for all American students. *Focus on Exceptional Children, 26*(5), 1–19.

Stateline.org (2005). Available at: http://www.stateline.org/live/ViewPage.action?siteNodeId=136&languageId=1&contentId=33244.

T. S. v. Board of Education of the Town of Ridgefield and State of Connecticut Department of Education, 10 F.3d 87 (2nd Cir. 1993).

Thomas, S. B., & Russo, C. J. (1995). *Special education law: Issues & Implications for the '90s.* Topeka, KS: National Organization on Legal Problems of Education.

Yell, M. L., & Drasgow, E. (2000). Litigating a free appropriate public education: The Lovaas hearings and cases. *Journal of Special Education, 33,* 206–215.

Yell, M. L., & Drasgow, E. (2001). Legal requirements for assessing students with emotional and behavioral disorders. *Assessment for Effective Intervention, 26,* 5–17.

Ysseldyke, J. E., & Algozzine, B. (1995). *Special education: A practical approach for teachers* (3rd ed.). Boston: Houghton Mifflin.

Ysseldyke, J. E., Thurlow, M. L., McGrew, K., & Vanderwood, M. (1994). *Making decisions about the inclusion of students with disabilities in large-scale assessments* (Synthesis Report 13). Minneapolis: University of Minnesota and National Center on Educational Outcomes.

CHAPTER ELEVEN

The Individualized Education Program

The importance of the IEP [should not] be understated . . . [it is] the
fundamental prerequisite of any FAPE.

Justice Huntley, *Thorndock v. Boise Independent School District*
(1988, p. 1246)

The individualized education program (IEP) is the keystone of the Individuals with Disabilities Education Act (IDEA) (*Honig v. Doe*, 1988). All aspects of the student's special education program are directed by the IEP and monitored throughout the IEP process (Smith, 1990). The goals of a student's program, the educational placement, the special education and related services, and the evaluation and measurement criteria that are developed in the IEP process are contained in the document.

The IEP process develops and formalizes the free appropriate public education (FAPE) for a student with disabilities (Bateman & Linden, 1996; Eyer, 1998; Huefner, 2000; Katsiyannis, Yell, & Bradley, 2001). The IEP is so important that the failure to properly develop and implement it may render a student's entire special education program invalid in the eyes of the courts (Horsnell & Kitch, 1996; Yell, Drasgow, Bradley, & Justesen, 2004).

Schools must follow both the procedural and substantive requirements of the IEP to ensure that a student receives an appropriate education. Procedural requirements compel schools to follow the law when developing an IEP and include such things as (a) providing notice to parents, (b) adhering to state mandated timelines, (c) involving the student's parents in educational decision making, (d) conducting complete and individualized evaluations, (e) ensuring that all the necessary IEP team members attend the IEP meetings, (f) including the appropriate content in the IEP, and (g) ensuring that the IEP is implemented as written. Substantive requirements compel schools to provide an education that confers meaningful educational benefit to a student. To ensure that our IEPs confer meaningful educational benefit we need to (a) thoroughly assess a student's academic and functional needs; (b) base our goals on those needs; (c) write goals that are complete, appropriate, and measurable; (d) provide special education and related services that are effective and based on scientific research; and (e) monitor the student's progress toward his or her goals and make instructional changes when necessary. The procedural and substantive requirements of the IEP form the framework that guides the development and implementation of an individualized FAPE for a student.

Since their inception in 1975, however, IEPs have been fraught with problems (Drasgow, Yell, & Robinson, 2001; Huefner, 2000; Lake, 2000, 2002). For example, Smith (1990) identified several problems with IEP development: lack of adequate teacher training in developing IEPs, poorly developed team processes, mechanistic compliance with the burdensome paperwork requirements, and excessive demands on teacher time. Additional problems with the IEP requirements are minimal coordination with general education (Lipsky & Gartner, 1992), the failure to link assessment data to instructional goals (Smith & Simpson, 1989), and (c) the failure to develop measurable goals and objectives to evaluate student achievement (Bateman & Herr, 2003). Furthermore, the IEP process has been replete with such legal errors as (a) failure to report current levels of educational performance; (b) lack of appropriate goals, objectives, and evaluation procedures; (c) absence of key personnel at IEP meetings; (d) placement decisions not based on the IEP; and (e) failure to include a student's access to the general curriculum in the IEP (Bateman & Linden, 1996; Huefner, 2000; Lombardo, 1999; Lynch & Beare, 1990; Martin, 1996; Smith, 1990). Similarly, Lake (2002) listed the 10 most common mistakes in IEP development as:

1. The IEP team membership is incorrect or incomplete.
2. The IEP lacks adequate parental input or consent.
3. Key IEP components are missing.
4. The IEP goals are incomplete, inadequate, or not measurable.
5. The IEP's transition component is lacking or deficient.
6. The IEP fails to adequately address the student's least restrictive environment.
7. The IEP placement offer and services are inadequate.
8. The school district fails to provide or fully implement the services under an existing IEP.
9. The IEP is not developed or revised in a timely manner.
10. The IEP fails to include positive behavioral interventions.

The challenges facing schools are further compounded by the recent changes in legislation. The federal government amended and reauthorized the Individuals with Disabilities Education Act (IDEA) in 1997 and again in 2004 in ways that have had, and will continue to have, an impact on the ways schools develop IEPs. The changes in these two authorizations emphasize accountability and the use of scientifically based practices in special education and hold schools to a higher level of responsibility for developing and implementing valid and beneficial IEPs.

Bateman and Linden (1996) asserted that:

> Sadly, most IEPs are horrendously burdensome to teachers and nearly useless to parents and children. Far from being creative, flexible, data-based, and individualized applications of the best of educational interventions to a child with unique needs, the typical IEP is empty, devoid of specific services to be provided. It says what the IEP team hopes to accomplish, but little if anything about the special education interventions and the related services or classroom modifications that will enable (the student) to reach those goals. . . . Many if not most goals and objectives couldn't be measured if one tried, and all too often no effort is made to actually assess the child's progress toward the goal. (p. 63)

Despite their assessment of the problems with IEPs in schools today, Bateman and Linden strongly believe that "a well-designed IEP can change a child's schooling experience from one of repeated failure, loss of self esteem, and limited options to one of achievement, directions, and productivity" (p. 2). If IEPs are to become such a tool, special educators must understand how to develop an IEP that is educationally meaningful and legally correct.

This chapter examines the IEP mandate of the IDEA, including (a) the purposes of the IEP; (b) the IEP development process, including the IEP team and content requirements; (c) the placement process; (d) substantive issues when developing IEPs; (e) litigation that has addressed the IEP mandate of the IDEA; and (f) procedures for developing legally correct IEPs.

Purposes of the IEP

The development of an IEP is a collaborative effort between school personnel and parents to ensure that a student's special education program will meet his or her individual needs and confer meaningful educational benefit. The IEP serves other important purposes, including communication, management, accountability, compliance and monitoring, and evaluation (IDEA Regulations, 34 C.F.R. § 300 Appendix C:1).

Communication

The IEP is developed during an IEP meeting or meetings. The IEP meeting serves as a communication vehicle between parents and school personnel, who are equal participants in IEP planning. This process is an opportunity for collaboration in planning the student's education. Together they determine a student's needs and the services the school will provide to meet those needs. Additionally, they decide what the anticipated outcomes will be. The IEP meeting can also be a forum for resolving differences that may arise regarding a student's educational needs. If differences cannot be resolved at the IEP meeting, procedural safeguards are available to either party. (See Chapter 13 for elaborations on procedural safeguards.)

Management

The IEP is a management tool in two major ways. First the IDEA sets forth procedures that govern how a school will determine the special education and related services that will provide a FAPE. This set of procedures is referred to as the *IEP process* (Gorn, 1997). Second, the IEP document lists the resources the IEP team determines are necessary for the student to receive an appropriate education. The IEP is a written commitment that the school will provide a student the special education and related services designed to meet the student's unique needs. The IEP is like a contract that obligates the school district to provide a FAPE by delivering specified special education and related services.

Accountability

The IEP is a legally constituted mechanism that commits the school to provide the student with an appropriate special education program. Schools are accountable for implementing the IEP as it was developed. The school is also accountable for revising and rewriting the IEP when necessary. The IEP is not, however, a performance contract that imposes liability on a teacher, the IEP team members, or school officials if a student does not meet the IEP goals (IDEA Regulations, 34 C.F.R. § 300 Appendix C:60). That is, the IEP is not a guarantee that the student will accomplish all goals and objectives within the stated time period. The IEP does, however, commit the school district to providing the special education and related services and to making good faith efforts to carry out its provisions. If parents believe that good faith efforts are not being made to properly implement the IEP, they may ask for revisions in the program or invoke due process procedures.

Compliance and Monitoring

The IEP may be used by state or federal governmental agencies to monitor the special education services provided by the school. The courts often use IEP to assess a school's compliance with the FAPE mandate of the IDEA. The IEP may be inspected to ensure that a student is receiving an appropriate special education and that the school is meeting all the legal requirements as agreed to by school personnel and parents in the IEP process.

Evaluation

Finally, the IEP is an evaluation tool. The annual goals in the document are measured using the criteria listed in the IEP to determine the extent of the student's progress. To evaluate student progress toward meeting goals, the IEP must contain goals that are measurable and the appropriate school personnel must ensure that the goals will be measured. Furthermore, the IEP must describe how a student's annual goals will be measured and include a schedule for reporting on a student's progress toward his or her goals. Parents must be informed of their child's progress at least every 9 weeks.

The IEP Mandate

The IEP is created in a planning process in which school personnel and parents work together to develop a program of special education and related services that will result in meaningful educational benefit for the student for whom it is developed. Because the IEP is the foundation of a student's FAPE, it must be individualized; that is, the IEP must be developed to meet the unique needs of a student. Schools cannot use standard IEPs, nor can IEPs be based on available services. Neither can IEPs be designed by disabling condition or any other categorical programming (IDEA Regulations, 34 C.F.R. § 300 Appendix C).

The IEP is defined in the IDEA as "a written statement for a child with a disability that is developed, reviewed, and revised in accordance with [the requirements of the law]" (IDEA, 20 U.S.C. § 1414(d)(1)(A)). An IEP must be developed for each student in special education. Furthermore, it must be in effect before special education and related services are provided to an eligible student (IDEA Regulations, 34 C.F.R. § 300.342(b)). The IEP is a written document that describes a student's needs and provides a blueprint of the services the district will provide to meet those needs (Bateman & Linden, 1996).

To summarize, the IEP is both a process in which an IEP team develops an appropriate program and a written document delineating the special education and related services to be provided to an eligible student. Although the process has no required format for holding an IEP meeting and no required form for the IEP, the IDEA spells out extensive mandatory procedural requirements schools must follow when developing IEPs. The purpose of these procedures is to help ensure that teams of individuals collaborate to create an individualized and meaningful IEP that provides a FAPE.

IEP Development

Strict adherence to IEP procedural requirements, including notice, consent, and participation in meetings, is extremely important, since major procedural errors on the part of a school district may render an IEP inappropriate (Bateman, 1996; Osborne, 1994). When procedural violations occur in the IEP process, the Individuals with Disabilities Education Improvement Act of 2004 (IDEA 2004) directs due process hearing officers to primarily consider the substantive aspects of a student's education. Nevertheless, when a procedural violation occurs, courts and hearing officers scrutinize the effects of the violation to see if it interfered with the student's FAPE, impeded the parents' participation, or deprived a student of educational benefit (IDEA 20 U.S.C. § 1415(f)(3)(E)). If the violations interfere with the student's education in these ways, the IEP may be ruled inappropriate.

The IEP Planning Process

When parents, teachers, or other school personnel believe that a student may need special education services, they can refer the student to a school's multidisciplinary team. It is the multidisciplinary team's task to obtain informed consent for the evaluation and,

Figure 11.1
The IEP Process

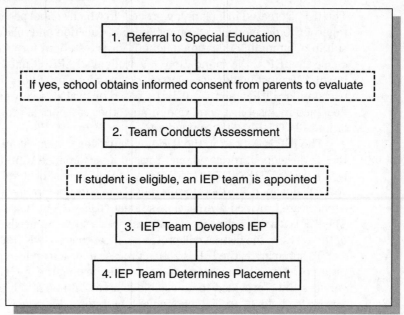

if obtained, to conduct the evaluation. If the student is determined to be eligible under IDEA then an IEP team is convened and an IEP developed. This process is depicted in Figure 11.1.

The referral process is generally initiated by school personnel, although if parents of a student with disabilities believe that their child's educational progress is not satisfactory or they disagree with the current IEP, they may request the meeting (IDEA Regulations, 34 C.F.R. § 300 Appendix C:11). If the referral process is initiated by the school, the parents of the referred student must be notified. Because the IDEA provides no specific requirements regarding the referral process, states and local school districts are free to develop their own referral procedures.

Following referral, if the multidisciplinary team (MDT) believes that the student may have a disability under the IDEA, the team contacts the student's parents to obtain informed consent to conduct an evaluation. If parents consent to the evaluation, the school assesses the student to determine the possible presence of a disability that adversely affects educational performance. The IEP team considers the results of the evaluation as well as the student's strengths and the parents' concerns for enhancing their child's education. IDEA 2004 requires that eligibility determination must be made within 60 days of consent for evaluation or within the timeframe set by a state (IDEA 20 U.S.C. § 1414(a)(1)(B)).

If the MDT finds a student is eligible for special education and related services, the next step is to convene the IEP team and develop the student's program of special education and related services. The school must convene an IEP team within 30 calendar days to develop the IEP (IDEA Regulations, 34 C.F.R. § 300.343(c)). The purpose of the time limit is to ensure that there will not be a significant delay between when a student is evaluated and determined eligible and when the student begins to receive services (IDEA Regulations, 34 C.F.R. § 300 Appendix C:7).

When developing the IEP, the participants discuss and develop a student's special education program. Regulations to the IDEA delineate the procedural requirements, including the required participants in the meeting and the actual content of the IEP, that must be followed in conducting the meeting and developing the IEP (IDEA Regulations, 34 C.F.R. §§ 300.340–300.350). During the meeting, participants review the results of the evaluation, the student's current records (including the current IEP if one exists), and other relevant information. The purpose of the meeting is to develop the student's educational program and document it in the IEP.

The actual format, procedures, and forms used in IEP meetings are not dictated by federal law but are the responsibility of the states and schools. School districts usually develop their own forms and procedures, although several states have developed forms for school districts' use. Federal statutes and regulations, however, mandate procedures that must be followed by schools in the IEP process.

A 1996 letter to OSEP queried the agency about a common practice in IEP meetings of bringing a completed IEP to the meeting and presenting it to the parents. This is not permissible (*Letter to Helmuth,* 1990). What is allowed, however, is bringing a draft IEP to the meeting as long as the parents understand it is draft only and the document does not interfere with the discussion of all aspects of the IEP before making final decisions about a student's educational program (Gorn, 1997).

The parents' signatures are not required on the IEP form; however, parental consent is required for the initial special education placement.* If parents have been told that a signature on the IEP constitutes consent for special education placement, the IEP can be used in this manner. Consent means that parents have been informed of all relevant aspects of the IEP, that they understand and agree in writing to the provision of a special education, and that they understand that the granting of consent is voluntary and can be revoked at any time. If the IEP is used to signify consent to placement in special education, language regarding the provision of consent should be included on the document. Furthermore, having the participants in the process sign the IEP is a way to document attendance.

The IDEA imposes no specific time limits within which the IEP must be implemented following its development, although the Office of Special Education Programs (OSEP) has indicated that generally no delay is permissible between the time the IEP is written and the provision of special education begins (OSEP Policy Letter, 1991b). Regulations specify only that the IEP must be implemented as soon as possible after the IEP meeting (IDEA Regulations, 34 C.F.R. § 300.342). A delay in implementation

---

*The Office of Civil Rights (OCR) found that a school district was not at fault for failing to implement an initial IEP when the parents refused to sign a consent form, which OCR stated was necessary for an initial placement in special education (*Davenport (IA) Community School District,* 1993).

is permitted in two situations: when the IEP meeting takes place during the summer or a vacation and when circumstances, such as arranging transportation, require a short delay. In most situations, however, the school should provide services immediately following IEP finalization (IDEA Regulations, 34 C.F.R. § 300 Appendix C:4). Regulations require that the IEP be in place at the beginning of the school year (IDEA Regulations, 34 C.F.R. § 300.342(a)). To ensure that this requirement is met, the school may hold the IEP meeting at the end of the preceding school year or during the summer months (*Myles S. v. Montgomery County Board of Education*, 1993).

IEP Planning Process Changes in IDEA 2004

IDEA 2004 includes six provisions intended to streamline the IEP planning process, especially during reviews and revisions. First, a member of the IEP team is not required to attend the IEP meeting or other meetings if the student's parents and the school personnel agree in writing that the person's attendance is not necessary because his or her area of curriculum or related services is not being modified or discussed at a meeting (§ 614(d)(1)(C)(i)). Second, a member of the IEP team may be excused from the IEP meeting if he or she submits a request in writing to the parents and the IEP team and both the parents and IEP team agree to excuse his or her attendance (§ 614(d)(1)(C)(ii)). These two provisions give IEP team members an opportunity to be excused from all or part of an IEP, thus releasing certain members, most likely general education teachers, from having to spend their time in meetings that do not directly concern them.

In the third provision, IDEA 2004 allows the IEP team to complete its work by means other than face-to-face meetings. Meetings can be held via conference calls, videoconferencing, or other means. Additionally, placement meetings, mediation meetings, resolution sessions, and the administrative aspects of due process hearings may be held using alternative means if the parents and school personnel agree this is acceptable. Fourth, if parents and school personnel agree, an existing IEP may be modified by writing a document to amend the IEP rather than convening a meeting to make the changes. Fifth, IDEA 2004 encouraged school districts to consolidate IEP meetings and reevaluation meetings whenever possible. Finally, IDEA 2004 allows the IEP team to make changes to the IEP by amending it rather than redrafting the entire document (IDEA, 20 U.S.C. § 1414(d)(3)(F)). These provisions were added in IDEA 2004 to make the IEP planning process more flexible and convenient for parents and school personnel.

In another provision in IDEA 2004, 15 states were allowed to apply to the U.S. Department of Education to be included in a program to pilot 3-year IEPs. The 3-year IEPs are comprehensive multiyear IEPs designed to coincide with natural transition points in the student's schooling (e.g., preschool to elementary school, elementary school to middle school, middle school to high school, secondary school to postsecondary activities) and allow IEP teams the opportunity to engage in long-term planning. States that take part in the program must allow parents to opt out of the 3-year IEP and use the traditional 1-year IEP. Additionally, parents who decide to use the 3-year IEP option must provide informed consent prior to being in the program. The required elements for a 3-year IEP include (a) measurable goals that coincide with natural transition points in a student's schooling, (b) measurable annual goals that will be used to measure progress toward the long-range goals, (c) a formal review by the IEP team of a student's IEP at the natural transition points, (d) an annual review of the IEP to determine a student's level of progress and whether the annual goals are being achieved, and (e) a thorough review of the IEP if the team decides the student is not making sufficient progress toward the goals in his or her IEP.

A provision in IDEA 2004 addresses what a school district's response should be when parents refuse to give their consent to special education placement or services. If parents of a student who has been determined to be eligible for special education services do not give their consent, the school may not provide service or use a due process hearing procedure to allow provision of services (IDEA, 20 U.S.C. § 1414(a)(1)(D)(ii)(II)). In such a situation, the school district will not be considered to be in violation of the requirement to make a FAPE available to the student because it did not provide special education and related services, even though the student may have needed them (IDEA, 20 U.S.C. § 1414(a)(1)(D)(ii)(III)(aa)). The school shall neither convene an IEP meeting nor develop an IEP.

Finally, IDEA 2004 includes provisions regarding students with IEPs who transfer into a school district from another school district or from another state. The school district that receives a transfer student with an IEP must provide the student with a FAPE. This means that the receiving school district must (a) provide the special education services that were in the student's previous IEP, (b) consult with the student's parents, (c) conduct an evaluation, and (d) develop a new IEP, if appropriate.

The IEP Team

The IDEA delineates the persons who are to compose the IEP team as well as persons who are permitted, but not required, to attend (IDEA Regulations 34 C.F.R. § 300.344(A)(1)–(3)). Figure 11.2 lists the required and discretionary participants of the IEP team. The school district is responsible for having the required participants at the IEP meeting. IEPs have been invalidated by the courts and by administrative law judges when the required participants were not involved in the process and their absence affected the document's development (*Girard School District*, 1992; *In re child with disabilities*, 1990; *New York City School District Board of Education*, 1992; OSEP Policy Letter, 1992; *W.G. v. Board of Trustees of Target Range School District No. 23*, 1992).

Generally the number of participants in the IEP meeting should be small because the meeting will tend to be more open and allow for more active parent involvement. Moreover, smaller team meetings may be less costly, easier to arrange and conduct, and more productive (IDEA Regulations, 34 C.F.R. § 300 Appendix C:20). Let's look next at the required participants.

The Student's Parents or Guardians

The IDEA clearly specifies that parents are to be equal partners in IEP development. Equal partnership includes the right to active participation in all discussions

Figure 11.2
IEP Team Members

Required Participants

- The student's parents or guardian
- A special education teacher (at least one)
- A general education teacher (at least one)
- A representative of educational agency(ies) (a) qualified to provide or supervise the provision of special education; (b) knowledgeable about the general education curriculum; and (c) knowledgeable about the availability of resources in the school
- A person who can interpret the instructional implications of the evaluation results (may be one of the preceding team members)
- The child, when appropriate (required for transition IEP)

Discretionary Participants

- Related services providers
- A person with expertise in assistive technology
- For a transition IEP, a representative of the agency that is likely to provide or pay for the transition services
- Other persons, at the discretion of the parents or the school. These individuals must have knowledge or special expertise about a student or his or her disability.
- Part C provider if a child is eligible for Part C

---

and decisions regarding their child's special education program. To this end, parents are an integral part of the IEP process. This includes meaningful participation in all special education decision making, including IEP development and placement decisions. IEPs developed without parental input have been invalidated (*New York City School District Board of Education,* 1992).

The school is required to follow specific procedures to ensure that parents attend and fully participate in the IEP meeting (IDEA Regulations, 34 C.F.R. § 300.345). Figure 11.3 contains the requirements to ensure parental participation. This includes giving parents a notice of the IEP meeting so they have an opportunity to attend and holding the meeting at a mutually agreeable time and location. The notice may be either written or oral and must include information about the time, purpose, and location of the meeting and the participants, by positions, who will be at the meeting. OSEP considers a notice given 10 days in advance of the meeting to be adequate. The bottom line is that schools must make good faith efforts to ensure that parents can be involved in the IEP planning process. If a parent cannot attend the meeting, the school may use alternative methods, such as conference calls, to hold the meeting. In such situations it is important that the IEP team keep detailed records of telephone calls, e-mails, letters, or other correspondence.

Figure 11.3
Parental Participation in the IEP Meeting

The educational agency shall take steps to ensure parental participation by:

1. Notifying parents of the meeting early enough to ensure participation
2. Scheduling the meeting at a mutually agreeable time and place
3. Including the following content in the notice:
   - The purpose, time, and location of the meeting and who will be in attendance
   - For a transition IEP, an invitation to the student and the name of the additional agencies invited
4. Using alternative methods if neither parent can attend (e.g., individual or conference telephone calls)
5. Giving the parents a copy of the IEP if they request it

When a student's parents are divorced, the school only has to invite the custodial parent. In such a situation, however, the IDEA's requirements would also be satisfied if the noncustodial parent attends. Unless parental rights have been terminated, a noncustodial parent has the right to attend all IEP-related meetings. If a parent's rights have been terminated, then the parent with custody of the child would have to give his or her permission for the noncustodial parent to attend IEP planning meetings.

If allowed by a state, school districts may recognize foster parents who are a child's primary caregivers as parents for IDEA purposes if the biological parents do not have authority to make legal decisions for their child (IDEA Regulations, 34 C.F.R. § 300.19). According to Bateman and Linden (1996), any errors in deciding who the parent is or which parent to include in the IEP process should be made on the side of inclusion rather than exclusion.

A Representative of the Local Educational Agency

The IEP team must include a representative of the school or school district. This individual must be qualified to provide or supervise the provision of the special education and to ensure that the educational services specified in the IEP will be provided. The representative of the agency must have knowledge regarding school district resources and the authority to commit them (IDEA Regulations, 34 C.F.R. § 300 Appendix C:13). If the representative can only commit resources within the school building, the IEP will not be valid (Martin, 1996). Moreover, the school district representative must be knowledgeable about the general education curriculum. This person cannot be the student's teacher or represent the student's teacher (OSEP Policy Letter, 1992). This position may be filled by the school principal, the special education administrator, or any member of the school staff designated by the principal or administrator. Furthermore, the representative must actually participate in the IEP meeting and not just appear briefly to sign documents (*Letter to Davilia*, 1992).

Furthermore, it is the duty of the representative of the school or school district to ensure that the IEP is not vetoed by other administrators who are not part of the team because OSEP has consistently held that school officials, such as school board members, may not change decisions made by the IEP teams (OSEP Policy Letter, 1991b, 1991c). As Bateman and Linden (1996) aptly state, "These requirements reveal that all the power to determine what services are needed, and therefore will be provided, rests with the IEP team and no one else."

The Student's Special Education Teacher

Until the passage of the IDEA Amendments of 1997, the IEP did not specify if the teacher on the core IEP team should be a student's general education or special education teacher. In the 1997 amendments, both were added as required participants on the IEP team. The participation of the student's special education teacher or provider is required to ensure that the person who will implement the IEP will be involved in its development. If a teacher directly involved in educating the student is not a member of the IEP team, the IEP may not be valid (*Brimmer v. Traverse City,* 1994). According to OSEP, at least one member of the IEP team must be qualified in the area of the student's disability (*Letter to McIntire,* 1989). Because the student's special education teacher usually has expertise in the student's disability, that person will typically fill this role.

Many school districts appoint case managers to coordinate the IEP process, and some states (e.g., Minnesota) require the appointment of a case or IEP manager, although case managers are not mandated by the IDEA. The manager's role usually is to coordinate the evaluation process, collect and synthesize all reports and relevant information, communicate with parents, and participate in and conduct the IEP meeting (IDEA Regulations, 34 C.F.R. § 300 Appendix C:24). The case manager is often the student's special education teacher.

The Student's General Education Teacher

The IDEA Amendments of 1997 added the student's general education teacher to the core IEP team if the student is participating, or may participate, in general education. Congress, finding that general education teachers often played a central role in the education of students with disabilities, stated that to the extent "appropriate," the general education teacher should participate in the development of the IEP, including the determination of appropriate behavioral interventions and strategies and supplementary aids and services, program modifications, and support for school personnel. Congress, however, did not intend that the general education teacher participate in all aspects of the IEP team's work (Senate Report, 1997). In fact, IDEA 2004 provides a means for IEP team members to be excused from all or part of IEP meetings.

When a student (e.g., a middle school or high school student) has multiple teachers, only one teacher is required to attend the IEP meeting. The school, however, may allow the other teachers to attend. Administrators may not take the place of teachers in IEP meetings (OSEP Policy Letter, 1992). Although the number of participants at the IEP meeting should generally be kept to a minimum, additional staff is required in some instances.

The primary purpose of having a regular education teacher on the team is to ensure input from someone who understands the general curricula. Additionally, general education teachers need to know what supplementary services will be provided for children in their classrooms.

A Person Who Can Interpret the Instructional Implications of the Evaluation Results

In the IDEA Amendments of 1997, an individual who can interpret the instructional implications of the evaluation data was added to the core IEP team. This role could be filled by one of the previously mentioned team members or by an additional member. Often school psychologists fill this role. The individual may have been added to the team to ensure that the IEP process begins with all members understanding the student's individual needs as determined in the evaluation.

The Student, When Appropriate

The school must inform parents that the student may attend the meeting. The student, however, should only be present when appropriate. Additionally, if parents decide that their child's attendance will be helpful, the child must be allowed to attend. Whenever possible, the school and parents should discuss the appropriateness of having the student attend prior to making a decision. In cases where transition services are discussed, the student must be invited (IDEA Regulations, 34 C.F.R. § 300.344(c)(i)). Beginning at age 16, students become an integral part of the IEP process because of transition requirements. Thus, they should attend the IEP meeting.

Related Services Personnel

When it is determined that the student will require related services, it is appropriate that related services personnel (e.g., social worker, school nurse, physical therapist) attend the IEP meeting and be involved in writing the IEP. The IDEA does not require that related services personnel attend the meeting; however, if related services personnel do not attend the IEP meeting, they should provide a written recommendation to the IEP committee regarding the nature, frequency, and amount of related services to be provided to the student (IDEA Regulations, 34 C.F.R. § 300 Appendix C:23). In IDEA 2004, Congress added school nursing services to the list of potential related services. Whenever needed, therefore, a registered school nurse should be a member of the IEP team to help define and make decisions about a student's education-related health needs.

Transition Services Personnel

When a student turns 16 years old, transition services must be included in his or her IEP. A previous IEP requirement to provide transition planning in the IEPs of 14-year-old students was removed when the IDEA was reauthorized in 2004. When transition services are to be considered at the IEP meeting, the school must invite the student and a representative of the agency likely to provide or pay for the transition services. If the student does not attend, the school must take steps to ensure that the student's interests and preferences are considered in designing the transition plan (IDEA Regulations, 34 C.F.R. § 300.344(c)(i)(2)).

Additionally, the IEP team must invite a representative of the agency that will be participating in transition services. If the agency does not send a representative, the school must take steps to ensure that the agency participates in the planning process.

According to Ray (2002), the transition members of a student's IEP team may not be regular participants on the team. They may be individuals from outside the school (e.g., business owners, managers, representatives from vocational schools) who can provide information about post-school services and assist in providing those services. When this information is available before the student graduates, the IEP team can modify the IEP in accordance with the information provided by transition team members (Ray, 2002).

Other Individuals at the Discretion of the Parents or School

Either the school or the parents may invite other persons to the meeting. Weber (2002) contends that confidentiality rules may prevent the attendance of persons who are not employed by the school district unless the parents give consent in writing. This rule would not apply to attorneys working for the school district or to related services personnel. The Department of Education, however, discourages the involvement of attorneys (Pitasky, 2002). In IDEA 2004, Congress specifically prohibited attorneys from collecting fees in IDEA cases for any time in which they attended IEP-related meetings, unless such meetings were required by a hearing officer or judge (IDEA 20 U.S.C. § 1415(i)(3)(B)).

It is inappropriate for representatives of teacher organizations to attend an IEP meeting (IDEA Regulations, 34 C.F.R. § 300 Appendix C:20). When the school does invite additional persons, it must inform the parents. Parents are not similarly required to inform the school districts of additional persons they will bring to the IEP meeting. It would be appropriate, however, for the school to inquire if the parents intend to bring other participants. Parents may also request the presence of school personnel at the IEP (Martin, 1996).

Lombardo (1999) suggested that school districts should seriously consider appointing "experts" to IEP teams. By doing this, especially when the school district does not have staff with meaningful expertise in a particular area, the district shows it is serious about developing a meaningful intervention program. In such situations it is also advisable that the school district get the experts to develop meaningful staff development activities.

Parents may bring anyone who is familiar with education laws or the student's needs, including, for example, independent professionals (e.g., psychologists, therapists). The school district is required to consider recommendations offered by the additional participants, but it is not required to accept the recommendations.

Content of the IEP

The IDEA requires that, at a minimum, eight components be present in the IEP (IDEA, 20 U.S.C. § 1401(a)(20); IDEA Regulations, 34 C.F.R. § 300.346). States and local agencies, however, may require additional elements. Failure to include all of these elements in IEPs is a frequent source of litigation (Martin, 1996). In fact, IEPs have been invalidated by the courts when the required elements were not written into the IEP and their absence affected the student's free appropriate public education (*Big Beaver Falls Area School District v. Jackson,* 1993; *Board of Education of the Casadaga Valley Central School District,* 1994; *Burlington School District,* 1994; *In re Child with Disabilities,* 1993; *New Haven Board of Education,* 1993; OSEP Policy Letter, 1991a; *School Administrative Unit #66,* 1993). It is crucial, therefore, that these elements be discussed at the IEP meeting and included in the document. Figure 11.4 lists the eight elements required in the IEP (IDEA Regulations, 34 C.F.R. § 300.346). Figure 11.5 is an example of an IEP form that meets the content requirements of the IDEA.

The IDEA also requires that the IEP team address participation and involvement in the general education curriculum. According to Congress, the addition of this language is not intended to result in an increase in the size of the IEP document (e.g., a greater number of goals and objectives); rather, the new focus is intended to place attention on the accommodations and adjustments needed for the student with disabilities to successfully participate in the general education curriculum (Senate Report, 1997). The new focus was written by Congress into the 1997 amendments because the IDEA presumes "that children with disabilities are to be educated in regular classes" (Senate Report, 1997, p. 21).

Present Levels of Academic Achievement and Functional Performance

The first component of an IEP is a statement of the student's present levels of academic achievement and functional performance (PLAAFP). This statement, which until the passage of IDEA 2004 was present levels of educational performance, must include information about how the student's disability affects his or her involvement and progress in the general education curriculum. For preschool children this statement should specify how the disability affects the child's participation in the appropriate activities. The purpose of the statement is to describe the problems that interfere with the student's education so that annual goals can be developed (Tucker & Goldstein, 1992). In effect, the statement of PLAAFP is the starting point from which teams develop the IEP and measure its success. The statement should contain information on the student's academic performance; test scores and an explanation of those scores; physical, health, and sensory status; emotional development; social development; and prevocational and vocational skills. In IDEA 2004, the new term for present levels emphasizes that in addition to academic achievement, IEP teams must also address other areas of student need, which may include "nonacademic areas such as behavioral problems, communication, difficulties, daily life activities, and mobility." This statement may include nonacademic areas, such as

Figure 11.4
Content of the IEP

The IEP for each IDEA eligible student must include:

1. A statement of a student's present levels of academic achievement and functional performance

2. A statement of a student's measurable annual goals, including academic and functional goals; short-term instructional objectives for students who take alternate assessments

3. A statement of how the student's progress toward meeting the annual goals will be measured and when periodic reports on the student's progress toward the goals will be provided to the parents

4. A statement of the special education, related services, and supplementary aids and services, based on peer-reviewed research, to be provided to the student and a statement of the program modifications or supports for school personnel

5. An explanation of the extent, if any, to which the student will not participate with students without disabilities in general education

6. A statement of any accommodations necessary to measure the academic and functional performance of the student on state- or district-wide assessment of student achievement or a statement of why a student cannot participate in the regular assessment and how the alternate assessment was selected

7. The projected date for beginning the services and modifications and the anticipated frequency, location, and duration of those services

8. A statement of appropriate measurable postsecondary goals based on age-appropriate transition assessments services and the transition services needed to assist the student in reaching those goals (Transition services must be included in the IEPs of students for students who are 16 years old.)

behavioral problems, communication difficulties, and mobility. Moreover, how these problems affect a student's performance in the general education curriculum should be specified. Labels (e.g., learning disabled, emotionally disturbed) are not appropriate substitutions for descriptions of educational performance.

The statement of current educational performance is a baseline from which the student's needs may be considered (Martin, 1979). The statement of needs should be written in objective terms using data from the multidisciplinary team's evaluation. When test scores are included in this section, an explanation of the results should be provided. The results of these scores should be understandable to all parties involved. Areas of educational performance in which the student has deficiencies should have corresponding goals and objectives, and any program or service must also relate to the current needs.

Figure 11.5
A Sample IEP

INDIVIDUALIZED EDUCATION PROGRAM (IEP)

IEP TEAM MEMBERS

Position	*Name*
LEA Representative:	_____ _____
General Education Teacher:	_____ _____
Special Education Teacher:	_____ _____
Evaluator:	_____ _____
Parents:	_____ _____
Others:	_____ _____
Transition Personnel:	_____ _____
Student:	_____

STUDENT

Name: _____   Date of Birth: _____

Sex: _____ Grade: _____   Social Security/Identification #: _____

Primary Disability: _____

Secondary Disabilities: _____

Student's Strengths:

Parental Concerns:

LENGTH AND DURATION OF IEP

Date of IEP Meeting: _____   IEP Initiation Date: _____

Annual Review Date: _____   IEP Expiration Date: _____

(Continued)

Figure 11.5
A Sample IEP—Continued

PRESENT ACADEMIC ACHIEVEMENT & FUNCTIONAL PERFORMANCE

Area of Need	Assessment Instruments	Date	Findings

How the student's disability affects the student's involvement and progress in the general education curriculum:

How the preschool student's disability affects the student's participation in appropriate activities:

For students who take alternate assessments aligned to alternate achievement standards, a description of the benchmarks or short-term objectives:

Figure 11.5
Continued

MEASURABLE ANNUAL GOALS, INCLUDING ACADEMIC AND FUNCTIONAL GOALS

Annual Goal:

How progress toward meeting the goal will be measured:

Review dates and results of progress monitoring:

Method of reporting progress:

Note: Attach as many goal pages as necessary.

SPECIAL EDUCATION AND RELATED SERVICES

Special Education Services	Location	Hours/Week

Related Services/Supplementary Aids and Services	Hours/Week

Modifications and Supports for School Personnel

_____
_____
_____
_____

(Continued)

Figure 11.5
A Sample IEP—Continued

LEAST RESTRICTIVE ENVIRONMENT
Extent to Which the Student Will Not Participate in General Education:

Rationale:

PARTICIPATION IN STATE- AND DISTRICTWIDE ASSESSMENTS
Will the student require modifications to participate
in assessments?   Yes _____   No _____
Testing accommodations

Will the student take an alternate assessment?
    Yes _____   No _____

Rationale for excluding the student from participation:

What alternate assessment will be administered?

TRANSITION SERVICES (Required in the first IEP after the student turns age 16)
Transition Assessment:

Postsecondary Goals:

Figure 11.5
Continued

Transition Services:

If the student has reached the age of majority, has the student been informed of his or her rights under the IDEA?

Yes _____   No _____

SPECIAL CONSIDERATIONS

Does the student's behavior impede learning
of self or others?   Yes _____   No _____

(If yes, the IEP should address behavior.)

Is the student limited in English proficiency?   Yes _____   No _____

(If yes, the IEP should address language needs.)

Does the student require assistive technology
devices or services?   Yes _____   No _____

(If yes, describe.)

Other special considerations:

Measurable Annual Goals

The IEP team determines annual goals for students in special education. The goals are written to reflect what a student needs to become involved in and to make progress in the general education curriculum and in other educational areas related to the disability. These goals focus on remediation of academic or nonacademic problems and are based on the student's current level of educational performance. At least one goal should be written for each identified area of need. Failure to write goals for each need area can render an IEP inappropriate (*Board of Education of the St. Louis Central School District*, 1993; *Burlington School District*, 1994; *New Haven Board of Education*, 1993).

Annual goals are projections the team makes regarding the progress of the student in one school year. In writing the annual goals, IEP teams should consider the student's past achievement, current level of performance, practicality of goals, priority needs, and amount of instructional time devoted to reaching the goal (Strickland & Turnbull, 1990). While goals should be written for a level that the student has a reasonable chance of reaching, courts have indicated that when goals are so un-ambitious that achieving them will not result in meaningful improvements in performance, such goals may render the IEP inappropriate (*Adams v. Hansen,* 1985; *Carter v. Florence County School District Four,* 1991).

If a teacher works with students who take the statewide test with or without testing accommodations (e.g., students with mild and moderate disabilities), benchmarks and short-term objectives (STOs) are no longer required by IDEA. Congress, in IDEA 2004, removed the STO requirement because they believed that (a) STOs were not necessary when an IEP contained measurable goals, (b) STOs were nonfunctional, and (c) STOs merely resulted in additional paperwork for teachers, with no corresponding benefit. Instead, Congress stressed the requirement that special education teachers monitor their students' educational progress during the school year and use that data to alter the program if necessary. Now, for each annual goal, the IEP must include information about how the student's progress toward each goal will be measured and when and how a student's progress will be reported to parents. In the report to the parents, the teacher must include information regarding how the goals are measured and whether the student is likely to achieve stated goals if his or her current rate of progress continues. Clearly, Congress intended that revisions to the IEP would be made if progress toward goals was inadequate (Huefner, 2000). If a student takes an alternate assessment based on alternate achievement standards, his or her IEP must include benchmarks or STOs. Furthermore, the STOs must describe expected student performance in measurable terms. The benchmarks are intermediate steps to be measured leading to the achievement of the annual goals (*Board of Education of the Whitesboro Central School District,* 1994). They are achievable components of the annual goal that allow monitoring of student progress on a short-term basis throughout the year. If a student achieves the STOs, therefore, he or she should also achieve the annual goals (*Pocatello School District #25,* 1991). The benchmarks describe what a student is expected to accomplish in a given time period.

The purpose of measurable annual goals and/or measurable annual goals and objectives is to help determine whether a student is making educational progress and if the special education program is providing meaningful educational benefit. Goals and objectives, correctly written, enable teachers and parents to monitor a student's progress in a special education program and make educational adjustments when necessary (Deno, 1992). In fact, Congress viewed the requirement of "measurable" annual goals as crucial to the success of the IEP (Senate Report, 1997).

It seems that one of the biggest challenges that IEP teams face is writing measurable annual goals (Bateman & Herr, 2003; Bateman & Linden, 1996; Lake, 2002). The purpose of annual goals is to develop an individualized metric to measure a student's program; goals are not meant to be applied to the average child (Lake, 2002).

The reauthorization of the IDEA in 1997 and 2004 placed an emphasis on developing measurable annual goals and then actually measuring them. The reauthorized IDEA requires that IEPs include a description of (a) how a student's goals will be measured and (b) when reports on how the student is progressing toward all the annual goals will be provided to his or her parents. The progress reports must be given to the students concurrent with the issuance of report cards. In other words, IEP teams must now ensure that a student's goals are measurable, say how they will measure the goals, and then actually measure them. Moreover, if a student is not progressing on a pace to meet his or her goals, the teacher must make instructional changes to the student's program and continue to monitor progress.

Following the passage of IDEA 1997, Huefner (2000) predicted that hearing officers and courts would now begin to carefully scrutinize student's IEPs and goals to see if a student had actually made progress toward the goals. She further asserted that for IEP teams, this meant if a student is not progressing at the expected rate, the team should be prepared to explain why the gap exists or to revise the IEP. Similarly, Lake (2002) stated that failing to change instructional procedures in the face of lack of student progress could lead to a ruling that a school had denied FAPE. Clearly, IDEA 2004 places even greater emphasis on the importance of IanceEP teams monitoring student progress on a frequent and ongoing basis and changing a student's educational program if he or she is not progressing toward the annual goals.

Special Education and Related Services and Supplementary Aids and Services

The third requirement is a statement of the specific educational services to be provided by the school. This includes special education, related services, and supplementary aids and services required to assist a student in attaining the IEP goals and objectives. The statement of services must be unambiguous so that the school's commitment of resources is clear to parents and other members of the team (IDEA Regulations, 34 C.F.R. § 300 Appendix C:51).

Statements of related services discuss the services and equipment provided to help students benefit from special education; that is, the services provided to students should enable them (a) to advance appropriately toward attaining annual goals; (b) to be involved in and progress in the general education curriculum and to participate in extracurricular and other nonacademic activities; and (c) to be educated with other children with and without disabilities. This requirement commits the school district to providing these services at no charge to parents. The team must determine the special education and related services needs of a student based on the student's needs, not on the availability of services. In addition to enumerating the types of services, the IEP should also include the amount, frequency, and duration of services. If the required services are not available in the district but are determined by the IEP team to be necessary, they must be provided through contracts or arrangements with other agencies.

In IDEA 2004, Congress added a requirement that a student's special education services be based on peer-reviewed research when possible. This aligns IDEA with NCLB's requirement regarding the importance of basing instruction on research validated practices.

The supplementary aids and services provided as part of a student's special education must be included in the IEP (IDEA Regulations, 34 C.F.R. § 300 Appendix C:48). It is not necessary, however, to include components of a student's educational program that are not part of the special education and related services required by the student. In fact, Gorn (1997) contends that nonmandatory educational services should not be included in the IEP, because adding particular nonmandated services to the IEP may create an obligation on the part of the school district to provide the services while the IEP is in effect. Moreover, in a report on the IDEA Amendments of 1997, the Senate Committee on Labor and Human Resources noted that while teaching and related services methodologies are appropriate subjects to discuss in an IEP meeting, they should not be written into the IEP (Senate Report, 1997).

The Extent to Which Students Will Not Participate in the General Education Classroom

The IEP must also delineate the amount of time the student will not participate in general education classes with students without disabilities. Students with disabilities must be allowed to interact with their peers to the maximum extent appropriate in both academic and nonacademic settings. When choosing the setting for a student's special education, the IEP team must place the student in the least restrictive environment (LRE) that is appropriate. A statement in the IEP regarding the extent of integration with students without disabilities is required to document the team's LRE decision (Strickland & Turnbull, 1990). A mere conclusionary statement that the multidisciplinary team has determined a particular setting to be the LRE would not pass legal scrutiny. According to the court in *Thorndock v. Boise Independent School District* (1988), a statement is required that describes a student's ability or inability to participate in a general education program and essentially provides justification for the team's decision.

If modifications in the general education classroom are necessary to ensure that the student participates in general education, the modifications must be incorporated into the IEP (OSEP Policy Letter, 1993). This applies to any general education programs in which a student participates (IDEA Regulations, 34 C.F.R. § 300 Appendix C:48).

Students' Participation in the Administration of State- or Districtwide Assessments of Student Achievement

The IDEA also requires that all students with disabilities be included in state- and districtwide assessments of student progress. Because students with disabilities may need individual accommodations to participate in these assessments, the IEP must include a statement detailing all such accommodations. If the IEP team determines that a student cannot be accurately assessed, even with modifications, using the regular assessment, the IEP must state why the assessment is not appropriate and list alternative assessments that will be used in place of the state- or districtwide assessments. Readers should check with their state departments of education regarding which accommodations are appropriate and what constitutes an alternate assessment. In other words, students with disabilities are to take the regular statewide assessment unless the IEP specifies how they will take the test or specifies that the student will take an alternate assessment and then justifies why this is necessary. Thus, the IEP does not determine if a student will take a statewide assessment, but rather how he or she will take it.

The Projected Date of Initiation and Anticipated Duration of the IEP

The IEP must be initiated as soon as possible after it is written. The only exceptions are if the IEP is written during a vacation period, over the summer, or when circumstance requires a short delay (such as working out transportation arrangements). When a student moves from another district, the delay should not be more than a week. A student must not be placed in a special education program prior to the initiation date in the IEP.

Transition Services

If a student is 16 years old, the IEP must contain a statement of needed transition services. Transition services are those services that help a student to prepare for life after school. This requirement was added to the IDEA in 1990. Transition services are

> a coordinated set of activities for a student, designed within an outcome-oriented process, which promotes movement from school to post-school activities, including post-secondary education, vocational training, integrated employment (including supported employment), continuing and adult education, adult services, independent living, or community participation. The coordinated set of activities shall be based upon the individual student's needs, taking into account the student's preferences and interests, and shall include instruction, community experiences, the development of employment and other post-school adult living objectives, and, when appropriate, acquisition of daily living skills and functional vocational evaluation. (20 U.S.C. § 1401(a)(19))

Congress was concerned that many high school age students in special education drop out of school or leave the school setting unprepared for adult life and responsibility (Gorn, 1997). Gorn (1997) noted that Congress added these requirements to the IEP to ensure that the IEP team would carefully consider where each student is heading after he or she leaves school and to determine what services will assist a student in reaching his or her post-school goals. The keystone of the transition services, like special education services in general, is individualization.

The purpose of including transition services in the IEP, therefore, is to (a) infuse a longer-range perspective into the IEP process; (b) assist each student to make a meaningful transition from the school setting to a post-school setting, which could include further education, employment, or independent living; and (c) help students better reach their potential as adults (Ray, 2002; Tucker & Goldstein, 1992). Most often the transition services focus on the transition from school to work. An IEP that includes transition services must address the areas listed in the IDEA's definition (i.e., instruction, community services, and employment and other adult-living objectives). If any of these required services are not included in a student's transition plan, the IEP must include an explanatory note detailing the reasons for exclusion (Goldstein, 1993).

According to Lake (2002), three of the most frequent mistakes made by schools are failing to (a) address transition in the IEP of a student who is 16 or older, (b) include the required or proper transition participants at the IEP meeting, (c) inform the parents about the role of transition planning, and (d) develop a transition plan that includes a coordinated set of activities to help the student meet his or her post-school

goals. Lake asserts that failing to comply with the aforementioned procedural requirements will usually result in a substantial deprivation of a student's right to a free appropriate public education.

Courts have not looked kindly on school districts that failed to include transition
requirements when they were needed, or when the school district develops a minimal
and largely meaningless transition plan. For example, a federal district court found
that a minimal approach to the IEP team's responsibility to include transition plans did
not meet the legal requirements of the IDEA. In this case, *Yankton S.D. v. Schramm*
(1995), the extent of the plaintiff's transition plan required that the student would
need public and private transportation with assistive devices when appropriate, and
that if the student was eligible for SSI, then she was also appropriate for Medicaid. In
all the other areas of the plaintiff's IEP, the team has just written "not applicable."
Clearly, the school district did not understand its responsibilities under IDEA.

In IDEA 2004, Congress altered the transition requirements in IEPs by requiring
that IEP teams include appropriate measurable postsecondary goals that are based
on appropriate transition assessments. Furthermore, these goals must be related to
training, further education, employment, and, when appropriate, independent living
skills. The law also includes a provision designed to facilitate the transition to a student's post-school life. IEP teams are no longer required to conduct an evaluation
prior to graduation from high school with a regular diploma or by aging out of IDEA
eligibility; now the IEP team is required to prepare recommendations and a summary
of the student's academic achievement and functional performance, which includes
recommendations on how to assist the student to meet his or her postsecondary
goals (IDEA 1414 § (e)(5)(B)(ii)). The student gives this summary to representatives of the postsecondary school he or she will attend or to future employers.

Reporting Requirements and Measurement Criteria to Determine Progress Toward the Annual Goals

The IEP must include a statement of how a student's progress toward the annual
goals will be measured. This requirement is a response to the movement toward
greater accountability in education. The measurement criteria and procedures must
be appropriate for evaluating progress toward the particular goal. The purpose of this
provision is to inform parents and educators how a student's progress toward his or
her annual goals will be measured. Additionally, this statement must delineate how a
student's parents will be regularly informed about their child's progress toward the
annual goals. Parents of students with disabilities must be informed about their
child's progress as regularly as are parents of children without disabilities (e.g.,
through regular report cards). Congress suggested providing an IEP report card
along with a student's general education report card (Senate Report, 1997). Furthermore, Congress suggested that such a report card could list the IEP goals and
rank each goal on a continuum (e.g., no progress, good progress, goal completed).

There is probably less substantive compliance with this component of the IEP than
any other (Tucker & Goldstein, 1992). Appropriate evaluation of a student's progress
toward meeting IEP goals and objectives is essential. Without such evaluation, the

goals and objectives are meaningless because it will be impossible to determine success or failure. If the goals and objectives of the IEP cannot be measured or evaluated, the IEP will not appropriately address the student's needs. The Idaho Supreme Court, in *Thorndock v. Boise Independent School District* (1988), held that because a student's IEP goals and objectives lacked objective measurement criteria, the IEP was inappropriate. Similarly, in *Board of Education of the Casadaga Valley Central School District* (1994), the IEP of a student classified as "other health impaired" was invalidated because it failed to set forth objective criteria and evaluation procedures.

Special Considerations in IEP Development

The IDEA includes a section that requires that five special considerations be included in an IEP, if necessary. First, in the situation of a student with behavioral problems, regardless of the student's disability category, the IEP should include a behavior management plan. This plan should be based on a functional behavioral assessment and include positive behavioral interventions, strategies, and supports to address the behavior problems proactively. Second, when an IEP is developed for a student with limited English proficiency, the student's language needs that relate to the IEP must be considered. Third, in developing an IEP for a student who is blind or visually impaired, the IEP must provide for instruction in Braille and the use of Braille unless the team determines that instruction in Braille is not appropriate. Fourth, when a student is deaf or hard of hearing, the IEP team must consider the student's language and communication needs, opportunities for direct communications with peers and professionals in the student's language and communication mode, academic level, and full range of needs, including opportunities for direct instruction in the student's language and communication mode. Finally, the IEP team should consider whether the student requires assistive technology devices and services.

Placement Decisions

The IDEA Amendments of 1997 require that in most cases the placement decision should be made by the IEP team. Until the 1997 amendments, the IDEA only required that the placement decisions be made by a knowledgeable group of persons. The parents must participate in the placement decision. When making a placement decision, it is important that IEP teams should only consider placement after the IEP has been developed and the school district has determined the student's least restrictive environment. Making preplacement decisions or final placement determinations outside of the proper forum is a serious mistake and can lead to a denial of FAPE (Lake, 2002).

Substantive Requirements

The crucial importance of the IEP was signified by the U.S. Supreme Court in *Board of Education of the Hendrick Hudson Central School District v. Rowley* (1982; hereafter *Rowley*). In part one of the two-part test developed to guide lower courts in determining compliance with the FAPE mandate of the IDEA, the high court directed the courts to examine the IEP. In the second part of the test, courts were directed to determine whether the IEP was "reasonably calculated to enable the [student with disabilities] to receive educational benefits" (*Rowley*, p. 207). (See Chapter 9 for elaborations of the *Rowley* test.) When courts are called on to determine whether a school district has offered an appropriate special education, the courts, acting on the directives from the *Rowley* decision, will often examine the IEP content.

Parental Participation

One of the most important of the IDEA mandates is that parents be equal partners in the IEP process. Parental participation is so crucial to the IEP process that the IDEA contains specific guidelines that schools must follow to ensure equal parental participation (IDEA Regulations, 34 C.F.R. § 300.345(a)–(f)). In fact, Congress considered strengthening the role of parents in the special education process one of the most important goals of the IDEA Amendments of 1997 (Senate Report, 1997).

The school must take steps to ensure that one or both parents are present at the IEP meeting or are afforded an opportunity to participate. The school must give parents or guardians sufficient notice of the IEP development meeting so that they have an opportunity to attend. The notice provided by the school must explain the purpose of the meeting, its time and location, and the persons to be in attendance. Participants in the meeting do not have to be identified by name; however, they must be identified by position (Gorn, 1997).

The meeting may be conducted without the parents in attendance if the school is unable to convince the parents to attend. The school must have a record of its attempts to arrange a meeting. Examples of the documentation of these attempts include items such as: (a) detailed records of telephone calls made or attempted, and the results of those calls; (b) copies of correspondence and any responses received; and (c) detailed records of visits made to the parents' home or place of employment, and the results of those visits (IDEA Regulations, 34 C.F.R. § 300.345(2)(d)).

The IDEA does not specify how far in advance the school district must notify parents, but it does state that notification must be early enough to ensure that parents have the opportunity to attend the IEP meeting (IDEA Regulations, 34 C.F.R. § 300.345(a)). Furthermore, school personnel have to work with parents to hold a meeting at a mutually agreeable time and place. The school does not have to honor every parental request to schedule the meeting, but the district must make good faith efforts to mutually agree on scheduling. In determining the meeting time and place, however, school personnel are allowed to consider their own scheduling needs (OSEP Policy Letter, 1992). An IEP meeting can be held without parents in attendance if the school is unable to convince them that they should attend. In such cases, the school personnel must keep a record of their attempts to arrange the meeting. If parents refuse to participate, the school district still has a responsibility to provide a FAPE to eligible students (Gorn, 1997).

The school must also make efforts to ensure that parents understand the proceedings, including arranging for an interpreter for parents who are deaf or whose native language is not English. If requested, the school must give the parents a copy of the IEP. The IEP meeting may be videotaped or audiotaped at the discretion of either the parents or the school (*Letter to Breecher,* 1990; IDEA Regulations, 34 C.F.R. § 300 Appendix C:12). The party taping the proceedings may obtain the consent of the other party, but consent is not required. Recordings must be kept confidential.

When the parents cannot be located, surrogate parents must be appointed to represent the interests of the student. Surrogate parents have all the rights and responsibilities of the parent; they are entitled to participate in the IEP meeting, view the student's educational records, receive notice, provide consent, and invoke a due process hearing (IDEA Regulations, 34 C.F.R. § 300.514). (For elaborations on appointing surrogate parents, see Chapter 13.) If the parents can be located but are unwilling to attend, the educational agency is not empowered to appoint a surrogate parent (*Letter to Perryman,* 1987). In such situations, the school should hold the meeting and document attempts to involve the parents.

Although parental participation is extremely important in the development of the IEP, parents do not have an absolute veto over the final results (*Buser v. Corpus Christi ISD,* 1994). When the parents and school personnel cannot reach agreement on an IEP, they should, when possible, agree to an interim special plan for serving the student until the disagreement is resolved (*Letter to Boney,* 1991; IDEA Regulations, 34 C.F.R. § 300 Appendix C:35). If no agreement is reached, the last IEP (if one exists) remains in effect until a final resolution. When the school and parents agree about basic IEP services but disagree about a related service, the IEP should be implemented in the areas of agreement. Additionally, the IEP should document the points of disagreement, and attempts to resolve the disagreement should be undertaken (IDEA Regulations, 34 C.F.R. § 300 Appendix C:35). If the disagreement concerns a fundamental issue, such as placement, the school should remind the parents of their right to call a due process hearing and attempt to develop an interim educational program. If agreements cannot be reached, the use of mediation or some informal means for resolving the disagreements prior to going to due process should be recommended (IDEA Regulations, 34 C.F.R. § 300 Appendix C:35). If a due process hearing is initiated, the school may not change the current educational placement unless the parents and school agree otherwise. For example, if the student is in a general education classroom and the parents cannot agree on a special education placement, even if they agree on the need for special education, the student must remain in the general education classroom unless the school and parents can agree on an interim placement. The same is true if the student is currently in a special education placement (IDEA Regulations, 34 C.F.R. § 300.513).

A completed IEP may not be presented to the parents in the IEP meeting. According to OSEP, presenting a completed document to the parents for review would minimize the parents' contributions, even if the document was to be used only as a basis for discussion (*Letter to Helmuth,* 1990). Schools may prepare a draft of an IEP, however, to present to the parents at the IEP meeting for discussion purposes. This draft may consist of evaluation findings, statements of present levels of performance, recommendations regarding goals and objectives, and the kinds of special education and related services recommended. This document may not be represented as the final IEP (*Letter to Helmuth*, 1990; IDEA Regulations, 34 C.F.R. § 300 Appendix C:55). At the beginning of a meeting in which the draft document is presented, it must be clarified that the document is only a working draft for review and discussion.

Reviewing and Revising the IEP

The IEP must be reviewed—and, if necessary, revised—at least annually (IDEA Regulations, 34 C.F.R. § 300.343(d)). The review must be conducted under the following circumstances: (a) the student has shown a lack of progress toward the annual goals, and in the general education curriculum where appropriate; (b) the results of a reevaluation need to be considered; (c) the parents have provided additional information about the child; (d) the student's needs are anticipated to change; and (e) other considerations as deemed appropriate.

The timing of these meetings is to be left to the school's discretion. The parents or the school, however, may initiate the IEP reviews as often as is deemed necessary (Gorn, 1997). If either the school or parents decide that components of the IEP (e.g., annual goals or short-term objectives) need revision, a new IEP meeting must be called.

The IEP remains in effect until it is revised or until a new IEP is written. The IEP cannot be revised unless the parents are notified about the proposed change and the reasons for the change. When a student moves from one district to another, the student's former IEP is to be implemented until the new district evaluates the student and writes a new IEP (IDEA Regulations, 34 C.F.R. § 300 Appendix C:6). If the current IEP is not forwarded by the student's former school district or is inappropriate, the new district should conduct an IEP meeting as soon as possible. If the IEP is appropriate and can be implemented as written, however, the new district can use it without developing a new IEP.

If a school district proposes to change any aspect of the student's special education program, or refuses to change aspects of the student's program, it must issue prior notification to the parent. The notice must include a full explanation of proposed actions, justification for the changes, reasons for the rejection of alternatives, parental appeal rights, and other procedural safeguards. As long as the school provides adequate notice and conducts meetings in accordance with procedures set forth in the IDEA, parental consent is not required for review and revision of the IEP. If parents reject revisions, they have the option of calling for a due process hearing (IDEA Regulations, 34 C.F.R. § 300.506).

Communicating the Requirements of the IEP

The IDEA requires that the IEP must be implemented as developed. This requirement applies to both special and general education. According to Martin (1996), some administrators misread the Family Educational Rights and Privacy Act (FERPA) as prohibiting release of IEP information to teachers because it is confidential. This is an incorrect understanding of the requirements of FERPA. (Chapter 14 elaborates the FERPA requirements.) Teachers working with a student who has an IEP are entitled to review the information contained in the document. Schools have an affirmative duty to inform these teachers of any requirements in the IEP.

Furthermore, if a teacher is not implementing an IEP as required, the school must take steps to correct the situation. In *Doe v. Withers* (1993), an IEP required general education teachers to modify testing by giving oral examinations to a student with learning disabilities. The student's social studies teacher deliberately chose not to modify tests, even though it was required by the IEP. The parents prevailed in a lawsuit against the teacher. The court assessed the teacher compensatory and punitive damages in the amount of $15,000.

Placement in Private Schools

When a school district places a student in a private setting, the IEP remains the responsibility of the district. Prior to placement, the school district should hold an IEP meeting that includes a representative of the private agency. In subsequent meetings the responsible school district may allow the private facility to conduct annual reviews, but the district retains responsibility for ensuring that the parents and a representative of the home school district participate and agree to any changes in the IEP (Weber, 2002). In situations where public schools provide special education services to students in private or parochial schools, the public school is responsible for the IEP. A representative of the private or parochial school attends the meeting.

Section 504 and the IEP

Section 504 of the Rehabilitation Act of 1973 (hereafter Section 504) does not require the preparation of an IEP for students protected under the law. Regulations to Section 504 allow a school district to use an IEP to fulfill the law's requirements, although this is only one method of meeting those requirements (Section 504 Regulations, 34 C.F.R. § 104.33(b)(2)). Consequently, it is good practice to prepare a written individualized plan, in the manner of an IEP, to document educational services the school district provides to a student under Section 504 (Fossey, Hosie, Soniat, & Zirkel, 1994; Gorn, 1997). Furthermore, Martin (1996) contends that when an IEP committee determines that a student is not eligible for services under the IDEA or that a student no longer requires services, the committee should automatically refer students for consideration for protection under Section 504. A student who does not qualify under the IDEA, or who no longer qualifies, might meet eligibility for services under Section 504.

Litigation on the IEP

In *Rowley*, the U.S. Supreme Court directed lower courts to review schools' IEP processes and written documents when determining compliance with the FAPE mandate of the IDEA. In using the high court's two-part test, lower courts are first to examine the procedural aspects of the IEP process; second, they must examine the IEP itself to determine whether the IEP is calculated to provide the student with educational benefit.

Cases reviewing procedural and substantive compliance with the FAPE mandate were summarized in Chapter 9 and will not be revisited here. It is instructive, however, to examine the FAPE cases for the specific attributes or defects in the IEPs that have led the courts to invalidate them.

The post-*Rowley* cases have indicated that procedural flaws may, but will not automatically, invalidate an IEP. Before a court will invalidate an IEP, the court must have reason to believe that the procedural error (a) compromised a student's right to an appropriate education; (b) resulted in the parents' being excluded from the IEP process; or (c) caused the student to be deprived of educational rights.

Substantively, the post-*Rowley* cases have held that the IEP must be reasonably calculated to produce educational benefit. An IEP that produces only trivial educational advancement or merely halts educational regression will not pass legal muster (Guernsey & Klare, 1993). To determine substantive compliance with the FAPE mandate, courts and administrative law judges have examined the following factors:

- The IEP's goals and objectives (*Carter v. Florence County School District Four*, 1991; *Chris D. v. Montgomery County Board of Education*, 1990; *Straub v. Florida Union Free School District*, 1991; *Susquenita School District v. Raelee S.*, 1996; *Thorndock v. Boise Independent School District*, 1988). For example, in *Carter v. Florence*, the U.S. Court of Appeals for the Fourth Circuit held that the school's IEP reading goal of 4 months' growth over a school year did not represent meaningful growth.

- The evaluation procedures used to measure a student's progress toward meeting IEP goals (*Board of Education of the Casadaga Valley Central School District*, 1994; *Chris D. v. Montgomery County Board of Education*, 1990; *Lewis v. School Board of Loudoun County*, 1992; *Susquenita School District v. Raelee S.*, 1996). In finding against the school district, the court in *Lewis v. School Board of Loudoun County* stated that, "significantly, the IEP also contained no evaluation procedures . . . to measure [the student's] progress towards meeting the goals and objectives of the IEP" (p. 528).

- Actual student progress in a school's special education program (*Adams v. Hansen*, 1985; *Hall v. Vance County Board of Education*, 1985; *Roland M. v. Concord School Committee*, 1990). In *Hall v. Vance County Board of Education*, the court invalidated a school's IEP, affirming the lower court's ruling that regardless of the goals and objectives in the IEP, the student had made no educational progress in 2 years. (For elaborations on court decisions regarding student progress, see Chapter 8.)

The litigation regarding the appropriateness of IEPs indicates the importance of carefully adhering to the requirements set forth in the IEP. The case law puts a premium on involving parents in the IEP process and in developing an IEP that will result in educational benefit to the student. To ensure that the IEP provides an appropriate education, school personnel must conduct thorough assessments, base goals on educational needs identified in these assessments, write meaningful goals and objectives, and measure student progress toward meeting these goals in ways that will allow educators to adjust educational procedures if they do not produce the desired outcomes within the time frame indicated in the IEP.

Summary

The IEP is the keystone of the IDEA, and special education is embodied in the IEP. The IEP is developed at a meeting that includes, at a minimum, a representative of the school or school district, the student's special education and general education teachers, the parents, and the student, when appropriate. Other persons may be invited at the discretion of the parent or school. If the student is being evaluated for the first time, a member of the evaluation team or a person familiar with the evaluation must be on the IEP team.

The IEP is developed in accordance with state and federal mandates. The program must include (a) the student's present level of educational performance; (b) annual goals and benchmarks or short-term objectives; (c) special education and related services to be provided; (d) the extent to which the student will not participate in the general education program; (e) student participation in state- or districtwide assessments and modifications if needed; (f) projected date of initiation and anticipated duration of the IEP; (g) transition services for students 16 years of age, or, when determined appropriate, 14 years or older; and (h) appropriate objective criteria and evaluation procedures for determining, on at least an annual basis, whether the IEP goals are being met.

The IDEA Amendments of 1997 emphasize the importance of involving a student's parents in the IEP process. The law delineates specific procedures that schools must follow to ensure meaningful parental participation. Schools must communicate the requirements of the IEP to a student's general and special education teachers. Moreover, courts have stressed the importance of following proper procedures in IEP development, writing meaningful goals and objectives, evaluating a student's progress toward the goals, and communicating the results of this progress.

For Further Information

IEP development

Bateman, B. (1996). *Better IEPs: How to develop legally correct and educationally useful programs*. Longmont, CO: Sopris West.

Bateman. B. D., & Herr, C. M. (2003). *Writing measurable IEP goals and objectives*. Verona, WI: IEP Resources.

Bateman, B. D., & Linden, M. (1998). *Better IEPs: How to develop legally correct and educationally useful programs*. Longmont, CO: Sopris West.

Chambers, A. C. (1997). Has technology been considered? A guide for IEP teams. In *CASE/TAM assistive technology policy and practice series*. Reston, VA: Council of Administrators of Special Education and the Technology and Media Division of the Council for Exceptional Children.

Gorn, S. (1997). *What do I do when . . . The answer book on individualized education programs*. LRP Publications.

Lake, S. E. (2000). *IEP procedural errors: Lessons learned, mistakes to avoid*. Horsham, PA: LRP Publications.

Lake, S. E. (2002). *The top 10 IEP errors: How to avoid them, how to fix them.* Horsham, PA: LRP Publications.

Lombardo, L. (1999). IEPs and the IDEA: What you need to know. Horsham, PA: LRP Publications.

Smith, S. W. (1990). Individualized education programs (IEPs) in special education—From intent to acquiescence. *Exceptional Children, 57,* 6–14.

Parental participation

Shea, T. M., & Bauer, A. M. (1991). *Parents and teachers of children with exceptionalities: A handbook for collaboration.* Boston: Allyn & Bacon.

Turnbull, A. P., & Turnbull, H. R. (1997). *Families, professionals and exceptionality: A special partnership* (3rd ed.). Upper Saddle River, NJ: Merrill/Prentice Hall.

References

Adams v. Hansen, 632 F. Supp. 858 (N.D. Cal. 1985).

Bateman, B. D., & Herr, C. M. (2003). *Writing measurable IEP goals and objectives.* Verona, WI: IEP Resources.

Bateman, B.D., & Linden, M. (1996). *Better IEPs: How to develop legally correct and educationally useful programs.* Longmont, CO: Sopris West.

Big Beaver Falls Area School District v. Jackson, 624 A.2d 806 (Pa. Cmwlth 1993).

Board of Education of the Casadaga Valley Central School District, 20 IDELR 1023 (SEA 1994).

Board of Education of the Hendrick Hudson Central School District v. Rowley, 458 U.S. 176 (1982).

Board of Education of the St. Louis Central School District, 20 IDELR 938 (SEA 1993).

Board of Education of the Whitesboro Central School District, 21 IDELR 895 (SEA NY 1994).

Brimmer v. Traverse City, 872 F. Supp. 447 (W.D. Mich. 1994).

Burlington School District, 20 IDELR 1303 (SEA 1994).

Buser v. Corpus Christi ISD, 20 IDELR 981 (S.D. Tex. 1994).

Carter v. Florence County School District Four, 950 F.2d 156 (4th Cir. 1991).

Chris D. v. Montgomery County Board of Education, 753 F. Supp. 922 (M.D. Ala. 1990).

Davenport (IA) Community School District, 20 IDELR 1398 (OCR 1993).

Deno, S. L. (1992). The nature and development of curriculum-measurement. *Preventing School Failure, 36,* 5–11.

Doe v. Withers, 20 IDELR 442 (W. Va. Cir. Ct. 1993).

Drasgow, E., Yell, M. L., & Robinson, T. R. (2001). Developing legally and educationally appropriate IEPs: Federal law and lessons learned from the Lovaas hearings and cases. *Remedial and Special Education, 22,* 359–373.

Eyer, T. L. (1998). Greater expectations: How the 1997 IDEA Amendments raise the basic floor of opportunity for children with disabilities. *Education Law Report, 126,* 1–19.

Family Educational Rights and Privacy Act (FERPA), 20 U.S.C. § 1232 *et seq.*

Fossey, R., Hosie, T., Soniat, K., & Zirkel, P. (1994). Section 504 and "front line" educators: An expanded obligation to serve children with disabilities. *Preventing School Failure, 39,* 10–14.

Girard School District, 18 IDELR 1048 (OCR 1992).

Goldstein, B. A. (1993). New regulations under Part B of the IDEA. In *Proceedings of the 14th National Institute on Legal Issues of Educating Individuals with Disabilities.* Horsham, PA: LRP Publications.

Gorn, S. (1997). *What do I do when: The answer book on individualized education programs.* Horsham, PA: LRP Publications.

Guernsey, T. F., & Klare, K. (1993). *Special education law.* Durham, NC: Carolina Academic Press.

Hall v. Vance County Board of Education, 774 F.2d 629 (4th Cir. 1985).

Honig v. Doe, 485 U.S. 305 (1988).

Horsnell, M., & Kitch, J. (1996). Bullet-proofing the IEP. In *Proceedings of the 15th National Institute on Legal Issues in Educating Individuals with Disabilities.* Alexandria, VA: LRP Publications.

Huefner, D. S. (2000a). Getting comfortable with special education law: A framework for working with children with disabilities. Norwood, MA: Christopher-Gordon Publications.

Huefner, D. S. (2000b). The risks and opportunities of the IEP requirements under IDEA '97. Journal of Special Education, 33, 195–204.

Individuals with Disabilities Education Act, 20 U.S.C. § 1401 et seq.

Individuals with Disabilities Education Act Regulations, 34 C.F.R. § 300.1 et seq.

Individuals with Disabilities Education Act Regulations, 34 C.F.R. § 300 Appendix C (1993).

In re Child with Disabilities, 16 EHLR 538 (SEA TN 1990).

In re Child with Disabilities, 20 IDELR 455 (1993).

Katsiyannis, A., Yell, M. L., & Bradley, R. (2001). Reflections on the 25th anniversary of the Individuals with Disabilities Education Act. Remedial and Special Education, 22, 324–334.

Lake, S. E. (2000). IEP procedural errors: Lessons learned, mistakes to avoid. Horsham, PA: LRP Publications.

Lake, S. E. (2002). The top 10 IEP errors: How to avoid them, how to fix them. Horsham, PA: LRP Publications.

Letter to Boney, 18 IDELR 537 (OSEP 1991).

Letter to Breecher, 17 EHLR 56 (OSEP 1990).

Letter to Davilia, 18 IDELR 1036 (OSERS 1992).

Letter to Helmuth, 16 EHLR 503 (OSEP 1990).

Letter to Livingston, 21 IDELR 1060 (OSEP 1994).

Letter to McIntire, 16 EHLR 163 (OSEP 1989).

Letter to Perryman, EHLR 211 438 (OSEP 1987).

Letter to Sheridan, 20 IDELR 1163 (OSEP 1993).

Lewis v. School Board of Loudoun County, 808 F. Supp. 523 (E.D. 1992).

Lipsky, D. K. & Gartner, A. (1992). Inclusive education and school restructuring. In W. Stainback & S. Stainback (Eds.), Controversial issues confronting special education: Divergent perspectives (pp. 3–15). Boston: Allyn & Bacon.

Lombardo, L. (1999). IEPs and the IDEA: What you need to know. Horsham, PA: LRP Publications.

Lynch, E. C., & Beare, P. L. (1989). The quality of IEP objectives and their relevance to instruction for students with mental retardation and behavioral disorders. Remedial and Special Education, 11 (2), 47–55.

Martin, R. (1979). Educating handicapped children: The legal mandate. Champaign, IL: Research Press.

Martin, R. (1996). Litigation over the IEP. In Proceedings of the 16th National Institute on Legal Issues in Educating Individuals with Disabilities. Alexandria, VA: LRP Publications.

Myles S. v. Montgomery County Board of Education, 20 IDELR 237 (M.D. Ala. 1993).

New Haven Board of Education, 20 IDELR 42 (SEA 1993).

New York City School District Board of Education, 19 IDELR 169 (SEA NY 1992).

Norlin, J., & Gorn, D. (1999). What do I do when. . . The answer book on special education law (4th ed.). Horsham, PA: LRP Publications.

Osborne, A. G. (1994). Procedural due process rights for parents under the IDEA. Preventing School Failure, 39, 22–26.

OSEP Policy Letter, 18 IDELR 530 (OSEP 1991a).

OSEP Policy Letter, 18 IDELR 627 (OSEP 1991b).

OSEP Policy Letter, 18 IDELR 969 (OSEP 1991c).

OSEP Policy Letter, 18 IDELR 1303 (OSEP 1992).

OSEP Policy Letter, 20 IDELR 541 (OSEP 1993).

Pitasky, V. M. (2002). What do I do when. . . The answer book on placement under the IDEA and Section 504. Horsham, PA: LRP Publications.

Pocatello School District #25, 18 IDELR 83 (SEA Idaho 1991).

Ray, J. M. (2002). Components of legally sound, high quality transition services planning under IDEA. Education Law Reporter, 170, 1–12.

Roland M. v. Concord School Committee, 910 F. Supp. 983 (1st Cir. 1990).

School Administrative Unit #66, 20 IDELR 471 (1993).

Section 504 of the Rehabilitation Act Regulations, 34 C.F.R. § 104.33(b)(2).

Senate Report of the Individuals with Disabilities Act Amendments of 1997, available on-line at wais.access.gpo.gov.

Smith, S. W. (1990). Individualized education programs (IEPs) in special education—From intent to acquiescence. Exceptional Children, 57, 6–14.

Smith, S. W., & Simpson, R. L. (1989). An analysis of individualized education programs (IEPs) for students with behavioral disorders. Behavioral Disorders, 14, 107–116.

Straub v. Florida Union Free School District, 778 F. Supp. 774 (S.D.N.Y. 1991).

Strickland, B. P., & Turnbull, A. P. (1990). *Developing and implementing individualized education programs* (3rd ed.). Upper Saddle River, NJ: Merrill/Prentice Hall.

Susquenita School District v. Raelee S., 25 IDELR 120 (M.D. Penn. 1996).

Thorndock v. Boise Independent School District, 767 P.2d 1241 (1988).

Tucker, B. P., & Goldstein, B. A. (1992). *Legal rights of persons with disabilities: An analysis of public law.* Horsham, PA: LRP Publications.

W. G. v. Board of Trustees of Target Range School District No. 23, 960 F.2d 1479 (9th Cir. 1992).

Weber, M. C. (2002). *Special education law and litigation treatise.* Horsham, PA: LRP Publications.

Yankton S.D. v. Schramm. (1995).

Yell, M. L., Drasgow, E., Bradley, R., & Justesen, T. (2004). Critical legal issues in special education. In A. McCray Sorrells, H. J. Reith, & P. T. Sindelar, *Issues in special education* (pp. 16–37). Boston: Allyn & Bacon.

CHAPTER TWELVE

Least Restrictive Environment

*We are concerned that children with handicapping conditions be educated in
the most normal possible and least restrictive setting, for how else will they
adapt to the world beyond the educational environment, and how else will the
nonhandicapped adapt to them?*

Senator Robert T. Stafford, *Congressional Record*, May 20, 1974

J ustice Potter Stewart, writing for the U.S. Supreme Court in *Sheldon v. Tucker*
(1960), stated that in a

> series of decisions this court has held, even though a governmental purpose be legitimate
> and substantial, that purpose cannot be pursued by means that broadly stifle fundamen-
> tal personal liberties when the end can be more narrowly achieved. The breadth of leg-
> islative abridgment must be viewed in the light of less drastic means for achieving the
> same purpose. (p. 482)

Although this decision did not involve the education of students with disabilities,
the Court set forth the following principle that has had a profound effect on special
education: that persons have a right to be free of unnecessary restrictions when the
government undertakes actions that have consequences for those individuals, even
though the actions are legitimate.

In 1954, the U.S. Supreme Court, in *Brown v. Board of Education,* declared that
the practice of segregation could not be used in public education. Again, although the
decision did not involve the education of students with disabilities, advocates argued
that the principles in *Brown* were true for all persons, including those with disabilities.
In *Hairston v. Drosick* (1976) the principles developed in *Brown* were used by the
Court in a case involving the education of a child with spina bifida. The Court stated that

> A child's chance in this society is through the educational process. A major goal of this ed-
> ucational process is the socialization process that takes place in the regular classroom,

with the resulting capability to interact in a social way with one's peers. It is, therefore, imperative that every child receive an education with his or her peers insofar as it is at all possible. (p. 184)

On May 20, 1974, Senator Robert Stafford of Vermont introduced an amendment to the Education of the Handicapped Act of 1974 intended to prevent the educational segregation of students with disabilities. The amendment required that school districts ensure that a student's placement be in the least restrictive appropriate educational setting (Stafford, 1978). This amendment was later incorporated into the Education for All Handicapped Children Act (EAHCA) in what has become known as the least restrictive environment (LRE) mandate.

The LRE mandate has been the subject of considerable controversy and debate. My purpose in this chapter is to examine the legislative basis of the LRE mandate and the major cases that interpreted it along with a model for determining the LRE for students.

LRE, Mainstreaming, and Inclusion

The terms *least restrictive environment, inclusion,* and *mainstreaming* are often used interchangeably. They are not, however, synonymous concepts. *Least restrictive environment* refers to the IDEA's mandate that students with disabilities should be educated to the maximum extent appropriate with peers without disabilities. The LRE mandate ensures that schools educate students with disabilities in integrated settings, alongside students with and without disabilities, to the maximum extent appropriate. Least restrictive environment is not a particular setting.

Champagne (1993) defines restrictiveness as "a gauge of the degree of opportunity a person has for proximity to, and communication with, the ordinary flow of persons in our society" (p. 5). In special education, this means that a student with disabilities has the right to be educated with students in the general education environment. The general education environment is considered the least restrictive setting because it is the placement in which there is the greatest measure of opportunity for proximity and communication with the "ordinary flow" of students in schools.

From this perspective, the less a placement resembles the general education environment, the more restrictive it is considered (Gorn, 1996). Specifically a student with disabilities has the right to be educated in a setting that is not overly restrictive considering what is appropriate for that student. Appropriateness entails an education that will provide meaningful benefit for a student. When the educational program is appropriate, a student with disabilities should be placed in the general education environment, or as close to it as is feasible, so long as the appropriate program can be provided in that setting. (For elaborations on an appropriate education, see Chapter 8.)

Inclusion refers to placement of students with disabilities in the general education classroom with peers without disabilities. Inclusion generally connotes more comprehensive programming than the somewhat dated term *mainstreaming.* The courts, however, tend to use the terms synonymously. Mainstreaming and inclusion are narrower terms than least restrictive environment (McColl, 1992). Although placement in the general education classroom may be the LRE for some students with disabilities, it is not required in all cases. The IDEA requires mainstreaming or inclusion when the general education classroom setting can provide an appropriate education. This view was also expressed by the U.S. Court of Appeals for the Fourth Circuit in *Carter v. Florence County School District Four* (1991):

> Under the IDEA, mainstreaming is a policy to be pursued so long as it is consistent with the Act's primary goal of providing disabled students with an appropriate education. Where necessary for educational reasons, mainstreaming assumes a subordinate role in formulating an educational program. (p. 156)

The LRE Mandate

The IDEA requires that, when appropriate, students with disabilities be educated in settings with children without disabilities. Specifically the law provides that,

> to the maximum extent appropriate, children with disabilities, including children in public or private institutions or other care facilities, are educated with children who are not disabled, and that special classes, separate schooling, or other removal of children with disabilities from the regular educational environment occurs only when the nature or severity of the disability is such that education in regular classes with the use of supplementary aids and services cannot be achieved satisfactorily. (IDEA, 20 U.S.C. § 1412)

There are two parts to the LRE requirement of the IDEA. The first addresses the presumptive right of all students with disabilities to be educated with students without disabilities. Schools must make good faith efforts to place and maintain students in less restrictive settings. This presumptive right, however, is rebuttable; that is, the principle sets forth a general rule of conduct (i.e., integration) but allows it to be rebutted when integration is not appropriate for a student (Turnbull & Turnbull, 2002). The IDEA favors integration, but recognizes that for some students more restrictive or segregated settings may be appropriate. Clearly, the law anticipates that placements in more restrictive settings may sometimes be necessary to provide an appropriate education.

To ensure that schools make good faith efforts to educate students in less restrictive settings, the LRE mandate also requires that before students with disabilities are placed in more restrictive settings, efforts must first be made to maintain a student in less restrictive settings with the use of supplementary aids and services. It is only when an appropriate education cannot be provided, even with supplementary aids and services, that students with disabilities may be placed in more restrictive settings.

The IDEA further requires that state educational agencies ensure that the LRE requirement extends to students in public schools, private schools, and other care facilities. States are required to ensure that teachers and administrators in all public schools are fully informed about the requirements of the LRE provision and are provided with the technical assistance and training necessary to assist them in this effort.

Continuum of Alternative Placements

Senator Stafford (1978), an original sponsor of the IDEA, stated that Congress included the LRE principle in the law in recognition that for some students an education in the general education classroom would not be appropriate. For these students, placements in more restrictive settings would be required to provide an appropriate education. The U.S. Supreme Court, in *Board of Education of the Hendrick Hudson School District v. Rowley* (1982), interpreted congressional intent similarly:

> Despite this preference for "mainstreaming" handicapped children—educating them with nonhandicapped children—Congress recognized that regular education simply would not be a suitable setting for the education of many handicapped children. . . the act thus provides for the education of some handicapped children in separate classes or institutional settings. (p. 192)

The Office of Special Education and Rehabilitation Services (OSERS) of the U.S. Department of Education also recognized "that some children with disabilities may require placement in settings other than the general education classroom in order to be provided with an education designed to address their unique needs" (*Letter to Goodling,* 1991, p. 214).

To ensure that students with disabilities are educated in the LRE that is most appropriate for their individual needs, the IDEA requires that school districts have a range or continuum of alternative placement options to meet their needs. The continuum represents an entire spectrum of placements where a student's special education program can be implemented (Bartlett, 1993; Gorn, 1996). Regulations require that

(a) Each [school district] shall ensure that a continuum of alternative placements is available to meet the needs of children with disabilities for special education and related services

(b) The continuum required. . . must:

    (1) Include the alternative placements. . . (instruction in regular classes, special classes, special schools, home instruction, and instruction in hospitals and institutions); and

    (2) Make provision for supplementary services (such as resource room or itinerant instruction) to be provided in conjunction with regular class placement. (IDEA Regulations, 34 C.F.R. § 300.551)

The purpose of the continuum is to allow school personnel to choose from a number of options in determining the LRE most appropriate for the student. OSERS has emphasized the importance of school districts' maintaining a continuum of placements "in order to be properly prepared to address the individual needs of all children with disabilities" (*Letter to Frost,* 1991, p. 594). If the local school district is unable to provide the appropriate placement, the state may bear the responsibility of ensuring the establishment and availability of a continuum of alternative placements (*Cordero v. Pennsylvania,* 1993). Figure 12.1 shows the continuum of placements (IDEA Regulations, 34 C.F.R. § 300.551).

Figure 12.1
Continuum of Placements

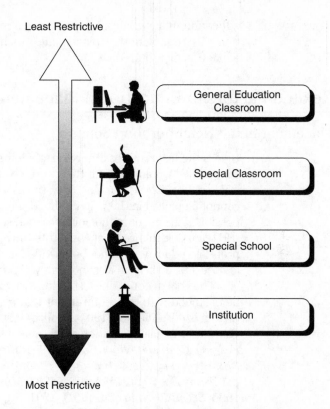

A school district may not refuse to place a child in an LRE because it lacks the appropriate placement option (Tucker & Goldstein, 1992). Moreover, if gaps in the continuum exist within a school district, the district must fill them through whatever means are required (e.g., consortium-type arrangements). This does not mean that each school district must provide for a complete continuum within its own boundaries. When the educational needs of a student cannot be met in district programs, however, the district is obligated to provide a placement where the student's needs can be met. The regulations implementing the IDEA require that the various alternative placements in the continuum of placements "are to be available to the extent necessary to implement the individualized education program" (IDEA Regulations, 34 C.F.R. § 300.552(b)). This may necessitate the district's sending the student to another school (public or private) that provides the needed placement. In such cases, the neighborhood school district retains financial responsibility for the student's education.

The IEP team determines the placement along this continuum that is the least restrictive setting in which a student will receive an appropriate education. Restrictiveness is defined, for purposes of the continuum, by proximity to the general education classroom. Education in the least restrictive setting (i.e., the general education classroom) is the preferred option so long as it is consistent with an appropriate education. If a student cannot receive a meaningful education in the general education classroom, another placement, in which the student will receive a meaningful education, is required.

Related Factors in Educational Placements

Placement in the Neighborhood School

Unless the IEP requires otherwise, students with disabilities should be educated in the school they would attend if they were not in special education (IDEA Regulations, 34 C.F.R. § 300.552(a)(3)). Moreover, the IDEA requires that if special education students cannot be placed in the neighborhood school, they must be placed as close to home as possible. Placement in the neighborhood school, however, is not an absolute right. The IEP team determines what constitutes an appropriate education for a student. If an appropriate education cannot be provided in the neighborhood school, the IEP team may choose a placement in a school that will provide an appropriate education.

The goal of educating a student with disabilities in the neighborhood school must be balanced with the requirement that a student's education be appropriate and individualized (Huefner, 1994). Courts have repeatedly held that the IDEA does not guarantee special education services in a student's neighborhood school (*Barnett v. Fairfax County School Board*, 1991; *Flour Bluff Independent School District v. Katherine M.*, 1996; *Hudson v. Bloomfield Hills School District*, 1995; *Lachman v. Illinois Board of Education*, 1988; *Murray v. Montrose County School District*, 1995; *Schuldt v. Mankato ISD*, 1991).

In *Schuldt v. Mankato ISD* (1991), the U.S. Court of Appeals for the Eighth Circuit ruled that a school district did not have to make the neighborhood school wheelchair-accessible for a student with spina bifida, since an elementary school only a few miles away was fully accessible. The court found that

> The school district satisfied its obligation under [IDEA] to provide [a student with disabilities] with a fully integrated public education by busing . . . the child to a nearby school, and therefore, did not violate the Act by refusing to modify neighborhood elementary school nearest to the child's home to make it accessible. (p. 1357)

If the neighborhood school cannot provide a free appropriate public education (FAPE), the school is not required to place a student with disabilities in that school. Schools retain the right to determine how to use their resources in the most efficient manner. If district administrators choose to concentrate resources at particular schools for particular needs and disabilities, it is allowed by the IDEA (Tucker & Goldstein, 1992).

The U.S. Court of Appeals for the Fifth Circuit, in *Flour Bluff Independent School District v. Katherine M.* (1996), ruled that the IDEA indicates a preference for placement in the neighborhood school but that this is not an entitlement. Furthermore, the court indicated that proximity is only one factor of many that the IEP team must consider in determining placement.

In *Murray v. Montrose County School District* (1995), the U.S. Court of Appeals for the Tenth Circuit held that although the IDEA gives a preference to education in the neighborhood school, the IDEA does not guarantee it. In *Urban v. Jefferson County School District R-1* (1994), the Tenth Circuit Court reaffirmed this principle and extended it to Section 504 and the Americans with Disabilities Act (ADA) as well as the IDEA.

Nonacademic Programming

Both the IDEA and Section 504 extend LRE requirements to nonacademic settings. Regulations implementing the IDEA extend the LRE requirements to areas such as extracurricular services, meals, recess periods, counseling services, athletics, transportation, health services, recreational activities, and special interest groups or clubs sponsored by the school (IDEA Regulations, 34 C.F.R. § 300.553). For example, if a student requires a restrictive placement to receive an appropriate education, but will not have contact with students without disabilities in that placement, the LRE requirement extends to other settings and situations in which students with and without disabilities can be integrated. Recess periods, physical education classes, or student meal times might be used to provide for the necessary integrated experiences.

Section 504 also extends the LRE requirement to nonacademic settings that include extracurricular activities:

> In providing or arranging for the provision of nonacademic and extracurricular services and activities . . . a [school] shall ensure that handicapped persons participate with non-handicapped persons in such activities and services to the maximum extent appropriate to the needs of the handicapped person. (Section 504 Regulations 34 C.F.R. § 104.34(b))

The Interests of Peers Without Disabilities

The IDEA indicates that a legitimate consideration in determining the LRE for a student with disabilities is the needs of the student's peers. According to the analysis in Section 504,

> it should be stressed that, where a [student with disabilities] is so disruptive in a regular classroom that the education of other students is significantly impaired, the needs of the [student with disabilities] cannot be met in that environment. Therefore regular placement would not be appropriate to his or her needs. (Section 504 Regulations, 34 C.F.R. § 104 Appendix, Paragraph 24)

The IDEA includes identical language in a comment to the LRE regulations (IDEA Regulations, comment following 34 C.F.R. § 300.552). The purpose of the comment is to provide guidance with respect to determining proper placement of the student with disabilities when the student is so disruptive that the education of other students is affected.

If the student has a health condition that poses an actual risk of contagion to other students, the student may be placed in a setting in which the risk is minimized. Such a placement would not violate the LRE mandate of either the IDEA or Section 504 (Zirkel, 2000).

Judicial Standards of Review

Few areas in special education law have been the subject of more debate and controversy than the LRE mandate. The issue of when an education in the general education environment constitutes the LRE for a given student with disabilities has proven to be a thorny legal issue (Huefner, 1994). Disagreements between parents and schools over LRE have led to a considerable amount of litigation. A number of these cases have made their way to the U.S. Courts of Appeals, but thus far the U.S. Supreme Court has not accepted a case interpreting the LRE mandate. Because the high court has not heard an LRE case, the LRE interpretations by the circuit courts are the highest authority available.

The results of these cases have been mixed, with some decisions favoring inclusive placements and others restrictive placements. The decisions of the circuit courts with respect to the proper standard of review to be used in determining a district's compliance with the LRE mandate, however, have begun to show some consistency. The following section will examine these cases and the methods they have adopted for determining a school district's compliance with the mainstreaming* requirement.

The *Roncker* Portability Test

One of the earliest LRE decisions was *Roncker v. Walter* (1983; hereafter *Roncker*). The decision is controlling in the Sixth Circuit, which covers the states of Kentucky, Ohio, Michigan, and Tennessee.

The case involved Neill Roncker, a 9-year-old classified as having moderate mental retardation. School personnel believed that the most appropriate placement for Neill was in a special school for children with disabilities. The parents objected, stating that their child would benefit from contact with his peers in a general education setting, and brought suit against the school district challenging the placement. The issue did not involve Neill's placement in a general education classroom; both sides agreed that he required special education. The Ronckers contended, however, that Neill could be provided the special education services in a setting that would allow greater integration and contact with students without disabilities.

The U.S. District Court for the Southern District of Ohio ruled in favor of the school district. The court stated that the mainstreaming requirement allowed schools

---

*The courts have tended to use the term *mainstreaming* in LRE cases. The term has been used to denote the practice in which children with disabilities are integrated into general education classrooms rather than a shorthand term for the LRE concept.

broad discretion in the placement of students with disabilities. The court, finding that Neill had not made significant progress while in an integrated setting, ruled that the school district had acted properly in determining Neill's placement.

The Ronckers appealed to the U.S. Court of Appeals for the Sixth District. The circuit court reversed the decision of the district court, stating that

> The act (PL 94-142) does not require mainstreaming in every case but its requirement that mainstreaming be provided to the maximum extent appropriate indicates a very strong congressional preference. (p. 1063)

Although the court noted the importance of balancing the benefits of segregated special education services against the benefits of mainstreaming, the *Roncker* decision is best known for what has been referred to as the *Roncker* portability test (Huefner, 1994):

> In a case where the segregated facility is considered superior, the court should determine whether the services which make that placement superior could feasibly be provided in a nonsegregated setting. If they can, the placement in the segregated school would be inappropriate under the Act. (*Roncker,* p. 1063)

Courts using this test must determine if the services that make the segregated setting more appropriate can be transported to the nonsegregated setting. If the services can be transported, the modification is required by the LRE mandate (Tucker & Goldstein, 1992). (See Figure 12.2 for the *Roncker* portability test.)

The *Daniel* Two-Part Test

Perhaps the seminal case regarding the LRE mandate came from the U.S. Court of Appeals for the Fifth Circuit in *Daniel R.R. v. State Board of Education* (1989; hereafter *Daniel*). The plaintiff in the case, Daniel, was a 6-year-old child with Down syndrome enrolled in the El Paso, Texas, Independent School District. At his parents' request, Daniel was placed in a prekindergarten class for half of the school day and an early childhood special education class for the other half. Shortly after the beginning of the school year, Daniel's teacher informed the school placement committee that Daniel was not participating in class and was failing to master any of the skills taught, even with almost-constant attention and instruction from the

Figure 12.2
The *Roncker* Portability Test

1. Can the educational services that make a segregated placement superior be feasibly provided in a unsegregated setting?
2. If so, the placement in the segregated setting is inappropriate.

teacher and aide. The committee met and decided that the prekindergarten class was inappropriate for Daniel. Daniel was removed from the prekindergarten class, attended only the early childhood special education class, and interacted with children from the prekindergarten class at recess and lunch. The parents exercised their right to a due process hearing. The hearing officer agreed with the school in concluding that Daniel could not participate in the prekindergarten class without almost-constant supervision from the teacher, that he was receiving little educational benefit, and that he was disrupting the class because his needs absorbed most of the teacher's time. The officer also noted that the teacher would have to modify the curriculum totally to meet Daniel's needs. The parents filed an action in the district and, eventually, the circuit court.

The circuit court stated that the imprecise nature of the IDEA's mandates were deliberate and that Congress had chosen to leave the selection of educational policy and methods in the hands of local school officials. However, Congress had created a statutory preference for mainstreaming while at the same time creating a tension between the appropriate education and mainstreaming provisions of the Act. By creating this tension, Congress recognized that the general education environment would not be suitable for all students with disabilities and, at times, a special setting or school may be necessary to provide an appropriate education. Essentially, the *Daniel* court said that when the provisions of FAPE and mainstreaming are in conflict, the mainstreaming mandate becomes secondary to the appropriate education mandate.

The *Daniel* court declined to follow the Sixth Circuit's analysis in *Roncker,* stating that the *Roncker* test necessitated "too intrusive an inquiry into educational policy choices that Congress deliberately left to state and local school districts" (p. 1046). Congress, according to the court, had left the choice of educational methods and policies to the schools. The court's task, therefore, was to determine if the school had complied with the IDEA's requirements.

The court believed that the statutory language of the LRE mandate provided a more appropriate test for determining a school's compliance with the mainstreaming requirement than did the *Roncker* inquiry. Relying on this language, the court developed a two-part test for determining compliance with the LRE requirement. (See Figure 12.3, the *Daniel* two-part test.)

First, the court must ask whether education in the general education classroom, with the use of supplementary aids and services, could be satisfactorily achieved.

Figure 12.3
The *Daniel* Two-Part Test

1. Can education in the general education classroom with supplementary aids and services be achieved satisfactorily?
2. If a student is placed in a more restrictive setting, is the student integrated to the maximum extent appropriate?

To make this determination, the court must decide whether the school has taken steps to accommodate a student with disabilities in the general education classroom. These attempts take the form of supplying supplementary aids and services and modifying the curriculum. In determining whether the school complied with this part of the test, the court must also decide if the student will receive benefit from the general education classroom and if the mainstreamed student will negatively affect the education of classroom peers. If the school has not attempted to mainstream the student to the maximum extent appropriate, the school will fail the first part of the test. The inquiry will thus end because the school district has violated the LRE mandate.

If the school passes the first part of the test, the court then moves to part two. Here the court asks whether the school has mainstreamed the student to the maximum extent appropriate; that is, by relying on the continuum of placements, the school must provide the student with as much exposure to students without disabilities as possible. The *Daniel* court suggested that students who are educated primarily in segregated settings should be placed in integrated settings outside the special education classroom when feasible (e.g., nonacademic classes, lunch, recess).

If the school meets both parts of the two-part test, then its obligation under the IDEA is fulfilled. After applying the two-part test in *Daniel,* the Fifth Circuit determined that Daniel's needs were so great and that he required so much of the teacher's time that it was affecting the education of the other students negatively. The court, finding that the school district had met the requirements of the two-part test, affirmed the decision of the district court that the school district has satisfied the LRE requirement of the IDEA.

In addition to the test, the *Daniel* court provided further direction for lower courts to follow in LRE cases in noting that the court's "task is not to second-guess state and local school officials; rather, it is the narrow one of determining whether state and local school officials have complied with the Act" (p. 1048). The *Daniel* decision is the legal authority on LRE in the states that comprise the Fifth Circuit: Louisiana, Mississippi, and Texas. It has proven to be a persuasive decision and has subsequently been adopted in the Third Circuit in *Oberti v. Board of Education of the Borough of Clementon School District* (1993), which is the legal authority in Delaware, New Jersey, and Pennsylvania, and in the Eleventh Circuit in *Greer v. Rome City School District* (1991), which is the legal authority in Alabama, Georgia, and Florida.

The *Rachel H.* Four-Factor Test

On January 24, 1994, the U.S. Court of Appeals for the Ninth Circuit affirmed a district court's decision in *Sacramento City Unified School District Board of Education v. Rachel H.** (1994; hereafter *Rachel H.*). This case is the legal authority for

---

*Because the child was a minor, the circuit court used Rachel H. rather than her full name, Rachel Holland. At the district level the case was *Sacramento City Unified School District v. Holland.*

the Ninth Circuit, which covers Alaska, Arizona, California, Hawaii, Idaho, Montana, Nevada, Oregon, and Washington.

The case involved Rachel Holland, an 11-year-old girl with moderate mental retardation. From 1985 to 1989, Rachel attended a number of special education programs in the Sacramento School District. In the fall of 1989, Rachel's parents requested that she be placed in a general education classroom during the entire school day. The district contended that Rachel's disability was too severe for her to benefit from being in a general education class and proposed that she be placed in special education for academic subjects, attending the general education class only for nonacademic activities (e.g., art, music, lunch, recess). The parents removed Rachel from the school and placed her in a private school. The parents also requested a due process hearing. The hearing officer held for the parents, stating that the school district had failed to make an adequate effort to educate Rachel in the general education classroom. The school appealed the decision to the district court. The court, relying on the decisions in *Daniel* and *Greer v. Rome City School District,* considered four factors in making its decision. (See Figure 12.4 for the *Rachel H.* four-factor test.)

The first factor concerned the educational benefits available to Rachel in the general education classroom with supplementary aids and services as compared with the educational benefits of the special education classroom. The court found that the district, in presenting evidence, had failed to establish that the educational benefits of the special education classroom were better than or even equal to the benefits of the general education classroom.

The second factor the court considered was the nonacademic benefits of each classroom. The court decided that the Hollands' testimony, that Rachel was developing social and communication skills as well as self-esteem, was more credible than the district's testimony that Rachel was not learning from exposure to other children and that she was becoming isolated from her peers. The second factor, therefore, was decided in favor of the Hollands.

Third, the district court examined the impact of Rachel's presence on others in the general education classroom—specifically, whether Rachel's presence was a

Figure 12.4
The *Rachel H.* Four-Factor Test

1. The educational benefits of the general education classroom with supplementary aids and services as compared with the educational benefits of the special classroom

2. The nonacademic benefits of interaction with students without disabilities

3. The effect of the student's presence on the teacher and on other students in the classroom

4. The cost of mainstreaming

detriment to others because she was disruptive or distracting, and if she would take up so much of the teacher's time that the other students would suffer. Both parties agreed that Rachel followed directions and was not disruptive. Also, the court found that Rachel did not interfere with the teacher's ability to teach the other children. The court ruled that the third factor was in favor of placement in the general education class.

The final factor in the court's decision involved evaluating the cost of placement in the general education classroom. The court found that the school district had not offered persuasive evidence to support its claim that educating Rachel in the general education class would be far more expensive than educating her in the combined general education and special education placement. Thus, the cost factor did not provide an impediment to educating Rachel in general education. Weighing the four factors, the district court determined that the appropriate placement for Rachel was full-time in the general education classroom with supplemental aids and services.

An appeal to the Ninth Circuit was heard on August 12, 1993, and the court delivered its opinion on January 24, 1994. The circuit court affirmed the decision of the district court. The higher court stated that the school district had the burden of demonstrating that its proposed placement provided mainstreaming to the maximum extent appropriate. The circuit court adopted the district court's four-factor test in determining that the school district had not met the burden of proof that Rachel could not be educated in the general education classroom. The court found the Hollands' position for inclusion to be more persuasive.

The school district filed a petition to have the U.S. Supreme Court review this case. The high court denied the petition, however, and did not hear the case, so the ruling of the appellate court stands.

Clyde K. v. Puyallup School District

In *Clyde K. v. Puyallup School District* (1994), the U.S. Court of Appeals for the Ninth Circuit applied its four-factor test to a case involving inclusion and a student with behavioral disorders. The case was especially noteworthy because it answered questions heretofore unexamined at the appellate court level.

The dispute involved Ryan K., a 15-year-old with Attention Deficit Hyperactivity Disorder (ADHD) and Tourette's syndrome. Ryan was receiving special education in the general education classroom with supplementary resource room help. His behavior, however, became increasingly disruptive. He used obscenities, was noncompliant, harassed female students with sexually explicit remarks, and physically assaulted classmates. Following two serious incidences of assaultive behavior, Ryan was suspended. When he returned, the school district had a paraprofessional observe his classroom behavior for 3 days. School officials met to review the IEP and concluded that Ryan's objectives could be met if he was placed in a segregated special education program called Students Temporarily Away from Regular Schools (STARS). His parents were notified of the proposed placement change. School personnel suggested that

Ryan be placed in STARS while they and his parents developed a plan to reintegrate Ryan in the general education classroom. The parents initially agreed but subsequently changed their minds concerning the placement in STARS. They requested a new IEP and a due process hearing.

Ryan's parents brought their attorney to the IEP meeting to discuss Ryan's return to the general education classroom. The parents contended that the STARS program was overly restrictive and that the appropriate placement would be the general education classroom with a personal aide. During the course of discussions, the parents' attorney abruptly ended the meeting, stating that Ryan would be in the general education class the next day. According to the court, the attorney insisted that the parents leave despite pleas by school district personnel that they continue the meeting.

A due process hearing was convened. The hearing officer concluded that the school district had complied with the requirements of the IDEA. The parents appealed to the district court, which, after reviewing the record of the administrative hearing and hearing additional testimony, affirmed the decision of the hearing officer. The parents then appealed to the U.S. Court of Appeals for the Ninth Circuit.

In its ruling, the circuit court applied the four-factor test it had established in *Rachel H.* The first factor considers the academic benefits of the general education classroom. The court noted that Ryan was not receiving academic benefits from the general education classroom and that testing had actually indicated academic regression. The court also noted that the school district had made efforts to provide supplementary aids and services to accommodate Ryan in the general education classroom (e.g., staff training about Ryan's disabilities, special education support in a resource room, and the involvement of a behavioral specialist). Because of the severity of Ryan's behavioral problems, the court did not believe that the presence of a personal aide would have made a meaningful difference.

The nonacademic benefits of the general education class setting are the second factor in the *Rachel H.* test. The court stated that testimony indicated that Ryan was a social isolate and seemed to benefit little from modeling. The court believed, therefore, that the nonacademic benefits of the general education class setting were minimal.

The third factor—the negative effects the student's presence had on the teacher and peers—was considered the most important by the court. Noting that Ryan's aggressive behavior, sexually explicit remarks, and profanity had an overwhelming negative effect on the teachers and peers, the court stated that the school had a statutory duty to ensure that all students with disabilities receive an appropriate education. This duty, however, did not require that schools ignore the student's behavioral problems. According to the court, schools have an obligation to ensure that all students are educated in safe environments:

> Disruptive behavior that significantly impairs the education of other students strongly suggests a mainstream placement is no longer appropriate. While school officials have a statutory duty to ensure that disabled students receive an appropriate education, they are not required to sit on their hands when a disabled student's behavioral problems prevent him and those around him from learning. (p. 1402)

In its ruling, the Ninth Circuit Court held that the STARS program was the LRE. The court also stated that the slow and tedious working of the court system made it a poor arena in which to resolve disputes regarding a student's education. The judgment of the district court was thus affirmed.

In an interesting and highly unusual move, the circuit court, in a footnote to the decision, criticized the attorney for the plaintiffs for "hardball tactics" and counterproductive dealings with the school district, which destroyed potential channels for constructive dialogue. The court noted that because of the litigation, Ryan spent 2 years in a self-contained placement that was originally intended to be a short-term interim placement, and that "Ryan's experience offers a poignant reminder that everyone's interests are better served when parents and school officials resolve their differences through cooperation and compromise rather than litigation" (p. 1402).

The *Hartmann* Three-Part Test

On July 8, 1997, the U.S. Court of Appeals for the Fourth Circuit handed down its decision in *Hartmann v. Loudoun County Board of Education.* Mark Hartmann was an 11-year-old child with autism. His family lived in Loudoun County, Virginia, where he attended Ashburn Elementary School. Based on Mark's previous IEP, school officials decided to place him in a general education classroom. To facilitate his educational progress, school officials hired a full-time aide, provided specialized training for his teacher and aide, provided 3 hours per week of instruction with a special education teacher (who also served as a consultant to Mark's teacher and aide), and provided 5 hours per week of speech therapy. Additionally, the entire staff at Ashburn Elementary received inservice training on autism and inclusion. The IEP team also included the supervisor of the Loudoun County program for children with autism to provide assistance in managing Mark's behavior. Finally, the IEP team received assistance from two consultants.

Despite the measures taken, the IEP team determined that Mark was making no academic or behavioral progress in the general education setting. Moreover, his behavior problems were extremely disruptive in class. Because of his aggression toward others (e.g., kicking, biting, punching), five families asked to have their children transferred to another classroom. The IEP team proposed that Mark be moved to a program for children with autism in a regular elementary school. Mark would receive his academic instruction and speech therapy in the special class and attend a general education classroom for art, music, physical education, library, and recess. The parents disagreed with the IEP, asserting that it violated the mainstreaming provision of the IDEA. The school district initiated a due process hearing. The due process hearing officer upheld the school district's IEP, and the state review officer affirmed the decision. The Hartmanns then challenged the hearing officer's decision in federal district court. The district court reversed the due process decision, specifically rejecting the administrative findings and ruling that the school had not taken appropriate steps to include Mark in the general education classroom. The school district filed an appeal with the U.S. Court of Appeals for the Fourth Circuit.

Figure 12.5
The *Hartmann* Three-Factor Test

Mainstreaming is not required when:

1. A student with a disability would not receive educational benefit from mainstreaming in a general education class.

2. Any marginal benefit from mainstreaming would be significantly outweighed by benefits that could feasibly be obtained only in a separate instructional setting.

3. The student is a disruptive force in the general education classroom.

Finding that the IDEA's mainstreaming provision established a presumption, not an inflexible mandate, the circuit court reversed the district court's ruling. The circuit court also admonished the district court for substituting its own judgment for that of educators. Additionally, the court reaffirmed a previous ruling that held that mainstreaming is not required when (a) a student with a disability would not receive educational benefit from mainstreaming in a general education class; (b) any marginal benefit from mainstreaming would be significantly outweighed by benefits that could feasibly be obtained only in a separate instructional setting; or (c) the student is a disruptive force in the general education classroom (see Figure 12.5). Finally, the circuit court stated that the LRE provision of the IDEA only created a presumption, and the presumption reflected congressional judgment that receipt of social benefits is a subordinate goal to receiving educational benefit.

Summary of Judicial Standards of Review

Although a number of LRE cases have been heard by the U.S. Courts of Appeals, there exists only four acknowledged tests for determining placement in the LRE. These tests, or judicial standards of review, are the *Roncker* portability test, the *Daniel* two-part test, the *Rachel H.* four-factor test, and the Fourth Circuit's three-part test. Of these tests, the *Daniel* test has proven the most persuasive, subsequently being adopted by the U.S. Courts of Appeals for the Third and Eleventh Circuits. These standards are important because they provide lower courts in the circuits with guidance in ruling on similar cases. They are also instructive to school districts because they indicate the relevant factors that courts will examine in LRE cases. Table 12.1 lists the standards of review and the states in which they are controlling authority.

The Burden of Proof

The question of which party bears the burden of proof in litigation has often been an area of conflict. *Burden of proof* refers to when parties, in taking a particular position, have to prove the correctness of their position to the satisfaction of a court. Decisions

Table 12.1
Judicial Standards of Review in LRE Cases

Roncker Portability Test	Daniel Two-Part Test	Rachel H. Four-Factor Test	Hartmann Three-Part Test
Kentucky	Alabama	Alaska	Maryland
Michigan	Delaware	Arizona	North Carolina
Ohio	Georgia	California	South Carolina
Tennessee	Florida	Hawaii	Virginia
	Louisiana	Idaho	West Virginia
	Mississippi	Montana	
	New Jersey	Nevada	
	Pennsylvania	Oregon	
	Texas	Washington	

in three circuits—the First Circuit in *Roland M. v. Concord School Committee* (1990), the D.C. Circuit in *Kerham v. McKenzie* (1988), and the Ninth Circuit in *Clyde K. v. Puyallup School District* (1994)—have held that the burden of proof rests with the party challenging the decision of the administrative agency. In *Clyde K.,* the court stated that because the IDEA does not contain language to the contrary, the burden of proof is placed on the parties challenging the ruling. Consequently, the parties that file a complaint with a court bear the burden of proving their case. The court in *Oberti v. Board of Education* (1993), however, stated that because of congressional preference for the integration of students with disabilities, the burden of proof should be placed on schools that have decided to educate a particular child in a segregated setting. The *Oberti* court stated that

> when IDEA's mainstreaming requirement is specifically at issue, it is appropriate to place the burden of proving compliance with the IDEA on the school. Indeed, the Act's strong presumption in favor of mainstreaming, 20 U.S.C. § 1422 (5) (B), would be turned on its head if parents had to prove that their child was worthy of being included, rather than the school district having to justify a decision to exclude the child from the regular classroom. (p. 219)

The parent was challenging the decision of the administrative agencies in *Oberti,* and would have borne the burden of proof in accordance with the *Roland, Kerham,* and *Clyde K.* decisions; however, the *Oberti* court placed the burden of proof on the school district. The Ninth Circuit court, in *Clyde K.,* specifically rejected the Third Circuit's ruling on burden of proof in *Oberti,* stating that the fact that a statute favors the rights of a certain group does not mean that the group is entitled to procedural advantage. Given the dicta and holdings in the previously cited court decisions, however, it is reasonable to assume that school districts' actions will be closely scrutinized when they place students with disabilities in more restrictive settings within the continuum of placements.

Standards for Determining the LRE

Clearly, several factors must be considered when determining placement. Ensuring that schools comply with the LRE mandate of IDEA is one of these factors. Additionally, it is important that IEP teams consider the standards established in the courts when determining placement. Figure 12.6 represents a multifactor decision-making model based on these three standards.

Figure 12.6
Determining the Least Restrictive Environment

School district decisions should be based on formative data collected throughout the LRE process.

1. Has the school taken steps to maintain the child in the general education classroom?
   - What supplementary aids and services were used?
   - What interventions were attempted?
   - How many interventions were attempted?
2. What are the benefits of placement in general education with supplementary aids and services versus special education?
   - Academic benefits
   - Nonacademic benefits (e.g., social, communication)
3. What are the effects on the education of other students?
   - If the student is disruptive, is the education of other students adversely affected?
   - Does the student require an inordinate amount of attention from the teacher, thereby adversely affecting the education of others?
4. If a student is being educated in a setting other than the general education classroom, are there integrated experiences with nondisabled peers to the maximum extent appropriate?
   - In what academic settings is the student integrated with nondisabled peers?
   - In what nonacademic settings is the child integrated with nondisabled peers?
5. Is the entire continuum of alternative services available from which to choose an appropriate placement?

From "Least Restrictive Environment, Inclusion, and Students with Disabilities: A Legal Analysis" by M. L. Yell, 1995, *Journal of Special Education, 28*(4), 389–404. Copyright 1995 by PRO-ED, Inc. Adapted by permission.

Individualization

The IEP team determines the least restrictive appropriate setting. The IDEA, its regulations, and comments to these regulations make it clear that the IEP team can only make this decision by examining students' needs and determining their goals based on this assessment. Federal regulations state that "the overriding rule . . . is that placement decisions must be made on an individual basis" (IDEA Regulations, 34 C.F.R. § 300.552, comment). In 1991, OSERS interpreted the LRE mandate as requiring that "children with disabilities should be educated with nondisabled children to the maximum extent appropriate; however, the determination of whether to place a child with disabilities in an integrated setting must be made on a case-by-case basis" (*Letter to Stutler and McCoy,* 1991, p. 308).

Because of the individualized nature of the LRE placement, there are no simple rules to guide IEP teams in making placement decisions. The legislation and litigation do, however, provide guidance regarding the decision-making process. Clearly, certain actions are never "appropriate," such as developing blanket policies regarding LRE decisions. For example, schools must never refuse to place particular categories of students with disabilities in general education classes; neither should they refuse more restrictive placements when required.

The decisions in *Greer v. Rome City School District* (1991) and *Oberti v. Board of Education* (1993) are particularly instructive, as the courts delineated the inappropriate actions by the school districts that resulted in the districts' losses in these cases. Perhaps the most important reason for these losses was the courts' unwillingness to accept assertions of appropriateness of restrictive settings without proof by school districts as to the inappropriateness of the general education classroom (Yell, 1995). In both *Greer* and *Oberti,* the school districts did not have data from direct experience to indicate that the general education class placement was not appropriate. For example, in *Oberti* the plaintiff was a student who exhibited significant behavior problems in the general education classroom. Although the school district's special education director testified that the school had attempted to keep the student in the general education classroom through various procedures, the IEP did not contain a behavioral plan. In *Greer,* the court ruled against the school district because (a) the IEP team failed to consider the full continuum of placements in determining the LRE; (b) the school made no attempt to assist the student to remain in the mainstream setting; and (c) the school district developed the IEP prior to the IEP meeting and did not clearly inform the Greers of the full range of services that may have been required to maintain their child in the general education classroom. Conversely, in the *Daniel, Hartmann,* and *Clyde K.* decisions, in which the school districts prevailed, school officials had attempted and documented a number of efforts to maintain the students in the general education classroom.

Benefits to the Student

The *Greer* court noted "several factors that a school district may consider in determining whether education in the regular classroom may be achieved satisfactorily" (p. 697). First, the school may compare the educational benefits of the general education classroom (with supplementary aids and services) with those received in the special education classroom. This comparison should include both academic and nonacademic (e.g., language, role-modeling) activities. If the school determines that the self-contained setting will provide "significantly" greater benefits and that in the general education classroom the student will fall behind peers in the self-contained class, the general education environment may not be appropriate.

Effect on Peers

School personnel may consider the effect the presence of a student with disabilities in a general education classroom would have on the education of other students in that classroom. A student who disrupts the education of others due to behavior problems or because of needing constant teacher attention may not be appropriately placed in a general education classroom. In weighing this factor, however, the school is cautioned by both the *Oberti* and *Greer* courts of their obligation to first consider the use of supplementary aids and services to accommodate a student.

The decision in *Clyde K.* further confirmed the legitimacy of considering the rights of other students in determining placement. In this case, a crucial factor in the school district's restrictive placement's being upheld was the use of supplementary aids and services. Similarly, school districts also prevailed in the removal of disruptive students in *MR v. Lincolnwood Board of Education* (1994) and *VanderMalle v. Ambach* (1987).

Appropriateness

The IDEA requires that schools provide a FAPE for all students with disabilities. The law also requires that to the maximum extent appropriate, students with disabilities should be educated with students without disabilities. When an appropriate education is not possible in the general education classroom, the FAPE and LRE provisions seem to be in conflict. This apparent conflict has provoked much controversy and confusion (Dubow, 1989). The FAPE and LRE requirements do not actually conflict; however, both are important elements in the special education decision-making process (McColl, 1992).

Legislation and litigation regarding LRE and FAPE indicate that the school's primary obligation is to provide the student with disabilities with a FAPE. The LRE principle, although important, is secondary (Champagne, 1993; Osborne, 1993; Tucker & Goldstein, 1992). The language of the law reinforces this by requiring that students with disabilities be educated in the LRE to the maximum extent appropriate, and by further requiring that schools have a continuum of alternative placements. In determining placement, the IEP team balances FAPE with the preference for educating students with disabilities with their peers in the general education classroom. The team selects the most integrated setting that is compatible with the delivery of an appropriate education. That setting is the LRE.

The IDEA appears unambiguous regarding LRE: The IEP team is to determine the setting with the greatest degree of integration in which an appropriate education is available. In practice, however, this requirement has proven to be difficult to apply (Champagne, 1993; Huefner, 1994; Osborne, 1993).

Integration

The IDEA clearly requires the maximum amount of integration that is appropriate given a student's needs. The LRE mandate was a clear expression of congressional preference for educating students with disabilities in the general education classroom when appropriate. As Champagne (1993) asserts, the IDEA requires the maximum integration that will "work" for a student. An appropriate interpretation of the LRE cases is that students with disabilities belong in integrated settings and that schools must make good faith efforts to make this possible.

The Use of Supplementary Aids and Services

According to the *Oberti* court, a key to meeting the LRE mandate is a school's proper use of supplementary aids and services. School districts must make good faith efforts to maintain students in a general education class placement, and the provision of various supplementary aids and services is a means by which schools can maintain students with disabilities in these settings. Supplementary aids and services may include prereferral interventions, consultation, behavior management plans, paraprofessionals, itinerant teachers, and resource rooms. According to the court in *Daniel*, schools are required to provide supplementary aids and services and to modify the general education classroom when they mainstream students with disabilities. If such efforts are not made, schools will be in violation of the IDEA. Furthermore, if the school has made these efforts, lower courts must examine whether the efforts are sufficient, because the IDEA

> does not permit [schools] to make mere token gestures to accommodate [students with disabilities], its requirement for modifying and supplementing regular education is broad. . . . Although broad, the requirement is not limitless. . . . [Schools] need not provide every conceivable aid or service to assist a child. . . . Furthermore, the [IDEA] does not require regular education instructors to devote all or most of their time to one [student with disabilities] or modify the curriculum beyond recognition. (p. 1048)

The question of the limit of supplementary aids and services that must be attempted or considered by the school remains undecided. In the *Daniel* decision, the court determined that the school district had fulfilled its requirements under the law, whereas the court's rulings in the *Greer* and *Oberti* cases held that the school districts had not.

In the *Oberti* case, the court believed that the school district had made negligible efforts to include the student, Rafael Oberti, in a general education classroom by mainstreaming him without a curriculum plan, behavior management plan, or special support to the teacher. The *Greer* court found that the school district failed to consider the full range of supplementary aids and services (including a resource room and itinerant instruction) that might have assisted the student, Christy Greer, in the mainstream placement. The court acknowledged that testimony by officials indicated that the school district had considered supplementary aids and services; however, this consideration was not reflected in the minutes of the IEP meeting or in the IEP itself. Neither had the school district made efforts to modify the mainstream curriculum to accommodate Christy.

The courts' direction regarding the importance of school districts' providing supplementary aids and services to place and maintain students in LREs is clear. Whether the school district needs to actually *attempt* a general education class placement with supplementary aids and services or is merely obligated to *consider* these services is, however, uncertain. Noting that the dicta in *Greer* and *Oberti* state that school districts must show that they have "considered" a range of supplementary aids and services, Huefner (1994) argues that school administrators may need to show that such considerations were made prior to concluding that an education in the general education classroom was not appropriate. Likewise, Maloney (1994) advises schools against failing to attempt general education classroom placements with adequate supplementary aids and services. Clearly, when there is a reasonable likelihood that a student can receive an appropriate education in the general education classroom with the use of supplementary aids and services, then the general education placement must be attempted (Gorn, 1996). When the general education classroom is clearly inappropriate for a student, however, it is not required that a student be placed in the general education classroom to fail prior to being moved to a more appropriate, restrictive placement (*Poolaw v. Bishop,* 1995).

A Model for Determining LRE

Notwithstanding the courts' guidance in making LRE decisions, placement teams find that determining the educational placement that constitutes the most appropriate and least restrictive setting for students with disabilities is tremendously difficult (Huefner, 1994). Champagne (1993) argues persuasively that school districts should adopt a sequential model in making placement decisions. The sequential model is an organized way of applying the LRE requirement to whatever facts a particular student's situation requires. Thus, the model preserves the "core statutory imperative" that placements are based on the student's educational needs. Additionally, Champagne has tested the model against the various LRE cases. According to his model, an IEP team should go through the following steps.

Step 1:   The team determines that a student is eligible for services.

Step 2:   The team defines what constitutes appropriate educational services for the student.

Step 3:   The team asks whether these appropriate educational services can be delivered in the general education classroom in its current form. If yes, then the general education setting becomes the student's primary placement. If no, go to step 4.

Step 4:   The team asks whether these appropriate educational services can be delivered in the general education classroom if the setting is modified through the addition of supplementary aids and services. If yes, then the general education setting with supplementary aids and services becomes the student's primary placement. If no, go to step 5.

Step 5:   If the team determines that the general setting, even with supplementary aids and services, is not appropriate, the team should determine placement by moving along the continuum of alternative placements one step at a time, from the least restrictive setting to more restrictive ones. At each step, ask whether the services called for in the IEP can be delivered in that setting. If yes, then the setting becomes the student's primary placement. If no, go to step 6.

Step 6:   The team asks whether the services called for in the IEP can be delivered in the slightly more restrictive settings if they are modified through the use of supplementary aids and services. If yes, that is the primary placement; if no, repeat step 5 for a placement on the continuum that is slightly more restrictive, and then, if necessary, go to step 6 for that setting. (In this manner, the placement team moves along the continuum of alternative placements, one step at a time, repeating steps 5 and 6 until a yes answer is obtained.)

Step 7:   In the context of the primary placement chosen, ask if there are additional opportunities for integration for some portion of the student's school day. If yes, design a split placement by including the student in the integrated setting for part of the school day and in the more restrictive setting for part of the school day.

Summary

The LRE mandate of the IDEA sets forth a clear congressional preference for integrating students with disabilities in general education classrooms. The LRE mandate has two specific components: First, students with disabilities must be educated along with students without disabilities to the maximum extent appropriate; second, students with disabilities should be removed from integrated settings only when the nature or severity of the disability is such that an appropriate education with the use of supplementary aids and services cannot be achieved satisfactorily in the general education setting. Recognizing that at times an integrated setting would not provide an appropriate education and thus a more restrictive setting may be necessary, IDEA regulations include a continuum of alternative placement options that vary in the degree of restrictiveness. The purpose of the continuum is to make appropriate educational placements available to students based on their individual needs. Recent decisions have indicated that the courts are unwilling to accept at face value a school district's assertions that a student cannot be educated in less restrictive settings. Schools will bear the burden of proof, therefore, when they choose more restrictive settings for students with disabilities.

For Further Information

Bartlett, L. D. (1993). Mainstreaming: On the road to clarification. *Education Law Reporter, 76,* 17–25.

Champagne, J. F. (1993). Decisions in sequence: How to make placements in the least restrictive environment. *EdLaw Briefing Paper, 9 & 10,* 1–16.

Huefner, D. S. (1994). The mainstreaming cases: Tensions and trends for school administrators. *Educational Administration Quarterly, 30,* 27–55.

Lewis, T. J., Chard, D., & Scott, T. M. (1994). Full inclusion and the education of children and youth with emotional and behavioral disorders. *Behavioral Disorders, 19,* 277–293.

Osborne, A. G., & DiMattia, P. (1994). The IDEA's least restrictive environment mandate: Legal implications. *Exceptional Children, 61,* 6–14.

Osborne, A. G., & DiMattia, P. (1994). Counterpoint: IDEA's LRE mandate: Another look. *Exceptional Children, 61,* 582–584.

Sharp, K. G., & Pitasky, V. M. (2002). *The current legal status of inclusion.* Horsham, PA: LRP Publications.

Yell, M. L. (1994). The LRE cases: Judicial activism or judicial restraint? *Exceptional Children, 61,* 578–581.

Yell, M. L. (1995). Least restrictive environment, inclusion, and students with disabilities: A legal analysis. *Journal of Special Education, 28,* 389–404.

Yell, M. L. (1995). *Clyde K. and Sheila K. v. Puyallup School District.* The courts, inclusion, and students with behavioral disorders. *Behavioral Disorders, 20,* 179–189.

References

Americans with Disabilities Act of 1990, 42 U.S.C. 12101 *et seq.*

Barnett v. Fairfax County School Board, 17 EHLR 350 (4th Cir. 1991).

Bartlett, L. D. (1993). Mainstreaming: On the road to clarification. *Education Law Reporter, 76,* 17–25.

Board of Education of the Hendrick Hudson School District v. Rowley, 458 U.S. 176 (1982).

Brown v. Board of Education, 347 U.S. 483 (1954).

Carter v. Florence County School District, 950 F.2d 156 (4th Cir. 1991).

Champagne, J. F. (1993). Decisions in sequence: How to make placements in the least restrictive environment. *EdLaw Briefing Paper, 9 & 10,* 1–16.

Clyde K. v. Puyallup School District, 35 F.3d 1396 (9th Cir. 1994).

Cordero v. Pennsylvania, 19 IDELR 623 (M.D. Pa. 1993).

Daniel R. R. v. State Board of Education, 874 F.2d 1036 (5th Cir. 1989).

Dubow, S. (1989). Into the turbulent mainstream: A legal perspective on the weight to be given to the least restrictive environment in placement decisions for deaf children. *Journal of Law and Education, 18,* 215–228.

Education for All Handicapped Children Act of 1975, 20 U.S.C. § 1401 *et seq.*

Education of the Handicapped Amendments of 1974, Pub. L. No. 93-380, 88 Stat. 580.

Flour Bluff Independent School District v. Katherine M., 24 IDELR 673 (5th Cir. 1996).

Gorn, S. (1996). *What do I do when . . . The answer book on special education law.* Horsham, PA: LRP Publications.

Greer v. Rome City School District, 950 F.2d 688 (11th Cir. 1991).

Hairston v. Drosick, 423 F. Supp. 180 (S.D. W.V. 1976).

Hartmann v. Loudoun County Board of Education (4th Cir. 1997). Available at http://www.law.emory.edu/4circuit/july97/962809.p.html.

Hudson v. Bloomfield Hills School District, 23 IDELR 612 (E.D. Mich 1995).

Huefner, D. S. (1994). The mainstreaming cases: Tensions and trends for school administrators. *Educational Administration Quarterly, 30,* 27–55.

Individuals with Disabilities Education Act of 1990, 20 U.S.C. § 1401 *et seq.*

Individuals with Disabilities Education Act of Regulations, 34 C.F.R. § 300 *et seq.*

Kerham v. McKenzie, 862 F.2d 884 (D.C. Gir. 1988).

Lachman v. Illinois Board of Education, 852 F.2d 290 (7th Cir. 1988).

Letter to Frost, 19 IDELR 594 (OSERS 1991).

Letter to Goodling, 18 IDELR 213 (OSERS 1991).

Letter to Stutler and McCoy, 18 IDELR 307 (OSERS 1991).

Maloney, M. (1994, May). *Full inclusion: Heaven or hell?* Paper presented at the National Institute on Legal Issues of Educating Individuals with Disabilities, San Francisco, CA.

McColl, A. (1992). Placement in the least restrictive environment for children with disabilities. *School Law Bulletin, 26,* 13–21.

MR v. Lincolnwood Board of Education, 20 IDELR 1323 (N.D. Ill. 1994).

Murray v. Montrose County School District, 22 IDELR 558 (10th Cir. 1995).

Norlin, J., & Gorn, S. (2005). *What do I do when . . . The answer book on special education law* (4th ed.). Horsham, PA: LRP Publications.

Oberti v. Board of Education of the Borough of Clementon School District, 995 F.2d 1204 (3rd Cir. 1993).

Osborne, A. G. (1993). The IDEA's least restrictive environment mandate: Implications for public policy. *Education Law Reporter, 74,* 369–380.

Poolaw v. Bishop, 23 IDELR 407 (9th Cir. 1995).

Roland M. v. Concord School Committee, 910 F.2d 983 (1st Cir. 1990).

Roncker v. Walter, 700 F.2d 1058 (6th Cir. 1983).

Sacramento City Unified School District Board of Education v. Holland, 786 F. Supp. 874 (E.D. Col. 1992).

Sacramento City Unified School District Board of Education v. Rachel H., 14 F.3d 1398 (9th Cir. 1994).

Schuldt v. Mankato ISD, 937 F.2d 1357 (8th Cir. 1991).

Section 504 Regulations, 34 C.F.R. § 104 *et seq.*

Sheldon v. Tucker, 364 U.S. 479 (1960).

Stafford, R. (1978). Education for the handicapped: A senator's perspective. *Vermont Law Review, 3,* 71–76.

Tucker, B. P., & Goldstein, B. A. (1992). *Legal rights of persons with disabilities: An analysis of public law.* Horsham, PA: LRP Publications.

Turnbull, H. R., & Turnbull, A. P. (2002). *Free appropriate public education: The law and children with disabilities* (6th ed.). Denver, CO: Love.

Urban v. Jefferson County School District R-1, 21 IDELR 985 (D. Col. 1994).

VanderMalle v. Ambach, 667 F. Supp. 1015 (S.D.N.Y. 1987).

Yell, M. L. (1995). Least restrictive environment, inclusion, and students with disabilities: Analysis and commentary. *Journal of Special Education, 28,* 389–404.

Zirkel, P. (2000). *Section 504 and the schools.* Horsham, PA: LRP Publications.

CHAPTER THIRTEEN

Procedural Safeguards

The history of liberty has largely been the history of the observance of procedural safeguards.

Justice Felix Frankfurter, *McNabb v. U.S.* (1943, p. 347)

When the Education for All Handicapped Children Act was passed in 1975, Congress wanted to ensure that students with disabilities would be treated fairly and provided with an appropriate education. One way in which they accomplished this was to provide students, and their parents, with procedural protections to ensure that they would be meaningfully involved with school districts when educational programs were being planned and implemented. These procedural protections relied on the 5th and 14th Amendments to the U.S. Constitution. According to the due process clause of these amendments, no state may deprive any person "of life, liberty, or property without due process of law." These amendments give persons, including students, two types of due process rights: procedural and substantive. According to Shrybman (1982), procedural safeguards are rules of law that govern the means by which individuals can maintain their substantive rights. In special education, procedural safeguards guide the method by which school officials make decisions regarding the education of students, and substantive due process rights are those personal rights that school officials may not abridge (Valente & Valente, 2005).

When writing the Individuals with Disabilities Education Act (IDEA), Congress created explicit procedural safeguards to be afforded students with disabilities and their parents. The purpose of these procedural safeguards is to ensure that parents of children with disabilities are meaningfully involved in their children's education (*Christopher P. v. Marcus,* 1990). According to the U.S. Supreme Court, Congress established the elaborate system of safeguards to "guarantee parents both an opportunity for meaningful input into all decisions affecting their child's education and the right to seek review of any decisions they think inappropriate" (*Honig v. Doe,* 1988, p. 598).

The procedural safeguards of the IDEA include (a) notice and consent requirements, (b) examination of relevant records, (c) procedures to protect the rights of a
student when parents are unavailable, (d) the independent educational evaluation,
(e) voluntary mediation, and (f) the due process hearing. Additionally, parents may
challenge the actions of a school district before a state educational agency (SEA) and
may eventually file suit in state or federal court.

Finally, parents challenging the special education services provided by a school
may use the procedures set forth in the Education Department General Administrative Regulations (EDGAR; 34 C.F.R. §§ 76.651–76.662). EDGAR requires states to establish procedures to resolve complaints regarding a school district's possible
violation of a federal law (EDGAR, 34 C.F.R. § 76.780). Under this law, parents may
resolve complaints that a school district has violated the IDEA. Moreover, parents
may exercise the EDGAR procedures as an alternative to the IDEA due process option (OSEP Memorandum 94-16, 1994). In a policy letter, the Office of Special Education Programs (OSEP) stated that the EDGAR procedures for resolving complaints
may be preferable to the IDEA due process hearing because they are less costly and
more efficient for resolving disputes (OSEP Memorandum 94-16, 1994).

This chapter reviews the procedural rights included in the IDEA, beginning with
a discussion of the procedural rights of parents and the general procedural requirements of the IDEA. In addition, I focus on the due process hearing and the different
types of remedies that courts can award to parents who prevail in the lawsuits
against schools.

Procedural Rights of Parents

Identification of Parents

Procedural safeguards must be extended to the parents of students with disabilities
under the IDEA. Because of the importance Congress attached to meaningful
parental involvement, it is obvious that the identification of a student's parents is an
important requirement under the law. The biological or adoptive parents who reside
with a child are considered parents for purposes of the IDEA. Additionally, other
adults may also be considered parents under the IDEA. Regulations to the IDEA define a parent as "a parent, a guardian, a person acting as a parent of the child, or a
surrogate parent" who has been appointed following the procedures of the law. In
IDEA 2004, Congress defined foster parents as parents under the law.

Regulations further "include persons acting in place of the parent, such as a
grandmother or stepparent with whom the child lives, as well as persons who are
legally responsible for a child's welfare" (IDEA Regulations, 34 C.F.R. § 300.13, note).
Gorn (1996) contends that there are two routes to parental eligibility under the law:
living with the child in a parental role or having legal responsibility for a child who resides elsewhere.

Because of the IDEA's encouragement of parental involvement, it seems likely
that noncustodial parents should also be allowed to participate in the development

of their child's special education program (Gorn, 1996). The IDEA, however, neither compels a school district to include a noncustodial parent in special education planning nor prohibits the inclusion of that parent. The decision to include noncustodial parents in the decision-making process is seemingly left to the school district. Gorn (1996) suggests that the involvement of noncustodial parents in the special education process is best resolved by agreement between the parents.

The IDEA does not address situations where parents of a student are divorced and live apart and one agrees with an individualized education plan (IEP) but the other disagrees. Greismann (1997) asserts that in such situations school districts should conclude the IEP process and proceed with implementing the IEP. According to Greismann, "[IDEA] regulations do not require both parents to be in agreement and if one parent believes the IEP is appropriate, that arguably satisfies the parental consent provision of the [IDEA]" (p. 3). The parent in disagreement with the IEP, however, should be notified of the IDEA due process rights.

In *Lower Moreland Township School District* (1992), a hearing officer in Pennsylvania ruled that a father who shared legal custody, but not physical custody, had the right to challenge an IEP agreed to by the mother, who had both legal and physical custody of their child. In this case, the father had been involved in educational planning until he objected to the school's proposed special education program. The school then asserted that he was not a "parent" under the IDEA. The hearing officer disagreed, ruling that the father had the right to participate under a court order that granted him legal custody of the child. The hearing officer, aware of the potential problems that such a ruling could cause school districts, stated that not every noncustodial parent could veto special education decisions, thereby burdening school districts with the difficult task of securing approval of special education decisions from absent, and possibly uninterested, parents. The hearing officer, nevertheless, recognized the right of the noncustodial father, who had been involved in previous education decisions, to make good faith objections to the proposed program.

Questions regarding the role of foster parents in the special education decision-making process remain unsettled (Guernsey & Klare, 1993). The role of foster parents is not addressed in the IDEA. The term "person acting as a parent of the child" does not include foster parents (*Letter to Baker,* 1993). Neither does the IDEA require that a state recognize a foster parent as a "parent." A state, however, may allow a foster parent to act as a parent for purposes of the IDEA if (a) a foster parent is legally responsible for a foster child's welfare and (b) the natural parents' authority to make educational decisions has been relinquished (Gorn, 1996). The primary question concerns when a foster parent becomes a parent under federal or state law. If a foster parent becomes a parent under the law, a surrogate parent need not be appointed to represent the student. The crucial determinant may be whether the foster care placement is permanent. OSEP has not established guidelines as to the length of time that a foster care relationship must exist to be considered permanent, but it has asserted that a state policy that considered foster placements in excess of 6 months to be long-term, and therefore permanent, had to be followed (Hargan Inquiry, 1990). There are no guidelines regarding the appointment of foster parents who do not meet the standards of permanent parents as surrogate parents for a child. Decisions regarding the use of foster parents as "parents" under the IDEA should be made on a case-by-case basis.

Surrogate Parents

The IDEA requires that parents be central participants in the special education decision-making process. If the child does not have a parent, the parent cannot be found, or the child is a ward of the state,* the IDEA requires that a surrogate parent be appointed (IDEA Regulations, 34 C.F.R. § 300.514). The surrogate parent is appointed to safeguard the educational rights of the child with disabilities by acting as an advocate for the child (Shrybman, 1982). Because a surrogate parent is considered a "parent" under the IDEA, he or she has all the rights, responsibilities, and procedural safeguards of a natural parent under the IDEA (Gorn, 1996). The surrogate parent must have no conflicts of interest, must have the requisite knowledge and skills to ensure that the child is adequately represented, and may not be an employee of the school or be involved in the education or care of the child (IDEA Regulations, 34 C.F.R. § 300.514 (c)–(d)). If a child is a ward of the state, a court appoints the surrogate of the child. IDEA 2004 extends the same surrogate parents' provisions to homeless children whose parents cannot be located. The appointment should take place within 30 days after it is determined that the child needs a surrogate.

If the parents' whereabouts are known but they do not make themselves available, there is no need to appoint a surrogate parent, even if the child is in a foster placement (Hargan, 1990). Under the IDEA, the appointment of surrogate parents does not terminate parental rights, nor do the surrogate parents act as replacements for parents in other matters.

The public agency responsible for the surrogate parent must have procedures for determining whether a student needs a surrogate parent and for assigning the surrogate parent. Regulations to the IDEA require that school districts determine the need for surrogate parents when the natural parents have not been located "after reasonable efforts" (IDEA Regulations, 34 C.F.R. § 300.514(a) (2)). What constitutes a reasonable effort, however, is not clear. A federal district court found that a school district had made reasonable efforts to locate parents when it made repeated telephone calls and sent letters to the child's residence and the parents' last known address (*Jesu D. v. Lucas County Children Services Board*, 1985).

If the parents can be located but seem to have no interest in their child's educational program or refuse to participate in the special education process, the IDEA does not empower school districts to appoint surrogate parents (*Letter to Perryman*, 1987). Neither can a school district appoint a surrogate parent to represent the interests of the child or obtain an injunction to prohibit parents from participating in

---

*A child is a ward of the state when the state has assumed legal responsibility to make decisions regarding the child (Shrybman, 1982).

the process, even if the parents act in bad faith or attempt to "sabotage" the process (*Board of Education of Northfield High School District, 225 v. Roy H. and Lynn H.,* 1995).

General Procedural Requirements

School districts must establish and maintain procedural safeguards in accordance with the IDEA and state law requirements (see Figure 13.1 for a list of IDEA's procedural safeguards). The safeguard notice and subsequent notices must (a) provide a full explanation of the procedural safeguards, (b) be written in the native language of the parents (unless it is clearly not feasible to do so), (c) be written in an easily understandable manner, and (d) be available to parents of students with disabilities. Additionally, a copy of the procedural safeguards must be made available to parents of a child with a disability one time a year. An additional copy shall be given to a child's parents when (a) a child is initially referred or the parent requests an evaluation, (b) a parent first files a complaint for a due process hearing, or (c) a parent requests a copy. A school district may place the procedural safeguard notice on its website.

Figure 13.1
Procedural Safeguards of the IDEA

The procedural safeguard notice to parents must fully explain the following safeguards:

1. The right to receive an independent educational evaluation

2. The right to receive prior written notice before a school poses or refuses to take a specific action

3. The right to access their child's educational records

4. The right and opportunity to present and resolve complaints (This includes (a) the time period in which to make a complaint, (b) the opportunity for the school to resolve the complaint, and (c) the availability of mediation.)

5. The placement of a child during the pendency of the due process hearing

6. The procedures for students who are placed in an interim alternative educational setting

7. The requirements for unilateral placement by parents of a child in private schools at public expense

8. The requirements for due process hearings, including information regarding the disclosure of evaluation results and recommendations

9. The requirements for state-level appeals (if applicable in the state)

10. The right to file a civil action, including the time period in which parents must file

11. The attorneys' fees requirements

Notice Requirements

The IDEA requires that schools notify parents at various stages in the special education process regarding their substantive and procedural rights. Notification means that the school must inform the parent of any actions proposed by the school district. The IDEA requires that written notice be provided to parents prior to the school's proposing to initiate or change the identification, evaluation, educational placement, or provision of a FAPE to the child, or prior to the school's refusing to make such changes (IDEA Regulations, 34 C.F.R. § 300.504–300.505). The purpose of notifying parents is to provide them with information to protect their rights and the rights of their child, to allow them to make informed decisions, and to enable them to fully participate in the special education process (Osborne, 1995). Notice must be provided to parents after an appropriate decision has been reached concerning identification, evaluation, or placement. Furthermore, notice must be given in a reasonable amount of time prior to the implementation of the decision (*Letter to Helmuth*, 1990). Because a school district's failure to provide notification is a serious matter, school districts often use various methods to document that the required notices have been sent (Shrybman, 1982). The IDEA, however, does not require that school districts have parents acknowledge the receipt of a notice in writing.

The notice must be written so that it is understandable to the general public. Sending parents a copy of the pertinent statutes and regulations is not an appropriate form of notice (*Max M. v. Thompson*, 1984). Moreover, the notice must provide enough information for parents to understand what the school district is proposing or why a particular option was chosen. Figure 13.2 lists the IDEA's specific requirements regarding the content of the notice (IDEA Regulations, 34 C.F.R. § 300.504–300.505).

Consent Requirements

The IDEA requires parental consent prior to the initial evaluation and placement of a student in special education (IDEA Regulations, 34 C.F.R. § 300.504(b)(1)). Before consent is obtained, a school district must inform parents of relevant information regarding the evaluation or placement. When a school obtains consent, it has parents' permission to carry out the action proposed in the notice. Once a student is initially placed in a special education program, the IDEA does not require that parental consent be obtained for subsequent evaluations or for changes in the student's special education program. In these situations, however, the school must provide notice of intent to evaluate or change placement, and must follow the requirements for changing the IEP (IDEA Regulations, 34 C.F.R. § 300.504, note 1). Moreover, consent is recommended, even though it is not legally required (Shrybman, 1982). States may have more stringent consent requirements, but they must not have the effect of excluding a child from special education (IDEA Regulations, 34 C.F.R. § 300.504(d)).

When obtaining consent, the school must ensure that the parents understand and agree to the proposal in writing (IDEA Regulations, 34 C.F.R. § 300.500(a)(3)). To be valid, consent must be given voluntarily by parents who have sufficient information to make an informed decision and have the capacity to give consent. Figure 13.3 lists the IDEA's specific requirements regarding consent and the content of the consent notice (IDEA Regulations, 34 C.F.R. § 300.504–300.505).

Parents must be told that the granting of consent is voluntary and may be revoked at any time (IDEA Regulations, 34 C.F.R. § 300.500(a) (3)). The right of revocation is somewhat limited because the opportunity to revoke consent is only available while the activity for which consent was given is taking place. For example, if consent is given for an evaluation, the time in which consent can be revoked ends

Figure 13.2
Content of Notice Requirements of the IDEA

1) A full explanation of all procedural safeguards and how parents may obtain a copy of the procedural safeguards

2) A description of the action proposed or refused by the school:

  (i) An explanation of why the action is being taken

  (ii) A description of any options considered

  (iii) Reasons why the school proposed or refused to take an action

3) A description of each evaluation procedure the school used to make its decision

4) A description of any other factors that were relevant to the school's decision

5) A description of where parents may obtain assistance to understand their procedural rights

6) If the language or mode of communication is not written, the school shall ensure that:

  (i) The notice is translated orally or by other means to the parents in their native language or mode of communication.

  (ii) The parent understands the content of the notice.

  (iii) There is written evidence that these requirements have been met.

Figure 13.3
Consent Procedures of the IDEA

Parental consent must be obtained before conducting a/an::

✓ Preplacement evaluation

✓ Initial placement in special education

✓ Reevaluation (unless the LEA can demonstrate that it took measures to secure parental consent but was unsuccessful) when the evaluation is completed (*Letter to Williams,* 1991). When given in a timely manner, a revocation of consent has the same effect as an initial refusal to consent. According to OSEP, when consent is withdrawn, members of the school staffing team should determine if they agree with the revocation. If they do not, they should continue providing appropriate educational services and pursue formal means to resolve the dispute, such as requesting mediation.

The Individuals with Disabilities Education Improvement Act of 2004 (IDEA 2004) addressed a situation that arises when parents refuse to grant consent for what school personnel believe are needed special education services or if parents fail to respond to the school's attempts to reach them. If the school is considering whether to conduct an initial evaluation of a student but does not have parental permission or a response from the parents of the student, the school district may pursue the initial evaluation by applying for mediation and due process procedures (IDEA 1414 § (D)(ii)(II)). If, however, the parent refusal to provide consent comes when the school district wants to provide special education services, the school district will not go to a hearing officer to order the parents to bring the child to the service center. Moreover, the school district will not be considered in violation of the FAPE requirement of the IEP because it did not provide a special education. Neither shall the school district be required to convene an IEP meeting for the student.

Opportunity to Examine Records

The IDEA contains specific requirements concerning parental access rights (IDEA Regulations, 34 § C.F.R. 300.562–300.567). The regulations state that

> the parents of a child with a disability shall be afforded. . . an opportunity to inspect and review all educational records with respect to—
>   (A) The identification, evaluation, and educational placement of the child, and
>   (B) The provision of FAPE to the child. (IDEA Regulations, 34 C.F.R. § 300.502)

Schools must permit parents to inspect and review all educational records collected, maintained, and used by the school concerning the student's special education (IDEA Regulations, 34 C.F.R. § 300.562). When parents ask to review educational records, they must be allowed to do so without unnecessary delay. Additionally, requests to inspect records must be granted prior to any meeting regarding the student's IEP or a due process hearing. The length of time between the parents' request to the school and the inspection or review of the records cannot exceed 45 days (IDEA Regulations, 34 C.F.R. § 300.562(a)). Figure 13.4 lists specific inspection and review rights granted to parents under the IDEA (IDEA Regulations, 34 C.F.R. § 300.562(b)).

The IDEA's confidentiality of information requirements directs schools to keep a record of parties obtaining access to the student records. The records maintained must include the name of the party obtaining access, the date access was given, and the purpose for which the records were used (IDEA Regulations, 34 C.F.R. § 300.563). This requirement, however, does not extend to parental access.

Figure 13.4
Parents' Inspection and Review Rights

- Schools shall permit parents to inspect and review any educational records relating to their child.
- The school must comply with the request without unnecessary delay and before any meeting regarding the child's education (45 days or less).
- The school must respond to reasonable requests for explanations and interpretations of records.
- Parents can request that the school provide copies of the records if failure to provide these copies would prevent the parents from exercising their rights.
- Parents can have a representative inspect and review the records.
- Schools must assume that parents have the right to inspect records unless they have been advised that the parents do not have the right under the applicable state laws.
- Schools must keep a record of parties obtaining access to educational records, including name of the party, date, and purpose.
- Schools shall provide parents with a list of types and locations of educational records used by the school.
- Parents who believe that information in the records is inaccurate or misleading may request that the school amend the information. If the school refuses to amend the records, the parents must be informed of their right to request a hearing.

Independent Educational Evaluation

The IDEA's procedural safeguards include the right of parents to obtain an independent educational evaluation (IEE) of their child (IDEA Regulations, 34 C.F.R. § 300.503). Under certain circumstances, the school may be required to provide this evaluation at public expense. (For elaborations on IEEs, see Chapter 11.)

An IEE is an "evaluation conducted by a qualified examiner who is not employed by the public agency responsible for the education of the child" (IDEA Regulations, 34 C.F.R. § 300.503(3)(i)). If the parents disagree with the school's evaluation, they may request an IEE at public expense. If, however, school personnel believe the evaluation to be appropriate, they may request a due process hearing. If the hearing officer determines that the school's evaluation was appropriate, the parents retain the right to an IEE, but not at public expense (IDEA Regulations, 34 C.F.R. § 300.503(b)). When parents obtain an evaluation at their own expense, school personnel must consider it in the special education decision-making process (IDEA Regulations, 34 C.F.R. § 300.503(c)). The IEE may also be presented as evidence at an impartial due process hearing (IDEA Regulations, 34 C.F.R. § 300.503(c)(2)).

Figure 13.5
Individual Educational Evaluations

- The parents of a child with disabilities have the right to obtain one IEE of the child at public expense.
- On request, schools shall provide to parents information about where an IEE may be obtained.
- Parents have the right to an IEE at public expense if they disagree with the school's evaluation.
- The school may initiate a hearing to show that its evaluation was appropriate. If the final decision is in favor of the school, the parents still have the right to an IEE, but not at public expense.
- If parents obtain an IEE at private expense, the results of the evaluation must be considered by the school.
- If a hearing officer requests an IEE, the cost must be borne by the school.

Parents have received reimbursement for IEEs when schools have violated procedural safeguards (*Akers v. Bolton*, 1981), when parents have taken unilateral actions that were later determined necessary (*Anderson v. Thompson*, 1981), and when the IEE was later used to determine placement (*Hoover Schrum Ill. School District No. 157*, 1980). The U.S. Court of Appeals for the Fourth Circuit has held that only one IEE at public expense is required (*Hudson v. Wilson*, 1987). A due process hearing officer may also request that an IEE be performed at public expense (IDEA Regulations, 34 C.F.R. § 300.503(d)). Specific requirements of school districts regarding IEEs are listed in Figure 13.5.

Dispute Resolution

When Congress passed the Education for All Handicapped Children Act in 1975, it included elaborate procedural protections to ensure that schools would include parents in all educational decision making involved in providing a free appropriate public education. However, if parents believe a school district has not followed the procedures or if they disagree with actions involving the identification, evaluation, or placement of the child, parents may follow a set of dispute resolution mechanisms.

Mediation

The IDEA Amendments of 1997 added voluntary mediation requirements to the procedural safeguards. Prior to the amendments, most states had already adopted some form of mediation. The federal standard, however, provided for greater uniformity among the states and furnished a model for the states that had not yet implemented mediation. IDEA 2004 retains the mediation requirements.

Mediation is a dispute-resolution and collaborative problem-solving process in which a trained impartial party facilitates a negotiation process between parties who have reached an impasse (Dobbs, Primm, & Primm, 1991; Goldberg & Huefner, 1995). The role of the mediator is to facilitate discussion, encourage open exchange of information, assist the involved parties in understanding each other's viewpoints, and help the parties to reach mutually agreeable solutions. The mediator has no authority to impose solutions on either party. In mediation sessions, the focus is on the negotiated resolution of the conflict rather than factual presentations, witnesses, or formal rules of evidence (Goldberg & Huefner, 1995). Mediation is an intervening step that may be used prior to conducting a formal due process hearing (Gorn, 1996).

When a mediation session is conducted, a neutral third party helps the parents and the school personnel arrive at their own solution to the disagreement. Although a mediation session is structured, it is less formal and adversarial than due process hearings or court proceedings. Advantages of mediation include the following: (a) takes less time, (b) costs less, (c) allows for greater discussion of the issues, and (d) helps to maintain a workable relationship between schools and parents (Dobbs et al., 1991; Primm, 1990). Dobbs, Primm, and Primm (1993) reported that a questionnaire given to parents and school personnel following special education mediation sessions revealed that 90% of the parents and 99% of the teachers who had been involved in the mediation would recommend the process to others to help resolve disputes.

States are required to offer mediation as a voluntary option for parents and school districts to resolve disputes. The law clearly specifies, however, that mediation cannot be used to delay or deny parents' right to an impartial due process hearing. If parents choose not to use mediation, school districts and state educational agencies may establish procedures to require parents to meet with a disinterested third party who would encourage and explain the benefits of mediation to them. Such meetings must be held at a time and place convenient to the parents.

Because states have been successful in using mediation systems that both allowed and disallowed attorneys at mediation sessions, Congress left to the states decisions regarding the attendance of attorneys at mediation. Procedurally, states are required to maintain a list of qualified mediators. When a school district and parents go to mediation, both parties should be involved in selecting a mediator from the list. The mediator must be impartial, so employees of the involved school districts or persons with personal or professional conflicts of interest are not allowed to mediate. Furthermore, the mediator must be experienced, trained, and knowledgeable about the law. Mediators do not have to be attorneys. When mediation is used, the states will bear the costs.

Mediation resolutions are to be put into a legally binding written agreement. The agreement states that discussions that occurred during mediation will be kept confidential. Furthermore, the agreement is signed by both parties and is enforceable in a state or federal court. The discussion from the mediation session cannot be used as evidence in subsequent due process hearings or civil actions. Parties in the mediation process may be required to sign a confidentiality pledge prior to the commencement of mediation.

Resolution Session

Congress, in IDEA 2004, developed the resolution session as an intermediary step between the meditation session and the due process hearing. Within 15 days of receiving a parent's complaint, the school district may convene a meeting with the parents and relevant members of the IEP team, including the school representative, to discuss the complaint and attempt to resolve it. Essentially, the parents give the school district 30 days in which to resolve the issue. If no resolution is reached within 30 days of filing the complaint, the due process hearing may take place. If the complaint is settled, both parties will sign a legally binding agreement. Moreover, this settlement agreement is enforceable in any state or federal court that has jurisdiction. According to Richards and Martin (2005), by including a resolution session prior to a due process hearing, Congress attempted to add a pre-hearing form to resolve parent complaints outside of the legal process.

The Due Process Hearing

According to the U.S. Court of Appeals for the Fourth Circuit, the IDEA contains a bill of rights for parents wishing to contest a school's special education decisions regarding their child (*Stemple v. Board of Education,* 1980). The sine qua non, or indispensable condition, of the IDEA's procedural safeguards is the due process hearing. The purpose of the due process hearing is to allow an impartial third party, the due process hearing officer, to hear both sides of a dispute, examine the issues, and settle the dispute (Anderson, Chitwood, & Hayden, 1990). Congress deliberately chose an adversarial system for resolving disputes, believing it was the best way to ensure that both parents and school officials would receive an equal opportunity to present their case (Goldberg & Huefner, 1995).

Parents may request a due process hearing to contest a school's identification, evaluation, educational placement, or provision of FAPE (IDEA Regulations, 34 C.F.R. § 506(a)) or to question the information in their child's educational records* (IDEA Regulations, 34 C.F.R. § 568). Parents must file within 2 years of the date of the action that forms the basis of the complaint. If the state has an explicit time limit, however, that time limit must be followed.

The due process hearing may also be used to seek resolution of procedural violations if the violations adversely affect a student's education (Guernsey & Klare, 1993). In addition to parents, students who have reached the age of majority can request hearings, as may schools (IDEA Regulations, 34 C.F.R. § 506(a)) when parents refuse consent to an evaluation.

---

*Disputes over educational records are subject to hearings under EDGAR rather than the due process hearing rules of the IDEA (EDGAR Regulations, 34 C.F.R. § 99.22).

The IDEA leaves the choice of the agency that conducts due process hearings to individual states (IDEA Regulations, 34 C.F.R. § 506(b)). Many states assign the conduct of hearings to the state educational agency, an intermediate educational agency, or the local school district. The agency responsible for the hearing is required to inform the parents of any free or low-cost legal and other relevant services if requested to do so by the parents (IDEA Regulations, 34 C.F.R. § 506(c)). The hearing must be conducted at a time and place that is convenient to the parents (IDEA Regulations, 34 C.F.R. § 300.512(d)).

No less than 5 days before the hearing, both parties are required to disclose any evaluations or information that the party intends to bring out at the hearing. If either party fails to file this information in time, the hearing officer may prevent the late party from introducing new evidence or raising new issues without the consent of the other party.

States also have the option of adopting a one-tier or two-tier hearing procedure. In a one-tier system, the initial level of review is conducted by the state educational agency. Judicial review of the state's decision is immediately available in a state or federal court. In a two-tier system, the initial review is usually conducted by the school district, and an appeal of the hearing officer's decision is made to the state for an intermediate administrative review. Following a decision at the second tier, a civil action can be filed in a state or federal court (Katsiyannis & Kale, 1991). In a survey of state practices in due process hearings, Katsiyannis and Kale (1991) found that 24 states and the District of Columbia used a one-tier system, while 26 states had a two-tier system.

State laws or regulations direct the method by which due process hearings are requested. If the due process hearing is conducted by the school district, the request normally goes through the district. Guernsey and Klare (1993) suggest that the request be made to the superintendent of schools, with a copy going to the director of special education. The nature of the disagreement and the names of the parties involved should be included in the request.

The U.S. Court of Appeals for the Ninth Circuit has ruled that due process hearings may be requested by parents even if their child has not been formally accepted into special education (*Hacienda La Puente Unified School District v. Honig*, 1992). Also, parents can request a due process hearing even if their child is not attending public school, but the reason that the child is not in the public school must be related to the public school's failure to provide a FAPE (*S-1 v. Turlington*, 1981).

The Impartial Hearing Officer

The integrity of the due process hearing is maintained by ensuring that the hearing officer is impartial. The officer must have no involvement with the child, the parent, the school system, or the state. That is, he or she must have no personal or professional interest that might conflict with his or her objectivity in the hearing (IDEA Regulations, 34 C.F.R. § 300.507(a) (1), (2)).

Potential hearing officers are not considered employees of the public agency if they are paid by the school only for the hearing and for no other reason. No guidelines for the training and evaluation of hearing officers are provided in the IDEA.

However, the hearing officer must understand the IDEA thoroughly. Additionally, the hearing officer must be knowledgeable about hearings, be able to conduct them, and know how to write decisions.

School districts must maintain a list of persons who may serve as due process hearing officers. If parents request a copy of the list, it must be provided by the school district. Although parents are given no right to participate in the selection of the hearing officer, they can challenge the selection of the officer. The majority of these challenges involve the impartiality of hearing officers (Guernsey & Klare, 1993). Challenges to the impartiality of a hearing officer must be made during the due process hearing or subsequent administrative or judicial reviews (*Colin K. v. Schmidt,* 1983).

The Role of the Hearing Officer

When a dispute concerning a student's special education reaches the due process hearing level, the authority to decide the issue passes from the parents and the school to the hearing officer (Shrybman, 1982). The primary duties of the hearing officer are to inform the parties of their rights during the hearing; allow all parties the opportunity to present their cases; conduct the hearing in a fair, orderly, and impartial manner; and render a decision in accordance with the law. According to the U.S. Supreme Court,

> the role of the [hearing officer]. . . is functionally comparable to that of a judge. . . . More importantly, the process of agency adjudication is currently structured so as to assure that the hearing examiner exercises his independent judgment on the evidence before him, free from pressures by the parties or other officials within the agency. (*Butz v. Economou,* 1978, p. 513)

In writing IDEA 2004, Congress repeatedly stressed the importance of providing educational services that confer meaningful educational benefit. In other words schools must produce results. This emphasis shows up in a section of IDEA 2004 that addresses the decision of a hearing officer, in which the law requires that educational results take precedence over procedural compliance. According to IDEA 2004, decisions of the hearing officer shall be made on substantive grounds. This means that the hearing officer must determine whether the student in question received a free appropriate public education (FAPE) that provided meaningful educational benefit. A hearing officer can only rule against a school on procedural grounds if the procedural violation (a) impeded the student's right to receive a FAPE, (b) impeded the parents' opportunity to participate in educational decision making, or (c) caused a deprivation of educational benefits.

Although the role of the hearing officer may be comparable to that of a judge, the hearing officer's authority to grant particular remedies is less extensive (Guernsey & Klare, 1993). A hearing officer may order an IEE, reimbursement of educational expenses, or compensatory education, but he or she may not award attorney's fees. Neither does the hearing officer have any authority over outside agencies. OSEP has stated that the hearing officer may order specific placements (*Letter to Big,* 1980), but OCR has held that hearing officers can only accept or reject a school's proposed placement (*District of Columbia Public Schools,* 1981). Guernsey and Klare (1993) assert that the better view is that the hearing officer is not limited to accepting or rejecting placements proposed by the school, but may consider placements sought by the parents.

The hearing officer must render a decision no later than 45 days after the request for the hearing. A copy of the decision must be mailed to each of the parties. The decision of the hearing officer is final unless it is appealed. In a two-tiered state, the decision is appealed to the state educational agency. In a one-tier state, the complainant may go directly to the courts.

Hearing officers cannot be held liable for actions taken in their official capacity. The U.S. Supreme Court, in *Butz v. Economou* (1978), held that hearing officers, like judges, have immunity from damages when fulfilling their duties as hearing officers. The high court held that "persons. . . in performing their adjudicatory functions. . . are entitled to absolute immunity for their judicial acts. Those who complain of error in such proceedings must seek agency or judicial review" (p. 514).

Hearing officers may, however, be sued for damages resulting from actions taken in their individual capacities. If hearing officers take actions that they know, or should have known, are violations of the student's constitutional rights, or if they take actions with malicious intent to deprive a student of his or her rights, they may be held liable for damages (Shrybman, 1982). The Supreme Court has ruled that hearing officers cannot be held liable for monetary damages if there were reasonable grounds for their actions and if they acted in good faith (*Schever v. Rhodes,* 1974), or if they merely made mistakes in judgment (*Butz v. Economou,* 1978).

Hearing Rights

The IDEA contains a set of procedural rights that must be afforded all parties in a due process hearing (IDEA Regulations, 34 C.F.R. § 300.508). These rights are listed in Figure 13.6.

Both parties in the hearing have the right to be represented by counsel if they desire. Additionally, schools must inform the parents of free or low-cost legal services if the parents request the information. The school's obligation, however, does not extend to obtaining these services for the parents or paying for them (Shrybman, 1982).

The parents have the exclusive right to open the hearing to the public. The school does not have the right to open the hearing (IDEA Regulations, 34 C.F.R. § 508(c)), nor can the school compel the attendance of the student (IDEA Regulations, 34 C.F.R. § 508(b)).

Either party in a hearing has the right to appeal the hearing officer's decision. In a two-tier state, the party files an appeal with the appropriate agency. Following review of the hearing officer's decision, the aggrieved party may file a civil action in state or federal court. In a one-tier state, the aggrieved party may file a civil action in state or federal court immediately following the decision in the due process hearing. Either party who plans to appeal a hearing officer's decision has 90 days in which to

Figure 13.6
Due Process Hearing Rights

Any party to a hearing has the right to:

Be accompanied and advised by counsel and by individuals with special knowledge or training with respect to special education.

Present evidence and confront, cross-examine, and compel the attendance of witnesses.

Prohibit the introduction of any evidence at the hearing that has not been disclosed to that party at least 5 days prior to the hearing.

Obtain a written or electronic verbatim record of the hearing.

Obtain written findings of fact and decisions.

Parents involved in the hearing have the right to:

Have the child who is the subject of the hearing present.

Require the LEA to provide an electronic verbatim record of the hearing.

Require the LEA to provide electronic findings of fact and decision.

Open the hearing to the public.

---

file an appeal. If the decision is appealed to a state or federal court, the court must receive the records of the hearing and shall hear additional evidence at the request of the party. The IDEA directs court officials to base its decision on the preponderance of the evidence and may grant relief to the prevailing parties.

The Stay-Put Provision

Unless the school and parents agree otherwise, when a request for a hearing is made the IDEA's "stay-put" provision is invoked. According to this provision,

> During the pendency of any administrative or judicial proceeding regarding a complaint, unless the public agency and the parents of the child agree otherwise, the child involved in the complaint must remain in his or her present educational placement. (IDEA Regulations, 34 C.F.R. § 300.513)

The U.S. Supreme Court, in *Honig v. Doe* (1988), stated that the stay-put provision prevents schools from unilaterally moving students from placement to placement. Essentially, the stay-put provision acts as an automatic preliminary injunction pending a resolution of a due process hearing or judicial action. The objective of the stay-put provision is to maintain stability and continuity for the student until the dispute is resolved (Gorn, 1996), but it can be suspended during the pendency of a review by an agreement between the schools and the parents regarding placement.

A comment to the regulation states that although the student's placement may not be changed, the school may use its normal procedures for dealing with students who are endangering themselves or others (IDEA Regulations, 34 C.F.R. § 300.513, Note). There is, however, no "dangerous exception" that allows the school to suspend the stay-put rule (*Honig v. Doe,* 1988).

The IDEA abrogates the stay-put amendment when a student with a disability (a) brings a weapon to school or a school function; (b) uses, sells, or solicits the sale of illegal drugs; or (c) inflicts serious bodily injury upon another person while at school or a school function. In such situations an administrator may immediately remove the student to an interim alternative setting for up to 45 *school* days. If a due process hearing is requested, the stay-put placement becomes the current setting, which is the interim alternative educational placement. During the pendency of the proceedings, therefore, the student remains in the interim alternative setting. (For elaborations on the discipline of students with disabilities, see Chapter 14.)

The U.S. Court of Appeals for the District of Columbia ruled that the stay-put provision applies during due process hearings, during state administrative reviews, and at the trial court level but does not apply to the appellate level (*Anderson v. District of Columbia,* 1989). According to the court, a school is not required to maintain the current educational placement if an appeal goes to the appellate court.

If students are not in special education and the hearing concerns their eligibility to receive special education services, they must remain in the general education placement until the dispute is resolved. Similarly, if students are in special education and the dispute concerns a change of placement, they must remain in the placement where they were when the request was made. If the dispute involves initial admission to public school, students must be placed in the public school program until the dispute is resolved.*

The Conduct of the Hearing

The purpose of the due process hearing is to provide a legally constituted forum in which the contending parties have an opportunity to present their cases to an impartial hearing officer. From the perspective of a hearing officer, the purpose of the hearing is to give the parties an opportunity to present the information necessary for an informed ruling to be made.

Although the conduct of hearings varies among hearing officers, usually hearings are conducted in a professional manner but with a more informal atmosphere than a trial court. There should be a structure to the hearing so that everyone clearly understands his or her role and participates fully. Shrybman (1982) warns that hearing officers must be in control of the proceedings and not allow any participants to abuse the process. Proceedings that erupt into acrimonious exchanges accomplish little.

Either party in a hearing has the right to a written record of the hearing. Parents may, at their option, require an electronic record of the hearing. In such situations,

---

*IDEA 2004 requires that if a student transfers into a school district within a state with an existing IEP, this is not to be treated as an initial admission and the school should continue to provide an FAPE by implementing the existing IEP until they either adopt the previous IEP or complete the IEP planning process.

court reporters must be used. In addition to meeting the legal mandate, the verbatim record is essential for hearing officers in writing their decision and, if the decision is appealed, for review of the hearing decision. According to Shrybman (1982), if no verbatim record is available, the case must be reheard.

The hearing room should be arranged in a manner that is conducive to the orderly presentation of evidence and testimony (Shrybman, 1982). The arrangement should allow all participants to see and hear each other clearly. Often hearing rooms are set up like a trial court, with the hearing officer in a central position and the respective parties on the sides.

The hearing officer typically opens the hearing with a call to order and an introductory statement. This statement should include the introduction of the hearing officer and the case, a statement of legal authority for the hearing, an explanation of the purpose of the hearing and the role of the hearing officer, an acknowledgment of persons present, an explanation of the rights of the parties in the hearing, and instructions on appropriate decorum and the structure and the procedures to be followed during the hearing (Ginn, Carruth, & McCarthy, 1988; Hamway, 1994; Shrybman, 1982).

Shrybman (1982) suggests a format to which hearings should adhere. The hearing should begin with preliminary matters such as questions, objections, or requests from participants. Following the preliminaries, representatives of each party should present a brief opening statement outlining their positions. During the opening statement, evidence is not presented. When opening statements have been completed, the evidence is presented. The formal rules of evidence that are used in courts do not apply to administrative hearings. Relevancy and reliability should be the rules for introducing evidence in the hearing (Guernsey & Klare, 1993). Because the school district is legally responsible for the student's placement and special education program and bears the burden of proof as to the appropriateness of the education, the school system should present its case first. Shrybman (1982) asserts that "it is the responsibility of the public schools to provide a [child with disabilities] with a free appropriate public education so they must always stand ready to prove that their conduct on behalf of the student meets this fundamental legal requirement" (p. 325). During the presentation, the school will present documents and testimony to support its position. The parents or their counsel, if they have one, may cross-examine the school district's witnesses after their testimony. After the school's presentation, the parents present their case. The school's counsel may cross-examine the parents' witnesses at this time. After both sides have completed their initial presentations and offered their witnesses and evidence, they should have the opportunity to cross-examine witnesses again and present additional evidence. Finally, both parties conclude with a closing statement that summarizes their positions.

Following the presentations and concluding statements, the hearing officer should close the hearing. This may be done by briefly stating when the decision will be available, telling how transcripts can be obtained, explaining the appeal procedures, and adjourning the hearing. Figure 13.7 outlines this format for the due process hearing.

Figure 13.7
Possible Format for a Due Process Hearing

Introduction of the officer and the case
- Hearing officer makes opening statements:
  - statement of legal authority for the hearing
  - explanation of the purpose for the hearing
  - explanation of the hearing officer's role
- Persons present are introduced.
- Parties are informed of due process rights.
- Instructions of decorum, structure, and procedures of the hearing are made.
- Preliminary matters are addressed.

Presentations
- Public school representatives present.
- Parents present.
- Cross-examinations are conducted and additional evidence is presented.
- Closing statements are made.

Closing the hearing
- The hearing officer:
  - explains the issuance of the decision
  - explains appeal procedures
  - thanks participants and closes the hearing

Appeals and Civil Actions

In states with a two-tiered process, the decision of the hearing officer can be appealed to the SEA. In an appeal, the agency reviews the entire hearing record, ensures that procedures were followed, seeks additional evidence if necessary, allows additional arguments at its discretion, and makes an independent decision (IDEA Regulations, 34 C.F.R. § 300.510). If additional evidence is heard at the state review, the protections available to parties in the original due process hearing are available at the review (e.g., disclosure of evidence 5 days prior to the hearing, the right to cross-examine witnesses).

The appeal is usually made to the office of special education of the state's department of education. The IDEA contains no timeline in which an appeal must be made, although individual states may address the issue (Guernsey & Klare, 1993). A written copy of the findings must be sent to both parties within 30 days of the date of the appeal to the state. Unless appealed, this decision is final and binding on all parties. Either party may appeal the SEA's decision and may file a civil action in a state or federal court (IDEA Regulations, 34 C.F.R. § 300.511). IDEA 2004 includes a time limit for filing civil actions. The party that brings the action, either the parent or school district, has 90 days from the date of the administrative decision to bring such an action. If the state has set a specific timeline, both parties must adhere to that schedule.

In a one-tier state, the civil action may be filed following the due process hearing. In a two-tier state, the civil action usually cannot be filed until all the administrative options have been exhausted; that is, both the due process hearing and the SEA hearing must have been completed before an action may be filed in state or federal court. An exception to the exhaustion rule may exist if administrative hearings would be futile or inadequate (*Honig v. Doe,* 1988). Although the time-consuming nature of a hearing is not, by itself, a basis for overturning the exhaustion rule (*Cox v. Jenkins,* 1989), situations such as the agency's failure to properly implement administrative appeal measures may provide such a basis.

The court will usually not rehear the case, nor will it focus on the entire case. Rather, the court will review the record to determine the presence of serious error of law at the hearing level. Following a review of pertinent materials, courts can affirm the decision of the lower authority, modify the decision of the lower authority, reverse the decision of the lower authority, or remand all or part of the lower authority's decision. To remand means that the court will order the lower authority to conduct further proceedings in accordance with the court's instructions (Weber, 1992).

A party in a due process hearing may also file a civil action if the other party fails to follow the decision of the hearing officer. In this case, the purpose of the civil action is to have the decision enforced. Enforcement actions are usually brought by parents against schools. Schools, however, have little legal leverage to force parents to comply with a decision (Shrybman, 1982).

Alternatives to the Due Process Hearing

Criticisms have been leveled at the system of procedural safeguards, especially due process hearings, as being too expensive, time consuming, adversarial, and emotionally draining for all parties involved (Goldberg & Huefner, 1995; Maloney, 1993; Zirkel, 1994). The hearings rarely solve problems and soothe anger; more often, they alienate and sustain antagonism and undermine cooperation (Beekman, 1993; Goldberg & Huefner, 1995). Parents also tend to view the due process system as unfair (Goldberg & Kuriloff, 1991). Finally, both sides have the right to be represented by attorneys (although it is not required), and the presence of attorneys may contribute to the adversarial nature of the proceedings (Shrybman, 1982). In a 1994 case from the U.S. Court of Appeals for the Ninth Circuit, the court upbraided an attorney for the use of "hardball tactics" in dealing with a school (*Clyde K. v. Puyallup School District*). The court also noted that the interests of schools, parents, and students would be more effectively served by compromise and cooperation rather than through adversarial positioning.

In the IDEA Amendments of 1997, Congress required states to adopt voluntary mediation systems to alleviate the overly adversarial nature of the dispute-resolution process. Mediation had been suggested by a number of legal scholars as an alternative to the due process hearing (Dobbs et al., 1991; Goldberg & Huefner, 1995; Goldberg & Kuriloff, 1991; Zirkel, 1994). In IDEA 2004, resolution sessions were added to reduce the amount of litigation.

Zirkel (1994) asserts that the current system of special education due process hearings serves the best interests of neither the school nor the child. He suggests a five-part solution to the problems inherent in the hearing process. First, the due process hearing should be the final stage for most special education disputes. The hearing officer's decision should be binding on both parties. Judicial review would only be available for an occasional case that presents an important legal issue. This suggestion would require an amendment to the IDEA to delete the option of a second tier. The single tier would be at the state level to remove the possible influence of the school district's paying the hearing officer. The selection, training, and payment of hearing officers would become the responsibility of an independent state agency. Zirkel's second suggestion is that because the due process hearing would escalate in importance under the first suggestion, regulations would specify that hearing officers must have expertise in special education. Third, the conduct of due process hearings would be changed to a problem-solving model rather than an adversarial model. To reinforce the less adversarial model, the fourth suggestion is that attorney's fees would be limited to the judicial stage. School districts could not be represented by counsel at the hearing unless the parents chose to be represented by counsel. This suggestion would require amending the attorney's fees provision of the IDEA. Finally, hearings in routing cases should be limited to one full day. Zirkel believes that by using this model the due process hearing would become a faster and less expensive problem-solving process.

School District Responsibilities in the Hearing

Guernsey and Klare (1993) found that the available evidence indicates that success in the due process hearing is critical to the ultimate outcome of the case. They further cite evidence that most decisions by due process hearing officers are upheld on review and that the vast majority of cases never go to court. It is critical to all parties, therefore, that they make the best possible case at this level.

Schools must prepare seriously when approaching a due process hearing. The results of the initial hearing are critical because appeals will often be based solely on the transcripts of the initial hearing (Reusch, 1993). If schools do not succeed in making their case at this level, they probably will not succeed on appeal (Zirkel, 1994).

Maloney (1993) listed "seven deadly sins" that frequently lead to due process hearings. Schools should attempt to avoid these errors. More often than not, these errors will also lead to losses in hearings or court and possible liability. The most common errors committed by schools leading to hearings, and the first "deadly sin," are procedural violations. A district's failure to fulfill the procedural protections of the

IDEA could be adequate grounds for finding that the school district has failed to provide a FAPE if the procedural violation (a) impeded the student's right to receive a FAPE, (b) impeded the parents' opportunity to participate in educational decision making, or (c) caused a deprivation of educational benefits.

A number of courts have ruled that serious procedural violations can subject a school district to liability for damages, compensatory education, or tuition reimbursement (*Burr v. Ambach*, 1988; *Evans v. Douglas County School District No. 17*, 1988; *McKenzie v. Smith*, 1985; *Salley v. St. Tammany Parish School Board*, 1993; *W.G. v. Board of Trustees Target Range School District No. 23*, 1992). However, minor procedural violations that do not deprive the student of a FAPE will not result in a due process hearing or a lost case. The procedural violations most likely to lead to due process hearings are (a) insufficient notice of proposal or refusal to change placement; (b) failure to obtain consent; (c) denial of an IEE; (d) incomplete or insufficient IEPs (especially regarding transition services, graduation, and the provision of assistive technology); (e) improper or insufficient evaluations; (f) substantially or procedurally deficient IEP committees; (g) unilateral change of placement; (h) restricted opportunity to examine student records; (i) improper suspension or expulsion; and (j) failure to implement or issue due process hearing orders.

The second violation likely to lead to due process hearings, and an error Maloney (1993) describes as the "kiss of death," is telling parents that a particular service or program is appropriate for their child but that the school district cannot afford it. Schools cannot deny appropriate services based on cost considerations.

The third error is rigidity (e.g., "We haven't done it in the past and we won't do it now"). Blanket statements that exclude the consideration of certain programs or services are clearly illegal. Rigidity on the part of schools (e.g., refusal to consider the provision of extended school services, to evaluate children with attention deficit disorders, or to provide certain related services) has led to many due process hearings and court cases.

The fourth error is giving in to parental demands when the demands will not provide the child with a FAPE. Because the right to a FAPE belongs to the child and not the parents, school districts must attempt to provide what they believe to be appropriate services, even if it requires requesting a due process hearing (Maloney, 1993).

The fifth error is acting on the basis of principle rather than reason. Schools should not act out of frustration or to prove a point. An example of this type of error was provided in *Rapid City School District v. Vahle* (1990). The school district determined that the services of an occupational therapist (OT) were necessary to provide a FAPE; however, the amount of services provided by the district was not sufficient to meet the student's needs. The parents purchased the services of an OT. The district then agreed that more services were necessary and agreed to provide them. The district refused, however, to reimburse the parents for the $861 they had paid for the OT services. The parents prevailed in federal court. The district's bill for attorney's fees was more than $30,000.

Sixth is the problem of burden of proof—the responsibility of proving a case. Although the IDEA does not address the issue, most hearing officers require school districts to assume the burden of proof in hearings (Maloney, 1993). Schools must assume that in a due process hearing they have the responsibility of proving they have provided the child with a FAPE.

Finally, the failure to act promptly to secure services recommended by the IEP team often leads to due process hearings. Procrastination may also lead to the schools being held liable for compensatory services. It is, therefore, an important school responsibility to ensure that the procedural safeguards in the IDEA are followed promptly.

Remedies

When a suit is filed, usually the court will defer to the facts as determined during the due process or administrative hearing, although the court may also hear additional evidence at the request of either party. The IDEA authorizes courts to provide relief (i.e., redress or assistance) to the prevailing party. According to the language of the IDEA,

> the court shall receive the records of the administrative proceedings, shall hear additional evidence at the request of a party, and basing its decision on the preponderance of the evidence, shall grant such relief as the court determines is appropriate. (IDEA, 20 U.S.C. § 1415 (e)(2))

The statute, however, does not clarify what exactly "appropriate relief" might entail. Determination of what constitutes appropriate relief has been left to the discretion of the courts. The types of relief provided by courts to redress violations of the law are referred to as *remedies* (Black, Nolan, & Nolan-Haley, 1990). Early interpretations of appropriate relief in special education cases were narrowly drawn; that is, relief was usually limited to ordering that a school refrain from a particular practice (e.g., expelling students with disabilities) or add a service to a student's educational program (e.g., provide extended school year services). Additionally, the courts often required the parties to arrive at a cooperative agreement regarding the matter (Dagley, 1995). In recent years, however, the courts have expanded the definition of appropriate relief.

The following sections examine five types of remedies: attorney's fees, injunctive relief, tuition reimbursement, compensatory education, and punitive damages. Prior to a discussion of these remedies, a brief explanation of sovereign immunity is in order.

Sovereign Immunity

In 1990, Congress passed the Education of the Handicapped Amendments (IDEA, 20 U.S.C. § 1403).* One of the results of the law was to allow parties to sue states

---

*P.L. 101-476 renamed the law the Individuals with Disabilities Education Act (IDEA).

and school districts under the IDEA. In effect, the law overturned the doctrine of sovereign immunity in actions brought under the IDEA. *Sovereign immunity* refers to the immunity of the states against damage suits. Under this doctrine, lawsuits against a governmental entity or its officials are prohibited. In *Dellmuth v. Muth* (1989), the U.S. Supreme Court ruled that while school districts could be sued under the IDEA, states were immune from liability regarding suits under the law by the 11th Amendment (see the Appendix). The case involved a student with a learning disability and emotional problems attending a Pennsylvania school. The student's father requested a due process hearing to challenge the school's IEP. The father also enrolled his son in a private school for students with learning disabilities. The hearing officer determined that the IEP was inappropriate. Subsequently, the IEP was rewritten and determined to be appropriate. While the lengthy hearing was underway, the father also filed a suit against the school district in federal district court. The court ruled against the school district, holding that the father was entitled to reimbursement for the private school tuition. The court further held that the state and school district were both liable. The IDEA, according to the court, had nullified the state's 11th Amendment immunity from damage suits. An appeal was filed with the U.S. Court of Appeals for the Third Circuit, which affirmed the lower court's ruling. The decision was then appealed to the U.S. Supreme Court.

In its ruling, the Supreme Court reversed the lower courts' rulings, noting that a congressional act does not abrogate sovereign immunity unless it specifically does so within the language of the act. Because the IDEA did not specifically mention state immunity from lawsuits, states were immune from suits for liability. The parents could not collect reimbursement from the state. The decision only involved state immunity, so the parents' ability to seek reimbursement from the school district was not affected. This decision was overturned by Congress in P.L. 101-476, the Education of the Handicapped Amendments of 1990. The law, as amended, specifically required that "states shall not be immune under the 11th Amendment to the Constitution of the United States from suit in Federal court for violation of this Act" (IDEA, 20 U.S.C. § 1403 (a)). This amendment, therefore, allows parties to sue states as well as schools for violations of the IDEA.

Attorney's Fees

When Congress passed the original EAHCA in 1975, the law contained no provision for reimbursement of attorney's fees. Parties who prevailed in suits against school districts prior to 1984, therefore, had to seek reimbursement for attorneys through other means. Reimbursement of attorney's fees was usually sought through Section 505 of the Rehabilitation Act of 1973 or Section 1988 of the Civil Rights Attorney's Fees Award Act, both of which allowed courts to grant reimbursement of attorney's fees to prevailing parties. In 1984, however, this practice was halted by the U.S. Supreme Court in *Smith v. Robinson* (1984; hereafter *Smith*).

Smith v. Robinson, 1984

In *Smith,* the parents of a child with cerebral palsy prevailed in their claim against a school district that had discontinued their child's special education program. The parents sued successfully for attorney's fees under Section 505 of the Rehabilitation Act in federal district court. On appeal, however, the attorney's fee award was overturned by the U.S. Court of Appeals. The appellate court ruled that attorney's fees were not available under the IDEA. The parents appealed to the U.S. Supreme Court. In a 5-4 ruling, the high court affirmed the ruling of the appeals court. In the majority opinion, Justice Blackmun stated that Congress had intended that the IDEA be the exclusive remedy for protecting the rights of students with disabilities. This law, therefore, was the only avenue by which special education actions could be pursued. Moreover, because the law contained no provisions for attorney's fees, none were available. In another special education decision handed down on the same day as Smith, *Irving Independent School District v. Tatro* (1984), the parents were denied attorney's fees even though they prevailed in their action.

Justice Brennan, in a dissenting opinion, asserted that the majority had misconstrued and frustrated congressional intent in their ruling. He stated that Congress would have to revisit the matter so that the parents of children who must sue for their rights under the law can be recompensed if they prevail. Congress did revisit the law and in 1986 passed the Handicapped Children's Protection Act (HCPA).

The Handicapped Children's Protection Act

The HCPA amended the IDEA to allow the provision of attorney's fees to parties prevailing in special education lawsuits (HCPA, 20 U.S.C. § 1415). The HCPA consisted of three major parts: (a) authorization of the courts to award reasonable attorney's fees to parents of a child with disabilities when they prevail in a lawsuit under the IDEA; (b) clarification of the effect of the IDEA on other laws; and (c) retroactive application of the HCPA (Yell & Espin, 1990). Thus in the HCPA, Congress overturned the Supreme Court's decision in *Smith.*

The major purpose of the HCPA is to allow parents to recover attorney's fees in successful actions under the IDEA without having to use other laws to sue. The HCPA provided that

> In any action or proceeding brought under [the HCPA], the court, in its discretion, may award reasonable attorneys' fees as part of the costs to the parents or guardian of a [child with disabilities] who is the prevailing party. (IDEA, 20 U.S.C. § 1415(e)(4)(B)(1990))

Issues in the Award of Attorney's Fees

The law, however, contained several stipulations regarding the reimbursement of these fees. A major proviso in the law was that parents could collect attorney's fees only if they were the prevailing party. If parents did not prevail on a major point of their suit, therefore, they were not entitled to attorney's fees. Subsequent cases have held that for plaintiffs to prevail they must succeed on any significant issue in their action (*Angela L. v. Pasadena Independent School District No. 2,* 1990; *Burr v. Sobol,* 1990; *Mitten v. Muscogee County School District,* 1989). That is, for parties to prevail it is not necessary that they are successful in obtaining all relief or even the primary relief sought, but merely that they succeed on some significant issue (Tucker & Goldstein, 1992). Findings of bad faith or unjustified conduct on the part of school officials are not required in the awarding of fees (*Mitten v. Muscogee County School District,* 1989).

In many cases brought to trial, school districts have made good faith efforts to provide services to students with disabilities, but parents and the schools have not been able to agree regarding the specific services required. In such cases, the determination of the prevailing party is decidedly more difficult for the courts (Dagley, 1994). In these instances, the courts have often turned to the U.S. Supreme Court's ruling in *Hensley v. Eckerhart* (1983; hereafter *Hensley*) for guidance. In *Hensley,* the Court defined a significant relief standard as relief on any significant issue that achieved some of the benefits the party sought in bringing the suit. Relief on a significant issue would result in that party's prevailing, and thus being awarded attorney's fees. In a later ruling by the high court in *Texas State Teachers Association v. Garland Independent School District* (1989), the *Hensley* standard was further clarified. According to the Court's decision, parties are considered to have prevailed when they succeed on a significant issue they raise. It is not necessary that the plaintiff prevail on the most significant issue or on the majority of issues raised. Furthermore, to be eligible for an award of attorney's fees, the plaintiff must be able to point to the resolution of the dispute that changes the legal relationship between the parties.

The HCPA addresses the calculation of fee awards as follows:

> For the purpose of [the HCPA], fees awarded shall be based on rates prevailing in the community in which the action or proceeding arose for the kind and quality of services furnished. No bonus or multiplier may be used in calculating the fees. (IDEA, 20 U.S.C. § 1415 (e)(4)(C) (1990))

In addition to the costs of litigating the case, attorney's fees may include costs of tests and evaluations, time spent in monitoring and enforcing a judgment, travel time, secretarial tasks, and the work of paraprofessionals (e.g., paralegals, law clerks). A decision out of the U.S. Court of Appeals for the Eighth Circuit in *Neosho R-V School District v. Clark* (2003), however, denied expert witness fees to a prevailing party in an IDEA case. The court granted attorney's fees to the prevailing party but declined to award fees for an expert witness. The U.S. Court of Appeals for the Seventh Circuit also denied expert witness fees to a prevailing party in *T.D v. LaGrange School District No. 102* (2003).

The law prohibits the awarding of attorney's fees in cases where parents have rejected a properly made settlement offer if they ultimately obtained essentially the same relief as originally offered. The HCPA also permits courts to reduce attorney's fees if they find that the parents or attorneys have unreasonably protracted the final resolution of the matter or if the fees unreasonably exceed the prevailing community rates. This provision of the law, which has been termed the *vexatious litigant provision,* provides schools with protection against parents and attorneys who become overly adversarial to the point of working to protract proceedings and undermine efforts at settlement (Dagley, 1994).

The HCPA also reversed the Court's ruling in *Smith* regarding the exclusivity of the IDEA in lawsuits. The high court had ruled that there was no option to sue school districts under Section 505 or Section 1988 because the IDEA was the exclusive remedy. The HCPA overturned this part of the decision, stating that nothing in the law should be construed as restricting or limiting the rights of parents to sue under another statute.

Finally, the law made the attorney's fees provision retroactive to cases pending on or brought after the date of *Smith* but before the passage of the HCPA. The effect of this clause was to allow plaintiffs to sue for attorney's fees if they had been denied fees because of the Smith ruling.

IDEA 1997 and the Attorney's Fees Provision

The 1997 amendments retained the HCPA's provisions regarding attorney's fees and added a few qualifications. These provisions served to limit the situations in which attorneys could seek reimbursement from school districts. Attorney's fees may be reduced in situations where the attorney representing the parents failed to provide the local educational agency with information regarding the specific nature of the dispute. The amendments also require that parents notify school officials in a timely manner about the problem and any proposed solutions. Additionally, because Congress believed that the IEP process should be devoted to considering students' needs and planning for their education rather than being used as an adversarial forum, the IDEA amendments specifically exclude the payment of attorney's fees for attorney's participation in the IEP process. The only exception is when the IEP meeting is ordered in an administrative or court proceeding. Similarly, attorney's fees are not available for mediation sessions prior to the filing of a due process action.

The amendments also specifically adopted the *Hensley* standard for determining the amount of any attorney's fees award. That is, in determining awards courts are required to assess the degree to which the plaintiff prevailed on significant issues (Senate Report, 1997).

Buckhannon Board & Care Home Inc. v. West Virginia Department of Health and Human Resources, 2001

In 2001, the U.S. Supreme Court issued a ruling in *Buckhannon Board & Care Home Inc. v. West Virginia Department of Health and Human Resources.* Although this case did not involve special education, the ruling has had a significant effect on attorney's fees available under the IDEA. The case involved an agency, Buckhannon Board & Care Home Inc, which operated assisted living facilities in West Virginia. The state would regularly conduct inspections of the facilities. Following one such inspection, the state ordered Buckhannon to close its facilities because they did not meet state requirements. Buckhannon sued the state of West Virginia claiming that the state statute violated the Fair Housing Act of 1988 and the Americans with Disabilities Act. During the time in which the lawsuit was pending, the state legislature of West Virginia eliminated the requirement that had led to the closing of the Buckhannon facility. The district court dismissed the lawsuit, declaring that the issue was moot. Buckhannon then sued for attorney's fees based on a legal concept called the *catalyst theory*.

According to the catalyst theory, a plaintiff may be considered the prevailing party, and be awarded attorney's fees, if it obtained its desired outcome because its legal action brought a voluntary change in the defendant's behavior, conduct, or policies. In this case Buckhannon claimed that because of its lawsuit the state of West Virginia dropped an illegal requirement from its laws. The case ultimately went to the U.S. Supreme Court. The high court ruled that the party could only be a prevailing party for purposes of awarding attorney's fees if it achieved the desired result in court or through a court-ordered consent decree. Even if the party's lawsuit brought about the desired change, unless a court ordered the change, attorney's fees cannot be awarded. The court, therefore, rejected the catalyst theory as a basis for attorney's fee awards. The court's opinion did not specifically mention attorney's fee awards under the IDEA; nevertheless, several circuit courts have applied the demise of the catalyst theory to IDEA-related cases.

For example, in *J.C. v. Regional School District #10, Board of Education* (2002), the U.S. Court of Appeals for the Second Circuit extended the scope of the Supreme Court's ruling in *Buckhannon* to claims for attorney's fees awards under both the IDEA and Section 504. Specifically, the court reversed a ruling awarding attorney's fees to parents who had successfully convinced a school district to fund an IEE because a hearing officer had not ordered the evaluation. Even though the voluntary funding of the IEE had led to a termination of an expulsion hearing, which may have been the direct result of the parents' complaint, according to *Buckhannon*, no fees were available.

IDEA 2004 and Attorney's Fees

In an effort to discourage IDEA-related litigation, Congress acted to alter the attorney's fees provision. According to IDEA 2004, in any IDEA-related action, a court may award reasonable attorney's fees to a prevailing party who is the parent of a child in special education. A court may also award attorney's fees to a school district against the parents' attorney who files a complaint or a subsequent cause of action that is frivolous, unreasonable, or without foundation, or if the parents' attorney continued to litigate after the litigation became unreasonable or without foundation. Additionally a court could award the state educational agency or the school district attorney's fees against the attorney of a parent, or against the parent, if the complaint or the cause of action was brought for an improper purpose such as harassment, causing unnecessary delay, or increasing the cost of litigation. Although this provision attracted quite a bit of attention, such awards may have already been allowed under Rule 11 of the Federal Rules of Civil Procedure.

Injunctive Relief

An injunction is a judicial remedy awarded for the purpose of requiring a party to refrain from or discontinue a certain action. An injunction is a preventive measure that guards against a similar action being committed in the future. Injunctions are not remedies for past injustices. For example, if parents believed that their child was not receiving an appropriate education and a court granted an injunction, typically the injunction might compel the school district to provide the education that the court deemed appropriate. Injunctive relief is available under the IDEA.

Two major types of injunctions are preliminary and permanent injunctions. Preliminary injunctions, which are temporary, are issued prior to a trial. To be granted a preliminary injunction, the plaintiffs (i.e., the party bringing the lawsuit) must convince the court that harm may result if the injunction is not issued. Plaintiffs must also show that there is a substantial likelihood that in a trial they would succeed in obtaining a permanent injunction, which is the second type of injunction. A permanent injunction is awarded when a court, after hearing the case, is convinced that such an injunction is required to prevent harm. The party seeking the injunction bears the burden of proof.

The U.S. Court of Appeals for the Eighth Circuit, in *Light v. Parkway School District* (1994), gave schools guidance in seeking an injunction for dangerous and disruptive student behavior. The circuit court developed a two-part test for obtaining an injunction. The court ruled that schools must first prove a child is substantially likely to cause injury. Second, the school must show that all reasonable steps have been undertaken to reduce the risk the student would cause injury.

When school officials attempt to obtain an injunction, they must convince the court that they will likely succeed on the merits of the case in trial (Mattison & Hakola, 1992). Furthermore, the district must persuade the court that without the injunction the school or students will suffer harm, that the harm to the student removed from school by the injunction does not outweigh the harm caused to the school district, and that the injunction is in the public interest.

Tuition Reimbursement

Tuition reimbursement is typically an award to compensate parents for the costs of a unilateral placement of their child in a private school when the public school has failed to provide an appropriate education. Tuition reimbursement is not a monetary award in the traditional sense, but rather is viewed by the courts as the school district's reimbursing the parents for the education that should have been provided in the first place. The appropriate education the parents had to obtain, therefore, is provided at no cost to the parents.

The U.S. Supreme Court examined the question of tuition reimbursement under the IDEA in *Burlington School Committee of the Town of Burlington v. Department of Education of Massachusetts* (1985; hereafter *Burlington*). In *Florence County School District Four v. Carter* (1993; hereafter *Carter*), the high court clarified further questions regarding tuition reimbursement. In the *Burlington* case, the high court ruled on a unilateral change of placement made by the parents of a child with learning disabilities. In *Carter,* the Court considered a unilateral placement in a school that was not approved by the state. In both instances, prior to the Supreme Court's ruling, the lower courts were split as to whether tuition reimbursement was available and if it was only available when the parents placed their child in an approved school.

Burlington School Committee v. Department of Education, 1985

Burlington involved a school district's education of a third grader, Michael Panico, who had learning disabilities and emotional problems. Michael's father became dissatisfied with his son's lack of progress and obtained an independent evaluation of the boy. The evaluation indicated that Michael should be placed in a private school for students with learning disabilities. When the Burlington school district offered placement in a highly structured class within the district, Michael's father withdrew him from the school and placed him at a state-approved facility in Massachusetts. Following a hearing, the state board of appeals found that the public school placement was inappropriate. The hearing officer ordered the school board to fund the private school placement and to reimburse the parents for expenses they had incurred.

The school district filed a lawsuit in a federal district court. While the case was being heard, the school district agreed to fund the cost of the private school education, though it refused to reimburse the parents. The court, determining that the proposed public school placement was appropriate, ruled in favor of the school district.

Michael's father appealed the decision. The U.S. Court of Appeals for the First Circuit reversed the ruling of the lower court. The appeals court ruled that the IDEA did not bar reimbursement when the parents of a child with disabilities had to unilaterally change the child's placement, if the court found that the parents' action was appropriate. Reimbursement was not available, however, when the school district had proposed and could implement an appropriate placement. The school district filed an appeal with the U.S. Supreme Court. The school district argued that the parents had violated the stay-put rule, which required that students remain in their current placement during the review process.

In unanimously affirming the ruling of the appeals court, the high court stated that parents who unilaterally place their children with disabilities in a private school setting are entitled to reimbursement for tuition and living expenses if a court finds that the school had proposed an inappropriate IEP. If the school's proposed placement, however, was found to be appropriate, the school would not have to reimburse the parents. Justice Rehnquist, writing for the majority, noted that the IDEA gave the courts broad discretion in granting relief. The majority opinion also stated that to deny reimbursement, when appropriate, would be to deny the parent meaningful input in the development of an appropriate education and would lessen the importance of the procedural safeguards. Rehnquist asserted that the decision requiring reimbursement did not constitute a damage award, but rather "required the [school district] to belatedly pay expenses that it should have paid all along and would have been borne in the first instance had it developed a proper IEP" (*Burlington,* pp. 370–371).

The high court also commented that if the school's placement was found to be appropriate, parents were not entitled to reimbursement. Parents who unilaterally change their child's placement, therefore, do so at their own risk.

In noting that the IDEA conferred broad discretion, the high court was saying that courts, in ordering appropriate relief, have a great deal of leeway. As the *Burlington* decision indicates, this discretion clearly includes the power to award tuition reimbursement. Parents are not required to bear the costs of providing an appropriate education for their children with disabilities (Mattison & Hakola, 1992).

Chief Justice Rehnquist negated the possibility of school districts' using the stay-put provision as a defense against unilateral placements made by parents. Rehnquist noted that if the stay-put provision was read in such a way as to prohibit parents from making unilateral placements, parents would be forced to either (a) leave their child in what may be an inappropriate placement or (b) obtain an appropriate education only by sacrificing any claim for reimbursement. The majority opinion stated that "the [IDEA] was intended to give handicapped children both an appropriate education and a free one; it should not be interpreted to defeat one or the other of these objectives" (*Burlington,* p. 372).

The Supreme Court also recognized that related expenses, in addition to tuition, may also be awarded to parents. Subsequent decisions have held that such expenses may include the following: cost of transportation and costs incurred during transportation (*Taylor v. Board of Education,* 1986); lost earnings by parents for time expended related to protecting their child's rights and interest on tuition loans (*Board of Education of the County of Cabell v. Dienelt,* 1988); costs of residential placement (*Babb v. Knox County School System,* 1992); expenses for related services (*Rapid City School District v. Vahle,* 1990); reimbursement for psychotherapy (*Max M. v. Illinois State Board of Education,* 1984); and insurance reimbursement when the parents had financed the tuition with their insurance (*Shook v. Gaston County Board of Education,* 1989).

Following the *Burlington* decision, a number of issues regarding tuition reimbursement were litigated. A primary issue involved reimbursement for parents who unilaterally placed their child in an unapproved school, one that had not been approved by the state educational agency. Lower courts were split on this issue. The Supreme Court put this controversy to rest in *Carter.*

Florence County School District Four v. Carter, 1993

Shannon Carter was a high school student in Florence County School District Four in Florence, South Carolina. Educational evaluations, done privately and by the school district, indicated that she had a learning disability and Attention Deficit Disorder (ADD). Her parents requested that Shannon be placed in a self-contained classroom in a neighboring school district. Because the Florence school district had no self-contained setting, it proposed that Shannon receive instruction from a special education teacher in a resource room. The parents refused the placement and requested a due process hearing. They continued to press for placement in a neighboring school district's self-contained classroom or placement at Trident Academy, a private school in Charleston, South Carolina. The hearing officer decided in favor of the school district. The Carters took Shannon out of the public school and placed her at Trident Academy. The Carters also appealed the hearing officer's decision to the state reviewing officer. The reviewing officer upheld the original decision. The Carters filed suit in the federal district court.

After hearing the evidence from court-appointed evaluators, the district court held that the school district's program was "wholly inadequate" and directed the school district to reimburse the Carters for expenses incurred at Trident Academy. The school district appealed the decision to the U.S. Court of Appeals for the Fourth Circuit. The circuit court ruled that even though Trident Academy was not on the state's list of approved special education schools, the school had to reimburse the Carters for tuition at Trident Academy. The school district appealed to the U.S. Supreme Court.

The Supreme Court requested that the solicitor general's office of the Department of Justice file a brief outlining the government's position. The Department of Justice filed a brief recommending that the Fourth Circuit court's decision be upheld (Wright, 1994). Seventeen states filed amicus curiae (friend of the court) briefs supporting the school district. The high court affirmed the circuit court's decision in ruling that the school district had to reimburse the parents for placement in the school, even though it was not on the SEA's approved list. The high court stated that limiting parental reimbursement to state-approved schools would be contrary to the IDEA when the school district had not complied with the law. Furthermore, the Court determined that applying state standards to parental placements would be fundamentally unfair in situations where parents have to find a private school that offers an appropriate education.

In *Carter,* the Supreme Court held that parents could be reimbursed for the use of unapproved personnel and schools for services obtained when school districts failed in their duty to offer an appropriate education for students with disabilities under Part B of the IDEA. The U.S. Court of Appeals for the Second Circuit, in *Still v. Debuono* (1996), ruled that the principles announced in *Carter* were equally applicable to Part H of the IDEA. Although Part H imposes a requirement that early intervention services are provided by qualified personnel, privately obtained services provided by unapproved personnel are reimbursable.

Compensatory Education

Compensatory educational services are designed to remedy the progress lost by students with disabilities because they were previously denied a free appropriate public education (FAPE) (Tucker & Goldstein, 1992). The award of compensatory education is the award of additional educational services, above and beyond the educational services normally due a student under state law (Gorn, 1996). Typically, compensatory education extends a student's eligibility for educational services beyond age 21 as compensation for inappropriate educational services (Mattison & Hakola, 1992). According to Gorn (1996), when students currently attending school are awarded compensatory education, it may take the form of extended-day programs, extended school year services, summer school, tutoring, compensatory related services (e.g., occupational or physical therapy), or future compensatory education (i.e., provision of educational services after the student turns 21). Following the *Burlington* decision, the issue of compensatory education received a great deal of attention in the courts. Even though the early decisions tended to rule that compensatory education was not available, the majority of recent decisions have ruled that compensatory educational services are remedies available in the IDEA (Zirkel, 1994).

Compensatory Awards Under the IDEA

An example of judicial thinking regarding compensatory education was delivered by the U.S. Court of Appeals for the Eighth Circuit in *Meiner v. Missouri* (1986). The appeals court ruled in favor of an award of compensatory education, explaining that

> Like the retroactive reimbursement in *Burlington,* imposing liability for compensatory educational services on the defendants "merely requires [them] to belatedly pay expenses that [they] should have paid all along." Here, as in *Burlington,* recovery is necessary to the child's right to a free appropriate public education. We are confident that Congress did not intend the child's entitlement to a free education to turn upon her parent's ability to front its costs. (p. 753)

In a policy letter, the Office of Special Education Programs (OSEP) stated a similar position on compensatory education: "In certain instances, compensatory education may be the only means through which children who are forced to remain in an inappropriate placement, due to their parents' financial inability to pay for an appropriate placement, would receive FAPE" (Letter to Murray, 1992, p. 496). OSEP further stated that compensatory education could be awarded by hearing officers or SEAs. Courts have also reached similar conclusions regarding a hearing officer's ability to award compensatory education (*Murphy v. Timberlane Regional School District,* 1993).

Compensatory education may be ordered if it is determined that a school district did not provide an appropriate education. Such a violation could involve programming or procedural violations (Mattison & Hakola, 1992). Additionally, compensatory education awards may take the form of either extending the student's eligibility beyond age 21 or providing summer programming (Letter to Murray, 1992). Zirkel (1995) asserts that compensatory education may also extend to educational services beyond the regular school day.

Zirkel (1995) refers to compensatory educational services as the "coin of the realm" (p. 483) in relief cases arising under the IDEA. This is because tuition reimbursement represents an up-front risk that many parents cannot afford; also, unlike attorney's fees awards, parents need not resort to litigation to receive an enforceable award of compensatory education. A due process hearing officer and the SEA may grant awards of compensatory educational services.

Punitive Damages

Punitive damage awards, which are monetary awards in excess of actual damages, are intended to serve as punishment and recompense for a legal wrong. Extensive litigation has examined whether courts can order the award of punitive damages in special education cases brought under the IDEA. The majority of these cases have held that these damages are not available (*Colin K. v. Schmidt,* 1983; *Hall v. Knott County Board of Education,* 1991; *Heidemann v. Rother,* 1996; *Hoekstra v. Independent School District No. 283,* 1996; *Meiner v. Missouri,* 1986).

In *Anderson v. Thompson* (1981), the U.S. Court of Appeals for the Seventh Circuit held that punitive damages were unavailable under the IDEA. In this influential ruling, the court stated that although there was no basis for awarding damages in the law's legislative history, damages might be available in exceptional circumstances. Such circumstances might include the school district's acting in bad faith in failing to comply with the IDEA (*Anderson v. Thompson*) or intentional violation of a student's right to a FAPE (*Taylor v. Honig,* 1992).

Recently, some legal developments have indicated that school districts can be held liable for punitive damages for violations of the IDEA (Guernsey & Klare, 1993; Mattison & Hakola, 1992). The first major development was the HCPA. In overturning the U.S. Supreme Court's decision in *Smith,* Congress restored parents' right to sue school districts under other laws beyond the IDEA. According to the statutory language, "Nothing in this chapter shall be construed to restrict or limit the rights, procedures, and remedies available under the Constitution, Title V of the Rehabilitation Act of 1973, or other federal statutes" (IDEA, 20 U.S.C. § 1415(e)(3)(f) (1994)). A number of observers have noted that because of the HCPA, Section 1983 of the Civil Rights Act (Civil Rights Act, 42 U.S.C. § 1983) may now be used by attorneys in special education lawsuits, although this is not specifically mentioned in the statute (Guernsey & Klare, 1993; Mattison & Hakola, 1992).

Section 1983

In their review of legislative history of the HCPA, Mattison and Hakola (1992) maintain that Congress clearly sought to restore plaintiffs' ability to use Section 1983 of the Civil Rights Act in special education lawsuits. The primary significance of Section 1983 to plaintiffs in special education lawsuits is the availability of monetary damages under the law. Section 1983 was derived from the Civil Rights Act of 1871. The basic purpose of this law, commonly referred to as the *Ku Klux Klan Act,* was to protect freed slaves from denial of their federal rights by state and local governments (Mattison & Hakola, 1992; Sorenson, 1992). This was accomplished by providing a legal action for damages and injunctive relief. In the last few decades, courts have extended the protections of Section 1983 to any person whose rights under the U.S.

Constitution or federal statutes are violated by a governmental entity or official. Thus, persons can sue for violations of their federal rights.

However, courts have not clearly answered whether Section 1983 claims can be based on violations of the IDEA. Although courts have recognized that Section 1983 is now available to plaintiffs as a result of the HCPA, the results of cases in which plaintiffs have used Section 1983 based on violations of the IDEA have been mixed. Some courts have concluded that plaintiffs can seek monetary damages based on violations of the IDEA (*Hiller v. Board of Education of the Brunswick Central School District,* 1988), while others have ruled that a Section 1983 violation cannot be based solely on IDEA violations (*Barnett v. Fairfax County School Board,* 1991). *Jackson v. Franklin County School Board* (1986) also recognized that suit could be brought under both the IDEA and Section 1983, thereby leading to awards of monetary damages.

In *Doe v. Withers* (1993) a jury assessed monetary damages against a teacher under Section 1983. In this case, a history teacher had refused to comply with the IEP requirement that tests be read orally to a student with learning disabilities. The teacher was aware of the requirement and deliberately ignored it. As a result of the teacher's action, the student failed the history course. The following semester, the history teacher was replaced by a substitute teacher. The substitute implemented oral reading of tests, and the student's grades improved dramatically. The parents brought an action under Section 1983 against the school district and the history teacher. A jury found in favor of the parents and awarded them damages against the history teacher in the amount of $5,000 in compensatory damages and $10,000 in punitive damages.

W. B. v. Matula, 1995

In an indication that monetary damages may be available, the U.S. Court of Appeals for the Third Circuit ruled that a lawsuit seeking punitive damages under the IDEA, Section 504, and Section 1983 against a school district and several educators was permissible. *W. B. v. Matula* (1995) reversed a decision by a federal district court granting summary judgment (i.e., a preverdict rendered by a court in response to a motion by a plaintiff or defendant) for the school district of Mansfield Township, New Jersey, regarding a question of damages because of a failure on the part of a school district to properly evaluate and educate a student with a disability. The circuit court remanded the case to the district court for a trial on the damages claim. The case involved a first-grade boy with behavioral problems and Attention Deficit Hyperactivity Disorder (ADHD). The student's parents wanted an evaluation, which the school district initially declined to conduct. When the district conducted an evaluation a year after first being requested to do so, it found that the student did have ADHD but did not qualify for special education. The school district did find the boy eligible for services under Section 504 but failed to provide the necessary services. An independent evaluation determined that the boy had Tourette's syndrome, severe obsessive-compulsive disorder, and ADHD. Several due process hearings were held and the district reclassified the student, implemented an IEP, and paid $14,000 to settle all the disputes with the parents. Following an administrative hearing in late 1994, the district was further ordered to pay for a private school placement for the student. The boy's parents sued in federal district court against nine school officials (including the school principal and two general education teachers). The case eventually was appealed to the circuit court, which, in dicta, rejected the school district's argument that damages were unavailable in a Section 1983 action premised on an IDEA violation. According to the court, when the IDEA was amended in 1986, Congress specifically allowed IDEA violations to be redressed by Section 504 and Section 1983 actions. The Third Circuit court's decision was widely seen as a strong indication that lawsuits seeking monetary damages for violations of the IDEA and Section 504 were available. Rather than going back to trial on the damages action, the school district agreed to an out-of-court settlement. The district paid a total of $245,000, including a $125,000 cash payment to the family in addition to court costs and attorney's fees.

In *Whitehead v. School Board of Hillsborough County* (1996), a federal district court agreed with the Third Circuit that compensatory and punitive damages were available under Section 504. The court disagreed regarding the IDEA, however, stating that relief under the law was generally limited to reimbursement that compensated parents for the cost of services the school should have provided.

Section 1403 of the IDEA

A second development indicating that monetary damages may be available was Section 1403 of the 1990 amendments to the IDEA, which overturned the U.S. Supreme Court's ruling in *Dellmuth v. Muth* (1989). This section of the 1990 amendments indicated that

> In a suit against a State for a violation of this act, remedies (including remedies both at law and in equity) are available for such a violation to the same extent as such remedies are available for such a violation in the suit against any public entity other than a state. (IDEA, 20 U.S.C. § 1403(B))

This language is significant in its recognition that remedies both at law and in equity are available under the IDEA. The phrase *remedies at law* generally includes monetary damages. Thus, a number of legal scholars have inferred that Congress has recognized that monetary damages are within the scope of appropriate relief (Guernsey & Klare, 1993; Mattison & Hakola, 1992; Tucker & Goldstein, 1992).

Franklin v. Gwinett County Public Schools, 1992

An important development occurred in the U.S. Supreme Court's ruling in *Franklin v. Gwinett County Public Schools* (1992; hereafter *Franklin*), even though the case did not involve special education. In *Franklin*, a high school student was repeatedly sexually abused and harassed by a teacher. The student brought suit against the school and the teacher under Title IX of the Education Amendments of 1972. Subsequently, the teacher resigned and charges against him were dropped. A federal district court then dismissed the suit against the school, ruling that Title IX did not allow an award of damages. The U.S. Court of Appeals for the Eleventh Circuit affirmed the district court's decision. On appeal, the U.S. Supreme Court reversed the lower courts' rulings, holding that monetary damages were available under Title IX, even though not specifically mentioned in the law. The Court stated:

> The general rule, therefore, is that absent clear direction to the contrary by Congress, the federal courts have the power to award any appropriate relief in a cognizable cause of action brought pursuant to a federal statute. (p. 1035)

Because the language of the IDEA does not prohibit monetary awards, it seems that they may be available in accordance with the high court's ruling in *Franklin*.

Hoekstra v. Independent School District No. 283, 1996

The U.S. Court of Appeals for the Eighth Circuit, in *Hoekstra v. Independent School District No. 283* (1996), refused to award parents punitive damages as a remedy in a case involving a district's delay in providing compensatory educational services for a student in special education. The court held that punitive damages were not available as a remedy under the IDEA. In an earlier decision, the Eighth Circuit court also held that punitive damages were not available under the IDEA (*Heidemann v. Rother,* 1996).

Goleta Union Elementary School District v. Ordway, 2001

In this case the parent of a student with learning disabilities sued a school district's special education director under Section 1983. The parent charged that the director had failed to investigate whether a junior high school was an appropriate placement for the student prior to transferring the student to that placement. The court determined that the parent could recover damages under Section 1983. On the merits of the case, the court found that the special education director was personally liable under Section 1983 for transferring the student without investigating the appropriateness of the new placement. *Goleta* is the most recent case to interpret Section 1983 as permitting monetary damages against individual representatives of the school district (Norlin, 2004).

The majority of courts have not granted punitive damages under the IDEA, although a few courts have indicated that such damages may be available. Some courts have found punitive damages available for violations of Section 504 or the ADA in cases involving bad faith or gross misjudgment. Courts are usually loath to open the public coffers to punitive damages unless Congress clearly makes such a remedy available under the law (Tucker & Goldstein, 1992). Congress has not expressly made punitive damages an available remedy under the IDEA. At present, the generally accepted view is that punitive damages are not available under the IDEA, although the issue is not settled and a few courts have ruled that punitive damages are available.

Summary

In the IDEA, Congress created substantive and procedural rights for students with disabilities. The substantive rights include the FAPE, an education that results in meaningful benefit, guaranteed to each student in special education. The procedural rights, referred to in the IDEA as *procedural safeguards,* are meant to ensure that schools follow proper procedures in planning and delivering a FAPE to students with disabilities. The procedural safeguards require involvement of both parents and professionals in the special education decision-making process.

The procedural safeguards consist of seven components: notice requirements, consent requirements, the opportunity to examine records, procedures to protect the rights of the child when the parents are unavailable, the independent educational evaluation, voluntary mediation, and the due process hearing. The heart of the procedural safeguards is the due process hearing. When there is a disagreement over identification, evaluation, placement, or any matters pertaining to a FAPE, parents may request a due process hearing. The purpose of the hearing is to resolve differences by presenting information to an impartial due process hearing officer. The task of the hearing officer is to make a final decision regarding the settlement of the disagreement. Either party can appeal the decision.

The due process hearing procedure has been the subject of much criticism. The process is time-consuming, expensive, and emotionally difficult, and tends to create an adversarial relationship between the parents and the school. In an attempt to alleviate the adversarial nature of many disputes between parents and school districts, the IDEA Amendments of 1997 required states to offer parents voluntary mediation. IDEA 2004 inserted a resolution session between mediation and the due process hearing.

In special education, not only are parents involved in the process of designing an appropriate education for their child, but they may also serve as the stimulus for forcing school districts to comply with the laws. When parents or school districts go to court, they often seek to determine the responsibilities for the delivery of educational services. Typically the parents, believing that the school district's IEP will not offer an appropriate education, will seek to have different services provided. If a court finds that a school district has committed statutory or procedural violations under either the IDEA or Section 504, it may award some form of relief to redress these violations. Such awards are usually in the form of injunctive relief, tuition reimbursement, and attorney's fees. Increasingly, courts are awarding compensatory educational services. The majority of courts have generally not granted punitive damages under the IDEA, although a few have indicated that such damages may be available. Some courts have found punitive damages available for violations of IDEA and Section 504 in cases involving bad faith.

School districts need not act in bad faith, however, to be directed to provide relief. When intentional violations do occur, they may lead to courts' ordering larger awards to plaintiffs. Minor or inconsequential violations will not lead to relief; however, violations that result in the provision of an inappropriate education or result in parents not being involved in the special education process will lead to relief. The best defense to prevent such awards is in providing an appropriate and meaningful education and collecting data to show educational progress.

For Further Information

Anderson, W., Chitwood, S., & Hayden, D. (1990). *Negotiating the special education maze: A guide for parents and teachers* (2nd ed.). Alexandria, VA: Woodbine House.

Dobbs, R. F., Primm, E. B., & Primm, B. (1991). Mediation: A common sense approach for resolving conflicts in special education. *Focus on Exceptional Children, 24,* 1–11.

Goldberg, S. S., & Huefner, D. S. (1995). Dispute resolution in special education: An introduction to litigative alternatives. *Education Law Reporter, 99,* 703–803.

Katsiyannis, A., & Kale, K. (1991). State practices in due process hearings: Considerations for better practice. *Remedial and Special Education, 12,* 54–58.

Osborne, A. G. (1995). Procedural due process rights for parents under the IDEA. *Preventing School Failure, 39,* 22–26.

Shrybman, J. A. (1982). *Due process in special education,* Rockville, MD: Aspen.

Zirkel, P. A. (1994). Over-due process revisions for the Individuals with Disabilities Education Act. *Montana Law Review, 55,* 403–414.

References

Akers v. Bolton, 531 F. Supp. 300 (D. Kan. 1981).

Anderson, W., Chitwood, S., & Hayden, D. (1990). *Negotiating the special education maze: A guide for parents and teachers* (2nd ed.). Alexandria, VA: Woodbine House.

Anderson v. District of Columbia, 877 F.2d 1018 (D.C. Cir. 1989).

Anderson v. Thompson, 658 F. Supp. 1205 (7th Cir., 1981).

Angela L. v. Pasadena Independent School District No. 2, 918 F.2d 1188 (5th Cir. 1990).

Babb v. Knox County School System, 965 F.2d 104 (6th Cir. 1992).

Barnett v. Fairfax County School Board, 927 F.2d 146 (4th Cir. 1991).

Beekman, L. E. (1993). Making due process hearings more efficient and effective (aka How to run a hearing—and get away with it!). In *Proceedings of the 14th National Institute on Legal Issues of Educating Individuals with Disabilities.* Horsham, PA: LRP Publications.

Black, H. C., Nolan, J. R., & Nolan-Haley, J. M. (1990). *Black's law dictionary* (6th ed.). St. Paul, MN: West Publishing Company.

Board of Education of County of Cabell v. Dienelt, 843 F.2d 813 (4th Cir. 1988).

Board of Education of the Hendrick Hudson School District v. Rowley, 458 U.S. 176 (1982).

Board of Education of Northfield High School District, 225 v. Roy H. and Lynn H., 21 IDELR 1171 (N.D. Ill, 1995).

Buckhannon Board & Care Home Inc. v. West Virginia Department of Health and Human Resources, 35 IDELR 160 (U.S. 2001).

Burlington School Committee of the Town of Burlington v. Department of Education of Massachusetts, 471 U.S. 359 (1985).

Burr v. Ambach, 863 F.2d 1071 (2nd Cir. 1988).

Burr v. Sobol, 888 F.2d 258 (2nd Cir. 1990).

Butz v. Economou, 438 U.S. 478 (1978).

Campbell Inquiry, 211 EHLR 265 (OSEP 1989).

Christopher P. v. Marcus, 16 EHLR 1346 (2nd Cir. 1990).

Civil Rights Act, 42 U.S.C. §2000 et seq. Section 1983, 42 U.S.C. §1983 (Civil Rights Act of 1871).

Clyde K. v. Puyallup School District, 35 F.3d 1396 (9th Cir. 1994).

Colin K. v. Schmidt, 715 F.2d 1 (1st Cir. 1983).

Cox v. Jenkins, 878 F.2d 414 (D.C. Cir. 1989).

Dagley, D. L. (1994). Prevailing under the HCPA. *Education Law Reporter, 90,* 547–560.

Dagley, D. L. (1995). Enforcing compliance with IDEA: Dispute resolution and appropriate relief. Preventing School Failure, 39(2), 27–32.

Dellmuth v. Muth, 491 U.S. 223 (1989).

District of Columbia Public Schools, 257 EHLR 208 (OCR 1981).

Dobbs, R. F., Primm, E. B., & Primm, B. (1991). Mediation: A common sense approach for resolving conflicts in special education. *Focus on Exceptional Children, 24,* 1–11.

Dobbs, R. F., Primm, E. B., & Primm, B. (1993). Mediation. In *Proceedings of the 14th National Institute on Legal Issues of Educating Individuals with Disabilities.* Horsham, PA: LRP Publications.

Doe v. Withers, 20 IDELR 442 (W. Va. Cir. Ct. 1993).

Education Department General Administration Regulations (EDGAR), 34 C.F.R. § 99.22.

Eig Inquiry, 211 EHLR 174 (OSEP 1980).

Evans v. Douglas County School District No. 17, 17 IDELR 559 (8th Cir. 1988).

Florence County School District Four v. Carter, 114 S.Ct. 361 (1993).

Franklin v. Gwinett County Public Schools, 112 S.Ct. 1028 (1992).

Ginn, M., Carruth, E., & McCarthy, G. (1988). *South Carolina handbook for hearing officers.* Columbia: South Carolina Department of Education.

Goldberg, S. S., & Huefner, D. S. (1995). Dispute resolution in special education: An introduction to litigative alternatives. *Education Law Reporter, 99,* 703–803.

Goldberg, S. S., & Kuriloff, P. J. (1991). Evaluating the fairness of special education hearings. *Exceptional Children, 57,* 546–555.

Goleta Union Elementary School District v. Ordway, 38 IDELR 64 (C.D. CA. 2001).

Gorn, S. (1996). *What do I do when . . . The answer book on special education law.* Horsham, PA: LRP Publications.

Greismann, Z. (1997, February 23). Question and answer. *The Special Educator, 12*(14), 3.

Guernsey, T. F., & Klare, K. (1993). *Special education law.* Durham, NC: Carolina Academic Press.

Hacienda La Puente Unified School District v. Honig, 976 F.2d 487 (9th Cir. 1992).

Hall v. Knott County Board of Education, 941 F.2d 402 (6th Cir. 1991).

Hamway, T. J. (1994). Presenting expert testimony in due process hearings: A guide to courtroom survival. In *Proceedings of the 15th National Institute on Legal Issues of Educating Individuals with Disabilities.* Horsham, PA: LRP Publications.

Handicapped Children's Protection Act of 1986, 20 U.S.C. § 1415.

Hargan Inquiry, 16 EHLR 738 (OSEP 1990).

Heidemann v. Rother, 84 F.3d 1021 (8th Cir. 1996).

Hensley v. Eckerhart, 461 U.S. 424 (1983).

Hiller v. Board of Education of the Brunswick Central School District, 687 F. Supp. 735 (N.D.N.Y. 1988).

Hoekstra v. Independent School District No. 283, 25 IDELR 136 (8th Cir. 1996).

Honig v. Doe, 479 U.S. 1084 (1988).

Hoover Schrum, Ill. School District No. 157, 257 EHLR 136 (OCR 1980).

Hudson v. Wilson, 828 F.2d 1059 (4th Cir. 1987).

Individuals with Disabilities Education Act (IDEA), 20 U.S.C. § 1400 *et seq.*

Individuals with Disabilities Education Act Amendments of 1997, Pub. L. No. 105-17, 105th Cong., 1st sess.

Individuals with Disabilities Education Act Regulations, 34 C.F.R. § 300.533 *et seq.*

Irving Independent School District v. Tatro, 468 U.S. 883 (1984).

Jackson v. Franklin County School Board, 806 F.2d 623, 630 (5th Cir. 1986).

J.C. v. Regional School District #10, Board of Education, 36 IDELR 31 (2nd Cir. 2002).

Jesu D. v. Lucas County Children Services Board, 1984–85, EHLR 556;484 (N.D. Ohio, 1985).

Katsiyannis, A., & Kale, K. (1991). State practices in due process hearings: Considerations for better practice. *Remedial and Special Education, 12,* 54–58.

Letter to Baker, 20 IDELR 1169 (OSEP 1993).

Letter to Big, 1980.

Letter to Grant, 17 EHLR 1184 (OSEP 1991).

Letter to Helmuth, 16 EHLR 550 (OSEP 1990).

Letter to Murray, 19 IDELR 497 (OSEP, 1992).

Letter to Perryman, EHLR 211: 438 (OSEP 1987).

Letter to Williams, 18 IDELR 534 (OSEP 1991).

Light v. Parkway School District, 41 F .3d 1223 (8th Cir. 1994).

Lower Moreland Township School District, 18 IDELR 1160 (SEA Pa. 1992).

Maloney, M. H. (1993). The seven deadly sins: Common mistakes which can lead to due process hearings. In *Proceedings of the 14th National Institute on Legal Issues of Educating Individuals with Disabilities.* Horsham, PA: LRP Publications.

Mattison, D. A. (1994). An overview in the development of procedural safeguards. In *Proceedings of the 15th National Institute on Legal Issues of*

Educating Individuals with Disabilities. Horsham, PA: LRP Publications.

Mattison, D. A., & Hakola, S. R. (1992). *The availability of damages and equitable remedies under the IDEA, Section 504, and 42 U.S.C. Section 1983.* Horsham, PA: LRP Publications.

Max M. v. Illinois State Board of Education, 629 F. Supp. 1504 (N.D. Ill. 1986).

Max M. v. Thompson, 592 F. Supp. 1450 (1984).

McKenzie v. Smith, 771 F.2nd 1527 (D.C. Cir. 1985).

McNabb v. U.S., 318 U.S. 332 (1943).

Meiner v. Missouri, 673 F.2d 969 (8th Cir. 1986).

Mills v. Board of Education of the District of Columbia, 348 F. Supp. 866 (D.C. 1972).

Mitten v. Muscogee County School District, 877 F.2d 932 (11th Cir. 1989).

Murphy v. Timberlane Regional School District, 819 F. Supp. 1127 (D.N.H. 1993).

Neosho R-V School District v. Clark (2003).

Norlin, J. W. (2004). *From Rowley to Buckhannon: 50 special education decisions special educators need to know.* Horsham, PA: LRP Publications.

Osborne, A. G. (1995). Procedural due process rights for parents under the IDEA. *Preventing School Failure, 39,* 22–26.

OSEP Memorandum 94-16, 21 IDELR 85 (OSEP 1994).

Powhatten, KS Unified School District No. 150, 257 EHLR 32 (OCR 1979).

Primm, E. B. (1990). Mediation: A comment under Part B; common sense for Part H. *Early Childhood Report, 1*(6), 4–6.

Rapid City School District v. Vahle, 733 F. Supp. 1364 (D.S.D. 1990).

Reusch, G. M. (1993). Special education disputes: Practical issues facing school board attorneys. In *Proceedings of the 14th National Institute on Legal Issues of Educating Individuals with Disabilities.* Horsham, PA: LRP Publications.

Richards, D. M., & Martin, J. L. (2005). The *IDEA amendments: What you need to know.* Horsham, PA: LRP Publications.

S-1 v. Turlington, 635 F.2d 342 (5th Cir. 1981).

Sachem N.Y. Central School District, 352 EHLR 462 (OCR 1987).

Salley v. St. Tammany Parish School Board, 20 IDELR 520 (E.D. La. 1993).

Schever v. Rhodes, 416 U.S. 232 (1974).

Section 504 of the Rehabilitation Act of 1973 Regulations, 34 C.F.R. § 104.36.

Shook v. Gaston County Board of Education, 882 F.2d 119 (4th Cir. 1989).

Shrybman, J. A. (1982). *Due process in special education.* Rockville, MD: Aspen.

Smith v. Robinson, 468 U.S. 992 (1984).

Sorenson, G. P. (1992). Special education discipline in the 1990s. *West's Educational Law Reporter, 62,* (2) 387–398.

Stemple v. Board of Education, 623 F.2d 893 (4th Cir. 1980).

Still v. Debuono, 25 IDELR 32 (2nd Cir. 1996).

T. D. v. LaGrange School District No. 102, 2003.

Taylor v. Board of Education, 649 F. Supp. 1253 (N.D.N.Y. 1986).

Taylor v. Honig, 910 F .2d 627, 629 (9th Cir. 1990).

Texas State Teachers Association v. Garland Independent School District, 489 U.S. 782 (1989).

Tucker, B. P., & Goldstein, B. A. (1992). Legal rights of persons with disabilities: An analysis of federal law. Horsham, PA: LRP Publications.

Valente, R., (1994). *Law in the schools* (3rd ed.). Upper Saddle River, NJ: Merrill/Prentice Hall.

Valente, R., & Valente, (2005). *Law in the schools* (6th ed.). Upper Saddle River, NJ: Merrill/Prentice Hall.

W. B. v. Matula, 67 F.3d 484 (3rd Cir. 1995).

W. G. v. Board of Trustees of Target Range School District No. 23, 960 F.2d 1479 (9th Cir. 1992).

Weber, M. (1992). *Special education law and litigation treatise.* Horsham, PA: LRP Publications.

Whitehead v. School Board of Hillsborough County, 932 F. Supp. 1393 (M.D. Fla. 1996).

Wright, P. W. (1994). Shannon Carter: The untold story. In *Proceedings of the 15th National Institute on Legal Issues of Educating Students with Disabilities.* Horsham, PA: LRP Publications.

Yell, M. L., & Espin, C. A. (1990). The Handicapped Children's Protection Act of 1986: Time to pay the piper? *Exceptional Children, 56,* 396–407.

Zirkel, P. A. (1991). Compensatory educational services in special education cases. *Education Law Reporter, 67,* 881–887.

Zirkel, P. A. (1994). Over-due process revisions for the Individuals with Disabilities Education Act. *Montana Law Review, 55,* 403–414.

Zirkel, P. A. (1995). The remedy of compensatory education under the IDEA. *Education Law Reporter, 67,* 881–887.

CHAPTER FOURTEEN

Disciplining Students with Disabilities

(Students with disabilities) are neither immune from a school's disciplinary process nor are they entitled to participate in programs when their behavior impairs the education of other children . . . school authorities can take swift disciplinary measures . . . against disruptive handicapped students.

Judge Daly, *Stuart v. Nappi* (1978, p. 1244)

Discipline refers to procedures teachers use to maintain a classroom climate that is conducive to learning (Walker, Ramsey, & Gresham, 2004). Teachers generally think of discipline as techniques they can use to manage misbehavior (Curwin & Mendler, 1999; Walker, 1995). However, discipline involves more than just using procedures to control student misbehavior; it is also a means to teach students about the effects of their behavior on others and to help them learn to control and manage their own behavior (Yell, Rozalski, & Drasgow, 2001). Indeed, discipline should maintain an effective classroom environment and positively affect the lives of students in that classroom.

Discipline has long been an important concern of administrators, teachers, and parents. It is not surprising, therefore, that courts and legislators have addressed issues regarding the use of disciplinary procedures with students in public schools. In fact, the law has been an important force in the development of how we use discipline. Thus, it is important teachers understand the legal requirements and constraints that guide school personnel when disciplining students.

The use of disciplinary procedures with students with disabilities has proven to be an especially controversial and confusing issue. Although the Individuals with Disabilities Education Act (IDEA) and the regulations implementing the laws are quite detailed, until recently no specific federal guidelines addressed the discipline of students with disabilities (Hartwig & Reusch, 2000). This lack of statutory or regulatory guidance resulted in uncertainty among school administrators and teachers regarding appropriate disciplinary procedures. A number of judicial decisions, however, have addressed this issue, and these decisions have led to the formation of a body of case law. Generally, the case law indicates that disciplinary actions against students with disabilities are subject to different rules and limitations than those applicable to students without disabilities (Tucker, Goldstein, & Sorenson, 1993). Maloney (1994) argued that because of these different rules, administrators, teachers, and school board members needed to acknowledge that a dual standard of discipline exists between students with and without disabilities. She further contended that for administrators to claim that all students were treated equally in terms of discipline and, thus, that there is no dual disciplinary standard would not be convincing to a court, because students with disabilities do, in fact, have special protections against certain types of disciplinary procedures.

In the IDEA Amendments of 1997, the subject of disciplining students with disabilities was finally addressed in federal legislation. In the process of drafting these amendments, Congress heard testimony regarding the difficulties school administrators and teachers faced when having to discipline students with disabilities. To ameliorate these problems, Congress added a section to the IDEA that specifically addresses discipline issues. In doing so, Congress sought to strike a balance between school officials' duty to ensure that schools are safe and conducive to learning and their continuing obligation to ensure that students with disabilities receive a free appropriate public education (FAPE).

The purpose of this chapter is to examine the discipline of students with disabilities. The chapter begins with a discussion of the right of schools to regulate the behavior of all students. An examination of the obligations of schools in disciplinary matters will be followed by a review of the use of disciplinary procedures specifically with students protected by the IDEA. It is important to note that many of these issues may also be addressed by state law.

Discipline in the Schools

To operate efficiently and effectively, schools must have rules to regulate student conduct. If students violate reasonable school rules, they should be held accountable. Student accountability to rules usually implies that violators will be subject to disciplinary sanctions. Courts have recognized the importance of student management and have granted latitude to teachers to exercise this control through the use of discipline.

The courts' recognition of the importance of school authority over student behavior originates from the English common-law concept of *in loco parentis* (i.e., in place of the parent). According to this concept, parents acquiesce in the control over their children when they are placed in the charge of school personnel (Alexander & Alexander, 2002). The principal and the teacher have the authority not only to teach, but to guide, correct, and discipline the child to accomplish educational objectives. *In loco parentis* does not mean that the teacher stands fully in the place of parents in controlling their child during the school day, but that school officials, acting in concert with appropriate laws and regulations, have a duty to maintain an orderly and effective learning environment through reasonable and prudent control of students. Although the concept does not have the importance it once did, it is nevertheless an active legal concept that helps to define the school–student relationship. With respect to the use of disciplinary procedures, the doctrine implies that teachers have the duty to see that school order is maintained by requiring students to obey reasonable rules and commands and to respect the rights of others.

All students, with and without disabilities, have rights in disciplinary matters based on the due process clause of the 5th and 14th Amendments to the U.S. Constitution (see Appendix). In practice, however, the due process protections afforded students are limited by the state's interest in maintaining order and discipline in the schools. The courts, therefore, have had to strike a balance between student rights and the needs and interests of the schools.

The two general areas of due process rights afforded students are procedural and substantive. In terms of discipline, procedural due process involves the fairness of methods and procedures used by the schools; substantive due process refers to the protection of student rights from violation by school officials and involves the reasonableness of the disciplinary processes (Valente & Valente, 2005). School authorities are vested with broad authority for establishing rules and procedures to maintain order and discipline. Unless a student can show that he or she was deprived of a liberty or property interest, there is no student right to due process. According to a federal district court in Tennessee, "teachers should be free to impose minor forms of classroom discipline, such as admonishing students, requiring special assignments, restricting activities, and denying certain privileges, without being subjected to strictures of due process" (*Dickens v. Johnson County Board of Education,* 1987, p. 157).

Procedural Due Process: The Right to Fair Procedures

School districts can meet these requirements by taking actions such as (a) developing reasonable and appropriate schoolwide discipline policies and procedures, (b) extending due process protections to students when using certain disciplinary procedures, and (c) ensuring that discipline sanctions are applied in a nondiscriminatory manner (Yell, Rozalski, & Drasgow, 2001).

Developing Schoolwide Discipline Policies

Schools must develop rules that regulate student conduct. This is necessary to maintain discipline and to operate efficiently and effectively. Students should clearly know which behaviors are acceptable and which behaviors are prohibited. If students violate reasonable school rules by behaving in ways that are prohibited, they will be held accountable. Student accountability to rules implies that violators will be subject to disciplinary sanctions or consequences (Yell, Rozalski, & Drasgow, 2001).

School officials understand that if students know what types of behavior are prohibited when they are in school and what the consequences of engaging in these prohibited behaviors are, then it is more likely students will conduct themselves appropriately and not engage in the prohibited behaviors. A number of courts have addressed the issue of schoolwide discipline policies and have tended to give great authority to teachers and school officials to write rules that govern student behavior when they are in school (Yell, Katsiyannis, Bradley, & Rozalski, 2000).

When schools develop policies that regulate student conduct, they must be careful the rules and consequences are rational and reflect a school-related purpose. Rules should be clear enough to allow students to distinguish permissible from prohibited behavior. School rules that are too vague or general may result in the violation of students' rights because students will not have a clear understanding of them. In fact, if a court finds that a school rule is so vague students may not understand what behavior is prohibited, it is likely the rule would be legally invalid. Thus, teachers and administrators must take care that their school rules are sufficiently clear and are communicated to students. Finally, rules must be school-related. School officials may not prohibit or punish conduct that is not related to their school's educational purposes.

Courts also have granted school officials the authority to impose reasonable consequences on students who break school rules. The most important requirement for schoolwide consequences for misconduct is that they are rational and fair. Consequences that are excessive and unsuitable to the particular circumstances may be legally invalid. School officials must use reasonable means to achieve compliance with a school's rules. Reasonableness refers to procedures that are rational and fair, not excessive or unsuitable to the educational setting. The disciplinary sanctions used in schools must not consist of penalties or restraints that are unnecessary or excessive for the achievement of proper school purposes (Hartwig & Ruesch, 2000).

Many school officials assume that because of the IDEA's restrictions on suspensions and expulsions, regular school district discipline policies do not apply to students with disabilities. This is a mistaken assumption. Students with disabilities who attend public school are subject to a school district's regular discipline policies and procedures (Gorn, 1999). In a few situations, however, general discipline policies must be changed when applied to students in special education. These situations are when the school district's disciplinary policy (a) deprives a student of their special education and related services (i.e., long-term suspensions or expulsions without providing educational services), (b) triggers the procedural safeguards of the IDEA (e.g., changes a student's placement without a change in the individualized education program (IEP) or without notice), or (c) interferes with a student's IEP, behavior intervention plan (BIP), or Section 504 accommodation plan.

If a student's IEP team determines that (a) he or she will be subject to the school district's regular disciplinary policy, and (b) the policy *does not* violate the requirements of IDEA 1997, the team may use the student's IEP or BIP to affirm that the student will be subject to the district's regular discipline policies and procedures (Gorn, 1999). Including a copy of the school's discipline policy along with the IEP or

BIP will accomplish this. If a student's parents agreed to the IEP or BIP, then they are consenting to using the school's regular discipline policy. The U.S. Department of Education seemingly supported such a view in a comment to the final IDEA regulations, "in appropriate circumstances the IEP team. . . might include specific regular or alternative disciplinary measures that would result from particular infractions of school rules" (OSEP Question and Answers, 1999, p. 12589). If an IEP team decides that a student will be subject to an alternative discipline plan, this plan should be included in the student's IEP or BIP.

Extending Due Process Protections to Students

The importance of education to a student's future requires that disciplinary actions resulting in students being deprived of an education (e.g., suspension, expulsion) are subjected to the standards of due process. The purpose of due process procedures is to ensure that official decisions are made in a fair manner. Due process procedures in school settings do not require the full range of protections afforded to persons in formal court trials, such as representation by counsel and cross-examination of witnesses (Sorenson, 1993). The procedures do, however, include the basic protections such as notice, hearing, and impartiality.

Due process protections in schools, which must be afforded to all students, were outlined by the U.S. Supreme Court in *Goss v. Lopez* (1975; hereafter *Goss*). The case involved nine high school students who had been suspended from school without a hearing. At issue was whether the students had been denied due process of law under the 14th Amendment. The Supreme Court ruled that the students had the right to at least minimal due process protections in cases of suspension. The high court stated that, "Having chosen to extend the right to an education. . . [the state] may not withdraw the right on grounds of misconduct absent fundamentally fair procedures to determine whether the misconduct had occurred" (p. 574). The Court, noting the broad authority of the schools to prescribe and enforce standards of behavior, held that states are constrained to recognize a student's entitlement to a public education as a property interest that is protected by the 14th Amendment. Because education is protected, it may not be taken away without adhering to the due process procedures required by the amendment. The school had argued that a 10-day suspension was only a minor and temporary interference with the students' education; the high court disagreed, stating that a 10-day suspension was not de minimus (i.e., trivial or minor) but was a "serious event in the life of the suspended child" (p. 576). The imposition of the 10-day suspension, therefore, must include "the fundamental requisite of due process of law. . . the opportunity to be heard" (*Grannis v. Ordean*, 1914, p. 388).

The opportunity to be heard, when applied to the school setting, involves the right to notice and hearing. The right to notice and hearing requires that students are presented with the charges against them and have an opportunity to state their case (Yudof, Kirp, & Levin, 1992). The due process protections to be afforded to students will not shield them from properly imposed suspensions, but they will protect them from an unfair or mistaken exclusion. The Court in *Goss* recognized the necessity of order and discipline and the need for immediate and effective action, stating that suspension is a "necessary tool to maintain order. . . [and] a valuable educational device" (p. 572). Although the prospect of imposing cumbersome hearing requirements on every suspension case was a concern, the Court felt that schools should not have the power to act unilaterally, free of notice and hearing requirements. The Court held that when students are suspended for 10 days or less, therefore, the school needs only to give them oral or written notice of the charges, an explanation of the reasons for the suspension, and an opportunity to present their side of the story.

The requirement does not imply a delay between the time notice is given and the time of a student's hearing. The disciplinarian could informally discuss the misconduct with students immediately after the behavior occurs and give them an opportunity to present their version of the facts. In such situations, notice and hearing would precede the disciplinary action. If, however, the behavior posed a danger to students or teachers or a threat to disrupt the academic process, a student could be immediately removed and the notice and hearing could follow as soon as possible. In this event, notice of disciplinary hearings should follow within 24 hours and the hearing be held within 72 hours. The basic due process protections prescribed by the high court in *Goss* applied solely to short suspensions of 10 days or less. Longer suspensions or expulsions, according to the Court, require more extensive and formal due process procedures. Figure 14.1 lists the due process protections that must be afforded to students in short- and long-term suspensions. In addition to these guidelines, it is permissible to immediately remove dangerous students from the school setting. Additionally, brief in-school sanctions do not require a due process hearing.

The due process protections outlined in *Goss* must be extended to *all* students who face suspensions, including students with disabilities. In fact, IDEA 1997 does not create more rigorous procedural protections for students with disabilities than

Figure 14.1
Due Process Protections for All Students

Short-Term Suspension (may be a formal or informal meeting)
- Written or oral notice of charges
- Opportunity to respond to charges

Long-Term Suspension and Expulsion (must be a formal meeting)
- Written notice specifying charges
- Notice of evidence, witnesses, and substance of testimony
- Hearing (advance notice of time, place, and procedures)
- Right to confront witnesses and present their own witnesses
- A written or taped record of the proceedings
- Right of appeal

the minimal protections in *Goss* (Gorn, 1999). If suspensions of students with disabilities exceed 10 consecutive school days or amount to a change in placement, however, the procedural protections of the IDEA apply.

These due process protections will not shield students from properly imposed suspensions. Rather, the purpose of the protections is to protect students from an unfair or mistaken suspension. The protections that must be afforded students who are suspended are limited by the school's interest in maintaining order and discipline.

Ensuring That Discipline Practices Are Nondiscriminatory

Recall from Chapter 6 that all students with mental or physical impairments that affect a major life function are protected from discrimination under Section 504 of the Rehabilitation Act of 1973 (hereafter Section 504). This includes students with disabilities who are not covered by the IDEA and students in special education who are covered. This means that all IDEA-eligible special education students are also protected by Section 504.

Discrimination refers to unequal treatment of qualified students with disabilities based solely on the basis of the disability. School districts may violate Section 504 when disciplining students with disabilities in four primary ways: (a) disciplining students with disabilities by using procedures that are not used with nondisabled students who exhibit similar misbehavior, (b) disciplining students with disabilities by using procedures that are more harsh than those used with nondisabled students who exhibit similar misbehavior, (c) suspending (long-term), expelling, or changing the placement of a student with disabilities for misbehavior that is related to the student's disability, or (d) disciplining a student using procedures that are prohibited in the IEP or behavior plan.

To ensure that discipline is not applied in a discriminatory manner, and thus violates Section 504, schools officials should adopt the following procedures (Yell, Rozalski, & Drasgow, 2001): First, schools must use the same disciplinary procedures for students with and without disabilities. In such situations, IEP teams or Section 504 teams should include the school's regular disciplinary policy in a student's IEP or Section 504 accommodation plan. Second, schools must conduct manifestation determinations to assess the relationship between a student's disability and misconduct before using long-term suspensions, expulsions, or making changes of placements (see the section on manifestation determinations). Third, administrators must ensure that all school officials and the student's teachers understand the contents of the IEP, BIP, or Section 504 plans and follow the interventions and disciplinary procedures listed in these documents. Discipline plans that are written into IEPs or Section 504 plans preempt a school district's regular disciplinary code (Gorn, 1999).

Substantive Due Process: The Right to Reasonableness

Courts have given schools great authority in promulgating rules governing student behavior. The power to establish rules and regulations, however, is not absolute, for when these regulations are developed, they must not violate constitutional principles.

Generally, this requires that the regulation of student behavior be reasonable. To be reasonable, rules must have a rationale and a school-related purpose, and the school must employ reasonable means to achieve compliance with the rule. Schools may not prohibit or punish conduct that has no adverse effect on public education. Neither may they employ disciplinary penalties or restraints that are unnecessary or excessive for the achievement of proper school purposes (Hartwig & Reusch, 2000). Reasonableness essentially means that procedures must be rational and fair and not excessive or unsuitable for the educational setting.

Rules must be sufficiently clear and specific to allow students to distinguish permissible from proscribed behavior. School rules that are too vague or general may result in the violation of students' rights. Appropriate school rules are specific and definitive; they provide students with information regarding behavioral expectations.

A federal district court in Indiana addressed the issue of the reasonableness of a school's use of discipline in *Cole v. Greenfield-Central Community Schools* (1986). The plaintiff, Christopher Bruce Cole, an elementary student, exhibited management and adjustment problems and was diagnosed as emotionally disturbed under Indiana state law. The school had attempted, and documented, numerous positive and negative procedures in efforts to control and modify Christopher's behavior. Included in the disciplinary procedures were time-out, response cost, and corporal punishment. The plaintiff sued the school, contending that in using these procedures the school had violated his civil rights.

The court recognized that although Christopher had a disability covered by the IDEA, he was not immune from the school's disciplinary procedures. The court held that the validity of the plaintiff's claim, therefore, rested on the "reasonableness" of the disciplinary procedures used by the school in attempting to manage Christopher's behavior. To determine reasonableness, the court analyzed four elements: (a) Did the teacher have the authority under state and local laws to discipline the student? (b) Was the rule violated within the scope of the educational function? (c) Was the rule violator the one who was disciplined? (d) Was the discipline in proportion to the gravity of the offense? Finding that all four elements of reasonableness were satisfied, the court held for the school district.

The IDEA and Discipline

Administrators and teachers face a different set of rules and limitations in using disciplinary procedures with students with disabilities who are protected by the IDEA (Maloney, 1994; Tucker et al., 1993). This dual standard only exists, however, when disciplinary procedures may result in a change of placement. The determination of what constitutes a change of placement under the IDEA is critical. Under the IDEA, changes of placement cannot be made without following the procedural requirements of the law.

In the IDEA Amendments of 1997, Congress addressed several issues related to discipline. According to the Office of Special Education Programs (OSEP) of the

Department of Education (Senate Report, 1997), the goals of the disciplinary provisions of IDEA 1997 were as follows:

1) all students, including students with disabilities, deserve safe, well-disciplined schools and orderly learning environments;
2) teachers and school administrators should have the tools they need to assist them in preventing misconduct and discipline problems and to address those problems, if they arise;
3) there must be a balanced approach to the issue of discipline of students with disabilities that reflects the need for orderly and safe schools and the need to protect the right of students with disabilities to a free appropriate public education (FAPE); and
4) students have the right to an appropriately developed IEP with well-designed behavior intervention strategies.

In IDEA 1997, Congress sought to expand the authority of school officials to protect the safety of all children by maintaining orderly, drug-free, and disciplined school environments, while ensuring that the essential rights and protections for students with disabilities were protected (*Letter to Anonymous,* 1999). In writing the discipline provisions, Congress sought to help school officials and IEP teams (a) respond appropriately when students with disabilities exhibit serious problem behavior and (b) appropriately address problem behavior in the IEP process (Yell, Katsiyannis, Bradley, & Rozalski, 2000). In the Individuals with Disabilities Education Improvement Act of 2004, Congress sought to give school districts more authority when disciplining students with disabilities.

In IDEA 2004, Congress made significant changes in four areas. First, the law now allows school personnel to consider any unique circumstances on a core-by-core basis when determining when they consider changing a student's placement who has violated a code of student conduct. According to Richards and Martin (2005), this language allows a school administrator to consider any unique circumstances when deciding to seek a long-term disciplinary removal. Furthermore, the authors assert that this language may be a response to school districts' zero tolerance policies in which administrators are required to take specified actions in certain circumstances. Second, Congress altered this manifestation requirement. Third, Congress added a behavior that can lead to a 45-day removal. Finally, the stay-put rule was modified in disciplinary situations. These changes will be covered in later sections of this chapter.

It is important that school personnel are aware of the law and regulations and are able to effectively implement their provisions. Three major points underlie the disciplinary changes of IDEA 1997 and IDEA 2004. First, the law emphasizes the use of positive behavioral interventions, supports, and services for students with disabilities who exhibit problem behaviors. The purpose of positive programming is to teach appropriate behaviors that increase the likelihood of a student's success in school and in post-school life, rather than merely using punishment-based programming to eliminate inappropriate behavior. These procedures must be included in students' IEPs when appropriate. Second, school officials may discipline a student with disabilities in the same manner as they discipline students without disabilities, with a few exceptions. A school's regular disciplinary procedures can be used with students with IEPs as long as they (a) are used with nondisabled students *and* students with disabilities (i.e., the procedures are not discriminatory), (b) do not result in a unilateral change in a student's placement (i.e., suspension in excess of 10 cumulative school days that constitutes a pattern of exclusion, change of educational placement made by school personnel and not the IEP team, suspension for 10 consecutive days, and expulsions from school) and (c) do not result in the cessation of educational services.

Third, discipline should be addressed through the IEP process. Yell et al. (2000) predicted that school districts were most likely to violate the disciplinary provisions of the IDEA by (a) failing to address problem behavior and discipline in the IEP process and (b) not following the behavioral plans and disciplinary procedures indicated in a student's IEP and in the IDEA (e.g., a principal unilaterally expels a student with disabilities rather than adhering to the discipline plan in the IEP).

An additional advantage of addressing discipline through the IEP process is that if school personnel and parents can arrive at solutions to a student's discipline problems through this process (e.g., changing a student's placement to an alternative school rather than moving to expel him or her), there is no need to invoke the disciplinary provisions of IDEA 1997. Let's examine the major changes in IDEA 1997 and IDEA 2004.

Addressing Problem Behavior in the IEP Process

The IDEA requires that if a student with disabilities exhibits problem behaviors that impede his or her learning or the learning of others, then the student's IEP team shall consider "strategies, including positive behavioral interventions, strategies, and supports to address that behavior" (IDEA, 20 U.S.C. § 1414 (d)(3)(B)(i)). Comments to the federal regulations indicate that if a student has a history of problem behavior, or if such behaviors can be readily anticipated, then the student's IEP must address that behavior (IDEA Regulations, 34 C.F.R. § 300 Appendix A question 39). This requirement applies to all students in special education, regardless of their disability category.

Neither the IDEA nor the regulations indicate what behaviors should be addressed in the IEP. The lack of specificity is consistent with the IDEA's philosophy of allowing IEP teams to make individualized decisions for each student (Gorn, 1999). It is up to the IEP team, therefore, to determine which behaviors are significant enough to require interventions formally written into the IEP. Drasgow, Yell, Bradley, and Shriner (1999) inferred from previous hearings and court cases that these problem behaviors may include (a) disruptive behaviors that distract teachers from teaching and students from learning, (b) noncompliance, (c) verbal and physical abuse, (d) property destruction, and (e) aggression toward students or staff.

These problem behaviors should be addressed in the following manner. First, when a student exhibits problem behavior, the IEP team must determine if the behavior impedes his or her learning or other students' learning. Second, if the team decides that the problem behavior does interfere with the student's learning, they must conduct an assessment of the behavior. Third, the IEP team must develop a plan based on the information gained from the assessment to reduce problem behaviors and increase socially acceptable behaviors.

The results of the team's decisions must be included in the IEP. This means that the IEP of a student with serious problem behaviors must include the information from the assessment in the present levels of performance section of the IEP. Because educational needs must be addressed by developing appropriate special education programming, the IEP must also include (a) measurable goals and objectives and (b) special education and related services that address the problem behavior. Moreover, if the student's behavioral program involves modifications to the general education classroom, these modifications must be included in the IEP. When an IEP team addresses a student's problem behavior, the needs of the individual student are of paramount importance in determining the behavior strategies that are appropriate for inclusion in the child's IEP (OSEP Questions and Answers, 1999).

If an IEP team fails to address a student's problem behaviors in the IEP, then that failure may deprive the student of a FAPE (Drasgow, Yell, Bradley, & Shriner, 1999). This could result in legal actions against the offending school district. The importance of including positive programming that addresses significant problem behavior in students' IEPs was emphasized by Thomas Hehir, former director of the U.S. Department of Education's Office of Special Education Programs, who stated that "the key provision in (IDEA) is using positive behavioral interventions and supports" (*Letter to Anonymous*, 1999, p. 707) in the IEPs of students who exhibit significant problem behaviors. Failure to do so "would constitute a denial of the free appropriate public education (mandate of the IDEA)" (IDEA Regulations, Appendix B, Question 38).

Functional Behavioral Assessment

The IDEA encourages, and sometimes demands, that IEP teams address problem behaviors by conducting functional behavioral assessments (FBAs) and by developing education programming based on the results of the assessment (Drasgow & Yell, 2002).

An FBA is a process that searches for an explanation of the purpose behind a problem behavior (OSEP Questions and Answers, 1999). Although the U.S. Department of Education has not defined an FBA, it is reasonable to assume Congress intended that the term be consistent with the meaning in the professional literature (Drasgow et al., 1999; Gorn, 1999). FBA is a process to gather information about factors that reliably predict and maintain problem behavior in order to develop more effective intervention plans (Horner & Carr, 1997; O'Neill et al., 1997). In essence, an FBA is used to develop an understanding of the cause and purpose of problem behavior (Drasgow et al., 1999).

The law intends that an FBA should be part of the process of addressing problem behavior. Moreover, the purpose of an FBA, or any special education assessment, is not merely to determine eligibility. Rather, its purpose is to determine the educational needs of students with disabilities and then to develop effective programming to meet those needs.

The IDEA does not detail the components of a FBA. Neither did the U.S. Department of Education include additional information on FBAs in the final regulations. This means that the composition of FBAs is left to states, school districts, and IEP teams. According to OSEP, a definition was not offered in the IDEA Regulations because IEP teams need to "be able to address the various situational, environmental, and behavioral circumstances raised in individual cases" (OSEP, 1999).

The decision to conduct an FBA, therefore, is left up to the professional judgment of the IEP team. In certain situations, though, an IEP team *must* conduct an FBA. These situations are when a student in special education is suspended for more than 10 days or placed in an interim alternative educational setting (IAES).

Functional Behavioral Assessments and Suspension.   The IDEA requires that the IEP team must meet and conduct or revise an FBA and BIP within 10 business days from when a student is (a) first removed for more than 10 school days in a school year, (b) removed in a manner that constitutes a change in placement, or (c) placed in an IAES for a weapons or a drug offense. In such situations, the IEP team must convene to conduct an FBA and develop a BIP. Martin (1999) suggests, however, that IEP teams should conduct an FBA if a student is approaching 10 cumulative days of suspension rather than waiting until the 10-day limit has been reached.

For subsequent removals of a student who already has an FBA and BIP, the IEP team members can individually review the BIP and its implementation. The review of the student's behavior may take place without a meeting unless one or more of the team members believe that the plan (or its implementation) needs modification (IDEA Regulations, 34 C.F.R. §300.520(c)). The regulations did not intend that school personnel develop behavioral interventions within 10 days of removing a student from the current placement. Instead, the regulations are intended to require that public schools expeditiously conduct the FBA. Moreover, the regulations ensure that the IEP team develops appropriate behavioral interventions based on the assessment. Those interventions must then be implemented as quickly as possible.

The purpose of conducting an FBA is to develop educational programming that is related to the cause and purpose of the problem behaviors. The IDEA Amendments of 1997 (hereafter IDEA 1997) refer to specific programming to address problem behavior as BIP. In IDEA 2004, the term BIP was dropped for "Behavioral Intervention services and modifications" (IDEA, 20 U.S.C. 1415 (k)(D)(ii)).

Behavior Intervention Plans

The IEP team develops a BIP based on the FBA. The IDEA does not provide details about the composition of the plan beyond indicating that the plan has to be individualized to meet the needs of different students in different educational environments. The U.S. Department of Education also refused to define a BIP. Congress and the Department apparently expected that the term *behavioral intervention plan* had a commonly understood meaning in special education (Gorn, 1999).

Behavior plans need to be proactive and multidimensional. This means that IEP teams should implement multiple strategies aimed at preventing problem behavior before it becomes severe enough to warrant sanctions such as suspension or expulsion (Drasgow et al., 1999; Gorn, 1999; Yell et al., 2000). In fact, behavioral plans that merely describe acts of prohibited misconduct and then specify consequences for misbehavior are almost certainly illegal because they are reactive and not proactive (Gorn, 1999).

The behavior change program should emphasize multiple strategies that include teaching prosocial behaviors. The key component of the plan is using positive behavioral interventions that do not rely on coercion or punishment for behavior change (Dunlap & Koegel, 1999).

When an IEP addresses behavior, the process for developing and writing the IEP is the same as would be for academics. First, the need for behavioral programming will be addressed in the present levels of educational performance. Second, measurable behavioral goals will be listed in the annual goal section along with the procedures that will be used to measure a student's progress toward the goals and the method for reporting a student's progress to his or her parents. Third, the behavioral programming will be addressed.

Despite the presence of positive behavioral intervention and support plans, Congress recognized that school officials still needed clarification of which disciplinary procedures could be used when students with disabilities exhibit serious misbehavior. Most discipline procedures used with students in public schools are permitted under the IDEA (e.g., time-out, in-school suspension). When the student misconduct is serious enough to warrant suspension or expulsion, however, the strictures of the IDEA must be followed.

Disciplinary Procedures

Most types of disciplinary procedures that are used as part of a schoolwide discipline plan may be used with students in special education. The exceptions are procedures that result in a student being suspended, expelled from school, or having his or her placement change.

Short-Term Disciplinary Removals

The IDEA authorizes school officials (i.e., building level administrators) to unilaterally suspend students with disabilities, or place students in an alternative educational program on a short-term basis, to the same extent that such suspensions or removals are used with students without disabilities. According to the U.S. Department of Education, the reason that school officials may make such decisions unilaterally (i.e., acting by themselves) is because maintaining safety and order in the school may sometimes require that students with disabilities be removed from the school environment immediately (*Letter to Anonymous,* 1999). To react quickly to such situations, the building level administrator can remove a student with disabilities from school without having to convene an IEP team, conduct a manifestation determination, or seek permission to do so from a student's parents. School officials, however, must afford a student of his or her due process rights (i.e., oral or written notice of the charges, an explanation of the evidence that support the charges, and an opportunity to present his or her side of the story).

The IDEA does not establish a specific limitation on the number of days in a school year that students with disabilities can be suspended from school. As a result of this lack of information in the statute and regulations, a great deal of confusion exists regarding the number of days that students with disabilities can be suspended without violating the IDEA. Students with disabilities may be removed from school for up to 10 cumulative or consecutive school days as long as such suspensions are used with nondisabled students as well.

School officials must keep two critical points in mind when using short-term suspensions. First, 10 consecutive days is the upper limit on out-of-school suspensions. If a suspension exceeds this limit, it becomes a change of placement. In this situation, if school officials do not follow the IDEA's change of placement procedures (e.g., written notice to the student's parents, convening the IEP team), the suspension is a violation of the law (see section on change of placement procedures for an explanation of this area of the law).

Second, when the total number of days that a student has been suspended equals 10 or more cumulative days in a school year, educational services must be provided. At this point the IEP team has to meet for a number of reasons. The team must determine what services will be provided and where, and conduct an FBA and develop a BIP. If an FBA and BIP are already a part of the IEP, they must be reviewed. Third, the IEP team must address the change of placement issue. In other words the team must examine the previous suspensions to see if they amounted to a unilateral change of placement. Finally, the team should conduct a manifestation determination.

If the manifestation determination finds that the misconduct was related to a student's disability, he or she cannot be suspended more than 10 consecutive days. If the misconduct was not related to a student's disability, he or she may be suspended for more than 10 consecutive days. Of course, the district must continue to provide educational services to the suspended student and his or her parents can challenge the decision of no relationship (see the section on manifestation determination).

Provided Educational Services.   Educational services must be provided after the 10th cumulative day of removal. For example, if a student is suspended for 10 cumulative days in the fall semester and is then suspended for 3 more days in the spring term, educational services must be provided from the first day in which cumulative suspensions exceed 10 days or, in this case, the first day of suspension in the spring. School officials may implement additional short-term suspensions for separate incidents of misconduct, therefore, as long as they provide educational services to the suspended student. Although not directly addressed in the IDEA, if a student is suspended for less than 10 school days, a school district is not required to continue educational services (IDEA Regulations, 34 C.F.R. § 300.121(d)(1)). School officials in consultation with the student's special education teacher should determine the content of the educational services, if the suspensions equal less than 10 cumulative days.

When suspensions exceed 10 cumulative days, the IEP team must determine educational services. The educational services provided to students must allow them to (a) progress in the general education curriculum, (b) receive special education and related services, and (c) advance toward achieving their IEP goals.

Because of limits on the number of days in which a student with disabilities may be removed from the school setting, school officials should use out-of-school suspensions judiciously and in emergency situations. Moreover, school personnel should keep thorough records of the number of days in which students with disabilities are removed from schools for disciplinary reasons so they do not inadvertently violate IDEA provisions.

The frequency and number of short-term removals, if they are excessive, may be indicative of a defective IEP. Martin (1999) asserts that the greater the number of short-term disciplinary removals, the greater the likelihood that a hearing officer will find that the behavior portion of the IEP is inappropriate and a deprivation of the student's right to a FAPE. Indeed, if a student is approaching 10 cumulative days of suspension, the IEP team should be convened to review the student's behavioral plans, conduct a functional behavioral assessment, and develop or review the student's BIP. Martin (1999) also suggests that the IEP team should also conduct a manifestation determination prior to the 11th day of accumulated short-term removals.

When a Short-Term Disciplinary Removal Becomes a Change of Placement.   A long-term suspension of more than 10 consecutive days is a change of placement under IDEA 1997. Because such a suspension is a change of placement, the school district must follow IDEA's change of placement procedures. This means that a school district must provide the parents of the suspended student with written notice prior to initiating the change. The purpose of such a notice is to give the parents an opportunity to object if they disagree with the placement change. The written notice should include an explanation of the applicable procedural safeguards (OSEP Questions and Answers, 1999). If a student's parents object to the change of placement, the school district may not suspend the students beyond the 10 consecutive days. The only exception to this rule is when the IEP conducts a manifestation determination and decides the student's misconduct is not related to his or her disability (see a later section for elaborations on the manifestation determination).

A series of short-term suspensions may also become a change in placement. The question of when disciplinary removals amount to a change of placement, however, can only be determined by a student's IEP team. To determine if a series of short-term suspensions have become a change in placement, an IEP team must determine the circumstances surrounding the suspension, including (a) the length of each removal, (b) the total amount of time the student is removed, and (c) the proximity of the removals to one another (IDEA Regulations, § 300.520, Note 1). Nevertheless, neither IDEA 1997 nor the regulations provide clear guidance as to when repeated short-term suspensions of fewer than 10 school days amount to a change of placement. Ultimately, this question will be answered by due process hearing officers and judges. The decision to classify a series of suspensions as a change in placement can only be decided on a case-by-case basis. It is important, therefore, that when a series of short-term suspensions amount to more than 10 cumulative school days, the IEP team be convened to determine whether these suspensions may be a change in placement.

Removal of a student for fewer than 10 cumulative or 10 consecutive school days probably will not amount to a change in placement. Similarly, if a series of short-term suspensions of not more than 10 days each are used for separate incidences of misbehavior, they probably will not be a change of placement, as long as the suspensions do not create a pattern of exclusion. However, school officials must not assess repeated short-term suspensions as a means of avoiding the change of placement procedures required when using long-term suspensions. According to Gorn (1999), subterfuge of this nature, if detected, will invariably result in a finding that a school district violated the procedural requirements of the IDEA.

Gorn (1999) reviewed decisions from the U.S. Department of Education's Office of Civil Rights (OCR) regarding when accumulated short-term suspensions become a change of placement. She listed eight decisions from 1990 to 1997 in which OCR decided that multiple suspensions leading to between 13 and 31 days of removal were significant changes of placement and thus violated the law. However, OCR also decided that a district's removal of a student on two separate occasions resulting in a total of 15 days of removal and another district's removal of a student on five separate occasions for a total of 38 days of removal did not result in a change of placement. It should be noted that OCR decisions only address violations of Section 504 and not of the IDEA. Nonetheless, because the rules regarding disciplinary removals are similar under Section 504 and IDEA 1997, these decisions are useful indicators of when multiple suspensions may become a change of placement.

Finally, readers are cautioned that state law regarding suspensions of students with disabilities should be consulted because some states put a ceiling on the number of days that students with disabilities can be suspended during a school year. If state law allows fewer days of suspension than does IDEA 1997, then school officials must adhere to the state guidelines.

Change in Placement.   The case law clearly indicates that schools may not unilaterally change the placement of a student with disabilities. If the school proposes a change in placement, and the proposal is contested by the student's parents, the stay-put provision comes into play and the student cannot be removed from the then-current educational placement. The only exception is when a student brings a weapon to school or uses, possesses, or sells illegal drugs. In such situations, school officials may immediately and unilaterally move a student to an interim alternative educational setting.

The determination of what constitutes a change of placement is important to understanding the limits of discipline under the IDEA (Tucker & Goldstein, 1992). Minor changes in the student's educational program that do not involve a change in the general nature of the program do not constitute a change in placement. For example, in *Concerned Parents and Citizens for Continuing Education at Malcolm X v. The New York City Board of Education* (1980), a circuit court held that a change in the location of the program, in and of itself, did not constitute a change of placement.

A change in the educational program that substantially or significantly affects the delivery of education to a student constitutes a change in placement and is not permissible. *Honig v. Doe* (1988) established that any suspension of more than 10 days constitutes a change. The 10-day rule became the federal norm with the IDEA 1997. Indefinite suspensions or expulsions in excess of 10 days, therefore, constitute a change in placement. In a 1988 memorandum, OCR issued a policy statement indicating that a series of suspensions cumulatively totaling more than 10 days would constitute a change of placement if the result was a pattern of exclusions that effectively changed a student's placement. The Office of Special Education Programs (OSEP) of the U.S. Department of Education issued a statement regarding short-term suspensions that adopted the OCR interpretation of short-term suspensions and change of placement (OSEP Memorandum 95-16, 1995). A 1989 OCR memorandum clarified the factors to consider in determining whether a series of suspensions would constitute a pattern of exclusions; these factors include the length of each suspension, the proximity of the suspensions to each other, and the total amount of time the student is excluded from school.

Long-Term Disciplinary Removals

Long-term suspension and expulsion qualify as a change of placement. A federal district court in Connecticut held that expulsion was a unilateral change of placement inconsistent with the IDEA (*Stuart v. Nappi*, 1978). Because expelling a student with disabilities would result in a placement change, the procedural safeguards of the IDEA would automatically be triggered. The U.S. Courts of Appeals for the Fourth Circuit, in *Prince William County School Board v. Malone* (1985); for the Fifth Circuit, in *S-1 v. Turlington* (1981); for the Sixth Circuit, in *Kaelin v. Grubbs* (1982); and for the Ninth Circuit, in *Doe v. Maher* (1986) reached similar conclusions. Not all courts, however, have agreed with this interpretation. The U.S. Court of Appeals for the Eleventh Circuit, in *Victoria L. v. District School Board* (1984), held that a school district could—unilaterally, if necessary—transfer a dangerous student to a more restrictive setting. The question was settled in 1988, when the U.S. Supreme Court issued a ruling in *Honig v. Doe.*

Honig v. Doe, **1988.**   *Honig v. Doe* (1988; hereafter *Honig*) involved the proposed expulsion of two students with emotional disabilities from the San Francisco public school system. Both students, following separate behavior incidents, had been suspended from school and recommended for expulsion. In accordance with California law, the suspensions were continued indefinitely while the expulsion proceedings were being held. Attorneys for the students filed a joint lawsuit in federal district court. The district court issued an injunction that prevented the school district from suspending any student with disabilities for misbehavior causally related to the student's disability. The school district appealed. The U.S. Court of Appeals for the Ninth Circuit, in *Doe v. Maher* (1986), held that expulsion is a change in placement, triggering the procedural safeguards of the law. The California superintendent of public instruction, Bill Honig, filed a petition of certiorari with the U.S. Supreme Court. One of the issues raised on appeal concerned the stay-put provision. Honig contended that the circuit court's interpretation of the rule—that no student with a disability could be excluded from school during the pendency of the administrative review regardless of the danger presented by the student—was untenable. A literal reading of this provision, according to *Honig,* would require schools to return potentially violent and dangerous students to the classroom, a situation Congress could not have intended.

Ruling in Honig.   On January 20, 1988, the U.S. Supreme Court issued a ruling in the case renamed *Honig v. Doe.* Justice Brennan, writing for the majority, rejected Honig's argument that Congress did not intend to deny schools the authority to remove dangerous and disruptive students from the school environment. Stating that Congress had intended to strip schools of their unilateral authority to exclude students with disabilities from school, the high court declined to read a dangerousness exception into the law. The Court ruled that during the pendency of any review meetings, the student must remain in the then-current placement unless school officials and parents agree otherwise. Expulsion, the Court held, constituted a change in placement.

The Court noted that this decision regarding the stay-put provision did not leave educators "hamstrung." While the ruling would not allow a school to change a student's placement during proceedings, it did not preclude the use of a school's normal disciplinary procedures for dealing with students with disabilities. Such normal procedures included time-outs, the use of study carrels, detention, restriction of privileges, and suspension for up to 10 days. These procedures would allow the prompt removal of dangerous students. During the 10-day period, school officials could initiate an individualized education program (IEP) meeting and "seek to persuade the child's parents to agree to an interim placement" (*Honig,* p. 605). If a student was truly "dangerous" and the parents refused to agree to a change, school officials, according to the high court, could immediately seek the aid of the courts. When seeking the aid of the courts, the burden of proof would rest upon the school to demonstrate that going through the IDEA's procedural mechanisms (i.e., due process hearing) would be futile and that in the current placement the student was "substantially likely" to present a danger to others. The stay-put provision, therefore, does not preempt the authority of the courts from granting an injunction to temporarily remove the student from the school. In effect, the court did read a dangerousness exemption into the stay-put rule; however, this determination could only be made by a judge and not by school officials.

The IDEA does not establish a specific limitation on the number of days in a school year that students with disabilities can be suspended from school for disciplinary reasons. Thus, the law offers no clear answer as to the number of days a student can be suspended before schools change a student's placement by using long-term suspensions. Neither is there an absolute limit on the number of school days students with disabilities can be removed from their current placement in a school year (OSEP Questions and Answers, 1999).

Suspensions over 10 days long require that the suspended student receive appropriate educational services. Furthermore, the IEP team must be convened to conduct an FBA, develop or revise a BIP, and conduct a manifestation determination.

Removal for 45 School Days

School officials may unilaterally exclude a student with disabilities from school for up to 45 *school* days without regard to whether the misbehavior was a manifestation of the student's disability if the student (a) brings, possesses, or acquires a weapon at school, on school premises, or at a school function (e.g., school dances, class trips, extracurricular activities); (b) knowingly possesses, uses, or sells illegal drugs, or sells a controlled substance at school, on school premises, or at a school function; or (c) has inflicted serious bodily injury to another person while at school, on school premises, or at a school function (IDEA, 20 USC § 1415(k)(1)). A weapon is defined as a "weapon, device, instrument, material, or substance . . . that is used for, or is readily capable of, causing death or serious bodily injury" (IDEA, 20 U.S.C. § 615(k)(10)(D)). (For a list of weapons covered under the IDEA, see the Federal Criminal Code, 18 U.S.C. § 930(g)). A controlled substance refers to a legally prescribed medication (e.g., Ritalin) that is illegally sold by a student. (For a list of controlled substances covered by the IDEA, see the Controlled Substances Act, 21 U.S.C. § 812(c)). *Serious bodily injury* refers to any physical injury that results in risk of death, physical pain, disfigurement, or loss of impairment of a bodily function. In the event of such exclusions, students must be placed in an appropriate IAES.

The Manifestation Determination

IDEA 2004 requires that within 10 school days of any decision to change the placement of a student with a disability because of a violation of a code of student conduct, the school, the parents, and relevant members of the IEP team (as determined by the parent and school administrator) shall review all relevant information in the student's file, including the student's IEP, any teacher observations, and any relevant information provided by the parents.

The purpose of this review will be to gather information necessary to conduct the manifestation determination. The reasoning behind the manifestation determination is that students should not be denied special education services because of misbehavior that could be anticipated as a result of their disabilities (Dagley, McGuire, & Evans, 1994; Tucker et al., 1993).

The school-based team conducts a manifestation determination to establish if the misbehavior of a student with a disability was caused by or was directly related to his or her disability (Hartwig & Reusch, 2000; Katsiyannis & Maag, 1998; Yell et al., 2001). IDEA 2004 (IDEA, 20 U.S.C. § 1415(k)(4)(B)) requires that when team members conduct a manifestation determination hearing, they must answer the following two questions: First, was the conduct in question caused by or did it have a *direct and substantial relationship* to the student's disability and second, was the conduct in question the *direct result* of the local educational agency's failure to implement the student's IEP.

This manifestation determination may not be made by administrators or school officials who lack the necessary expertise to make special education placement decisions (*S-1 v. Turlington,* 1981). Courts have consistently held that these decisions may not be made using normal school procedures for disciplining students without disabilities (Guernsey & Klare, 1993); that is, school boards, members of school boards, administrators acting unilaterally, or any one school representative may not make the manifestation determination (OSEP Memorandum 95-16, 1995).

If the determination is made that the disability was not related to the misbehavior and that the IEP is appropriate, the student can be disciplined as any other nondisabled student would be disciplined. For example, the student could be placed on a long-term suspension, expelled, or placed in an interim alternative educational setting (IAES). Students must continue to receive educational services. That is, they must continue to work on their IEP goals and on the general curriculum, although in a different setting. The actual IAES is determined by the IEP team.

If a team determines that a relationship between behavior and disability existed or that a student's IEP was not implemented, the student may not be expelled, although school officials will still be able to initiate change-of-placement procedures. The standard specifies that if a relationship exists between a student's misbehavior and the school's failure to provide or properly implement the IEP or placement, the IEP team must conclude that the misbehavior was a manifestation of the student's disability. In such a situation, the student's IEP team must conduct an FBA and implement a BIP for the student, or review the BIP if one was already in place. Also, the student must be returned to the setting from which he or she was removed, unless the IEP team and the parents agree to a change in placement when they develop the new BIP.

Conducting the Manifestation Determination

Although numerous cases have referred to the manifestation determination, the courts have offered little guidance to schools regarding standards for making this determination. As Dagley, McGuire, and Evans (1994) remarked, "a careful reading of court cases implicating the relationship test creates the suspicion that no one really knows how to conduct the relationship test" (p. 326). In the IDEA Amendments of 1997, Congress provided guidance to IEP teams in conducting manifestation determinations.

When conducting the test, the IEP team shall consider the behavior subject to the disciplinary action and relevant information, including evaluation and diagnostic results and the student's IEP and placement. Moreover, all decisions must be based on an individualized inquiry informed by up-to-date evaluation data. Team members responsible for collecting and interpreting the data should be qualified and knowledgeable regarding the student, the misbehavior, and the disability. Moreover, the data used to inform the decision-making process should be recent and collected from a variety of sources. Data collection procedures should include review of records of past behavioral incidences, interviews, direct observation, behavior rating scales, and standardized instruments. Finally, the team must consider any other relevant information supplied by the student's parents.

Assessing the Relationship

When conducting the manifestation determination, the team should first answer the following question to assess the relationship between misconduct and disability: Was the misconduct caused by the disability, or was there a direct and substantial relationship between the misconduct and the disability? A direct and substantial relationship is a very rigorous standard; the relationship cannot be indirect, such as the student's disability caused low self-esteem, which, in turn, led to the misconduct. Therefore, proving that a student's misconduct was a manifestation of his or her disability may be a difficult standard to meet. Next, the team must address the implementation of the student's IEP (e.g., special education services, related services, supplementary aids and services, program modifications). If the IEP was not implemented as written, the determination is essentially over because such problems indicate the presence of a causal relationship between the misbehavior and the disability.

Courts have clearly indicated what will not constitute proper lines of inquiry in the manifestation determination. First, the determination must be independent of a student's disability classification. The *Turlington* court noted that a causal relationship between misconduct and behavior can occur in any disability area, not just in students with behavioral disabilities; that is, the test should be conducted when suspending or expelling any student protected by the IDEA, regardless of the student's disability classification. Second, the manifestation determination is not an inquiry into whether a student knew the difference between right and wrong. According to the Fifth Circuit Court in *Turlington,* determining whether students are capable of understanding rules or regulations or right from wrong is not tantamount to determining that the student's misconduct was or was not a manifestation of the disability.

The Burden of Proof

If school personnel decide there is no relationship between the behavior and the disability and expel a student, the burden of proof will be placed on the school district to prove there is no relationship. Hartog-Rapp (1985) argues that if the school district is questioned regarding a decision of expulsion, it must prove that there is no causal relationship. Sorenson (1993) contends, however, that if an appropriate group of knowledgeable persons follows appropriate procedures in conducting the manifestation determination, the decision will probably be upheld in the appeals process. Recent rulings by OCR (*Hopewell (VA) Public Schools,* 1994) and the Texas Department of Education (*Beaumont Independent School District,* 1994) upheld school districts' expulsion of students with disabilities for bringing weapons to school. The IEP teams in both cases found no relationship between the behavior and disability, which supports this contention. In conducting the determination, it is important that teams keep thorough documentation of the process.

Interim Alternative Educational Settings

The IDEA requires that a FAPE must be made available to all eligible students with disabilities, even those who have been suspended or expelled from school (IDEA, 20 U.S.C. § 1412(a)(1)). According to the regulations (IDEA Regulations, 34 C.F.R. § 300.520(a)(1)(ii)) and Department of Education guidance (OSEP Questions and Answers, 1999) when a student is suspended in excess of 10 cumulative days in a school year, the school district must continue to provide a FAPE. This means that on the 11th cumulative day of a student's removal from school, educational services must begin. These services are provided in an IAES (IDEA, 20 U.S.C. § 1415(k)(3)).

The IDEA describes three specific circumstances when an IAES may be used for disciplinary purposes. First, an IAES may be used for a short-term disciplinary removal from school for 10 days or less. School officials may unilaterally impose a short-term suspension on a student with a disability for less than 10 consecutive days for violating school rules and for additional removals for not more than 10 consecutive days in a school year for separate incidences of misconduct, as long as these removals do not constitute a change in placement. After 10 days of removal in a school year, educational services must be provided to suspended children. An alternative to out-of-school suspension is placement in an IAES. There is not an absolute limit on the total number of short-term placements in an IAES, as long as FAPE is provided and the proximity and pattern of removal does not constitute a change in placement (Telzrow & Naidu, 2000). Second, an IAES may be used in situations when a student with disabilities is removed from school for a longer term (e.g., long-term suspension, expulsion). Third, an IAES placement can be ordered by a hearing officer.

When a student is placed in an IAES for a short-term disciplinary removal, school officials, in consultation with the student's special education teacher, can determine the content of his or her educational programming (IDEA Regulations, 34 C.F.R. § 121(3)(1)). In such short-term removals it is not required, therefore, that the IEP team determines the services. For a long-term removal in an IAES, however, the student's IEP team must determine the setting and services that will be offered. In both situations, the IAES must (a) allow the student to continue to participate in the general curriculum, although in a different setting; (b) provide the services necessary to allow the student to meet his or her goals from the IEP; and (c) include services designed to keep the misbehavior from reoccurring. Additionally, the school must continue to receive the special education services, supplementary aids and services, program modifications, and related services listed in the IEP, including the interventions to address the student's problem behavior.

Although the use of homebound instruction or tutoring as an IAES is not specifically prohibited by IDEA 1997, homebound placements are problematic (Katsiyannis & Maag, 1998). This is because school districts must continue to provide the services listed in a student's IEP while he or she is in the IAES. For example, if a student receives related services such as counseling, physical therapy, or speech, these services must be part of the student's program in the IAES. Clearly, providing these services in a homebound setting would be difficult. Furthermore, a comment in the proposed regulations suggests that a homebound placement will usually be appropriate for a limited number of students, such as those who are medically fragile and not able to participate in a school setting (IDEA Regulations, 34 C.F.R. § 300.551, Note 1). In answers to a series of questions regarding discipline, the Office of Special Education and Rehabilitative Services (OSERS) noted that in most circumstances homebound instruction is inappropriate as a disciplinary measure; however, the final decision regarding placement must be determined on a case-by-case basis (Department of Education Answers Questions, 1997). Gorn (1999) notes that in hearings, it will be up to school districts to justify homebound placements. If districts have in-school suspension programs or alternative schools, and instead opt for placing a student in a homebound setting, it may be difficult to justify to a hearing officer the use of the more restrictive homebound setting. Finally, in one state level hearing, a school's use of a homebound placement was overturned when the hearing review officer ruled that the homebound placement was inappropriate because it failed to provide the services that previously were included in a student's IEP (*Board of Education of the Akron Central School District,* 1998).

Telzrow and Naidu (2000) suggest that for short-term IAES placements, schools should develop and use in-school suspension programs as their IAESs. Using such programs for an IAES means that students continue to work on their individualized goals and objectives and receive the special education, related services, and behavioral programming that are required by their IEPs. These authors also suggest that school districts consider the use of alternative programs or schools for long-term IAES placements, as long as these programs include the academic and behavioral programming and parental involvement as required in a student's IEP.

The procedural safeguards of the IDEA allow parents who wish to contest a school's special education decisions regarding their child to request a due process hearing. The purpose of a due process hearing is to allow an impartial third party (i.e., the due process hearing officer) to hear both sides of a dispute, examine the issues in relation to the law, and then settle the dispute by imposing a solution on the parties involved. If a parent disagrees with the interim placement or the manifestation determination, or if the school wants to remove a student to a new placement, either party may request a due process hearing. At his or her discretion, the hearing officer can choose to send the student back to his or her current placement or order a change in placement to an IAES for 45 school days if the student is likely to injure others or him or herself.

The Stay-Put Provision

When parents disagree with a change in placement proposed by a school district, the IDEA's stay-put provision prohibits the district from unilaterally changing placement. This provision states that "during the pendency of any proceedings. . . unless the [school] and the parents. . . otherwise agree, the child shall remain in the then current placement of such child" (IDEA, 20 U.S.C. § 1415(e)(3)). The purpose of the stay-put provision is to continue students in their current placement (i.e., their placement before the dispute arose) until the dispute is resolved. The stay-put provision effectively operates to limit the actions of the school district (Tucker et al., 1993). The court in *Zvi D. v. Ambach* (1982) stated that the stay-put procedures operated as an automatic preliminary injunction because a request for a hearing automatically requires that schools maintain a student's placement. It is only permissible to move a student during the pendency of a hearing when the parents and school agree on an interim change of placement.

IDEA 2004 significantly altered the stay-put rule. First, school officials may move a student to an interim alternative educational setting (IAES) for no more than 45 school days for the aforementioned infractions. If a parent objects to this placement change and requests a due process hearing, the stay-put rule would normally function to keep a student in the previous placement during the hearing. With the new language in IDEA 2004, the stay-put placement is the IAES; that is, a student will remain in that setting during the pendency of the hearing.

If school personnel maintain that a student with disabilities is dangerous to other students if he or she remains in the current placement, the school district may request an expedited hearing to challenge the continued placement. The hearing officer may change a student's placement to an interim alternative setting for 45 school days if school officials convince the hearing officer that the student, in the current placement, is very likely to injure him- or herself or others. In making this decision, the hearing officer will consider whether the school has made reasonable efforts to minimize the risk of harm in the student's current placement and if the current placement enables the student to continue to participate in the general education curriculum.

Disciplining Students Not Yet Eligible for Special Education

IDEA 2004 provides protections for students with disabilities who have not been determined to be eligible for services under the IDEA and who violated a code of student conduct. If a student's parents assert that their child is protected by the IDEA, the student will only be protected by the law if the school had knowledge that the child had an IDEA disability before the behavior incident that precipitated the disciplinary action.

For a school to be determined to have prior knowledge, school personnel must have known of or suspected that the child had a disability because the parent expressed a concern in writing to school administrative or supervisory personnel or to the child's teacher that the child had a disability and needed special education services. Additionally if the parents referred their child for a special education evaluation, a school will be determined to have prior knowledge. Finally, if the child's teacher or other school personnel had expressed specific concerns about the child's behavior directly to the special education director or to other supervisory personnel, the school will be deemed to have prior knowledge. In such situations students may be protected under the IDEA even if they are not currently eligible. The only exception to this rule is if the child's parent refused to consent to an evaluation that the school sought. If the school had no prior knowledge of a possible disability, the school may discipline the child who exhibited similar problem behavior. If a parent of a child who is being disciplined requests an evaluation for special education during the disciplinary period, the school must conduct the evaluation in an expedited manner.

In a memorandum, OSEP took the position that students not previously identified as eligible under the IDEA could not invoke the stay-put provision to avoid disciplinary sanctions such as expulsion (OSEP Memorandum 95-16, 1995). In situations in which a request for an evaluation or due process hearing was made following a disciplinary suspension or expulsion, school districts were not obligated to reinstate students to in-school status during the pendency of the evaluation or hearing. The stay-put setting in such situations would be the out-of-school placement.

Rodiriecus L. v. Waukegan School District, 1996

In an important ruling, the U.S. Court of Appeals for the Seventh Circuit upheld the OSEP position regarding students' avoiding discipline by invoking the procedural protections of the IDEA. In *Rodiriecus L. v. Waukegan School District* (1996), the circuit court held that a student in general education could not avoid expulsion by claiming protection under the IDEA unless school district officials knew or reasonably should have known that the student had a disability. The court held that

> If the stay-put provision is automatically applied to every student who files an application for special education, then an avenue will be open for disruptive, nondisabled students to forestall any attempts at routine discipline by simply requesting a disability evaluation and demanding to "stay-put," thus disrupting the educational goals of an already overburdened . . . public school system. . . . However . . . there may arise circumstances where a truly disabled child, who has not as yet been identified by the school . . . or has been misidentified, is improperly denied appropriate public education. In those situations, the stay-put provision is necessary to keep the student in school until a hearing officer has resolved the dispute. (p. 562)

In this case, the court believed that the school district had no reason to suspect that the student had a disability, even though he had a poor academic record and a history of disciplinary contacts. That the student may have had a disability had never been suggested until he was recommended for expulsion.

Additionally, the Seventh Circuit Court offered guidance to other courts in determining if school officials should have known that a student had a disability and was therefore entitled to the procedural protections of the IDEA. Courts should weigh the following four factors in making such decisions: (a) the likelihood that the student will succeed on the merits of his or her claim; (b) the irreparability of the harm to the student if the stay-put provision is not invoked; (c) the relative harm to the student in comparison to the harm to the district; and (d) the public interest. Furthermore, students must show they reasonably would have been found eligible for special education through the IDEA's administrative procedures.

Honig Injunctions

If the parents refuse to agree to a change of placement, however, and the school is convinced that the student is truly dangerous, school officials can request an injunction or temporary restraining order (TRO) from a hearing officer to remove the student from the school environment. A TRO issued to remove a dangerous student with disabilities from school has been frequently referred to as a *Honig* injunction. When an injunction is issued, schools may use the time when a student is not in school to determine if a change of placement is needed or to conduct a manifestation determination.

Obtaining an Injunction

In *Honig,* the Supreme Court stated that any action brought by a school district to obtain a TRO will carry a presumption in favor of a student's current educational placement. School officials can only overcome this preference by "showing that maintaining [the] child in his or her current placement is substantially likely to result in injury either to himself or herself, or to others" (p. 606). Prior to the IDEA Amendments of 1997, *Honig* injunctions could only be granted by courts, but now such injunctions can be granted by hearing officers. School officials must convince a hearing officer that unless a student is removed from the current placement, the student is dangerous and substantially likely to injure himself or others. Additionally, school officials must prove that reasonable steps have been taken to minimize the risk of harm in the current setting; that the current IEP is appropriate; that the interim setting allows the student to participate in the general education curriculum, although in a different setting; and that the student can continue to work on IEP goals. Furthermore, the school must demonstrate these factors with substantial evidence, which the IDEA defines as being beyond a preponderance of the evidence (IDEA Amendments, 1997).

The substantial evidence requirement would seem to be a difficult threshold to meet. Nevertheless, in a number of post-*Honig* rulings schools have been granted discipline-related TROs (e.g., *Binghamton City School District v. Borgna,* 1991; *Board of Education of Township High School District No. 211 v. Corral,* 1989; *Board of Education of Township No. 211 v. Linda Kurtz-Imig,* 1989; *Prince William County School Board v. Willis,* 1989; *Texas City Independent School District v. Jorstad,* 1990).

Texas Independent School District v. Jorstad, 1990

In *Texas Independent School District v. Jorstad* (1990), a school was granted a TRO after parents refused a change in placement. The student, classified as seriously emotionally disturbed (SED), was placed in a regular classroom with an individual aide and resource room services. Following a number of serious behavioral problems in the classroom, the student's IEP team met to change the student's placement to a more restrictive setting. The student had been physically aggressive to the teacher and other students and had attempted to escape the classroom by jumping from a second-story window. All school personnel working with the student believed that he was an extreme danger to himself and others. The parents did not agree with the more restrictive placement, and neither did the boy's psychologist, who believed placement in a more restrictive setting would cause a regression in his social skills. The parents requested an administrative hearing. The case went before the federal district court for the Southern District of Texas.

The federal court, citing the stay-put rule, held that only under limited circumstance could a school change the placement of a student during the pendency of a due process hearing. A change of placement would only be permitted if the school could show that maintaining a student in the current placement was substantially likely to result in injury to the student or others in the environment. The court concluded that in this situation the student would not suffer any realistic harm by being placed in the more restrictive setting pending completion of the administrative hearing. However, the court viewed the potential for harm to others as substantial. Thus, a TRO was issued and the school district was allowed to change the student's placement.

Light v. Parkway School District, 1994

In *Light v. Parkway School District* (1994), the U.S. Court of Appeals for the Eighth Circuit established a two-part test for determining the appropriateness of removing a disruptive student with disabilities from school. In its ruling, the court interpreted the U.S. Supreme Court's decision in *Honig v. Doe.* The court delineated circumstances under which a school can seek an injunction to remove a disruptive student. The case involved a 13-year-old girl, Lauren Light, with moderate mental retardation, autism, and a history of aggressiveness toward students and staff. The student was enrolled in a self-contained classroom with full integration in art, physical education, and computer education. A full-time aide and a special education teacher were assigned to the student during the school day. Despite the presence of the aide, special education teacher, regular classroom teacher, and a consultant selected by the girl's parents, Lauren's aggressiveness escalated. The parents of other students in the class began to complain that Lauren's behavior was disrupting the educational environment and creating a dangerous situation. The IEP team met and recommended a change in placement. The girl's parents requested a due process hearing, thereby invoking the stay-put rule. Before the due process hearing was held, Lauren hit a student. She was suspended from school for 10 days.

Following the suspension, the Lights sued in federal court, contending that Lauren had been denied due process. The school district also went to court to seek an injunction to remove Lauren as a substantial risk to herself and others. The federal district court granted the injunction. The Lights appealed to the Eighth Circuit Court, contending that the school had to prove that Lauren was truly dangerous before the school could remove her. They also stated that under *Honig,* the school could only remove a student who intended to injure another student.

The court, citing the records kept by the school regarding Lauren's behavior, asserted that students do not actually have to cause harm before a school may remove them; rather, students only have to be substantially *likely* to cause harm. The court pointed to the school district's record of efforts to modify Lauren's behavior as an attempt to accommodate the student. Finally, the court established a two-part test to determine the appropriateness of a student removal (see Figure 14.2 for the *Light v. Parkway* two-part test). First, the school must determine and show that the student is substantially likely to cause injury. Second, the school must show that it has done all that it reasonably can to reduce the risk of injury and to modify a student's behavior. If a school can prove these two points, it will be issued a temporary injunction to remove a student from school.

Referral to Law Enforcement and Courts

School personnel may report to police a crime committed by a student with a disability who is protected by the IDEA. Moreover, law enforcement and judicial authorities can exercise their authority under the law when confronted with a crime committed by a student who is in special education. Furthermore, the school personnel can transmit copies of all the student's special education and disciplinary records to law enforcement.

Figure 14.2
The *Light v. Parkway* Two-Part Test

Part One: Maintaining the student in the current educational placement is likely to result in injury to the student or peers (actual injury is not required).

Part Two: The school district has made reasonable attempts to minimize the risk of injury.

The Legal Status of Disciplinary Procedures

In *Honig,* the U.S. Supreme Court ruled that typical disciplinary procedures—those that are often used for establishing school discipline, such as restriction of privileges, detention, and removal of students to study carrels—may be used with students with disabilities. Such disciplinary procedures do not change placement and are generally not restricted by the courts. A significant restriction exists, however, against certain types of discipline that may result in a unilateral change in placement. To clarify which disciplinary practices are legal and which are not, disciplinary procedures may be placed into one of three categories: permitted, controlled, and prohibited (Yell, Cline, & Bradley, 1995; Yell & Peterson, 1995).

Permitted Procedures

Permitted disciplinary procedures include those practices that are part of a school district's disciplinary plan and are commonly used with all students. These procedures are unobtrusive and do not result in a change of placement or the denial of the right to a FAPE. Such procedures include verbal reprimands, warnings, contingent observation (a form of time-out where the student is briefly removed to a location where he or she can observe but not participate in an activity), exclusionary time-out, response cost (the removal of points or privileges when a student misbehaves), detention, and the temporary delay or withdrawal of goods, services, or activities (e.g., recess, lunch). As long as these procedures do not interfere significantly with the student's IEP goals and are not applied in a discriminatory manner, they are permitted. In general, if the disciplining of a student with disabilities does not result in a change of placement, the methods of discipline available to schools are the same for all students (Guernsey & Klare, 1993). In the case of emergency situations, procedures such as physical restraint or immediate suspension are permissible.

Controlled Procedures

Controlled procedures are those interventions that the courts have held to be permissible as long as they are used appropriately. The difficulty with these practices is that if they are used in an inappropriate manner, they can result in interference with

IEP goals or objectives or in a unilateral change in placement. Controlled procedures include disciplinary techniques such as seclusion/isolation time-out, in-school suspension, and out-of-school suspension.

Seclusion/Isolation Time-out

Time-out is a disciplinary procedure frequently used by teachers of students with disabilities. Time-out generally involves placing a student in a less reinforcing environment for a period of time following inappropriate behavior. A type of time-out that should be classified as a controlled procedure is seclusion/isolation time-out (Yell, 1994): The student, contingent on misbehavior, is required to leave the classroom and enter a separate time-out room for a brief period. Two federal court cases considered the legality of seclusion/isolation time-out.

In *Dickens v. Johnson County Board of Education* (1987), a federal district court ruled that the use of time-out with the plaintiff, Ronnie Dickens, was only a de minimus (trivial or minor) interference with the student's education. The use of time-out did not, therefore, violate the plaintiff's right to an education. While extremely harsh and abusive use of time-out may violate a student's rights, the court found that the legitimate and reasonable use of time-out was a particularly appropriate disciplinary procedure to use with students with disabilities because it would not deprive them of their right to an education.

Hayes v. Unified School District No. 377 (1987) involved the use of seclusion/isolation time-out with two students with behavioral disorders. The teacher used a system of written warnings to allow the students time to alter their behavior to escape time-out. If the students received three warnings, they were placed in a time-out room. The court ruled that the teacher had used time-out to ensure the safety of others, protect the educational environment from disruptive behavior, and teach the students more appropriate behavior. According to the court, the appropriate use of seclusion/isolation time-out is not prohibited by the IDEA.

OCR affirmed the use of time-out following an investigation of a complaint against a school district's use of this procedure (*Marion County (FL) School District,* 1993). The investigation revealed that the school district properly followed state and local educational policies, established a disciplinary policy that included time-out procedures for students with and without disabilities, incorporated behavior management plans into students' IEPs that included the use of time-out, and kept records on the use of time-out. Furthermore, parents were informed about the possible use of time-out and agreed to its use. Concluding that the school district was not in violation of Section 504 or the Americans with Disabilities Act, OCR stated that time-out prevented the necessity of using more restrictive measures to control behaviors. When time-out escalates to the level of punishment that infringes on a student's personal safety rights and appropriate education, however, it may be a violation of Section 504 or the IDEA (Cline, 1994). In a 1991 OCR ruling, for example, the excessive and prolonged use of time-out was ruled a violation of Section 504 (*McCracken County School District,* 1991).

In-School Suspension

In-school suspension (ISS) programs require the suspended student to serve the suspension period in the school, usually in a classroom isolated from schoolmates. During ISS, the student works on appropriate educational material provided by the teacher. Several advantages of using ISS are that (a) it avoids the possibility of the suspended student roaming the community unsupervised; (b) the student being disciplined is segregated from the general school population; and (c) the student continues to receive an education during the suspension period (Yell, 1990). In *Hayes v. Unified School District No. 377* (1987), a school district's use of ISS was challenged. The plaintiffs, who had not consented to its use, argued that ISS, which sometimes lasted as long as 5 days, constituted an illegal change of placement and a deprivation of due process. The court noted that the school had clearly specified the behaviors that would lead to ISS, thereby providing the students with adequate notice to protect themselves from being placed in ISS. The court also ruled that as long as the school continued to provide an appropriate education, ISS for 5 days did not constitute an illegal change of placement.

In a ruling regarding a school district's use of ISS, OCR determined that ISS was being used appropriately (*Chester County (TN) School District,* 1990). The complainant alleged that the district had improperly placed special education students in ISS for periods in excess of 10 days and had failed to provide adequate notice of these disciplinary actions to parents. OCR determined that the district had established formal procedures regarding their disciplinary policies (including the use of ISS), provided parents with written explanations of these procedures, and adequately notified parents prior to the use of ISS. OCR also stated that the ISS program, when used for 10 days or more (in this case 28 days), did not constitute a change in placement because the school district provided a program that was "comparable, in nature and quality, to the educational services regularly provided to special education students" (p. 301). The ISS instructor was a certified special education teacher, usually the number of students in ISS was less than six, and lesson plans were sent daily or weekly from the student's regular and special education teachers. OCR confirmed that the goals and objectives on the students' IEPs were followed when students were in ISS. Figure 14.3 lists the necessary components of a legally sound ISS program.

Despite the fact that ISS programs remove students with disabilities from their classrooms, the courts have not considered them either long-term suspensions, expulsions, or changes of placement as long as the programs are comparable to the educational program regularly offered to students (Gorn, 1999). Schools, however, must not use ISS as a de facto long-term suspension or expulsion. In such cases, ISS may be viewed as an illegal change of placement.

Out-of-School Suspension

Out-of-school suspension generally refers to a short-term exclusion from school for a specified period of time, accompanied by a cessation of educational services. Numerous cases have ruled on the use of out-of-school suspension with students with disabilities (*Doe v. Koger,* 1979; *Doe v. Maher,* 1986; *Honig v. Doe,* 1988; *Kaelin v. Grubbs,* 1982;

Figure 14.3
Legally Sound In-School Suspension Policies

- Have written policy informing students and parents when violation of rules may result in student being placed in ISS.
- Provide a warning to students when their behavior may lead to ISS.
- Inform parents when student is placed in ISS.
- Supervise ISS with paraprofessional or a teacher.
- Continue to provide an appropriate education (e.g., have student's teacher prepare lesson plans, provide materials).
- Document in-school suspension.

S-1 v. Turlington, 1981; *Stuart v. Nappi,* 1978; *Victoria L. v. District School Board,* 1984). According to the courts, expulsion and indefinite out-of-school suspensions are changes in placement and cannot be made unilaterally even in cases where students present a danger to themselves or others. Courts have stated, however, that schools can use short-term suspensions of up to 10 days. Suspension from transportation to school, unless alternative means of transportation are available, should be treated as part of the 10 days (*Mobile County (AL) School District,* 1991). Sorenson (1993) suggests that schools adopt a 10-day suspension policy. The IDEA Amendments of 1997 specifically allow school officials to suspend students with disabilities for up to 10 school days. Suspensions for longer than 10 days constitute a change of placement under the IDEA, and if a student's parents do not agree to a change in placement, the IDEA procedural safeguards must be followed.

Time-out, in-school suspension, and out-of-school suspension are permitted if used appropriately. Basic due process rights, such as notice and hearing, must be given to students prior to the use of suspension. It is important in using such procedures that schools not abuse or overuse them, as these could be interpreted as unilateral changes of placement or discriminatory by the courts.

Prohibited Procedures

Disciplinary procedures that result in a unilateral change in placement are prohibited. Thus, expulsions (i.e., the exclusion from school for an indefinite period of time) and long-term suspensions are illegal if made without following the IDEA's procedural safeguards. In many states, corporal punishment is illegal and, therefore, a prohibited procedure.

Long-Term Suspension and Expulsion

If the IEP team determines that a student's misbehavior and his or her disability are not related, long-term suspensions and expulsions are legal. However, even when no relationship is found and an expulsion is made in accordance with procedural rules, there cannot be a complete cessation of educational services. If the IEP team determines that the misbehavior and disability are related, long-term suspensions and expulsions are not legal.

Attempts to bypass the suspension and expulsion rules have not been looked upon favorably by the courts or administrative agencies. OCR has stated that a series of suspensions cumulatively totaling more than 10 days constitutes a change of placement if the results create a pattern of exclusion (OCR Memorandum, 1988). Serial and indefinite suspensions, therefore, are prohibited. A series of five suspensions totaling 22 days over a school year was found to be a pattern of exclusions that created a significant change of placement for a student with disabilities (*Cobb County (GA) School District,* 1993). In *Big Beaver Falls Area School District v. Jackson* (1993), a Pennsylvania court ruled that a school district, in violation of the IDEA and state law, had effectively suspended a student by continually assigning her to ISS. Rather than serve the ISS, the student was allowed to leave school, which she usually did. According to the court, the school continually assigned the ISS knowing that the student would leave school; therefore, the action amounted to a de facto expulsion in violation of the IDEA.

Corporal Punishment

One of the most controversial disciplinary procedures is corporal punishment. Courts have heard many challenges to the use of this type of disciplinary action in schools. In 1977 the U.S. Supreme Court, in *Ingraham v. Wright,* held that corporal punishment in public schools was a routine disciplinary procedure not proscribed by constitutional law. The U.S. Court of Appeals for the Fourth Circuit, in *Hall v. Tawney* (1980), stated that brutal, demeaning, or harmful corporal punishment would be a violation of a student's substantive due process rights. The court applied the standard of reasonableness in holding that corporal punishment that is reasonable is legitimate, but if it is not reasonable (e.g., excessive) it is illegal.

Many states have made the use of corporal punishment illegal. Furthermore, in states where corporal punishment is not prohibited, many local school districts proscribe its use. In many schools throughout the country, therefore, corporal punishment is illegal. According to Weber (2002), even in states where corporal punishment is legal, its use might be a violation of Section 504 and the IDEA.

Weapons

A topic that has received a great deal of attention recently is the issue of school officials' authority in disciplining students with disabilities who bring weapons to school. The Gun-Free Schools Act (GFSA), which was enacted as part of the Goals 2000: Educate America Act (20 U.S.C. § 5801 *et seq.*), essentially required school districts to expel any student who brings a gun to school. According to the statutory language,

No assistance may be provided to any local educational agency under this Act unless such agency has in effect a policy requiring the expulsion from school for a period of not less than one year of any student who is determined to have brought a weapon to school under the jurisdiction of the agency except such policy may allow the chief administering officer of the agency to modify such expulsion requirement for a student on a case-by-case basis. (Gun-Free Schools Act, 20 U.S.C.S. § 3351(a)(1))

The Gun-Free Schools Act and Students with Disabilities

A policy guidance statement issued by the U.S. Department of Education stated that the FAPE and stay-put requirements of the IDEA prohibited the automatic removal of any student with a disability for disability-related misbehavior (Gun-Free Schools Act Guidance, 1995). This position appeared to be at odds with the expulsion requirement of the GFSA. According to the statement, no conflict between the laws existed because administrators were allowed to consider discipline on a case-by-case basis; therefore, administrators could take the laws affecting students with disabilities into account. Congress sought to alter this apparent discrepancy with the Jeffords amendment to the IDEA (IDEA, 20 U.S.C. § 1415(e)(3)). This amendment allowed schools to immediately and unilaterally remove students with disabilities who bring guns to school to an interim alternative setting for up to 45 days. The primary effect of the law was to modify the stay-put provision of the IDEA. During the 45-day period, the school and parents may decide on a permanent placement. The school may also convene a team to conduct a manifestation determination. If the result of the determination is that the misbehavior was not a manifestation of the disability, a student may be expelled or receive a long-term suspension. If parents request a due process hearing to contest the placement in the interim setting or an expulsion, the school may keep the student in the alternative placement during the pendency of the hearing.

School District Responsibilities

From the body of case law on discipline, as well as the IDEA 1997 and 2004, several important school district responsibilities can be extrapolated. These responsibilities are listed in Figure 14.4.

Formulate and Disseminate Discipline Policies and Procedures

School districts should develop policies and procedures for ensuring that schools maintain safe and orderly environments where teachers can teach and students can learn. Procedures for disciplining students to maintain safety and order, to reduce misbehavior, and to teach appropriate behavior are essential. Such policies must clearly delineate behavioral expectations of students and the consequences for not conforming to these expectations. If the consequences include suspension and expulsion, all students are entitled to basic due process rights before exclusion occurs. For suspensions of 10 days or less, students must be afforded oral or written notice of the charges and the opportunity to respond to these charges. For suspensions in

Figure 14.4
School District Responsibilities in Discipline for Students with Disabilities

1. Formulate and disseminate discipline policies and procedures. Ensure that parents have access to and understanding of the school district policies.

   - *Expectations for student conduct.* Should include statements regarding student property and the diminished right of student privacy in regards to lockers and school property.

   - *Rules and consequences.* Delineate inappropriate student behavior and conduct through school rules. Specify consequences for violating school rules.

   - *Due process rights.* If students are suspended for 10 days or less, notify students of charges and give them an opportunity to respond. If suspended more than 10 days or expelled, notification, opportunity to respond, and more formalized hearing procedures are required.

2. Recognize the dual disciplinary standard.

   - *IDEA* students. Suspension of change of placement for 10 days is allowed. No long-term suspension or expulsion is allowed unless the behavior is unrelated to the disability (can only be determined in a manifestation hearing). No cessation of educational services. If a student brings a weapon or uses or sells drugs, he or she may be placed in an IAES for up to 45 days.

   - *Section 504* students. Suspension of change of placement for 10 days is allowed. No long-term suspension or expulsion is allowed unless the behavior is unrelated to the disability (can only be determined in a manifestation hearing). Cessation of educational services is allowed (check state guidelines).

3. Include a behavior intervention plan in students' IEPs or Section 504 accommodation plans. The plan should be based on a functional assessment, including positive procedures and consequences. Delineate consequences that may be used (e.g., in-school suspension, time-out) and a crisis intervention plan.

4. Document behavioral incidents. In situations involving problem behavior, document in writing disciplinary actions. Notify school administrators and parents.

5. Evaluate the effectiveness of disciplinary procedures and interventions.

excess of 10 days, in addition to a notice and hearing, students must be provided with the opportunity for a more formal hearing process. When students present a danger to themselves or others, they can be removed from the school immediately, with notice and hearing to follow. When students violate the law, the legal authorities should be informed (Maloney, 1994).

Schools should also develop policies regarding search and seizure of students and property. Such policies should include statements addressing the diminished right of student privacy in school lockers and on school property.

It is extremely important that school administrators, teachers, and other personnel understand the district's disciplinary policies and procedures. Steps should

Figure 14.5
Manifestation Determination

- The school district, parent, and relevant members of the IEP team must determine if

    (1) the conduct in question was caused by, or had a direct and substantial relationship to, the students' disability, or

    (2) the conduct in question was the direct result of the school district's failure to implement the IEP.

---

also be taken to ensure that parents have access to, and understand, information in the school district's discipline policy. Methods to ensure parental access include mailing discipline policy brochures to district parents and having teachers explain the procedures in parent-teacher conferences.

Recognize the Dual Disciplinary Standard

Courts have repeatedly held that students with disabilities are not immune from a school's normal disciplinary procedures. Students with disabilities, however, have special protections against any procedures that result in a unilateral change of placement. Expulsions and long-term or indefinite suspensions are changes in placement and cannot be made without following the procedural safeguards of the IDEA or Section 504. If a school decides to use long-term suspension or expulsion, the IEP team must meet to determine the relationship between the behavior and the student's disability. A school district cannot expel a student on the basis of misbehavior caused by the disability.

Because of these additional protections, it is crucial that school officials know which students are classified as having disabilities under the IDEA and Section 504. A disciplinary meeting may involve many issues and concerns. Two issues that must be resolved in the meeting concern the appropriateness of the IEP and the manifestation determination (Cline, 1994). Figure 14.5 summarizes the questions teams must answer when conducting a manifestation determination.

Students with disabilities who have a tendency to misbehave must have behavior goals and objectives and a disciplinary plan included in their IEP (Hartwig, Robertshaw, & Reusch, 1991; Senate Report, 1997). This requirement, which applies to all students in special education regardless of their disability category, was included in the IDEA Amendments of 1997. The plan must be based on a functional behavioral assessment and should cover strategies, including proactive positive behavioral interventions and supports, to address the behavior problems. Additionally, because these elements would be discussed at an IEP meeting, the plan would have an increased probability of success because of parental support and participation. The intervention plan would also be less likely to be legally challenged and more likely to meet legal muster if challenged.

The discipline plan for each student should delineate expected behaviors, inappropriate behaviors, and positive and negative consequences for the behaviors (Hartwig & Reusch, 2000). The disciplinary process that will be followed, including intervention techniques, should be outlined in the plan. The plan should also include procedures for dealing with a behavioral crisis. A sample behavior intervention plan is represented in Figure 14.6.

Behavior intervention plans must be based on legitimate disciplinary procedures. To ensure that procedures are used reasonably, schools should use disciplinary methods in accordance with the principle of hierarchical application. According to Braaten, Simpson, Rosell, and Reilly (1988), this principle requires that school officials use more intrusive disciplinary procedures (e.g., in-school suspension) only after less intrusive procedures (e.g., warnings and reprimands) have failed.

Document Disciplinary Actions Taken and Evaluate Their Effectiveness

Maloney (1994) contends that in the law, "if it isn't written down, it didn't happen" (p. 4). In disciplining students with disabilities, therefore, it is crucial to keep written records of all discussions and of all disciplinary actions taken. An examination of court cases and administrative rulings in disciplinary matters indicates that in many instances, decisions turned on the quality of the school's records. For example, in *Cole v. Greenfield-Central Community Schools* (1986), *Dickens v. Johnson County Board of Education* (1987), and *Hayes v. Unified School District No. 377* (1987), the thoroughness of the schools' record keeping played a significant part in the court's decisions in favor of the schools. In *Oberti v. Board of Education of the Borough of Clementon School District* (1993), the court decided against the school district, partly because no behavior intervention plan to improve the student's behavior in the regular classroom was included in the IEP. Although the school district maintained that it did have a behavior intervention plan, because it was not written down, it did not exist in the eyes of the court.

Records on emergency disciplinary actions are also important. Such records should contain an adequate description of the incident and disciplinary action taken, as well as the signatures of witnesses present. Figure 14.7 is an example of a behavior incident report.

Finally, it is important that teachers evaluate the effectiveness of disciplinary procedures used. There are a number of reasons for collecting data on an ongoing basis. To make decisions about whether an intervention is reducing target behaviors, teachers need data collected during the course of the intervention. If formative data are not collected, teachers will not know with certainty if a given procedure is achieving the desired results. Teachers are accountable to supervisors and parents, and data collection is useful for accountability purposes. From a legal standpoint, it is imperative that teachers collect such data. Anecdotal information is not readily accepted by courts, but data-based decisions certainly are viewed much more favorably.

Figure 14.6

A Sample Behavior Intervention Plan

Behavior Intervention Plan

Student: _____   Date of Meeting: _____

Teacher: _____   Administrator: _____

Teacher: _____   _____

Parents: _____   _____

Others: _____   _____

Operational description of the problem behaviors:

Antecedents of problem behaviors:

Positive procedures to teach replacement behaviors:

Procedures to ensure that inappropriate behavior is not reinforced:

Methods of evaluation:

Criteria for success:

Date the plan will be evaluated:

Figure 14.7
A Sample Behavior Incident Report

Behavior Incident Report

Student: _____   Date: _____

Teacher: _____   Time: _____

Observed behavior prior to the incident:

Description of incident:

Parents notified: Yes   No

Description of positive approaches to correct behavior:

Did behavior endanger the safety of students or disrupt the learning environment?
If yes, how?

Summary

Specific guidelines regarding the discipline of students with disabilities were not written into federal law (e.g., the IDEA, Section 504) until the IDEA Amendments of 1997. Prior to that time, school districts had to operate on guidelines extrapolated from the decisions of administrative agencies (e.g., OSEP, OCR) and case law.

Students with disabilities are not immune from a school's disciplinary procedure. Schools may use procedures such as reprimands, detention, restriction of privileges, response cost, in-school suspension (if the student's education is continued), and out-of-school suspensions (10 days or less) as long as the procedures are not

Figure 14.7
Continued

Intervention(s) used:
- ☐ Warning
- ☐ Response cost
- ☐ Exclusion time-out
- ☐ Isolation/seclusion time-out
- ☐ Overcorrection
- ☐ Physical restraint
- ☐ In-school suspension
- ☐ Out-of-school suspension
- ☐ Other

Reasons for the choice of intervention:

Results of intervention:

Remarks:

Signatures

Teacher: _____   Witness: _____

Principal: _____   Parents: _____

abused or applied in a discriminatory manner. Disciplinary procedures that effectively change a student's placement are, however, not legal if not done in accordance with the procedural safeguards afforded students with disabilities by the IDEA and Section 504. Such procedures include suspension (if over 10 days) and expulsion.

When determining whether or not to use a long-term suspension or expulsion, the school must convene the student's IEP team and other qualified personnel to determine the relationship between the student's misbehavior and the disability. If there is a relationship, the student cannot be expelled. If the team determines that no relationship exists, the student may be expelled. Even when an expulsion follows a determination of no relationship and is done in accordance with procedural safeguards, there cannot be a complete cessation of educational services.

A school district cannot unilaterally exclude a student with disabilities from school, regardless of the degree of danger or disruption. School districts may go to court, however, to obtain a temporary restraining order to have the student removed from school. The school will bear the burden of proof when attempting to get a TRO. If students with disabilities bring weapons to school or use, possess, or sell illegal drugs, school officials may unilaterally remove them to an interim alternative setting for 45 school days. During this time the IEP team should meet to consider appropriate actions.

Disciplining students with disabilities is a complex issue. In addition to observing the due process rights that protect all students, administrators and teachers must be aware of the additional safeguards afforded students with disabilities by the IDEA. In using disciplinary procedures with students with disabilities, educators should be aware of state and local policies regarding discipline, develop and inform parents of school discipline policies, and continuously evaluate the effectiveness of disciplinary procedures. When disciplinary procedures are used, proper documentation is critical. Teachers must collect formative data to determine if the procedures are having the desired effect on student behavior. Finally, disciplinary procedures should be used reasonably and for legitimate educational purposes; they must not compromise a student's FAPE or be applied in a discriminatory manner.

For Further Information

Gorn, S. (1999). *What do I do when: The answer book on discipline.* Horsham, PA: LRP Publications.

Hartwig, E. P., & Reusch, G. M. (2000). *Discipline in the schools.* Horsham, PA: LRP Publications.

Yell, M. L., Rozalski, M. E., & Drasgow, E. (2001). Disciplining students with disabilities. *Focus on Exceptional Children, 33*(9), 1–20.

References

Alexander, K., & Alexander, M. D. (1984). *The law of schools, students, and teachers in a nutshell.* St. Paul, MN: West Publishing.

Alexander, K., & Alexander, M. D. (2002). *American public school law* (3rd ed.). St. Paul, MN: West Publishing.

Bartlett, L. (1989). Disciplining handicapped students: Legal issues in light of *Honig v. Doe. Exceptional Children, 55,* 357–366.

Beaumont Independent School District, 21 IDELR 261 (SEA TX, 1994).

Big Beaver Falls Area School District v. Jackson, 624 A.2d 806 (Pa. Cmwlth. 1993).

Binghamton City School District v. Borgna, 1991 W. L. 29985 (N.D.N.Y. 1991).

Board of Education of the Akron Central School District, 28 IDELR 909 (SEA 1998).

Board of Education of Township High School District No. 211 v. Corral, 441 EHLR Dec. 390 (N.D. Ill. 1989).

Board of Education of Township No. 211 v. Linda Kurtz-Imig, 16 EHLR Dec. 17 (N.D. Ill. 1989).

Braaten, S., Simpson, R., Rosell, J., & Reilly, T. (1988). Using punishment with exceptional children: A dilemma for educators. *Teaching Exceptional Children, 20,* 79–81.

Chester County (TN) School District, 17 EHLR 301 (OCR, 1990).

Cline, D. (1994). *Fundamentals of special education law: Emphasis on discipline.* Arden Hills, MN: Behavioral Institute for Children and Adolescents.

Cobb County (GA) School District, 20 IDELR 1171 (OCR 1993).

Cole v. Greenfield-Central Community Schools, 657 F. Supp. 56 (S.D. Ind. 1986).

Concerned Parents and Citizens for Continuing Education at Malcolm X v. The New York City Board of Education, 629 F.2d 751 (2nd Cir. 1980).

Curwin, R., & Mendler, A. (1999). *Discipline with dignity.* Alexandria, VA: Association for Supervision and Curriculum Development.

Dagley, D. L., McGuire, M. D., & Evans, C. W. (1994). The relationship test in the discipline of disabled students. *Education Law Reporter, 88,* 13–31.

Dickens v. Johnson County Board of Education, 661 F. Supp. 155 (E.D. Tenn. 1987).

Dise, J. H., Iyer, C. S., & Noorman, J. J. (1996). *Searches of students, lockers, and automobiles.* Detroit: Educational Risk.

Doe v. Koger, 480 F. Supp. 225 (N.D. Ind. 1979).

Doe v. Maher, 793 F.2d 1470 (9th Cir. 1986).

Doe v. Rockingham School Board, 658 F. Supp. 403 (W.D. Va. 1987).

Drasgow, E., & Yell, M. L. (2002). School-wide behavior support: Legal implications. *Child and Family Behavior Therapy, 24,* 129–145.

Drasgow, E., Yell, M. L., Bradley, R., & Shriner, J. G. (1999). The IDEA Amendments of 1997: A school-wide model for conducting functional behavioral assessments and developing behavior intervention plans. *Education and Treatment of Children, 22,* 244–266.

Dunlap, G., & Koegel, R. L. (1999). Welcoming Introduction. *Journal of Positive Behavior Interventions, 1,* 2–3.

Eric J. v. Huntsville City Board of Education, 22 IDELR 858 (N.D. Ala. 1995).

Goals 2000: Educate America Act, 20 U.S.C.S. § 5801 *et seq.*

Gorn, S. (1999). *What do I do when: The answer book on discipline.* Horsham, PA: LRP Publications.

Goss v. Lopez, 419 U.S. 565 (1975).

Grannis v. Ordean, 234 U.S. 383 (1914).

Guernsey, T. F., & Klare, K. (1993). *Special education law.* Durham, NC: Carolina Academic Press.

Gun-Free Schools Act, 20 U.S.C. § 1415(e)(3).

Gun-Free Schools Act Guidance. (1995, January 20). U.S. Department of Education, Office of Elementary and Secondary Education, Assistant Secretary, Thomas W. Payzant. Washington, DC: Author.

Hacienda La Puente Unified School District of Los Angeles v. Honig, 976 F.2d 487 (9th Cir. 1992).

Hall v. Tawney, 621 F.2d 607 (4th Cir. 1980).

Hartog-Rapp, F. (1985). The legal standards for determining the relationship between a child's handicapping condition and misconduct charged in a school disciplinary proceeding. *Southern Illinois University Law Journal, 2,* 243–262.

Hartwig, E. P., & Reusch, G. M. (2000). *Discipline in the schools.* (2nd ed). Horsham, PA: LRP Publications.

Hartwig, E. P., Robertshaw, C. S., & Reusch, G. M. (1991). Disciplining children with disabilities: Balancing procedural expectations and positive educational practice. In *Individuals with disabilities education law report, special report #8.* Horsham, PA: LRP Publications.

Hayes v. Unified School District No. 377, 669 F. Supp. 1519 (D. Kan. 1987).

Honig v. Doe, 479 U.S. 1084 (1988).

Hopewell (VA) Public Schools, 21 IDELR 189 (OCR 1994).

Horner, R., & Carr, E. (1997). Behavioral support for students with severe disabilities: Functional assessment and comprehensive intervention. *Journal of Special Education, 31,* 84–101.

Huefner, D. S. (1991). Another view of the suspension and expulsion cases. *Exceptional Children, 57,* 360–393.

Illinois v. Pruitt, 64 USLW 2575 (Ill. App. 1996).

Individuals with Disabilities Education Act (IDEA), 20 U.S.A. § 1400 *et seq.*

Ingraham v. Wright, 430 U.S. 651 (1977).

In the Interests of Isaiah B., 500 N.W. 2d 637 (Wis. 1993).

Kaelin v. Grubbs, 682 F.2d 595 (6th Cir. 1982).

Katsiyannis, A., & Maag, J. W. (1998). Disciplining students with disabilities: Practice considerations for implementing IDEA '97. *Behavioral Disorders, 23:* 276–89.

Letter to Anonymous, 30 IDELR 707 (OSEP 1999).

Letter to Zirkel, 22 IDELR 667 (OCR 1995).

Light v. Parkway School District, 21 IDELR 933 (8th Cir. 1994).

M. P. v. Governing Board of the Grossmont Union School District, 21 IDELR 639 (S.D. Cal. 1994).

Maloney, M. (1993). Strip search for drugs did not violate student rights. *The Special Educator, 9*(3), 42.

Maloney, M. (1994). How to avoid the discipline trap. *The Special Educator,* Winter Index, 1–4.

Marion County (FL) School District, 20 IDELR 634 (OCR 1993).

Martin, J. L. (1999, May). Current legal issues in discipline of disabled students under IDEA: A section by section comment of §1415(k), discipline regulations, and initial core law. Paper presented at LRP's Annual Conference on Special Education Law. San Francisco, LRP.

McCracken County School District, 18 IDELR 482 (OCR 1991).

Mineral County (NV) School District 167, 16 EHLR 668 (OCR 1990).

Mobile County (AL) School District, 18 IDELR 70 (OCR 1991).

New Jersey v. T.L.O., 469 U.S. 325, 105 S.Ct. 733 (1985).

Oberti v. Board of Education of the Borough of Clementon School District, 995 F.2d 1204 (3rd Cir. 1993).

O'Connor v. Ortega, 480 U.S. 709 (1987).

OCR Letter of Finding, EHLR 307:06 (OCR 1988).

OCR Letter of Finding, EHLR 353:205 (OCR 1989).

OCR Memorandum, EHLR 307:05 (OCR 1988).

OCR Memorandum, 16 EHLR 491 n. 3 (OCR 1989).

OSEP Memorandum 95-16, 22 IDELR 531 (OSEP 1995).

OSEP Questions and Answers (1999, March 12). *Federal Register, 64,* 12617–12632, Volume 64, no. 48.

O'Neill, R. E., Horner, R. H., Albin, R. W., Sprague, J. R., Storey, K., & Newton, J. S. (1997). *Functional assessment and program development for problem behavior: A practical handbook.* Pacific Grove, CA: Brooks/Cole.

People v. Dilworth, 661 N.E.2d 310 (Ill. 1996).

People v. Overton, 249 N.E.2d 366 (NY 1969).

Prince William County School Board v. Malone, 762 F.2d 1210 (4th Cir. 1985).

Prince William County School Board v. Willis, 16 EHLR 1109 (VA Cir. Ct. 1989).

Richards, D. & Martin, J. (2005). *The IDEA Amendments: What you need to know.* Horsham, PA: LRP Publications.

Rodiriecus L. v. Waukegan Rodiriecus L. v. Waukegan School District, 24 IDELR 563 (7th Cir. 1996).

S-1 v. Turlington, 635 F.2d 342 (5th Cir. 1981).

Section 504 of the Rehabilitation Act of 1973, 29 U.S.C. § 794 *et seq.*

Senate Report of the Individuals with Disabilities Act Amendments of 1997, available at wais.access.gpo.gov.

Sorenson, G. (1993). Update on legal issues in special education discipline. *Education Law Reporter, 81,* 399–411.

State of Washington v. Slattery, 787 P.2d 932 (Div. 1 1990).

Stuart v. Nappi, 443 F. Supp. 1235 (D. Conn. 1978).

Telzrow, C. F., & Naidu, K. (2000). Interim alternative educational settings: Guidelines for prevention and intervention. In C. Telzrow & M. Tankersley (Ed.). *IDEA Amendments of 1997: Practice guidelines for school-based teams* (pp. 199–204). Bethesda, MD: National Association of School Psychologists.

Texas City Independent School District v. Jorstad, 752 F. Supp. 231 (S.D. Tex. 1990).

Thomas v. Carthage School District, 87 F.3d 979 (8th Cir. 1996).

Tinker v. Des Moines Independent Community School, 393 U.S. 1058 (1969).

Tucker, B. P., & Goldstein, B. A. (1992). *Legal rights of persons with disabilities: An analysis of federal law.* Horsham, PA: LRP Publications.

Tucker, B. P., Goldstein, B. A., & Sorenson, G. (1993). *The educational rights of children with disabilities: Analysis, decisions, and commentary.* Horsham, PA: LRP Publications.

Valente, W. D., & Valente, C. (2005). *Law in the schools* (6th ed.). Upper Saddle River, NJ: Merrill/Prentice Hall.

Victoria L. v. District School Board, 741 F.2d 369 (11th Cir. 1984).

Virginia Department of Education v. Riley, 25 IDELR 309 (4th Cir. 1996).

Walker, H. M. (1995). *The acting out child: Coping with classroom disruption* (2nd ed.). Longmont, CO: Sopris West.

Walker, H. M., Ramsey, E., & Gresham, F. M. (2004). *Antisocial behavior in school: Evidence-based practices.* Belmont, CA: Thomson/Wadsworth.

Weber, M. (2002). *Special education law and litigation treatise* (2nd ed.). Horsham, PA: LRP Publications.

Yell, M. L. (1989). *Honig v. Doe: The suspension and expulsion of handicapped students. Exceptional Children, 56,* 60–69.

Yell, M. L. (1990). The use of corporal punishment, suspension, expulsion, and timeout with behaviorally disordered students in public schools: Legal considerations. *Behavioral Disorders, 15,* 100–109.

Yell, M. L. (1994). Timeout and students with behavior disorders: A legal analysis. *Education and Treatment of Children, 17,* 293–301.

Yell, M. L., Cline, D., & Bradley, R. (1995). Disciplining students with emotional and behavioral disorders: A legal update. *Education and Treatment of Children, 18,* 299–308.

Yell, M. L., Katsiyannis, A., Bradley, R., & Rozalski, M. E. (2000). Ensuring compliance with the discipline provisions of IDEA '97: Challenges and opportunities. *Journal of Special Education Leadership, 13,* 204–216.

Yell, M. L., & Peterson, R. L. (1995). Disciplining students with disabilities and those at risk for school failure: Legal issues. *Preventing School Failure, 39*(2), 39–44.

Yell, M. L., Rozalski, M. E., & Dragow, E. (2001). Disciplining students with disabilities. *Focus on Exceptional Children, 33(9),* 1–20.

Yudof, M. G., Kirp, D. L., & Levin, B. (1992). *Educational policy and the law* (3rd ed.). St. Paul, MN: West Publishing.

Zvi D. v. Ambach, 694 F.2d 904 (1982).

CHAPTER FIFTEEN

Additional Issues

The [IDEA] does not define appropriate education but leaves to the courts and the hearing officers the responsibility of giving [it] content.

Chief Justice William Rehnquist, *Board of Education of the Hendrick Hudson Central School District v. Rowley* (1982, p. 187)

Special education was born in the arena of advocacy, litigation, and legislation. Previous chapters have delineated many of these highly regulated and litigated issues. Other issues in special education, however, have only recently begun receiving attention in the courts. The purpose of this chapter is to review some of these issues. First, I examine the accessibility and confidentiality of student records. Second, I discuss an issue that is increasingly important to special educators in public schools—public schools' responsibility for students with disabilities attending private schools. Third, I review searches of students and their property, an issue of increasing importance in today's public schools. Finally, the topic of teachers' legal liability for student injury is discussed.

Issue #1: Student Records

Prior to 1974, it was common for schools to deny parental access to educational records. Granting access was time consuming and costly and often was seen in a negative light because it increased a school's potential liability by opening up records to public scrutiny. Additionally, students' educational records, although denied to parents, were often made available to third parties without regard to student confidentiality (Thomas & Russo, 1995).

In 1974, Congress enacted the Family Educational Rights and Privacy Act (FERPA) to address concerns regarding the confidentiality and accessibility of student records. The law, also known as the Buckley Amendment, was introduced by Senator James

Buckley of New York. Senator Buckley introduced this act to (a) ensure that parents and students would have access to their educational records and (b) protect student's right to privacy by not releasing records without consent.

When the Education for All Handicapped Children Act (now the Individuals with Disabilities Education Act or IDEA) was passed in 1975, the confidentiality and access provisions of FERPA were incorporated into the law. The regulations implementing the student records provisions of the IDEA can be found at 34 C.F.R. § 300.560–300.577. State educational agencies must notify parents of students with disabilities about their rights under the IDEA's records provisions. Figure 15.1 includes the information that must be included in this notice.

Family Educational Rights and Privacy Act

The Family Educational Rights and Privacy Act applies to all students who attend public schools that receive federal financial assistance. The law requires that these institutions adhere to the following requirements: (a) school districts must establish written policies regarding student records and inform parents of their rights under FERPA annually; (b) parents are guaranteed access to their children's educational records; (c) parents have the right to challenge the accuracy of the records; (d) disclosure of these records to third parties without parental consent is prohibited; and (e) parents may file complaints under FERPA regarding a school's failure to comply with the law.

Figure 15.1
Confidentiality Notice

The IDEA requires that public schools supply this information to parents of students with disabilities.

1. The extent to which the notice is provided in the native language of the different population groups within the state

2. The children and youth on whom the state maintains records that contain personally identifiable information

3. The types of information the state maintains

4. The methods the state uses to gather the information

5. The ways in which the information will be used

6. The policies and procedures schools follow with respect to storing, disclosing, retaining, and destroying records with personally identifiable information

7. The rights of parents, children, and youth regarding this information, including their rights under FERPA

This confidentiality notice must be published or announced in newspapers and through other outlets before identification, location, or evaluation activities are undertaken.

Definition of Educational Records

FERPA and IDEA cover all records, files, documents, and other materials that contain personally identifiable information directly related to a student and that are maintained by the school district or by a person acting for the district. Records not covered by the FERPA disclosure rules include (a) those records made by educational personnel who are in sole possession of the maker and are not accessible or revealed to other persons except substitutes (e.g., personal notes made by a child's teacher, a school psychologist's interview records) and (b) records of the law enforcement unit of an educational agency (e.g., a school's police liaison officer) that are maintained solely for law enforcement purposes. Additionally, schools need not obtain parental consent when records are made available to correctional facilities (*Alexander v. Boyd,* 1995), school attorneys, or special education service providers (*Marshfield School District,* 1995), or when disclosure of information is related to child find activities under the IDEA (Letter to Schipp, 1995). A school district's release of confidential information to a family doctor without parental permission, however, was ruled a violation of FERPA (*Irvine Unified School District,* 1995).

The IDEA adopted the definition of educational records found in FERPA. The U.S. Department of Education has determined that educational records include (a) individualized education programs (IEPs) and treatment plans; (b) test forms, providing that the school districts retains personally identifiable test forms; (c) school evaluations, medical evaluations, and independent evaluations, and any other documents that pertain to a student's educational performance; (d) recordings of IEP meetings; (e) transcripts of due process hearings; (f) complaints filed with the state educational agency; and (g) correspondence and investigative findings regarding a complaint if they contain personally identifiable information and are maintained by the school district. The following items are not considered educational records by the Department of Education: (a) personal notes or teacher papers, and other records of instructional, supervisory, and educational personnel that are not revealed to others; (b) test protocols that do not contain personally identifiable information; and (c) documents, such as tests, instruments, and interpretive materials that do not contain a student's name (Pitasky, 2000).

Accessibility Rights

Parents and eligible students over 18 years of age have the right to see, inspect, reproduce, and challenge the accuracy of educational records. These rights extend to custodial and noncustodial parents, unless a court order has been issued that denies the noncustodial parent access rights. Additionally, schools must explain and interpret records to parents if they ask school officials to do so. School officials must comply promptly with parental requests to inspect educational records. The response must be made "in a reasonable time frame"—within 45 days of the parent's request.

Similarly, the IDEA requires that upon request a school district allow parents of students with disabilities to inspect and review educational records related to their child that are collected and maintained by the school district. Moreover, they are required to reply to any requests in less than 45 days. The access rights apply to educational records and not to classroom visits because state and school district rules govern access to classrooms (Pitasky, 2000).

Amending Records

If parents believe educational records are misleading or incorrect, they may request that the school amend the records. The school may deny the parents' request. The parents may contest this refusal in a due process hearing. The task of the hearing officer in this situation is to determine whether the information in the file is accurate and appropriate. If the officer determines that the information is not accurate or does not belong in the file, it must be removed from the file immediately. If the hearing officer determines that the files are accurate and appropriate, the school does not need to amend the records. The parents, however, may attach a statement regarding their objection to the educational record. This statement must be kept in the student's records.

Confidentiality of Information

Third-party access to educational records is permitted only if the parents provide written consent. The exceptions to these confidentiality provisions include (a) school personnel with legitimate educational interests; (b) officials representing schools to which the student has applied; (c) persons responsible for determining eligibility for financial aid; (d) judicial orders for release; and (e) in emergency situations, persons who act to protect the student's health and safety. Additionally, FERPA allows a school to use and make public directory information, including the name and address of a student, if the school gives parents prior notice of the type of information to be released and gives them adequate time to respond if they disagree. The content of directory information is left to school districts. Courts have held that the directory information provision of the law is the one significant exception to FERPA's confidentiality requirements (Johnson, 1993).

Destruction of Records

Finally, when the local educational agency (LEA) no longer needs the records, it must notify the parents. The parents may request copies of the file or may request that the records be destroyed. If destruction is requested, the LEA may retain a permanent record of the student's name, address, telephone number, grades, attendance, grade level, and the last year of school the student completed.

IDEA also gives parents the right to request the destruction of personally identifiable educational records. Additionally, the school has to inform parents when the records are no longer needed to provide educational services to the student. The school may retain permanent records of students, including information such as name, address, phone number, grades, attendance record, classes, and grade level completed. Also, records that are used to demonstrate compliance with the IDEA, including IEPs, evaluations, and other records that prove a FAPE has been provided, must be kept for at least 3 years. When parents of students in special education request destruction of records, they should be informed that the records may be useful at a later date.

Enforcement of FERPA

Schools receiving federal financial assistance are in violation of FERPA when they deny parents their rights to inspect and review records or if third parties that are not exempt from FERPA's requirements are allowed to view records without parental permission. If a school district does not take steps to voluntarily remedy the violation, the Department of Education may terminate federal aid to the district. Under FERPA, however, there is no private right of action, which means that a person cannot sue a school under the law (Johnson, 1993; Mawdsley, 1996; Norlin, 2002). In fact, in 2002 the U.S. Supreme Court in *Gonzaga University v. Doe* (2002) ruled that individuals could not file private lawsuits against schools or colleges for violations of FERPA. If schools and colleges violate FERPA, individuals can only file a complaint with the U.S. Department of Education. If a FERPA violation occurs with a student also covered by the IDEA, however, the parent may, following exhaustion of due process remedies, initiate a lawsuit under the latter law. The Department is empowered to withhold federal funds if a school or college violates FERPA and fails to correct the violation.

Summary of Student Records

The IDEA contains all of the components of FERPA, and both laws apply to the educational records of students with disabilities. The IDEA requires that state and local educational agencies formulate policies that are consistent with FERPA regarding the educational records of students with disabilities. Furthermore, school districts must inform parents of students with disabilities of district policies on educational record access, confidentiality, and maintenance and destruction of records, and explain to parents their rights regarding their children's records.

Additionally, the IDEA requires that school districts assign a qualified person at each school to protect the confidentiality of all personally identifiable educational records. Persons who have access to these records must be trained in the policies and procedures of the state as well as FERPA requirements. The school must also keep a record of persons obtaining access to educational records. The information that must be collected for accessing records includes the name of the party reading the records, the date of access, and the purpose.

Issue #2: Providing Special Education Services in Private Schools

The IDEA guarantees a free appropriate public education (FAPE) to eligible students with disabilities. A question that has vexed special educators—and one that has no clear answer in the IDEA—concerns the extent of the public schools' responsibilities to students with disabilities whose parents enroll them in private schools. Do these students have the same right to special education and related services under the IDEA as do students attending public school? According to the IDEA Amendments of 1997, children with disabilities attending private schools are entitled to a proportionate amount of IDEA funds. Moreover, these funds may be provided to students on the premises of the private schools, including parochial schools, to the extent consistent with existing law. The IDEA unquestionably extends some benefits to private school students with disabilities; however, the extent of these benefits is unclear.

Congress again addressed the issue of private schools in the Individuals with Disabilities Education Improvement Act of 2004. The relationship between public schools and private schools has been clarified in this reauthorization. IDEA 2004 addresses the issue of children in private schools at 1412(a)(10) *et seq.* This section includes the following three subsections: (a) children enrolled in private schools by their parents; (b) children placed in, or referred to, private schools by public agencies; and (c) payment for education of children enrolled in private schools without consent of or referral by the public agency.

Defining Private Schools

Although private schools or facilities are not specifically defined in the IDEA, the Office of Special Education Programs (OSEP) has indicated that the definition is to be determined by individual state laws (*Letter to Williams,* 1992). Bartlett, Weisenstein, and Etscheidt (2002) note that because some states have passed laws requiring certain special education services to be provided to children enrolled in public schools, state laws should determine how an individual state approaches public special education services for private school students. Nonetheless, private schools are typically understood to encompass schools of either a nonsectarian (not church-related) or sectarian (church-related) nature that are not publicly financed. If a state defines home schooling as a private school, these children will also be included under state law and thus included by the IDEA (Mehfoud, 1994).

Children Enrolled in Private Schools by Their Parents

The child find mandate requires that schools locate, identify, and evaluate all students with disabilities within their jurisdiction, including students with disabilities who attend private elementary and secondary schools, even those in religious schools. After children who attend private schools are identified as eligible under the IDEA, the public school district must provide special education and related services to children in their district who have been placed in private schools by their parents. Such services may include direct services provided to parentally placed private school students, even in religious-oriented private schools. Moreover, school districts are required to spend a proportionate amount of a districts' Part B funds to provide appropriate services.

Personnel from the public school district are required to engage in meaningful consultation with private school representatives during the design and development of special education and related services for the children in a private school. Representatives of parents of private school children, teachers, and private school officials must be informed of and included in this process. In the consultation process the proportionate amount of federal funds that will be available to serve parentally placed private school children will be determined. Additionally, public school officials and private school representatives must also decide how the special education delivery system will operate during the school year to ensure that parentally placed private school children identified through the child find process can meaningfully participate in special education and related services. The discussion of how, where, and by whom the special educations will be provided should include issues such as (a) the type of service to be offered, including direct services and alternate service delivery mechanisms; (b) how such services will be apportioned if funds are insufficient to serve all children; and (c) how and when these decisions will be made. The special education services may be provided directly by the public school or they can be provided through contracts. Moreover, any services, including material and equipment, must be provided to parentally placed private school children with disabilities in a secular, neutral, and nonideological manner. The funding, and any materials or equipment purchased, will be controlled by the public agency.

If the public school officials and their private school counterparts cannot agree on the provision of services or type of services, the officials of the public school will provide a written explanation of the reasons for their decisions to the private school officials. Furthermore, following the consultation the school district personnel must obtain written affirmation signed by the private school officials that the consultation process has occurred. If the private school officials do not sign the affirmation within a reasonable amount of time, the representatives of the public school will send documentation of the consultation process to the state educational agency.

If private school officials do not believe that the public school representatives engaged in meaningful consultation, they may submit a complaint to the state. This complaint must include the information about why the public school representatives did not engage in meaningful consultation. The public school personnel may then forward their documentation of the process to the state educational agency. If the private school representatives then become dissatisfied with the way the state is handling the situation, they may send a complaint to the Secretary of the U.S. Department of Education.

The exact nature of the public school services provided to parentally placed private school students with disabilities, therefore, is not specified by IDEA 2004. What is mandated is that the public school (a) locate these students through the child find process, (b) identify and evaluate these children, and (c) provide special education and related services, the exact nature of which will be determined in discussions between public and private school officials.

Mehfoud (1994) reports that many school districts choose to offer special education services to private school students; however, these services are usually offered in the public school setting. According to an OSEP policy letter (1991), in such situations the transportation of the private school student to the public school may be required under the IDEA (*Felter v. Cape Girardeau School District,* 1993). School districts may also choose to provide the services at the private school. In these instances, however, public money cannot be expended to benefit the private school (Education Department General Administrative Regulations, 34 C.F.R. § 76.658(a)). For example, educational equipment may only be used for students served under the IDEA when this equipment is put in the private school to provide special education and related services to a student.

Children Placed in, or Referred to, Private Schools by Public Schools

The IDEA requires local public school districts that place students with disabilities in private schools to provide special education and related services to these students at no cost to their parents (IDEA 1412 § (a)(10)(B); IDEA Regulations, 34 C.F.R. §§ 300.401–300.402). The public school's responsibility is to "initiate and conduct meetings to develop, review, and revise an individualized education program for the child" (IDEA Regulations, 34 C.F.R. § 300.348). Furthermore, case law clearly indicates that if a school district fails to provide an appropriate education to a student with disabilities and the parents unilaterally place the child in a private school to receive an appropriate education, the school has to reimburse the parents for private school placement (*Burlington School Committee v. Department of Education,* 1985).

Payment for Educating Children Enrolled in Private Schools Without the Consent of, or Referral by, the Public School

A more difficult issue arises when students for whom the school district would normally have been obligated to provide a special education are directly placed in a private school by their parents. That is, when parents choose a private school placement rather than the public school (and the special education services that the public school would have provided), does the public school still have an obligation to provide these services? In such situations the public school will not be required to pay for the cost of the private school placement, if the public school made a free appropriate public education (FAPE) available to the student and the parents elected to place their child in a private school. Also, if a child had previously received special education and related services from a public school, and the child's parents enrolled him or her in a private school without the consent or referral of the public school, only a court or hearing officer could require the public school to pay for the services, and only if the public school special education services had not been appropriate.

Hearing officers or judges can also order tuition reimbursement if a parent placed a student with disabilities in a private school because the public school did not provide the child with a FAPE. The amount of the reimbursement can be reduced, however, if (a) at the most recent IEP meeting held between the parents and public school officials, the parents did not notify the school district of their intent to move their child to a private school to obtain a FAPE for their child; (b) the parents did not provide the public school with a written notice of their intent to move their child to a private school 10 business days before the removal; (c) prior to the removal to a private school the school notified the parents of their intent to evaluate the child, and the parents did not make their child available for the evaluation; and (d) the hearing officer or judge found that the parent's action was unreasonable.

In *Greenland School District v. Amy N.* (2004), the U.S. Court of Appeals for the First Circuit ruled that the failure of parents to give a school district prior notice of their intent to place their child in a private school precluded them from recovering tuition reimbursement for the placement. The circuit court explained that the reason for the notice requirement was to give the public school district time to (a) assemble a team, (b) evaluate the child, (c) devise an appropriate plan, and (d) determine whether a FAPE could be provided in the public school.

Public School Responsibilities Under EDGAR

Regulations to the IDEA (IDEA Regulations, 34 C.F.R. § 300.451) cite the Education Department General Administrative Regulations (EDGAR, 34 C.F.R. §§ 76.651–76.662) regarding the obligations of public schools to privately placed students. EDGAR requires that private school students must be given a "genuine opportunity for equitable participation" (EDGAR, 34 C.F.R. § 76.651(a)(1)). To fulfill these obligations, a public school district must consult with representatives from the private schools (e.g., administrators, teachers). Furthermore, EDGAR indicates that private school students must receive benefits comparable to those provided to students in public schools. The regulations, however, do not include a directive to provide a FAPE to privately placed students when a FAPE is available in a public school.

School District Responsibilities to Private School Students

Clearly, public schools are obligated to include parent-enrolled private school students in the child find process. If the school suspects the existence of a disability, it is obligated to evaluate the private school student. If the student is found to have a disability covered by the IDEA, the school is required to write an IEP that provides a FAPE.

Mehfoud (1994) states that a beginning point for public schools to meet their obligations to private school students with disabilities is to consult with representatives of the private school. With the signing of IDEA 2004 into law, this clearly remains good advice. The purpose of the consultation is to determine which students will be provided services, as well as how, where, and by whom. Prior to IDEA 2004, OSEP indicated that the state or local educational agency was responsible for determining the private school representative, although the IDEA contained no guidelines as to whom this representative must be (*Letter to Cernosia,* 1994). IDEA 2004 calls for a consultation process. Mehfoud suggests that public schools send annual letters to private schools advising them of services available and requesting notification regarding the presence of students with disabilities in the private schools (Know Your Obligations, 1995). Also, the public school needs to inform the private schools of the consultation process and arrange opportunities for private school participation. The school district may not have to provide the same special education and related services in a private school that it would have had to provide students if they were placed in a public school; however, these services have to be determined in the consultation process. The district must offer comparable special education and related services. At present, it seems that if the public school offers special education services on-site at the parochial school, at a neutral site, or at the public school, thereby giving the private school student with disabilities a genuine opportunity to participate, the public school will have met its responsibilities under the IDEA.

Summary of the IDEA and Private Schools

The child find provisions of the IDEA require that school districts locate all children with disabilities within their jurisdiction, including students in a private school. If public school officials place a student in a private school, the public school is responsible for writing, reviewing, and revising the IEP, as well as paying for the schooling, unless the private school decides to assume this responsibility. In the latter case, the public school must have a district representative at IEP meetings. If children are parentally placed in private schools, the public school district's responsibilities include (a) identification, (b) evaluation, (c) writing the IEP, and (d) offering the special education services. The specifics of the services that will be provided must be determined in discussions between the public and private school representatives.

If parents remove their child from the public school even though the public school offered a FAPE to a student with disabilities, the public school will not be responsible for paying for the schooling. Additionally, if parents remove their child to a private school without providing proper notification to the public school, a hearing officer or judge could reduce any award for reimbursement.

The extent of school districts' responsibility to provide a special education to students with disabilities placed by their parents in private schools seems to have been clarified by IDEA 2004. Future litigation will no doubt further clarify the law.

Issue #3: The IDEA and the Establishment Clause

An additional level of legal complexity exists when the private school in question is sectarian or church-sponsored. Sectarian schools are also referred to as parochial schools. The primary legal question involves the extent to which the Constitution permits the use of public funds for services to students with disabilities who are attending parochial schools (Linden, 1995). The constitutional concern is that special education services, when made available in parochial schools, may be construed as state aid to parochial schools and, thus, violate the First Amendment. The First Amendment requires that governmental relations with religions be guided by two fundamental principles: the government cannot make a law establishing a religion, nor can it deny the free exercise of any religion (see the Appendix). This amendment contains two separate elements regarding the government and religion. The first, referred to as the establishment clause, was summarized by Justice Black in *Everson v. Board of Education* (1947):

> Neither a state nor the Federal Government can set up a church. Neither can pass laws which aid one religion, aid all religion, or prefer one religion over another. . . . No tax in any amount, large or small, can be levied to support any religious activities or institutions . . . to teach or practice religion. (p. 15)

The second element, the free exercise clause, constrains state governments and the federal government from intruding upon an individual's religious beliefs and practices. Educational practices involving church/state issues primarily concern the establishment clause.

The exact meaning of the establishment clause has been the subject of much debate. The U.S. Supreme Court has recognized only two instances in which education becomes intertwined with the establishment clause. The first involves religious activities within the public schools (e.g., school prayer), and the second concerns public aid to sectarian schools (e.g., providing educational materials). Special education services, when provided in parochial school, involve the latter.

Everson v. Board of Education, 1947

The U.S. Supreme Court first addressed the question of state aid to a parochial school in *Everson v. Board of Education* (1947; hereafter *Everson*). The case involved a New Jersey statute that authorized the state to reimburse the parents of public and parochial school children for bus fares paid for the purpose of transporting their children to and from school. The statute was challenged on the grounds that it violated the First Amendment by providing state support to church-sponsored schools. In the majority opinion, Justice Black wrote a lengthy historical analysis of the establishment clause. Black cited Thomas Jefferson's writings regarding the establishment clause as being intended to erect a "wall of separation between church and state." Based on this analysis, Black concluded that the primary concept underlying the establishment clause was the principle of neutrality. The establishment clause "requires the state to be neutral in its relations with groups of religious believers and nonbelievers, it does not require the state to be their adversary" (*Everson*, p. 18). The high court held that the New Jersey statute did not violate the establishment clause because the bus fares were paid directly to the parents, regardless of whether or not their children attended a church-sponsored school, thereby not breaching the "wall" between church and state. In fact, the Court stated that to deny parents of children attending parochial schools the reimbursement would be tantamount to denying children their rights based on their parents' religious convictions.

Under the *Everson* neutrality test, the question of special education aid to parochial school students would probably have passed constitutional muster because the IDEA requires that special education services be provided to all students with disabilities whether they attend public, private, or parochial schools (Guernsey & Klare, 1993; Linden, 1995). The high court, however, has analyzed cases involving state aid to students in parochial schools not according to whether these services should be provided, but rather according to how those benefits can be provided so as not to violate the establishment clause.

The EDGAR requirements mirror the *Everson* standard in setting forth limitations on the use of public education funds at sectarian schools. According to the EDGAR requirements, the use of funds for religion is prohibited, and

  (a) No State or subgrantee may use its grant or subgrant to pay for any of the following:
       (1) Religious worship, instruction, or proselytization
       (2) Equipment or supplies to be used for any activities specified (EDGAR, 34 C.F.R. § 76.532(a))

Lemon v. Kurtzman, 1971

In *Lemon v. Kurtzman* (1971), the U.S. Supreme Court devised a test to determine the validity of laws that may violate the establishment clause. The test consisted of a three-part analysis. To be judged permissible, federal or state laws must (a) have a secular purpose; (b) have a primary effect that neither advances nor inhibits religion; and (c) avoid excessive government entanglement with religion (see Figure 15.2). The test was used to rule on the constitutional validity of programs in both Rhode Island and Pennsylvania. The program in Rhode Island authorized salary supplements for teachers of secular subjects in nonpublic schools. In reality, the program benefited only 250 teachers in Catholic schools in the state. The Pennsylvania statute authorized the reimbursement of private schools for teacher salaries, texts, and instructional materials in secular subjects. The majority of the schools that received the reimbursement were parochial schools. In both instances the laws were ruled unconstitutional because they would result in excessive church-state entanglement due to the necessary administration and surveillance they would require.

The Supreme Court subsequently applied the *Lemon* test to a number of programs that provided state aid or assistance to parochial schools. The Court has struck down direct monetary reimbursement to parochial schools for state-mandated educational expenditures such as testing (*Levitt v. Committee for Public Education,* 1973) and maintenance of school facilities (*Committee for Public Education v. Nyquist,* 1973). Additionally, the purchase or loan of instructional materials or equipment to parochial schools and the provision of guidance counseling and remedial and accelerated instruction in parochial schools were found to be violations of the *Lemon* test (*Meek v. Pittenger,* 1975).

A common fault of many of these state statutes was the lack of control of state monies once they were given to the parochial schools. If the state could not guarantee that the money was used only for sectarian purposes, it was in violation of the second prong of the *Lemon* test because the monies could possibly be used to advance a religion. The test created a problem in instances where the state set up monitoring systems to ensure that state monies would not be used for religious purposes. In such situations, the third part of the Lemon test, prohibiting excessive entanglement of church and state, would be violated.

Figure 15.2
The *Lemon* Test

1. Does the policy or practice have a secular purpose?
2. Is the primary effect of the policy or practice one that neither advances nor inhibits religion?
3. Does the policy or practice avoid excessive entanglement with religion?

Because special education and related services under the IDEA are provided directly to the student, not the parochial school, it would seem less likely that the provision of these services would violate the establishment clause. Two Supreme Court decisions from 1985, however, seemed to counter this notion.

Grand Rapids School District v. Ball, 1985

The high court's decision in *Grand Rapids School District v. Ball* (1985; hereafter *Grand Rapids*) involved a program to enrich the curriculum of private schools through the provision of supplementary classes conducted by state-paid teachers. The classes were held in rooms in private schools that were leased for these classes. Parochial schools were required to remove all religious symbols from the classrooms and post signs on the classroom doors noting that the rooms were public school classrooms. The Supreme Court found that these programs violated the establishment clause because the sectarian atmosphere might influence the state-paid teachers to indoctrinate the students at public expense. The Court also stated that the symbolic union of the state and the parochial school might convey a message of state support for religion and noted that the programs were actually subsidizing parochial schools by freeing up the resources they would normally spend on the teaching of the secular classes for religious purposes.

Aguilar v. Felton, 1985

Aguilar v. Felton (1985; hereafter *Aguilar*) concerned the implementation of Title I of the Elementary and Secondary Education Act of 1965. Title I provides federal funds to assist schools to provide remedial instruction for educationally deprived children from low-income families. Aguilar involved the implementation of these programs in New York. The state was offering Title I services in parochial schools in clearly designated classrooms. As in Grand Rapids, the classrooms were devoid of all religious materials. New York had also instituted a surveillance system for monitoring the Title I classes to keep them free of religious content. The high court held that the Title I program violated the establishment clause because the monitoring system resulted in an excessive entanglement of church and state.

The decisions in *Grand Rapids* and *Aguilar* seem to portend possible violations of the establishment clause when special education and related services are provided on site to students with disabilities in parochial schools. Justice O'Connor's dissent in *Aguilar* was an indication of a new direction the Court may be headed regarding the establishment clause. O'Connor examined the decision and specifically questioned the value of the *Lemon* test. Her dissent viewed educational services less as a form of aid to parochial schools and more as a general government program designed to benefit all children without reference to religion (Linden, 1995). This has been called the child benefit theory. According to this theory, if a governmental practice is neutral toward religion, the program or activity will pass constitutional muster if it benefits a child's general welfare, even if it aids the sectarian function of the parochial school (McKinney, 1993).

Opinions in a few decisions in the early 1990s indicated that a majority of the Supreme Court justices shared Justice O'Connor's view or held similar views. In an important development, the Court agreed to reexamine its decision in *Aguilar* (renamed *Agostini v. Felton*).

Zobrest v. Catalina Foothills School District

The Supreme Court, in *Zobrest v. Catalina Foothills School District* (1993; hereafter *Zobrest*), ruled that there is no general prohibition against providing services at parochial schools. The case involved a deaf student, James Zobrest, who received special education and related services while attending a public middle school. He was mainstreamed with resource room services and was provided with a sign language interpreter in his classes. When he reached high school age, his parents unilaterally enrolled him in a Catholic high school. While in the parochial high school, James received speech therapy in a public school classroom. James's parents requested that the public school provide the services of the interpreter in the parochial school. The public school board declined to provide the services, although it indicated that these services would be provided if James were still in the public school. The Zobrests filed suit in federal district court, seeking provision of an interpreter by the public school. The court held that the provision of the interpreter violated the establishment clause of the First Amendment. The decision was upheld on appeal to the U.S. Court of Appeals for the Ninth Circuit. The Zobrests appealed to the U.S. Supreme Court, which chose to hear the case. In a 5 to 4 decision, the high court reversed the decision of the lower courts and ruled in favor of the Zobrests. The Court ruled that the public financing of James's sign language interpreter did not conflict with the establishment clause of the Constitution.

The Court developed a three-part test to determine whether a program of governmental services would survive an establishment clause challenge (see Figure 15.3). First, the services must be provided in a neutral manner, without regard to religion; that is, the services provided must assist the student without regard to the religious nature of the school. Second, the services cannot be provided at the sectarian school as a result of legislative choice but rather as a result of private choice of the person using

Figure 15.3
The *Zobrest* Three-Part Test

1. Services to the parochial school student must be provided in a religiously neutral manner.
2. Services can only be provided when the placement in the parochial school is the result of parental choice.
3. IDEA funds must not find their way into the parochial school's coffers.

the services. A student, therefore, must be placed in the parochial school because of parental choice and not from the choice of school district officials. Finally, the funds traceable to the government must not find their way into the sectarian school's coffers. The funds must not provide direct assistance to the parochial school, although indirect aid may be difficult to avoid.

The Establishment Clause and the IDEA

Chief Justice Rehnquist, writing for the majority in *Zobrest,* noted that the IDEA conferred benefits on the student and that these benefits were neutral; that is, the public funds were distributed to an eligible child without regard to the nature of the school the child attended. Also, the public school funds did not go directly to the parochial school, so no public assistance was provided to the parochial school. The student, not the school, was the primary beneficiary of the public school's funds. The Court held that the establishment clause does not bar religious organizations from participating in publicly sponsored welfare programs that neutrally provide benefits to a broad class of citizens defined without reference to religion. Neither does the establishment clause create an absolute bar to placing a public employee at a sectarian school. Because an interpreter for James Zobrest would do no more than accurately interpret the material presented to the student's class, the interpreter would neither add to nor subtract from the sectarian environment of the school.

The high court held that the IDEA is a program distributing benefits neutrally to students with disabilities without regard to the religious or secular nature of the school they attend. Neither does the law encourage religion, because it creates no incentive for parents to select a sectarian school. Finally, the IDEA funds only benefit sectarian schools indirectly, at best. In providing IDEA funds, the government is not subsidizing costs that the sectarian school would otherwise have assumed in educating its students.

The Court also noted that the duties of the sign language interpreter were considerably different from the duties of a teacher or counselor. Because the role of the interpreter was to relay instructional content, the provision of the interpreter was not prohibited by the establishment clause.

The Court did not answer whether the IDEA requires or permits public schools to provide interpreters on site in parochial schools. Rather, the Court dealt exclusively with the establishment clause issue. The holding of the high court in *Zobrest* was a narrow one. The Court simply stated that certain services that can only be provided on site may be provided without violating the First Amendment. In this decision the Court seemed firmly to adopt the child benefit theory.

Post-*Zobrest* Cases

The *Zobrest* court, in dicta, indicated that the services of a teacher or guidance counselor may be prohibited by the establishment clause. Following *Zobrest,* the issue facing the courts involved questions of what on-site services could be provided by personnel other than interpreters.

A decision in the U.S. Court of Appeals for the Second Circuit provided some direction regarding the scope of services that were not barred by the establishment clause. In *Russman v. Sobol* (1996), a school district had written an IEP for an 11-year-old girl with moderate mental disabilities. The IEP called for an inclusive placement with the services of a consultant teacher and a teacher's aide. The girl was subsequently placed in a parochial school, where the parents demanded that she receive the services called for in the IEP. The parents won a judgment at the district court level, and the school district appealed. The Second Circuit Court affirmed the lower court's decision, holding that the special education services sought by the parents (i.e., the services of a consultant teacher and the teacher's aide) were limited to core academic subjects and were permissible under the First Amendment. The court held that the purpose of the consultant and the aide, like the sign language interpreter in *Zobrest*, was to make material intelligible to the student, not to advance a religious viewpoint.

In a policy letter following the *Zobrest* decision, OSEP wrote that the provision of a personal computer for in-school use by a student with disabilities attending a sectarian school was not prohibited by the establishment clause (*Letter to Moore*, 1993). According to OSEP,

> Part B funds [may be used] to purchase a computer if the personal computer, like the sign language interpreter at issue in *Zobrest*, is provided to overcome the child's disability by enhancing his ability to communicate, not for religious worship, instruction, or proselytization. (p. 1213)

Board of Education of Kiryas Joel Village School District v. Grumet, 1994

In 1994, the U.S. Supreme Court issued a ruling in *Board of Education of Kiryas Joel Village School District v. Grumet* (hereafter *Kiryas Joel*). Kiryas Joel is a village in New York comprised of about 8,500 Satmar Hasidim. Members of this Orthodox Jewish sect speak Yiddish and choose to remove themselves from certain aspects of modern society (e.g., they wear traditional religious clothes and do not watch television). Children generally attend sex-segregated parochial schools. In the mid-1980s, the local public school district began to provide special education services for the children with disabilities from Kiryas Joel in an annex to their religious school. In 1985, however, the public school suspended this practice after the Supreme Court's decisions in *Aguilar* and *Grand Rapids*. The Satmar children who needed special education services were forced to attend public schools to continue to receive these services. Within a short period of time, most of the children were withdrawn from these services because of the trauma the children suffered from attending the public schools. The village elders sought help from the New York legislature. The legislature created a public school district in Kiryas Joel. The district consisted of one school, which served the children with disabilities from the village. The school was secular, no religious classes were included in the curriculum, boys and girls were educated together, and there were no religious symbols in the school. The New York State School Boards Association claimed that the state-sponsored special school district violated the establishment clause of the Constitution. The association prevailed in the lower courts. An appeal was filed with the U.S. Supreme Court, which agreed to hear the case.

In a 6 to 3 decision, the high court ruled that the establishment of the special school district in Kiryas Joel was unconstitutional. The Court issued a narrow ruling (i.e., a ruling on a fine point of law) based on the principle of government neutrality toward religion (Schimmel, 1994). The greatest significance of Kiryas Joel, however, was in the concurring and dissenting opinions issued by the justices. These opinions indicated possible directions the Court may take in future establishment cases. A majority of the justices seemed to believe that *Aguilar* was wrongly decided and that it should be overturned. Schimmel (1994) asserted that if the Court overruled *Aguilar,* it would be a victory for those advocating greater governmental accommodation for religion and a lower wall of separation between church and state.

Agostini v. Felton, 1997

In a 5 to 4 ruling in *Agostini v. Felton* (1997), the U.S. Supreme Court reversed *Aguilar.* The petitioners emphasized the costs of complying with the decision and the assertions of five high court justices that *Aguilar* should be reconsidered because it was no longer good law. According to the Court's opinion, written by Justice O'Connor, federally funded programs that provide supplemental, remedial instruction to disadvantaged students on site in parochial schools are valid under the establishment clause when such instruction contains safeguards such as those of the New York program (i.e., sending a school supervisor into the parochial schools on unannounced monthly visits). The Court also noted that the portion of the decision in *Grand Rapids* that addressed a similar program in Grand Rapids, Michigan, was also invalid. The opinion was based on the Court's more recent decisions regarding this issue. These cases had served to undermine the assumptions of *Aguilar* and *Grand Rapids.* The majority opinion stated that placing full-time government employees on parochial school campuses did not, as a matter of law, have the effect of advancing religion through indoctrination. The Court did not believe that the mere presence of public employees in parochial schools would inevitably inculcate religion or that their presence would constitute a symbolic union between government and religion. Neither would the presence of public school teachers in parochial schools illegally support religion. The teachers would benefit the students, not the parochial school.

Clearly, the decision allows public school districts to use public money to provide services on site in parochial schools. Nevertheless, the decision does not create a new entitlement for parochial school students. Essentially, the Court ruled that there is no First Amendment problem when public schools send teachers into parochial schools.

Summary of the IDEA and Parochial Schools

Conclusions regarding the IDEA and the church-state issue must be considered tentative at best. School districts have a significant obligation to children with disabilities in parochial schools. Public school districts must identify all children with disabilities living in the district's attendance area, including those attending parochial schools, and must offer special education and related services to eligible parochial school students. The primary question that remains unanswered is how the students should be served. The Supreme Court's decision in *Zobrest* indicates that school districts may provide supportive services to students with disabilities in parochial schools. This decision does not indicate, however, that districts are allowed to provide all types of services on site at parochial schools (e.g., counseling or direct teaching). The U.S. Supreme Court's decision in *Agostini* seems to enlarge the *Zobrest* decision to include other types of supportive services.

Neither *Zobrest* nor *Agostini* indicates that public schools are required to provide special education and related services to parochial school students; they merely indicate that certain services may be offered on site at parochial schools without violating the establishment clause. Post-*Zobrest* decisions, such as *Russman,* expanded the types of related services that may be provided in private schools without violating the establishment clause.

Regarding the actual services that should be extended by public schools to parochial school students, the standard is whether the student with disabilities is provided with a genuine opportunity for meaningful participation. The private school requirements in IDEA 2004 may serve to increase the amount and type of special education services offered in parochial school.

Issue #4: Liability for Student Injury

In the past few years, there has been a substantial increase in the number of lawsuits filed on behalf of students with disabilities injured while at school. These suits are usually filed against the schools and school personnel (Pitasky, 1995). Typically these cases involve injuries, either physical or emotional, that occur either accidentally or intentionally. Often these suits involve tort claims of negligence.

Tort Laws

Tort laws are laws that offer remedies to individuals harmed by the unreasonable actions of others. Tort claims usually involve state law and are based on the legal premise that individuals are liable for the consequences of their conduct if it results in injury to others (McCarthy & Cambron-McCabe, 1992). Tort claims involve civil suits, which are actions brought to protect an individual's private rights. Civil suits are different from criminal prosecution. Criminal prosecutions are actions brought by the state to redress violations of the law. Two major categories of torts are typically seen in education-related cases: intentional torts and negligence.

Intentional Torts

Intentional torts are usually committed when a person attempts or intends to do harm. For intent to exist, the individual must know with reasonable certainty that injury will be the result of the act (Alexander & Alexander, 2002). A common type of intentional tort is assault. Assault refers to an overt attempt to physically injure a person or to create a feeling of fear and apprehension of injury. No actual physical contact need take place for an assault to occur. Battery, however, is an intentional tort that results from physical contact. For example, if a person picks up a chair and threatens to hit another person, assault has occurred; if the person then actually hits the second person, battery has occurred. Both assault and battery can occur if a person threatens another, causing apprehension and fear, and then actually strikes the other, resulting in injury. According to Alexander and Alexander (2002), teachers accused of assault and battery are typically given considerable leeway by the courts. This is because assault and battery cases often result from attempts to discipline a child, usually by some manner of corporal punishment, and courts are generally reluctant to interfere with a teacher's authority to discipline students (Alexander & Alexander, 2002; McCarthy & Cambron-McCabe, 1992; Valente & Valente, 2005).

Courts have found teachers guilty of assault and battery, however, when a teacher's discipline has been cruel, brutal, excessive, or administered with malice, anger, or intent to injure. In determining if a teacher's discipline constitutes excessive and unreasonable punishment, courts will often examine the age of the student; the instrument, if any, used to administer the discipline; the extent of the discipline; the nature and gravity of the student's offense; the history of the student's previous conduct; and the temper and conduct of the teacher. For example, a teacher in Louisiana was sued and lost a case for assault and battery for picking up a student, slamming him against bleachers, and then dropping the student to the floor, breaking his arm (*Frank v. New Orleans Parish School Board,* 1967). In Connecticut, a student was awarded damages when a teacher slammed the student against a chalkboard and then a wall, breaking the student's clavicle (*Sansone v. Bechtel,* 1980). Clearly, teachers may be held personally liable for injuries that occur to students because of teachers' behavior. The legal principles that apply to teachers whose behavior causes injury are the same principles that apply to all citizens (Fischer, Schimmel, & Kelly, 1994).

A small body of case law also indicates that school districts and school officials may be liable for damages in cases alleging teacher abuse of students. In *C. M. v. Southeast Delco School District* (1993), the Federal District Court for the Eastern District of Pennsylvania ruled that a student could proceed with a suit for damages against a school district and school officials because of injuries incurred as a result of alleged abuse perpetrated by a special education teacher. The abuse in this case included verbal harassment (e.g., name calling, ridiculing, profanity), physical abuse (e.g., slapping, hitting, grabbing and slamming into a locker, spraying with water and Lysol), and sexual abuse. The court ruled that the state had an affirmative duty to protect people from its own employees. Furthermore, the court stated that this was particularly true of teachers, because they are in positions of great sensitivity and responsibility. Later that year, the same court heard another damage claim against the same school district and teacher for sexual, physical, and verbal abuse. In *K. L. v. Southeast Delco School District* (1993), the court reiterated that the student had an appropriate claim for damages based on the school district's actions or inaction that resulted in injuries to the student. Again the court noted that school districts and school officials have a heightened duty to supervise and monitor teachers. Pitasky (1995) posited that these cases, although legally binding only in their districts, have created a potential for damages to be imposed on school districts and school officials for liability claims against teachers and other school personnel.

Teachers have also won assault and damage suits against students. A Wisconsin court awarded a teacher compensatory and punitive damages for a battery case he brought against a student who physically attacked and injured him as he brought the student to the principal's office for a rule violation (*Anello v. Savignac*, 1983). An Oregon court assessed damages against a student who struck and injured his teacher for not allowing him to leave the classroom during a class period (*Garret v. Olson*, 1984).

Negligence

The second type of tort seen most frequently in education-related cases is negligence. The difference between negligence and an intentional tort is that in negligence the acts leading to injury are neither expected nor intended (Alexander & Alexander, 2002). Negligence arises in instances where conduct falls below an acceptable standard of care, thereby resulting in injury. For negligence to occur, an injury must have been avoidable by the exercise of reasonable care. The ability to foresee injury or harm is an important factor in determining negligence. Unforeseeable accidents that could not have been prevented by reasonable care do not constitute negligence.

Four elements must be present for negligence to occur:

1. The teacher must have a duty to protect another from unreasonable risks.

2. The teacher must have failed in that duty by failing to exercise a reasonable standard of care.

3. There must be a causal connection between the breach of the duty to care and the resulting injury.

4. There must be an actual physical or mental injury resulting from the negligence.

In a court all four elements must be proven before a court will award damages for negligence (Freedman, 1995; McCarthy & Cambron-McCabe, 1992).

Duty to Protect.   The first element, the duty to protect, is clearly part of a teacher's responsibilities. Teachers have a duty to anticipate foreseeable dangers and take necessary precautions to protect students in their care from such dangers (McCarthy & Cambron-McCabe, 1992). Specifically, teachers' duties include adequate supervision, maintenance of equipment and facilities, and heightened supervision of high-risk activities. In the majority cases of negligence against teachers, the duty to protect is easily proven (Fischer et al., 1994). Clearly, this duty applies to activities during the school day; however, courts have also held that this duty may extend beyond regular school hours and away from school grounds (e.g., after-school activities, summer activities, field trips, bus rides).

Failure to Exercise a Reasonable Standard of Care.   The second element occurs when teachers fail to exercise a reasonable standard of care in their duties to students. If a teacher fails to exercise reasonable care to protect students from injury, then the teacher is negligent. In negligence cases, courts will gauge a teacher's conduct on how a "reasonable" teacher in a similar situation might have acted (Alexander & Alexander, 2002). The degree of care exercised by a "reasonable" teacher is determined by factors such as (a) the training and experience of the teacher in charge; (b) the student's age; (c) the environment in which the injury occurred; (d) the type of instructional activity; (e) the presence or absence of the supervising teacher; and (f) a student's disability, if one exists (Mawdsley, 1993; McCarthy & Cambron-McCabe, 1992). For example, a primary-grade student will require closer supervision than a secondary student; a physical education class in a gymnasium or an industrial arts class in a school woodshop will require closer supervision than a reading class in the school library; and a student with a mental disability will require closer supervision than a student with average intelligence. In *Foster v. Houston General* (1981), a student with a moderate mental disability was struck and fatally injured when she darted into traffic while being escorted, along with nine other students from her special education class, to a park three blocks from the school. The court held that the teacher had failed to select the safest route to the park and to maintain the close supervisory duties required in this situation. The court also found that the general level of care required for all students becomes greater when the student body is composed of students with mental retardation. Finally, the court stated that the standard of care was heightened because the children were being taken off the school campus. A number of cases have held that the student's IEP, disability, and unique needs are all relevant factors in determining a reasonable level of supervision (Daggett, 1995). Additionally, school officials may be liable for damage claims resulting from a failure to supervise a student with a disability when that student injures another student. In *Cohen v. School District* (1992), a federal district court ruled that a liability claim could go forward when a behaviorally disordered student with known violent tendencies was placed in a general education classroom without adequate supervision and subsequently attacked and injured another student.

Proximate Cause.   The third element that must be proven in a negligence case is a connection between the breach of duty by the teacher (element two) and the subsequent injury to the student (element four). This element, referred to as *proximate cause,* often hinges on the concept of foreseeability; that is, was the student's injury something that a teacher could have anticipated? If the injury could have been foreseen and prevented by a teacher if a reasonable standard of care had been exercised, a logical connection and, therefore, negligence may exist. To answer questions regarding proximate cause, courts will ask, "Was the injury a natural and probable cause of the wrongful act (i.e., failure to supervise), and ought [it] to have been foreseen in light of the attendant circumstances?" (*Scott v. Greenville,* 1965). Negligence claims will not be successful if the accident could not have been foreseen. In *Sheehan v. St. Peter's Catholic School* (1971), a teacher was supervising a group of students at recess when some of the students began throwing rocks. The rock throwing had continued for almost 10 minutes when a student was struck in the eye and injured. The court found the supervising teacher liable for negligence because a reasonable teacher would have anticipated or foreseen potential harm arising from the incident and stopped it. In a Wyoming case, *Fagan v. Summers* (1978), a teacher's aide was determined not to be the proximate cause of a playground-related injury that occurred during her supervision. Immediately after the aide walked by a group of students, one child threw a rock, which was deflected and hit another child. The court concluded that the injury was unforeseen and could not have been prevented even with the aide providing stricter supervision.

Actual Injury.   The final element that must be proven in negligence cases is that there was an actual physical or mental injury. Even in instances where there is negligence, damage suits will not be successful unless there is provable injury.

Teachers' Defenses Against Liability

If it can be shown that a student contributed to the injury, the teacher may use a defense of contributory negligence. If the court finds that contributory negligence was present, the teacher will not be held liable. With younger students (i.e., under age 6), it is difficult to prove contributory negligence because the tort laws in many states hold that young children are incapable of contributory negligence. In these instances, therefore, students can collect damages even if they did contribute to the injury. If students are between the ages of 7 and 14, unless it can be shown that they are quite intelligent and mature, contributory negligence is difficult to prove.

With older students, assumption of risk can also be used as a defense against negligence claims. Assumption of risk has been recognized as a defense against claims of liability in activities such as competitive sports (Fischer et al., 1994). If a student is mature enough to recognize the dangers of certain activities and still volunteers to participate, the student assumes a certain amount of risk. For example, in *Kluka v. Livingston Parish Board* (1983), an 11th-grade student challenged his basketball coach to a wrestling match. The student was injured during the match and subsequently sued the coach for damages. The student testified that he had not contributed to the injury because he had not known he could be injured wrestling. The court found the teacher not liable for damages, stating that there were some risks that everyone must appreciate. As is the case with contributory negligence, it is unlikely that young and less mature students would be found by a court to assume the risk in activities, since they are often seen as not able to understand or appreciate the consequences of high-risk activities.

Finally, it is often assumed that teachers and schools can release themselves from damages by having parents sign waivers or releases. This is untrue, because parents cannot waive their children's claims for damages (Fischer et al., 1994; Freedman,

1995; McCarthy & Cambron-McCabe, 1992). Teachers always have a duty to their students to supervise them to prevent foreseeable injury. Parental releases, waivers, and permission slips do not relieve teachers or schools of liability if they fail to appropriately discharge their duties. According to Fischer, Schimmel, and Kelly (1994), such waivers may be useful for public relations purposes, but they will not relieve teachers or school officials of possible liability for negligence.

School District Responsibilities Regarding Student Care and Supervision

Schools, school officials, and teachers may have a heightened standard of care for students with disabilities (Mawdsley, 1993). School districts should take actions to make certain that administrators, special education and regular education teachers, and other personnel are aware of their care and supervisory duties under the law (Daggett, 1995; Freedman, 1995; Mawdsley, 1993). (These responsibilities are listed in Figure 15.4). The following are suggestions to assist administrators and teachers in meeting these responsibilities:

- School districts should develop policies regarding standards of care and supervision. These policies should be in writing. Because this area of law changes rapidly, legal developments should be monitored and school policies should be updated when necessary. Additionally, tort laws vary by state, so it is extremely important that school district officials understand tort laws in their states prior to developing policies.

- Special education and regular education teachers, as well as administrators and other staff, should be trained in their responsibilities under the law. Training may be important in convincing a court that a school district acted with care and good faith.

- The IEP team should address potential safety risks and plan for them when appropriate. The IEP should include actions that will be taken to minimize these risks. The listing of precautionary procedures in the IEP provides convincing evidence that a school district has made an effort to prevent student injury. If, however, procedures listed in the IEP are not followed and an injury results, the school's negligence can more easily be proven (Daggett, 1995).

Figure 15.4
Avoiding Liability for Student Injury

- Develop written school district policies regarding care and supervision of students.
- Train administrators, teachers, paraprofessionals, and other staff in responsibilities for care and supervision of students.
- Have the IEP team address potential safety risks for students with disabilities.

Issue #5: Search and Seizure

Stating that students do not "shed their Constitutional rights . . . at the schoolhouse gate," the U.S. Supreme Court held that "school officials do not possess absolute authority over their students . . . students in school as well as out of school are 'persons' under the Constitution . . . possessed of fundamental [constitutional] rights" (*Tinker v. Des Moines Independent Community School,* 1969, p. 511). These rights include freedom of expression, bodily security, and privacy. If these rights are regulated, school officials must be able to justify the regulations.

Another category of student rights is the right to be free of unreasonable searches. Student searches have assumed increasing importance in recent years due to the introduction of drugs and other contraband into public schools and the increasing levels of violence. The Fourth Amendment to the Constitution prohibits unreasonable searches of persons. This amendment protects student privacy rights and must be respected by school officials. The frequency of student searches and locker searches by school officials without warrants has led to litigation decrying this practice as an invasion of students' constitutional rights. Application of the Fourth Amendment to the schools has also caused a great deal of disagreement among the lower courts.

New Jersey v. T.L.O., 1985

Recognizing the division among the courts, the U.S. Supreme Court, in *New Jersey v. T.L.O.* (1985; hereafter *T.L.O.*), addressed warrantless searches in the schools. The case involved a teacher in a New Jersey high school who discovered two students smoking in the school lavatory. The students were taken to the principal's office. One student, called T.L.O. by the court, denied smoking. The vice principal took T.L.O.'s purse to examine it for cigarettes. In addition to the cigarettes, the purse also contained cigarette rolling papers, a pipe, a small amount of marijuana, a substantial amount of money, and two letters implicating her in marijuana dealing. The principal notified T.L.O.'s parents and the police. Delinquency charges were brought against T.L.O. in juvenile court. Based on this evidence, a juvenile court in New Jersey declared T.L.O. delinquent. T.L.O.'s lawyer defended her by asserting that the search was improper under the Fourth Amendment and that the evidence was inadmissible. The case went to the New Jersey Supreme Court, which reversed the decision and ordered the evidence obtained during the school's search suppressed on the grounds that the warrantless search was unconstitutional.

The case was eventually heard by the U.S. Supreme Court. The high court ruled that the Fourth Amendment applied to school personnel. However, the Court also noted the need to balance the school's responsibility to conduct a search against a student's legitimate expectation of privacy. Noting that a student's privacy interest must be weighed against the need of administrators and teachers to maintain order and discipline in schools, the U.S. Supreme Court reversed the New Jersey Supreme Court, stating that

> the fourth amendment applies to searches conducted by school authorities, but the special needs of the school environment require assessment of such searches against a standard less exacting than probable cause . . . . [C]ourts have . . . upheld warrantless searches by school authorities provided that they are supported by a reasonable suspicion that the search will uncover evidence of school disciplinary rules or a violation of the law. (p. 333)

The *T.L.O.* decision affirmed the constitutional protection of students against searches. The court, however, granted a great deal of latitude to schools by holding them to the standard of *reasonable suspicion,* a standard less exacting than the standard of *probable cause* (the standard required of police before a warrant can be obtained). Reasonable suspicion, nonetheless, does place some degree of restraint on school personnel. There must be reasonable grounds to lead school authorities to believe a search is necessary, and the search must be related to the original suspicion. Situations that justify a reasonable suspicion include information from student informers, police tips, anonymous tips and phone calls, and unusual student conduct. The intrusiveness of the search is also a relevant factor.

The high court stated that school personnel did not need a search warrant before searching a student or his or her property. The Court also developed a two-part test for determining whether a school search is valid. First, the search must be justified at inception; that is, the search must be based on reasonable suspicion that exists prior to the search. Second, the reason for conducting the search must be related to the violation of the law or the school rules. The scope of the search, therefore, must be reasonably related to the circumstances leading to the search. Finding that the school had satisfied both parts of the test, the high court overturned the New Jersey Supreme Court's ruling that evidence collected against T.L.O. during the school search was inadmissible.

Court decisions have also recognized situations in which searches and seizures in school environments do not give rise to Fourth Amendment concerns as long as the search meets the two-part *T.L.O.* test. These situations include (a) searches to which a student voluntarily consents; (b) searches of material left in view of school authorities; (c) emergency searches to prevent injury or property damage; (d) searches by police authorities that are incidental to arrests; (e) searches of automobiles on school property; (f) searches of students' desks; (g) searches of students' personal belongings (e.g., book bags, briefcases, purses); and (h) searches of lost property (Dise, Iyer, & Noorman, 1996).

Cornfield v. Consolidated High School District No. 230, 1993

In a decision by the U.S. Court of Appeals for the Seventh Circuit, *Cornfield v. Consolidated High School District No. 230* (1993), a high school student classified as seriously emotionally disturbed (SED) brought suit alleging that a strip search conducted by the teacher and dean was a violation of his constitutional rights. Suspecting that the student was hiding drugs, the dean phoned the student's mother, who refused to consent to a search of the boy. The teacher and dean then escorted the student to the boys' locker room, where they conducted a strip search and physically inspected his clothing. No drugs were found. The student sued the school district, the teacher, and the dean. The district court ruled in favor of the defendants.

On appeal, the circuit court affirmed the decision of the district court, stating that the strip search met the Fourth Amendment standard of reasonableness for searches conducted by school officials. The court noted that prior drug-related incidents involving the student, combined with the personal observations of the teacher and aide, created a reasonable suspicion that the student was concealing drugs. According to Maloney (1993), this ruling indicates that students, with or without disabilities, who are actively using or dealing drugs are subjected to the same search procedures. Because of the highly intrusive nature of these types of student searches, they should only be used as a last resort, should employ the least intrusive means, and should be based on reasonable suspicion (Miller & Ahrbecker, 1995). When strip searches are necessary, they should be conducted by persons of the same sex as the student, in a private area, and in the presence of school personnel also of the same sex as the student.

Thomas v. Carthage School District, 1996

Finally, the U.S. Court of Appeals for the Eighth Circuit, in *Thomas v. Carthage School District* (1996), ruled that the exclusionary rule does not apply in school settings. The exclusionary rule is a judicially created rule that bars the admission of unlawfully seized evidence in criminal trials. The case involved a student who was expelled from school after school officials found crack cocaine in his possession during a random search for weapons. A federal district court had awarded the student $10,000 in damages for wrongful expulsion because the school had violated the student's Fourth Amendment rights. The circuit court reversed the lower court, holding that the exclusionary rule does not apply to school disciplinary matters.

According to the court, school officials are not law enforcement agents, and students have reduced expectations of privacy at school. The court saw the societal costs of applying the exclusionary rule in schools as unacceptably high. The court's opinion gave the example of a school unable to expel a student who confessed to killing another student if the school failed to inform the student of his or her Miranda rights. The court also held that individual suspicion is not required to conduct minimally intrusive searches of students.

Locker Searches

In *O'Connor v. Ortega* (1987), the U.S. Supreme Court upheld searches of government-supplied offices, desks, and file cabinets based on reasonable suspicion. Courts, using this decision as precedent, have upheld school officials' searches of student lockers, whether targeted or random, based on reasonable suspicion (*In the Interest of Isaiah B.,* 1993, hereafter *Isaiah B.; People v. Overton,* 1969). Searches by school authorities may also extend to students' cars and locked brief-cases (*State of Washington v. Slattery,* 1990), as well as objects, such as back-packs, in which contraband may be hidden (*People v. Dilworth,* 1996). The use of metal detectors to search students even though there is no suspicion or consent to a search is permitted (*Illinois v. Pruitt,* 1996). The use of random searches has also been determined to be constitutionally permissible (McKinney, 1994).

In *Isaiah B.,* the Wisconsin Supreme Court ruled that a student did not have rea-sonable expectations of privacy in his school locker. The court based its decision largely on the existence of a school policy regarding student lockers. According to the school policy,

> School lockers are the property of Milwaukee Public Schools. At no time does the Mil-waukee School District relinquish its exclusive control of lockers provided for the con-venience of students. Periodic general inspections of lockers may be conducted by school authorities for any reason at any time, without notice, without student consent, and with-out a search warrant. (*Isaiah B.,* p. 639, n. 1)

Miller and Ahrbecker (1995) suggest that schools develop—unless they are pro-hibited from doing so by state law—policies regarding locker searches, such as the Milwaukee Public Schools' policy. This policy should notify students and parents that there is no reasonable expectation of privacy in a student locker and that both ran-dom and targeted searches of the locker may be conducted without student or parental consent. Bjorklun (1994) likewise concludes that random locker searches may be conducted without individualized suspicion. Figure 15.5 lists procedural sug-gestions for conducting searches of students and their property.

Summary

Students are persons under the Constitution who possess the constitutional rights of free-dom of expression, bodily security, and privacy. This includes being free of unjustified searches of themselves or their property. When school of-ficials seek to regulate these rights, they must be able to justify the regulations.

Schools need to balance the need to con-duct a search against a student's legitimate ex-pectation of privacy. A student's privacy interest must be weighed against the need of adminis-trators and teachers to maintain order and dis-cipline in schools. Although students have constitutional protections against unreasonable

searches, schools have a great deal of latitude to conduct searches.

Prior to conducting searches of students and their property, school officials must have reasonable grounds to believe a search is neces-sary. Moreover, the search must be related to the original suspicion. Situations that justify a reasonable suspicion include information from student informers, police tips, anonymous tips and phone calls, and unusual student conduct. The U.S. Supreme Court also developed a two-part test for determining whether a school search is valid. First, the search must be justi-fied at inception; that is, the search must be

Figure 15.5
Legally Sound Searches

1. Draft a public policy regarding searches and seizures:
   - Describe circumstances that will lead to searches of property.
   - State that lockers are the property of the school and not students.
   - Describe circumstances that will lead to student searches.
   - Specify when police will be notified regarding searches.
   - Notify public regarding district policy (e.g., parent manual).
2. Officials must have reasonable suspicion to search a student.
3. The scope of the search must be reasonable in relation to the age of the student and the circumstances.
4. Require that strip searches be conducted only when school officials possess reliable information and as a last resort.
5. Strip searches should be conducted by at least two officials of the same gender as the student.
6. Random searches should only be conducted when school officials possess reliable information.
7. Document student searches and seizures.

based on reasonable suspicion that exists prior to the search. Second, the reason for conducting the search must be related to the violation of the law or the school rules. The scope of the search, therefore, must be reasonably related to the circumstances leading to the search.

In addition to conducting searches of students, school authorities may search students' cars, locked briefcases, and backpacks. The search must be conducted in a reasonable, and not overly intrusive, manner. Schools should develop policies regarding searches of students and student property. Schools should develop such policies and notify students and parents that there is a lower expectation of privacy during school hours or at a school function and that both random and targeted searches of the locker or backbacks may be conducted without student or parental consent.

For Further Information

FERPA

Johnson, T. P. (1993). Managing student records: The courts and the Family Educational Rights and Privacy Act of 1974. *Education Law Reporter, 79,* 1–16.

Mawdsley, R. D. (1996). Litigation involving FERPA. *Education Law Reporter, 110,* 897–914.

Norlin, J. W. (2002). *Beyond FERPA: A guide to student records under the IDEA.* Horsham, PA: LRP Publications.

Providing special education services in private schools (secular and nonsecular)

Linden, M. A. (1995). Special educational services and parochial schools: Constitutional constraints and other policy considerations. *Journal of Law and Education, 24,* 345–375.

Mehfoud, K. S. (1994). *Special education services for private school students.* Horsham, PA: LRP Publications.

Teacher liability

Mawdsley, R. D. (1993). Supervisory standard of care for students with disabilities. *Education Law Reporter, 80,* 779–791.

Pitasky, V. M. (1995). *Liability for injury to special education students,* Horsham, PA: LRP Publications.

References

Agostini v. Felton, 65 LW 4524 (Supreme Court, June 24, 1997).

Aguilar v. Felton, 473 U.S. 402 (1985).

Alexander, K., & Alexander, M. D. (2002). *American public school law* (3rd ed.). St. Paul, MN: West Publishing.

Alexander v. Boyd, 22 IDELR 139 (D.S.C. 1995).

Anello v. Savignac, 342 N.W. 2d 440 (Wis. Ct. App. 1983).

Barnett v. Fairfax County School Board, 927 F.2d 146 (4th Cir. 1991).

Bartlett, L. D., Weisenstein, G. R., Etscheidt, S. (2002). *Successful inclusion for educational leaders.* Upper Saddle River, NJ: Merrill/Prentice Hall.

Bjorklun, E. C. (1994). School locker searches and the Fourth Amendment. *Education Law Reporter, 92,* 1065–1071.

Board of Education of the Hendrick Hudson School District v. Rowley, 458 U.S. 176 (1982).

Board of Education of Kiryas Joel Village School District v. Grumet, 114 S.Ct. 2481 (1994).

Burlington School Committee v. Department of Education, 471 U.S. 359 (1985).

C. M. v. Southeast Delco School District, 19 IDELR 1084 (E.D. Pa. 1993).

Cefalu v. East Baton Rouge Parish School Board, 25 IDELR 142 (5th Cir. 1996).

Cohen v. School District, 18 IDELR 911 (1992).

Committee for Public Education v. Nyquist, 413 U.S. 756 (1973).

Cornfield v. Consolidated High School District No. 230, 991 F.2d 1316 (7th Cir. 1993).

Daggett, L. M. (1995, April). *Reasonable schools and special students: Tort liability of school districts and employees for injuries to, or caused by, students with disabilities.* Paper presented at the International Conference of the Council for Exceptional Children, Indianapolis, IN.

Dise, J. H., Iyer, C. S., & Noorman, J. J. (1996). *Searches of students, lockers, and automobiles.* Detroit: Educational Risk, Inc.

Dreher v. Amphitheater Unified School District, 19 IDELR 315 (D.C. AZ, 1992).

Education Department General Administrative Regulations (EDGAR), 34 C.F.R. §§ 76.651–76.662.

Everson v. Board of Education 330 U.S. 1 (1947).

Fagan v. Summers, 498 P.2 457 1227 (1978).

Family Educational Rights and Privacy Act (FERPA), 20 U.S.C. § 1232 *et seq.*

Felter v. Cape Girardeau School District, 810 F. Supp. 1062 (E.D. Mo., 1993).

Fischer, L., Schimmel, D., & Kelly, C. (1994). *Teachers and the law* (3rd ed.). White Plains, NY: Longman.

Foster v. Houston General, 407 So.2d 758 (1981).

Fowler v. Unified School District, 25 IDELR 348 (10th Cir. 1996).

Frank v. New Orleans Parish School Board, 195 So.2d 451 (La.Ct. App. 1967).

Freedman, M. (1995, August). *Substance and shadows: Potential liability of schools and school personnel in special education cases.* Paper presented at the Seventh Utah Institute on Special Education Law and Practice, Salt Lake City, UT.

Garret v. Olson, 691 P.2d 123 (Or.Ct. App. 1984).

Gonzaga University v. Doe. 536 U.S. 273 (2002).

Gorn, S. (1996). *What do I do when . . . The answer book on special education law.* Horsham, PA: LRP Publications.

Grand Rapids School District v. Ball, 473 U.S. 373 (1985).

Greenland School District v. Amy N. 358 F .3d 150 (1st Cir. 2004).

Guernsey, T. F., & Klare, K. (1993). *Special education law.* Durham, NC: Carolina Academic Press.

Illinois v. Pruitt, 64 USLW 2575 (Ill. App. 1996).

In the Interests of Isaiah B., 500 N.W. 2d 637 (Wis. 1993).

Individuals with Disabilities Education Act (IDEA), 20 U.S.C. § 1401 *et seq.*

Individuals with Disabilities Education Act Regulations, 34 C.F.R. § 300.1 *et seq.*

Irvine Unified School District, 23 IDELR 911 (FPCO, 1995).

Johnson, T. P. (1993). Managing student records: The courts and the Family Educational Rights and Privacy Act of 1974. *Education Law Reporter, 79,* 1–16.

K.L. v. Southeast Delco School District, 20 IDELR 244 (E.D. Pa. 1993).

Kluka v. Livingston Parish Board, 433 So.2d 213 (1983).

Know your obligations to serve private school students. (1995, August 8). *The Special Educator, 11*(2), 5.

Lemon v. Kurtzman, 403 U.S. 602 (1971).

Letter to Aschenbrenner, EHLR 211:110 (1979).

Letter to Cernosia, 22 IDELR 365 (OSEP 1994).

Letter to Mentink, 18 IDELR 276 (OSERS 1991).

Letter to Moore, 20 IDELR 1213 (OSEP 1993).

Letter to Schipp, 23 IDELR 442 (OSEP 1995).

Letter to Schmidt, 20 IDELR 1224 (OSERS 1993).

Letter to Williams, 18 IDELR 742 (OSEP 1992).

Letter to Wing, EHLR 211:414 (OSEP 1986).

Levitt v. Committee for Public Education, 413 U.S. 472 (1973).

Linden, M. A. (1995). Special educational services and parochial schools: Constitutional constraints and other policy considerations. *Journal of Law and Education, 24,* 345–375.

Maloney, M. (1993). Strip search for drugs did not violate student rights. *The Special Educator, 9*(3), 42.

Marshfield School District, 23 IDELR 198 (SEA ME 1995).

Mawdsley, R. D. (1993). Supervisory standard of care for students with disabilities. *Education Law Reporter, 80,* 779–791.

Mawdsley, R. D. (1996). Litigation involving FERPA. *Education Law Reporter, 110,* 897–914.

McCarthy, M. M., & Cambron-McCabe, N. H. (1992). *Public school law: Teachers' and students' rights* (3rd ed.). Boston: Allyn & Bacon.

McKinney, J. R. (1993). Special education and the establishment clause in the wake of *Zobrest:* Back to the future. *Education Law Reporter, 85,* 587–599.

McKinney, J. R. (1994). The Fourth Amendment and the public schools: Reasonable suspicion in the 1990s. *Education Law Reporter, 91,* 455–463.

Meek v. Pittenger, 421 U.S. 349 (1975).

Mehfoud, K. S. (1994). *Special education services for private school students.* Horsham, PA: LRP Publications.

Miller, M. B., & Ahrbecker, W. C. (1995). *Legal issues and school violence.* Paper presented at Violence in the Schools, a conference of LRP Publications, Arlington, VA.

New Jersey v. T.L.O., 469 U.S. 325 105 S. Ct. 733 (1985).

Norlin, J. W. (2002). *Beyond FERPA: A guide to student records under the IDEA.* Horsham, PA: LRP Publications.

O'Connor v. Ortega, 480 U.S. 789 (1987).

OSEP policy letter, 17 IDELR 1117 (OSEP 1991).

People v. Dilworth, 661 N.E.2d 310 (Ill. 1996).

People v. Overton, 249 N.E.2d 366 (NY 1969).

Pitasky, V. M. (1995). *Liability for injury to special education students.* Horsham, PA: LRP Publications.

Pitasky, V.M. (2000). *The complete OSEP handbook.* Horsham, PA: LRP Publications.

Russman v. Sobol, 22 IDELR 1028 (N.D.N.Y. 1995), *aff'd,* 85 F.3d 1050 (2nd Cir. 1996).

Sansone v. Bechtel, 429 A.2d 820 (Conn. 1980).

Schimmel, D. (1994). *Kiryas Joel Village School District v. Grumet:* The establishment clause controversy continues. *Education Law Reporter, 94,* 685–697.

Scott v. Greenville, 48 S.E. 2d 324 (1965).

Sheehan v. St. Peter's Catholic School, 188 N.W. 2d 868 (Minn. 1971).

State of Washington v. Slattery, 787 P .2d 932 (Div. 1 1990).

Thomas v. Carthage School District, 87 F.3d 979 (8th Cir. 1996).

Thomas, S. B., & Russo, C. J. (1995). *Special education law: Issues and implications for the 90s.* Topeka, KS: National Organization on Legal Problems in Education.

Tinker v. Des Moines Independent Community School, 393 U.S. 1058 (1969).

Valente, W. D., & Valente, C. (2005). *Law in the schools* (6th ed.). Upper Saddle River, NJ: Merrill/ Prentice Hall.

Work v. McKenzie, 661 F. Supp. 225 (D.D.C. 1987).

Zobrest v. Catalina Foothills School District, 113 S.Ct. 2462 (1993).

Major Changes of IDEA 2004

Title & Part	Area of Change	Description
Title I, Part A	Assistive technology device	• Adds language to clarify that the term does not include surgically implanted medical device or replacement of that device.
	Core academic subjects	• Adds the definition from NCLB that core academic subjects are English, reading, language arts, mathematics, science, foreign language, civics and government, economics, arts, history, and geography.
	Homeless children	• Adds the definition of homeless children from the McKinney-Vento Homeless Assistance Act. "Children who don't have a regular night time residence, including children (a) sharing others' housing due to loss of housing, economic hardship, or similar reason; living in motels, hotels, trailer parks, or campgrounds due to lack of alternative adequate accommodations; living in emergency or transitional shelters; abandoned in hospitals; or awaiting foster care placement.
	Limited english proficient	• Adds definition of limited English proficient from NCLB: "An individual, aged 3–21, enrolled or preparing to enroll in an elementary or secondary school, 1. (a) who wasn't born in the U.S. or whose native language isn't English: (b) who is a Native American or Alaskan Native, or native resident of the outlying areas and comes from an environment where a language other than English has significantly impacted level of English language proficiency; or (c) who is migratory, with a native language other than English, from an environment where a language other than English is dominant; and

	2. whose difficulties in speaking, reading, writing, or understanding English may be sufficient to deny the child (a) ability to meet proficiency level of achievement on State assessments; (b) ability to successfully achieve in class where instruction is in English; or (c) opportunity to participate fully in society."
Parent	• Adds natural, adoptive, or foster parent; guardian (but not the state if child is a ward of the state); or a person acting in place of a natural or adoptive parent with whom the child lives or who is legally responsible for the child.
Related services	• Adds school nurse services and interpreting services to the list of related services.
Transition services	• Adds that services must be focused on improving academic and functional achievement, and that student's strengths must be taken into account.
Universal design	• Adds definition from the Assistive Technology Act of 1998: "A concept or philosophy for designing and delivering products and services that are usable by people with the widest possible range of functional capabilities, which includes products and services that are directly usable (without requiring assistive technology) and products and services that are made usable with assistive technologies."
Highly qualified special education teachers	• The new highly qualified special education teacher requirements do not create a right of action if a teacher is not highly qualified. • All special educator teachers must: a) Be certified by the state to teach in special education. b) Hold at least a bachelor's degree. c) Demonstrate competency in all core academic subjects in which they teach. • Special education teachers teaching students with significant cognitive disabilities, who are assessed on alternative achievement standards, must: a) Be certified by the state to teach in special education. b) Hold at least a bachelor's degree.

		c) Demonstrate competency in (a) core academic subjects they teach or (b) in subject knowledge appropriate to level of instruction.
		• Currently teaching special education teachers who teach two or more academic subjects may meet the highly qualified standards of the NCLB by passing a single, multi-subject, high objective, uniform state standard of evaluation (HOUSSE).
		• New special education teachers who teach two or more academic subjects and are highly qualified in math, language arts, or science may meet the highly qualified standards by passing a state's HOUSSE within two years of the date they were hired.
		• Certification/licensure requirements cannot be waived on emergency, temporary, or provisional basis.
	Paperwork reduction	• Fifteen states can apply to a pilot program in which states may develop and implement three-year IEPs. States that are in the program may offer parents the option of developing a comprehensive three-year IEP designed to coincide with natural transition points in their child's education (e.g., preschool to kindergarten, elementary school to middle school, middle school to high school). Parents have to agree to this option.
		• Pilot programs must also include a process for reviewing and revising the IEP, including (a) review at natural transition points, (b) annual review to determine levels of progress and whether progress is sufficient for goals to be met, (c) a requirement to review and amend the IEP if the student is not making sufficient progress to meet his or her goals.
Title I, Part B	Local educational agency risk pool	• Adds language that every year allows states to reserve 10% of funds reserved for State-level activities to establish a high-cost fund and to support innovative ways of cost sharing.
	Prohibition on mandatory medication	• Adds language that prohibits State and local educational agency personnel from requiring a child to obtain a prescription for medications covered by the Controlled Substances Act (e.g., Ritalin) as condition of school attendance or receiving an evaluation or services.
	IEPs	• Special education services must be based on peer-reviewed research.

Initial evaluation	• Parent, school district, SEA, or other state agency may request initial evaluation.
	• Although IDEA 2004 requires school districts to obtain parental consent before conducting an initial evaluation, there are circumstances in which an initial evaluation can be completed without parent consent. Unless parental consent is required by a state, a school district may use mediation or due process to conduct an initial evaluation even when parents refuse to provide their consent or fail to respond to a request to evaluate.
	• Eligibility determination must be made within 60 days of consent for evaluation or within the timeframe set by the state if it is less than 60 days.
	• Timeframe does not apply if the child's parents repeatedly fail to produce the child for evaluation or if the parents refuse to provide consent to evaluate.
	• If a school screens a student to determine appropriate instructional strategies, it is not considered evaluation for special education eligibility.
Evaluation procedures	• Assessments of a student who has transferred from another school district must be coordinated between prior and new school.
	• An evaluation is not required before dismissing a student from special education if the dismissal was due to graduation with a regular diploma or if he or she exceeds the state age at which FAPE is no longer required (usually 21).
	• If a student ages out of special education, a school district is required to provide a summary of the student's academic achievement and functional performance. This includes recommendations on how to assist the student to meet his or her postsecondary goals.
	• A student cannot be determined to have a disability if the student's primary problem was a lack of appropriate instruction in reading, including instruction in the essential components of reading instruction.
Identification of students with learning disabilities	• When determining if a student has a learning disability, a state cannot require a school district to use a discrepancy formula.
	• A school district may use a process, referred to as a *response to intervention model,* in which an IEP

	team is used to determine if a student responds to scientific, research-based intervention.
IEPs	• Parents and educators can agree to change an IEP without holding a formal IEP meeting. Annual IEP reviews are still required. If a meeting is not held, parents and teachers may develop a written document to amend or modify the current IEP.
	• The IEP team can agree to conduct IEP meetings by conference calls, video conferencing, or other means instead of face-to-face meetings.
	• A member of the IEP team won't be required to attend the IEP meeting or other meetings if the student's parents and the local education agency personnel agree that the person's attendance is not necessary because his or her area of curriculum or related services is not being modified or discussed at a meeting. To be excused the team member must submit a request in writing to the parents and the IEP team, and the parents and IEP team must agree to excuse the team member.
	• For transfer students in the same state who had an IEP in that year, a school district shall provide services comparable to the previous IEP until the district adopts the previous IEP or develops a new one.
	• IDEA 2004 no longer requires that benchmarks or short-term objectives be included in the IEP, except for students with severe disabilities who take alternate assessments.
	• IDEA 2004 emphasizes the importance of writing measurable annual goals and then measuring progress toward each goal during the course of the year. The IEP must describe how the student's progress toward the annual goals will be measured. The IEP must also include the schedule for reporting a student's progress. A student's parents must be informed of their child's progress at least every 9 weeks.
	• When an IEP is developed for a child who was in a Part C program, the parent may request that the Part C service coordinator shall be invited to the IEP team meeting.
	• After a student reaches 16 years of age, his or her IEP must include (a) measurable postsecondary transition goals based on age-appropriate

	transition assessments related to training, education, employment, and when appropriate, independent living skills and (b) transition services, including courses, needed to assist a student to reach his or her goals.
Providing a special education	• A school district shall seek to obtain parents' consent before providing special education services. • A school district shall not be required to develop an IEP or provide special education and related services to a child in the absence of parental consent. If a parent doesn't consent to placement, the school district cannot be held liable under the IDEA for failing to provide special education and related services.
Scientifically based instruction	• Special education services must be grounded in scientifically based research.
Discipline	• A school district may remove a student who violates a student code of conduct from his or her current placement to an interim alternative educational setting (IAES) or another setting, or suspend him or her for not more than 10 school days to the extent that similar procedures would be used with a student who did not have a disability. • If a school district wants to order a disciplinary change of placement that exceeds 10 school days, the district must conduct a manifestation determination. • When conducting a manifestation determination, the misbehavior can be determined to be a manifestation of a student's disability only if the conduct in question was "caused by" or had a "direct and substantial relationship" or if a school fails to implement a student's IEP as written. • If a student's misbehavior was not a manifestation of his or her disability, the school may use disciplinary procedures that are used with students who do not have a disability. These procedures may also be used for the same duration of time although educational services must continue for any period beyond 10 school days. • A student with a disability who is removed from his or her current placement in excess of 10 school days must continue to receive educational services that enable him or her to progress toward IEP

	goals and continue to participate in the general education curriculum. Additionally a functional behavioral assessment must be conducted as appropriate, and the student must continue to receive behavioral interventions and supports.
	• Students can be moved to an IAES if they possess or use weapons or drugs in school or at a school function or if they inflict serious bodily injury on another person while at school or a school function, without regard to whether the behavior was a manifestation of the student's disability.
	• Students can be placed in an IAES for up to 45 school days (this is longer than the previously allowed 45 calendar days).
	• The stay-put placement during hearings in which a disciplinary sanction is challenged will be the IAES, not the setting the student was in before the dispute.
	• Children or youth who are not currently in special education can receive protections under the disciplinary provisions of the IDEA if (a) the child's parents expressed their concern that their child needed special education services, *in writing,* to an administrator, supervisor, or teacher, or (b) the child's teacher or other school personnel expressed concerns about the child's behavior directly to the special education director or other supervisory personnel.
Mediation	• If at the conclusion of mediation, both parties agree to and sign a legally binding agreement, that agreement will be enforceable in state or federal court.
Personnel qualifications	• Related services personnel must meet state-approved certification or licensure requirements.
	• Certification or licensure cannot be waived on an emergency, temporary, or provisional basis.
	• Special education teachers must be highly qualified by the NCLB deadline of no later than the 2005–2006 school year.
	• States must have policies that require school districts to take measurable steps to recruit, hire, train, and retain highly qualified personnel.
	• Parents may file a complaint with the state regarding a teacher's qualifications.
Overidentification of minority students	• School districts that have high rates of minority students in special education are required to

	implement early identification services and eliminate the IQ discrepancy model to reduce overidentification of minority students.
Parental empowerment	• School districts may use state IDEA funds to support supplemental services chosen by parents for their children with disabilities in schools that are identified as needing improvement under No Child Left Behind.
Attorneys' fees	• State educational agencies and school districts that are prevailing parties in hearings and court cases may collect reasonable attorneys' fees when parents' attorneys file or litigate cases found to be frivolous, unreasonable, or without foundation. • Courts may levy a fine against parents if they bring actions against school districts for improper purposes such as harassment, causing unnecessary delay, protracting the final resolution, or increasing the cost of litigation. • Attorneys' fees are not available for prehearing resolution sessions.
Administrative proceedings	• If either the parents or school district decide to bring a civil action following a due process hearing, they will have 90 days from the date of the decision to file the action.
State performance plans	• States must develop performance plans that evaluate the SEA's efforts to implement IDEA and describe how implementation will be improved. The plan must be approved by the Secretary of the U.S. Department of Education and reviewed at least once every 6 years. • In this plan the state must: a) Establish measurable goals and rigorous targets regarding the provision of FAPE in the LRE, the state's general supervisory authority, and disproportionate representation of racial and ethnic minorities, and collect data on these goals. b) Collect data on these goals and targets, analyze the data, report to the public annually on school district's performance, and file a report with the U.S. Department of Education. The U.S. Department of Education will review these reports annually and determine if the state needs assistance, intervention, or

		substantial intervention to implement the IDEA.
		• The U.S. Department of Education will enforce this plan to determine the state's status in implementing IDEA.
		• If for 2 consecutive years the Department determines that the state needs assistance in implementing the IDEA, the Secretary may (a) advise the state of technical assistance sources, (b) direct use of state funds to where the assistance is needed, or (c) identify the state high risk and impose conditions on the state's grant under Part B.
		• If for 3 consecutive years the Department determines that the state needs intervention, the Secretary may (a) require a new improvement plan or that the state take corrective action, (b) require a compliance agreement, (c) withhold state funds until the problem is corrected, (d) seek to recover funds, (e) withhold some or all IDEA payments to the state, or (f) refer the state to an appropriate agency for enforcement.
		• If the Department determines that the state needs substantial intervention, the Secretary may: (a) recover funds, (b) withhold some or all IDEA payments to the state, (c) refer to the U.S. Department of Education Inspector General, or (d) refer the state to an appropriate agency for enforcement.
	Education of students with autism	• Part D authorizes support for developing and improving programs to train special education teachers to work with students who have autism spectrum disorders.
	Funding	• Schools may redirect a share of their local resources for activities consistent with NCLB. • IDEA 2004 establishes a 6-year path to reach the 40% percent funding goals originally set in 1975.
Title I, Part C	Scientifically based research	• Early childhood special education services must be grounded in scientifically based research.
	Early childhood special education	• Children with disabilities who are served under Part C can continue in the same program from birth to kindergarten.

Title I, Part D	State personnel development grants	• In years when appropriations for this category of grants is less that $100 million, competitive grants are awarded to states for personnel development. Priority will be given to states that demonstrate the greatest difficulty meeting personnel needs. • In years when appropriations for this category of grants exceeds $100 million, formula grants will be awarded to all states. • To receive a grant, a state must have a personnel development plan and spend at least 90% of the grant for professional development.
	Accountability for alternative achievement standards	• National studies are authorized to examine the (a) criteria that states use to determine eligibility for alternative assessments, (b) reliability and validity of states' instruments and procedures, (c) alignments with a state's content standards, and (d) effectiveness of measuring progress on outcomes specific to instructional needs.
	IAES, behavioral supports, and systemic schoolwide interventions	• Authorizes grants to support safe learning environments that foster academic achievement by improving quality if IEASs and providing behavioral supports and systemic schoolwide interventions. • Funds from these grants must be used to support activities such as staff training on: (a) identification, prereferral, and referral procedures; (b) positive behavioral supports and interventions; (c) classroom management; (d) linkages between school-based and community-based mental health services; and (e) using behavioral specialists and related services personnel to implement behavioral supports • Funds may also be used to improve IAESs through (a) staff training, (b) referrals for counseling, (c) instructional technology, and (d) interagency coordination.
Title II	National Center for Special Education Research	• Establishes the National Center for Special Education Research within the Institute for Education Sciences. • The center's mission is to (a) expand the knowledge base in special education, (b) improve services under the IDEA, and (c) evaluate implementation and effectiveness of the IDEA. • A commissioner of special education research will direct the center.

Relevant Sections of the U.S. Constitution

* * *

Preamble

We the people of the United States, in order to form a more perfect union, establish justice, insure domestic tranquility, provide for the common defense, promote the general welfare, and secure the blessings of liberty to ourselves and our posterity, do ordain and establish this Constitution for the United States of America.

* * *

Article 1

Section 8. [1] The Congress shall have the power to lay and collect taxes, duties, imposts and excises, to pay the debts and provide for the common defense and general welfare of the United States; . . .

* * *

Article III

Section 1. The judicial power of the United States shall be vested in one supreme Court, and in such inferior Courts as the Congress may from time to time ordain and establish. . .

* * *

Article VI

This constitution, and the laws of the United States which shall be made in pursuance thereof; . . . shall be the supreme law of the land; and the judges in every state shall be bound thereby, any thing in the Constitution or laws of any state to the contrary not withstanding.

* * *

Amendment I

Congress shall make no law respecting an establishment of religion, or prohibiting the free exercise thereof; or abridging the freedom of speech, or of the press; or the right of the people peaceably to assemble, and to petition the Government for a redress of grievances.

* * *

Amendment IV

The right of the people to be secure in their persons, houses, papers, and effects, against unreasonable searches and seizures, shall not be violated, and no warrants shall issue, but upon probable cause, supported by oath or affirmation, and particularly describing the place to be searched, and the persons or things to be seized.

* * *

Amendment V

No person shall be . . . compelled in any criminal case to be a witness against himself, nor be deprived of life, liberty, or property, without due process of law; nor shall private property be taken for public use, without just compensation.

* * *

Amendment X

The powers not delegated to the United States by the Constitution, nor prohibited by it to the states, are reserved to the states respectively, or to the people.

* * *

Amendment XIV

Section 1. All persons born or naturalized in the United States, and subject to the jurisdiction thereof, are citizens of the United States and of the state wherein they reside. No state shall make or enforce any law which shall abridge the privileges or immunities of citizens of the United States; nor shall any state deprive any person of life, liberty, or property, without due process of law, nor deny to any person within its jurisdiction the equal protection of the laws.

GLOSSARY OF KEY TERMS AND ACRONYMS

ADA   Americans with Disabilities Act.

Affirm   When a higher court upholds the opinion of a lower court in an appeal.

Amicus curiae   "Friend of the court"; a person or organization that is allowed to appear in court or file arguments with the court even though the person or group is not a party to the suit.

Appeal   A request to a higher court for a review of the decision of a lower court to correct mistakes or an improper ruling.

Appellate court   A court that has jurisdiction to review decisions by lower courts but that does not have the power to hear a case initially.

Case law   Law developed by courts; also called *common law.*

Certiorari   A request to a higher court to review a decision of a lower court; the request can be refused.

C.F.R.   Code of Federal Regulations.

Civil case   All lawsuits other than criminal proceedings; usually brought by one person against another and usually involves monetary damages.

Class action   A lawsuit brought by a person on behalf of all persons in similar situations as well as himself; to bring such a suit, the person must meet certain statutory criteria.

Consent decree   An agreement by the parties in a lawsuit, sanctioned by the court, that settles the matter.

De minimus   Trivial or unimportant matter.

Defendant   The person against whom a legal action is brought; at the appeals stage this person is the appellee.

Dicta   The part of an opinion in which the court discusses the reasoning behind the court's ruling; it is not binding. The singular is dictum.

DOE   Department of Education.

EAHCA   Education for All Handicapped Children Act; in 1990, renamed the Individuals with Disabilities Education Act.

En banc.   "In the bench"; when a full panel of judges hears a case.

Et al.   "And others"; when it appears in the opinion, it signifies that unnamed parties went before the court.

Et seq.   "And following"; it is used in a legal citation to indicate the sections that follow the cited section.

F. 2d   Federal reporter, second series; the reporter contains selected rulings of the U.S. Court of Appeals. Published by West Publishing Company.

F. 3d   Federal reporter, third series; the reporter contains selected rulings of the U.S. Court of Appeals. Published by the West Publishing Company.

F. Supp.   The Federal Supplement; the supplement contains selected decisions of federal district courts. Published by the West Publishing Company.

FAPE   Free appropriate public education.

FERPA   Family Educational Rights and Privacy Act.

Guardian ad litem   A guardian appointed by the court to represent a minor.

HCPA   Handicapped Children's Protection Act.

Holding   The part of a judicial opinion in which the law is applied to the facts of the case; the ruling.

IDEA   Individuals with Disabilities Education Act.

Informed consent   When a person agrees to let an action take place; the decision must be based on a full disclosure of the relevant facts.

Injunction   A court order requiring a person or entity to do something or refrain from taking a particular action.

In re   "In the matter of"; this prefix is often used in a case in which a child in involved.

LRE   Least restrictive environment.

NCLB   No Child Left Behind Act of 2001.

OCR   Office of Civil Rights.

Opinion   Judges' statement of a decision reached in a case, consisting of the dicta and the ruling.

OSEP   Office of Special Education Programs.

OSERS   Office of Special Education and Rehabilitative Services.

P.L. 94-142   The number of the Education of All Handicapped Children Act of 1975; the bill was a public law, the 142nd bill passed by the 94th Congress.

Section 504   Section 504 of the Rehabilitation Act of 1973.

Petitioner   A person who initiates a judicial proceeding and requests that relief be granted.

Plaintiff   A person who initiates a lawsuit.

Precedent   A court decision that gives direction to lower courts on how to decide similar questions of law in cases with similar facts.

Remand   To send back; a higher court may send back a ruling to a lower court with directions from the higher court.

Respondent   A person who responds to a lawsuit.

Sectarian   Church related.

Sine qua non   An indispensable part or condition.

Stare decisis   "To stand by that which was decided"; similar to precedence.

Tort   A civil wrong done by one person to another.

U.S.C.   United States Code.

Vacate   When a higher court overturns or sets aside the opinion of a lower court in an appeal.

INDEX OF CASES

A U T H O R
I N D E X

SUBJECT INDEX

....